THE CHANGING ROLE OF UNIONS

ISSUES IN WORK AND HUMAN RESOURCES

Daniel J.B. Mitchell, Series Editor

THE CHANGING ROLE OF UNIONS

New Forms of Representation

Edited by

Phanindra V. Wunnava

M.E.Sharpe
Armonk, New York
London, England

Library of Congress Cataloging-in-Publication Data

The changing role of unions : new forms of representation / Phanindra V. Wunnava, editor.
    p. cm. — (Issues in work and human resources)
Includes bibliographical references and index.
ISBN 0-7656-1237-2 (alk. paper)
    1. Labor unions—United States. I. Wunnava, Phanindra V. II. Series.

HD6508.C453 2004
331.88´0973—dc22   2003061819

Printed in the United States of America

The paper used in this publication meets the minimum requirements of
American National Standard for Information Sciences
Permanence of Paper for Printed Library Materials,
ANSI Z 39.48-1984.

♾

MV (c)   10   9   8   7   6   5   4   3   2   1

To my late beloved parents,

Sri Venkateswararao and Ranganayakamma Wunnava

Contents

III. Union Wage and Employment Effects:
U.S. Evidence

IV. Union Wage and Employment Effects:
International Evidence

V. Desire to Unionize and Union Impact on
Workplace Practices and Performance

VI. U.S. Union Organizing: Any Hope for a Rebound?

Figures, Tables, and Appendices

Figures

Tables

Appendices

Series Editor's Foreword

The decline in unionization in the United States and elsewhere in the devel
oped world has not dimmed the academic appetite for studying unions and
their effects. At the Middlebury Economics Conference of April 2002, on
which this book is based, a variety of economic perspectives was presented.
None of the participants saw the environment as especially favorable to growth
in unionization as a percentage of the workforce. But possibilities for growth
in particular sectors, or for using nontraditional approaches to organizing
and representation, were highlighted. And the variation in experience internationally, and over time, was stressed.

Readers will have different motives for reading this volume. First, it points
to the various research tools now in use, or which can be used, to study
unions. It also points to some data puzzles that continue to produce ambiguous outcomes for empirical researchers. Second, the book naturally directs
attention toward the future. If indeed unions are going to be increasingly
associated with a limited number of sectors, what is the implication for the
larger workforce that will be increasingly nonunion in many countries?

This book joins other volumes in the series Issues in Work and Human
Resources that illuminate developments in union and nonunion employment.
In *Working in Silicon Valley,* for example, Alan Hyde explores a largely nonunion sector in which employees have nonetheless found various ways to
network and to associate in order to resolve job-related problems. In *Nonunion Employee Representation,* by Bruce E. Kaufman and Daphne Gottlieb
Taras, readers can find studies of alternative approaches to the need for employee "voice" in a variety of industries. Evolution of the American indus-

trial relations system over the entire twentieth century is examined in *Industrial Relations to Human Resources and Beyond*. The contrast between public and private unionization—as noted by several contributors in this volume—is developed in *Collective Bargaining in the Public Sector* and *The Future of Private Sector Unionism in the United States* (James Bennett and Bruce Kauffman). Leo Troy's *Beyond Unions and Collective Bargaining* foreshadows the sectoral variation that is highlighted in this book and Arthur Shostak's two *Cyberunion* volumes suggest high-tech tools available to unions.

Obviously, there are many perspectives contained in this volume and those in the series that have preceded it. But the bottom line for all of them, including this book in particular, is that the various forms of workers' representation and union activities within this category are undergoing constant evolution. The 1950s' model of "big labor" setting wage patterns and personnel practices across national economies is no more. Speeds of adjustment vary internationally across the developed world. But the process is unrelenting. Only studies such as the ones presented in this book can keep abreast of the change and provide analyses of future scenarios.

Daniel J.B. Mitchell

Preface

This volume is a refined product of the Twenty-third Annual Conference on Economic Issues: "Changing Role of Unions," held April 13–14, 2002, at Middlebury College. Our annual conference series has had a very rich history of bringing together diverse researchers working on a set of issues of common interest, with the aim of expanding the frontiers of knowledge. Such an ambitious event cannot take place without the generosity of donors. I would like to formally acknowledge that the Christian A. Johnson Endeavor Foundation has been providing us funding over the years.

A few words about my interest in unions: I would say that I have had a love-hate relationship with unions. My first impressions were very negative. Growing up in southern India, for me "unions" and "strikes" were synonymous! I remember a number of school closings due to union-initiated strikes and work stoppages. My late father, who was in middle management at a public-sector commercial bank, was once manhandled for crossing a union picket line—indeed, he was out of circulation for over a week. On another occasion, I was at the receiving end. I was just about to make my maiden voyage to the United States in the fall of 1978, and I had to endure the wrath of a group of unionized airport workers when I tried to help an elderly fellow-passenger carry her luggage. That was the last straw for me. I said to myself that I did not want to have anything to do with those "damn" unions!

So why am I now interested in unions? When I was a graduate student at the University of Miami economics department, Professor Ronald Ehrenberg of Cornell University came to give a talk to the faculty and graduate students in January 1982. Around that time, I was also getting interested in labor economics, with professors Phil Robins and David Blau joining the faculty ranks of the economics department. The theme of Ehrenberg's talk was the relative productivity of public-sector union and nonunion workers. His talk was a revelation to me, because it demonstrated that after one controls for some of the observed differences, union workers on average could be more productive than nonunion workers. Ehrenberg's work was subsequently published in a leading economics journal. I was willing to give unions a second chance.

As I was completing my studies at the University of Miami, my interest in an applied economics Ph.D. program with a labor economics focus grew, but I missed the deadline to apply for admission at Cornell Industrial Labor Relations School (ILR) in the spring of 1982. It was suggested that I look into the State University of New York (SUNY), Binghamton, which also had a good group of labor economists, as a stopgap alternative. Since the chair at the University of Miami at that time was a former chair of the SUNY economics department, with his recommendation, I managed to get into the SUNY economics program with funding in the late spring of 1982 and started my studies at Binghamton that fall. Initially, my plan was to stay for a year at Binghamton and than apply to Cornell the following year. Around the same time, a distinguished labor economist from the University of North Carolina, Chapel Hill, was in the process of joining the economics department at SUNY. That distinguished economist is none other than my mentor, Professor Solomon Polachek. Given my East Asian heritage, maybe it was my "good karma" that I managed to work under Professor Polachek.

When I was looking for a topic on which to write a term paper for an advanced econometrics course, one of Dr. Polachek's suggestions to me was that I expand one of his working papers. Interestingly, the paper was an investigation of the effect of unions on age-earnings profiles. His suggestion was like a mantra to me. Subsequently, that particular econometrics term paper evolved into my doctoral dissertation. Since then, unions have been one of my favorite areas of research. Over the years, I have learned a lot about unions from the writings of most of the researchers who contributed to this volume. I would like to acknowledge that I am immensely grateful to Dr. Polachek for being such a lively mentor, professional colleague (by coauthoring a number of journal articles), and true friend. His interest in his current and former students is boundless. If some of my students think that I am a bit hard on them, I want them to know what I had to endure working under Professor Polachek! But the bottom line is that he is my hero.

A brief overview of this conference volume follows. One of the caveats of this volume is the exclusion of public-sector unionism and the degree to which government employment standards and regulation substitute for unionism.

The chapters in part I by Richard B. Freeman and Christopher L. Erickson et al. focus on reasons for the success of union drives in certain sectors against the odds. In the words of Freeman, "With the Internet offering great opportunities to deliver services to workers who otherwise cannot gain collective bargaining at their workplace and permitting the development of new organizational forms, I expect unions to morph into something akin to the open source described herein." Erickson et al. present a very interesting case study of janitors (Justice for Janitors [JfJ]) in Los Angeles to provide a union success story. Despite the obstacles, the JfJ campaign of the Service Employees International Union succeeded in reunionizing the cleaning service industry in Los Angeles. The tactics and successes have spread to other areas. The JfJ is seen by organized labor as a model to be emulated. Moreover, janitorial unionization in Los Angeles has survived ups and downs in the business cycle and three bargaining rounds, suggesting that the JfJ strategy is sustainable. Key factors that contributed to the success of the JfJ approach are its application in a nontradable service industry, the surprising industrial concentration of the cleaning services industry despite its low capital requirements, union use of pressure on building owners and managers—rather than on the contractors—that surmounts legal barriers, union enlistment of key political and community figures in the organizing and bargaining campaigns, and public sympathy for the plight of the working poor. In addition, a union strategy of coordinated bargaining across cities appears able to leverage success in one area to achieve gains in others.

In part II, the chapter by Bruce E. Kaufman gives us a historical perspective of American unionization and the critical lessons to be learned, contrasting union growth in two earlier periods: the 1920s and the 1930s. In the words of Kaufman, "[T]hese two decades are particularly instructive, because they illustrate two 'end points' with respect to the private and social demand for union WRAP [wealth redistribution, aggrandizement, and protection] and CGI [constitutional government in industry] and thus provide examples of possible outcomes for the early twenty-first century." Rafael Gomez and Morley Gunderson propose a novel approach to modeling unionization; specifically, as an "experience" good. Such an approach will enable one to account for major empirical findings of union literature, such as the intergenerational transmission of union status and preferences, the persistence of union membership or its decline, the observed postpurchase satisfaction among workers who have sampled union membership, and the effect of social networks in influencing the desire for unionization on the part of the young and those with less market experience.

Parts III and IV consist of mostly empirical chapters focusing on union wage and employment effects based on both U.S. and international data.

Barry T. Hirsch, David A. Macpherson, and Edward J. Schumacher present conflicting evidence on trends in private-sector union and nonunion wages. The U.S. Bureau of Labor Statistics's quarterly Employment Cost Index (ECI), constructed from establishment surveys, uses fixed weights applied to wage changes among matched job quotes. The ECI shows a substantial decrease in wage growth for union relative to nonunion workers. The annual Employer Costs for Employee Compensation (ECEC), drawn from the same survey data as the ECI, provides wage-level estimates constructed from the full sample of job quotes using current sector weights. Surprisingly, the ECEC shows no trend in the relationship between union and nonunion wages. The authors conclude that there has been a closing in the union-nonunion wage gap since the mid-1980s, but that the magnitude of the closing is anything but clear.

Bradley T. Ewing and Phanindra V. Wunnava's chapter is concerned with identifying the differing responses of union and nonunion wages to shocks to real output growth, inflation, and the stance of monetary policy. Theoretical macroeconomic models imply that wages will respond in certain ways to unanticipated changes in aggregate measures of economic activity. Given the differences in compensation levels of union and nonunion workers, and the link to the stage of the business cycle and industry, it is expected that the aggregate wage differentials both for the entire private sector and by industry will respond to macroeconomic shocks in a predictable manner. The relationship among these wages differentials and the macroeconomy is examined in the context of a vector autoregression. Ewing and Wunnava's results show the extent and the magnitude of the relationship between the union-nonunion wage differentials and several key macroeconomic factors.

Francine D. Blau and Lawrence M. Kahn examine microeconomic evidence on the impact of collective bargaining on the wage structure and on the relative employment of different skill groups in the United States and the Organization for Economic Cooperation and Development countries. They find abundant evidence that collective bargaining and minimum wage laws lead to wage compression and help explain the higher level of wage inequality in the United States than we see in other countries. Collective bargaining appears to have stronger effects on the overall labor market than do minimum wages. However, their examination of the impact of institutions on employment yields less clear-cut results than those for the wage structure. In many cases, union- or minimum-wage–induced wage compression is seen to lower the relative employment of the less skilled. The negative employment effects of unions appear to be concentrated on the young.

Sarah Brown and John G. Sessions investigate the relationship between international competition and the labor market prospects of a representative sample of British workers. Their analysis, which sets out the first explicit test of both the wage *and* employment implications of increased international competition, highlights an interesting asymmetry. Competition negatively affects the wage, but not the employment, prospects of unionized workers and the employment, but not the wage, prospects of nonunion workers.

The chapters in part V are solely based on British data. Clive R. Belfield and John S. Heywood focus on how the desire to unionize impacts human resource management practices, while John T. Addison and Clive R. Belfield's chapter focuses on the strength of unions and establishment performance. Specifically, Belfield and Heywood investigate the desire of nonunion workers in the United Kingdom (UK) to become represented by unions. Comparing their results to those from the United States, they find those in the UK are less likely to desire unionization and express lower dissatisfaction with their influence at work. The determinants of the desire for unionization are estimated, controlling for a wide variety of individual and workplace variables. The role of human resource management, and employee involvement in particular, is isolated. They identify a direct effect of these practices in reducing the desire for unionization and an indirect effect operating through the influence of employee relations, a major determinant of the desire for unionization. Also, they identify characteristics of coworkers that are associated with a desire for unionization and examine the role information revelation may play in managerial strategies to forestall unions.

An interesting aspect of British research on unions based on the Workplace Industrial Relations Surveys and Workplace Employment Relations Surveys has been the apparent shift in union impact on establishment performance in the 1990s compared to the 1980s—and the recent scramble to explain the phenomenon. Addison and Belfield chart these changes along the dimensions of financial performance, labor productivity, employment, quits, absenteeism, industrial relations climate, and plant closings. Using the most recent workplace survey, they also investigate the controversial notion that union influence is positive where unions are strong and is negative where unions are weak. This notion, encountered in recent research in Britain, emphasizes the benefits of the collective voice of unions, arguing that this voice is only "heard" when the union is strong or is a credible agent. They examine this contention for a fuller array of definitions of union influence and workplace performance measures. Overall, their discussion reveals some evidence that is consistent with reduced bargaining power in the wake of antiunion reform measures and heightened product market competition. On the other hand, there is little support for the recherché notion that stronger unions have a beneficial impact, yet weaker ones do not.

Finally, the chapters in part VI focus on union organizing trends in the United States (Henry S. Farber and Bruce Western) and in other selected countries (Solomon W. Polachek). The lessons from these two chapters will have far-reaching consequences for the future of union organizing across the globe. It is common knowledge that rates of private-sector union membership are declining in the United States. However, not known is why union density in the United States is declining. Farber and Western illustrate the powerlessness of the "usual suspect" causes usually linked to declining private-sector unionism. As such, they find that U.S. labor law matters little, and that Ronald Reagan and the Republicans made little difference. Certification and decertification issues were not the culprits either, because both affect too few workers to matter. Thus, U.S. union density is declining almost solely because of nonneutral U.S. economic growth. Since this growth is taking place mostly in the nonunion sector, union employment is getting relatively smaller. Accordingly, union membership relative to workforce size is dwindling drastically. Put simply, the economy is divided into two parts: a union segment, which appears to be shrinking, and a nonunion segment, which by contrast is expanding. From a policy perspective, Farber and Western's conclusion is important because it implies a rather pessimistic view of future U.S. union power. Over the 1973–99 period, unions would have had to organize at a rate more than twenty times their actual new-organization rate to be able to yield a union membership equal to the U.S. 1950s' peak. The amount of resources needed for this endeavor would have been over $2 billion, or about $200 in organizing expenses per union member, compared to the current $20. But it is not even clear that expending this much on organizing would yield the necessary replacement rates of union membership, especially if globalization and other factors caused the economy to sustain structural changes. So, for example, if workers have become skeptical of unions' abilities to provide high wages, job security, and other worker benefits, then the process of organizing workers would have become even more difficult and expensive. Thus, according to Farber and Western, the future of unionism is bleak.

It is to be noted that declining union membership patterns are not the norm for all countries. In the words of Polachek, "[I]t is not obvious the same conclusions would be reached if international data were explored." The purpose of Polachek's chapter is to employ international data, albeit with a different empirical methodology, to see if conclusions similar to those of Farber and Western can be obtained. In addition, his chapter suggests an interesting reason based on international relations research why certain economic sectors tend to be union, while others tend to be nonunion.

Hence, the main goal of this conference volume is to bring together the multifaceted efforts of a number of researchers working on different aspects of unions. We hope that the resulting mixture of perspectives will help shed light on the evolving role of unions in the twenty-first century.

I would like to thank my colleagues in the economics department of Middlebury College for giving their unstinting support on this project. I would like to thank our academic coordinator, Amy Holbrook, for her timely assistance when this project was getting off the ground. Although initially I thought our events coordinator, Marie Winner, was my sidekick, I very quickly realized that maybe I am her sidekick! I would not hesitate to say that her scrupulous attention to every possible detail was outstanding. I do not think we could have had the gathering of conference participants in April 2002, and the subsequent publication of this volume, without her hard work, dedication, and planning.

Our students here at the college are an integral part of our intellectual lives, and they actively take part in the proceedings of our annual conferences. I would like to thank the student moderators (Jessica Wasilewski, Dusan Petrovic, Laura Zarchin, Valerie O'Hearn, Brendan McCauley, and Justin Dreschler) for their meticulous time management of the conference sessions; the student drivers (Nathan Anderson, Ammad Faisal, Kevin Immonje, Ryan Birtwell, and Laura Zarchin) for transporting the conference participants safely; director of media services Dean Cadoret, technician W. Stewart Lane, digital specialist Scott Witt, and video camera operator Bernadette Gunn for their outstanding professional support in running this conference; and our dining staff for putting together excellent meals. I would like to thank our dean of library and information services, Barbara Doyle-Wilch, and her colleagues, reference librarian Brenda Ellis, collections specialist William Warren, and project coordinator Tess Deddo and educational tech specialist Alex Chapin, for their unwavering support and encouragement in running this conference and in getting this manuscript ready for publication. I would like to thank our college computer center consultants Amy Hoffman, Nathan Burt, Sasha Huntley, Dimitar Koparov, Khurram Jamali, and Ngheta Waithaka for their timely help in translating files from one format to another, and 2003 Christian A. Johnson Economics summer interns Laurel Houghton and John Oliver, who provided invaluable assistance when the details of organizing the tables, notes, and references required focused, careful labor. In fact, it is not an exaggeration that without the sustained effort of Laurel on the copyedited manuscript as well as the page proofs, this volume would not have appeared in print in a timely fashion. I was also very fortunate to work with Lynn Taylor (executive editor), Esther Clark (editorial assistant), Henrietta Toth (project editor), Steven Long (copyeditor), and Daniel J.B.

Mitchell (series editor) of M.E. Sharpe. Aside from contributing a chapter to this volume, Hirsch was instrumental in pulling the major themes of this conference (and volume) together—I am very grateful for his additional contribution to this volume. I gratefully acknowledge the timely and meticulous indexing by Helen Reiff.

I need to thank my family (Vijaya, Geetha, and Sanjay) for their loving support—especially my better half for not carrying out her threat of throwing the deadbolt when I was holed up in my office late at night working on some aspect of this conference (and volume). Finally, I would like to thank my spiritual guru, Bhagawan Sri Satya Saibaba, for giving me strength in making this project a reality.

I

Unions and New Constituents

1

The Road to Union Renaissance in the United States

Richard B. Freeman

If they were an animal or plant, private-sector unions would fall on the endangered species list of the U.S. Fish and Wildlife Service. Private-sector union density is in single digits—comparable to the level at the turn of the twentieth century. Despite the "organize, organize, organize" mantra of the American Federation of Labor and Congress of Industrial Organizations (AFL-CIO) leadership, density fell throughout the 1990s, even in states whose rates of unionization would seem to have reached rock bottom. In 1990, for example, Mississippi had an 8 percent unionization rate for all workers, public as well as private. In 2001, it had a 5.5 percent unionization rate.[1] The AFL-CIO commitment to organizing may have helped staunch the rate of union decline in the 1990s,[2] but it did little to bring unionism to the millions of workers who want union representation but who are either a minority at their workplace or who cannot win a collective bargaining contract in the face of massive employer opposition.

Unionism looked healthier in the public sector, where density is four times as high as it is in the private sector and where density is holding steady rather than falling over time. But the public sector accounts for no more than 15 percent of the U.S. workforce, and the terms and conditions public-sector unions negotiate are unlikely to spill over to the private sector. Unions have to expand in the private sector to play a significant role in the economy.

The difficulty facing unions can be seen in statistics on organizing. To balance off the loss of members due to the normal birth and death of firms and changes in employment in union and nonunion workplaces and maintain their 2001 9 percent share of the private workforce, unions must add about 500,000 new members annually. To add a point of density, unions must organize close to 1 million new members. But National Labor Relations Board (NLRB) election statistics show that unions win less than 100,000 workers annually, of whom perhaps two-thirds eventually end up with collective bargaining contracts. The AFL-CIO's *Work in Progress* reports higher numbers, due largely to the inclusion of the affiliations of previously organized workers into the federation. Of the 463,000 new members reported in 2001, for example, about 310,000 came from such affiliations.[3] The actual number of new unionists for the year was a bit over 150,000, and the number of new members in the private sector was close to the NLRB numbers.

Moreover, to fund a massive organizing campaign it would take huge union resources. Turning Paula Voos's (1983) estimates of the marginal cost of organizing a new member into 2001 dollars, the cost of organizing a new member would appear to be on the order of $2,000—though it could be as low as the $1,000 that is the rule of thumb for some unions and as high as $3,000.[4] Adding a half-million new members annually at $2,000 per member would then require spending $1 billion, or about 20 percent of total annual union dues. Adding 1 million members would take about 40 percent of total dues.[5] These figures bracket the AFL-CIO's goal that unions dedicate 30 percent of revenues to organizing. Most unions, however, come nowhere close to spending 30 percent of dues money on organizing. Some, like the Teamsters, have cut their organizing budgets. Others, like the Steelworkers, have trouble finding campaigns where large expenditures will pay off. In election years, many unions put aside organizing efforts and allot their discretionary resources to politics, where they have greater success. But political success does not improve union density. When the Democrats control the White House and appoint members of the NLRB, the fall in density is nearly as great as when the Republicans control the White House and appoint the NLRB.

Given these facts, most analysts see little future for unions outside of the public sector. Many regard private-sector unions as highly endangered species on their way to fossilization in the new global economy, where markets rule the roost. But unionism has been at the abyss before, and expert analysts have been wrong in proclaiming union failure before. In 1933, right before the Great Depression-era spurt in the United States, George Barnett, the president of the American Economic Association, declared that unions had no future, much as many analysts of the U.S. scene do today. In the 1950s, before unionism came to the public sector, George Meany, the president of the AFL-CIO, declared public-sector workers nonorganizable in the United States, despite unionization of the public sector in other countries. Labor relations scholars concurred with Meany, seeking reasons why unionism fit better with the private sector.

Labor experts and leaders are not exceptionally lame-headed or blind. The empirical problem is that, historically, unions have grown in spurts in periods of social crisis that are exceedingly difficult to foresee (Freeman 1998). Union density grew in nearly all advanced countries during World War I, when governments needed labor cooperation to prosecute the war. Density grew in advanced countries in the aftermath of the Great Depression, when workers lost faith in business leadership and the market system. It grew in World War II in advanced countries that were not conquered by the Nazis. During the 1970s' oil crisis inflation, it grew in most European Union countries and in the U.S. public sector, though not in the U.S. private sector, where density continued to fall. Experts who base their forecasts on an extrapolation of the recent past inevitably miss these spurts.

Spurts in union growth are, moreover, often associated with new union forms that attract previously nonorganizable groups of workers or with the development of new ways of operating that greatly weaken employer opposition. In the depression-era spurt, the new form was the industrial union, which the CIO pushed and which the AFL eventually adopted as well. In the 1880s, the new form was the geographic lodge associated with the Knights of Labor. In the World War I and World War II periods, the new way of operating was through various war labor boards and compulsory arbitration. If there is one message from labor history for the future of unions, it is that *if unionism manages to recover from the endangered species list, it will be through a new growth spurt associated with some new union form and new mode of operating.*

Since only a stockbroker or astrologer would have the chutzpah to predict the timing of a new spurt in unionism, if any, I will analyze what a new union form might do better in the information economy than the current form and thus contribute to any possible new union spurt. The form I will describe makes extensive use of information communication technologies, particularly the Internet, to deliver services to members and surmount employer opposition. In a series of articles, Richard B. Freeman and Joel Rogers (2002a, 2002b) call the new form "open-source unionism," making an analogy with the open-source computer programming movement.[6] To show that the new union form is more than blue-sky abstraction, I give examples of innovative unions operating in an open-source manner today and of past union practice that provide historic precedent for open-source unions.

Toward a New Union Form: Open-Source Unionism

The argument for a new form of unionism in the United States is straightforward. As long as management remains as strongly opposed to unionism as it was in the last two decades of the twentieth century and national labor law does not change dramatically, unions have little or no chance of gaining substantial new membership. The conventional game of battling for majority status in NLRB representation elections and trying to get often-recalcitrant employers into collective bargaining contracts is a losing one for trade unions. It is not a matter of "leveling the playing field," as some union leaders believe, but of changing the game of unionization from one where employers can effectively veto the desire of workers to one where the decision to unionize rests exclusively with workers. To accomplish this, unions must create new forms of membership and develop services for workers outside of majority-status workplaces where they win collective contracts with employers. There are enough workers who desire workplace representation and advice and sufficient legal rights for non-majority–based union organizations that unions operating outside of majority-status collective bargaining could substantially increase the reach of unions and improve the working lives of millions of workers.

The major reason unions have shied away from providing services and organizing workplaces that cannot gain majority status is that historically the cost of such activity exceeded the benefits. Workers lacking collective bargaining contracts could not be expected to pay full dues for membership, and without such dues, unions could not afford union services that members would truly value. As a result, when workers approached a union to seek an organizing drive, organizers would refuse to try to organize them if the union felt that the organizing drive was unlikely to lead to a contract. The result was that workers who wanted union services would go away with nothing.

But modern computer technology, particularly the advent of the Internet as a major source of information and communication, greatly alters this benefit-cost calculation for unionizing workers outside of collective bargaining. The Internet makes it cost effective for unions to deliver union services to minorities of workers across workplaces and for individual workers or groups of workers to coordinate with each other regardless of the collective bargaining status of their workplace. The Internet offers a near zero marginal cost technology for providing information to workers, for interactive communication with them, and for pressuring management on their behalf. Organizing and the nature of union activity should be rethought in light of this.

By itself, of course, information and communication over the Web is not a magic elixir for creating a new union form. The dot.com bubble shows that going online does not guarantee success in business, and the same is true for unionization. Any new union form must create the face-to-face human interactions that build the trust and solidarity that lie at the heart of any collective organization. Since the least-cost way for such interactions to occur is in a local geographic area, Freeman and Rogers argue that the new union form would need a strong local basis—be it through city labor councils or community organizations or some other units that would transcend particular workplaces (2002a, 2002b). It is the combination of local organization with broader Internet-based global linkages that provide the basis for open-source unionism.

In open-source programming, programmers create and share modules that others can build on and add to. So, too, we see open-source unionism building a common collaborative platform, language, and practice among workers and union activists—often operating at some distance from one another, or at different work sites, or moving across multiple sites over their working lifetimes. The key to open-source unionism is that union membership is defined more by shared values and actions than by the collective bargaining status of the present employment. Membership would take different forms in different settings and with different union affiliations. It would involve a more graduated dues structure than is the norm today. Lacking collective bargaining, open-source members would pay lower dues than workers in traditional majority-status union settings—perhaps just a nominal amount. But such workers would still be full-fledged members of the labor movement. They would not be "associate members" of the type that the AFL-CIO tried to enroll briefly through non work related services, such as low-interest credit cards. Rather, open-source unionism would deliver what unions do best: the representation and servicing of workers in their employment and role as workers. It would, however, perform this traditional function outside collective bargaining in majority-status settings, as well as in traditional ways. Members outside a majority-status position could bargain for themselves, seek enforcement of statutory worker rights, provide support for actions outside their workplace, conduct campaigns in their community or in the political world, and so on.

The meaning of being a union member would widen and grow fuzzier under the open-source form. Under current practice, union membership is limited to workers in a given unit that has a collective contract. Under open-source unionism, that limit on membership would fall, and there would be greater variation in the types of membership and in the service fees associated with membership. Consider someone who supports the union by providing it with contact detail such as e-mail or who backs the union in a particular campaign—such as student or community activists—but who pays no dues. Or someone who receives services provided largely through the Internet at low cost to the union and who pays just nominal dues. Or the activist who obtains a new job or promotion and leaves his or her former coworkers but wants to remain part of the movement. All could be members of an open-source union.

Historical Precedent

Defining union membership outside a majority collective bargaining situation has considerable historical precedence in the United States. In the 1880s, the Knights of Labor established "mixed lodges" that included workers from many occupations and firms in the same geographic area as well as single craft-based lodges. This form underlies the 1880s' spurt in unionization. The first constitution of the AFL, adopted at its founding in 1886, stated that membership was open to any "seven wage workers of good character and favorable to Trade Unions, and not members of any body affiliated with this Federation." Many such groups applied for and received direct affiliation with the national federation—migrating later to one or another international union. Direct affiliation and membership in minority- or members-only unions was also important in the 1930s, when workers who did not fit well into established forms sought to join unions. In the early organizing of the industrial trades of the mineworkers and steelworkers, such nonmajority unions provided a union presence in the workplace well before an employer recognized a collective bargaining unit. After World War II, however, unions abandoned both direct affiliation and minority unionism as common practices in the private sector.

But they did not do this in the public sector. In the 1960s and 1970s, public-sector unionism developed from minority representation in organizations that did not bargain collectively. Teachers' unions grew to several million in membership, initially off agreements negotiated only for members of nonmajority associations. The same is true of many state and local employee unions, which developed under meet-and-confer provisions in state laws. These provisions did not impose binding duties to bargain on employers or restrict the bargains made to majority organizations. Indeed, many states did not allow for collective bargaining in their labor laws. And over 1 million employees in the federal government have joined unions, even though the federal government does not bargain over wages and working conditions. Union density was higher in 2001 among federal employees (32 percent), who are unlikely ever to have a collective bargaining contract, than among private-sector workers (9 percent).

In short, the notion that unionism means membership in an organization that has demonstrated majority support among workers at a particular work site recognized by an employer as the exclusive bargaining representative of workers is not the historic norm in the United States. It is a union self-imposed limit that creates an unnecessary barrier to union influence and growth.

Legal Standing

Many unionists seem to believe that U.S. labor law privileges majority-status unions. With one possible exception, however, workers in unions lacking majority support have the same legal standing and protections (for what they are worth) as workers who win an NLRB election. This is because section 7 of the National Labor Relations Act protects the concerted activity of workers, regardless of minority or majority status. It states that "[e]mployees shall have the right to self organization, to form, join and assist labor organizations, to bargain collectively through representatives of their own choosing, and to engage in other concerted activities, for the purpose of collective bargain or other mutual aid and protection." The key phrase is "concerted action." The law is open-ended on the form and function of protected collective activity. Legal protection applies *identically* to members of minority unions or to workers acting together, absent any formal union organization, as it does to members of majority unions.

The one legal advantage that majority status unions may have is that the law imposes on firms a *duty to bargain* in good faith with a majority-status union. As the statute does not say nor have the NLRB or courts ruled that employers can refuse to bargain with minority unions, it is not clear whether an employer would have to bargain in good faith with a minority union or not. Some legal scholars think that the firms would be so required, but no one can be sure.[7] Even if duty to bargain applies only to majority-status unions, however, this does not bring great advantage to these unions. There is no punitive remedy to violation of the provision, and no requirement that bargaining should produce a contract or be resolved by arbitration. The duty to bargain is, at best, a duty to talk and talk. Union strength, not the statute, forces unwilling employers to agreement.

In short, the issue with open-source unionism is not whether unions based on a minority of workers at given workplaces have less legal support than majority-status unions, but whether such unions can deliver valuable services to workers and can develop sufficient strength to contest employers' decisions, absent collective bargaining.

What Can They Do?

Assuming no collective bargaining, open-source unions have to deliver cost-effective services to workers outside the workplace, where any particular management is irrelevant, and have to find ways to pressure particular managements to respond to employee demands.

The Internet is the cost-effective tool for delivering services to members.

An open-source union would use the Internet to provide members with accurate and up-to-date information about economic conditions affecting them. At firm-based locals, the union would gather information from members as well as from the regular business and economic news services about the firm. At locals in a given occupation or industry, the union would gather information about wage and employment developments in the specified job markets. Since the union's first product would be information, the union Web site would have to provide utterly trustworthy information and minimize the spin it might want to put on that information. It could also give information about unionism in the world writ large, for instance through access to www.labourstart.org.

Going beyond the provision of information, the open-source union would have to develop the capacity to provide advice to members about economic problems. It could do this through frequently asked questions (FAQs) and queriable online knowledge-base systems, as many unions do today. If people wanted to know what they might do if an employer mistreated them or how they might best get their employer to offer more options for defined contribution pension moneys or if some bill before the Congress was likely to help or harm their economic position, the union Web site would offer answers.

In the United Kingdom, UNISON, the largest single union, has pioneered providing information and giving personalized advice to members. Working with the National Union of Students, UNISON has developed a Web site that provides information and advice on work-related problems to student workers (www.troubleatwork.org.uk). The site contains contact information to unions, but because the vast bulk of students are not union members, the essence of this site is a free provision of union expertise to a largely non-union group. For its own members, UNISON has UNISON-Direct, a helpline call service that provides advice and support eighteen hours a day, six days a week, except Sunday. The advice system uses a seventeen-seat call center to respond to members' problems; the call-center workers use computerized access to more than 300 scripts to guide members through common problems, as well as a database holding personal membership details. Union members made approximately 150,000 calls to the center in 2001, stretching its capacity with a demand that surprised the union. In the United States, where a larger proportion of workers are on the Internet than in the United Kingdom, the natural way to deliver many of these services would be the Internet.

The natural end product of this line of services is an artificial-intelligence (AI) union expert system ("Walter Reuther," "Sam Gompers," "Bob the Builder," or whatever) that would respond to specific queries. Members would click on the union AI expert program for interactive sessions that would bring union expertise to workplace problems. As unions develop such services for members with collective bargaining contracts, they can readily extend them at low cost for members without contracts. The services would be broader than those covered by a particular contract, extending to information about training outside the workplace, family services, and so on. Developing computerized data files on members' skills, needs, career goals, and so on, the open-source union would provide personalized information and advice that no other organization could or would want to do.

But how would an open-source union confront management at a particular workplace? As it would typically not have the clout inside the firm of a majority-status collective bargaining union, it would have to use different tactics. It could use its reputation for providing accurate information to set the agenda in disputes with management, to shape public discourse, and to marshal resources from outside a unit to support workers in disputes. When young law associates felt that they were getting an unfair deal from major law firms in 1998, they set up a Web site (www.greedyassociates.com) that provided information to potential recruits to firms about salaries and working conditions. Fearful that complaints on the site could adversely affect future recruitment, the major law firms quickly improved conditions, raising pay massively in some cities to remedy one of the major problems (there are differential rates of pay between associates working in Silicon Valley and those working in other locales). In the space of one year, the law associates won larger gains in pay than almost any union has won through collective bargaining (Taras and Gesser 2003). Since workers seeking employment often use the Internet to find out about a prospective employer, open-source unions could provide the venue for current workers to inform potential new employees about working conditions and problems at the workplace. If existing workers were upset about a problem, it could harm recruitment, pressuring firms to resolve the issue. If workers felt management treated them fairly, this would help the firm in its recruitment.

The absence of clout inside the firm would also induce an open-source union to forge meaningful alliances with community groups outside itself and engage in local political activity, much as public-sector unions did when they were governed by meet-and-confer legislation. Unlike unions based on collective bargaining, open-source unions would not be able to turn inward when they faced struggle, but would have to look outward. They would have to develop a more coherent and attractive public face and become a more visible source of stewardship and moral value in the broader economy. Open-source unions would gain the political and social influence that comes from playing a broader public role, as a substitute for traditional sources of muscle in disagreements with management.

Does all this sound like "pie in the sky"? If I had offered this vision of a new union form when I was on the Commission on the Future of Labor/Management Relations in the early 1990s, John Dunlop, the chair of the commission, would undoubtedly have called for the white coats to cart me away. Labor relations are a highly practical world, which disdains blue-sky speculations. But in the latter part of the 1990s, through the early years of the twenty-first century, innovative unions in the United States and countries with similar labor relations systems—the United Kingdom, Australia, and Canada—began developing cutting-edge practices that exploit modern technology and enlarge the meaning of membership along the lines of open-source unions.

Cutting-Edge Practices

The most striking examples of the new union form[8] are found in the communication and information technology (IT) sectors, where workers have greater familiarity and expertise with the Internet and related IT technologies than workers in most other sectors. The exemplar open-source union is Alliance@ IBM (www.allianceibm.org), a chartered local of the Communication Workers of America (CWA) at the historically nonunion (at least in the United States) IBM. Alliance@IBM developed from Web-based protests by IBM employees in response to IBM's 1999 unilateral change in the company pension system, which greatly harmed some future retirees. The workers protested in chat rooms and sounding boards around the Web, impelling IBM to restore some of the pension benefits. Alliance@IBM has a small number of voting members, a large number of "subscribers" to e-mail messages, and several visitors to its Web site. The Alliance site provides discussion groups, mailing lists, links to related sites, and information about company issues of concern to workers—all developed by local members. Among the accomplishments of IBM workers was an e-mail campaign to raise the allowance per mile driven for IBM customer engineers, who pay for their own vehicle costs when traveling to repair customer machines. When management did not respond to individual complaints about rising costs, the customer engineers planned a one-day e-mail and phone-call campaign to contact the manager in charge. The one-day campaign succeeded in getting the mileage allowance increased.[9]

An extended union that is closer to a craft union or occupational association is WashTech (www.washtech.org), also associated with the CWA, which represents the interests of Silicon Valley and related high-tech industry workers. This organization raised the issue of overtime pay for contract employees at Microsoft and other firms that hire many software engineers as contractors. It provides discounted-cost training courses, information about developments in the industry on its Web site, contract advice, and legislative advocacy. It publishes the *WashTech News,* a free digest of news that is delivered bimonthly via e-mail to subscribers who are promised that the membership list will be kept confidential. The form for subscribing says, "Yes! I support the basic goals of WashTech and believe that workers need a collective voice in the high-tech industry. Please subscribe me to the *WashTech News,"* which aligns the subscribers with the union.

Outside the United States, in October 2001 the Australian union movement established the IT Workers Alliance (www.itworkers-alliance.org). As their Web site explains, "The idea of the IT Workers Alliance is to provide a space for IT workers to share information and ideas and receive advice on workplace issues" and to "create a culture that workers will want to be part of," rather than simply "attempting to recruit members up front." It includes a forum for discussion, news about the IT sector, information on independent contractor issues, and numerous FAQ sections so that the IT workers learn about their rights and ways to redress problems. Three weeks after the launch of the IT Workers Alliance, the Australian Computer Society formed a special-interest group for contractors in New South Wales, indicating that the IT specialists took the new union seriously.

But innovative union use of the Internet goes beyond the high-tech sector. The National Writers Union (NWU; www.nwu.org), which is part of the United Automobile Workers, has organized some 7,000 freelance writers, for whom it provides information and generic assistance via the Web. The writers are spread out around the country and across the world, so the union almost has to deliver services to them via the Internet. The NWU views its Web site as the "cyberspace equivalent of the union hall where members (and prospective members) can find the information they need and conduct union business." In addition to constantly updating its Web site, which averaged some 125,000 page views a month in early 2001, the NWU e-mails the entire membership several times a month. The site includes a Web-maintained national job hotline that lists freelance writing projects for which members can apply. In 2001, the NWU won a U.S. Supreme Court case on copyrights of written material on the Web against the *New York Times.*[10]

Workers in many of these settings are unlikely to gain a collective contract, and some have no such long-run goal. But unions that become permanent fixtures in their company or occupation can affect the way the companies treat those workers. They can also be tied to unions with majority collective bargaining status, perhaps organized at the same employer. The CWA developed Workers at GE (WAGE; www.geworkersunited.org) for workers not covered by collective bargaining at General Electric (GE), in part by linking them to the minority of GE's national workforce that is under a collective bargaining contract. This shows the natural links between an ongoing union-organizing drive and the extension of the reach of that drive through new services and networking to unorganized workers, supported by the established core of union workers under contract. WAGE invites GE workers from around the world to "join us in building worker power at this mammoth corporation" and offers them online ability to sign on as members. On the geographic front, King County Labor Council in Seattle (www.kclc.org) developed a Web site that increasingly functions as a broader community means of communication around political programs, organizing, and other activities; Progressive Wisconsin (www.progressivewisconsin.org) extends the bounds of traditional union activity to embrace a wider community; and many central labor committees and community groups also use the Web to strengthen local area linkages among workers and groups. By bringing different pro-labor groups together, these organizations represent the extension that characterizes open-source unionism.

In disputes with management, many unions now use the Internet to present their case to members, businesses, and the general public. In the 2001 communication workers' strike against Verizon, the union posted daily bargaining updates on its Web site, with access restricted to members. Other unions have used the Internet to organize wider protests to help workers in disputes in particular localities. In the 2000 Steelworkers' strike in North Carolina against German-owned Continental General Tire, the union provided information to activists around the United States via Internet postings that led the activists to pressure tire distributors and purchasers of Continental products, including Wal-Mart and Ford. Some 80 to 100 Internet postcards were sent to the headquarters in Germany. Changing the locus of the dispute from one of the least union-friendly states in the United States to the wider world helped the union win its dispute. In the 2000 strike by the Society of Professional Engineering Employees at Boeing, one of the largest white-collar strikes in U.S. history, the union used its Web page to keep members alert to the latest twists and turns of the negotiations.

In the organizing area, the NWU is far from the only union that conducts organizing campaigns over the Web and that enrolls members online. The United Food and Commercial Workers describes its site (www.walmart workerslv.com) as follows: "Although we do print publications as well, we've found most of our members use the Internet and enjoy this medium. They have learned about the process and keep up-to-date on current Wal-Mart activities online. It's also a vehicle for the community to see how our campaign is running and what we're really up against so that Wal-Mart Corporate is not the only one talking." The Hotel and Restaurant Employees Union site (www.eyesonsodexho.com) provides data on Sodexho-Marriot's record in food safety and labor relations that will help gain community support in any organizing drive.

These examples are just the tip of an iceberg of what innovative unions, union activists, and union-associated groups are doing in the early twenty-first century. They show that some unions are moving in the direction of open-source unionism and using the Internet to mobilize and organize workers, labor, and broader communities and to deliver union services that did not exist even a few years ago. While no single union has put all the pieces together to create the full-fledged new form, the picture of that form that I have laid out is grounded in reality.

The AFL-CIO and Enron

The 2002 Enron scandal in the United States galvanized the AFL-CIO into a set of actions that fits well the open-source union form, save in one critical respect. A brief review of what the AFL-CIO did highlights the way unions can aid workers, absent collective bargaining and the seemingly small step needed to create the new form.

To begin with, the top officials of the federation and constituent union presidents were among the most outspoken supporters of Enron's laid-off nonunion employees. They spent money and staff resources on behalf of these workers. Supported by the federation, the Harris County (Houston, Texas, the headquarters of Enron) central labor council provided direct support to former Enron employees. The AFL-CIO paid for lawyers to fight for a larger severance package for the workers; organized a public campaign to support this action; pressured other companies to remove from their boards members of the Enron board; and lobbied Congress to change its laws to protect employees with 401k monies.

Since neither the AFL-CIO nor any constituent union had a collective bargaining contract for the laid-off workers, the union campaign was based on providing information, galvanizing community action, and giving legal support to the workers. The federation provided a highly informative Web site on the Enron situation (www.aflcio.org/enron/connections.htm). It called on its membership countrywide to support the Enron workers by leafleting creditor banks in cities throughout the country and sending more than 55,000 faxes and phone calls to creditor committees and Enron executives. Its legal staff submitted petitions to the Securities and Exchange Commission to tighten its rules and investigate diverse aspects of the Enron disaster. All this for a group of workers who were not organizable when they were employed and who were not union targets once they were laid off.

The AFL-CIO campaign had some notable success. In June 2002, former Enron employees and their court-appointed Employee Committee reached an agreement with the firm that increased the amount of severance pay going to the workers by an estimated $34 million. In addition, the AFL-CIO pressured and shamed other companies where the directors at Enron sat on the board to the extent that these men resigned directorships at other firms and institutions, including Harvard University.

The one thing that separates the AFL-CIO effort from open-source unionism is that the federation did not have any place in the union movement for the many former Enron workers that it was helping, much less for the millions of other workers around the country troubled over the safety of their retirement moneys or jobs due to top management malfeasance or criminal behavior. The federation could not enroll the workers it supported as members, not because they would refuse to join, but because they were not in a majority-status collective bargaining situation! Open-source unionism would say to these workers, "We have helped you, we will help you and workers like you in the future. Join our movement. There is a place (at nominal dues) for laid-off workers and others without collective contracts in the house of labor."

How Many Open-Source Members?

A key question about any new union form is whether it would attract a sufficient number of workers to be viable and to be able to influence labor outcomes.

There is evidence that many nonorganized workers want unions or union services at their workplace, but no one to my knowledge has examined whether workers would be attracted to a union that would deliver much of its services through the Internet. The *What Workers Want* survey that Joel Rogers and I developed in 1999 shows that the vast majority of nonorganized workers want some organization speaking to their everyday concerns at work, ranging from unions to workplace committees of various forms. Our estimate was that 32 percent of nonunion nonsupervisory workers would vote for a trade union in an NLRB election if it was the only option available. In a split sample design, we found that 20 percent of workers favored a union over other forms of representation or participation, while 29 percent favored "employee organizations that negotiate or bargain with management"—a union without the appellation. The majority of employees preferred joint committees that met with management, with most wanting those committees to be independent of management. A 1999 AFL-CIO–sponsored Hart survey shows that a larger proportion (43 percent) would vote union in an NLRB in that year (www.aflcio.org/labor99/am_attitude.htm), suggesting that our study of workers' demands for greater representation and participation may underestimate the desire for unions. But whether these workers would respond positively to an organization with the characteristics of an open-source union, we cannot say.

Still, extrapolating from the *What Workers Want* survey, I believe that a sizable number of workers would find such an organization attractive. The representation gap in American workplaces extends beyond the "bread and butter" issues of pay and benefits to better enforcement of statutory rights, more control and say in the organization of work and use of new technology, better access to training or other career assistance, and better information on the company, among other concerns on which an open-source union could be particularly helpful. Applying the *What Workers Want* estimates to the 2001 workforce, about 42 million workers want an organization with elected representatives and arbitration of disputes with management; while an equal number want an organization focused on information, career assistance, or consultation with management. Even if an open-source union could not gain these two groups of workers all that they would want, if just 1 percent elected to join such an organization at nominal dues, private-sector unions would have their greatest organizing success since the 1940s; if 5 percent joined, union density would rise by nearly 50 percent!

Going beyond surveys, consider the number of workers who contact unions, vote for union representation in NLRB elections that unions lose, or report favorable past experience with unions, even though they now hold a nonunion job. Today, these pro-union workers disappear almost entirely from membership. In the private sector, there are approximately twice as many past union members as present ones. These former members are modestly more inclined than other nonunion workers to say they would "vote union tomorrow" if given a chance. Thirty-eight percent report their past experience with unions as "very good" (14 percent) or "good" (24 percent).[11] That there are two-thirds as many former members (excluding retirees) who had good or very good experiences with unions as there are current members cries out for unions to develop a place for former members in the house of labor.

These calculations are suggestive at best. When push comes to shove, perhaps all the workers who say they want some form of union representation or services would reject joining an explicit organization; perhaps all the satisfied members going to nonunion jobs would not want any link to the union that represented them. But since it only takes a small proportion of these groups to increase greatly the reach of trade unions, unions cannot afford to simply neglect them. What is needed is for some union to build on the cutting-edge examples given earlier to see if it could sign up workers in a failed organizing drive or sign up workers whom organizers would normally turn away because of the low probability of being able to attain a majority-status collective bargaining contract. The AFL-CIO or some affiliates ought to experiment with developing some way the former Enron employees and their peers throughout the United States could attach themselves to the union movement—at minimal cost.

Can Unions Beat the Competition?

As anyone who surfs the Internet knows, there are many Web sites that provide information about jobs and the world of work at no cost to workers. Internet recruitment firms such as Monster.com or Hotjobs.com offer career advice to workers as well as listings of jobs. Government Web sites contain information on laws and workplace issues, and will increasingly become the medium for disseminating information via "e-government." Labor law firms have FAQs on legal issues in the hope of attracting clients. Nonprofit groups provide information and advice on labor matters as on other aspects of life. Particular groups of workers or human rights activists concerned with worker problems use the Web and other forms of communication to provide advice and assistance to affected parties. The anti-sweatshop movement in particular has organized campaigns that go from the Internet to the streets. And many of the Web sites of these groups are more attractive than those of trade unions.

But unions have a comparative advantage for helping workers with labor problems. As representatives of workers, unions have greater credibility than commercial interests, the state, or other groups in informing workers about what is happening at their workplace and in the labor market at large. Members trust their union in ways they would not trust other organizations. In the Web world, where firms pay millions to develop a brand, unions already have the high visibility and network gains that come from that. In addition, unions have the expertise to advise and lead workers about how to handle problems through collective action—to conduct campaigns against employers, the state, or whomever. And unions have a bricks-and-mortar reality—live members who would benefit from exchanging information and experiences. Unions are better suited to combine the human network with the digital network, to provide representation as well as information, than commercial sites or nonprofit or government sites. No other organization in the United States could have carried out the campaign for the Enron workers that the AFL-CIO did.

The biggest barrier to unions developing a new open-source union form is not external. It is internal. Moving to a new union form will likely require unions to make sweeping organizational changes that shift internal incentives and power relations and to adopt different political and organizing strategies. Whether existing unions are up for such change, or would survive it in a recognizable form, is an open question (see Voss and Sherman 2000). Unions that choose to experiment with open-source unionism, or any comparable innovative way to engage workers in nontraditional settings, will have to fully integrate these workers into the membership status and representational routine of a broader labor movement. They will have to learn to accept younger and less orthodox people as major players in labor's affairs without destabilizing their bureaucracies. Just as the AFL unions refused to accept industrial unionism in the 1930s until the CIO forced this on them, it could take some major struggle inside the union movement to impel unions to respond to the challenge of developing services and membership for workers outside of collective bargaining. Alternatively, perhaps the arguments in this chapter and the innovative activities at some unions that others and I are beginning to study will strike a chord with union leaders en masse and produce the kind of experimentation that could set the stage for a new union spurt.

Conclusion

As U.S. unionism continues on its downward trajectory, the study of unionism has been moving from the province of labor and industrial relations experts into the hands of paleontologists. Economists, who stress the benefits that unions give to workers, society, and to some firms, find this pattern disheartening or sad. Economists, who stress the costs that unions bring to firms, society, and to some workers, take heart at this pattern. In both cases, however, there is a widespread feeling that unionism is heading toward extinction outside the public sector and a few private-sector ghettos.

I reject this consensual view of the likely future for unions. With the Internet offering great opportunities to deliver services to workers who otherwise cannot gain collective bargaining at their workplace and permitting the development of new organizational forms, I expect unions to morph into something akin to the open-source union form described herein. If unions fail to take advantage of new technologies, I expect that some nontraditional worker organization will replace them by successfully adapting the open-source union form. Whether adopted by organized labor or other worker-based institutions, the new technologies and forms will strengthen the voice and face of union or union-like organizations and improve the potential contribution these groups can make to capitalist economies. Thus, I expect that the study of unionism in the twenty-first century will be more social science than paleontology. The key papers will be entitled: "Union Morphing in Cyberspace" or "The Mutation of Worker Organizations" not "Why Did Unions Go Extinct?"

Notes

Parts of this chapter are based on work done with Joel Rogers and parts on work done with Wayne J. Diamond, as referenced. I have benefited from comments by Larry Kahn and discussions at the Centre for Economic Performance (CEP) Trades Union Congress on "Unions and the Internet," May 2001.

1. See www.trinity.edu/bhirsch/Monthly%20Labor%20Review%20Article.htm (accessed August 12, 2002), and see also Hirsch et al. (2001).

2. The decline in the private sector from 1996 to 2001 was just 1.2 percentage points compared to 1.7 percentage points from 1991 to 1996. But many factors affect the change in union density, and the rate of decline was already leveling off in the early 1990s compared to the 1980s.

3. The largest such affiliations that year came from the California State Employees Association (175,000) and the United American Nurses (100,000).

4. Voos's (1983) estimates vary depending on her model. Average costs were $729 in 1967 dollars. Her marginal cost figures range from $176 to $579 in 1967 dollars. This translates into a range of $933 to $3,100 in 2001 dollars. Taking the midpoint and rounding, I use $2,000 as my estimate of the marginal cost of gaining a new member with a collective bargaining contract.

5. Organizing at this scale would likely change the cost rules, but the direction of that is unclear. On the one hand, economies of scale could reduce per new-member costs. On the other hand, the likely antiunion management campaign that such an effort would stimulate might easily raise the per capita costs. In any case, the money needed vastly exceeds what is currently being spent or that unions as a whole show any intention of spending.

6. But you can label it whatever you wish. Osterman et al. (2001) call a new union movement with some similarity to what Freeman and Rogers describe as "extended unionism."

7. Summers (1990) thinks that contrary understanding or practice has gone on long enough that explicit statutory amendment is required to clarify this right. Morris (2003), while welcoming NLRB clarification of it, emphatically disagrees on any need for such amendment.

8. For detailed discussion, see Diamond and Freeman (2001). See also reports on and proceedings from the May 2001 conference, jointly sponsored by the Harvard Trade Union Program, the London School of Economics, and the British Trades Union Congress on "Unions and the Internet," www.trinity.edu/bhirsch/Monthly%20 Labor%20 Review%20Article.htm (accessed August 12, 2002).

9. See Guyer (2001).

10. See Hartford (2001).

11. The majority of former members viewed their experience as mixed, while 13 percent described it as bad and 12 percent as very bad (Freeman and Rogers 1999, 74). In our 1994–95 survey, there were 1.45 times as many former members as members, but since then, private-sector density has fallen from 10.9 percent to 9 percent, which would raise the number of former members and lower the number of members. Our estimate is a crude one.

References

Diamond, Wayne J., and Richard B. Freeman. 2001. "Will Unionism Prosper in Cyber-Space? The Promise of the Internet for Employee Organization." Working Paper, no. 8483. Cambridge, MA: National Bureau of Economic Research, www.nber.org/papers/w8483.

Freeman, Richard B. 1998. "Spurts in Union Growth: Defining Moments and Social Processes." In *The Defining Moment: The Great Depression and the American Economy in the Twentieth Century*, ed. Michael Bordo, Claudia Goldin, and Eugene White, 265–295. Chicago: University of Chicago Press.

Freeman, Richard B., and Joel Rogers. 1999. *What Workers Want*. Ithaca, NY: Cornell University Press.

———. 2002a. "A Proposal to American Labor: Let's Create 'Open-Source Unions,' and Welcome Millions into the Movement." *The Nation* 274 (June 24): 18–21.

———. 2002b. "Open Source Unionism: Beyond Exclusive Collective Bargaining." *WorkingUSA* 5 (Spring): 8–40.

Guyer, Linda. 2001. "Real World Experiences of Online Organizing." Unions and the Internet Conference (May), www.allianceibm.org.

Hartford, Bruce. 2001. "Riding the Internet." Unions and the Internet Conference (May), www.allianceibm.org.

Hirsch, Barry T., David A. Macpherson, and Wayne G. Vroman. 2001 "Estimates of Union Density by State, 1964–2002." *Monthly Labor Review* 124, no. 7 (July): 51–55.

Morris, Charles J. 2003. "Returning Members-Only Collective Bargaining to the American Workplace." *Industrial Relations Research Association Proceedings of the 55th Annual Meeting*, January 3–5, Washington, DC: 165–176.

Osterman, Paul, Thomas A. Kochan, Richard M. Locke, and Michael Piore. 2001. *Working in America: A Blueprint for the New Labor Market*. Cambridge: MIT Press.

Summers, Clyde. 1990. "Unions Without Majority—A Black Hole?" *Chicago-Kent Law Review* 66: 531–548.

Taras, Daphne, and A. Gesser. 2003. "How New Lawyers Use E-Voice to Drive Firm Compensation: The 'Greedy Associates' Phenomenon." *Journal of Labor Research* 24 (Winter): 9–29.

Trades Union Congress. 2001. *Reaching the Missing Millions: Report of TUC's Promoting Trade Unionism Task Group*. London: Trades Union Congress.

Voos, Paula. 1983. "Union Organizing: Costs and Benefits." *Industrial and Labor Relations Review* 36 (July): 576–591.

Voss, Kim, and Rachel Sherman. 2000. "Breaking the Iron Law of Oligarchy: Union Revitalization in the American Labor Movement." *American Journal of Sociology* 106 (September): 303–349.

2

Justice for Janitors in Los Angeles and Beyond

A New Form of Unionism in the Twenty-first Century?

*Christopher L. Erickson, Catherine Fisk,
Ruth Milkman, Daniel J.B. Mitchell, and
Kent Wong*

The decline of unionization in the United States is a well-known fact of the labor market.[1] In 1980, the union representation rate stood at 25.7 percent. By 2001, it had fallen to 14.8 percent. The drop over that twenty-one-year period was concentrated almost exclusively in the private sector. Simple analysis suggests this loss was not just the product of industrial restructuring of the U.S. workforce. Had all major industry groups simply retained their 1980 unionization rates, only about one-fourth of the drop would have occurred.[2] Thus, other explanatory forces were at work.

Even before the 1980s, downward pressure on unionization was apparent. Although consistent data are not available, union membership stood at about 35 percent of the workforce as of the mid-1950s.[3] Because union-represented workers are more likely to be full time and higher paid than average, collective bargaining may have directly determined over 40 percent of the private national labor compensation bill at that time (Jacoby and Mitchell 1988).[4] Unions and their activities were important concerns of public policy makers. Their wage-setting activities were the de facto focus of the anti-inflation wage-price guidelines and controls of the 1960s and 1970s. Unions were seen as key determinants of macroeconomic outcomes. As late as 1978, a high official in the Jimmy Carter wage-price guidelines program cited an upcoming Teamsters settlement as an important target of government policy (Rowan 1978).

But by the mid-1990s, public interest in union wage setting had diminished to the point that the U.S. Bureau of Labor Statistics discontinued data collection related to union settlements. Predictions of continued union decline became common in the academic literature (Troy 1999). And slippage of foreign unionization rates—especially in the 1980s and beyond—indicated that the malady afflicting U.S. unions was international in scope, suggesting that "globalism" might be a causal factor (Organization for Economic Cooperation and Development 1994; International Labor Office 1997). Generally, formality and long-term employment relationships—often characteristic of union contractual relations with employers—seemed under attack worldwide.

The union decline story was also partially linked to the broader literature on increased wage and income inequality. There is no general consensus on the degree to which international trade has contributed to downward pressure on wages of unskilled and lesser-educated workers in the United States. But there is a widespread view that at least some part of the growth in wage inequality can be attributed to trade (Katz and Murphy 1991; Levy and Murname 1992). Indeed, trade theory—the standard Heckscher-Ohlin model—suggests that the workforces of different countries are placed in indirect competition with one another through world product markets. The U.S. trade deficit—as opposed to generic trade—may also play a role by weakening worker bargaining power in the manufacturing sector, where much of the trade deficit occurs (Freeman 1995; Erickson and Mitchell 1998). More generally, downward pressure on wages and weakened union bargaining positions could contribute to union representation loss as unionized employers lost market share—or tried to become nonunion—and as nonunion employers sought to retain their status as unilateral determiners of wages and conditions. Yet, unionization of low-wage employees with some exceptions (e.g., Freeman 1991b) has not been much discussed as a response. Policy discussions have tended to focus on minimum wages, "living wage" laws, and income redistribution through the tax system.

Given this gloomy background for labor unions, it might be assumed that there is little hope for expanded unionization—especially in the private sector. Yet, the story that follows is in fact a union success story in a seemingly unlikely setting. California has generally experienced a greater growth of wage inequality than the rest of the United States (Reed 1999). Southern California in particular has been recipient of substantial low-wage immigration, legal and illegal and heavily Latino in origin. In 1990, Latinos accounted for 38 percent of the population of Los Angeles County. In 2000, the figure was about 45 percent.[5] The unionizing of a heavily immigrant workforce poses several problems. Other things being equal, a large low-wage labor inflow can be expected to put downward pressure on unskilled wages. In addition, immigrants may be hard to unionize due to lack of English-language ability, fear of immigration authorities, high turnover rates characteristic of low-wage employment, and lack of permanent roots in the United States. The last two factors may discourage worker "investment" in unionization and its longer-run payoff of higher future earnings streams and other benefits. Someone not expecting to be on the job for a long period might well be reluctant to undertake the risks inherent in participating in union organizing.

Janitorial labor in Los Angeles—the topic of this chapter—places still more burdens on potential union organizers. Janitors are employed in small groups scattered around the metropolitan area. They are thus difficult to reach, unlike—say—workers at a large manufacturing plant. Cleaning service firms, as will be noted in more detail later on, are labor-intensive operations. Labor is a larger portion of total costs in such firms compared to many other industries, a classic cause of high labor demand elasticity.[6] Cleaning services are under short-term contracts with building owners and managers; they can be quickly replaced should labor costs cause them to bid uncompetitive prices.

In the Los Angeles area in particular, unionized cleaning service firms either gave way to nonunion competitors in the 1980s or became nonunion themselves through "double-breasted" subsidiaries. An attempt to reunionize those janitors might have seemed a lost cause from the outset. Yet, Los Angeles janitors were reunionized through a combination of unconventional tactics that have been further developed over time and that have spread to other urban areas. Beyond that accomplishment, the union involved—the Service Employees International Union (SEIU)—has become the largest union in the American Federation of Labor and Congress of Industrial Organization (AFL-CIO) and the second largest union in the United States.[7] Its Justice for Janitors (JfJ) tactics were the centerpiece of *Bread and Roses,* a full-length motion picture that played around the country in 2000.[8] In something of a palace coup, the former president of the SEIU became head of the AFL-CIO, in part on the strength of the JfJ campaign in Los Angeles. One concrete change that occurred thereafter was a shift in official AFL-CIO policy away from an anti-immigration stance. Another was encouragement of greater allocation of resources toward new union organizing.

If a new model of private-sector union organizing is emerging, the SEIU and its JfJ campaign is an obvious candidate. In what follows, we describe the evolution of the campaign, factors and tactics that appeared to contribute to its success, and issues of its robustness in the face of the business cycle. Although there has been research on the impact of federal labor legislation in the United States compared to that of other countries (Freeman 1991b), our story suggests that state law, too, can play a significant role in organizing and bargaining outcomes.

Background

The SEIU began as the Building Service Employees International Union (BSEIU) in 1921, consolidating preexisting unions in Chicago and elsewhere (Jentz 1997). Los Angeles, in sharp contrast to San Francisco, was long known as an antiunion city. But unionization began to develop in Los Angeles in the 1930s, as in the rest of the country. The wartime boom of employment in military-related industries during World War II fostered still more unionization and helped make organized labor a major political force. Thus, when the BSEIU entered the city and began organizing janitors, it faced less management resistance than would have been seen prior to the Great Depression. In addition, it had potential allies in other unions and in the political arena. Faced with growing unionization in a broad range of industries and occupations, employers were more willing to accept union demands for recognition than would have been the case earlier.

Local 399, the chief BSEIU branch in Los Angeles, had 5,000 members in 1950, 7,000 in 1955, and 11,000 in 1960. By 1959, Local 399 was the second largest local in the entire BSEIU. During this period, the union began to expand beyond building service workers, organizing in the public sector as well as among health care workers. By 1960, the BSEIU had 20,000 members in the Los Angeles area, over a third of them on government payrolls (Beadling et al. 1992, 21, 34, 43; Building Service Employees International Union [BSEIU], *Proceedings,* 1950, 10; 1955, 133; 1960, 190; BSEIU, *Report to Locals,* November 1950, 2).

About a third of the city's large office buildings were unionized by the early 1950s. Most building owners at the time hired janitors and other service employees directly, rather than using outside contractors. In 1956, a management survey found that 72 percent of the city's office cleaners, 88 percent of its elevator operators, and 93 percent of its watchmen were directly employed by building owners (BSEIU, *Report to Locals,* June 1956, 2). However, the BSEIU organized many of Los Angeles's large-scale janitorial contractors, mainly those that were profitable enough to make concessions (Mines and Avina 1992, 435).

Los Angeles BSEIU members benefited substantially from union representation. Janitorial work often had been part time. But the union successfully pressed to transform jobs into full-time positions (Mines and Avina 1992, 436). Pay was raised and by the mid-1950s health and welfare plans had become standard benefits for BSEIU members. For some workers, pension plans were added as well (BSEIU, *Proceedings,* 1955, 134). However, pay remained higher in New York, Chicago, and San Francisco, where union coverage in building services was more extensive (BSEIU, *Report to Locals,* October 1955, 2–3). African Americans were the center of janitorial unionization at the time. In 1950, half the members of Los Angeles's main janitorial local were African American; another 9 percent were Mexican (Greer 1959, 175).

Developments in the 1980s

Janitorial membership in Local 399 peaked at about 5,000 in 1978; total compensation in the union sector rose to $12 an hour by 1982, compared to $4 in the nonunion buildings. During the 1980s, Los Angeles experienced an office construction boom, particularly in the central city area. Tax breaks and foreign investment (especially Japanese) played an important role in downtown development. Other things being equal, the building boom should have been favorable to the unionization of janitorial workers since it created more demand for cleaning personnel in the new office complexes. But in fact the 1980s were a period of deunionization of Los Angeles's building services. By 1985, Local 399's janitorial membership in Los Angeles fell to 1,800.

As with other economic phenomena, the causes of union decline can be decomposed into demand and supply influences. There were changes in employer structure in the industry (demand) and changes in the workforce (supply). Outsourcing of building services by owners and managers to contractors had become the general rule, in Los Angeles and elsewhere.[9] Cleaning labor costs as a fraction of total building operating costs are small.[10] But *direct* labor expenses are a major element of the cleaning services themselves. As Figure 2.1 shows, for the smallest cleaning service firms in 2000, such costs absorbed about 50 percent of total revenue; for the largest, 69 percent. The positive correlation with size is due to the spread of overhead expenses (administration, marketing, and so on) over a larger volume of sales for the bigger firms.[11] Note that such economies of scale are conducive to competitive advantage of large firms. As will be noted, there are also other factors that tilt competitive advantage toward larger firms—an important element in the JfJ campaign.

Contracts between building owners or managers and their cleaning services are written to permit short notice of termination, typically thirty days. Thus, union members can lose work almost overnight if a building owner or manager switches from a union to a nonunion cleaning service. SEIU Local 399's past ability to improve or maintain conditions and compensation relative to lower nonunion standards provided an incentive for cleaning contrac-

Figure 2.1 **Direct Labor Expenses as a Percent of Revenue, 2000**

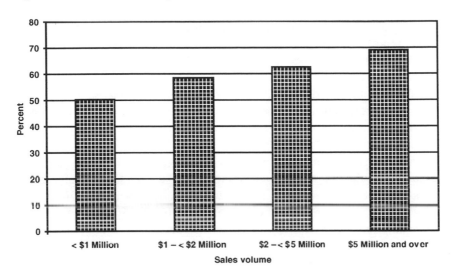

tors to explore nonunion options by the early 1980s. The unionized part of the industry made up of the larger buildings—was put under particular cost pressure, as building owners and managers sought cheaper cleaning services. The big cleaning service operators, as noted earlier, enjoy advantages of economies of scale by spreading overhead. But once a firm meets a certain size/asset threshold (needed to cover payroll and insurance costs), there are few additional incremental economies of scale, and none on the labor side. It is hard to pass wage increases to building owners and managers in a fiercely competitive industry.

The last Los Angeles master union agreement before the JfJ campaign sparked a union revival which was signed by SEIU Local 399 in 1983. Shortly thereafter, all increases in wages and benefits were frozen in response to the slide toward nonunion building services. The union agreed to a proliferation of concession side agreements. Only the downtown retained a unionized workforce of significant proportions. But even there, union ranks barely attained 30 percent of the major buildings. Countywide, less than one janitor in ten was a member of the union. The union's local leadership saw the janitorial labor market as a lost cause and focused on health care. While it would not abandon the janitors it had, Local 399's leadership did not favor mounting a major effort to reorganize those it lost. About 38 percent of downtown Los Angeles's office space as of the end of 2000 was built during the 1979–88 period.[12] But this building boom, with its derived growth in demand for janitors, did not seem to present a feasible organizing target.

The JfJ Campaign in Los Angeles

The JfJ campaign in Los Angeles began in the downtown area in the hands of union representatives who were placed by the national SEIU into the reluctant local. These implants had to deal with both representing the atrophied union base of janitors and organizing janitors in nearby nonunion buildings. Their plan entailed targeting the nonunion wings of "double-breasted" cleaning service companies and other nonunion operators, while continuing concessions for those contractors that remained unionized. Gradually, a variety of unorthodox tactics were adopted.

JfJ tactics aim at building owners and managers, even though the formal employer of the janitors is the cleaning service contractor. The object is to pressure owners or managers to use union contractors paying union-scale wages. Direct pressure on the contractors was not effective, since they could be readily replaced by lower-cost nonunion contractors, even if they should agree to union representation and terms. The approach to organizing ensconced in labor law—a National Labor Relations Board (NLRB) election held for workers of the formal employer—became infeasible once building services were detached from owners and managers through contracting. But if owners and managers were persuaded to use only unionized contractors, the barrier to the union would be removed. A reserved market for union contractors would be created by agreement.

Industry Concentration in Cleaning Services

Even if there were a reserved market, organizing one cleaning service at a time would appear to be impractical, given the many cleaning services that operate in Los Angeles. What makes the strategy work is the surprising fact that only a few contractors have large numbers of janitors in their employ. The capital costs of operating in building services are low—essentially acquisition of vacuum cleaners and waxing machines—so entrance to the industry is technically easy. However, the industry is surprisingly concentrated in the submarket that exists for major buildings and complexes. In the mid-1990s, the two largest firms—American Building Maintenance (ABM) and International Service Systems (ISS)—accounted for over a fourth of all janitorial employment in the Los Angeles area; the top twenty-one firms accounted for over a third, and the proportion was much higher if only janitors at major "Class A" buildings are included. In the large building submarket, ABM and ISS were the major players.

As noted earlier, there appear to be certain economies of scale in the cleaning service industry related to fixed administrative overhead. However, the chief reason for the high concentration is "trust." Cleaning service personnel are given the keys at night to buildings containing valuable equipment (and valuable tenants who would be upset if their equipment disappeared or was damaged). Mom and pop operators cannot necessarily be trusted to do the cleaning while also preventing theft or damage. Owners and managers of major complexes want to entrust their buildings to firms with a reputation for proper service that will keep tenants pleased.[13] And since such owners and managers often have properties in more than one city—even more than one country—they look for building service firms that they have dealt with satisfactorily elsewhere. The union reasoned that if agreement could be obtained from ABM and ISS, other smaller contractors would follow and Los Angeles's major office centers could be reunionized.

Turning Point: Century City

By April 1989, Local 399 had negotiated a new master agreement, the first in downtown Los Angeles since the early 1980s. In the summer of 1989, the campaign's focus shifted to Century City, a large Westside office complex, employing 400 janitors, of whom about half were employed by ISS. The union marshaled a variety of tactics to put pressure on ISS. As it had done downtown earlier on, the JfJ staged various "in your face" public relations stunts to draw the attention of Century City building tenants to the janitors' economic plight. Tenants complained to building managers about JfJ activities, but also expressed sympathy for the janitors. By the end of the 1980s, the issue of wage inequality and the situation of the working poor was already becoming salient in the Los Angeles area. Tenant complaints and sympathies intensified pressure on ISS.

In late spring 1990, the union decided to stage a strike. On June 15, 1990, Los Angeles police attacked a peaceful march of JfJ strikers and supporters as they walked from adjacent Beverly Hills to Century City. With the media spotlight on Century City (and recorded on videotape), police charged the crowd, injuring many participants, including children and pregnant women. By the late 1980s, Los Angeles had become a politically liberal city. Public outrage at the televised police attack brought local politicians into the janitors' dispute, including Mayor Tom Bradley. In New York City, after seeing a video of police beating strikers, Gus Bevona, the powerful president of SEIU Local 32B-32J (who was facing a significant dissident movement in his local at the time), took action. Previously, he had been unwilling to pressure ISS, which was unionized in New York. Bevona reportedly called the president of ISS into his office and insisted that a deal for Los Angeles be reached.[14] The Los Angeles contract with ISS was signed on that day and later extended to ABM and other cleaning services.

Secondary Boycott Issues

One of the most important legal obstacles to organizing and economic pressure for janitors is the federal labor law's prohibition on secondary boycotts. Federal labor law in principle protects the rights of workers to use strikes and picketing to pressure their own employer; for janitors, this is the cleaning contractor. But it prohibits the use of pressure against any other business for the purpose of inducing it to cease doing business with the employees' employer. This prohibition on secondary pressure is an acute problem for janitors for two reasons. First, janitors work in office buildings where there are a number of employers. Protests outside the building may be deemed to put pressure against employers other than the janitors' own. Second, building owners and managers might be deemed to be secondary employers. This is the more critical problem.

While the NLRB, contractors, owners, and unions have litigated relatively few JfJ secondary boycott cases all the way to a final decision, many secondary boycott charges have been filed (most were settled).[15] In a 1993 ruling on the permissibility of JfJ tactics in San Francisco, the NLRB decided that picketing outside the office buildings in which nonunion firms had been hired to replace unionized janitors was an illegal secondary boycott (*West Bay Building Maintenance Company,* 312 NLRB, 1993, 715). However, learning by doing has occurred and, as will be explained later on, the union succeeded in remaining on the right side of the law in Los Angeles (including during the 2000 strike).

The First Contract

The contract with ISS resulting from Century City ran for 22 months and involved only 200 workers.[16] These workers averaged $4.50 an hour at the time the agreement was concluded. The first contract provided for a $0.30 increase or a wage of $5.20, whichever was greater. A second increase of $0.20 or $5.50 was scheduled for April 1991. By the time the second increase was due, the ISS contract was superseded in March 1991 by an extended three-year agreement also covering ABM's nonunion Bradford subsidiary.[17] This new contract covered 5,000 to 6,000 workers. It added dental and drug coverage to the health plan for those covered by that benefit and provided wage increases of $0.20 to $0.45 per hour in each of the three years, depending on location.

One notable aspect of the early contracts (the downtown master agreement negotiated in April 1989, and the ISS and ABM contracts negotiated after the Century City events) is that they allowed for a tiered wage/benefit structure. The highest wages and benefits covered the downtown and the Century City areas. As contract coverage moved away from the core areas to the Wilshire corridor, Santa Monica, Culver City, the South Bay, the San Fernando Valley, the San Gabriel Valley, and other outlying areas of Los Angeles County, lower wages and benefits were allowed. The lower tiers reflected the reality of stronger nonunion competition away from the core areas. However, this tiered wage/benefit structure—and the union's objective of wage/benefit parity across the region—became a major issue in later contract negotiations.

Even with tiers, the new contract settlements were hailed as a major victory for the Southern California labor movement and for immigrant unionism. When the new regime took over at the AFL-CIO in the mid-1990s, Los Angeles was seen as a model for unions in the rest of the United States.[18] All did not go smoothly for Local 399, however. Not long after the initial JfJ organizing victory, Local 399 broke into feuding factions. The division was partly along health care versus janitor lines and partly along ethnic lines; many of the original JfJ organizers were Anglos, albeit Spanish-speaking Anglos. Ultimately, the internal disputes became so severe that the national SEIU put Local 399 into trusteeship in 1995.[19] The janitors were separated from Local 399 and made part of Local 1877, a San Jose-based local for janitors in the Silicon Valley, Oakland, and Sacramento, which also utilizes JfJ tactics.

Immigrant-related issues are reflected in JfJ contracts with employers. Employers are obligated to notify the union by phone if an Immigration and Naturalization Service (INS) agent appears on or near the premises. Employers are forbidden to disclose information about employees to the INS unless required by law. Reinstatement to his or her job is required for an employee who is absent from work for up to seven days due to immigration proceedings. Employees who change their names or their Social Security numbers cannot be penalized. And there is a catch-all protection against discharge or discipline in the case of a worker absent from work for up to seven days due to circumstances beyond his or her control.

Round II: The Second Contract

At the time of the second round of contract negotiations in 1995, uncertainties existed for the outcome.[20] It was unclear as to whether the first successful round of contracts was sustainable or whether it was the result of a fluke. The Los Angeles economy was in a major slump with high vacancy rates prevailing in commercial office buildings. But total employment of janitors in Los Angeles County was about at the level it had attained in 1990. Rents for office space in Los Angeles County were beginning to recover after a four-year decline, but were still below 1990 levels. This economic factor was a wild card in the negotiations. On the one hand, it could be argued that building owners pinched by excess capacity would put pressure on cleaning contractors to hold down labor costs. But on the other hand, owners would not like to have their scarce tenants unnerved by demonstrations of angry janitors.

The identity of the building owners was changing. Buildings that had been bought or developed in the booming 1980s were not yielding the expected rates of return in the mid-1990s that would allow repayment of lenders. Foreign investors, especially Japanese, had paid inflated prices for Los Angeles real estate and were losing control of their properties to financial institutions (creditors). By 1997, only two major Japanese firms—Shuwa and Matsui—remained in Los Angeles County with eleven buildings. And they were trying to bail out. In contrast, by that time Met Life, John Hancock, and TIAA—all financial institutions—had seventeen buildings.[21] The new owners did not have the experience of dealing with the union in the first round. Would they be less sensitive to public pressure entailed in JfJ tactics?

As it turned out, the negotiations for the second contract went smoothly. The result was a five-year agreement—a duration longer than the typical union agreement. But the outcome of Round II raised new uncertainties for Round III, scheduled to take place in 2000. As Table 2.1 (see pp. 34–35) shows, the contract broke Los Angeles County down into various regions with different wage and benefit levels for each area. The more outlying geographical locations had lower wages and benefits specified than the core downtown/Century City area. Outlying areas tend to have smaller buildings, smaller owners, and smaller cleaning companies, competitive factors reflected in the pay differential. However, the Round II contract contained a significant element of backloading in the form of the addition of health insurance in early 2000, shortly before the contract expired. It also equalized pay in several noncore areas, effectively reducing the number of wage-differentiated regions to three, down from the prior six.

Health insurance probably added about $2 per hour in costs, a considerable percentage increase for janitors earning $6 to $7 per hour. Thus, a key complicating factor going into Round III of bargaining would be the recent bump up in labor costs preceding those negotiations. Would the management side be willing to accept new contract improvements in Round III, having just provided a significant benefit for many workers under the expiring Round II?

Background to Round III

As in Round II, the state of the real estate market and the identity of the building owners that would indirectly pay for any janitorial contract improvements had changed by 2000. The downtown office was built on corporate headquarters of companies such as ARCO and Security Pacific Bank that no longer existed thanks to mergers and acquisitions. On the other hand, areas of the Westside, such as Santa Monica, had become red hot centers of multimedia activity and dot.coms, as had other regional markets such as Burbank. The dot.com boom peaked coincidentally with the janitors' 2000 negotiations that took place before the tech bust. As a result, relatively high vacancy rates in the downtown area coexisted with a scarcity of space in the hot areas. On average, rents in Los Angeles County had risen 50 percent since 1995. But in an odd doughnut phenomenon, rental costs for downtown were reportedly one-third below average commercial rates for office space in the greater Los Angeles area. By 2000, cheaper downtown space was attracting spillover tenants priced out of the hot areas. Despite the slow market equilibration, the SEIU leadership had to be concerned with the move of office location away from the downtown core area and into nonunion Orange County.

New Ownership and New Employers

The buildings themselves were no longer in the hands of reluctant lenders—as was the case in Round II—but had been taken over by real estate investment trusts, partnerships, and similar institutions. The Japanese investors who had found themselves burned by the "irrational exuberance" of the 1980s were largely gone from the market. It was unclear how the new owners would react to the public pressure the janitors could bring. However, local politicians had become more sensitive to Latino interests as the Latino electorate increased in numbers.

The two big cleaning contractors in 2000 were the same as those in the prior two Los Angeles negotiations. ABM Janitorial Services, based in San Francisco, operates throughout the United States and in Canada. It is part of a still-larger enterprise providing other building services such as security, parking, and elevator repair. The parent company has 57,000 employees, over 40 percent unionized. ABM had been a relatively stable corporation throughout the 1990s. One Source, the former ISS, had a more complex history.

At the time of the first negotiation in the early 1990s, ISS was an autonomous arm of a Danish multinational parent that focused its attention on the European market. Autonomy, however, apparently led to financial "irregularities" by managers of the North American subsidiary from 1989

Table 2.1

Wages and Wage Adjustments Specified in 1995–2000 Maintenance Contractors Agreement: Cleaners

	4/1/95	9/1/95	4/1/96	9/1/96	4/1/97	4/1/98	4/1/99	2/1/00
Area 1								
Start	$6.80	$6.80	$6.80	$6.80	$6.80	$7.00	$7.20	$7.20
Minimum	$6.80	$6.80	$6.80	$6.80	$6.80	$7.00	$7.20	$7.20
Increase	$0.15	$0.00	$0.15	$0.00	$0.15	$0.25	$0.30	$0.00
Health	Yes	Yes	Yes	Yes	Yes	Yes	Yes	Yes
Pension	Yes	Yes	Yes	Yes	Yes	Yes	Yes	Yes
Area 2								
Start	$5.40	$5.40	$5.50	$5.50	$5.65	$5.90	$6.30	$6.30
Minimum	$5.60	$5.60	$5.80	$5.80	$6.00	$6.30	$6.80	$6.80
Increase	$0.20	$0.00	$0.20	$0.00	$0.20	$0.30	$0.50	$0.00
Health	LT Area 1	LT Area 1	LT Area 1	LT Area 1	LT Area 1	LT Area 1	LT Area 1	Yes
Pension	No	No	No	No	No	No	No	No
Area 2A								
Start	$4.70	$4.70	$4.85	$4.85	$5.10	$5.55	$6.05	$6.40
Minimum	$4.95	$4.95	$5.20	$5.20	$5.75	$6.30	$6.80	$6.80
Increase	$0.25	$0.00	$0.25	$0.00	$0.55	$0.55	$0.50	$0.00
Health	No	No	No	No	No	No	No	Yes
Pension	No	No	No	No	No	No	No	No
Area 3								
Start	$4.70	$4.70	$4.85	$4.85	$5.10	$5.55	$6.05	$6.40
Minimum	$4.90	$4.90	$5.10	$5.10	$5.55	$6.05	$6.40	$6.80
Increase	$0.20	$0.00	$0.20	$0.00	$0.45	$0.50	$0.35	$0.40
Health	No	No	No	No	No	No	No	Yes
Pension	No	No	No	No	No	No	No	No

Area 4							
Start	—	$4.45	$4.45	$4.75	$5.15	$5.65	$6.15
Minimum	—	$4.45	$4.75	$5.15	$5.65	$6.15	$6.80
Increase	$0.00	$0.20	$0.30	$0.40	$0.50	$0.50	$0.65
Health	No	No	No	No	No	No	Yes
Pension	No	No	No	No	No	No	No
Area 5							
Start	—	$4.50	$4.50	$4.65	$4.90	$5.20	$5.20
Minimum	—	$4.50	$4.75	$5.00	$5.30	$5.65	$5.65
Increase	$0.00	$0.25	$0.00	$0.25	$0.30	$0.35	$0.00
Health	No	No	No	No	No	No	No
Pension	No	No	No	No	No	No	No

Source: "Maintenance Control Agreement: April 1, 1995 through March 31, 2000." U.S. Department of Labor.

Notes: LT Area 1 = Health plan but less generous than Area 1.

Pension: Minimum of $.10 or continuation of contributions of $.33 or $.35.

Increase refers to existing employee receiving at or above minimum.

Area 1 = Downtown Los Angeles, Century City.

Area 2 = Wilshire Corridor, Beverly Hills, Los Angeles International Airport, Westwood.

Area 2A= Santa Monica, Culver City.

Area 3 = Pasadena, Hollywood, Long Beach, Glendale/Burbank, South Bay, City of Commerce.

Area 4 = Studio City/Sherman Oaks, Woodland Hills/West Valley.

Area 5 = Other areas of Los Angeles County.

to 1995, leading to unanticipated charges against income and the departure of ISS's chief financial officer. The Danish parent divested its problem in 1997, selling its subsidiary to a Montreal-based firm known as Aaxis on the condition that the ISS name be dropped. Aaxis was sold to BHI, a Belize-based multinational, in 1998. BHI merged with another firm, Carlisle Holdings, in 1999 to form Carlisle Holdings Limited. The three firms—Aaxis, BHI, and Carlisle—are all linked to Michael Ashcroft, a high-ranking official in the British Conservative Party and who was Belize's ambassador to the United Nations at one point.[22]

The new One Source enterprise operates in the United States and has 42,000 employees; Carlisle also operates in Britain, Ireland, and Belize. But while the operation of One Source is more opaque than ABM's because of the former's external ownership, both ABM and One Source are vulnerable to pressures by the SEIU in cities other than Los Angeles. Both ABM and Carlisle suffered drops in stock price at around the time of the 2000 strike in Los Angeles and other cities. However, ABM's price recovered while Carlisle's did not.

Round III: Political Conditions in Los Angeles

At the time the first contract was signed, the office of the mayor was held by Tom Bradley, a Democrat with ties to organized labor. Bradley was succeeded in 1993 by Richard Riordan, a Republican without those ties. The new mayor's reaction to the janitors' tactics was untested in the 1995 negotiations. Those negotiations went surprisingly smoothly and there was little call for mayoral involvement. However, by 2000 Riordan had developed amicable relations with Miguel Contreras, the executive secretary-treasurer of the Los Angeles County Federation of Labor.[23] Riordan also had close ties with the Catholic Church in Los Angeles and with Cardinal Roger M. Mahony in particular. Mahony had developed ties to organized labor in the Los Angeles area despite a dispute in the 1980s about unionization of Catholic cemetery workers. And the Church was, of course, sensitive to the growing representation of Latinos in its parishes. In a precursor of the 2000 janitorial negotiations, Mahony had played a role in settling a long and bitter dispute between the University of Southern California and its food service and janitorial workers in 1999.[24]

Mayor Riordan also had ties to influential developer Robert F. Maguire III.[25] Maguire has been involved in major projects in downtown Los Angeles. These include the seventy-three-story Library Tower (zapped by creatures from outer space in the 1996 film *Independence Day*), the Wells Fargo Center, and the Gas Company Tower. He has also been a player in Westside projects such as Playa Vista—a development with much involvement by Los

Angeles—and MGM Plaza in Santa Monica. Maguire, Mahony, and Riordan were all to play significant roles in the 2000 janitors' negotiation.

Round III: Legal Strategy

As noted earlier, the illegality of using economic pressure on any "neutral" employer—other than the janitors' own employer (the building services contractor)—is a serious obstacle to effective labor protest. In practice, however, the union designed the 2000 JfJ campaign in Los Angeles to ensure a maximum of publicity and political pressure, while minimizing potential liability under the secondary boycott laws. Indeed, the success of the JfJ campaign in Los Angeles was due, at least in part, to the union's care in planning its various protests.

Several features of this planning are important from the legal standpoint. First, in the weeks leading up to the 2000 strike, cleaning contractors had allegedly committed a variety of unfair labor practices, including threatening employees and refusing to bargain in good faith with the union. The union filed at least thirty unfair labor practice charges about the employers' prestrike conduct with the NLRB. These pending charges could help bolster the union's position that the strike was precipitated or prolonged by the employers' unfair labor practices. If the NLRB was to agree that the strike was to protest the unfair labor practices, the employers could not permanently replace the striking janitors. Thus, the filing of charges provided some assurance that the contractors could be forced to reinstate the striking janitors at the end of the strike.

Second, the union picketed at buildings only at night, when replacement workers were inside doing the cleaning that the union janitors were striking. This was necessary to avoid the charge that the janitors were pressuring other tenants, or the building owner, rather than their cleaning service employers who had hired replacement workers. Nightly picketing and protest marches through the streets of downtown became a regular feature of the strike.

Creative Street Theater in Round III

Limitations imposed by secondary boycott rules partially explain the creativity and unconventional nature of the JfJ protest tactics. The need to picket only at night and only at targeted buildings may have simplified the task of staffing and coordinating the picketing. Rather than rely on picketing at the workplace during the ordinary business hours (which might be an unlawful secondary boycott), the union chose to make its daytime protests in the form of marches across town and rallies in public spaces. These mass protests have the advantages of being protected speech under the U.S. Constitution, unlike labor picketing, which does not enjoy unqualified First Amendment protection. More important, the marches and rallies are more conspicuous than traditional picketing and likely to elicit media attention.

Round III: Management Perspective

Building service contractors considered the janitors' decision not to rely just on traditional strikes and picketing an important and successful strategic choice. Management disputed the union's claims about the success of the strike in keeping janitors out of the building. It was noted that, especially by the end of the strike, many unionized janitors were crossing the picket lines to go to work. But whether the strike remained strong and whether the picketing was effective was not determinative. Much of the union's negotiating leverage came from the strong public sentiment supporting the janitors' efforts, rather than from preventing buildings from being cleaned.

Building owners chose not to insulate themselves from involvement in, or responsibility for, the janitors' working conditions. They participated directly in the negotiations and evidently wanted to have a direct relationship with the union (since they would ultimately pay for the labor cost outcome). The owners' involvement had the legal consequence of making it difficult for them to assert that pressure against them was a secondary boycott.[26]

Support from Other Unions in Round III

Union leaders we interviewed attributed some of the success of the strike to the support they gained from other unions, including those of elevator repair workers, painters, carpenters, garbage collectors, and United Parcel Service drivers. The building owners or cleaning contractors made efforts in the first two days of the strike to establish separate gates for replacement janitors. These gates were designed to preclude picketing at other entrances and thus make it difficult for other unions to observe the janitors' picket line.

In a workplace shared by many employers, one employer can legally insulate itself from picketing directed at other employers by establishing a separate gate (entrance) for the exclusive use of the striking employees. However, the separate gates strategy failed in this case. The replacement janitors and the other employees persisted in using each others' gates, thus preventing insulation.

Round III: State Political Climate

In November 1996, the Democrats captured the governor's seat for the first time in sixteen years and both houses of the state legislature. Incoming Governor Gray Davis enjoyed strong support from the California labor unions, although he ran on a moderate Democratic platform and was anxious not to be perceived as a union captive. On the janitors' front, in June 1999 Davis proposed to hire eighty-seven workers to clean state government buildings in place of private janitorial services, a symbolic action that reversed the policy of former Governor Pete Wilson, who had privatized many government functions. Davis's spokesperson characterized the decision as one of equity, entitling workers to fair wages and benefits. But when the SEIU supported legislation to protect the jobs of janitorial workers in situations where building owners change service contractors, Governor Davis exercised his veto. Senate Bill 1877, numbered after the janitors' local union, would have required the successor contractors to employ the janitors already working at a site for at least ninety days. After ninety days, they would be offered continued employment if their work performance was satisfactory. In issuing his veto, Davis said that the bill would set a "troubling precedent in regulating private-sector employment relationships."[27] Nonetheless, another bill dealing with labor injunctions was signed by the governor that assisted the janitors during the 2000 strike.

Labor Injunctions Background

By the Round III negotiations, the union and its lawyers were evidently so accustomed to the restrictions imposed on their tactics by the secondary boycott law that they did not even describe potential secondary boycott charges as a major concern. What they seemed to think far more significant was the previously mentioned change in California law limiting the ability of employers to obtain injunctions against labor picketing. To understand why this law mattered as much as it did, it is necessary to explore some of the legal background to regulating labor protest and the related risks of union liability.

The tort and criminal law of California prohibits workers from using violence or intimidation in conducting protests. Among the prohibited conduct is actual or threatened violence or property damage, mass protests, trespass, and blocking ingress to, or egress from, employer property. Such conduct is prohibited under state law even if it takes place as part of an otherwise permissible strike or picket line. Federal labor law protections for peaceful picketing and protest do not immunize labor protesters from criminal or tort liability for misconduct.

One of the hallmarks of JfJ campaigns is large, ebullient, and noisy street protests. Building owners and managers often respond to the arrival of large numbers of red T-shirted janitors and their supporters by seeking court orders limiting the size, location, and noise level of the demonstration. If a court issues an injunction, violation is punishable by contempt sanctions, which can be speedy, harsh, and devastating to protesters as well as to the union's treasury. Thus, availability of injunctions could be a significant element in the success or failure of a JfJ campaign. While the most high-profile public demonstrations in the 2000 JfJ campaign were not traditional picketing of work sites, the union felt it had to do at least some conventional picketing to connect the demonstrations (and the demonstrators) with the actual locations of the dispute.

Until the 1930s, federal courts routinely enjoined strikes and related labor protests. In 1932, however, Congress enacted the Norris–La Guardia Act, which stripped federal courts of jurisdiction to issue injunctions in most labor disputes.[28] The Norris–La Guardia Act did not, however, affect the power of state courts to issue injunctions. Many states, therefore, enacted their own "little Norris–La Guardia" statutes, divesting their courts of jurisdiction. Although California enacted some protection for labor picketing, the protection it adopted was relatively weak. Not until 1999, under Governor Davis, did California adopt a law that is virtually identical to Norris–La Guardia.

The 1999 California statute imposes several requirements to restrict the ability of courts to enjoin strike activity. No state court may issue an injunction unless there is a showing that the police or other officers charged with the duty to protect the complainant's property are unable or unwilling to do so. No state court may issue an injunction except after hearing testimony of witnesses in open court, with an opportunity for cross-examination. A person or business seeking an injunction must show that it has not committed any violations of labor or other laws and has made "every reasonable effort" to settle the labor dispute "either by negotiation or with the aid of any available governmental machinery of mediation or voluntary arbitration." A person or business seeking an injunction must post a bond to compensate those enjoined for damages caused by an erroneously issued injunction. Finally, the court must determine that a person or business seeking the injunction will suffer immediate and irreparable injury to its property from ongoing or threatened unlawful actions. Moreover, the harm to the complainant if the unlawful actions are not enjoined must be greater than the harm to the persons enjoined.

Impact of the New State Anti-injunction Statute

SEIU Local 1877 and its lawyers believed that the new anti-injunction statute made a difference in how the courts responded to the strike and the related nightly protests. While it was not practical to picket every affected janitorial work site in the area, as noted earlier, the union believed that it had to do some picketing to link the more general street demonstrations to the buildings and contracted employees involved in the dispute. Building owners and their allies tried on five separate occasions to have a state court enjoin the protests; each time the court rejected their request, based on the new law. Thus, the new state legal requirements evidently made a difference in how state courts perceived the strike.

Under prior law, courts would have entertained and often granted requests for injunctions based only on sworn affidavits describing allegedly illegal protests and asserting threatened harm to business or property due to potential blockage of access, noise, and other factors. Union lawyers had felt that cross-examination of the employer witnesses was necessary to reveal that the harm allegedly caused by the protest was often significantly exaggerated and that the protests did not pose any real threat to property. But under the old law, they were not necessarily granted the right to present such evidence.

The requirement that courts not issue injunctions without finding that the police were unable or unwilling to control any threatened injury to property also benefited the union. Union lawyers were able to show the court that Los Angeles police officers had been briefed and were present (and prepared) to deal with any illegal protests that might occur. As one union lawyer said to us, the union and the police essentially agreed that the police got the streets and "we got the sidewalks." The final feature of the new state law that made life easier for the union side was a new restriction on the ability to hold a union responsible for the unlawful conduct of individual members. An often-successful management tactic is for an employer to obtain an injunction, wait for some picketers to violate the terms of the injunction, and then seek to hold the union officers in contempt of court for the violations. Penalties for contempt of court can include large fines that are payable out of the union treasury if union officials were involved in, or approved of, the enjoined illegal activities.

The new California law provides that injunctions may not be issued except "against the person or persons, association, or organization making the threat or committing the unlawful act or actually authorized those acts." Furthermore, the statute provides that no union officer or member, nor any union, can be held liable for unlawful acts of individual union officers or members "except upon clear proof of actual participation in, or actual authorization of those acts." Taken together, these new provisions prevent a union that had not authorized illegal acts, or members who were not involved in illegal acts, from being enjoined (and thus from being held in contempt of court). They also provide that persons who are not named in the injunction cannot be held liable for the violations of others without clear proof that the union officially authorized the conduct. These new requirements provided some assurance to the union that the illegal protest of individual picketers would not become the basis for the entire union to be enjoined. As a result, violations of an injunction by union members would not become the basis for a huge fine against the union.

Round III Union Strategy

SEIU union leaders and negotiators profess a strong preference for having the janitorial contracts across the country expire at approximately the same time, and are clearly pushing in the direction of a "de facto national contract." There would be closely coordinated bargaining, if not an explicit "national contract," on certain issues. The goal seemed to be to extend the contract pattern from a set of regional labor/product markets to the entire country. As Stephen Lerner, the former director of building services organizing for SEIU and an architect of the JfJ strategy, said about the initial basic plan, JfJ sought to compel employers "to fight on our terms, not theirs" (1991, 8). Thus, it is worth exploring the nature of the current national pattern, as well as the conditions under which this coordinated strategy might make sense for the union. Such a strategy effectively joins the California negotiations in particular cities to those in other cities within the state and elsewhere.

A New Form of Pattern Bargaining Emerges

Many of the JfJ contracts around the country were settled in the months after the April 2000 Los Angeles settlement. Some examples include contracts in New York, Cleveland, Portland, and San Diego in May; Silicon Valley in June; Seattle in July; Milwaukee in August; and Hartford and Philadelphia in October. Yet, it is also worth noting that a number of janitorial contracts were settled in the months *before* the Los Angeles settlement. These contracts include San Francisco in August 1999, Minneapolis in January 2000, and downtown Chicago just before the Los Angeles settlement in April 2000.[29] Despite these agreements, union and management sources, as well as some press sources, labeled the Los Angeles settlement as the "pattern setter." And Lerner was explicit about the delicate balance the union sought: to "make strides in establishing minimum standards" for more full-time jobs, health care coverage, a living wage, and the employer's respect for the employees' right to organize, but at the same time acknowledging that "we never claimed the standards should be the same" for all markets (Walpole-Hofmeister 2000, C1).

The Contrast with Traditional Pattern Bargaining

Pattern bargaining is a well-known phenomenon in the labor relations literature Thomas A. Kochan and Harry C. Katz define pattern bargaining as "an

informal means for spreading the terms and conditions of employment negotiated in one formal bargaining structure to another. It is an informal substitute for centralized bargaining aimed at taking wages out of competition"
(1988, 136–137). This pattern approach seems to work best where a union
can organize a set of companies that share product and labor markets, as in
the domestic automobile industry.[30] And traditional pattern bargaining was
clearly applied by SEIU *within* individual regions. When the JfJ first came to
Los Angeles, the strategy was to organize all the major cleaning companies
and have them sign identical contracts, thus avoiding wage competition.

Yet, the product and labor markets of (nontraded) janitorial services are
geographically distinct. Raising wages in Chicago does not "take wages out
of competition" for building services contractors in Los Angeles. So, the
SEIU clearly envisions a different kind of pattern setting. It is necessary to
look beyond "taking wages out of competition" for explanations of the operation and potential effectiveness of the cross-region coordination tactic.

Reputation Effects in Bargaining

Even though contractors in one city are not in direct competition with contractors in another city, a high-profile strike and settlement has the effect of
establishing reputational effects throughout the state and country. It signals to the contractors and building owners elsewhere that union strike
threats are credible. It also creates a point of comparison, or "benchmark"
for workers as well as contractors and building owners. Arthur M. Ross
long ago argued for the importance of what he termed "orbits of coercive
comparison" in the formation of workers' wage demands. Ross argued that
workers make comparisons to the wages obtained by other workers in similar
situations; they then set their expectations accordingly (1948). Thus, Spanish-
language television seems to have played an important role in spreading
information concerning the Los Angeles strike and settlement to janitorial
workers across the country.

Some of the effects of the alternative pattern approach are connected to
the distinctive structure of the industry described earlier. Given the complexities of the relationships between the building owners and the managers, a pattern-setting agreement might alter the negotiations between these
two parties over the terms of the cleaning contracts. The vice president for
labor relations at the major contractor One Source was quoted as saying
that the contractors' strategy was to use the Los Angeles settlement as a
benchmark to take to building owners who were putting their cleaning service contracts out to bid in other cities (Walpole-Hofmeister 2000). Thus,
the Los Angeles strike and settlement may have given building contractors

a compelling argument to take to the owners in other cities as to why the owners should accept the costlier cleaning contracts that would go along with higher janitorial wages.

It is important to recall that several of the larger building maintenance companies (including One Source and ABM) have operations in cities across the country. Thus, for example, One Source workers in one city might naturally compare their wages to the wages obtained by One Source workers in another city. ABM might know from direct experience the willingness of the union to launch a strike and the efficacy of those efforts in other cities. These national contractors may also be induced to settle quickly in one city in order to avoid sympathy strikes and work slowdowns in their operations elsewhere. This outcome could occur if the union's efforts are sufficiently well-coordinated across cities and if the contract expiration dates are sufficiently close together. Union officials argue that simultaneous contract expiration provides them with the opportunity to achieve the same level of coordination at the national level as that which routinely exists within the cleaning companies.

Splits Between Large Versus Small Contractors

There are significant differences between the operations of large contractors and the smaller contractors; these differences can lead to disagreements over management's bargaining approach. Smaller companies are less susceptible to threatened actions in other cities. And—as they tend to clean smaller buildings—they are also more likely to fear losing their contracts to nonunion contractors. Smaller contractors are less likely to be concerned about pattern-setting implications of a settlement for subsequent deals in other cities. These differences contributed to a split at the bargaining table between larger and smaller contractors in Los Angeles, a split that the union was able to use to its advantage.

Remaining Questions on Union Strategy

The unions' hope to achieve a "de facto national contract" leaves some questions unanswered. There is seemingly nothing to be gained by "taking wages out of competition" across regions, as there is in tradable goods industries; Chicago janitors are not in competition with Los Angeles janitors, nor are their local employing establishments. So it is not immediately clear why simultaneous contract expiration and the drive for minimum national standards is a strategy strongly favored by the union. The official answer lies in the union's desire to match the internal coordination and national-level presence of the large contractors. But simultaneous contract expirations could give an advantage to the contractors in some future negotiations, that is, the ability to lock out unionized workers across dispersed operations. More rounds of bargaining will have to occur before a definitive assessment of the union's alternative pattern-bargaining approach can be made. Both sides are still learning. The union may find ways to coordinate more effectively, and management may find ways to react more effectively than it did in 2000 to union coordination. In any event, future negotiations in Los Angeles and California are likely to become more and more part of a national process.

Round III: The Strike of 2000

Local 1877 began to prepare for a strike months before the 2000 contract expiration. Shop stewards and other rank-and-file leaders devoted many hours of work and discussion to "internal organizing" among the union's members. Their goal was to prepare the membership for mass protests for which the JfJ had become known a decade before during the organizing that led to the 1990 victory in Century City. Since 1990, there had been considerable turnover of union members. Many workers had no direct memory of the 1990 events. Such efforts may also have been intended to show that the union could consolidate its hold on the industry with as much energy as it had a decade earlier.

In the prestrike training sessions, stewards and other union activists were briefed about the economics of the janitorial industry and the commercial real estate market in Los Angeles. They also engaged in detailed discussions of union strategies. The goal was to build workers' confidence and to develop an organizational structure that was primed for a strike if an impasse developed in the negotiations.

The Strike Commences

A key feature of earlier JfJ campaigns had been disruption: mass street protests, rallies in public places, and aggressive efforts to garner media attention, together with strategic pressures on major players in the janitorial industry. The three-week strike that began on Monday, April 3, 2000, followed this scenario. A week before the strike began, the union staged a boisterous rally. And the strike itself started with a public membership vote rejecting management's most recent settlement offer. The vote was combined with mass picketing of downtown Los Angeles buildings.

Each day of the week brought another geographical focus, a part of what the union termed a "rolling strike." On April 4, the picketing spread to Los

Angeles's affluent Westside; by week's end, janitors walked off the job in major office buildings throughout the metropolitan area. On April 5, the strikers paraded through Beverly Hills's shopping area to dramatize the plight of working poor janitors. On Thursday, April 6, Jesse Jackson led a march of more than 2,000 janitors through Century City, the site of the union's earlier breakthrough. On April 7, strikers wearing photogenic red JfF T-shirts marched ten miles in an all-day event that drew support from many citizens.

Union Relations with the Los Angeles Police

Strike leaders went to great lengths to ensure that public protests were peaceful and orderly. Union officials obtained permits required by law for each march and rally. They worked with the Los Angeles Police Department's (LAPD) labor detail to minimize potential confrontation. There was only one occasion, early in the strike, when a conflict loomed. One night in Los Angeles's otherwise empty downtown, a security guard panicked at the sight of a large group of strikers and called 911. The LAPD tactical squad responded to the call and—after a tense standoff—Local 1877 president Mike Garcia persuaded the police that the union could control the protesters.

During the three-week walkout, there were arrests (including some of local politicians) in response to civil disobedience undertaken in support of the strikers. A few incidents of police beatings were reported. However, strike organizers managed to avert major conflicts. The outcome was in contrast to the police violence against janitors that had taken place in 1990 at Century City. Organized labor's political clout in the city that had developed over the intervening decade played a role. Also, the strike occurred just months before the Democratic National Convention in Los Angeles and the city was anxious to show it could manage public demonstrations in an orderly fashion.[31]

Union Legal Strategy

The union managed to offset legal maneuvers by building owners during the course of the strike. Management hired workers in some buildings to replace strikers. But this employer tactic—which can be devastating for striking unions in many instances—was not a disaster from the union perspective in this case. In fact, it was actually helpful to the SEIU in legal terms. If no one had been working in a building targeted by picketers, the union was more vulnerable to charges of engaging in illegal secondary boycotts. There was only one secondary boycott charge filed with the NLRB during the three-week strike (and which resulted in an NLRB complaint). Building owners did try to enjoin the mass protests on other grounds, however. On five separate occasions, they went to state court to seek an injunction on picketing, arguing that blocking ingress or egress to private property was a violation of state tort law. Each time the judge refused to enjoin the strikers. In each case, the court found that the requirements of the state's newly enacted "little Norris–La Guardia Act" for an injunction had not been met.

External Financial Support for the Union Side

Well before the walkout began, the SEIU International raised $1 million from its other locals around the country to support the walkout. In addition, Local 1877 had its own strike fund of $500,000 (Gilroy and Walpole-Hofmeister 2000). Along with the mobilization of its membership for picketing and other high-profile strike activities, the local undertook extensive efforts to develop an effective public relations strategy. Local 1877 conducted polls and focus groups to this end (Meyerson 2000, 28).

Public opinion responded to the strike far more positively than in the organizers' most optimistic projections, and not only because of the prestrike preparations. In a city that was enjoying unprecedented prosperity at the turn of the twenty-first century, yet where inequality between the rich and poor was pronounced, the striking janitors were symbols of the plight of the working poor. They were immigrant workers laboring nightly at low wages to clean glitzy offices occupied by wealthy executives, lawyers, and other professionals during the day. The janitors' demand for a raise of $1 an hour seemed eminently reasonable in this context and the contractors' offer of $0.50 an hour seemed heartless. Public sympathy was overwhelmingly prostriking janitor.

Drivers regularly honked their horns in support of picketers as they went past. Those on foot sometimes spontaneously thrust dollar bills into the hands of the strikers. The janitors' signature red T-shirts became local fashion icons; passersby bought them off the strikers' backs. (There were even knockoff shirts appearing on the spot market.) In one of the more unusual events of the strike, during the second week of the walkout an anonymous donor delivered $1 million to Local 1877 to help defray the strike expenses.[32] A contribution of that magnitude was undoubtedly unprecedented in labor history.

Media coverage of the strike was extensive and generally sympathetic. Reports in the *Los Angeles Times* and elsewhere highlighted the difficult living conditions endured by the city's low-wage immigrants. "Even L.A.'s TV newscasts—the most substance-free in the land—were compelled to cover the janitors' daily marches and mention the wage rates at which they worked," one commentator noted (Meyerson 2000, 28).

Union, Political, and Religious Support for the Janitors

Prestrike planning paid off in the form of support from a wide array of organized groups. Teamster members refused to make deliveries or collect trash from struck buildings. The Los Angeles Building Trades Council also voted to honor the janitors' picket lines. Operating Engineers—workers who do elevator repair and other skilled building maintenance—also supported the strike. The Los Angeles County Federation of Labor organized a food distribution program for strikers and helped to coordinate other support activities.

Even before the walkout began, the Los Angeles City Council voted unanimously to support the janitors. The Los Angeles County Board of Supervisors voted to back the janitors on the second day of the strike. The California State Assembly passed a resolution in support of the janitors by a huge margin. In the third week of the walkout, Vice President Al Gore spoke at a union demonstration, as did Senators Edward Kennedy and Diane Feinstein. Local politicians were especially visible at union rallies and demonstrations—and not just Democrats. Republican mayor Richard Riordan intervened in various ways on behalf of the janitors.[33] Riordan was influenced by a tradition of Catholic teachings on social justice as well as the growth of the Latino electorate. Local 1877, along with the Los Angeles County Federation of Labor, had already emerged as a vehicle of Latino political mobilization.

Support from the Catholic Church played a very important role throughout the conflict. Cardinal Mahony—who had long had friendly relations with AFL-CIO president and former SEIU head John Sweeney—voiced sympathy for the strikers' cause. The cardinal celebrated a mass in honor of the janitors and publicly offered to mediate the dispute. Behind the scenes, both he and Mayor Riordan were in contact with Miguel Contreras, head of the Los Angeles County Federation of Labor. They helped start serious settlement negotiations by making direct appeals to building owners, managers, and other key players in the industry.[34]

Pressures Felt on Both Sides

As the walkout moved into its third week, workers and their families were beginning to feel the loss of wages a strike entails. Janitors lived paycheck to paycheck on wages of $7.20 an hour (and that much only in core area buildings). Few janitors had savings on which to draw. Even with food provision and strike funds helping to provide alternative support, economic pressures became intense. Some workers did eventually cross picket lines. However, unlike conventional strikes, the union goal was not the halting of production. Rather, it was carrying out demonstrations and obtaining external support, combined with whatever disruption of service could be attained. In any event, the union continued to demonstrate. When the Jewish holiday of Passover took place during the strike's third week, the janitors held a Seder in front of the headquarters of TrizecHahn, one of the city's largest commercial property owners. A local rabbi compared the strike to the Jews' exodus from Egypt. And a candlelight vigil in downtown's Pershing Square drew thousands of members and supporters together and bolstered flagging spirits.

The SEIU organized its janitorial division on a nationwide basis, and in the final week of the strike it increased the pressure on the contractors by flexing its muscles across the nation. Local 1877 members went to Seattle, Denver, San Francisco, and San Jose to picket buildings cleaned by the major contractors. Their picket lines were honored by SEIU janitors in the other cities. "We just did a couple of buildings in each city for one night, but we planned to escalate considerably if the strike had to go into its fourth week," Lerner explained to a reporter (Meyerson 2000, 28). As it turned out, there was no fourth week.

The End of Round III: A Deal Is Struck

A few key building owners, led by Maguire, finally brokered a strike settlement. Maguire, as noted earlier, is one of the area's largest real estate magnates. He threatened to make his own arrangement with the union if the contractors did not agree to settle the dispute. Cleaning contractors themselves were divided between the two major firms—One Source and ABM—that employed the bulk of the janitors downtown and at Century City, and an assortment of smaller firms. These smaller firms had distinct economic interests and were not vulnerable to the geographic pressures One Source and ABM faced. They did not have SEIU members cleaning their buildings in other cities since they did not service a national market. As a result, the smaller firms still had hopes of defeating the strike well into the third week of the walkout. They took a more intransigent posture than the major contractors that by all accounts prolonged the conflict.[35] But eventually, the big industry players prevailed and the strike was settled at the end of its third week, a widely celebrated victory for the union. As they had at Century City a decade before, the janitors in 2000 once again emerged as an inspiration to the labor movement.

Key Features of the Round III Agreement

The Los Angeles settlement of 2000 has a three-year duration, unlike the prior five-year agreement.[36] (Three years is a more typical duration than five for a labor contract.) Due to the strike, wage increases were delayed until May 1, 2000, a month after the new agreement's retroactive start date.

As Table 2.2 illustrates, the de facto consolidation of geographic zones for pay under the prior contract was formally recognized with new area designations.[37] Employment in the core Area 1 remains the highest paid with pension and health insurance benefits. The surrounding Area 2 continues the health insurance that was backloaded into the prior settlement. Outlying Area 3 features smaller increases than the other two and does not provide for health insurance coverage. However, the agreement includes a provision guaranteeing that employees are paid no less than $0.30 above the federal or state minimum wage. This provision—which nominally covers all areas—would most likely affect only Area 3. Unionized cleaning contractors who take over a previously nonunion location are allowed a graduated phase-in period before the application of full area wages and benefits comes into force. A $0.01-per-hour contribution to a training fund is mandated. Contractors are protected from union concessions to other employers through a "most-favored nations" clause.[38]

Although there were some complaints by employers about the expedited grievance/arbitration system, it was retained in the 2000 agreement, along with a conventional arbitration system. The expedited system essentially calls for rapid hearings and bench decisions.[39] A hiring hall or referral system— under which employers fill vacancies from workers referred by the system— is applied to temporary and permanent employees for the core area. Standard union shop and checkoff language is included along with a management rights clause.[40] Employers are required to notify the union about impending investigations by immigration authorities of which they are aware; they are prohibited from providing more information to such authorities about employees than is legally required. Various protections are provided for employees who are absent from work due to immigration-related proceedings.

While not part of the new contract, two "spillover" effects followed from the Round III negotiations. Supermarkets in the Los Angeles area had contracted out their janitorial services to nonunion contractors. A press exposé of this practice appeared and complaints were filed with state and local authorities alleging labor law violations. The litigation and adverse publicity, combined with the general public sympathy for janitors that the strike of 2000 had evoked, led the supermarkets to agree to contracts with the SEIU requiring a phase-in of union cleaning contractors (or the equivalent wages and benefits). About 2,100 janitors were covered by the new supermarket agreements. Some chains reemployed their janitors directly as part of the settlement rather than use outside contractors.

Several building service companies under union contract in Los Angeles operated on a nonunion basis in historically conservative Orange County,

Table 2.2

Wages and Wage Adjustments Specified in 2000–2003 Maintenance Contractors Agreement: Cleaners

	4/1/00	5/1/00	10/1/00	4/1/01	4/1/02
Area 1					
Start	$7.20	$7.90	—	—	—
Minimum	$7.20	$7.90	$7.90	$8.50	$9.10
Increase	$0.00	$0.70	$0.00	$0.60	$0.60
Health	Yes	Yes	Yes	Yes	Yes
Pension	Yes	Yes	Yes	Yes	Yes
Area 2					
Start	$6.30	$6.30	$6.90	—	—
Minimum	$6.80	$6.80	$7.20	$7.80	$8.40
Increase	$0.00	$0.00	$0.40	$0.60	$0.60
Health	Yes	Yes	Yes	Yes	Yes
Pension	No	No	No	No	No
Area 3					
Start	$5.20	$6.10			
Minimum	$5.65	$6.10	$6.10	$6.30	$6.50
Increase	$0.00	$0.45	$0.00	$0.20	$0.20
Health	No	No	No	No	No
Pension	No	No	No	No	No

Source: "Maintenance Contract Agreement: April 1, 2000 through April 30, 2003." U.S. Department of Labor.

Area 1 = Downtown Los Angeles and Century City.

Area 2 = Wilshire Corridor, Beverly Hills, Los Angeles International Airport, Westwood, Westside Area, Pasadena, Hollywood, Long Beach, Glendale/Burbank, South Bay, City of Commerce, Studio City/Sherman Oaks, Woodland Hills/West Valley.

Area 3 = Greater Los Angeles County.

including ABM, One Source, and another firm—Diversified Maintenance Services. While the Orange County government suffered from a bankruptcy crisis in the mid-1990s, the private economy boomed thereafter and commercial real estate participated in the upswing. At the same time, a severe labor shortage developed in the county for low-wage labor, despite continuing immigration. During the Los Angeles strike, Orange County janitors were also mobilized by the union to attend rallies and demonstrations.

Nonetheless, the speed at which actual recognition was obtained took union leaders by surprise. The SEIU obtained a neutrality agreement from the major building owners and contractors that had buildings in Orange County.[41] Owners and managers agreed informally that employers would recognize the union if it could obtain signed authorization cards from a majority of the employees. In January 2001, 3,000 new janitors were brought under union contract, pursuant to this understanding and constituting a major breakthrough for the labor movement of Orange County.

Lessons and Questions from the Janitors' Experience
in Three Rounds

It is easy to tick off the reasons why the JfJ campaign in Los Angeles should not have succeeded. But with the benefit of hindsight, the logic of the JfJ strategy is clear. The tactics basically do not depend on a strike that halts production of services. Instead, they enlist public opinion, political support, and sympathy from community leaders. While building service labor costs are important for competing cleaning contractors, they are a relatively minor portion of the overall costs of operating a building. Once building owners and managers agree to use unionized contractors, a highly elastic demand for labor becomes relatively inelastic. And the low-tech nature of building services does not allow much option for capital/labor substitution. Capital is mops, brooms, vacuum cleaners, waxing machines, and trash carts. In theory, management might step up the intensity of work to try and raise productivity. But there are some limits on that option; notably that ultimately building owners/managers want their structures to be properly cleaned. Moreover, in our interviews with union officials, the issue of "speedups" did not arise, suggesting that such strategies had not been undertaken by management.

As for sustainability, JfJ tactics in Los Angeles have survived three rounds of bargaining and the ups and downs of the business cycle. They seem in addition to have provided a wedge for organizing in nonunion areas such as Orange County via a demonstration effect. The demonstration effect also appears to make possible a loose form of pattern bargaining that spreads from one urban area to another. Potential legal concerns—primarily related to the secondary boycott issue—have proved not to be insurmountable barriers. Indeed, the political connection—which led to a change in state law regarding injunctions—helped overcome another possible legal obstacle.

But there are limits to the JfJ approach. It was not applied in an industry in which international trade, or even competition from other areas of the United States, was a consideration. Cleaning services must be performed on site. JfJ strikes do not create a major inconvenience or have important economic ripple effects that could erode supportive public opinion. The trust factor that fosters industry concentration and thus limits the number of key players was also a significant helping influence from the union perspective. Substitution of capital for labor is not a current option.

Like other industries, unionization of building services at the national level was on the decline in the 1980s and into the 1990s, as Figure 2.2 shows. Data on unionization of that industry from the Current Population Survey (CPS) are erratic on a year-to-year basis due to small sample size. Nonetheless,

Figure 2.2 **Percent Union Representation Rate of All-Industry Janitors and of All Employees in the Building Services Industry, 1983–2000**

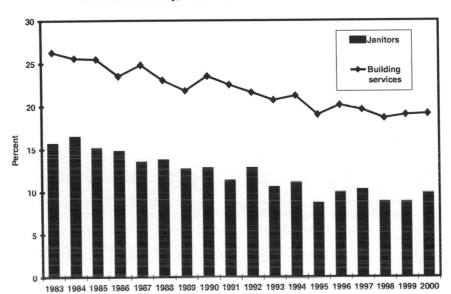

Source: Hirsch and Macpherson (2001 and earlier editions).

there seems to be a leveling out of the decline in the second half of the 1990s, the period in which the second and third contract rounds occurred in Los Angeles. There may also be a leveling off of the decline of unionization in the janitor occupation. Most janitors do not work for cleaning contractors, but an increasing proportion do so.[42]

The JfJ approach is not applicable to all industries and occupations. Use of the political connection did lead to unionization of home health care workers in Los Angeles County by the SEIU.[43] Progress was also made in unionizing workers at private concessions operated at the municipally owned Los Angeles International Airport. Similarly, workers at the Staples Center were organized on the eve of the Democratic National Convention in 2000. But in apparel manufacturing, another low-wage industry with a heavily Latino workforce in the Los Angeles area, unionization has made little headway due to import competition.

There is a temptation to overinterpret the wisdom gained from hindsight. Hotels in Los Angeles—also with a heavily Latino workforce and with a service that must be performed on site—have been more resistant to unionization than janitorial services. Reasons for the differential union success in hotels versus janitorial services are not entirely obvious.[44] Still, the JfJ case does suggest that union organizing in the future will take a political route where feasible. And in organizing and bargaining, strikes will be used more as a way of seeking public support than of putting direct pressure on employers by halting production.

Notes

1. This chapter is part of an ongoing research effort by the authors and others on the Justice for Janitors campaign in Los Angeles. Prior references to this effort are Fisk, Mitchell, and Erickson (2000) and Waldinger et al. (1998). Some information for this chapter was obtained from the news media, especially the *Los Angeles Times* and the *Daily Labor Report.* Due to space limitations, such source citations are omitted except for direct quotes.

2. The figures on union representation come from the CPS. The one-fourth estimate comes from applying 1980 union representation rates to the following industry sectors: agriculture; mining; construction; durables; nondurables; transportation; communications and public utilities; wholesale trade; retail trade; finance, insurance, and real estate services; and government. Changes in industry composition explained 26.8 percent of the total drop in unionization from 1980 to 2001. For the private sector only, it explained 23.6 percent of the drop.

3. The U.S. Bureau of Labor Statistics estimate of 35 percent refers only to membership—not representation—and covers the nonfarm sector. Because public-sector unionization was not prominent at the time, the private-sector representation may well have been higher.

4. Union workers have a disproportionate weight in total compensation relative to employment because of their pay premiums and propensity to work full time.

5. Nationally, over a fourth of employment in "services to dwellings and other buildings" was of Hispanic origin by 2000, according to CPS data, and over half was female. About one-sixth of the workforce in that industry was black. Thus, the stereotype of a janitor as a black male is no longer valid in the United States and certainly not valid in Los Angeles.

6. A high ratio of labor costs to total costs is one of the standard Marshallian factors leading to high labor demand elasticity. As is well known, under some circumstances—essentially a high degree of substitutability of other factors for labor—the ratio may not lead to high elasticity. However, in the case of cleaning service production, there is no evident other factor that is highly substitutable for labor. "Capital" in the industry consists of such items as vacuum cleaners, waxing machines, mops, and so on.

7. The unaffiliated National Education Association, representing teachers, is the largest labor organization in the United States.

8. The film was made in 1999, that is, before the 2000 negotiations took place. It was nominated for the Golden Palm Award at the Cannes Film Festival.

9. The number of employees in "services to dwellings and other buildings"—not all of whom are janitors—increased at an annual rate of 3.9 percent from 1983 to 2000. The number of employees in the "janitors and cleaners" occupation increased

only 0.5 percent at an annual rate over this period. The ratio of the former to the latter in 2000 was 30 percent, so a large majority of janitors in the overall U.S. workforce are still employed directly by private and public employers other than cleaning contractors. However, this characteristic is not true of office complexes in major urban areas (Hirsch and Macpherson 2001 and earlier editions).

10. It is difficult to obtain reliable estimates. However, in 2000 prime commercial office space in Los Angeles rented for roughly $20 per square foot. Based on various—and not necessarily unbiased—Internet sources, cleaning costs were likely $1 to $2 per square foot, putting the expense of cleaning in the range of 5 to 10 percent of revenue.

11. This figure's data come from trade association estimates and appear to change notably from period to period, probably because of the unscientific nature of the survey. However, the economies of administrative scale phenomenon highlighted by the figure seem to be robust. Direct labor expenses on the figure are defined as pay for direct labor, supervision, and related expenditures for Social Security, unemployment insurance, workers' compensation, and health and welfare. Excluded are labor expenses for such overhead functions as administrative, sales, and office personnel.

12. Data based on square feet of Class A building space in the downtown central business district is reported in the online quarterly newsletter of Cushman Realty. No buildings were completed during 1989. A few more came on line between 1990 and 1992 and none thereafter. Construction of such space in the 1990s took place outside the downtown area.

13. Cleaning contractors provide service to a variety of buildings. Office buildings comprise over half the market. The rest is made up of facilities such as apartment complexes, industrial plans, shopping malls, supermarkets, hospitals, educational institutions, and so on. See the Web site of the Small Business Development Center, University of Georgia, at http://research.cbdc.uga.edu (accessed July 1, 2002).

14. Bevona was later forced out of office by dissidents who wanted JfJ tactics used in New York City to avert membership losses. He retired amid a scandal over a $1.5 million severance package.

15. Under federal law, a union engaged in a secondary boycott may be subject to charges that it has committed an "unfair labor practice." If the NLRB finds the union has committed such a practice, it will issue a "cease and desist" order requiring the union to stop the behavior.

16. Union contracts typically run for more than a year. Three-year durations are quite common. Multiyear agreements usually include staged wage and benefit improvements, often at the anniversary date of the agreement.

17. Although union contracts usually have a fixed duration, during which both parties are bound to the terms of the agreement, both sides can mutually agree to modify or scrap an existing contract before it expires.

18. One symbolic result of this view is that the AFL-CIO moved its biennial convention to Los Angeles. Such conventions had previously been held at a Florida resort.

19. National unions may take control of local unions that have administrative problems through trusteeships. However, federal law regulates the process and tilts toward returning trusteed locals to member control within a reasonable time.

20. As noted earlier in the text, the contract with ISS after Century City was superseded by another contract also covering ABM. For ISS, therefore, the contract negotiated in 1995 was technically the third contract.

21. Shuwa's centerpiece downtown Los Angeles property—the ARCO Plaza—was put up for sale in 1999 and then withdrawn. It was again put up for sale in late 2001. It originally purchased the property for $620 million in 1986, reportedly the second largest real estate transaction in California. At the time of the 2001 offering, brokers estimated that Shuwa would take a nominal loss of at least $270 million on the sale.

22. Ashcroft was involved in a widely publicized libel suit against the *Times* of London. The newspaper had published allegations of money laundering at a bank in Belize that is part of his enterprise. After negotiations with Rupert Murdoch, whose News Corporation owns the *Times*, the suit was settled.

23. Contreras became head of the Los Angeles County Federation of Labor in 1996, the first Latino in that position, reflecting the changing demographics of the Los Angeles labor force.

24. The University of Southern California dispute, which had gone on since 1995, involved the university's assertion of a right to contract out the jobs covered by an expired agreement with the Hotel Employees and Restaurant Employees. A compromise was reached that protected job security of the affected workers but that allowed subcontracting.

25. Maguire is a political liberal who, for example, was a donor to Democrat Bill Bradley's unsuccessful campaign for his party's presidential nomination in 2000, according to Federal Election Commission records.

26. Given the contractors' involvement, they would likely be found to be joint employers with the building contractors. A joint employer is not considered a neutral or secondary entity and therefore is a permissible target for labor protest.

27. "California Governor Signs Bills to Bolster Labor Laws, Limit Fund Use in Organizing." *Daily Labor Report*, October 3, 2000, A2.

28. Later U.S. Supreme Court decisions have determined that the courts retained authority to enjoin unfair labor practices, including secondary boycotts. George Norris was a Republican progressive senator from Nebraska. Fiorello La Guardia was a Republican congressman from New York City and later the city's colorful mayor.

29. The *Daily Labor Report* carried reports of these various settlements.

30. General Motors, Ford, and DaimlerChrysler usually sign contracts that are virtually identical in terms of their basic conditions. The United Auto Workers selects one company as the target and, after settling with it, takes the pattern to the other two.

31. Street protests were expected at the Democratic convention slated for Los Angeles. Overreaction by the police during the earlier janitors' strike might have created anxiety about what would ensue at the convention, something the city wanted to avoid.

32. The identity of the donor remains unknown to the union.

33. The mayor of Los Angeles is legally a nonpartisan position, as are many local offices.

34. The cardinal's actions in the janitors' strike effectively buried unpleasant memories of his role—noted earlier in the text—in a refusal by the Church to recognize a union of grave diggers in Catholic cemeteries in the 1980s.

35. In situations in which employers join together for purposes of collective bargaining in the labor market, it is still the case that they are commercial rivals in the product market. Thus, disputes *within* the employer side where multiemployer bargaining is practiced are not uncommon.

36. Although the contractors effectively negotiate as a group, after a settlement each contractor signs an individual—but identical—master agreement with the union.

37. Smaller buildings are treated as Area 3, regardless of their geographic location.

38. These clauses—whose odd name derives from similar clauses found in international trade treaties—provide that one party or the other give the benefit of any more favorable agreements to its contractual partner. In this agreement, the clause applies to the union side.

39. In a standard arbitration system, the arbitrator holds a formal hearing on the grievance. The parties, often represented by lawyers, submit briefs, call witnesses, and so on. After the hearing, the arbitrator writes a decision, often several weeks later. Under expedited arbitration, the hearing is much less formal and the arbitrator makes an immediate ruling from the bench.

40. Under a union shop, new hires must join the union or pay a representation fee. A check-off clause provides that union dues are automatically deducted from a worker's paycheck and forwarded to the union. Management rights clauses are often placed in union agreements. They affirm management's right to run the business and carry out normal functions, such as hiring, discipline, and discharge, subject to any limitations that the contract otherwise provides.

41. In a neutrality agreement, employers agree not to campaign against the union as the union seeks to organize workers.

42. See note 9 for more details.

43. Recipients of public funding to hire health care aides originally employed such aides directly. With Los Angeles County, the "industry" was restructured by creating an entity that acted as the employer. Employees of that entity were then unionized.

44. Labor costs in hotels account for roughly half of revenues, a factor that may account for stronger employer opposition to unionization than in the janitors' case. The estimate is drawn from the national income accounts and input-output accounts.

References

Beadling, Tom, Pat Cooper, Grace Palladino, and Peter Pieragostini. 1992. *A Need for Valor: The Roots of the Service Employees International Union, 1902–1992.* Washington, DC: Service Employees International Union.

Building Service Employees' International Union. *Proceedings.* Various issues. Privately published.

———. *Report to Locals.* Various issues.

Erickson, Christopher L., and Daniel J.B. Mitchell. 1998. "Labor Standards and Trade Agreements: U.S. Experience." *Comparative Labor Law and Policy Journal* 19 (Winter): 147–183.

Fisk, Catherine L., Daniel J.B. Mitchell, and Christopher L. Erickson. 2000. "Union Representation of Immigrant Janitors in Southern California: Economic and Legal Challenges." In *Organizing Immigrants: The Challenge for Unions in Contemporary California,* ed. Ruth Milkman, 199–224. Ithaca, NY: ILR Press.

Freeman, Richard. 1995. "Are Your Wages Set in Beijing?" *Journal of Economic Perspectives* (Summer): 15–32.

———. 1991. "On the Divergence in Unionism Among Developed Countries." Working Paper, no. W2817. Cambridge, MA: National Bureau of Economic Research.

Gilroy, T., and Elizabeth Walpole-Hofmeister. 2000. "SEIU Janitors Threaten Strike in Los Angeles to Begin April 3, Locals Pledge $1 Million." *Daily Labor Report,* April 3.

Greer, Scott. 1959. *Last Man In: Racial Access to Union Power.* Glencoe, IL: Free Press.

Hirsch, Barry T., and David A. Macpherson. 2001 and earlier editions. *Union Membership and Earnings Data Book: Compilations from the Current Population Survey.* Washington, DC: Bureau of National Affairs.

International Labor Office. 1997. *World Labour Report, 1997–98: Industrial Relations, Democracy and Social Stability.* Geneva: International Labor Office.

Jacoby, Sanford M., and Daniel J.B. Mitchell. 1988. "Measurement of Compensation: Union and Nonunion." *Industrial Relations* 27 (Spring): 215–231.

Jentz, John B. 1997. "Citizenship, Self-respect, and Political Power: Chicago's Flat Janitors Trailblaze the Service Employees International Union, 1912–1921." *Labor's Heritage* 9: 4–23.

Katz, Lawrence F., and Kevin M. Murphy. 1991. "Changes in Relative Wages, 1963–1987: Supply and Demand Factors." Working Paper, no. W3927. Cambridge, MA: National Bureau of Economic Research.

Kochan, Thomas A., and Harry C. Katz. 1988. *Collective Bargaining and Industrial Relations.* Homewood, IL: Irwin.

Lerner, Stephen. 1991. "Let's Get Moving." *Labor Research Review* 18 (Fall): 1–15.

Levy, Frank, and Richard J. Murname. 1992. "U.S. Earnings Levels and Earnings Inequality: A Review of Recent Trends and Proposed Explanations." *Journal of Economic Literature* 30 (September): 1333–1381.

Meyerson, Harold. 2000. "A Clean Sweep: How Unions Are Once Again Organizing Low-Wage Workers." *The American Prospect* 11 (June 19–July 3): 24–29.

Mines, Richard, and Jeffrey Avina. 1992. "Immigrants and Labor Standards: The Case of California Janitors." In *U.S.-Mexico Relations: Labor Market Interdependence,* ed. Jorge A. Bustamante, Clark Reynolds, and Raul Hinojosa-Ojeda, 429–448. Stanford, CA: Stanford University Press.

Organization for Economic Cooperation and Development. 1994. *Employment Outlook (July).* Paris: Organization for Economic Cooperation and Development.

Reed, Deborah. 1999. *California's Rising Income Inequality: Causes and Concerns.* San Francisco: Public Policy Institute of California.

Ross, Arthur M. 1948. *Trade Union Wage Policy.* Berkeley: University of California Press.

Rowan, Hobart. 1978. "Bosworth Says U.S. Fumbles Rail Talks." *Washington Post,* June 16.

Troy, Leo. 1999. *Beyond Unions and Collective Bargaining.* Armonk, NY: M.E. Sharpe.

Waldinger, Roger, Chris Erickson, Ruth Milkman, Daniel J.B. Mitchell, Abel Valenzuela, Kent Wong, and Maurice Zeitlin. 1998. "Helots No More: A Case Study of the Justice for Janitors Campaign in Los Angeles." In *Organizing to Win: New Research on Union Strategies,* ed. Kate Bronfenbrenner et al., 102–119. Ithaca, NY: ILR Press.

Walpole-Hofmeister, Elizabeth. 2000. "100,000 Janitors Covered in SEIU Pacts Bargained During 2000 in Two Dozen Cities." *Daily Labor Report,* November 28.

II

Lessons from the Past and New Frontiers in Modeling Unionism

3

The Two Faces of Unionism

Implications for Union Growth

Bruce E. Kaufman

In their book *What Do Unions Do?* (1984), Richard B. Freeman and James Medoff argue that unions have two faces, each of which lead to a different view of the institution. They call these the "monopoly face" and "collective voice face." The monopoly face arises from the ability of unions to use their market power to raise wages and other terms and conditions of employment above the competitive level. The collective voice face is the ability of unions to articulate and communicate to management the collective opinions and preferences of the workforce and to effectively speak up and represent the workers' interests in workplace decisions. Although the boundaries between the two faces are not entirely separable, they can be thought of as the exercise of "muscle" and "voice."

Freeman and Medoff use the "two faces" dichotomy to examine the economic and social impact of labor unions on firms and the economy. In this chapter, I apply this conceptual framework to a modestly different issue: the growth prospects of unions in the early twenty-first century. My conclusions are twofold. The first is that Freeman and Medoff's conceptual model needs to be revised and broadened in several important respects in order to provide a well-rounded explanation of past patterns of union growth and a prediction of future trends. The revisions I suggest come from the work of early twentieth-century labor economist John R. Commons. The second conclusion is that consideration of both the "muscle" and "voice" faces of unions leads to the same prediction—absent a major socioeconomic upheaval, union membership and (particularly) density will continue to decline in the years ahead. I develop this conclusion with the help of detailed examination of the role of union muscle and voice in two earlier historical periods, the 1920s and the 1930s.

The Pattern of Union Growth

Before prognosticating on future union growth, a brief examination of past trends provides a useful context and perspective. Toward that end, the pattern of change in union membership and density (membership as a percent of nonagricultural employment) is shown in Figures 3.1 and 3.2. Figure 3.1 presents the level of union density in the American economy from 1900 to 2000 and in the private and public sectors, respectively, for 1950 to 2000. Figure 3.2 (see p. 64) does the same, but for membership.

The dominant pattern that emerges from Figure 3.1 is the half-century rise in union density from 1900 to the early 1950s, followed by a significant decline in the succeeding half-century. Union membership in Figure 3.2 shows the same sharp upward trend for the first half of the century, but then continues to slowly grow until finally cresting in the late 1970s, after which it, too, declines. In 1900, only 7 percent of nonagricultural workers belonged to unions, comprising slightly less than 1 million workers. Over the next five decades, membership and density increased substantially, particularly in three "spurt" periods around World War I, the New Deal years of the 1930s, and World War II. At midcentury, union density had increased 450 percent to one-third of the workforce and 14 million American workers held union cards.

From the vantage point of midcentury, unions had made remarkable gains and collective bargaining was firmly established as the dominant method of wage determination and workforce governance in the United States. And most experts at the time predicted that this pattern would continue well into the future. But history proved otherwise. Density peaked in 1953 at 33 percent of the workforce, declined slowly for the next two decades, and then fell more sharply in the 1980s and 1990s, reaching the lowest level in six decades in 2000 (14 percent). Although union membership continued to grow until the late 1970s, it then dropped by 5 million during the next two decades, leaving union membership in 2000 at nearly the same level (16 million) it had reached in the mid-1950s.

The trends in membership and density since the 1950s mask, however, highly divergent developments in the private and public sectors. Unionism in the public sector increased dramatically over this period, while it contracted sharply in the private sector. In the 1950s, only slightly more than 10 percent of government workers belonged to unions, but expansion of collective bargaining rights to federal, state, and local employees in the intervening years fueled a major surge in union growth. As a result, public-sector membership

Figure 3.1 **Union Density, 1900–2000**

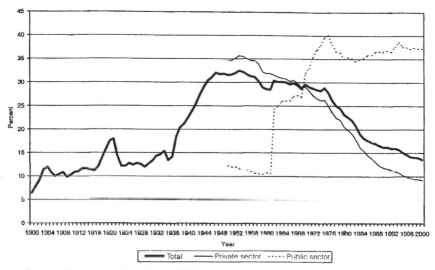

Source: Bennett and Kaufman (2002a).

grew from 1 million to 6 million and public-sector density jumped to 40 percent by the mid-1970s—a level then largely maintained up to 2000.

Unionism in the private sector, on the other hand, has badly eroded. While one in four private-sector workers belonged to unions in the mid-1970s, this ratio fell to less than one in ten in 2000. Indeed, it is noteworthy that private-sector density had fallen to a level in 2000 (9 percent) that was quite close to the density figure that existed exactly 100 years ago at the start of the twentieth century (7 percent). Union membership in the private sector also reflected a marked deterioration, falling by nearly 5 million since the early 1970s.

The Two Faces of Unionism

A popular model in labor economics portrays the level of union membership and density as a product of the demand and supply of union services (Pencavel 1971; Farber 1983). The demand for union services comes from employees, and, other things being equal, the stronger this demand is, the higher union membership and density will be. Likewise, union membership and density will also be larger the greater the supply of collective bargaining services provided by labor unions, or the lower the price at which they provide these services. Behind demand and supply lie government labor policy and court rulings, as they exert considerable influence on the structure, operation, and activities of unions.

With this model in mind, forecasting the future growth of the labor movement

Figure 3.2 **Union Membership, 1900–2000**

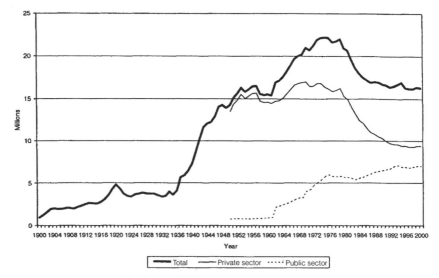

Source: Bennett and Kaufman (2002a).

evidently requires attention to shifts in both the demand and supply curves for union services. The thesis of this chapter is that both are directly related to the question posed by Freeman and Medoff's book: "What do unions do?" That is, the answer to this question—and correlatively to another question: "How much do they do it?"—directly impacts employees' demand for union services and the stance taken by government and the courts with respect to regulating the supply of union services. Thus, if workers perceive that unions provide highly desirable services and are effective in delivering them, the demand for unions will be large and membership and density will grow accordingly. Similarly, if voters and their elected government leaders and appointed judges perceive that what unions do bestows large benefits on society, they are more likely to pass legislation and write court opinions that encourage union-joining and union activities, thereby promoting higher membership and density.

These considerations directly lead to Freeman and Medoff's proposed two faces of unionism. The essence of their typology is that unions serve two functions: a bargaining (muscle) function and a communication (voice) function. The bargaining function of unions is to use their market power to gain above-market wages and other terms and conditions of employment; the communication function is to aggregate and express workers' preferences and opinions to management and government officials. The strength of workers' demand for unions rests, in turn, on the size of the net benefits they perceive unions can deliver from the exercise of muscle and voice, as well as the "price" that goes with obtaining these net benefits. Similarly, the degree government leaders and judges are motivated to encourage union-joining and collective bargaining is directly related to their judgment about the size of the net benefits to the economy and society from union muscle and voice.

I find Freeman and Medoff's "two faces" dichotomy an interesting and insightful framework for thinking about the benefits and costs of unions, and I will apply it in this chapter to the issue of union growth. But, at the same time, the "two faces" as Freeman and Medoff present them have several limitations and shortcomings for the purpose at hand. To remedy these problems, I draw on the work of early twentieth-century economist and industrial relations scholar John R. Commons (Kaufman 2001a, 2002a).

Freeman and Medoff attribute the intellectual inspiration for the "two faces" framework to the work of Albert Hirschman and, in particular, his book *Exit, Voice, and Loyalty* (1971). But in large measure, the bargaining and voice functions of unions is clearly identified in the work of the early institutional labor economists nearly a century ago. Commons, for example, claims that unions have both an economic and noneconomic purpose. The economic function is "wealth redistribution," "joint aggrandizement," and "protection." According to Commons (1905, reprinted in Commons 1913, 121), unions accomplish these goals by acting much as a cartel of firms in the product market—they organize as many of the sellers of labor as possible, establish rules that allocate the available work among members, and use their market power to set a common price for all sellers that is above the prevailing market rate. By doing so, they redistribute income from capital to labor, increase the wage bill for labor ("aggrandizement"), and shield workers from adverse consequences of market competition, such as wage cuts, speed-ups, and long hours.

The noneconomic function of unions, according to Commons, is to provide what he called "constitutional government in industry" (CGI) (1905, vii), or what Sidney Webb and Beatrice Webb (1897) earlier called "industrial democracy." According to Commons (1951), every organization is a form of "government," in that each is a product of collective action, is governed by working rules that specify authority relations and the distribution of rights, liberties, duties, and exposures, and employs sanctions to enforce the working rules. In the work world, the most important organization is the business firm and, parallel to modern writings of new institutional economists such as Oliver Williamson (1985), Commons suggests that we view firms as a form of industrial government or a "governance structure."

Looked at from the vantage point of the early twentieth century, the governance structure of most firms was closely akin to that of fourteenth-century England, that is, a system of unvarnished autocracy in which a monarch rules with largely undisputed authority (Kaufman 2000a). Commons thinks this system of industrial government to be obviously despotic (but perhaps benevolently so), and thus favors trade unions as a way to introduce democracy or representative government into the workplace. By "democracy," he does not necessarily mean majority voting, but he does envision the representation of workers' interests (or voice, a term he explicitly uses [Commons 1919, 43]), the substitution of "rule by law" for "rule by men" in the governance of the workplace, and due process and impartial adjudication in the resolution of disputes.

Are the differences between Freeman and Medoff and Commons substantive or semantic? To a significant degree, both sets of authors are describing the same aspects of unionism, but I think for the purposes of predicting union growth Commons's conceptualization of the "two faces" has several advantages.

With regard to the bargaining function of unions, for example, the monopoly metaphor used by Freeman and Medoff tends to focus attention on the role of unions in raising the price of labor (wages and benefits), while Commons's notion of wealth redistribution, aggrandizement, and protection (WRAP) broadens the goal of unions to include "protection"—that is, using bargaining power to maintain gains already achieved or to shield workers from actions of firms and/or markets. Although wealth redistribution is certainly implicit in the monopoly metaphor, Commons's framework likewise gives it explicit attention. A second problematic aspect of Freeman and Medoff's monopoly metaphor is that it assumes the exercise of union bargaining power takes place within a system of competitive labor markets. Thus, Freeman and Medoff state, "Most, if not all, unions have monopoly power, which they can use to raise wages above *competitive* levels" (1984, 6, emphasis added). Given the assumption that markets are competitive, Freeman and Medoff are necessarily led to concede that most of what unions do in their bargaining function is against the social interest—per this statement, "If one looks only at the monopoly face, most of what unions do is socially harmful" (246). Commons, by way of contrast, develops the function of union WRAP in the context of labor markets that may be competitive but more often contain various forms of market imperfections and failures. Doing so opens the possibility that the exercise of union bargaining power, rather than harming social welfare, can improve it by offsetting employer domination in wage determination and the adverse consequences of externalities, public goods, and asymmetric information.

The second function of unions is captured by Freeman and Medoff in the metaphor of "voice," while Commons uses the term "constitutional government in industry." The two conceptions are certainly related, per Freeman and Medoff's characterization of "voice" as a "political mechanism" (1984, 8). But Freeman and Medoff's emphasis regarding union voice is nonetheless on the communication aspect, per their statements, "'Voice' refers to the use of direct communication to bring actual and desired conditions closer together" and "voice means discussing with an employer conditions that ought to be changed, rather than quitting the job" (8). Commons, however, provides a broader and more legal/political science-oriented conception of the voice function of unions. As noted earlier, he views firms as a form of industrial government with executive, legislative, and judicial functions, and the role of unions is to introduce rule of law and a measure of democracy into a system of industrial absolutism and "rule by men" (Kaufman 2000a). Attention is thus shifted from the communication function of unions to the governance function and, in particular, the role of unions in giving workers political voice in the determination of the terms and conditions of employment (the legislative function) and in the interpretation and enforcement of the rules of the workplace (the judicial function). For Commons, the written union contract is the most tangible and far-reaching expression of union voice.

Both Freeman and Medoff and Commons suggest that unions have "two faces" in the workplace, one related to muscle and the other related to voice. The difference between the two conceptualizations is one of emphasis, interpretation, and nuance. Freeman and Medoff suggest that the private and social demand for unions is fundamentally tied to the answer of the question "what do unions do?"—a proposition Commons would certainly support. I also think, however, that Commons would suggest that a modestly broader and more inclusive conceptualization of the two faces of unions would provide a more accurate and insightful framework for evaluating the future growth prospects of unions. It is to the task of demonstrating this conjecture that I now turn.

Looking Back: The Decade of the 1920s

Before using the "two faces" framework to examine future union growth, valuable lessons and implications are gained by first using it to understand the pattern of union growth in two earlier periods of American history: the 1920s and the 1930s. Although separated from the early twenty-first century by seven decades, these early periods exhibit many close parallels with modern times regarding prospects and contingencies for union growth.

The 1920s was a period of union stagnation and decline. Density fell from 17 percent in 1920 to 12 percent in 1929, while membership dropped by over 1 million. What accounts for this pattern in union growth? Why did union fortunes decline in the 1920s, only to rebound in the 1930s?

Judging from past experience, the 1920s should have been a period of union growth (Wolman 1936; Kaufman 2001a). Union membership and density had increased markedly during the previous two decades of the century,

and particularly during periods of economic prosperity similar to the buoy-
ant times of the 1920s. Government policy had also turned favorable to unions
in the World War I period and pressure was exerted on employers to hold
representation elections, recognize unions where a majority of employees
expressed desire, and engage in good-faith collective bargaining. But, paradoxically, unions fell on hard times in the 1920s and both the public and
government reverted to an indifferent-to-hostile attitude. A review of the historical literature suggests that a significant part of the explanation lies with a
much-diminished appeal of union WRAP and CGI.

Consider first union WRAP. The demand of workers for union services
comes in part from their desire to use collective bargaining to redistribute
wealth from profits to wages, increase the wage bill paid to labor (aggrandizement), and protect previously won gains in compensation and working
conditions. But both the need of workers for WRAP, and the ability of unions
to deliver WRAP, declined in the 1920s. The reasons include the following:

Economic Conditions

For the first time in the twentieth century, the 1920s featured strong economic
growth with stable prices—a product of robust productivity growth in the "new
economy" industries of that era (e.g., automobiles and electrical equipment)
and declining agricultural prices. The result was a gently rising real wage. In
years past, observes Selig Perlman, "with the barking dog of the rising cost of
living steadily at his feet, the wage earner could not afford to be anything but
profoundly wage conscious and an attentive listener to the gospel of unionism" (1928, 212). But, observes economist Lyle Cooper, with advancing real
wages and living standards, "large numbers of wage earners felt they were
'getting ahead' . . . without any direct assistance from organized labor [so]
workers could well ask why they should bother to join unions" (1932, 646).

Changing Industrial/Occupational Structure

Another factor undercutting the appeal of union WRAP in the 1920s was the
changing industrial and occupational distribution of employment. Unions
were concentrated in certain industries, such as mining, apparel, construction, and printing. These were slow-growth industries in the 1920s, register-
ing employment growth of only 10 percent. By way of contrast, employment
grew by 40 percent in the largely unorganized sectors of the American
economy, including the new economy industries concentrated in durable
manufacturing. Not only did employment growth bypass union strongholds,
union WRAP had less appeal because many of the new economy jobs of the

1920s paid high wages and offered good working conditions. Reflective of these trends are the following comments of Leo Wolman:

> In business and industry the period was marked by an immense shift in the centers of economic activity. . . . It is rare that the rate of change in this respect has been so great as it was in this brief spell of seven years. . . . With few exceptions the industries and trades comprising the most prosperous sections of the American economy had in the past been the least penetrated by trade unionism and retained their immunity to organization probably through their capacity to pay high wages and to offer satisfactory conditions of employment. (1936, 35)

Craft Union Structure

Most unions of the period were organized along craft (occupational) lines and catered to the skilled elite of the workforce. The process of technological change and growth of the mass-production industries seriously undercut the bargaining effectiveness and appeal of unions, however. George Barnett remarks on these trends:

> The rapid introduction of labor saving machinery accompanied as it almost always is by the replacement of skilled labor with unskilled has lessened the membership of many of the most important American trade unions. . . . Many writers have counseled the leaders of the American trade-union movement to abandon their present forms of organization and to move in the direction of industrial trade unionism. There are no indications that anything of this kind will happen in the near future. (1933, 4)

Cooper offers similar thoughts, saying that the craft unions of the period were "confined to the aristocracy of the skilled and inclined to view the unskilled with aloof indifference if not arrogant condescension" (1932, 654).

Welfare Capitalism

Prior to World War I, employers typically treated labor as a commodity to be bought for as little as possible, utilized to the maximum extent, and then discarded (Jacoby 1985; Kaufman 2001b). Naturally, this system of labor management created a large demand for union WRAP on the part of workers. After the war, however, progressive employers crafted a new labor policy that looked at workers not as a commodity but a human resource. This new strategy was called welfare capitalism. The goal of welfare capitalism was to attain competitive advantage by fostering cooperation and loyalty among employees, and to do this firms paid above-market wages, provided employee benefits (e.g., paid vacations and life insurance), and instituted job security measures. The impact of welfare capitalism on worker demand for unions is explained in these words by Perlman:

> This program of "welfare capitalism" is the new labor program of American capitalism. . . . [T]his "new" capitalism which fights unionism with a far-sighted "preventive" method . . . leaves it [trade unionism] stunned and bewildered. . . . Welfare capitalism appears to voluntarily offer to the worker a "fair wage," a reasonable working day, and the security from unemployment, from injury to health, and from unjust discrimination, which unionism has always endeavored to obtain for him through its "job control." (1928, 210–211)

The second face of unionism is voice or CGI. In the traditional employment model prevalent through World War I, the workplace was run in an autocratic and often heavy-handed manner. The legal doctrine underlying the employment relation was "master and servant"—the employer was the master and had unfettered rights to command the worker (the servant) to do his bidding. A corollary of the master-servant doctrine was "employment-at-will"—the ability of the employer to fire the worker without notice and for whatever reason. A third accoutrement of the traditional employment model was the "drive" system of motivation—the use of threats, verbal abuse, and constant supervision to drive employees to exert maximum work effort. Sumner Slichter speaks about the oppressive and unjust features of this system of employment in this observation:

> [T]hey [employers] maintained as a matter of policy a brusque, more or less harsh, distant, and stern attitude toward their men. They resorted to discharge on fairly slight provocation. They discouraged the airing of grievances. The man with a complaint was told, "If you don't like things here, you can quit. . . ." Above all, it was felt that the men must be made to feel that the management was strong and powerful, determined to have its way and not to be trifled with. (1920, 44)

Not unexpectedly, many workers and citizens were attracted to the union cause in this period by the prospect that unions and collective bargaining could replace unvarnished workplace autocracy with a measure of industrial democracy. The appeal of industrial democracy was particularly pronounced in the World War I years, a period marked by a surge in union-joining, strike action, and appeals from labor leaders, church groups, progressive intellectuals, and liberal businessmen for more enlightened employment practices

(Lichtenstein and Harris 1993; Barnett 1922). But, as noted earlier, the appeal of unions waned in the 1920s and union membership and density dropped noticeably. Why?

Part of the answer, as just described, is attributable to the decline in worker demand for, and union effectiveness in supplying, WRAP. Similar considerations apply to union-provided CGI. Two developments, in particular, undermined the allure of union CGI.

Personnel Management and Employee Representation

The advent of welfare capitalism heralded an entirely different labor strategy on the part of employers. Part of this strategy, as noted earlier, was to pay above-market wages and provide new types of employee benefits, thus undercutting the appeal of union WRAP. But there were also other features that did much to undercut the appeal of union CGI. During the World War I years, employers realized that the traditional "commodity/autocratic management" model of managing employees had numerous negative repercussions, such as high rates of labor turnover, bitter feelings and low morale among the workforce, and continual strikes and threats of unionization, all of which were detrimental to productivity and firm performance. Progressive, forward-looking employers decided to try a different approach to competitive advantage—one that would gain higher productivity and product quality by winning employees' goodwill, loyalty, and cooperation. In this vein, Slichter observes, "unwilling to try driving, one course remained—to increase efficiency by developing a stable work force and by winning the good will and cooperation of the men. This alternative was widely adopted" (1929, 401).

In an effort to win employees' goodwill, welfare capitalist employers reformed workforce governance and management methods in a number of respects, all of which reduced the demand of employees for union CGI. Examples include limits on the authority of foremen to fire workers, training of foremen in "human relations," use of job evaluation procedures to remove inequitable wage differentials, and provision for job security and promotion from within. Most important, however, was a nonunion form of industrial democracy in the form of an employee representation plan (ERP). Derided by critics as "company unions," ERPs provided an alternative method for employee voice in the enterprise (Kaufman 2000b). Set up by management, they were joint councils composed of elected employee representatives and appointed management representatives that met monthly or quarterly to discuss and resolve problems of mutual interest relating to production, working conditions, wages/benefits/ hours, and discipline and discharge. The negative impact progressive management methods had on worker demand for union CGI is attested to in this observation by William Leiserson, "[T]he Personnel Managers are leading the great masses of unskilled, semiskilled, and clerical workers away for the official labor movement, and attaching them with various devices more or less loyally to the management of the corporations which employ them" (1929, 141). Of the various management devices referred to by Leiserson, he states that ERPs "are perhaps the most significant contribution" (154).

Autocracy and Corruption in Unions

The demand for union CGI was also impaired by shortcomings in the internal governance practices of the unions themselves. While union leaders denounced the autocratic practices of employers and the denial of basic civil liberties and human rights in the workplace, frequently their own organizations were marred by these same problems. Illustrative of this conundrum is this query by Willard Hotchkiss, "Why should we overthrow the autocracy of the employer, an autocracy which doubtless oftener than not is a benevolent autocracy . . . [i]n order to establish a meddlesome oligarchy whose interests are frequently quite different from the interests of the workers for whom it speaks?" (1920, 113–114).

Union CGI in the 1920s was afflicted with a number of specific shortcomings. For example, most unions of that period catered to the skilled elite of the workforce and excluded the broad mass of unskilled and semiskilled workers and openly discriminated against the foreign born, women, and nonwhites. These practices led Leiserson to comment, "[T]he history of handling these workers by the trade unions is not something to impress on their minds that the unions are particularly desirous of promoting their interests" (1929, 157). Nor were the internal governance practices of many unions democratic—per the observation of Leiserson, that many unions resembled a "one party system of industrial democracy" (1959, 74), and the observation by Robert Hoxie, that "unionism in its own organization and conduct is hardly to be called democratic" (1917, 177). Unions were also troubled by self-interested, sometimes corrupt leadership. A contemporary witness lamented, for example, that the leaders of a number of the building trades unions were "a bunch of racketeers in league with a lot of the building contractors" (quoted in Elliot 1992, 56–57). The problem of union corruption in the 1920s is also noted by Cooper when he remarked, "particularly in large cities, where unionism reaches its greatest strength, shady practices involving the racket and accompanying graft flourish" (1932, 654).

Looking back on the 1920s, my contention is that the decline of unionism was directly tied to two developments: a diminished need on the part of workers for union WRAP and CGI, and growing doubts about the efficacy of union WRAP and CGI and the ability of unions to effectively deliver them. In effect, neither of the "two faces" of unionism in the 1920s looked as appealing or blemish-free as in earlier years, leading to a decline in worker demand for collective bargaining. Then, compounding this problem, was public indifference to unions and a national labor policy that allowed employers practically free rein to resist union recognition and bargaining. Court injunctions, blacklists, yellow-dog contracts, imported strikebreakers, large-scale terminations for union activity, and armed company police were among the favored and often-used weapons. The injustices of these acts were evident to many observers, but public officials were under little pressure to curb their use given the low regard the public had for unions and the exercise of WRAP and CGI. In this regard, Perlman observes that "American unionism faces the problem of winning back the public support which it has lost. The material rise in real wages and the disappearance of the more glaring abuses has robbed the labor movement of grounds for telling appeal to public sympathy. But public sympathy has been slipping from organized labor much more on account of the aggressiveness of many union groups" (1928, 215).

Union Resurgence: The Decade of the 1930s

In the fall of 1929, the outlook for organized labor looked relatively bleak—per an article devoted to the trade union movement in the *Nation* entitled "Labor Asleep" (October 23, 1929, 455). Even supporters of trade unionism, such as Leiserson, were forced to admit that the labor movement seemed increasingly marginalized by the employers' strategy of welfare capitalism, per this observation: "The weakening of trade unionism that has resulted is an undesirable consequence, but who will say then that we should go back to the days when management neglected its social responsibilities toward its employees. . . . The labor movement must have a mission beyond the program which personnel management has shown itself willing to adopt. If it is weakened by the activities of personnel management, it needs to look to its larger program" (1929, 146–147).

Shortly after these words were written, the nation plunged into the Great Depression. Although a calamity for the nation, the Great Depression in a perverse way posed an opportunity for the labor movement—perhaps it could turn misfortune for the nation into good fortune for itself. To do so, however, it would have to follow Leiserson's advice and "look to its larger program," demonstrating to the nation's workforce and polity that union WRAP and CGI were indeed able to deliver economic and social benefits that employers and their welfare capitalism strategy could not.

For the first three years of the depression, the union movement enjoyed little success at this task and, indeed, continued on a downward trajectory in both membership and public confidence. From 1929 to 1932, official union membership shrunk by another 350,000 people, but in reality by far more (since unions continued to count as members many workers who retired or were laid off). Despite the hard times visited on the nation's workers, there was little overt interest in organizing and for several years only modest and sporadic evidence of substantial discontent with employers. In early 1932, Cooper remarked on labor's impotency by saying, "something in the nature of a defeatist psychology has seized the minds of many labor leaders and members of the rank and file" (650), while columnist Louis Adamic observed in a similar vein that the organized labor movement "is undoubtedly a sick body. It is ineffectual—flabby, afflicted with the dull pains or moral and physical decline. The big industrialists and conservative politicians are no longer worried by it" (1932, 167). Even after the election of Franklin D. Roosevelt in November 1932, the labor movement remained becalmed, per the lament of one union president in early 1933, "[E]verything that the Socialists predicted in the way of breakdown of the capitalist system is coming to pass. [Still,] the great mass of wage earners seem to be as difficult to reach as ever" (quoted in Zieger 1984, 67).

From the vantage point of the early 1930s, two economists prognosticated on the future of the organized labor movement and saw little about which to be hopeful. Cooper stated, for example, "Little reason appears to exist for the expectation that a weak labor movement will be replaced soon by one that will be strong" (1932, 641), while George Barnett prophesied, "I see no reason to believe that American trade unionism will so revolutionize itself within a short period of time as to become in the next decade a more potent social influence. . . . We may take it as probable that trade unionism is likely to be a declining influence in determining conditions of labor" (1933, 6).

But the ink was barely dry on these words when suddenly, beginning in the summer of 1933, a wave of union organizing and strikes erupted across the nation, the nation's labor law and elected government officials swung solidly behind the cause of organized labor, and union membership rolls more than doubled in the space of a few years. What happened to so suddenly and swiftly revitalize trade unionism?

The answer, I contend, has much to do with a dramatic shift in the private and public views about the two faces of unionism and, in particular, the efficacy and desirability of union WRAP and CGI. Consider first WRAP.

In the context of the (relatively) prosperous and full employment era of the 1920s, union WRAP was regarded by many as exerting on net a harmful influence, per Perlman's observation in the late 1920s that unions "force upon industry uneconomic wage scales" and are associated with "rules that hamper output, prevent promotion on merit, raise costs of production, and bring on strikes" (1928, 215). Likewise, individual workers had little interest in WRAP, per Cooper's previously cited observation that "large numbers of wage earners felt they were 'getting ahead' . . . without any direct assistance from organized labor" (1932, 646).

After several years of depression, however, attitudes began to change. Repeated wage cuts, layoffs, and speed-ups took their toll, as did a hardening of discipline and supervision in the shops. Academics, such as Leiserson (1931) and Slichter (1931), began to take a more critical perspective on employers, questioning the justice of maintaining and even expanding stock dividends, while at the same time cutting wages and laying off long-time employees. Some astute business observers also saw potential trouble on the horizon. The welfare capitalist employers had pledged to maintain wages and provide job security—a pledge they mostly lived up to through the fall of 1931. But then U.S. Steel, under pressure of millions of dollars of losses, cut wage rates, causing numerous other firms to follow suit in what turned out to be a revolving series of wage cuts through the winter of 1932. These wage cuts, while perhaps forced by economic necessity, destroyed the "social contract" between employers and workers and led to much bitterness and sense of exploitation on the part of the latter. *Business Week* observed, "To risk satisfactory employee relationships, maintained only with considerable difficulty under present conditions, for a wage cut which can have only a minor effect upon costs at the best and is just as likely to increase them as to lower them appears to many managers with modern views on employee relationships a gamble against reasonable odds" (October 7, 1931, 6). How prescient the writer was!

The growing appeal of union WRAP and CGI also becomes apparent from the personal accounts of workers who experienced the Great Depression firsthand. Illustrative, for example, is this remembrance by a blue-collar worker:

> There was quite a buzz in the machine shop in Brooklyn when we got our first pay cut. . . . During lunch hour, while we were talking about the cut, the fellows agreed to get a committee together to see the superintendent. We tried to pick out skilled people who would be least likely to be fired. . . . We tried it. The boss went right past us out of the office and said, "All you guys better go back to work or the whole shebang will be fired." Without another word we picked up our tools and got busy on the job. A while later, we were discussing the things and we agreed that the reason we didn't get anywhere was because we didn't have a union. (Quoted in Matles and Higgins 1974, 22–23)

A second illustration is captured in this fiddle song of a black coal miner:

> In nineteen hundred an' thirty-two
> We wus sometimes sad an' blue,
> Travelin' roun' from place to place
> Tryin' to find some work to do.
> If we's successful to find a job,
> De wages wus so small,
> We could scarcely live in de summertime—
> Almost starved in de fall. (Quoted in Alexander 1999, 62)

These conditions, by leading to a profound sense of suffering and injustice, created a readiness among workers for collective action. Where in the 1920s workers had faith in the fruits of individual initiative and the employers' promise of a "square deal," the experience of the early 1930s seemed much more like a "raw deal" and showed the futility of individual action. Collective action thus grew in appeal, and one form of collective action was union-joining. While union WRAP and CGI seemed to offer modest-to-little benefit in the 1920s, they suddenly looked much more attractive in the depths of the depression.

But a predisposition to unionize does not necessarily translate into actual union organizing activity. Workers have to also believe that organizing will be successful and that unions can effectively deliver WRAP and CGI (Wheeler and McClendon 1991). This requirement was provided by the newly elected Roosevelt administration in 1933, when it switched government labor policy toward a position supportive and protective of unions. The opening move in this direction was in June 1933, when the president signed into law the National Industrial Recovery Act (NIRA), followed in July 1935 by the passage of the National Labor Relations Act (NLRA).

The NIRA contained the now-famous section 7(a) which, for the first time in American law, made it national policy that workers have the right to join unions free of coercion and intimidation (Bernstein 1950). Within weeks of its passage, a wave of union organizing and strikes erupted across the nation. The NIRA suffered from two defects, however, which required additional legislation. The first shortcoming was that it did not specify actions that contravened the guarantee of free choice, nor did it contain an enforcement mechanism; the second was that the law was declared unconstitutional in early 1935 by the U.S. Supreme Court. To remedy these shortcomings, President Roosevelt swung his support behind Senator Robert Wagner's proposed NLRA and it was quickly enacted. The NLRA proscribed a series of employer antiunion "unfair labor practices," established the secret ballot, set up a majority vote union representation election to decide the issue of union recognition and bargaining rights, and created a National Labor Relations Board to enforce and administer the provisions of the law. Among the employer unfair labor practices outlawed was the establishment and operation of a "company union"—a provision that wiped out the crown jewel of the welfare capitalism strategy: the employee representation plan.

It is widely accepted that passages of the NIRA and NLRA were major contributors to the surge of unionism in the 1930s. They did so by shifting rightward both the demand and supply curves for union services—the demand curve because these laws appeared to give the stamp of government approval to union-joining and made it much more likely that unions could successfully organize, collectively bargain, and strike; the supply curve because union organizing and collective bargaining now had legal protection and encouragement. The interesting issue in all of this is why government policy shifted from indifferent/hostile toward unions to a supportive/protective position. The answer, I claim, involves a marked shift in the view of workers and policy makers regarding the private and social benefits of the two faces of unionism: union WRAP and CGI.

In documenting this claim, it is necessary to go back and examine the reasons the NIRA was adopted and, in particular, why section 7(a) and its support and protection of collective bargaining was inserted. As I have described elsewhere (Kaufman 1996), President Roosevelt and Senator Wagner had a common diagnosis of the cause of the depression and the economic measures needed to end it. The initial cause, they perceived, was the growing maldistribution of income in the 1920s as profits increased faster than wages, which led to excessive stock market speculation, overinvestment in industrial capacity, and insufficient household purchasing power and aggregate demand, all of which in 1929 precipitated the stock market crash and the beginning phase of the downturn. The downturn then turned into a deflationary plunge due to "destructive competition," as excess supplies in product and labor markets drove down prices and wages, further reducing purchasing power and threatening wide-scale bankruptcy and impoverishment.

The solution Roosevelt and Wagner engineered was the NIRA. It sought to stabilize the wage-price structure by cartelizing markets through price fixing and production quotas in product markets (contained in "codes of fair competition," and drafted and monitored by industry associations) and through unions, collective bargaining, and minimum wage laws in labor markets. Not only would unions put a floor under competition and stanch destructive competition, but by pursuing WRAP they would also redistribute income from profits to wages and thereby augment household purchasing power, stimulate aggregate demand, and move the economy back toward full employment. Greater unionization thus came to be seen by government leaders as beneficial for economic performance, rather than harmful as in the 1920s, and out of this change of perspective sprang the change in labor policy.

The change in labor policy that brought about the NIRA encouraged greater unionization in other important ways. As already noted, the events of the depression created significant feelings of dissatisfaction and injustice among workers. Robert Zieger, in a case study of the International Brotherhood of Pulp, Sulphite, and Paper Mill Workers, notes in this regard, "Workers surged into the Brotherhood in 1933 and 1934 primarily in hopes of increasing their wages. . . . Discipline on the job, deterioration of working conditions, and callousness on the part of managers also impelled pulp and paper workers toward the union" (1984, 69–70). But he goes on to note how the passage of the NIRA further fueled the drive to organize by wrapping personal gain in the flag of patriotic duty, "The broader goals that workers brought to local union formation usually had less to do with commitment to organized labor than the desire to support the New Deal, President Roosevelt, and the NRA [National Recovery Act]. . . . Workers in every sector seized upon the NRA promise, as a means both of bettering their individual lot and of revitalizing the country. Patriotism fused with self-interest" (71). Another place the comingling of public and private purpose in union-joining was on display in 1933 was the coal industry, where union organizers paraded through towns in cars and trucks carrying signs "The President wants you to joint the union!"

'The NIRA also increased workers' demand for union CGI. A premise behind the NIRA was that a competitively organized market economy is inherently unstable and wasteful. The New Deal thus sought to move to an alternative, Americanized version of "corporatism"—a system of economic organization in which the economy is managed by organized interest groups under the leadership of the government (somewhat akin to the fascist model adopted in the 1930s in Italy). Senator Wagner articulated this vision by explicitly tying it to a political conception of CGI:

> Modern nations have selected one of two methods to bring order into industry. The first is to create a super-government. Under such a plan, labor unions are abolished or become the creatures of the state. . . . The second method of coordinating industry is the democratic method. . . . Instead of control from on top, it insists upon control from within. It places the primary responsibility where it belongs and asks industry and labor to solve their mutual problems through self-government. This is industrial democracy. (Quoted in Keyserling 1945, 13)

Union CGI thus complemented union WRAP in Roosevelt's and Wagner's perspective and gave a double rationale for the promotion of greater unionism under the NIRA. But the social rationale for greater union CGI, and the corporatist model that underlay it, also fueled greater private demand for union CGI on the part of workers. Under the NIRA, wages and hours were determined in part through a quasi-political process in Washington, D.C., where government officials and representatives of employers' associations—and union officials in cases where the workers were organized—negotiated minimum and maximum levels of these items and included them in the codes of fair competition. It thus quickly became obvious to unorganized workers that they had no effective voice in this process and needed to organize to be represented. Union organizers, in turn, skillfully used this message to induce union-joining—per this statement of organizer William Collins to a group of Detroit auto workers, "[T]he automobile workers can only secure the maximum benefits to which they are entitled under the Industrial Recovery Act through collective action" (*Business Week,* July 15, 1933, 8).

The weaknesses of the NIRA led Wagner to propose new legislation that would put teeth into section 7(a). In testimony to the Senate Committee on Education and Labor in early 1935, Wagner justified the proposed NLRA by citing the economic and social virtues of union WRAP and CGI. He said:

> It is well recognized today that the failure to spread adequate purchasing power among the vast masses of the consuming public disrupts the continuity of business operations and causes everyone to suffer. . . . Two years ago, we set forth upon a new program, openly and completely reversing our earlier policies. Industrial cooperation was given sanction in order to limit the evils of destructive competition. Employees were guaranteed protection in their cooperative efforts, in order that they might help the Government to insure a sufficient flow of purchasing power through adequate wages. . . . This process of economic self-rule must fail unless every group is equally well represented. In order that the strong may not take advantage of the weak, every group must be equally strong. Not only is this common sense; but it is also in line with the philosophy of checks and balances that colors our political thinking. It is in accord with modern democratic concepts. (National Labor Relations Board 1985, 1410–1411)

Elsewhere, he couched the rationale for the NLRA expressly in terms of reforming what he regarded as an autocratic, almost feudal form of industrial government in the shop. He told the Senate, "It [the NLRA] seeks merely to make the worker a free man in the economic as well as the political field. . . . There can be no freedom in an atmosphere of bondage" (1312–1313).

Wagner was not alone in touting the virtues of union WRAP and CGI in the depression years. Many economists now swung over to a like-minded position. Paul Douglas of the University of Chicago testified to Congress:

> I should like to submit that the organization of labor should be welcomed instead of feared. We might get along with purely individual bargaining in a period of small-scale competitive capitalism. When large-scale enterprises appeared, individual bargaining, even under competition, became inadequate. Now that we are replacing competitive capitalism by strong associations of employers who are given the power of united action, and who are coming to have even greater control over prices and production under the codes, it is, in my opinion, essential to build up organizations of labor as a counterpoise. . . . We must grant reciprocal rights to both parties and not exclusive rights to one. (National Labor Relations Board 1985, 239)

Similar remarks were offered by fellow labor economist Harry Millis, "The truth, as I see it, is, however, that the competitive demand for labor, while important, does not go far in protecting the workers against long hours, excessive overtime, fines, discharges without sufficient cause, and objectionable working standards. . . . One is thus driven to the conclusion that hours of work and conditions of work—things which intimately concern workmen, are best decided collectively" (1555).

Or, finally, consider Leiserson. As previously noted, Leiserson had generally taken a positive position during the 1920s on accomplishments of employers' personnel management programs and employee representation plans and, with respect to the latter, portrayed them as a valuable way to improve joint relations and achieve a mutual gains outcome for employers and workers. But in the 1930s, he changed his point of view and became a staunch supporter of the NLRA and the need for expanded collective bargaining. In his congressional testimony on the NLRA, Leiserson shifted the focus of his attention to emphasize how the relative bargaining strength of capital and labor determines the split between profits and wages. For example, in discussing the role of labor organizations he stated, "[W]hat we want here is to make a contract [between labor and the firm], a commercial contract" (National Labor Relations Board 1985, 2267). And, viewed from this perspective, he found the company union fatally flawed, "For a company to come in and say [to the workers], 'I want to be on the selling end of this through my personnel manager' . . . is obviously to defeat the purpose of the contract." And what is the purpose of the contract? He stated, "the whole theory of the N.R.A., it seems to me, rests on the idea that what we need is collective organization of the people in industry, whether . . . laborers, or [as] businessmen. . . . We have discovered that if we let each individual businessman, doing business on his own . . . then all sorts of unfair practices creep in. We find that if laborers compete alone, wages go down to $4 a week" (2260).

The surge of union membership during the 1930s was thus the product of two simultaneous trends. The first blade was that the prolonged deterioration in workplace conditions caused by the Great Depression created a large demand for union WRAP and CGI on the part of individual workers. The second was that the depression also led policy makers to take a much more favorable view of union WRAP and CGI, bringing with it new legislation that greatly stimulated both the demand for and supply of union services. Where the two faces of unionism were viewed with indifference and suspicion in the 1920s, they became agents of both private and social progress in the 1930s. Not unexpectedly, union membership stagnated in the former period and mushroomed in the latter.

A host of other developments, I should briefly note, also contributed to the mass unionization of industry in the 1930s (Freeman 1998). Among the most important are the

- formation of the Congress of Industrial Organizations in 1935,
- spread of industrial unionism,
- dynamic union leaders, such as John L. Lewis and Sydney Hillman.

While unionism was weighed down in the 1920s by reliance on an outmoded craft union model and a stodgy, sometimes corrupt leadership, the resurgence of unionism in the 1930s was greatly promoted by new innovations in union structure and the appearance of a more forceful, progressive leadership.

Union Growth Prospects in the Early Twenty-first Century

I now wish to fast-forward the discussion seven decades to the early twenty-first century. As noted earlier, union density peaked at one-third of the workforce in the early 1950s and then slowly declined over the next four decades until at the end of the century it reached 14 percent in the total economy and 9 percent in the private sector. Union membership continued to grow up to the late 1970s, but then dropped by 5 million over the next two decades. So, the question is: What will happen to union membership and density in the early part of the twenty-first century—will it continue to decline, or will trade unionism either stabilize or rebound in the years ahead?

My thesis is twofold: first, that the answer is directly tied to the private and social appeal of the two union faces of WRAP and CGI in the early twenty-first century and, second, that the experience of unionism in the 1920s and 1930s provides many clues for the likely direction of change.

As was true in the 1920s and 1930s, unions provide two essential services: WRAP and CGI. The challenges in forecasting union growth are, first, to accurately estimate employees' strength of demand for union WRAP and CGI in the years ahead and, second, to estimate public policy makers' demand for union WRAP and CGI and, thus, the likelihood that they will utilize a change in labor law and judicial opinion to promote more of both union demand and supply. Framed another way, the task is to determine whether the next one to two decades will more closely resemble the 1920s or the 1930s.

The evidence suggests that the next one to two decades are more likely to resemble the 1920s and thus the prospect for union growth in the years ahead has to be judged as relatively gloomy. This forecast is obviously contingent on an important assumption, however—that the United States avoids in future years a major disruptive event such as the Great Depression that substantially boosts both the private and public demand for union WRAP and CGI. Let me briefly amplify on these thoughts.

In a recent article, Henry Farber and Bruce Western (2002) demonstrate that changes in the stock of union membership over time arise from differential flows of people into and out of unions. The trend in union density, in turn, depends on the growth rate of union membership relative to the growth of the labor force. Their data show that the decline in union membership and density in the last part of the twentieth century in the private sector arose because the outflow of workers from union membership greatly exceeded the inflow. Extrapolating forward, Farber and Western conclude that should present trends continue, the equilibrium level of private-sector density is approximately 2 percent. One need not subscribe to this exact number to nonetheless agree with their fundamental point: "other things being equal," union membership and density in the private U.S. economy is headed downward. These trends are partially offset by the stability in public-sector union membership and density, but further growth prospects appear limited.

This conclusion then raises the obvious next question: Why is the outflow of union members so much greater than the inflow? Put in terms of the framework developed in this chapter, the answer has two parts (Bennett and Kaufman 2002a). The first is that the private and social benefits of union WRAP and CGI have declined over the last several decades and are likely to continue to do so; the second part is that the private and social costs of union WRAP and CGI have risen over time and are also likely to continue to do so. The combination of declining benefits and rising costs from WRAP and CGI form a pincer movement that together lead to a diminished inflow of new members and an accelerated outflow of existing members, while at the same time they cause citizens and policy makers to remain relatively indifferent to and often skeptical of the union cause and thus unsympathetic to efforts by organized labor to amend the nation's labor law to enhance their organizing and bargaining effectiveness. Let me briefly elaborate on these points.

Benefits of WRAP and CGI

My contention is that the benefits of union WRAP and CGI have declined in recent years and are likely to remain of modest size, thus providing reduced incentive for unorganized workers to seek union representation and for policy makers to liberalize the nation's labor law. This conclusion rests on the following considerations.

Smaller Dissatisfaction with Nonunion Jobs

As emphasized previously, workers are "pushed" into a high demand for union WRAP and CGI by work conditions viewed as onerous and unjust. Feeling dissatisfied, workers look for a solution to their problems and one attractive option is unionization. From decade to decade, a gradual improvement has taken place in the quality of work life for American employees. Whether one works in a factory, an airline, a school, or an office building, for the vast majority of American workers, jobs in 2000 paid better, provide better benefits, involve more interesting and less onerous work, and are managed in a more professional and equitable manner than at any time in the previous century (Federal Reserve Bank of Dallas 2001). The apex of these trends is the "high performance workplace," with its self-managed teams, gain-sharing compensation, egalitarian culture, and formal dispute resolution system.

Of course, there are still many workplaces that are an exception to this generalization and, indeed, recent evidence suggests that one-third of American workers are dissatisfied at work and would vote for a union if given the opportunity (Freeman and Rodgers 1999). Also, there are trends that on net foster greater dissatisfaction or fears of insecurity, such as diminished guarantees of lifetime jobs, increased pension (401k) risk, greater economic restructuring, and the threat to American jobs and living standards from global integration (Kaufman 1997a). But, on net, if the nation avoids a major economic/social disruption along the lines of the Great Depression and the locus of employment continues to shift from blue-collar/goods-producing industries to services and "new economy" industries of the 1990s (e.g., information technology), I have to conclude that employee satisfaction with work conditions at nonunion firms will certainly not worsen in years ahead and most likely will slowly improve. The implication of the foregoing is that as the breadth and depth of employee dissatisfaction recedes, so do the net benefits of union WRAP and CGI and, hence, the need and desire of employees for unions and the pressure on policy makers to support union WRAP and CGI through new legislation.

Diminished Effectiveness in Delivering WRAP and CGI

Workers are also "pulled" into unions by the potential of prospective gain in the form of higher wages and benefits, reduced hours, improved working conditions, and protection from unfair discipline and discharge. Recent trends, however, work against the ability of unions to deliver these items as effectively as in earlier years. The primary constraint is more open, competitive product markets brought about by globalization, deregulation of key industries, greater geographic mobility of capital, and the heightened pressure on companies from financial markets. These factors collectively undercut union bargaining power and make it difficult for unions to "deliver the goods" for members (Troy 2002). As a result, even if workers have a high level of dissatisfaction with nonunion employment conditions, they may nonetheless shy away from seeking union representation to the degree they perceive unions are powerless to make things better. A second important factor in this regard is the decline in the effectiveness of the strike threat, caused by things such as the growing willingness of employers to relocate production to other plants or countries and to hire nonunion replacement workers. A third factor is heightened management opposition to unions—a factor that makes employers take a stronger stance against union organizing and bargaining demands and, correlatively, makes it more difficult for unions to win in these matters (Kleiner 2001).

More Effective Substitutes for Union WRAP and CGI

A third factor diminishing worker and public demand for unions is the increased availability of good substitutes for WRAP and CGI. The three major substitutes are "good markets," progressive management, and government legislation (Bennett and Kaufman 2002b). "Good markets" means labor markets that are relatively competitive, wide open, and close to full employment. Given these conditions, workers can obtain wages commensurate with their skills and abilities, have opportunities for advancement, and have protection from unfair treatment (by quitting and seeking work elsewhere), thus reducing their demand for unions. An alternative substitute is progressive management. Employers can voluntarily provide through their human resource programs many of the things that unions provide, such as above-market wages, attractive benefit programs, job security, an employee involvement program, and a formal alternative dispute resolution process (Fiorito 2002; Kaufman 1997b). A third substitute is government legislation (Bennett and Taylor 2002). Government can mandate reasonable wages and hours, protect employee pension rights, provide help in retraining, and prohibit unfair discrimination through legislation and court review. All three union substitutes have grown in breadth and depth in the last several decades and I see no reason to believe that they will not collectively continue to advance in the decades ahead, thus further reducing the demand for union services. Of course, prosperity appeared ensured in the late 1920s but then quickly crumbled, so if there is a wild card here, it is in the ability of the American economy to remain close to full employment on a relatively sustained basis in the years ahead.

Employee Preferences for Unions

A fourth factor determining the strength of demand for unions is employees' preferences or "tastes" for union membership. The United States has always been marked by a social ethos that stresses the virtues of individualism and competition; correlatively, it has also scored low on a strong working-class identity and solidarity (Lipset and Katchanovski 2002). These psychological/social predispositions have strengthened over the decades in this country and thus work to further reduce the attractiveness of union-joining. There remains, admittedly, a large if not always stereotypical working class that continues to have working-class concerns, but so far unions—despite greater efforts to transform themselves from inward-looking business unions to an outward-looking social movement (Turner, Katz, and Hurd 2001), have not been able to substantially broaden their appeal. Employee preferences for union membership are also hurt by continued concerns over union corruption and nondemocratic practices, as well as a more general negative image of unions as stodgy, out-of-date institutions more relevant to a smokestack/blue-collar economy.

Costs of WRAP and CGI

One blade of the metaphorical scissors that leads to predicted union decline in future years is a continued fall in the benefits unions can deliver in the form of WRAP and CGI. The second blade is a predicted rise in the costs that go with obtaining WRAP and CGI. Several factors are important here.

More Elastic Labor Demand Curves

Greater competition in product and financial markets and increased mobility of capital have made labor demand curves in many industries/firms more elastic over time. This statement is particularly true of firms in the private, for-profit sector, but even government organizations in the public sector have greater opportunities for substitution in production (through privatization). Given that unions raise wage and benefit costs 15 to 25 percent above market levels, the result is to force firms up their labor demand curves, leading to a diminution of jobs over time. As labor demand curves become more elastic, the threat of job loss that goes with the exercise of WRAP and CGI increases, making it less attractive for new workers to organize and more likely that the existing stock of union members will shrink in the future (Bennett and Kaufman 2002b; Hirsch and Schumacher 2002; Nissen 2002).

Union Insensitivity to Employment Loss

Not only have labor demand curves become more elastic, unions evince considerable insensitivity in taking the increased costs of WRAP and CGI into account in their bargaining behavior. Union wage policy is often determined through a "median voter" mechanism that in effect gives considerable weight to the preferences of the more senior members in the union (Kaufman 2002b). As long as these workers are not threatened by the prospect of drastic employment losses at the company (thus threatening their jobs), their preference is for "more" in WRAP and CGI even if it comes at the expense of fewer jobs for less senior workers. Barry Hirsch (1991) characterizes union behavior in this regard as "rational myopia." While perhaps rational, this type of wage policy hastens the shrinkage of the union sector and causes nonunion workers to be more leery of union-joining out of fear the union will cost them their jobs.

Greater Management Opposition

The cost of WRAP and CGI has also increased because of heightened management opposition to unions (Kleiner 2001). American management has always preferred to operate union-free, but in recent times this preference has become more pronounced. Reasons include a greater need for flexibility as economic and organizational change quickens, less ability to pass on union-imposed costs to consumers, and greater desire to promote a cooperative work environment and avoid the adversarial atmosphere that goes with collective bargaining. Increased management opposition takes a variety of forms, such as closing unionized plants, shifting capital investment away from unionized facilities, using replacement workers during a strike, waging a "hardball" campaign to remain union-free, and terminating union activists. All of these things raise the cost of WRAP and CGI to workers.

Reduced Strike Effectiveness

A fourth factor increasing the cost of WRAP and CGI is the reduced effectiveness of unions' strike threat (Bennett and Kaufman 2002b). The diminished success of strikes not only reduces the benefits to union membership, but it also increases the costs. The most important cost is potential job loss, such as from striker replacement, closing of the plant, or layoffs. These factors have increased in severity in recent times and will most likely continue to remain high in the future.

Conclusion

Freeman and Medoff point out that unions have two different functions or "faces"—a bargaining or "muscle" function and a governance or "voice" function. I broadened these modestly to incorporate the insights of Commons. He characterizes the aim of the bargaining function as WRAP—wealth redistribution, aggrandizement, and protection—and the goal of the voice function as CGI—constitutional government in industry. My contention is that the growth prospects for unions in the early twenty-first century hinge critically on the private demand of workers for WRAP and CGI and the social utility citizens and policy makers see in union WRAP and CGI, as this perception critically influences the legal support and encouragement given to unions.

In this chapter, I contrasted union growth in two earlier periods of American history: the 1920s and the 1930s. These two decades are particularly instructive, because they illustrate two "end points" with respect to the private and social demand for union WRAP and CGI and thus provide examples of possible outcomes for the early twenty-first century.

The 1920s witnessed stagnation in union growth; the 1930s saw a surge in unionism. Why? A full answer involves numerous diverse factors, but surely a significant part of the explanation lies with shifts in private and public attitudes about the virtues and necessities of union WRAP and CGI. In the 1920s, union WRAP and CGI were widely seen in the American polity as economically harmful and serving the self-interested goals of a labor elite, while among workers the demand for WRAP and CGI was considerably diminished by a combination of good markets, improved employment practices in industry, defects and shortcomings of unions, and lack of protection from antiunion discrimination by employers. In the 1930s, by way of contrast, public sentiment and policy shifted toward a much more supportive and protective position regarding unions, based on the perception that union WRAP and CGI were vital contributors to the public welfare by promoting economic recovery, balanced growth, and democracy in industry. Likewise, the experience of the Great Depression created widespread feelings of deprivation and injustice among a large portion of the workforce and, hence, interest in union WRAP and CGI—a latent interest that then became manifest when the New Deal labor policies of the Roosevelt administration gave support and protection to union-joining.

The record of union growth in the 1920s and the 1930s provides two alternative scenarios for union growth in the early part of the twenty-first century. What is the likely outcome? My impression is that the future will more closely resemble the 1920s—assuming the nation avoids another depression, full-scale wartime mobilization, or other such socioeconomic disruptions (Bennett and Kaufman 2002b). Certainly, in the years ahead significant pockets of dissatisfaction and, hence, interest in union-joining will continue to exist in the workforce. But, more generally, broad-based interest in union-joining is likely to remain anemic, partly because many workers have only a small intrinsic interest in union WRAP and CGI and partly because of doubts about the ability of unions to successfully carry out organizing campaigns and deliver WRAP and CGI through collective bargaining. At the same time as the inflow of new people into unions remains relatively small in size, the outflow of people from union membership is likely to stay several times larger as unionized firms continue to shed employees through layoffs, downsizings, plant closings, and union decertifications. These trends together spell a further decline in union density in the years ahead, while unions—particularly in the private sector—will face a major struggle simply to maintain the present level of membership.

Several academic observers in the early 1930s wrote similarly pessimistic forecasts of the future of the union movement and history soon showed them to be spectacularly wrong. Such a union rebound may also occur in the early twenty-first century, and I certainly do not rule it out. What I think the analysis in this chapter suggests, however, is that the conditions of the 1920s are, historically viewed, in many respects a close parallel to the present-day situation facing unions in the United States (Kaufman 2002a). Hence, any reversal of unionism's long-term decline in the early twenty-first century requires a significant disruption to the socioeconomic status quo, as took place in the 1930s when the social contract between workers and companies was broken under the weight of the Great Depression or in the World War I and World War II periods, when inflation and the need for labor peace necessitated a government policy regime accommodative to the interests of organized labor. These disruptions to the status quo dramatically increased both the private and public demand for union WRAP and CGI, and led to government policies that facilitated union organizing and bargaining.

In the present economic and social environment, however, the private and public demand for union WRAP and CGI is soft and "spotty" due to a confluence of circumstances—an overall strong economy, improvement in employer human resource management practices, expansion in government protection of workers' rights and labor conditions, and various shortcomings of unions. This constellation of forces is likely to continue in the years ahead, unless displaced by some substantial "shock," and hence the prospects for union growth have to be rated as relatively gloomy—other things being equal. Of course, other things rarely stay equal (witnessed by the outbreak of corporate scandal and the plunge of the stock market in 2002 and 2003) and a large-scale economic or social disruption may well occur in the years ahead. But until such occurs, the status quo is likely to prevail, at least in broad outline, and the best forecast is thus continued hard times for unions.

References

Adamic, Louis. 1932. "The Collapse of Organized Labor." *Harper's Magazine* (January): 167–178.

Alexander, Peter. 1999. "Rising from the Ashes: Alabama Coal Miners, 1921–1941." In *It Is Union and Liberty: Alabama Coal Miners and the UMW*, ed. Edwin Brown and Colin Davis, 62–83. Tuscaloosa: University of Alabama Press.

Barnett, George. 1922. "The Present Position of American Trade Unionism." *American Economic Review* 12 (March): 44–55.

———. 1933. "American Trade Unionism and Social Insurance." *American Economic Review* 23 (March): 1–15.

Bennett, James, and Bruce Kaufman. 2002a. "Introduction." In *The Future of Private Sector Unionism in the United States*, ed. James Bennett and Bruce Kaufman, 3–8. Armonk, NY: M.E. Sharpe.

———. 2002b. "Conclusion: The Future of Private Sector Unionism in the U.S.—Assessment and Forecast." In *The Future of Private Sector Unionism in the United States*, ed. James Bennett and Bruce Kaufman, 359–386. Armonk, NY: M.E. Sharpe.

Bennett, James, and Jason Taylor. 2002. "Labor Unions: Victims of Their Own Political Success?" In *The Future of Private Sector Unionism in the United States*, ed. James Bennett and Bruce Kaufman, 245–259. Armonk, NY: M.E. Sharpe.

Bernstein, Irving. 1950. *The New Deal Collective Bargaining Policy*. Berkeley: University of California Press.

Commons, John R. 1905. *Trade Unionism and Labor Problems*. Boston: Ginn.

———. 1913. *Labor and Administration*. New York: Macmillan.

———. 1919. *Industrial Goodwill*. New York: McGraw-Hill.

———. 1951. *The Economics of Collective Action*. Madison: University of Wisconsin Press.

Cooper, Lyle. 1932. "The American Labor Movement in Prosperity and Depression." *American Economic Review* 22 (December): 641–659.

Elliot, Thomas. 1992. *Recollections of the New Deal: When the People Mattered*. Boston: Northeastern University Press.

Farber, Henry. 1983. "The Determinants of the Union Status of Workers." *Econometrica* 51 (September): 21–31.

Farber, Henry, and Bruce Western. 2002. "Accounting for the Decline of Unions in the Private Sector, 1973–1998." In *The Future of Private Sector Unionism in the United States*, ed. James Bennett and Bruce Kaufman, 28–58. Armonk, NY: M.E. Sharpe.

Federal Reserve Bank of Dallas. 2001. *Have a Nice Day: The American Journey to Better Working Conditions.* Dallas: Federal Reserve Bank of Dallas.

Fiorito, Jack. 2002. "Human Resource Management Practices and Worker Desires for Union Representation." In *The Future of Private Sector Unionism in the United States*, ed. James Bennett and Bruce Kaufman, 205–226. Armonk, NY: M.E. Sharpe.

Freeman, Richard B. 1998. "Spurts in Union Growth: Defining Moments and Social Processes." In *The Defining Moment: The Great Depression and the American Economy in the Twentieth Century*, ed. Michael Bordo, Claudia Goldin, and Eugene White, 265–295. Chicago: University of Chicago Press.

Freeman, Richard B., and James Medoff. 1984. *What Do Unions Do?* New York: Basic Books.

Freeman, Richard B., and Joel Rodgers. 1999. *What Workers Want.* Ithaca, NY: Cornell University Press.

Hirsch, Barry. 1991. *Labor Unions and the Economic Performance of Firms.* Kalamazoo, MI: Upjohn Institute.

Hirsch, Barry, and Edward Schumacher. 2002. "Private Sector Union Density and the Wage Premium: Past, Present, and Future." In *The Future of Private Sector Unionism in the United States*, ed. James Bennett and Bruce Kaufman, 92–128. Armonk, NY: M.E. Sharpe.

Hirschman, Albert. 1971. *Exit, Voice, and Loyalty.* Cambridge, MA: Harvard University Press.

Hotchkiss, Willard. 1920. "Participation in Management—Discussion." *American Economic Review* 10 (May): 110–115.

Hoxie, Robert. 1917. *Trade Unionism in the United States.* New York: Appleton.

Jacoby, Sanford. 1985. *Employing Bureaucracy: Managers, Unions, and the Transformation of Work in American Industry, 1900–1945.* New York: Columbia University Press.

Kaufman, Bruce. 1996. "Why the Wagner Act?: Reestablishing Contact with Its Original Purpose." In *Advances in Industrial and Labor Relations*, vol. 7, ed. David Lewin, Bruce Kaufman, and Donna Sockell, 15–68. Greenwich, CT: JAI Press.

———. 1997a. The Future of the Labor Movement: A Look at the Fundamentals." *Labor Law Journal* 48 (August): 474–484.

———1997b. "The Growth and Development of a Nonunion Sector in the Southern Paper Industry." In *Southern Labor in Transition, 1945–95*, ed. Robert Zieger, 295–329. Knoxville: University of Tennessee Press.

———. 2000a. "The Early Institutionalists on Industrial Democracy and Union Democracy." *Journal of Labor Research* 21 (Spring): 189–209.

———. 2000b. "The Case for the Company Union." *Labor History* 41 (August): 321–350.

———. 2001a. "The Prospects for Union Growth in the United States in the Early 21st Century." Paper presented at the International Conference on Union Growth. Toronto: University of Toronto.

———. 2001b. "Strategic HRM and Participative Management: Antecedents in Early Industrial Relations." *Human Resource Management Review* 11, no. 4: 505–533.

———. 2002a. "The Future of U.S. Private Sector Unionism: Did George Barnett

Get It Right after All?" In *The Future of Private Sector Unionism in the United States*, ed. James Bennett and Bruce Kaufman, 330–358. Armonk, NY: M.E. Sharpe.

———. 2002b. "Models of Union Wage Determination: What Have We Learned since Dunlop and Ross?" *Industrial Relations* 41 (January): 110–158.

Keyserling, Leon. 1945. "Why the Wagner Act? In *The Wagner Act: After Ten Years*, ed. L. Silverberg, 5–33. Washington, DC: Bureau of National Affairs.

Kleiner, Morris M. 2001. "Intensity of Management Resistance: Understanding the Decline of Unionization in the Private Sector." *Journal of Labor Research* 22, no. 3: 519–540.

Leiserson, William. 1929. "The Contributions of Personnel Management to Improved Industrial Relations." In *Wertheim Lectures on Industrial Relations*, 125–164. Cambridge, MA: Harvard University Press.

———. 1931. "Who Bears the Risks?" *Survey Graphic* (March): 596–600, 622.

———. 1959. *American Trade Union Democracy*. New York: Columbia University Press.

Lichtenstein, Nelson, and Howell Harris, ed. 1993. *Industrial Democracy in America: The Ambiguous Promise*. New York: Cambridge University Press.

Lipset, Seymour Martin, and Ivan Katchanovski. 2002. "The Future of Private Sector Unions in the U.S." In *The Future of Private Sector Unionism in the United States*, ed. James Bennett and Bruce Kaufman, 9–27. Armonk, NY: M.E. Sharpe.

Matles, James, and James Higgins. 1974. *Them and Us: Struggles of a Rank-and-File Union*. Englewood Cliffs, NJ: Prentice-Hall.

National Labor Relations Board. 1985. *Legislative History of the National Labor Relations Act 1 and 2*. Washington, DC: U.S. Government Printing Office.

Nissen, Bruce, ed. 2002. *Unions in a Globalized Environment*. Armonk, NY: M.E. Sharpe.

Pencavel, John. 1971. "The Demand for Union Services: An Exercise." *Industrial and Labor Relations Review* 22 (January): 180–191.

Perlman, Selig. 1928. *A Theory of the Labor Movement*. New York: Kelley.

Slichter, Sumner. 1920. "Industrial Morale." *Quarterly Journal of Economics* 35 (November): 36–60.

———. 1929. "The Current Labor Policies of American Industries." *Quarterly Journal of Economics* 43 (May): 393–435.

———. 1931. "Pharaoh Dreams Again." *Atlantic Monthly* 148 (August): 248–252.

Troy, Leo. 2002. "Twilight for Organized Labor." In *The Future of Private Sector Unionism in the United States*, ed. James Bennett and Bruce Kaufman, 59–76. Armonk, NY: M.E. Sharpe.

Turner, Lowell, Harry Katz, and Richard Hurd, eds. 2001. *Rekindling the Movement: Labor's Quest for Relevance in the 21st Century*. Ithaca, NY: ILR Press.

Webb, Sidney, and Beatrice Webb. 1897. *Industrial Democracy*. London: Longmans Green.

Wheeler, Hoyt, and John McClendon. 1991. "The Individual Decision to Unionize." In *The State of the Unions*, ed. George Strauss et al., 47–83. Madison, WI: Industrial Relations Research Association.

Williamson, Oliver. 1985. *The Economic Institutions of Capitalism*. New York: Free Press.

Wolman, Leo. 1936. *Ebb and Flow in Trade Unionism*. New York: NBER.

Zieger, Robert. 1984. *Rebuilding the Pulp and Paper Workers Union, 1933–1941*. Knoxville: University of Tennessee Press.

4

The Experience Good Model of Trade Union Membership

Rafael Gomez and Morley Gunderson

The terms "experience" and "search" have been part of most economists' vocabulary for nearly thirty years.[1] Experience goods, according to Nelson (1970), are goods and services whose attributes and quality are hard to discern prior to purchase, whereas search goods are composed of attributes that can be easily identified before purchase. These concepts are so ubiquitous that they form part of almost every introductory industrial organization (IO) textbook and have appeared in countless other management and marketing contexts as well (Kotler 2000). Indeed, they are even applicable in nonproduct market settings.

In the field of labor economics, for example, one of the longest standing debates has centered around the human capital versus signaling explanation of wages (Weiss 1995). The debate has its origins in Spence's (1973) seminal paper on job market signaling that, in turn, drew its inspiration from Nelson's (1970) pioneering work on experience goods. Spence argued that the selection of a prospective worker—from an employer's standpoint—resembles the purchase of an experience good, since worker quality and performance are only fully revealed after the worker has been hired. This chapter is similar in spirit to that of Spence's (1973) original formulation, in that the logic of experience good theory, we argue, can be applied to the services that trade unions offer workers. Put simply, if a majority of "what unions do" is largely unobservable to workers, then from an employees' standpoint, trade union membership can be treated as an experience good.

An implication of the experience good model is that unless a worker has sampled unionization (i.e., actually been employed in a unionized job), or has access to reliable information about the pros and cons of union membership (i.e., has family and friends who are union members), then he or she will be unable to form an accurate assessment of whether or not the benefits of being in a union outweigh any potential costs. This makes recruitment of union members—even in the absence of employer opposition and other obstacles—perpetually difficult.

The aims of this chapter therefore are as follows:

1. To show that workers view unionization as a multiattribute product with certain qualities that are easily discernable before purchase and others that are less observable and therefore are high in experience qualities,
2. To illustrate that, on balance, the experience good properties of union membership outweigh the search characteristics, such that union membership can be labeled an "experience good" for workers,
3. To show that trade unions can be viewed as suppliers of employee voice to workers,
4. To examine empirical evidence on union status and desired union representation in order to determine whether it is consistent with the experience good model of trade union membership,
5. To add to the rather paltry empirical record of the experience good model by examining whether the model's predictions hold true when transposed to the individual's choice of union status.

In particular, we point to four recent findings in the unionization literature, which are accounted for by the experience good model. These include: (1) the intergenerational transmission of union status and preferences, (2) the persistence of trade union membership or its decline, (3) the observed postpurchase satisfaction of workers who have sampled union membership, and (4) the effect of social networks in influencing the desire for unionization on the part of the young and those with less labor market experience.[2]

Some Background to the Experience Good Model

Despite becoming part of the lexicon of economics, the experience good model has produced considerable debate within the field of IO. Questions still remain over the nature of what the terms "experience" and "search" actually mean, which is perhaps why the model has generated surprisingly little rigorous empirical work (Laband 1991).

Porter (1974, 1976) was the first to explore the subjective nature of the

Figure 4.1   **Continuum of Search and Experience Characteristics**

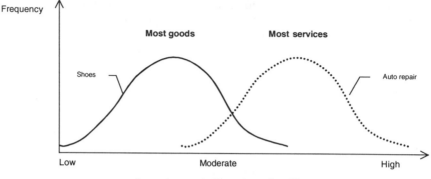

Prepurchase evaluation and sampling difficulties

Source: P. Kotler and G. Armstrong. *Principles of Marketing*. (Englewood Cliffs, NJ: Prentice Hall, 2004).

"experience" versus "search good" dichotomy. His analysis proposes an objective way of classifying goods on the basis of price and frequency of purchase. According to Porter, a consumer deciding whether to purchase a low-cost nondurable item (i.e., a low-involvement convenience good) will have an easier time discerning product quality via sampling, regardless of whether or not the good in question is an experience good by "design." The opposite, of course, holds true for high-cost, infrequently purchased items (i.e., high-involvement shopping goods). In Porter's model, whether a product is labeled an "experience" or "search" good is actually dependent on the costs to the buyer of acquiring product-quality information.

These costs can be incurred either before purchase through information gathering, or after purchase, through sampling. The cost of gaining product-quality information is therefore a function of both *price* (i.e., the cost of sampling) and *frequency of purchase* (i.e., the durable/nondurable nature of the product).

Under the previous interpretation, the terms "experience" and "search" merely represent two extremes of a continuum, with goods capable of being low in sampling costs and high in search qualities (characteristics the buyer can evaluate easily before purchase), or high in price and experience qualities (characteristics the buyer can only evaluate at high cost after purchase). Most goods, naturally, display a mixture of both qualities and therefore fall somewhere in-between the two extremes (see Figure 4.1). It should also be noted that personal services (such as those offered by unions) are skewed toward the experience spectrum, primarily because of the difficulties surrounding evaluation of their prepurchase attributes.

The modified experience good model—amended so that the classification of an experience good is based on the costs of acquiring information—appears plausible in most product markets. It is our contention that the model is also applicable to labor markets, and more specifically to the determination of the union status of workers.

The Experience Good Model of Union Membership Determination

Assumptions

The experience good model of trade union membership is premised on four assumptions, three of which are standard in the consumer theory literature and one that is drawn from the literature on labor relations systems. In the first three cases, the assumptions need to be translated from their product market origins to our particular labor market setting.

We begin with a basic assumption of consumer theory found in marketing and industrial organization: that consumers are not interested in products per se, but care only about the function or the solution to a problem that a product is likely to provide (Lambin 1997). Someone does not (typically) purchase a concert ticket for its own sake, but instead purchases it for the inherent function it fulfils; namely, musical entertainment.[3] This simple idea has important implications for our model of trade union membership, since it speaks to the motives that workers have for becoming unionized or desiring unionization.[4]

In a product market setting, different goods can often meet the same function or need. This second assumption seems obvious. For example, if the basic function required is to heat food, then there are at least two alternatives: an oven or a microwave. Less obvious, perhaps, is the labor market analogue of this assumption since it implies that substitutable jobs can originate from employment prospects that outwardly appear very different. For example, if a requirement of work is to have promotional prospects, then a worker may choose between two alternatives: a unionized job where decisions on whether to promote are typically based on objective standards such as seniority, versus a nonunionized job where a mixture of performance and less objective criteria are often used.

In the product-market literature, this assumption is often used as a justification for the existence of "solution markets." Solution markets are where specific customers seek a solution to satiate a particular demand, but where the technology used to satiate that demand can vary (Lambin 1997). The virtue of this market definition, as opposed to the more widely known product market definition, is that it incorporates the existence of substitute technologies that can satisfy the same need or perform the same function. In our case, employee "voice" is the need in question and union and nonunion jobs compete for its provision to workers.

The third assumption appropriated from consumer theory is that union membership contains a bundle of characteristics or attributes. In the literature, this assumption is referred to as "the multiattribute product" model of consumer choice (Lancaster 1966, 1971). The multiattribute model examines the relationship between product attributes and consumer preferences and assumes that consumers evaluate a product along several dimensions, which (in the model's more relaxed form) can be real or perceived (Jagpal 1999).

The notion that union membership contains multiple attributes can also be conceived as a restatement of standard compensating differential theory, which implicitly assumes that employees perceive the benefits of a job along several dimensions. This is why employers can trade off wage and nonwage benefits when offering different employment contracts to workers, and why shadow prices can be estimated for each of these attributes (Rosen 1974). In the union versus nonunion setting, the multiattribute model is analogous to the union wage premium, being only one attribute among many (mostly unobserved benefits) that unionized employment can provide.

The fourth and final assumption is that in decentralized employment relations systems (such as in the United States), the market for employee voice is open to competition.[5] Workers have scope (albeit circumscribed) in determining their choice of union status or alternative forms of representation at the workplace. If they desire unionization, they can apply for a unionized job or if employed in a nonunionized setting, they can organize the workplace for the purposes of collective bargaining. Alternatively, if they prefer to negotiate individually with their employers, they will sort themselves into nonunionized sectors or refuse to cooperate in organizing campaigns.[6]

Implications of Our Four Assumptions

Thus far, we have assumed (1) that workers demand unionization only to the extent that it can satiate a set of generic needs,[7] (2) that unionization competes in a solution market where substitutes for union services, such as progressive nonunion workplace practices, exist, (3) that unionization contains multiple attributes, most of which are hard-to-observe prior to purchase, and (4) that in systems where workplace statutory recognition prevails, there exists a solution market for "employee voice." When these four assumptions are applied to the question of the determination of the union status of workers, they make clear that unions are collectively operating in a crowded marketplace (see Figure 4.2).

Figure 4.2 **Consumer Choice Framework and Union Membership**

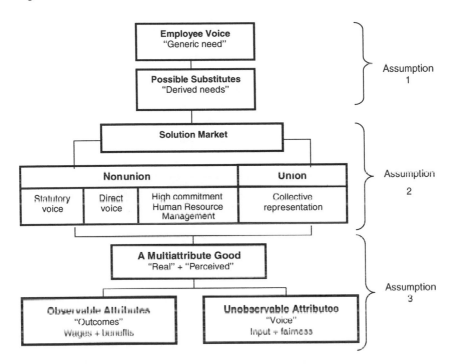

It may very well be true that unions are the only independent guarantors of employee voice, but, to appropriate another industrial organization term, the market for voice is more "contestable" than ever before. Many attributes of unionized employment—from wage premiums to formal grievance procedures—have been appropriated by firms under the nomenclature of human resource management practices (Ichniowski, Shaw, and Prennushi 1997). The progressive adoption of these employee voice attributes by nonunion firms in the United States over the last twenty-five years has long been cited as one reason for the decline in unionization observed over the same period (Kochan, Katz, and McKersie 1986).

The question, therefore, is whether unions still have a role in an economy where the monopoly over employee voice provision has been eroded. We feel that the answer to the question is decidedly "yes," but that the relevance of trade unions emerges only when union membership is conceptualized in a specific way. We begin with the simplest view of union membership—that it is a search good affecting only the wage premium—and then examine the instance where unions affect more than just the wage, what we term "the experience good" case.

The Model

Union Membership As a "Search Good"

The purchase of a particular good is a function of decisions made independently by consumers and producers. Similarly, the determination of union status is a function of decisions made separately by workers, unions, and employers. Consider an employee choice model where unions affect the wage received by workers (this assumption will be relaxed later). In more precise terms, unions impart a wage premium such that each worker i has a nonunion wage of W_{ni} and a union wage of W_{ui}, where the gross benefit of being a union member is $R_i = W_{ui} - W_{ni}$. If there is a cost associated with union membership C_{ui} (the membership fee, organizing cost, or possible strike costs), then worker i is unionized when the net benefit V_i is positive, $V_i > R_i - C_{ui}$, and remains nonunion otherwise.[8]

The previous model is identical to the framework used by Farber in two other papers (see Farber 1983, 2001). Interestingly, the same approach can be transposed to a product market setting rather easily. If we assume that the size of the wage premium is known to workers before the hiring decision, or learned as workers go through the interview process, then a unionized job that only affects the wage is akin to a "search good" with a single attribute. This means that union "quality" can be evaluated before purchase without the need for prior experience or sampling. Union membership is therefore a search good when the gross benefit in question (R_i) is known to workers before applying for a job (i.e., when the wage premium is known before "purchase").

Applications of the Search Good Case

If unionization is a search good, then any combination of individual labor market experience, prior knowledge, and/or exposure to union membership should have no significant effect on the desire for unionization. This first proposition emerges from the search good case when union benefits are easily identifiable by workers, irrespective of labor market experience and prior knowledge.

Search goods, because their quality is easily observed or sampled, have low to nonexistent switching costs (Klemperer 1995). If union benefits are easy to observe, then learning and uncertainty play a small role in the job-sorting process, ensuring that the costs of switching between unionized and nonunionized jobs should be relatively the same. That is to say, those who desire union membership should have no reason to remain nonmembers and vice versa. However, if a significant number of workers do not conform to these predictions, we have to ask ourselves one of two questions: Are workers simply irrational, or do they face substantial switching costs from changing their union status? If it is the latter, then the product model of union membership may require amending. One obvious way to amend it is simply to argue that unionization is more like an experience good, which is what we will do.

Union Membership As an Experience Good: The Multiattribute Case

Unions, because they negotiate with employers on behalf of employees, are the suppliers of wage premiums to workers. But the size of that wage premium is largely determined by factors outside of the control of an individual union. Indeed, the wage premium is determined to a large extent by factors even outside of the control of any given firm. Deregulation and global competition have left many firms with few if any rents and little bargaining space. Not surprisingly, recent evidence indicates that the union wage premium may have all but disappeared in Britain (see Bryson and Gomez 2002a; Blanden and Machin 2003) and fallen dramatically in the United States (Hirsch and Schumacher 2001). If union membership were a pure search good, one would expect workers to perceive fewer benefits from unionization—given that unions have been unable to deliver a wage markup as large as before—and begin to lessen their desire for unionization. Yet, roughly 40 percent of workers in Britain, Canada, and the United States still prefer to be unionized, which speaks to the perceived value of unionization on other grounds (Bryson et al. 2001).

A more realistic model of union status determination should consider not only the wage premium, but also the nonpecuniary benefits that union membership provides. These attributes, which include protection from unfair labor practices, access to formal grievance procedures, and even pension advice, are acknowledged by labor economists (Farber 1983; Freeman 1980) and are particularly well documented in the industrial relations literature·(Meltz 1989; Barbash 1987). What is mentioned less often is that it is nearly impossible to discern these benefits without experiencing them first. The sampling of union membership, therefore, is akin to the purchase of an experience good—which in our model is a function of (1) the cost of becoming a union member and (2) the frequency of job turnover.[9] The experience good properties of union membership, we argue, vastly outweigh the observable search characteristics.[10] Unionization is therefore a high-involvement, infrequently purchased, durable good that is high in experience characteristics.

The experience good model of union choice can be represented analytically by adapting standard notation found in Farber and Western (2001).[11] Let each worker i have a benefit derived from union employment (which includes the observed wage premium and all the hard-to-observe aspects of union voice) of B_{ui} and nonunion benefits B_{ni}, so that the advantage of unionization is $R_i + B_{ui} - B_{ni}$. Given a cost of becoming a union member (e.g., the search costs involved in applying for a unionized job, the membership fee, or the cost of organizing) C_i, the value to the worker of being unionized is

$$V_i = R_i - C_i \tag{1}$$

and worker i desires unionization if $V_i > 0$ and does not otherwise.

However, equation 1 is still only applicable to unionization in the search good case. This is so for two reasons. First, there is no risk attached to the benefit from unionization R_i. If unionization is a highly priced, infrequently purchased experience good (i.e., a "durable" employment prospect), then the payoff from unionization is only imperfectly observed. Hence, there is always a chance that the unionized job will not deliver its expected payoff. Denote this probability as θ_i, such that if unionization is an experience good, then $0 \leq \theta_i \leq 1$, whereas if it is a search good this probability would approach unity, $\theta_i \sim 1$.

Second, if unionized employment is an experience good, then there must be some positive switching cost S_i involved once it is sampled.[12] Adding these two additional elements to our initial search choice model (equation 1), we arrive at the following experience good version of equation 1:

$$V_i = \theta_i R_i - C_i + S_i \tag{2}$$

where a worker will desire unionization if $V_i > 0$ and will remain unionized even if $V_i < \theta_i R_i - C_i$, so long as $S_i \geq C_i$. This implies that the condition for a union to successfully unionize a given worker is

$$\theta_i > \frac{C_i - S_i}{R_i} \tag{3}$$

The right-hand side of equation 3 defines a critical value for the probability of a worker desiring unionization. The critical value is

$$\theta_i^* = \frac{C_i - S_i}{R_i}, \tag{4}$$

and unions will successfully target workers for whom $\theta_i > \theta_i^*$.[13]

Applications of the Experience Good Case

Now, consider differences in labor market experience, social environment, managerial opposition, or the effectiveness of union organizing tactics. These can affect any of the four elements of equation 2. We will now consider changes in each.

A change that makes workers more certain of the benefits derived from unionization is represented by an increase in θ_i, and this will make the effectiveness of union organizing higher by increasing the number of workers where $\theta_i > \theta_i^*$. A change in θ_i can occur when the experience good properties of unionization are revealed to workers. That is, workers with greater labor market experience should have higher values of θ_i, as should workers who have been exposed to the benefits of unionization through social interactions either at the home or in the community. If unionization were a pure search good, the value of θ_i would of course be 1.

A change that makes it more costly to leave a unionized job is represented by an increase in S_i. Though switching costs make union membership "sticky," they also make it harder for a forward-looking worker to be successfully organized, since the gross benefits have to be greater than the direct costs plus the costs of switching $(R_i > C_i + S_i)$. Switching costs do not have to be static, and can correlate positively with tenure and age of worker. Likewise, because of higher values for S_i, union members with greater levels of experience are therefore more likely to *remain* unionized even if the benefits of unionization begin to fall. Examples of switching costs applied to the union voice case include the transaction cost of quitting a job with a unionized employer and starting work in a job that is nonunion; the learning cost incurred by switching to a new work environment after having adapted to an existing unionized environment; and the uncertainty about the quality of work environment with the "untested" nonunion employer.

A change that makes it more costly to become or remain a union member but keeps a worker's assessment of the potential benefits derived from unionization fixed (i.e., does not change θ_i) is represented by an increase in C_i. This can occur for any number of reasons. The most obvious is an increase in managerial opposition to unionization for workers seeking to organize. For employees already working for a union employer, this may include an increase in the costs of membership dues or participation in industrial action.

A change that reduces the benefit to unionization for workers is represented by a reduction in R_i. Following Farber and Western (2001), a reduction in the benefit of union membership could result from more militant employers that are unwilling to negotiate improvements in compensation and benefits or, alternatively, from poor negotiating on the part of the union.

Conceiving of unionization as a high-involvement experience good opens the door to several strands in the IO literature and presents an even more interesting set of problems in terms of our central concerns in this chapter. For example, are workers with high labor market knowledge and low switching costs more likely to favor union voice? Do workers engage in low-cost sampling of jobs in order to discern the quality of employee voice provision? Can a worker be "fooled" into applying for, or remaining in, a nonunion job with poorer quality voice provision, believing that the employee voice is of higher quality than an otherwise similar unionized job? And what mechanisms exist to aid the independent supplier of employee voice (the union) in convincing workers of the quality of union voice provision, such that they will be willing to pay membership dues if already unionized or accept the associated organizing costs of unionization in nonunionized settings?

All of these questions are important and have been addressed in some cases elsewhere. But they have scarcely been organized in any systematic fashion, because the conception of what union membership actually is has yet to be explored in much depth. In our final section, we assemble existing literature to see if any of the predictions of the experience good model have received (unwitting) empirical confirmation.

Empirical Evidence of the Experience Good Model of Unionization

The experience good model of unionization generates several propositions that are consistent with the facts established in the literature on union employment. We loosely organize our discussion around the applications of the experience and search good cases discussed earlier. We begin by identifying the key properties of experience goods, which are:

1. Durability
2. High brand loyalty
3. High postpurchase satisfaction
4. High switching costs
5. Low levels of formal advertising.

We then analyze whether each of these properties conforms to the empirical features found in the unionization literature. Each of the five propositions and their relation to the empirical evidence is also summarized in Table 4.1 (see p. 104).

Properties Shared by Experience Goods and Union Membership

Durability: Union Jobs Exhibit Longer Tenure Than Nonunion Jobs

Experience goods tend to be durable (Porter 1974), in the sense that they have a long shelf life. Their infrequent purchase generates higher sampling costs and hence creates more uncertainty over benefits before purchase. Nondurables are purchased frequently and hence make better search good candidates, even if their attributes are sometimes experience laden (fizzy drinks are the classic example).

All employment opportunities are durable, in the sense that people are rarely employed in spot markets. The key, however, is that "union jobs" are relatively more durable than comparable nonunion jobs. Employment durability can be measured by turnover and job tenure and in these respects, unionization displays just such a durable quality. Union members tend to have longer job spells with one employer than similar nonunion workers, and unionized firms have lower quit rates than comparable nonunion firms. These findings have been confirmed in the United States and in Britain (Freeman and Medoff 1984; Fernie and Metcalf 1995).

Brand Loyalty: People Who "Purchase" Membership Stick with It

Another characteristic of union membership is that it is sticky, in the sense that if a person has ever been a union member, he or she is more likely to remain so in any new job as compared to an otherwise similar worker who has never sampled membership (Booth and Arulampalam 2000). This is akin to what is known about experience goods in product market settings, in that they tend to generate greater levels of brand attachment once sampled (Kotler 2000). The reasons for this may be psychological (as some in the marketing profession argue) or they may owe their origin to switching costs as economists tend to believe.

What is true, in any case, is that for first-time users of products heavy with experience characteristics, there is an inherent uncertainty (θ_i) between the needs of a consumer and the characteristics of a product (Villas-Boas 2002). Once the product is purchased, however, an informational advantage arises for the good that the consumer has purchased as compared to its alternatives. Therefore, a consumer will only consider switching if he or she has a particularly bad experience with the service or a cheaper alternative is present or both. The certainty of user-product specific relationships may be costly to replace or reacquire, which is perhaps why a consumer who buys a

Table 4.1

Evidence for the Experience Good Model of Trade Union Membership

Feature	Empirical evidence	
	Product market	Labor market
1. Durability: Product has "long-shelf" life. Infrequently purchased.	**Porter (1976):** Infrequently purchased items increase demand for prepurchase information in keeping with experience model.	**Freeman and Medoff (1984):** Tenure is longer for unionized workers. **Bryson and Lucíofora (2002):** Same result as above from Britain. (Britain)
2. Brand Loyalty: Purchase "stickiness" is more common among experience goods than search goods. People remain loyal to their brand despite similar (often less costly) alternatives.	**Klemperer (1987):** First-mover advantages and existing market share in experience good markets are strongest predictors of future market share.	**Bryson and Gomez (2002a):** Workers who sample membership stick with it. The rate of exit from membership has remained constant in Britain since 1980. (Britain) **Blanden and Machin (2003):** Derecognition is rare. Majority of union density decline in Britain due to lack of uptake on the part of new workers and workplaces. (Britain)
3. Postpurchase Satisfaction: Once sampled, experience goods exhibit higher levels of satisfaction than search goods.	**Greer (1992:117–147):** Reviews evidence on higher consumer ratings of experience goods once purchased.	**Freeman and Diamond (2001):** Identify the "incumbency effect." Workers initially exposed to either unionized or nonunion forms of employee voice remain more favorable to those forms throughout their careers. (Britain) **Bryson and Gomez (2002):** Desire for unionization increases with exposure (individual and workplace). (Britain, Canada, United States)

4. Switching Costs: Once purchased, experience goods generate informational advantages and other frictions inducing higher switching costs.

Klemperer (1995): Many instances of where switching costs appear in product markets settings.

Freeman and Medoff (1984): Quit rates are lower for unionized jobs. (United States)
Fernie and Metcalf (1995): Union recognition associated with reduction in quits. (Britain)
Booth and Arulampalam (2000): The persistence of union status in a longitudinal study of British youth. (Britain)
Farber and Krueger (1993); Riddell (1993); Bryson and Gomez (2002): There is significantly more frustrated demand than oversupply of unionization. A condition which is hard to explain without switching costs. (Britain, Canada, United States)

5. Personal Referrals:
Experience goods commonly promoted via informal advertising channels, social networks, and word of mouth.

Stigler (1962); Rees (1966): Employees are like "experience goods" for employers. Tend to be hired on the basis of personal referrals.
Reinstein and Snyder (2000): Strong evidence for movie reviews affecting box-office intake.
Kotler (2000): Most experience goods (auto repair, movies) tend to be promoted via social networks and personal referrals.

Blanden and Machin (2003): Strong intergenerational transmission of union status independent of industry and occupation. (Britain)
Gomez, Gunderson, and Meltz (2002): Strong social network effect (having a family or peer group who is supportive of unionization) associated with greater desire for unionization. (Canada)
Charlwood (2002): Socioeconomic characteristics of the community where a person lives have significant effects on desired unionization. (Britain)

particular experience good may find it optimal to keep consuming the product, even when there are cheaper or more valuable alternatives available. If the consumer were unattached or had perfect knowledge (i.e., $\theta_i = 1$), then he or she would consider switching.

Postpurchase Satisfaction: Approval for Unions Increases with Exposure

The preferences that one has for union membership are more likely to be positive if one has ever been exposed to unions. This so-called incumbency effect remains significant even when one controls for sets of individual attributes, which could (positively or negatively) bias attitudes toward unions (Freeman and Diamond 2001). Studies of consumer satisfaction with experience goods generate similar results, in that experience goods often display higher than expected levels of postpurchase satisfaction, something that is not consistent with the traditional model of consumer behavior (Greer 1992).

When purchasing experience goods, consumers are more likely to "learn to like what they buy" than "buy what they like." Such behavior is often called "attribution error" by social psychologists and is part of a more general set of phenomena that can be explained by "cognitive dissonance" theory (Ajzen 1991). Cognitive dissonance can occur even when consumers carefully weigh their options before purchase. For example, if Sally thinks that brands X, Y, and Z are equally attractive before purchase, her positive judgment of Y, if selected, will rise after purchase merely because of its selection. The reasons for such behavior are still not well understood.

Switching Costs: Quit Rates Are Lower for Union Jobs

A fourth characteristic of experience goods is that they are usually accompanied by high switching costs (S_i).[14] This is also a feature of our own experience good model in equation 4, where it is argued that initial exposure to union voice will lower uncertainty for that particular form of voice and as a by-product will set up informational advantages that make it less likely for a worker to switch out of membership. The switching in this case could take the form of either quitting or actively decertifying a nonunionized workplace.

An empirical confirmation of the presence of switching costs in the unionized setting are the lower quit rates observed for unionized jobs (Freeman and Medoff 1984). Second is the persistence of union status, which was also an example of brand loyalty (Booth and Arulampalam 2000). A third, albeit indirect confirmation, is the fact that significant levels of frustrated demand and oversupply of unionization have been found to coexist in Britain, Canada, and the United States.[15] In other words, there are nonunion workers (possibly 40 percent in Britain and the United States) who desire union representation but who are not getting it. Likewise, there is a smaller though equally important segment of unionized workers who would prefer to be in the unorganized sector but who are not. Put simply, a significant proportion of workers do not appear to be getting what they want in terms of workplace voice. The implication is that either workers are not rational, or that there are costs associated with changing from a unionized to a nonunionized employer and vice versa (Bryson and Gomez 2002c).

Social Networks and Personal Referrals: Informal Advertising and Unions

A final feature of experience goods relates to the economics of information, a research stream originating with Stigler (1961) that was later applied to the topic of job search by Stigler (1962) and only recently has been applied to the unionization literature (Charlwood 2002; Gomez, Gunderson, and Meltz 2002). In short, theory suggests that knowledge about the potential benefits of experience goods is optimally disseminated via personal recommendations, rather than through formal advertising channels (Kotler 2000). A mechanic or doctor does not generally advertise his or her services on television. Indeed, we tend to be suspicious of any doctor or mechanic who does. Instead, they acquire their patient lists and customer base through personal referrals, or more generally, by "word of mouth." This is because "trust" is highly correlated with "reputation" and a personal referral is akin to someone staking his or her "reputation" on the product in question. Thus, when product characteristics are hard to observe before purchase, personal recommendations become the preferred channel by which potential customers are informed about quality.[16]

The information asymmetries generated by experience goods are replicated in the union case if we note the strong intergenerational transmission of union status observed in panel data (Blanden and Machin 2003). Sons and daughters of union workers are 20 percent more likely than are comparable individuals to become union members later in life. This effect is independent of occupation, region, and industry. Similarly, having a social environment consisting of friends and relatives who support unions makes the probability of desiring unionization higher, as compared to those lacking access to such social networks (Gomez, Gunderson, and Meltz 2002). This effect is even larger when youths and adults are separated into subsamples and analyzed separately. In other words, the positive effect of a social circle that is supportive of unionization is twice as large for those with less labor market experience (2003).

Older workers, it seems, rely on their accumulated labor market experience to form opinions about unionization, whereas younger workers with less labor market experience rely on social networks and personal referrals. This is consistent with our model, since it implies that those with a lower (higher) degree of certainty regarding unionization's potential benefits (θ_i) will be influenced to a greater (lesser) degree by external indicators of product quality, such as social relations and familial union status.

Conclusion

Unionization confers certain benefits to workers. Some of these benefits, like the union wage premium, are easily observable, whereas most others, such as procedural justice and job security, are less observable and harder to quantify. If a majority of "what unions do" is largely unobservable to workers, then they may never learn of the true stream of benefits to be derived from unionization. It is only when a worker is actually employed in a unionized environment for a long enough duration or has access to reliable information about union membership that he or she can form an accurate assessment of whether the value of these benefits outweighs any of the costs. This, we argue, is the basis for treating unionization as an experience good for workers.

In this chapter, several testable propositions were implied by the experience good model of trade union membership, and, in each case, they conformed to the established facts. Overall, the message for unions arising from the experience good model is simple: although those with less labor market experience such as the young and immigrants may be less likely to join a union, sensitizing them to the benefits of unionization may pay off since opportunities for unionization increase over one's lifetime. This may explain why declines in unionization caused by exogenous shifts in antiunion legislation, for example, have a snowballing effect over time as fewer and fewer individuals become exposed to unionization through social networks and personal referrals. This makes uncertainty over the expected payoff of unionization greater (lowering θ), thus lessening the chance that someone will demand unionization or seek to organize a nonunionized employer.

Notes

We thank the Leverhulme Trust's "Future of Trade Unions in Modern Britain" and Social Sciences and Humanities Research Council (SSHRC) in Canada for their funding and support of this chapter. We are also grateful to David Metcalf for encouragement of this research and to Bruce Pearce and Konstantinos Tzioumis for their helpful research assistance. An earlier version of this chapter was prepared as a paper for the

Twenty-third Annual Middlebury Conference on Economic Issues: "Changing Role of Unions." We especially appreciate the useful comments of the conference participants, in particular those of our discussant Edward J. Schumacher and the detailed comments supplied by Henry S. Farber.

1. Nelson (1970) was, to our knowledge, the first to identify the search versus experience dichotomy present in product markets. To be more precise, Nelson was the first to expand on Stigler's (1961) earlier and now seminal paper on search costs and the first to use the terms "experience" and "search goods."

2. In this chapter we will state that the young have higher costs in gaining information about union voice quality and hence will be less likely to "purchase" membership but just as likely to desire it.

3. A generic need or demand is based on a need that is an inherent requirement of natural or social life. Inherent needs are not satiable, but derived needs are, because they are based on a particular technological response to a generic need. An example of this distinction is the generic need for instant forms of communication, which never declines, but the derived need for fax machines, which are a particular solution to the inherent need for communication, has been progressively replaced by e mail.

4. Employment, as opposed to a specific job, can also be thought of as a solution to a set of inherent or generic needs. Therefore, it is in the employee's self-interest to first delimit the objective (and perhaps even subjective) requirements that employment (in general) can provide, as opposed to those needs that are derived from a particular job in a particular sector.

5. This last assumption is one that is not a hallmark of all labor markets. In some countries, collective representation is still commonly provided to all workers as a default option. Indeed, even within countries with workplace statutory recognition like Canada and the United States, certain sectors (nonresidential construction or the public sector) compel workers to be unionized in many environments. This, we argue, is akin to a regulated monopoly or a product market that is not open for competition.

6. The purchase analogy here is really the decision of a given worker to actively apply for a job in a unionized setting or to actively organize in the nonorganized sector. Indeed, to the extent that employers begin to match the wage and nonwage aspects of unionized jobs, then even workers with favorable attitudes toward unions will have less of an incentive to "purchase" or "desire" unionization.

7. This is the same as saying that employees have no intrinsic desire for union membership.

8. The product market analogy is not perfect since not all workers who desire union employment are employed in unionized jobs, whereas most consumers who desire a certain search good can find a willing supplier. In countries with Wagner-style collective bargaining legislation, workplaces are "born" nonunion and it takes the combined effort of unions and workers to organize a given workplace. If an employer is hostile to union organizing, then the cost of becoming a union member is higher for those workers who desire union jobs in a nonunionized setting than for those who find employment in an existing unionized establishment. This dual cost structure is what gives rise to the so-called queuing model of unionization (Farber 2001), which states that a worker will be in a union job only if the worker prefers union employment to nonunion employment and a union employer hires the worker.

9. Despite widespread claims that the long-term job is dead, job duration studies in Canada and the United States show that tenure with the same employer is roughly the same length that it was twenty years ago (Riddell 1993).

10. The wage premium is the most obvious and indeed, although it only represents one attribute, it may outweigh the other nonpecuniary benefits for some workers.

11. Farber suggests a better way of conceptualizing this decision by using a formal two-period model, where R is unobserved ex ante and the second-order conditions show an ambiguous effect arising from switching costs. Though the model is superior, for the purposes of this chapter the same result can be seen using the simple cost-benefit equation. We pursue Farber's two-period approach elsewhere.

12. These insights are adapted from Klemperer's (1987) work on the switching costs associated with experience goods. The switching cost may also be an "expected value" if workers are aware that unionization is an experience good requiring some up-front investment.

13. Unfortunately for unions in systems with workplace statutory recognition, a majority of employees in a workplace must have $\theta_i > \theta_i^*$ before they are targeted for organizing drives.

14. The reason for these switching costs in the union case were spelled out earlier and for products can be found in more detail in Klemperer (1995).

15. For work on Canada and the United States, see Riddell (1993), Farber and Krueger (1993), and Gomez, Lipset, and Meltz (2001). For work comparing Britain, Canada, and the United States, see Bryson et al. (2001). And for work on Britain, see Bryson and Gomez (2002b) and Charlwood (2002).

16. An interesting confirmation of this effect has been found for movies and movie reviews. In a study by Reinstein and Snyder (2000), it was found that a positive movie review by Siskel and Ebert raises the box office gross of a film by 10 percent. This effect is larger for films reviewed prior to opening—in keeping with the predictions of the experience good model.

References

Ajzen, Icek. 1991. "The Theory of Planned Behavior." *Organizational Behavior and Human Decision Processes Special Issue: Theories of Cognitive Self-Regulation* 50, no. 2: 179–211.

Barbash, J. 1987. "Like Nature, Industrial Relations Abhors a Vacuum." *Relations Industrielles* 42: 168–179.

Blanden, Jo, and Stephen Machin. 2003. "Cross-Generation Correlations of Union Status for Young People in Britain." *British Journal of Industrial Relations* 41, no. 3: 391–415.

Booth, A., and R. Arulampalam. 2000. "Union Status of Young Men in Britain: A Decade of Change." *Journal of Applied Econometrics* 15 (May–June): 289–310.

Bryson, A., and R. Gomez. 2002a. "Marching on Together? Reasons for the Recent Decline in Union Membership." In *British Social Attitudes: The Xth Report,* ed. Park C. Bromley and K. Thompson. London: London School of Economics, mimeograph.

———. 2002b. "You Can't Always Get What You Want: Frustrated Demand for Unionization in Britain." London: London School of Economics, mimeograph.

———. 2002c. "Why Have People Stopped Joining Unions?: The Rise of Never-Membership in Britain." London: London School of Economics, mimeograph.

Bryson, A., R. Gomez, M. Gunderson, and N. Meltz. 2001. "Youth-Adult Differences in the Demand for Unionization." Discussion Paper, no. 515. London: Centre for Economic Performance, London School of Economics.

Charlwood, Andy. 2002. "Why Do Non-union Employees Want to Unionize? Evidence from Britain." *British Journal of Industrial Relations* 40, no. 3: 463–491.

Farber, H. 1983. "The Determination of the Union Status of Workers." *Econometrica* 51: 1417–1438.

———. 2001. "Notes on the Economics of Labor Unions." Working Paper, no. 452. Princeton, NJ: Industrial Relations Section, Princeton University.

Farber, H., and A.B. Krueger. 1993. "Union Membership in the United States: The Decline Continues." In *Employee Representation: Alternatives and Future Directions,* ed. B. Kaufman and M. Kleiner, 70–79. Madison, WI: Industrial Relations Research Association.

Farber, H., and B. Western. 2001. "Ronald Reagan and the Politics of Declining Union Organization." Working Paper, no. 460. Princeton, NJ: Industrial Relations Section, Princeton University.

Fernie, Sue, and David Metcalf. 1995. "Participation, Contingent Pay, Representation and Workplace Performance: Evidence from Great Britain." *British Journal of Industrial Relations* 33, no. 3: 379–415.

Freeman, R.B. 1980. "The Exit Voice Trade-Off in the Labor Market: Unionism, Job Tenure, Quits, and Separations." *Quarterly Journal of Economics* 94: 643–674.

Freeman, R.B., and W. Diamond. 2001. "Liking the Workplace You Have: The Incumbency Effect in Preferences towards Unions." Working Paper, no. 1115. London: Centre for Economic Performance, London School of Economics.

Freeman, R.B., and J. Medoff. 1984. *What Do Unions Do?* New York: Basic Books.

Gomez, R., M. Gunderson, and N. Meltz. 2002. "Comparing Youth and Adult Desire for Unionization in Canada." *British Journal of Industrial Relations* 40, no. 3: 521–542.

Gomez, R., S.M. Lipset, and N. Meltz. 2001. "Frustrated Demand for Unionization: The Case of the United States and Canada Revisited." Fifty-third Annual Proceedings of the Industrial Relations Research Association (IRRA), October, 163–177.

Greer, D. 1992. *Industrial Organization and Public Policy,* 3rd ed. New York: Macmillan.

Hirsch, Barry T., and Edward J. Schumacher. 2001. "Private Sector Union Density and the Wage Premium: Past, Present, and Future." *Journal of Labor Research* 22, no. 3: 487–518.

Ichiniowski, C., K. Shaw, and G. Prennushi. 1997. "The Effects of Human Resource Management Practices on Productivity." *American Economic Review* 87 (May): 291–313.

Jagpal, S. 1999. *Marketing Strategy and Uncertainty.* London: Oxford University Press.

Klemperer, P.D. 1987. "Markets with Consumer Switching Costs." *Quarterly Journal of Economics,* 102: 375–394.

———. 1995. "Competition When Consumers Have Switching Costs: An Overview with Applications to Industrial Organization, Macroeconomics, and International Trade." *Review of Economic Studies* 62: 515–539.

Kochan, T.A., H.C. Katz, and R.B. McKersie. 1986. *The Transformation American Industrial Relations.* New York: Basic Books.

Kotler, P. 2000. *Marketing Management: International Edition.* London: Prentice Hall.

Laband, D.N. 1991. "An Objective Measure of Search versus Experience Goods." *Economic Inquiry* 29 (July): 497–509.

Lambin, J.J. 1997. *Strategic Marketing Management.* London: McGraw-Hill.

Lancaster, K. 1966. "A New Approach to Consumer Theory." *Journal of Political Economy* 74: 132–157.

———. 1971. *Consumer Demand: A New Approach.* New York: Columbia University Press.

Meltz, N. 1989. "Industrial Relations: Balancing Efficiency and Equity." In *Theories and Concepts in Comparative Industrial Relations,* ed. J. Barbash and K. Barbash, 109–113. Columbia: University of South Carolina Press.

Nelson, P. 1970. "Information and Consumer Behavior." *Journal of Political Economy* 78: 311–329.

Porter, M. 1974. "Consumer Behavior, Retailer Power and Market Performance in Consumer Goods Industries." *Review of Economics and Statistics* 56 (November): 419–436.

———. 1976. *Interbrand Choice, Strategy and Bilateral Market Power.* Cambridge, MA: Harvard University Press.

Reinstein, D., and C. Snyder. 2000. "The Influence of Expert Reviews on Consumer Demand for Experience Goods: A Case Study of Movie Critics." Working Paper. Berkeley: University of California.

Riddell, C. 1993. "Unionization in Canada and the United States: A Tale of Two Countries." In *Small Differences That Matter: Labor Markets and Income Maintenance in Canada and the United States,* ed. David Card and Richard Freeman. Chicago: University of Chicago Press.

Rosen, S. 1974. "Hedonic Prices and Implicit Markets: Product Differentiation in Pure Competition." *Journal of Political Economy* 82: 34–55.

Spence, M.A. 1973. "Job Market Signaling." *Quarterly Journal of Economics* 87 (August): 355–374.

Stigler, G.J. 1961. "The Economics of Information." *Journal of Political Economy* 69: 213–225.

———. 1962. "Information in the Labor Market." *Journal of Political Economy* 70: S94–S104.

Villas-Boas, J. M. 2002. "Competing with Experience Goods." Working Paper. Berkeley: University of California.

Weiss, A. 1995. "Human Capital vs. Signaling Explanations of Wages." *Journal of Economic Perspectives* 9 (Fall): 133–154.

III

Union Wage and Employment Effects

U.S. Evidence

5

Measuring Union and Nonunion Wage Growth

Puzzles in Search of Solutions

Barry T. Hirsch, David A. Macpherson, and Edward J. Schumacher

Few subjects in labor economics have received more attention than the estimation of union-nonunion wage differentials (Lewis 1986; Jarrell and Stanley 1990; Andrews et al. 1998; Blanchflower 1999). Although there is a consensus that union density and organizing strength in the United States have declined over time, there is no agreement as to how union wage premiums have changed. The theoretical relationship between union density and the union wage gap is ambiguous. For any given level of union labor demand, there exists an inverse relationship between union density and the wage premium, while declining union premiums are more likely if demand curves for union labor are shifting inward.[1]

There is general agreement that union wage premiums increased during the late 1970s, but there is no consensus as to whether the premium has been stable or falling since the early 1980s. David G. Blanchflower (1999) estimates union wage gaps from the Current Population Survey (CPS) from 1983 to 1995. He finds little evidence of a trend and concludes that the economy-wide union gap has remained constant. Bernt Bratsberg and James F. Ragan Jr. (2002) also examine this issue using the CPS, concluding that dispersion in the union premium across industries has substantially declined as the U.S. economy has become more competitive, but that there has been only a modest decline in the average premium.[2] An annual data book from Barry T. Hirsch and David A. Macpherson (2002) provides estimates of CPS union wage premiums for all years since 1973 using a time-consistent specification. They obtain an economy-wide premium estimate of 0.172 log points in 1983 and 0.136 in 2001, suggesting modest decline. For the private sector, however, they obtain estimates of 0.218 in 1983 and 0.143 in 2001, a large −0.75 log point drop in the union premium. Some of the decline evident in the CPS, however, results from an increase in the number of workers with earnings allocated by the census.[3]

Although academic studies typically use the CPS or other household microdata, the U.S. Bureau of Labor Statistics (BLS) provides published wage indices for union and nonunion wages (and benefits) based on establishment data. The BLS provides a quarterly index of employer wage cost changes using fixed sector weights (the Employment Cost Index [ECI]) and annual data providing dollar figures on employer costs using current employment weights (the Employer Costs for Employee Compensation [ECEC]). The ECI and ECEC measures are derived from the same underlying survey data, the ECI-ECEC program being one of three that form the comprehensive National Compensation Survey (NCS) statistical program (the other two are the Occupational Compensation Survey and the Employee Benefits Survey).

Despite their common source, union-nonunion wage trends seen in published ECI and ECEC statistics are consistent neither with each other nor with the CPS. Depending on the data series examined, one can conclude that there has been a steep decline, a modest decline, or no decline in relative union-nonunion wages. Conflicts arise primarily owing to different rates of nonunion wage growth in the surveys. Hence, the puzzles highlighted in this chapter have important implications not only for union wage gaps, but also for economy-wide wage and productivity growth. In this chapter, we first examine the seemingly conflicting evidence, identifying which pieces can be readily reconciled and which present real puzzles. We then examine more carefully the puzzles, attempting to identify solutions. In the process, we examine changes over time in the industry-occupational structure and demographic characteristics of union and nonunion workers. In a concluding section, we provide an assessment of what can be reliably inferred about changes in union wage gaps.

An Overview of the Evidence: Uncovering the Puzzles?

In this section, we provide evidence on changes over time in the union-nonunion wage gap. We examine four types of data: quarterly ECI wage (and compensation) indices; annual ECEC wage (and compensation) levels; the CPS unadjusted for worker, job, and location controls; and CPS union wage gap estimates using a variety of approaches. To provide an overview of the

Figure 5.1   **CPS, ECI, and ECEC Changes in the Union-Nonunion Wage Gap, 1986–2001**

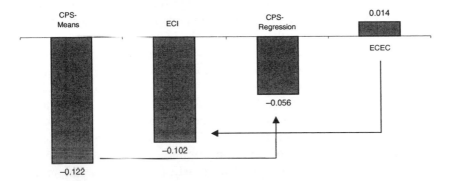

Notes: Figures taken from Tables 5.1 and 5.3. See the text and table notes for details. For the Employer Costs for Employee Compensation (ECEC), mean dollar values are converted to a wage index by taking the ratio of 2001 to 1986 wages, and the change in the log wage gap is approximated by the difference in the logs of the union and nonunion indexes. The change in the wage gap from the Employer Cost Index (ECI) is approximated by the difference in the logs of the relative 2001/1986 index values for union and nonunion jobs. Current Population Survey (CPS) log wage calculations are based on CPS union-nonunion mean wage differences in 2001 minus 1986, and on the change between 1986 and 2001 in regression-based union wage gap estimates. The arrows represent movement from the current employment weighted ECEC means to the ECI using fixed-sector weights, and movement from current weighted CPS means to CPS regression estimates with sectoral (and other) controls.

puzzles present in the data, we first show changes in the union wage gap over the period 1986 to 2001 based on these four approaches, using either data published by BLS or results calculated by us from the CPS.[4] Although we subsequently examine union-nonunion wage patterns in the ECI, ECEC, and CPS in depth, this quick overview nicely illustrates the issues at hand.

In Figure 5.1, changes in the union log wage gap for the U.S. private sector are shown, based on calculations from published ECI and ECEC figures, and from the CPS based on mean wages (i.e., no controls) and standard regression models. Details are provided in the figure note and in analysis discussed later in this chapter. Based on the quarterly fixed-weight ECI wage indices for union and nonunion work units, nonunion wages have grown substantially faster than union wages, with the log wage gap closing by –0.102 log points between 1986Q2 and 2001Q2 (the end of the second quarter corresponds most closely to annual averages from the ECEC and CPS). The ECEC is based on the same survey data as the ECI, but provides average annual dollar figures on pay using current weights. In contrast to the ECI evidence, the ECEC shows union wage levels growing slightly faster than nonunion, with the union-nonunion wage gap increasing by approximately 0.014.[5]

Evidence from the CPS monthly earnings files introduces even more puzzles. CPS mean wage rates for union and nonunion workers should produce a result comparable to that seen using the ECEC, with the use of current employment weights and no controls for worker or job characteristics. Yet, the unadjusted CPS union log wage gap closes by –0.122 log points between 1986 and 2001, far different from the ECEC result showing no closing. Ironically, the pattern shown using the unadjusted CPS is highly similar to that obtained with the ECI, even though the latter has fixed employment weights and uses a very different methodology. The puzzles accumulate when we turn to regression estimates of the union premium, which include control for industry, occupation, and worker characteristics. The regression premium falls by –0.056 log points between 1986 and 2001, a bit less than half of the decline evident in the raw CPS wage data.[6]

In short, evidence indicates that between 1986 and 2001 changes in the union wage gap ranged between a closing of as much as –0.12 log points and a widening of 0.01 points. Moreover, methods that are seemingly similar (the ECEC and unadjusted CPS) provide very different answers. "Control" for employment, albeit in a noncomparable fashion (fixed weights in the ECI and sector dummies in the CPS regression), has seemingly opposite effects (seen by the direction of the arrows in Figure 5.1), with a large narrowing of the gap moving from the ECEC to ECI and exactly the opposite pattern moving from the unadjusted CPS to CPS regressions with controls. We will provide more comprehensive discussion and evidence later on in an attempt to find solutions to the puzzles so clearly demonstrated in Figure 5.1.

The Employment Cost Index

The quarterly ECI is part of the BLS's comprehensive NCS of employers. The ECI is a Laspeyres-type index intended to measure average increases in employer wage (or compensation) costs for a fixed composition of jobs. It is constructed from average pay increases for "linked" jobs (i.e., jobs that have remained in the sample in consecutive quarters). Quarterly pay ratios among "job quotes" are first averaged within 700 industry-occupation cells (70 industries by 10 broad occupations) using compensation shares as weights. Average wage or compensation changes across industry-occupation cells are then averaged using cost shares employing fixed employment weights from a base period. In short, the ECI is intended to represent average pay increases for existing jobs, being invariant to changes in employment shifts.[7]

The ECI is available for union and nonunion workers beginning in 1975:3.[8] Figure 5.2a provides the published private-sector union and nonunion ECI

Figure 5.2a **Union and Nonunion Private ECI Wage Index Values, 1975:3–2001:4 (1989:2 = 100)**

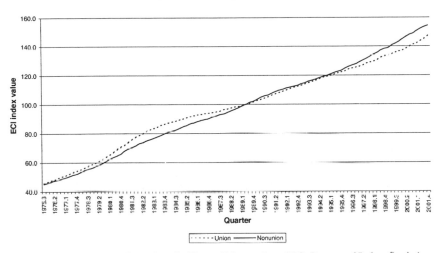

Source: ECI Wage index values in Figure 5.2a are from U.S. Bureau of Labor Statistics, Office of Compensation Levels and Trends, Employment Cost Index: Historical Listing, January 31, 2002, Table 5.7.

for wages for the period 1975:3 through 2001:4 (with 1989:2 = 100). Figure 5.2b (see p. 120) provides the same information in different form, showing each quarter's (approximate) difference in union-nonunion log wage growth from the previous twelve months. The pattern is clear. Union workers displayed substantially faster wage growth than did nonunion workers during the late 1970s and early 1980s. Converting the ECI to changes in log points, there was a 0.073 widening of the union log wage gap between 1975:3 and 1983:2. The quarter 1983:2 approximates the time period when union wage growth fell below nonunion wage growth and corresponds most closely to the January–December 1983 CPS average.

Beginning in the early 1980s, union wages increased more slowly than nonunion wages, with the exception of the early 1990s and the latter half of 2001.[9] During the period 1983:2 and 2001:2 (the midpoint of the 2001 CPS), the ECI indicates that the union log wage gap closed by a remarkable –0.139 log points! To put this into perspective, note that the consensus opinion among labor economists is that the union wage premium is approximately 15 percent.[10] If both the profession's consensus and the ECI wage patterns were correct, then there would no longer exist a union wage premium. We will argue subsequently that neither assumption is correct. By the early 1980s, the union wage premium (measured by standard cross-sectional wage equations) was substantially larger than 15 percent. Moreover, the relative wage changes evident in the ECI are likely to overstate the decline in the union premium.

Figure 5.2b **Union Minus Nonunion Private-Sector ECI Fourth-Quarter Wage Changes, 1976:3–2001:4**

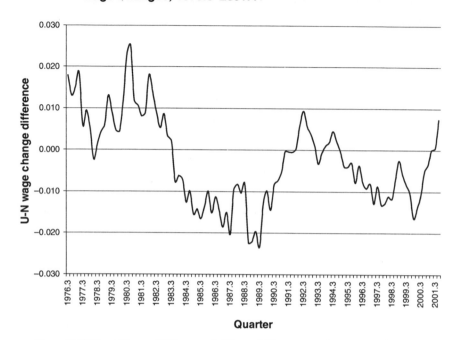

Quarter

Notes: U-N Wage Change Differences in Figure 5.2b represent the fourth-quarter change in log values for the union ECI index minus the nonunion change. A positive (negative) value represents an increase (decrease) in the union-nonunion wage gap.

Beginning in 1979:4, the ECI provides evidence on union and nonunion compensation as well as wages. The ECI compensation indices for union and nonunion workers are shown in Figure 5.3. As compared to the –0.139 closing in the ECI wage gap between 1983:2 and 2001:2, the compensation gap closed by –0.111. This difference reflects a faster rate of growth in union than in nonunion benefits, partially offsetting the slower union growth in wages.

Articles by BLS economists appearing in *Compensation and Working Conditions* report the slower growth of union than nonunion wages evident in the ECI (Schwenk 1996; Foster 2000). But they neither note nor address in print the substantial discrepancies between the ECI and ECEC in relative union-nonunion wage growth.

BLS economists recognize that the ECI displays faster economy-wide wage growth than does the ECEC and attempt to reconcile these series (Schwenk

Figure 5.3   **Union and Nonunion Private ECI Compensation Index Values, 1979:4–2001:4**

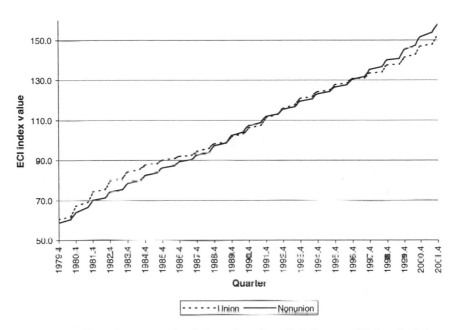

Source: ECI total compensation index values from U.S. Bureau of Labor Statistics, Office of Compensation Levels and Trends, Employment Cost Index: Historical Listing, January 31, 2002, Table 4.

1997; Lettau, Loewenstein, and Cushner 1997).[11] The analysis by Michael K. Lettau, Mark A. Loewenstein, and Aaron T. Cushner (1997) accounts for much but not all of the difference. They show that faster ECI growth results from both calculation of wage change within cells and aggregation of average growth across cells. First, "job quote" wage growth between quarters is based on linked jobs that remain in the survey. Average wages among jobs entering the survey, however, are lower than among those continuing in the survey. Were composition allowed to vary (as in the ECEC), job cells would show slower wage growth. Secondly, the ECI's use of fixed rather than current employment to construct the cost share weights that aggregate industry-occupation cells into an average leads to faster wage growth. Although Lettau, Loewenstein, and Cushner cannot provide an exact decomposition, they conclude that both sources are important. The implications of their analysis are that within ECI-ECEC industry-occupation cells, employment has been moving toward lower-paying jobs, and that over time employment has been shifting toward lower-paying industry-occupation cells. It is important to note that the ECI and ECEC have no measures of worker characteristics such as schooling, age, and gender, a point we return to in our analysis using the CPS.

Following the logic of Lettau, Loewenstein, and Cushner, one can speculate on potential explanations for divergence between the ECI and ECEC in relative union and nonunion wage growth. One possible explanation would be that union employment has become more concentrated over time across industry-occupation cells displaying rapid wage growth. Whereas the ECI (where relative union wage growth has been slow) holds sectoral employment fixed, the ECEC (where union and nonunion wage growth are similar) reflects these shifts in employment. A second possibility is that union employment has grown (or declined least) among those jobs *within* industry-occupation cells displaying rapid wage growth. A third possibility, following the logic of Lettau, Loewenstein, and Cushner (1997), is that entering job quotes, which the ECI fails to account for, not only are lower paying on average, but are also likely to be nonunion since there are lower rates of attrition and creation in union job quotes. Hence, as compared to the ECEC, the ECI may overstate wage growth most substantially for nonunion jobs where there is rapid entry, but far less so for union jobs where entry is limited.[12] This explanation is also consistent with the countercyclical pattern of the union wage gap, since creation of new jobs and quits are likely to fall during recessions relatively most in the nonunion sector. A final possibility is that the ECI-ECEC sample (or at least its nonunion component) has unintentionally shifted toward lower wage jobs. That is, low-wage jobs were either previously underrepresented or are now overrepresented. This would result in artificially slow growth in ECEC mean (nonunion) wages over time, but have little systematic effect on rates of ECI wage growth among continuing job quotes.[13] Although we cannot literally replicate the ECI and ECEC using the CPS, the plausibility and importance of alternative explanations can be investigated.[14]

Employer Costs for Employee Compensation

The ECEC is an annual series that provides dollar costs for employee wages and benefits as of March of each year. The series is available for years beginning in 1986. The ECEC is part of the NCS and based on the same survey data that form the basis for the quarterly ECI. The ECEC is intended to measure average wages and compensation at a point in time for a representative cross-section of workers (jobs). Unlike the ECI, the ECEC utilizes current employment weights and accounts for the wages of new workers (those not

Figure 5.4a **Union and Nonunion ECEC Annual Wage Changes, 1986–2001**

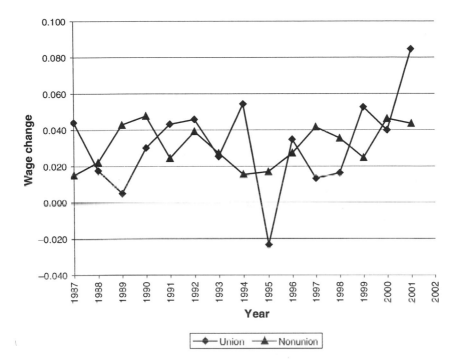

employed in the job the previous quarter). Changes in the ECEC across years thus reflect changes in the average wage across all workers (jobs), following employment shifts within and across industry-occupation job cells.

In contrast to the ECI, trends from the ECEC indicate that union and nonunion wages have grown at similar rates. As seen previously in Figure 5.1, between 1986 and 2001 ECEC union wages increased by 0.014 more than did nonunion wages, in contrast to the –0.10 slower union growth indicated by the ECI. If we focus instead on total compensation, average pay and benefits increased by 0.026 more than did nonunion compensation, as compared to –0.07 slower union compensation growth suggested by the ECI. Figure 5.4a shows the union and nonunion (approximate) year-to-year change in log wages (using the log of the ratio of year t to year $t–1$ wages) between 1986–87 and 2000–01. Figure 5.4b (see p. 124) provides the identical information for union and nonunion total compensation. Consistent with the full-period trends, union wage growth during the overall period is not systematically higher or lower than for nonunion workers.

In line with discussion in the previous section, explanations that could

Figure 5.4b **Union and Nonunion ECEC Annual Compensation Change, 1986–2001**

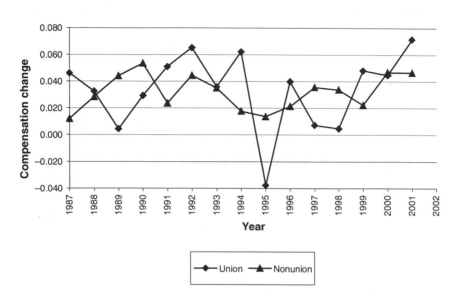

Notes: ECEC mean dollar wage (compensation) values are from U.S. Bureau of Labor Statistics, Office of Compensation Levels and Trends, Employer Costs for Employee Compensation Historical Listing, August 29, 2001, Table 5. Wage (compensation) change is an approximate log change, measured by union status as the log of the ratio of year *t* to year *t*–1 wages (compensation).

help reconcile the ECEC and ECI evidence include a finding that union employment has become less concentrated over time in industry-occupation cells displaying slow wage growth, that union employment has declined most sharply among those jobs within industry-occupation cells displaying slow wage growth, that the ECI failure to give weight to entering job quotes causes the ECI to overstate wage growth for nonunion jobs relative to union jobs, or that the composition of the ECEC (and ECI) has shifted over time toward greater representation of low-wage nonunion jobs. It is important to note that circumstances that internally reconcile the ECI and ECEC need not be consistent with external evidence from the CPS.

Current Population Survey

Much of the published research on levels of and changes in union premiums comes from the CPS. The CPS reports worker union membership status in

the May 1973–81 earnings supplements and, beginning in 1983, during all
months (for a quarter sample) in the CPS-ORG (outgoing rotation group)
earnings files.[15] CPS regression estimates of the union premium show little
decline through the mid-1990s (but decline thereafter), leading some authors
to conclude that there has been stability in the overall union premium
(Blanchflower 1999). Barry T. Hirsch and Edward J. Schumacher (2002a)
point out that private-sector regression-based premiums decline, particularly
in the late 1990s. They also show that the "raw" or unadjusted CPS union
wage gap changes over time in a fashion roughly similar to the ECI, with
substantial decline since the early 1980s. The oddity of this result is that the
unadjusted CPS should closely mimic the ECEC and not the ECI.

Meaningful comparison of CPS wage trends with those in the ECI and
ECEC requires that we construct consistent time-series of CPS union wage
gap estimates. This cannot be done without taking into account the substantial effect of "allocated earnings" on relative union-nonunion wages. In the
CPS, individuals who either refuse or are unable to report weekly earnings
have earnings imputed (i.e., allocated) using a "cell hot deck" method. The
cell hot deck method matches each nonrespondent to an earnings "donor"
with an identical mix of match characteristics (this differs from the method
used in the March CPS). There are just under 15,000 "cells" or combinations
of match variables. The match criteria include schooling, age, gender, occu
pational category, hours, and gender, but *not* sectoral variables such as industry or union status.

As shown in Hirsch and Schumacher (2002b), even if the census matching provides an unbiased measure of average earnings, wage differential estimates are systematically understated when the attribute being studied is *not*
a criterion used by the census to match donors to nonrespondents. These
include, among others, union-nonunion, industry, and public-private wage
gap estimates. Hirsch and Schumacher refer to this as "match bias" and derive a general expression for the bias. They show that in the case of union
wage gap estimates, the bias is closely approximated by $\Omega\Gamma$, where Ω is the
proportion of workers with imputed earnings and $\Omega\Gamma$ is a log wage gap estimate free of match bias. Standard wage gap estimates from CPS samples
including allocated earners must be multiplied by $1/(1-\Omega)$ to approximate a
wage gap free of match bias. For example, if a quarter of the estimation
sample has allocated earnings, the union wage gap estimate is attenuated by
roughly 25 percent (i.e., a quarter of the sample displays no gap); thus, gap
estimates should be adjusted upward by 1.33.[16]

Prior to the 1994 revision in the CPS, approximately 20 percent of the
earnings sample had their earnings allocated. Since 1994, in excess of 25
percent have allocated earnings, with particularly high rates (about 30 per-

cent) in the most recent years. Hirsch and Schumacher (2002b) show that union gap estimates understate actual wage gaps by about 5 percentage points, owing to a large downward bias in imputed earnings for union nonrespondents, matched primarily to nonunion donors, and a small upward bias for non-union nonrespondents. Moreover, changes over time in the number and iden-tification of allocated earners makes it difficult to estimate time-consistent union wage gap estimates. For example, the 1973–78 May CPS files do not provide allocated earnings for nonrespondents (earnings are recorded as miss-ing), but beginning in May 1979 allocated earnings are included. The appar-ent sharp decline in CPS union wage premium estimates between 1978 and 1979, long a puzzle in the literature (Freeman 1986; Lewis 1986), is found to result in large part from the inclusion of imputed earnings in CPS earnings records beginning in 1979 following their exclusion from 1973 to 1978. There are additional problems. During the period from 1989 to 1993, only about a quarter of those with allocated earnings are identified in the CPS-ORG files. There are no valid allocated earnings flags in the CPS-ORG for all of 1994 and most of 1995. The proportion of the sample with allocated earnings in-creased with the 1994 CPS redesign (valid allocation flags begin in late 1995), and has been particularly large since 1999. Thus, standard estimates of CPS union wage differentials substantially understate the size of the gaps (due to inclusion of allocated earners), while overstating recent declines in the gap (due to the increasing number of allocated earners).

In Figure 5.5, we reproduce the time-consistent estimates of the regression-adjusted private nonagricultural sector union wage gap from 1973 to 2001, as shown in Hirsch and Schumacher (2002b).[17] Presented are regression union wage gaps, with control for worker characteristics, job sector, and location. The solid line corrects for match bias. The dotted line shows what a researcher would obtain using the full CPS sample, with downward bias beginning in 1979 following inclusion of allocated earners. Their regression estimates of the union premium (corrected for match bias) indicate a decline of –0.051 log points from the 1984 peak through 2001. Their unadjusted (nonregression) figures measuring the union-nonunion wage gap (not shown here) show a –0.122 log point closing between 1984 and 2001.[18]

Having examined evidence on union wage gaps from the CPS, ECI, and ECEC, puzzles abound. The pattern since the mid-1980s ranges from evi-dence of no closing in the union-nonunion wage gap (the ECEC) to evidence of a substantial narrowing of the wage gap (the ECI and raw CPS). CPS regression estimates indicate a moderate closing of the gap. The ECEC and CPS results are based on the use of current industry-occupation employment weights, whereas the ECI uses fixed weights. CPS regression estimates pro-vide controls for worker characteristics (e.g., schooling, age, and gender)

Figure 5.5 **Union-Nonunion Private-Sector Wage Premiums: With and Without Match Bias from Earnings Allocation, 1973–2001**

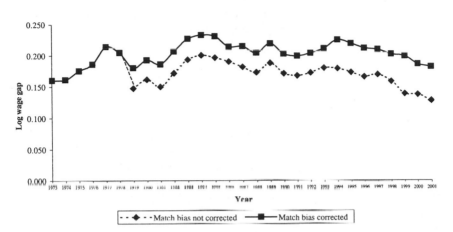

Notes: Estimate taken from Hirsch and Schumacher (2002a), measuring regression log wage gaps for the private nonagricultural sector, based on 1973–2001 CPS earnings files. See section II-C and footnote 14 for estimation details. The "squared" line corrects for imputation match bias by removing allocated earners in years possible and approximating unbiased gaps in years where allocated earners cannot be reliably identified (1989–95). The "diamonds" represent estimates attenuated by match bias. Researchers who use all valid earnings records in publicly available CPS files would obtain wage gap estimates similar to the "squares" for 1973–78, when CPS files do not include imputed earnings, and the "diamonds" beginning in 1979, when CPS files include imputed earnings values.

and sector of employment (industry-occupation). The ECEC and raw CPS results provide no worker or sectoral controls, whereas the ECI provides fixed sectoral weights but no worker controls. Given the common method used by the ECEC and the raw CPS, one expects to see a similar pattern, yet the ECEC and raw CPS results are at opposite ends of the spectrum.

One also expects to see the use of fixed sectoral weights (as in the ECI) or regression controls (in the CPS) drive results in the same direction. Just the opposite occurs. Use of fixed weights in the ECI (compared to the ECEC) produces slower union than nonunion wage growth; use of sectoral controls in CPS regressions (compared to the raw CPS) results in a far less marked pattern of union wage decline. There is no shortage of puzzles.

Are There Solutions to the Puzzles? Reconciling the Evidence

In this section, we attempt to reconcile conflicting evidence on the trends in union and nonunion wages. We focus on three areas. First, we tackle what is inherently the most difficult puzzle—why there exist completely different patterns in the ECEC and the raw CPS. Because both use similar methods, with current employment weights and no statistical controls, there is little that we can do to reconcile the surveys, absent access to microdata from the ECI-ECEC as well as the CPS. We do discuss possible differences in the surveys that might account for the different pattern. The second area of focus is the discrepancy in wage patterns between the ECEC and ECI. In principle, we can simulate changes that occur as one moves from the ECEC to ECI through the adoption of similar adjustments within the CPS. Specifically, using the CPS one can switch from current year weights to fixed employment weights and switch from measurement of changes in mean wages across years to the measurement of the mean change in year-to-year wages among individual union and nonunion job stayers. This analysis has the potential to shed light not only on union wage gap patterns in the CPS, but also on differences in behavior of the ECEC and ECI. Finally, we analyze the CPS using standard decomposition techniques. Starting with the total (raw) change in the union-nonunion wage gap over time, we examine how much of the change is accounted for by changes in worker and sectoral characteristics (and their payoff in the labor market) and how much by a changing union wage premium. An important by-product of this analysis will be our examination of how the private-sector union workforce has changed over time.

The CPS Versus the ECEC

Were the CPS and ECEC to have identical wage measures and an identical sample frame, they would likely display the same pattern of change in the union-nonunion wage gap. Of course, neither is the case. The CPS samples households, with wage figures based on the reported earnings of employed wage and salary workers who report that they are and are not union members (or covered by a collective bargaining agreement). The wage measure represents usual weekly earnings (including overtime, tips, commissions, and shift pay) divided by usual hours worked per week. The ECEC and ECI, however, are based on establishment surveys. Sampled are "jobs" or "job quotes" within establishments classified by occupation and work level ("leveling factors" include knowledge required, supervision received, complexity, physical demands, work environment, and so on). Based on current employment weights, job quotes are averaged into 700 cells (70 industries by 10 occupations), which in turn are averaged based on current weights. The wage measure represents the straight time wage, inclusive of tips, commissions, and other productivity-related incentive pay but, in contrast to the CPS, excludes overtime and shift supplements (these are included in the benefits measure). Thus, one avenue to explore is whether rootrioting the CPS analysis to straight-time pay has a substantial effect on union-nonunion wage trends.

A second issue is the classification of jobs as union or nonunion. In the CPS, this is based on individual workers' reported union status. In the ECEC and ECI, it is based on whether the job within an establishment is reported as primarily covered by a union contract. Although union density in the ECEC is not reported, the one piece of evidence that we located suggests that differences in the union measure may not be important. Ann C. Foster (2000) reports that in 1997, 23 percent of her total NCS-ECEC sample was unionized, as compared to a coverage rate of 15.6 percent in the 1997 CPS. In the private-sector NCS-ECEC sample, there was a 16 percent unionization rate, as compared to 10.6 coverage density in the CPS. Most of this difference can be explained by the fact that unlike the full ECEC or ECI, her NCS-ECEC sample excluded establishments with fewer than fifty employees. In the private sector, establishments with over fifty employees accounted for only 58 percent of total employment in March 1998 (based on Employment Statistics 202 state unemployment insurance reports, published in *Employment and Wages, Annual Averages 1998*). Using the extreme assumption that no employees in small establishments were unionized, this would increase the CPS private-sector figure from 10.6 to 18.3 percent (10.6/0.58), a bit higher than the ECEC union density of 16 percent. In short, the very limited evidence that we find does not lead us to worry about the representativeness of the ECEC (and ECI) samples with respect to union density.

We can also assess the plausibility of mean wage estimates from the ECEC and CPS. On the one hand, CPS wages including overtime and shift pay should be higher than ECEC straight-time wages. On the other hand, ECEC hours for salaried workers are effectively truncated at forty based on a standard workweek, which should cause ECEC wages to exceed CPS implicit hourly earnings for those with greater than forty usual hours worked per week. Table 5.1 (see p. 131) presents mean union and nonunion wages from the ECEC and CPS for 1986 and 2001, with CPS wages calculated for all workers based on earnings inclusive of overtime and shift pay, and for workers for whom straight-time pay can be isolated.[19] Mean union wages reported in the ECEC are $18.36 in 2001, nearly identical to the $18.39 we calculate from the CPS. Nonunion wages, on the other hand, are lower in the ECEC than in the CPS, $14.81 versus $15.87. Equally disturbing is that 1986 wages are not similar, with ECEC union wages being a bit higher than in the CPS ($11.32 versus $11.09), and nonunion wages now being substantially higher in the ECEC than in the CPS ($9.26 versus $8.51), the opposite of what is observed in 2001. These are puzzling patterns. As compared to the CPS (and the ECI), the ECEC substantially understates nonunion (but not union) wage growth between 1986 and 2001. We do not know why.[20]

For many workers, hourly earnings in the CPS are implicit, being calculated as the ratio of usual weekly earnings on the principal job divided by usual hours worked per week on that job. Some have argued that many workers overreport hours worked, reporting scheduled rather than actual hours, and that this overreporting has increased over time (see Abraham, Spletzer, and Stewart 1999; Hamermesh 1990; Robinson and Bostrum 1994), causing CPS growth in hourly earnings (and productivity) to be understated. For the moment, assume that this is correct for the overall labor force. In order to explain a declining union wage gap in the CPS as compared to the ECEC, it must be the case that there has been an increase in the overreporting of hours for union relative to nonunion workers, thus understating union wage growth. This seems unlikely. Typically, union jobs have less flexibility in hours than do nonunion jobs and, if anything, we would think there has been less variation in hours reporting over time in the union than in the nonunion sector.

Evidence reported in Table 5.1 addresses some of these issues. By examining wage changes among hourly union and nonunion workers reporting their straight-time wage, wage trends should be largely purged of bias resulting from misreporting of hours worked. Comparing 1986 and 2001, we find that there has been a closing in the union wage gap for hourly workers of –0.121 in the CPS, similar to the –0.118 for the more comprehensive wage measure for all wage and salaried workers combined. We also use our standard wage measure (including tips, commissions, and overtime) for the full sample, but for workers with greater than forty usual hours worked per week, we calculate the wage by dividing weekly earnings by forty. This mimics the ECEC-ECI assumption of forty hours for full-time workers (but unlike the ECEC-ECI, this mixes in overtime wages for hourly workers). As seen in line 3, wages are higher (by construction) using this measure and, owing to an increase in hours over time among high-wage workers, we also see more rapid wage growth. Closing in the union gap, however, is affected little, being nearly identical to that seen in line 1 (a closing of –0.12). In short, differences in the wage measure between the ECEC and CPS fail to explain even a modest portion of the large divergence in wage growth (particularly for nonunion workers) between the ECEC and CPS. Even if it could, this would tell us nothing about differences between the ECEC and ECI.

Finally, the bottom panel of Table 5.1 provides the CPS calculations in log wages as well as dollars, thus allowing us to assess how closely our approximation to log wage changes comes to actual log wage changes. They are reasonably close, with the log approximation calculated from mean dollar wages slightly understating the actual closing in union-nonunion log wages (e.g., for all private workers, a –0.118 approximation versus the –0.122 actual change in the log wage).

Table 5.1

Private-Sector Mean Wages and Union-Nonunion Wage Gap Change, 1986–2001

	Union 1986	Union 2001	Wage growth index	Nonunion 1986	Nonunion 2001	Wage growth index	Union-nonunion change in log wage gap
Employment Cost Index (ECI)							
Index values (1989:2 = 100)	93.1	143.7	154.4	89.0	152.2	171.0	−0.102
Employer Costs for Employee Compensation (ECEC)							
Current dollar mean wages, private sector	11.32	18.36	162.2	9.26	14.81	159.9	0.014
Current Population Survey (CPS)							
Current dollar mean wages:							
Full hourly earnings, all private sector	11.09	18.39	165.8	8.51	15.87	186.5	−0.118
Straight-time wage, hourly workers only	10.60	16.72	157.7	6.23	11.09	178.0	−0.121
Full hourly earnings, assuming maximum 40 hours	11.53	19.48	169.0	9.07	17.28	190.5	−0.120
Current dollar mean log wages:			$\Delta \ln W$			$\Delta \ln W$	
Full hourly earnings, all private sector	2.307	2.787	0.480	1.950	2.552	0.502	−0.122
Straight-time wage, hourly workers only	2.276	2.717	0.442	1.724	2.294	0.570	−0.129
Full hourly earnings, assuming maximum 40 hours	2.339	2.831	0.492	1.995	2.606	0.611	−0.119

Notes: Mean dollar wages are converted to a wage index by taking the ratio of 2001 to 1986 wages times 100. The change in the union-nonunion log wage gap is approximated by the difference in the logs of the indexes. For the CPS log wage calculations, the change in the wage gap is measured by the difference in log wage growth for union and nonunion workers. For the ECI, we report the index values of union and nonunion wages for 1986:2 and 2001:2 (with 1989:2 = 100). The ECI wage growth index represents the ratio of 2001 to 1986 index values times 100, with the change in the log wage gap approximated by the difference in the log of the index values.

Emulating ECEC and ECI Wage Growth Methods with the CPS

Wage growth in the ECI differs in several fundamental ways from that calculated in the ECEC and CPS. First, ECI wage growth within jobs is based on a continuing sample of matched job quotes, ignoring jobs that have exited or entered the sample. Second, wage growth in the ECI is averaged across cells using fixed industry-occupation (I/O) weights (wage bill shares). A third difference—use of alternative wage growth metrics— is more apparent than real. For the ECEC and CPS, wage growth is measured by the change between periods in average wages. In the ECI, growth is measured by the average of wage growth rates over time. However, because the latter is payroll weighted, these wage growth metrics are equivalent (see note 14).

Although we cannot precisely replicate ECI methods using the CPS, we can use methods in the spirit of the ECI. First, we can utilize the panel nature of the CPS and measure wage growth based on wage changes of matched workers in adjacent years (i.e., workers who are union job cell stayers or nonunion stayers in adjacent years). Second, average wage growth across cells can be calculated using payroll shares based on fixed industry-occupation employment weights. And third, long-term wage change can be calculated from linked year-to-year wage growth ratios rather than relying on just beginning- and end-point wages. By making changes one step at a time, we may identify the impact of specific methodological differences.

We report the outcome of this investigation in Table 5.2. Recall that previously we found a closing of the union gap of –0.118 using CPS means absent disaggregation (see Table 5.1). Using the 1986 and 2001 CPS, we disaggregate union and nonunion private-sector workers into eighty-five job cells based on a division into five broad occupational categories cross-classified with seventeen broad industry groupings. We measure union and nonunion wage growth separately in all calculations. In lines 1 and 2, we examine the effect of using 1986 versus 2001 fixed employment weights. We measure wage growth for each group within the eighty-five industry-occupation cells by taking the mean wage for 1986 and mean wage for 2001 (each calculated using CPS employment weights) and then taking the ratio of the 2001 to 1986 mean wages. We then average across the eighty-five job cells using current (2001) employment weights. Letting 1986 = 100, the union wage index in 2001 is 163.2 (i.e., a 2001–1986 wage ratio of 1.632); the nonunion wage index is 179.1. Taking the log difference of the index values, we approximate closing of the union-nonunion log differential to be –0.093. In line 2, we switch from using current year to base year employment weights

Table 5.2

Emulating ECI Methods Using the CPS: Union and Nonunion Wage Growth, 1986–2001

Calculation method	Union wage index	Nonunion wage index	U-N log gap change
1. Average across I/O cells using 2001 employment weights	163.2	179.1	−0.093
2. Average across I/O cells using 1986 employment weights	161.3	177.7	−0.097
3. Average across I/O cells using 1986 payroll share weights (employment x wages x hours)	161.0	177.4	−0.097
4. Average within I/O cells calculated with worker payroll shares; average across cells with 1986 payroll share weights	166.4	186.4	−0.114
5. Average within I/O cells from CPS panel cell stayers. Wage ratios by year averaged across individuals using worker payroll weights. The ratios are multiplied across years to measure 1986–2001 cell growth. The average growth ratio across cells is calculated using 1986 payroll share weights, as in Line 4	308.5	412.9	−0.291

Notes: Data sources for Lines 1–4 are the 1986 and 2001 CPS-ORG files. Union and nonunion workers are grouped into 85 broad occupation (5) by industry (17) cells. In Lines 1–3, within-cell means are calculated by the ratio (times 100) of 2001 to 1986 mean wages, where means are calculated using individual employment weights. In Line 4, within-cell means are calculated using individual payroll shares (employment weight times wage time hours worked). Aggregation across the 85 I/O cells is based on 2001 employment in Line 1, 1986 employment in Line 2, and 1986 payroll in Lines 3–4. In Line 5, within-cell wage growth is measured separately among union and nonunion workers who remain in the job cell during adjacent years. Individual workers' wage ratios are calculated for the year pairs 1987–86, 1988–87, …, 2001–00. Cell-specific wage growth for each year pair is averaged using worker payroll weights from the initial year. Each cell's wage growth for 1986–2001 is calculated by multiplying the 15-year pair ratios. The average across cells, reported in Line 5 for union and nonunion workers, is calculated using 1986 cell payroll share weights from the full sample (as in Line 4) and multiplying by 100. The union-nonunion log gap change is approximated by the difference in the logs of union and nonunion wage growth. Union workers include those who are union members and non-members covered by a collective bargaining agreement.

to aggregate across cells, which increases (in magnitude) the union wage gap closing to −0.097.

We next switch to aggregation across cells using payroll rather than employment weights (payroll weights account for employment times wages times

hours worked), since payroll weighted wage ratios across cells are equivalent to the change in means. The use of 1986 payroll weights across cells
(line 3) indicates a closing in the wage gap of –0.097. We next modify the
calculation by compiling within-cell wage growth based on individual shares
in cell payroll rather than employment (line 4). This leads to faster union and
nonunion wage growth, suggesting that wage growth within cells has been
highest among those with larger earnings (wages times hours), and shows
more rapid closing of the union wage gap, to –0.114. The pattern found so
far is consistent with differences in the ECEC and ECI, with the use of base
year and cell payroll weights leading to a finding of a shrinking union wage
gap (slower union than nonunion wage growth). The differences found so far
are rather trivial, however: an order of magnitude different than the huge
disparity between the ECEC and ECI.

The final set of calculations (line 5) is potentially important, but statistically problematic. We focus exclusively on wage changes among job cell
stayers. We form worker-year pairs based on CPS panels and then restrict
our analysis to the subset of the panel comprising workers who do not change
industry, occupation, or union status across the year. These calculations are
intended to approximate the effect that use of matched job quotes (and omission of new quotes) and linked wage indices have on the ECI measure of
wage change, as compared to the ECEC. We first measure wage changes (the
ratio of the year 2 to year 1 wage) for each individual stayer in the CPS
panel. We then calculate the mean of the wage growth ratio within each
industry-occupation-union-year job cell (based on year 1 worker payroll
weights). Because some cells, particularly union cells, are empty or very
small, and individual wage changes vary enormously (in part due to measurement error), small cells ($N < 6$) are assigned the mean wage growth for
their industry and union status during that year (i.e., occupations are collapsed). Next, we form a linked 1986–2001 index for each cell, in the spirit
of the ECI, by multiplying for each of the industry-occupation-union cells
the wage ratio for 1987–86 times the ratio for 1988–87, and so forth, continuing through 2001–00. Having calculated wage growth over the 1986–
2001 period for each of the eighty-five union cells and eighty-five nonunion
cells, we next calculate the average across these cells using 1986 payroll
weights calculated from the full CPS file, as used previously in line 4 (this
ensures adequate cell sample sizes).[21]

The results of our calculations are shown in line 5 of Table 5.2. Rates of
implied wage growth are implausibly high, with a 1986–2001 index of
308.5 for union growth and of 412.9 for nonunion growth. These index
numbers imply an unrealistic –0.291 log point closing in the union premium.
The extremely high rates of wage growth for both union and nonunion

wages in line 5, however, are consistent with the higher growth rates in ECI than in ECEC wages. But our methods do not identify the extent to which this outcome is the result of using a sample of job cell stayers or from measurement error producing extreme values whose errors are compounded as they are multiplied across years. Lettau, Loewenstein, and Cushner (1997) show the first explanation (i.e., a matched sample) to be important using ECI-ECEC data. We suspect that the second explanation also matters, although we do not know the extent of error in ECI job quotes. In contrast to BLS calculations using matched job quotes, our CPS analysis is overwhelmed by individual variability in wage changes resulting in part from measurement error and compounded by small cell sizes. The most that we can say is that our panel analysis imitating ECI methods is at least suggestive of an explanation for ECI-ECEC differences in the pattern of union and nonunion wages.

In short, the large difference in relative union-nonunion wage growth in the ECEC and ECI remains a mystery. Given that both rely on the same survey data, the different outcomes are obviously a result of different methodologies. But neither economic intuition nor methodological differences appear readily consistent with such large differences. Our suspicion, based in part on the results in line 5, is that multiplication of wage ratios across years tends to produce larger rates of wage growth than taking the change in average wages. Any tendency toward higher measures of wage growth using ECI than ECEC methods must be strongest for nonunion workers, thus leading to a substantial closing in the union gap using the ECI but not the ECEC. Again, such an explanation is largely conjecture. Even if this were to account for differences between the ECEC and ECI, it does not explain the large discrepancy in union-nonunion results between the ECEC and CPS. As discussed previously, a change in the representativeness of the ECEC-ECI nonunion sample (but not union sample) toward more low-pay jobs and fewer high-pay jobs would simultaneously help account for ECEC-ECI differences and ECEC-CPS differences. But, again, we have no evidence that such a shift has occurred.

Decomposing Union and Nonunion Wage Changes in the CPS

Our third general approach involves decomposition of CPS union and nonunion total wage changes into those resulting from employment shifts, changes in worker characteristics, and in the residual union wage premium. We provide this analysis for the 1986–2001 period in order to shed light on the puzzles created by the contradictory evidence from the ECEC, ECI, and CPS.

Simple annual wage regressions provide measures of the union wage gap based on a union intercept shift, with a common set of parameters attaching to worker and sectoral variables.

$$w_{it} = \Sigma\beta_t x_{it} + \Sigma\theta_t z_{it} + \Gamma_t u_{it} + \xi_{it} \tag{1}$$

Here, w is the log wage for individual i in year t, x is a set of individual characteristics (those not measured or fixed within the ECI) with β the corresponding parameter set, z is a set of sectoral dummies measuring occupation, industry, location, and part-time status variables (those fixed within the ECI) with θ their coefficients, u is union membership, Γ_t represents the logarithmic union-nonunion wage gap in year t, and ξ is an error term assumed to have zero mean and constant variance.

Letting W, X, Z, and U represent the mean values in year t, the total change in the log union-nonunion wage gap between any two years 0 and 1 is equal to:

$$(W_{u1} - W_{n1}) - (W_{u0} - W_{n0}) = \Sigma\beta_1(X_{u1} - X_{n1}) - \Sigma\beta_0(X_{u0} - X_{n0})$$

$$+ \Sigma\theta_1(Z_{u1} - Z_{n1}) - \Sigma\theta_0(Z_{u0} - Z_{n0}) + \Gamma_1 - \Gamma_0 \tag{2}$$

Designating Δ as the change operator between years 0 and 1, the equation simplifies to:

$$\Delta(W_u - W_n) = \Delta\Sigma\beta(X_u - X_n) + \Delta\Sigma\theta(Z_u - Z_n) + \Delta\Gamma \tag{3}$$

The total change in the union-nonunion wage gap is decomposed into the change in the regression gap Γ, the change in relative union-nonunion worker characteristics over time, and the change in relative union-nonunion sectoral employment. Note that the "explained" effects of changes in worker characteristics and employment sector are "priced" based on their current prices (coefficients) in years 0 and 1 rather than using fixed prices. Thus, the explained changes in the union-nonunion wage gap reflect not only changes in relative characteristics and sector of employment, but also changes over time in how these are rewarded in the labor market.

Table 5.3 shows the results of this decomposition for the 1986–2001 period. The total change in the union-nonunion mean log wage gap between 1986 and 2001 is –0.122. The change in the regression wage premium Γ is –0.056, from –0.238 in 1986 to –0.182 in 2001, with the remaining –0.066 of the total decline "explained" by measurable control variables and their coefficients. Changes in individual characteristics (and their coefficients) account for –0.020 of the decline in the union wage gap, reflecting factors

Table 5.3

Decomposition of Private-Sector Union-Nonunion CPS Wage Change, 1986–2001

Change in total union-nonunion log wage gap	−0.1220
Change due to worker characteristics and payoffs	−0.0198
Change due to sectoral shifts and payoffs	−0.0458
Change in union log wage premium	−0.0564
Estimated union log wage premium: 1986	0.2383
Estimated union log wage premium: 2001	0.1818

Notes: Private-sector wage and salary workers, 1986 and 2001 CPS-ORG. Worker characteristics include schooling, experience and its square, gender, race, and marital status. Sectoral variables are part-time, metropolitan area, region (8), occupation (5), and industry (12). Calculation of the decomposition is shown in equations 2 and 3 in the text. Changes attributed to worker characteristics and sector reflect changes over time in relative union-nonunion values times their payoffs (coefficients).

not measured or held constant in the ECI or ECEC. The decomposition indicates that −0.046 of the decline is accounted for by a change in employment sector (industry, occupation, large metro, region, and part-time) factors held constant within the ECI owing to fixed sector weights with matched job quotes to calculate percentage changes. The employment sector is allowed to vary within the ECEC because it uses current weights and its sample of job quotes changes (slowly) over time.

The decomposition is informative in that it helps us understand why the unadjusted CPS union gap decline exceeds the estimated decline in the regression wage gap. Table 5.4 (see p. 138–139) shows means of the regression controls for 1986 and 2001 (plus 1973–74). Among individual characteristics, part of the decline in the unadjusted union gap between 1986 and 2001 is due to an increase in the union relative to nonunion percentage of private-sector female workers and slower growth in mean experience for union compared to nonunion workers. Working in the opposite direction is higher growth in mean schooling for union than for nonunion workers. Among the sectoral changes, two stand out as important: first, a substantial decline in union relative to nonunion employment in durable manufacturing and, second, a decline in relative pay (i.e., the coefficient) in transportation, communications, and utilities (TCU), a sector with a large share of total union employment (18.0 percent in 1986 and 18.7 percent in 2001).[22]

Although enhancing our understanding of union premiums and the CPS, the decomposition analysis does little to solve the puzzling discrepancies among the data sets. The −0.02 difference that results from control of individual characteristics accounts for a modest share of the large difference

Table 5.4

Private-Sector Union and Nonunion Worker Characteristics, 1973–74, 1986, and 2001

	Union			Nonunion		
	1973–74	1986	2001	1973–74	1986	2001
Wage (current dollars)	5.01	11.09	18.39	4.02	8.51	15.87
Log wage (current dollars)	1.5205	2.3068	2.7865	1.1824	1.9499	2.5515
Schooling (years completed)	10.99	12.05	12.87	11.94	12.74	13.16
Age 39.38	39.12	41.15	36.35	35.04	37.73	—
Experience (age-schooling-6)	22.39	21.07	22.29	18.42	16.32	18.63
Female	0.206	0.284	0.318	0.439	0.453	0.480
White	0.877	0.833	0.807	0.900	0.851	0.840
African American	0.110	0.136	0.149	0.086	0.091	0.110
Other race	0.013	0.031	0.044	0.014	0.028	0.050
Married spouse present	0.765	0.674	0.600	0.631	0.556	0.527
Separated, divorced, widowed	0.093	0.145	0.173	0.116	0.141	0.156
Never married	0.143	0.181	0.227	0.252	0.304	0.317
Part-time	0.108	0.082	0.101	0.255	0.215	0.196
Occupations:						
Managers/professionals	0.044	0.081	0.144	0.189	0.212	0.277
Technicians/sales/admin support	0.136	0.184	0.179	0.345	0.355	0.322
Service	0.059	0.075	0.100	0.146	0.145	0.140
Farming/forestry/fishing	0.006	0.005	0.005	0.031	0.022	0.018
Precision production/craft and repair	0.261	0.255	0.253	0.109	0.110	0.102
Operators/laborers	0.494	0.400	0.319	0.181	0.157	0.141
Industry:						
Agriculture	0.003	0.003	0.003	0.027	0.021	0.018
Mining	0.016	0.013	0.007	0.009	0.010	0.005
Construction	0.103	0.095	0.133	0.050	0.056	0.060
Durable manufacturing	0.335	0.272	0.179	0.146	0.130	0.102

Nondurable manufacturing	0.185	0.156	0.105	0.112	0.091	0.066
Transportation, communication, utilities	0.160	0.130	0.187	0.047	0.052	0.061
Wholesale trade	0.027	0.025	0.027	0.056	0.051	0.047
Retail trade	0.092	0.102	0.103	0.222	0.217	0.213
Finance, insurance, real estate	0.010	0.019	0.021	0.082	0.091	0.081
Business and repair services	0.015	0.024	0.033	0.039	0.063	0.067
Personal services	0.015	0.018	0.020	0.059	0.047	0.037
Entertainment and recreation	0.007	0.038	0.016	0.010	0.012	0.019
Professional services	0.031	0.034	0.165	0.141	0.162	0.154
Large metropolitan area	0.462	0.393	0.407	0.399	0.336	0.348
Region:						
New England	0.055	0.051	0.046	0.070	0.064	0.053
Middle Atlantic	0.232	0.214	0.207	0.161	0.146	0.129
East North Central	0.283	0.250	0.250	0.184	0.166	0.163
West North Central	0.068	0.074	0.080	0.074	0.073	0.072
South Atlantic	0.086	0.100	0.098	0.172	0.184	0.151
East South Central	0.053	0.050	0.045	0.065	0.058	0.059
West South Central	0.051	0.056	0.052	0.104	0.112	0.112
Mountain	0.029	0.034	0.041	0.044	0.053	0.064
Pacific	0.143	0.172	0.180	0.125	0.142	0.156
Sample size (wages, w/o allocated earners)	22,009	19,507	9,441	72,641	112,100	87,981
Sample size (total)	26,826	21,710	13,802	90,106	125,967	128,380

Notes: Data are from the 1973–74 May CPS and 1986 and 2001 CPS-ORG files. Employment weights are used to calculate means. The full sample includes all employed private-sector wage and salary workers. The wage sample excludes workers with earnings allocated by the Census. Union workers in 1973 include members only; in 1986 and 2001 union includes members plus covered nonmembers.

between the unadjusted CPS and the ECEC. More fundamentally, sectoral controls clearly move CPS outcomes toward the result of less closing over time in the union wage gap, just the opposite of the result seen as one moves from the ECEC toward the fixed-weight ECI.

As discussed earlier, in order to reconcile differences in the ECI and ECEC union wage gap trends, it should be the case that union employment became less concentrated (relative to nonunion employment) in sectors with slow wage growth. An implication from the CPS decomposition, however, is that relative sectoral shifts (at a very aggregate level) have been mildly unfavorable for union workers. This should lead to a slower relative union wage growth in the ECEC (where employment weights vary) than in the ECI (with fixed employment weights), the opposite of what is seen in these series.[23] In work not shown, we examined this issue further. Recall from Table 5.2, line 2, that the ratio of 2001 to 1986 union wages averaged across cells using 1986 union employment weights is 1.613, or an index of 161.3. Substituting 1986 nonunion weights we obtain an index of 164.9, indicating that union employment in 1986 was disproportionately concentrated in those industry-occupation cells exhibiting slow union wage growth. Likewise, we find little correlation (−0.012) between the proportion unionized in a sector in 1986 and that cell's overall wage growth between 1986 and 2001 (weighted by 1986 total employment).

We do find some evidence consistent with greater union employment decline (growth) where union wage growth is small (large). We find a positive correlation across the eighty-five sectors between union employment change during the 1986–2001 period and union wage change (0.351), stronger than the correlation between nonunion employment growth and union wage change (0.174) over the same period. Likewise, union employment change is more highly correlated with nonunion wage change (0.437) than is nonunion employment and nonunion wage change (0.312).[24]

We find evidence from the CPS that is both supportive and not supportive of the qualitative discrepancies between the ECEC and ECI regarding union and nonunion wage trends. But at best, these findings might account for a tiny share of the vast difference between the ECI and ECEC in union-nonunion wage growth. In short, we identify many puzzles, but few solutions. Despite our lack of progress, the questions being asked are important and clearly warrant a more detailed and systematic analysis than we can provide in this chapter.

Changes over Time in Union and Nonunion Workforces

One element of our investigation has been the importance of changes in relative union-nonunion employment weights and worker characteristics.

This section summarizes these changes. As seen in the previous section, over half of the total −0.122 log wage gap change in the CPS is accounted for by changes in relative union-nonunion attributes and their valuation. That is, shifts in sectoral employment and wages adversely affected relative union-nonunion wages during the 1986–2001 period. In Table 5.4, we provide a demographic and sectoral profile of union and nonunion wage and salary workers over the past twenty-eight years, with descriptive statistics for 1973–74, 1986, and 2001.

Notable are changes in gender composition. Whereas the percentage of women in private nonunion employment was effectively constant between 1986 and 2001, after rising between 1973 and 1986, the percentage of women in unionized employment rose from 20.6 percent in 1973, to 28.4 percent in 1986, and to 31.8 percent by 2001. Although the unionized private sector remains disproportionately male, this has become less true over time. Growth in the proportion of women is most readily evident when we include private- and public-sector employment, the latter being heavily female. Among public and private union wage and salary workers, the proportion of women increased from 23.8 percent in 1973 to 42.4 percent by 2001 (versus 45.2 to 49.0 percent among nonunion workers). Union workers have also increased relative schooling over time. Whereas union workers averaged nearly 1.0 year less schooling in 1973, the gap narrowed to 0.3 years by 2001.

Also worthy of mention are trends in part-time work. Part-time employment decreased among nonunion workers, from 25.5 percent in 1973, to 21.5 percent in 1986, and to 19.6 percent in 2001, yet remained close to 10 percent among private-sector union workers, despite the increase in female workers who comprise roughly two-thirds of all part-time workers.

When we turn to industry and occupational composition, several changes are notable. Nearly half (49.4 percent) of all union workers were in operative or laborer occupations in 1973, but by 2001 the share had fallen to 31.9 percent (for nonunion workers, shares fell from 18.1 percent to 14.1 percent). Whereas only 4.4 percent of union workers in the private sector were in managerial and professional occupations in 1973, the share rose to 14.4 percent in 2001 (for nonunion workers, shares rose from 18.9 percent to 27.8 percent). Focusing on broad industry, the share of union workers in manufacturing (durable plus nondurable) fell from 52.0 percent in 1973 to 28.4 percent in 2001, as compared to a decrease among nonunion workers from 25.7 percent to 16.8 percent. The share of union employment rose most markedly in professional services, from 3.1 percent to 16.5 percent between 1973 and 2001, and to a far lesser extent in construction and transportation, communications, and utilities.

What Can We Conclude About Changes in the Union Wage Gap?

Knowledge of wage growth in an economy is fundamental to our understanding of economic performance and the operation of labor markets. This chapter emphasized the large and puzzling differences found in relative union-nonunion private-sector wage growth using different data sets and methods. Focusing primarily on the period from 1986 to 2001, we find that the evidence on the wage gap between union and nonunion workers varies enormously. BLS's widely used ECI indicates a substantial narrowing of the union wage gap, by roughly 10 percentage points (–0.10 log points). Yet, published annual wages from the ECEC, based on the same underlying survey as the ECI, indicate that private-sector union wages have grown slightly faster than nonunion wages. The ECEC and ECI are based on employer surveys among establishments. Evidence on mean hourly earnings across individual workers in the CPS shows that mean wages for union relative to nonunion workers have fallen by about –0.12 log points between 1986 and 2001. This is highly similar to evidence from the ECI. Yet, the computational methods used to compile the CPS mean figures differ substantially from ECI methods and closely match ECEC methods. CPS regression analysis, which controls for worker characteristics and sector of employment, suggests that the union wage premium has declined by less than –0.06. Just over half of the decline in the mean union wage gap can be accounted for by measured changes (and the payoffs) in worker characteristics and employment sector.

Although the puzzles presented in this chapter are clear cut, solutions are not. We presented evidence that accounts for bits and pieces of the differences across surveys, but cannot provide a comprehensive reconciliation of CPS, ECI, and ECEC evidence. Differences between the CPS and ECEC are the result of substantially slower wage growth among nonunion workers in the ECEC than in the CPS (and ECI). Thus, these differences present a troubling puzzle for economy-wide wage (and productivity) growth. Analysis with the CPS using ECEC and ECI-type methods provides results both consistent and inconsistent with the pattern of differences reported in the ECEC and ECI. Little in our CPS analysis helps us in understanding the magnitude of the difference between the ECEC and ECI.

In the end, we find ourselves relying most heavily on results from the CPS. First, the CPS data are publicly available so that researchers may use the data in a way suited for the specific question at hand and disaggregate economy-wide union and nonunion wage trends into their component parts. Second, CPS results conform most closely to our priors and economic intuition. Relative union wages have declined substantially during a period of shrinking unionization, but the decline reflects in part the slow wage growth occurring in those occupations and industries in which private-sector union employment is concentrated. Decreases in the union wage premium are far more modest. Third, ECI methods are complex, making it difficult to understand the large and puzzling differences between the ECEC and ECI. The closing union wage gap seen in the ECI simply appears too large to represent changes in the union wage premium. ECEC methods are more straightforward, but the ECEC results of slow growth in nonunion wages and a slight increase in the relative union-nonunion wage are counterintuitive and the clear outlier among the various pieces of evidence.

The weight of the evidence indicates that the union-nonunion wage gap in the private sector has declined, perhaps substantially, since the early to mid-1980s.[25] The magnitude of the decline is anything but certain, although the six percentage point decline in the CPS regression estimate of the union premium (since 1986) appears plausible, certainly more so than evidence from the ECEC of no decline or from the ECI of a huge decline. Of course, a −0.06 log point decline since 1986 is quite sizable if one believes the conventional wisdom among labor economists that the union premium (as typically measured in wage level equations) is close to 15 percent, a figure long associated with the work of H. Gregg Lewis (1986). By the early 1980s, however, the private-sector union premium had risen to a level around 25 percent, a finding hidden in part by the large downward "match bias" (due to inclusion of allocated earners) present in most CPS union gap estimates. By 2001, however, private-sector union wage gaps in the CPS had fallen below 20 percent. Such a level is not so far from 15 percent, making Lewis and the conventional wisdom reasonable once again. In a chapter that is long on puzzles and short on solutions, it is perhaps appropriate to conclude on this comforting note.

Notes

We particularly appreciate the detailed comments received from Mark Loewenstein of BLS, as well as remarks from our discussant, Darren Grant, and other conference participants on earlier drafts of this chapter.

1. For a more complete discussion, see Hirsch and Schumacher (2002a). These conclusions follow strictly if bargaining settlements are on labor demand curves. Similar conclusions are likely to follow when outcomes are off the demand curve. To the extent that union-nonunion wage gaps differ across labor markets, sectoral employment shifts can affect the average union premium.

2. Bratsberg and Ragan provide an update and extension of the industry analysis presented in Linneman, Wachter, and Carter (1990).

3. Hirsch and Schumacher (2002b) show that the census match procedure used to impute missing earnings causes a large downward bias in union wage gap estimates.

The increase in recent years in numbers of allocated earners implies that standard CPS estimates overstate the decline in union wage gaps.

4. The 1986–2001 period is chosen since 1986 is the first year for which ECEC figures are available.

5. Changes in the log wage gap cannot be calculated precisely based on the ECI index values or ECEC mean dollar wages for union and nonunion workers. We approximate the log wage changes for union and nonunion workers by calculating $ln(I_1/I_0)_u - ln(I_1/I_0)_n$, where I is the ECI index value, u and n index union and nonunion, and 0 and 1 represent years 1986 and 2001. Letting W represent the mean wage, $ln(W_1/W_0)_u - ln(W_1/W_0)_n$ is used to approximate the log change in the union-nonunion wage gap based on mean wage figures by year. Using the CPS, we subsequently show that this approximation is close to the actual log wage change (Table 5.1).

6. Hirsch and Macpherson (2002) provide annual computations from the CPS monthly earnings files. For years from 1973 to 2001, they include both mean hourly earnings for union members and nonmembers, and a logarithmic union wage gap based on a wage regression with standard controls. They report a ratio of unadjusted mean union to nonunion wages that falls from 1.26 in 1986 to 1.12 in 2001. Regression estimates of the union premium fall by –0.076 log points between 1986 and 2001. Because allocated earners are included in their samples and the proportion of these workers has increased over time, the decline in the wage gap is overstated (Hirsch and Schumacher 2002a).

7. For details on construction of the ECI, see Wood (1982) and Lettau, Loewenstein, and Cushner (1997).

8. The union and nonunion subindices are not pure Laspeyres indices, as is the overall ECI. Rather, relative union-nonunion employment is updated each period. Rates of wage change for longer periods are calculated by chaining together subperiod wage growth. By construction, the weighted sum of the union and nonunion indices equals the change in the overall index. See Wood (1982) for details.

9. Although not the focus of this chapter, it is worth noting that union wage growth exceeded nonunion growth during the recessions of the early 1980s and early 1990s. A similar pattern is evident for the early twenty-first-century slowdown, with faster union than nonunion wage growth during 2001:3 and 2001:4. Grant (2001) provides a comprehensive analysis of union-nonunion wage cyclicality using CPS panels. He concludes that beginning in the early 1980s, reduced bargaining power of unions was associated with union wages becoming less procyclical than in the past and as compared to nonunion wages. This conclusion is consistent with patterns seen in the ECI. Likewise, evidence from the Panel Survey of Income Dynamics (PSID) indicates greater nonunion than union procyclicality during the 1980s (Wunnava and Okunade 1996). For a summary of relevant literature, see Grant (2001).

10. A survey by Fuchs, Krueger, and Poterba (1998) measured the views of labor economists at top universities. In response to the question—"What is your best estimate of the percentage impact of unions on the earnings of their average member?"— the median response was 15 percent and mean response 13.1 percent.

11. More broadly, Bosworth and Perry (1994) examine differences in wage growth seen in different data series, including the ECI and CPS.

12. Lettau, Loewenstein, and Cushner (1997), however, conclude that nonrandom rates of attrition can explain little of the discrepancy in overall rates of ECI and ECEC wage growth.

13. The appeal of this final explanation is that it can simultaneously help resolve

differences between the ECEC-ECI and the ECEC-CPS. Unfortunately, we cannot follow up on such speculation, absent a comparison of ECEC microdata with other data sets believed to have maintained representativeness over time.

14. The ECI can be thought of as an average of percentage changes (payroll weighted across cells), whereas wage changes calculated from the ECEC measure percentage changes in average wages (employment weighted across cells within years). The average of percentage changes, weighted by payroll shares in the initial year, is equivalent to the percentage change across years in employment weighted mean wages.

15. In May 1973–80, all rotation groups were asked union questions, but in May 1981 only a quarter of the sample was administered the questions. There were no union questions in the 1982 CPS.

16. Hirsch and Schumacher (2002b) provide the general expressions for bias (attenuation), with and without covariates. A similar (albeit more complex) match bias exists for longitudinal estimates of wage gaps. Longitudinal analyses of union wage gaps based on CPS panels include Card (1996) and Hirsch and Schumacher (1998). Both studies omit workers with allocated earnings.

17. The estimates correct for match bias by omitting all allocated earners in those years possible (from 1973 to 1988 and from 1996 to 2001) and making adjustments in other years based on the expected difference in the wage gap with and without allocated earners. This is done by adjusting 1989–93 estimates based on differences observed from 1983 to 1988 (0.031 log points) and adjusting 1994–95 estimates (following revisions in the CPS that increased the number of allocated earners) based on differences observed from 1996 to 1998 (0.046 log points). Hirsch and Schumacher (2002b) also conduct their own earnings imputation, in which union status is used as a match criterion (i.e., union nonreporters are assigned the reported earnings of matched union donors and nonunion nonreporters earnings of nonunion donors). Estimates obtained omitting allocated earners are similar to those obtained retaining all workers and relying on their own imputation method.

18. Hirsch and Schumacher (2002b) estimate union membership gaps for the nonagricultural private sector. CPS results calculated for this chapter are union coverage gaps for the entire private sector. Union premium decline economy wide is less pronounced than in the private sector. The conclusion reached in some studies of no change in the union premium is not surprising, especially if analysis begins after the peak of the early 1980s and ends prior to the late 1990s' decline.

19. Union and nonunion workers in the CPS are identified based on union coverage rather than membership, since this corresponds more closely to the union measure in the ECI and ECEC. Covered workers include all union members plus nonmembers stating they are covered by a collective bargaining agreement. Union wage premiums using coverage as the union measure are about 0.01 log points lower than using membership. For an analysis of the "membership premium," see Schumacher (1999) and Budd and Na (2000).

20. As previously mentioned, a possible explanation (for which we have no evidence) would be that over time the ECEC-ECI nonunion (but not union) sample has increased the proportion of low-wage jobs (or decreased high-pay jobs). This would account for ECEC-CPS differences and different growth rates for the ECEC and ECI, since change in sample representativeness need not affect the ECI measures of wage growth among matched jobs.

21. Absent data quality restrictions, the magnitude of these rates of wage growth blow up, being highly sensitive to individuals with extreme ratios of wage growth

(a very low first-year wage followed by a large second-year wage). There is no easy way to identify whether extreme values are real or result from reporting error. We arbitrarily truncate wage growth at 100 percent and -50 percent in the calculations reported.

22. Bratsberg and Ragan (2002) provide an analysis of union wage gaps across industries, finding that the dispersion in gaps has decreased over time due, in part, to declines in high-premium sectors such as TCU.

23. Recall that use of fixed sectoral employment weights in the ECI wage index is not equivalent to use of regression controls for sector of employment. Moreover, sectoral changes in the CPS decomposition are the product of relative employment and union wage gap changes.

24. All correlations weight cells by 1986 total employment.

25. Recall that this conclusion applies to the private sector. Public-sector union wage gaps, if anything, have increased, while the share of unionized (covered) workers employed in the public sector rose to 45 percent by 2001 (Hirsch and Macpherson, 2002, Tables 1a, 1f, 2a). Moreover, both the ECEC and ECI indicate faster growth in private-sector nonwage benefits among union than nonunion workers.

References

Abraham, Katharine G., James R. Spletzer, and Jay C. Stewart. 1999. "Why Do Different Wage Series Tell Different Stories?" *American Economic Review Papers and Proceedings* 89 (May): 34–39.

Andrews, Martyn J., Mark B. Stewart, Joanna K. Swaffield, and Richard Upward. 1998. "The Estimation of Union Wage Differentials and the Impact of Methodological Choices." *Labour Economics* 5 (December): 449–474.

Blanchflower, David G. 1999. "Changes over Time in Union Relative Wage Effects in Great Britain and the United States." In *The History and Practice of Economics: Essays in Honor of Bernard Corry and Maurice Peston,* vol. 2, ed. Sami Daniel, Philip Arestis, and John Grahl, 3–32. Northampton, MA: Edward Elgar.

Bosworth, Barry, and George L. Perry. 1994. "Productivity and Real Wages: Is There a Puzzle?" *Brookings Papers on Economic Activity* 1: 317–344.

Bratsberg, Bernt, and James F. Ragan Jr. 2002. "Changes in the Union Wage Premium by Industry." *Industrial and Labor Relations Review* 56 (October): 65–83.

Budd, John W., and In-Gang Na. 2000. "The Union Membership Wage Premium for Employees Covered by Collective Bargaining Agreements." *Journal of Labor Economics* 18 (October): 783–807.

Card, David. 1996. "The Effect of Unions on the Structure of Wages: A Longitudinal Analysis." *Econometrica* 64 (July): 957–979.

Foster, Ann C. 2000. "Union-Nonunion Wage Differences, 1997." *Compensation and Working Conditions* 5 (Spring): 43–46.

Freeman, Richard B. 1986. "In Search of Union Wage Concessions in Standard Data Sets." *Industrial Relations* 25 (Spring): 131–145.

Fuchs, Victor R., Alan B. Krueger, and James M. Poterba. 1998. "Economists' Views about Parameters, Values, and Policies: Survey Results in Labor and Public Economics." *Journal of Economic Literature* 36 (September): 1387–1425.

Grant, Darren. 2001. "A Comparison of the Cyclical Behavior of Union and Nonunion Wages in the United States." *Journal of Human Resources* 36 (Winter): 31–57.

Hamermesh, Daniel S. 1990. "Shirking or Productive Schmoozing: Wages and the Allocation of Time at Work." *Industrial and Labor Relations Review* 43 (February, Special Issue): S121–S133.

Hirsch, Barry T., and David A. Macpherson. 2002. *Union Membership and Earnings Data Book: Compilations from the Current Population Survey.* Washington, DC: Bureau of National Affairs.

Hirsch, Barry T., and Edward J. Schumacher. 1998. "Unions, Wages, and Skills." *Journal of Human Resources* 33 (Winter 1998): 201–219.

———. 2002a. "Private Sector Union Density and the Wage Premium: Past, Present, and Future." In *The Future of Private Sector Unionism in the United States,* ed. James T. Bennett and Bruce E. Kaufman, 92–128. Armonk, NY: Sharpe.

———. 2002b. "Match Bias in Wage Gap Estimates Due to Earnings Imputation." Trinity University, available at www.trinity.edu/bhirsch/ or www.ssrn.com

Jarrell, Stephen B., and T.D. Stanley. 1990. "A Meta-analysis of the Union-Nonunion Wage Gap." *Industrial and Labor Relations Review* 44 (October): 54–67.

Lettau, Michael K., Mark A. Loewenstein, and Aaron T. Cushner. 1997. "Explaining the Differential Growth Rates of the ECI and the ECEC." *Compensation and Working Conditions* 2 (Summer): 15–23.

Lewis, H. Gregg. 1986. *Union Relative Wage Effects: A Survey.* Chicago: University of Chicago Press.

Linneman, Peter D., Michael L. Wachter, and William H. Carter. 1990. "Evaluating the Evidence on Union Employment and Wages." *Industrial and Labor Relations Review* 44 (October): 34–53.

Robinson, John P., and Ann Bostrom. 1994. "The Overestimated Workweek? What Time Diary Measures Suggest." *Monthly Labor Review* 117 (August): 11–23.

Schumacher, Edward J. 1999. "What Explains Wage Differences Between Union Members and Covered Nonmembers?" *Southern Economic Journal* 65 (January): 493–512.

Schwenk, Albert E. 1996. "Trends in the Differences Between Union and Nonunion Workers in Pay Using the Employment Cost Index." *Compensation and Working Conditions* 1 (September): 27–33.

———. 1997. "Measuring Trends in the Structure and Levels of Employer Costs for Employee Compensation." *Compensation and Working Conditions* 2 (Summer): 3–14.

Wood, G. Donald. 1982. "Estimation Procedures for the Employment Cost Index." *Monthly Labor Review* (May): 40–42.

Wunnava, Phanindra V., and Albert Ade Okunade. 1996. "Countercyclical Union Wage Premium? Evidence for the 1980s." *Journal of Labor Research* 17 (Spring): 289–296.

6

Union-Nonunion Wage Differentials and Macroeconomic Activity

Bradley T. Ewing and Phanindra V. Wunnava

This research identifies the differing responses of union and nonunion wages to shocks to real output growth, inflation, and the stance of monetary policy. The literature documents the existence of a union wage premium; however, previously the focus has primarily been at the microlevel and on whether or not a union worker receives greater compensation than an otherwise comparable nonunion worker (e.g., Freeman and Medoff 1984; Hirsch and Addison 1986; Lewis 1986; Wunnava and Ewing 1999, 2000). Research also links the wage differential to the stage of the business cycle (Wunnava and Honney 1991; Wunnava and Okunade 1996) and to industrial structure (Okunade, Wunnava, and Robinson 1992).

Theoretical macroeconomic models imply that the response of employment to changes in aggregate measures of economic activity depends on the degree to which wage and price rigidities exist (e.g., see Romer 1996). For example, in explaining the labor market dynamics of Keynesian-type models when wages are rigid relative to output prices, Sargent (1987) shows that employment rises with an increase in the price level.[1] Sargent goes on to say that "sticky" money wages might occur in the presence of long-term labor contracts, such as those often found in the union sector. Certainly, it is possible that the degree to which this stickiness exists differs by union and nonunion status, as well as by economic sector. Given the differences in compensation level of union and nonunion workers, and the link to the stage of the business cycle and industry, it is expected that the response of union-nonunion wage differentials to macroeconomic shocks may vary by industrial sector.

The relationship between the union-nonunion differential and macroeconomic factors is examined by computing generalized impulse response functions derived from the estimation of vector autoregression models.[2] These response functions allow us to compare and contrast the effects of unanticipated changes in the macroeconomic factors on the wage differential within an industrial sector as well as between industrial sectors. An innovation to any of the variables may be interpreted as (unexpected) economic news. Clearly, firms and workers, and thus the wage gap, may be affected by movements in any of these macroeconomic variables. Knowledge of what leads to movements in the union-nonunion wage gap and how long shocks may last might be of concern to workers, firm owners and managers, as well as policy makers.

Macroeconomic Factors and the Union-Nonunion
Wage Differential

An event (i.e., economic news) that affects either the union labor market or the nonunion labor market should influence the union-nonunion wage gap. Interestingly, Heywood and Deich (1987) studied the effect of unions on economic activity. According to their investigation, there is no evidence that unionism deters economic activity. At the aggregate level, the stage of the business cycle—whether the economy is in a growth period or recession— affects demand for labor. Therefore, news about upturns (downturns) in the economy should correspond to a general rise (fall) in labor demand. Hsing (2001) and Neumark and Wachter (1995) discuss the behavior of union wages vis-à-vis nonunion wages during different stages of the business cycle. When the economy is near full employment, an increase in union wages may place upward pressure on nonunion wages due to the threat effect. During a recession, firms have an incentive to lay off high-paid union workers in an effort to lower costs. However, the accompanying increase in the pool of labor may lower nonunion wages. Consequently, changes in real output can be expected to affect the union-nonunion wage gap. Moreover, a number of papers have suggested a relationship between aggregate economic activity and the union-nonunion wage gap. For example, Medoff (1979) and Wachter (1986) suggest a countercyclical wage gap based on theories of wage rigidities in long-term (multiyear) union contracts (Wunnava and Okunade 1996), as well as the prevalence of union seniority rules for assigning layoffs in recessions. Unless the recession threatens the very existence of the union itself, as per the "wage norm" hypothesis of Perry (1986) and Mitchell (1986), unions may not concede to wage reductions. In contrast, Rees (1989) suggests that recessions induced by price shocks may widen the wage gap. Moreover, it is possible that the wage gap is unresponsive to the business cycle, either because firms are able to adjust their employment of labor and productive factors at relatively low cost or because nominal price and wage rigidities do not exist, as might be suggested by real business cycle models. Since union representation and strength varies by industry, the effect of changes in real output on aggregate measures of the wage gap should be examined by the industrial sector (Okunade, Wunnava, and Robinson 1992).

The expected rate of inflation affects the real wage and would, therefore, affect employment decisions. In the presence of nominal wage rigidity, an inflation shock lowers the real wage. If constraints such as contracts and so on make union compensation less flexible than nonunion compensation, then the fall in the real wage of nonunion workers will exceed that of the union workers and the wage gap will widen. Note that the widening may occur with a lag in the presence of contracts and employment wage agreements or when wages are set at the beginning of the period, as in Sargent's (1987) depiction of the Keynesian model. Over time, as contracts are renegotiated and new wage agreements are made, the money wage is expected to adjust upward and the equilibrium real wage is restored. Furthermore, there is another avenue in which inflation shocks may affect the wage gap. Unanticipated inflation, by creating volatility and uncertainty in price changes, may restrict production activity and, thus, firm hiring. Union firms may have less ability to optimally adjust employment levels due to seniority or layoff rules and contract provisions. Consequently, if low wage (short tenure) union workers and nonunion workers are the first to be let go, then the wage gap should widen. Moreover, if it takes some time for the price uncertainty to be resolved, perhaps as economic information is revealed and processed by agents, then the response of the wage gap to the inflation shock may persist for a number of periods. Hendricks and Kahn (1983), in their seminal work on cost of living agreements, also predict that the union-nonunion wage differential widens during the periods of unanticipated inflation.

Thorbecke (1997) and Ewing (2001) argue that money may have real effects and that monetary policy may represent a significant source of business cycles. Tighter monetary policy tends to reduce aggregate demand through an interest rate effect and, in the presence of rigidities, output falls and employment is affected. In general, a rise in the federal funds rate places upward pressure on rates to rise. In the short run, the Federal Reserve's actions may have a more pronounced effect on nonunion wages than on union wages. If nonunion wages fall relatively more than union wages, the differential becomes wider. This might be the case if union firms face restrictions on their ability to optimally adjust employment levels. Thus, it is expected that the wage gap will rise with a sudden monetary tightening, and the response will be more pronounced in those sectors that are sensitive to interest rate movements.

As the previous discussion attests, the union-nonunion wage gap may be linked to macroeconomic factors. This chapter adds to the literature on unions and macroeconomic activity by providing insight into the response of the wage gap to innovations in real output growth, monetary policy, and inflation.

A Simple Reduced-form Model of the Union-Nonunion Wage Differential

In this section, we briefly outline a reduced-form model of the union-nonunion wage differential derived from general specifications of supply and demand in the market for union and nonunion workers. We specify supply and demand in the nonunion worker market as follows:

$$N^S = N^S(X^{NS}, w_N) + v^{NS}$$
$$N^D = N^D(X^{ND}, w_N, (w_U - w_N)) + v^{ND}$$

where X^{NS} and X^{ND} are vectors of exogenous variables that affect the supply and demand for nonunion workers, respectively, w_N is the nonunion (log) real wage and w_U is the union (log) real wage. v^{NS} and v^{ND} are shocks to supply and demand for nonunion workers that are assumed to have zero mean and are uncorrelated.

Similarly, the supply and demand for union workers may be represented as:

$$U^S = U^S(X^{US}, w_U) + v^{US}$$
$$U^D = U^D(X^{UD}, w_U, (w_U - w_N)) + v^{UD}$$

where X^{US} and X^{UD} are vectors of exogenous variables that affect the supply and demand for union workers. v^{US} and v^{UD} are shocks to supply and demand that are assumed to have zero mean and are uncorrelated.

The underlying structural equations can be solved to obtain the reduced-form equation for the union-nonunion wage differential:

$$GAP = (w_U - w_N) = F(X^{NS}, X^{ND}, X^{US}, X^{UD}) + E$$

The size of the wage gap will respond to changes in the exogenous variables that affect supply and demand in the markets for union and nonunion workers. Based on the reasons given earlier, we treat real output growth, inflation, and the stance of monetary policy as these variables.

The Data

Shocks to real output, monetary policy, and inflation are examined over the period 1976Q3 through 2001Q1 to see how union-nonunion wage differentials respond to innovations in these macroeconomic variables.[3] Following the work of Bernanke and Blinder (1992), Thorbecke (1997), and Ewing (2001), we use changes in the federal funds rate as a proxy for the stance of monetary policy. The consumer price index for all urban consumers is used to compute the inflation rate (Park and Ratti 2000). Real economic activity is gauged by the growth rate in real gross domestic product. We use the Employment Cost Index (ECI) series for wages and salaries of (private industry) union workers and nonunion workers to construct the union-nonunion wage gaps. Wage gaps are computed for total private industry, goods-producing industries, manufacturing industries, nonmanufacturing industries, and service-producing industries. Each ECI index is seasonally adjusted. The five wage gaps are defined as the log difference between wages and salaries of union workers and nonunion workers. Thus, the quarterly data consist of changes in the federal funds rate, growth in real gross domestic product, consumer price inflation, and five union-nonunion wage differentials. All data were extracted from the Economagic database. Table 6.1 provides more detailed information on data and variable definitions.

Table 6.2 presents descriptive statistics for the variables. Somewhat surprisingly, the largest mean wage gap is found in service-producing industries, while the smallest is in manufacturing. Table 6.3 (see p. 154) shows the associated estimated (contemporaneous) correlation matrices. Generally speaking, union-nonunion wage gaps are negatively correlated with changes in real output and positively correlated with inflation. Monetary policy changes are negatively correlated with the wage gaps in nonmanufacturing and service-producing industries as well as with (total) private industry. In contrast, monetary policy is positively correlated with the wage gaps in manufacturing and goods-producing industries.

Tests of Stationarity

The proper specification of a vector autoregression (VAR) model depends on the univariate properties of the variables under investigation. In particular, it is important to ascertain the data-generating process of each series. The purpose of this section is to make a distinction between a trend-stationary process and a unit-root process. In the former case, the (perhaps detrended) level of a series would be appropriate to use in the VAR, while if the series has a unit root, it is necessary to first-difference the series to render a station-

Table 6.1

Variable Definitions

GAPGP   Log difference between (seasonally adjusted) wages and salaries of
             union workers and nonunion workers in goods producing industries

GAPMF   Log difference between (seasonally adjusted) wages and salaries of
             union workers and nonunion workers in manufacturing industries

GAPNMF   Log difference between (seasonally adjusted) wages and salaries of
             union workers and nonunion workers in nonmanufacturing industries

GAPPI   Log difference between (seasonally adjusted) wages and salaries of
             union workers and nonunion workers in (total) private industry

GAPSP   Log difference between (seasonally adjusted) wages and salaries of
             union workers and nonunion workers in service-producing industries

GROWTH   Growth rate in (seasonally adjusted) Gross Domestic Product,
             billions of chained 1996 dollars, computed as $(x_t - x_{t-1})/(x_{t-1})$

MPOLICY   Change in the federal funds rate

INF   Growth rate in consumer price index, all urban consumers, com-
             puted as $(x_t - x_{t-1})/(x_{t-1})$

Note: Wages and salaries data are from Employment Cost Index and are for private
industry.

Table 6.2

Descriptive Statistics (adjusted sample period is 1976Q3–2001Q1)

	Mean (×100)	Standard deviation (×100)
GAPGP	0.3622	3.2565
GAPMF	0.3364	3.3515
GAPNMF	2.0964	4.4952
GAPPI	1.5258	4.0977
GAPSP	2.1445	4.1026
GROWTH	0.7889	0.8134
INF	1.1511	0.7921
MPOLICY	−0.9663	110.7479

Note: Number of observations: 99.

Table 6.3

Estimated Correlation Matrices

Panel A: Private industry

	ΔGAPPI	GROWTH	MPOLICY	INF
DGAPPI	1.0000	—	—	—
GROWTH	−0.2855	1.0000	—	—
MPOLICY	−0.0636	0.2188	1.0000	—
INF	0.2657	−0.0794	0.2565	1.0000

Panel B: Goods-producing industry

	ΔGAPGP	GROWTH	MPOLICY	INF
ΔGAPGP	1.0000	—	—	—
GROWTH	−0.1720	1.0000	—	—
MPOLICY	0.0480	0.2188	1.0000	—
INF	0.2173	−0.0794	0.2565	1.0000

Panel C: Manufacturing industry

	ΔGAPMFI	GROWTH	MPOLICY	INF
ΔGAPMF	1.0000	—	—	—
GROWTH	−0.1035	1.0000	—	—
MPOLICY	0.0670	0.2177	1.0000	—
INF	0.2975	−0.0780	0.2583	1.0000

Panel D: Nonmanufacturing industry

	ΔGAPNMF	GROWTH	MPOLICY	INF
ΔGAPNMF	1.0000	—	—	—
GROWTH	−0.2139	1.0000	—	—
MPOLICY	−0.1524	0.2177	1.0000	—
INF	0.1524	−0.0780	0.2583	1.0000

Panel E: Service-producing industry

	ΔGAPSP	GROWTH	MPOLICY	INF
ΔGAPSP	1.0000	—	—	—
GROWTH	−0.2083	1.0000	—	—
MPOLICY	−0.0703	0.2188	1.0000	—
INF	0.2114	−0.0794	0.2565	1.0000

ary process. Furthermore, if two or more series are each integrated of order one (e.g., contain unit roots), it is possible that a linear combination of them is stationary. In this case, the appropriate VAR to be estimated would be of the class of error correction models.

In order to determine whether or not a series is stationary, we perform unit root tests based on the method of Dickey and Fuller (1981). The augmented

Table 6.4

Tests of Stationarity

Variable	ADF	Phillips-Perron
ΔGAPGP	-7.13[a]	-9.25[a]
ΔGAPMF	-6.27[a]	-9.31[a]
ΔGAPNMF	-5.32[a]	-8.62[a]
ΔGAPPI	-5.58[a]	-8.00[a]
ΔGAPSP	-4.95[a]	-9.75[a]
GROWTH	-5.52[a]	-7.41[a]
MPOLICY	-2.36	-2.63[b]
INF	-7.79[a]	-8.56[a]

Notes: Superscripts a, b denote significance at the 1 percent and 10 percent levels based on critical values in MacKinnon (1991). Δ denotes the first-difference operator. One lag was used on the augmenting term, as suggested by Akaike's information criterion, and was sufficient to ensure the absence of autocorrelation in the residuals.

Dickey-Fuller (ADF) test is used to check for the presence of unit roots and is based on the ordinary least squares regression of equation 1.

$$\Delta X_t^j = \rho_0 + (\rho_1 - 1) X_{t-1}^j + \rho_2 t + \sum_{k=1}^{m} \alpha_k \Delta X_{t-k}^j + e_t \qquad (1)$$

where X^j is the individual series under investigation, Δ is the first-difference operator, t is a linear time trend, e_t is a covariance stationary random error, and m is determined by Akaike's information criterion to ensure serially uncorrelated residuals. The null hypothesis is that the variable is a non-stationary time series and is rejected if $(\rho_1 - 1) < 0$ and statistically significant. The finite sample critical values for the ADF test developed by MacKinnon (1991) are used to determine statistical significance.

An alternative unit root test developed by Phillips and Perron (1988) allows for weak dependence and heterogeneity in the error term and is robust to a wide range of serial correlation and time-dependent heteroskedasticity. The test is based on the following regression:

$$X_t^j = \eta_0 + \eta_1(t - T/2) + \lambda X_{t-1}^j + v_t \qquad (2)$$

where $(t - T/2)$ is the time trend with T representing the sample size and v_t is the error term. The null hypothesis of a unit root, $H_0: \lambda = 1$, is tested against the alternative hypothesis that X_t^j is stationary around a deterministic trend $(H_a: \lambda < 1)$. As in the ADF test, MacKinnon critical values may be used to determine statistical significance for the Phillips-Perron test.

The results of the unit root tests are presented in Table 6.4. The first-difference of each wage gap measure is stationary and, thus, a shock to a change in the union-nonunion wage gap will revert to the mean. Consistent with previous research, such as Ewing (2001) and Park and Ratti (2000), GROWTH, MPOLICY, and INF[4] are all found to be stationary series.[5]

Vector Autoregression and Generalized Impulse Response Analysis

Dynamic analysis of VAR models can be conducted using innovation accounting methods, such as impulse response functions. However, this method has been criticized because results from impulse response analysis are subject to the "orthogonality assumption" and may differ markedly depending on the ordering of the variables in the VAR (Lutkenpohl 1991). To overcome this problem, we employ the "generalized" impulse response function developed by Pesaran and Shin (1998) and Koop, Pesaran, and Potter (1996). This method is not sensitive to the ordering of the variables in the VAR. Ewing, Levernier, and Malik (2002) provide additional explanation on the use of this method.

Pesaran and Shin (1998) describe the generalized impulse response analysis in the following way.[6] Consider the infinite moving average representation of the VAR:

$$x_t = \Sigma_{j=0}^{\infty} A_j u_{t-j} \tag{3}$$

where x_t is an $m{\times}1$ vector of the variables under investigation, $A_j = \Phi_1 A_{j-1} + \Phi_2 A_{j-2} + \ldots + \Phi_p A_{j-p}$, $j = 1, 2, \ldots$, with $A_0 = I_m$ and $A_j = 0$ for $j < 0$.[7]

Let us denote the generalized impulse response function (G) for a shock to the entire system, u^0_t, as:

$$G_s = E(x_{t+N} \mid u_t = u^0_t, \Omega^0_{t-1}) - E(s_{t+N} \mid \Omega^0_{t-1}) \tag{4}$$

where the history of the process up to period $t-1$ is known and denoted by the information set Ω^0_{t-1}. Assume $u_t \sim N(0, \Sigma)$, and $E(u_t \mid u_{jt} = \delta_j) = (\sigma_{1j}, \sigma_{2j}, \ldots, \sigma_{mj})' \sigma^{-1}_{jj} \delta_j$, where $\delta_j = (\sigma_{jj})^{-1/2}$ denotes a one standard error shock. Furthermore, e_i is $m{\times}1$, with the ith element equal to one and all other elements equal to zero. The generalized impulse response function for a one standard deviation shock to the ith equation in the VAR model on the jth variable at horizon N is:

$$G_{ij,N} = (e'_j A_N \Sigma e_i) / (\sigma_{ii})^{1/2}, \; i, j = 1, 2, \ldots, m \tag{5}$$

A key feature of the generalized impulse response function is that the generalized responses are invariant to any reordering of the variables in the VAR.[8] Thus, the generalized impulse response function provides more robust results than the orthogonalized method. Another key feature is that, because orthogonality is not imposed, the generalized impulse response function allows for meaningful interpretation of the initial impact response of each variable to shocks to any of the other variables.

Discussion of Results

A total of five VARs were estimated, one for each wage gap measure. Each VAR contained the four equations corresponding to MPOLICY, INF, GROWTH, and the particular ΔGAP. A constant term was included in each equation. The order of each VAR was determined to be one based on Akaike's information criterion, Schwartz Bayesian criterion, and likelihood ratio tests. If the shocks to the respective equations in a VAR are contemporaneously correlated, then orthogonalized and generalized impulse responses may be quite different. Reordering the variables may lead to a number of vastly different conclusions based on orthogonalized responses. Thus, before proceeding to an examination of the dynamic responses of the union-nonunion wage gaps to macroeconomic shocks, we performed tests to determine if innovations in the four individual equations in each of the VARs were contemporaneously correlated. The null hypothesis is that the off-diagonal elements in the covariance matrix equal zero and is tested against the alternative that none of the off-diagonal elements is equal to zero. Log-likelihood ratio test statistics are computed as $LR = 2(LL_u - LL_r)$, where LL_u and LL_r are the maximized values for the log-likelihood functions for the unrestricted and restricted models, respectively.[9] The LR statistic is distributed χ^2 with four degrees of freedom and was significant at less than the 5 percent level for each case examined. Thus, it is appropriate to examine generalized impulse response functions.

Figures 6.1 through 6.5 (see pp. 158–162) present the generalized impulse response functions and are plotted out to the tenth quarter. Figure 6.1 shows the response of the change in the (total) private industry union-nonunion wage gap to one standard deviation (SD) shocks to ΔGAPPI, GROWTH, MPOLICY, and INF. As can be seen in Figure 6.1, an unexpected positive change in the private industry wage gap fully dissipates after one quarter.[10] Neither a sudden monetary tightening, as evidenced by an unanticipated rise in the Federal Reserve funds rate, nor a shock to real output growth have a significant effect on ΔGAPPI. In fact, the only significant response occurs from a shock to INF, and that occurs with a lag. The response becomes positive and significant after one quarter and lasts for about five to six quarters before dying out.

Figure 6.1 **Private Industry**

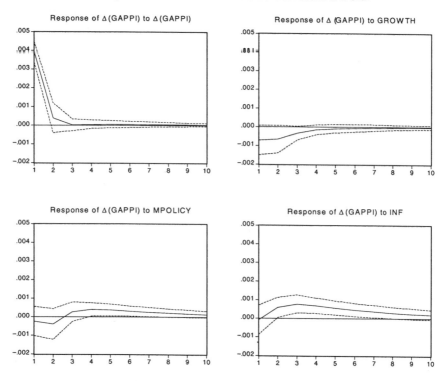

Response to Generalized One S.D. Innovations ± 2 S.E.

Notes: Horizon is measured in quarters. Δ denotes first-difference operator.

The responses of ΔGAPGP to macroeconomic shocks are shown in Figure 6.2. Similar to the case of private industry, a real output growth shock does not significantly affect the change in the goods-producing wage gap. However, the response of ΔGAPGP to a monetary policy shock is actually negative and significant one quarter after the shock then, as expected, becomes positive and significant for two quarters. This suggests that the Federal Reserve's actions can affect the union-nonunion wage gap in the goods-producing sector. Moreover, the unexpected monetary tightening leads to an observed "cycling" of the wage gap. This type of response to monetary shocks of economic aggregates is found in many macroeconomic models that incorporate expectations that rely on a standard IS-LM framework with predetermined prices. A significant impulse response to MPOLICY sug-

Figure 6.2 **Goods-Producing Industries**

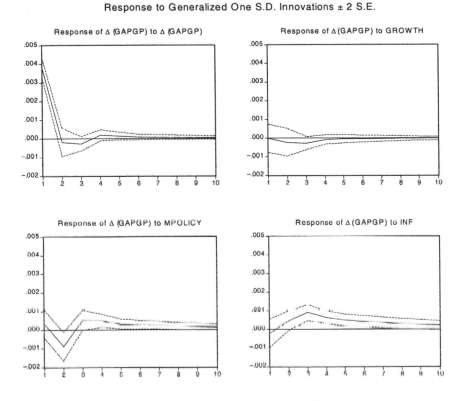

Response to Generalized One S.D. Innovations ± 2 S.E.

Notes: Horizon is measured in quarters. Δ denotes first-difference operator.

gests that firms in the goods-producing sector are sensitive to interest rate
changes. In particular, the labor market responses of firms in this sector may
result from a reliance on such things as inventory financing. A rise in borrowing costs and thus the user cost of capital, as would be the case with a
monetary tightening, may alter the optimal labor-capital mix. If firms in this
sector respond by increasing union worker hours and employment relative
to that of nonunion workers, then the wage gap should rise. The initial impact of an inflation shock on the goods-producing industry wage gap is insignificant, but is positive and significant at one quarter following the shock.
The effect of an inflation shock occurs with a short lag and lasts for five to
six quarters. As in the case of private industry, the own impulse response
lasts for one quarter.

Figure 6.3 **Manufacturing Industries**

Response to Generalized One S.D. Innovations ± 2 S.E.

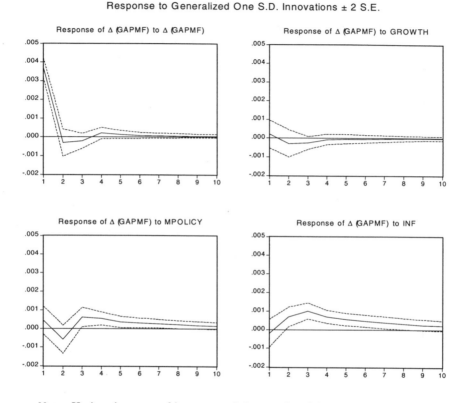

Notes: Horizon is measured in quarters. Δ denotes first-difference operator.

Figure 6.3 presents the responses of change in the manufacturing sector wage gap to the macroeconomic shocks. The responses are quite similar to those found in the goods-producing sector with few exceptions. A shock to GROWTH has no effect, while a shock to MPOLICY has a positive effect following a two-quarter lag. The MPOLICY effect then lasts for about four to five quarters (i.e., up to about seven quarters following initial impact). As in the case of the goods-producing wage gap, we attribute the response of the manufacturing sector wage gap to an unanticipated monetary tightening to these firms' interest rate sensitivity. Like the goods-producing sector, the response of ΔGAPGP to an inflation shock is positive and significant following a one-quarter lag. The response is a bit stronger than that found in the goods-producing sector but persists for

Figure 6.4 **Nonmanufacturing Industries**

Response to Generalized One S.D. Innovations ± 2 S.E.

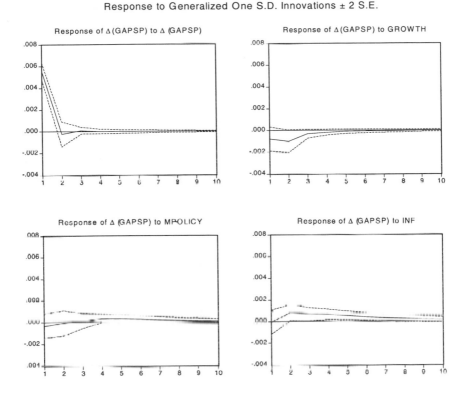

Notes: Horizon is measured in quarters. Δ denotes first-difference operator.

about the same length of time. Similar to the other wage gaps, the own impulse response lasts for one quarter.

Figure 6.4 shows how ΔGAPNMF responds to macroeconomic shocks. In contrast to the other sectors, the nonmanufacturing wage gap falls with a real output shock. In particular, the response is negative and significant one quarter after the shock and remains significant for about one quarter. This finding is consistent with the countercyclical wage gap theories. No significant response is found for MPOLICY, suggesting that the labor market actions of firms in this sector are relatively insensitive to interest rate changes. The wage gap responds positively and significantly to an inflation shock, after a two-quarter lag. The inflation effect, while smallest in magnitude compared to the other sectors, persists for around four

Figure 6.5 **Service-Producing Industries**

Response to Generalized One S.D. Innovations ± 2 S.E.

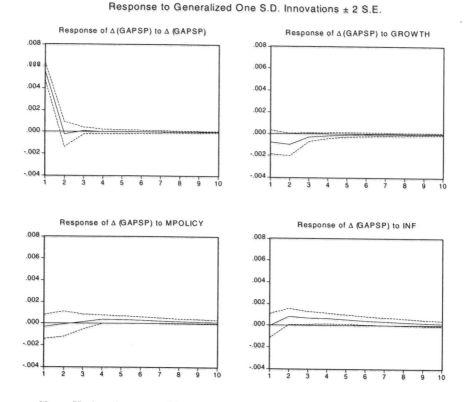

Notes: Horizon is measured in quarters. Δ denotes first-difference operator.

quarters. As with the other wage gaps, the own impulse response lasts for one quarter.

The response to macroeconomic shock of changes in the service-producing union-nonunion wage gap is presented in Figure 6.5. Shocks to GROWTH and to MPOLICY are insignificant, while an inflation shock is significant and positive following a two-quarter lag. The inflation effect persists for only about three quarters and is the shortest in duration of all the sectors. The relatively faster dissipation of inflation shocks suggests that the firms in the service-producing sector exist in a competitive market environment, in which price changes are absorbed into wages more quickly. Consistent with the other wage gaps, the own impulse response for this sector lasts for just one quarter.

Conclusion

This chapter examined and documented the response of union-nonunion wage differentials to shocks in three key macroeconomic variables using the newly developed technique of generalized impulse response analysis. The technique is robust in terms of the choice of ordering variables in the VAR, thus one can accurately examine and compare both the severity and extent of shocks to these variables on the wage gaps. The results add to the literature on the relationship between the macroeconomy and the union-nonunion wage gaps.

The results can be summarized as follows. For each sector as well as the total private industry, an inflation shock leads to a widening of the wage gap and occurs after a short lag and may last for several quarters. Generally speaking, a monetary policy shock is associated with a wider gap, which appears only after a couple of quarters, in each sector (and overall) except in nonmanufacturing and service-producing industries. Finally, growth shocks are found to be significant and negative only in the nonmanufacturing sector.

Notes

1. This simple analysis assumes diminishing marginal product of labor and no adjustment costs.

2. This chapter employs the recently developed econometric technique of generalized impulse response analysis (Koop, Pesaran, and Potter 1996; Pesaran and Shin 1998).

3. The raw data series start before this date, but due to data transformations (e.g., growth rates), the usable or adjusted sample period begins in 1976Q3.

4. The results for INF are not as clear as those for the other variables. However, given the findings of Engle (1982), the Phillips-Perron test is probably more appropriate than the ADF for the case of inflation.

5. It was determined that the variables were not cointegrated. The results of Johansen-Juselius cointegration tests, which allowed for deterministic trends in the (levels of the variables), are available on request.

6. For a more detailed discussion, including proofs, see Pesaran and Shin (1998). Additional background material on the development of generalized impulse response analysis can be found in Koop, Pesaran, and Potter (1996).

7. The traditional orthogonalized impulse response employs a Cholesky decomposition of the positive definite $m \times m$ covariance matrix, Σ, of the shocks (u_t).

8. Pesaran and Shin state that "generalized impulse responses are unique and fully take account of the historical patterns of correlations observed amongst the different shocks" (1998, 20). Thus, they caution against using orthogonalized responses, since there is generally no clear guidance as to which of many possible parameterizations to employ. Note that generalized and orthogonalized impulse responses coincide only when the covariance matrix is diagonal.

9. LL_u is the system log-likelihood from the VAR and LL_r is computed as the sum of the log-likelihood values from the individual equations in the VAR.

10. Significance is determined by the use of confidence intervals representing plus/minus two standard deviations. See Runkle (1987) for a discussion on confidence intervals.

References

Bernanke, B., and A. Blinder. 1992. "The Federal Funds Rate and the Channels of Monetary Policy." *American Economic Review* 82: 901–921.

Dickey, D.A., and W.A. Fuller. 1981. "Likelihood Ratio Statistics for Autoregressive Time Series with a Unit Root." *Econometrica* 49: 1057–1071.

Engle, Robert. 1982. "Autoregressive Conditional Heteroskedasticity with Estimation of the Variance of United Kingdom Inflation." *Econometrica* 50, no. 4: 987–1007.

Ewing, B.T. 2001. "Cross-effects of Fundamental State Variables." *Journal of Macroeconomics* 23: 633–645.

Ewing, B.T., W. Levernier, and F. Malik. 2002. "Differential Effects of Output Shocks on Unemployment Rates by Race and Gender." *Southern Economic Journal* 68: 584–599.

Freeman, R.B., and J. L. Medoff. 1984. *What Do Unions Do?* New York: Basic Books.

Hendricks, W.E., and L.M. Kahn. 1983. "Cost of Living Clauses in Union Contracts: Determinants and Effects." *Industrial and Labor Relations Review* 36: 447–460.

Heywood, J.S., and M.D. Deich. 1987. "Do Unions Discourage Economic Activity?" *Economics Letters* 25: 373–377.

Hirsch, B.T., and J.T. Addison. 1986. *The Economic Analysis of Unions.* Boston: Allen and Unwin.

Hsing, Y. 2001. "A Macroeconomic Analysis of the Impact of Union Wage Increases on Nonunion Wages." *Applied Economics Letters* 8: 803–806.

Koop, G., M.H. Pesaran, and S.M. Potter. 1996. "Impulse Response Analysis in Nonlinear Multivariate Models." *Journal of Econometrics* 74: 119–147.

Lewis, H.G. 1986. *Union Relative Wage Effects.* Chicago: University of Chicago Press.

Lutkenpohl, H. 1991. *Introduction to Multiple Time Series Analysis.* Berlin: Springer-Verlag.

MacKinnon, J. 1991. "Critical Values for Cointegration Tests in Long Run Econometric Relationships." In *Readings in Cointegration,* ed. R. Engle and C. Granger, 267–276. New York: Oxford University Press.

Medoff, J. 1979. "Layoffs and Alternatives Under Trade Unions in United States Manufacturing." *American Economic Review* 69: 380–395.

Mitchell, D.J.B. 1986. "Union vs. Nonunion Wage Norm Shifts." *American Economic Review Papers and Proceedings* 76: 249–252.

Neumark, D., and M.L. Wachter. 1995. "Union Effects on Non-union Wages: Evidence from Panel Data on Industries and Cities." *Industrial and Labor Relations Review* 49: 20–38.

Okunade, A., P.V. Wunnava, and M. Robinson. 1992. "Union-Nonunion Compensation Differentials and Industry Structure." *Economics Letters* 39: 329–337.

Park, K., and R.A. Ratti. 2000. "Real Activity, Inflation, Stock Returns, and Monetary Policy." *Financial Review* 35: 59–78.

Perry, G. 1986. "Shifting Wage Norms and their Implications." *American Economic Review Papers and Proceedings* 76: 245–248.

Pesaran, M.H., and Y. Shin. 1998. "Generalized Impulse Response Analysis in Linear Multivariate Models." *Economics Letters* 58: 17–29.

Phillips, P., and P. Perron. 1988. "Testing for a Unit Root in Time Series Regression." *Biometrika* 75: 335–346.

Rees, A. 1989. *The Economics of Trade Unions,* 3rd ed. Chicago: University of Chicago Press.

Romer, D. 1996. *Advanced Macroeconomics.* New York: McGraw-Hill.

Runkle, D.E. 1987. "Vector Autoregressions and Reality." *Journal of Business and Economic Statistics* 5: 437–442.

Sargent, T.J. 1987. *Macroeconomic Theory,* 2nd ed. Orlando, FL: Harcourt Brace Jovanovich, Academic Press.

Thorbecke, W. 1997. "On Stock Market Returns and Monetary Policy." *Journal of Finance* 52: 638–654.

Wachter, M. 1986. "Union Age Rigidity: The Default Setting of Labor Law." *American Economic Review* 76: 240–244.

Wunnava, P.V., and B.T. Ewing. 1999. "Union-Nonunion Benefit Differentials and Establishment Size: Evidence from the NLSY." *Journal of Labor Research.* 20: 177–183.

———. 2000. "Union-Nonunion Gender Wage and Benefit Differentials Across Establishment Sizes." *Small Business Economics* 15: 47–57.

Wunnava, P.V., and J. Honney. 1991. "The Union-Nonunion Wage Differential over the Business Cycle: Evidence from PSID." *Economics Letters* 37: 97–103.

Wunnava, P.V., and A. Okunade. 1996. "Countercyclical Union Wage Premium? Evidence for the 1980s." *Journal of Labor Research* 17: 289–296.

IV

Union Wage and Employment Effects

International Evidence

7

Collective Bargaining, Relative Wages, and Employment

International Microeconomic Evidence

Francine D. Blau and Lawrence M. Kahn

In this chapter, we examine research that studies the impact of labor market institutions, including collective bargaining, on the wage distribution and on the employment of particular labor force groups in relation to others. Much of this work is comparative in nature, and we believe that by looking at other countries' outcomes, we can better understand the U.S. labor market.

In particular, over the last thirty years, the United States went from being a relatively high unemployment country to one with relatively low levels of joblessness in the 1990s. In 1973, the unemployment rate standardized to a common Organization for Economic Cooperation and Development (OECD) definition was 4.8 percent in the United States but 3.2 percent or below in Australia, Austria, Belgium, France, West Germany, Japan, the Netherlands, Norway, Spain, Sweden, and the United Kingdom (UK). The unweighted average unemployment rate among these countries was 2.1 percent, an astonishingly low figure by today's standards.[1] Since the early 1970s, after two oil crises, vastly increased globalization, and rapid technical change, the unemployment position of the United States and the other Western countries has dramatically reversed. By 1999, the U.S. unemployment rate had fallen to 4.2 percent, and was as low as 3.9 percent as of October 2000 (see the U.S. Bureau of Labor Statistics Web site, www.bls.gov/). In contrast, unemployment had risen sharply in virtually every other Western country, and, by 1999, averaged 8.7 percent in the European Union and had been at comparable levels for nearly twenty years (Organization for Economic Cooperation and Development [OECD] 2000). While generous systems of social insurance in Europe cushion the income loss of the unemployed, surveys of Europeans show that, controlling for individual fixed effects, unemployment greatly lowers an individual's happiness (Winkelmann and Winkelmann 1998). This survey evidence suggests that the jobless in Europe view unemployment as a serious problem.

However, there is another side to this comparison. While the United States has fared well in recent years in creating jobs and maintaining low unemployment, its wage levels have deteriorated relative to those overseas, and wage inequality, always higher in the United States than in other advanced countries, has risen more sharply than it has elsewhere.

Institutional differences between the United States and other OECD countries provide a potential explanation for these outcomes. Compared to other countries, the United States has low levels of collective bargaining coverage and union density (the fraction of wage and salary workers who were union members), less centralized and less coordinated wage setting, less generous unemployment insurance (UI), greater employer freedom to hire and fire, lower mandated benefits, and lower labor taxes (Nickell and Layard 1999). As an illustration, in 1994 union density and collective bargaining coverage averaged 41 percent and 71 percent of wage and salary workers, respectively, among nineteen non-U.S. OECD countries, compared to much smaller figures of 16 percent and 18 percent, respectively, in the United States (OECD 1997).[2]

Some argue that these institutional differences have meant that, in the face of oil shocks of the 1970s and 1980s, the productivity growth slowdown that began in the 1970s, globalization and technical change that continue today, and contractionary monetary policies in the 1980s and 1990s, flexible U.S. labor market institutions allowed real and relative wages to adjust. U.S. unemployment was therefore allowed to stay low and even decline in the late 1990s. In contrast, according to this view, which has been termed the "unified theory" (Blank 1997), the institutions in many European countries kept real and relative wages rigid, contributing to their rising relative unemployment levels over the 1980s and 1990s.[3] This theory also implies that the less skilled should have had the greatest deterioration in their employment over this period in the countries whose institutions did not allow relative wages to change in response to changing supply and demand.[4] Moreover, the theory in principle works in reverse: the low European unemployment of the 1960s and early 1970s may have been facilitated by rigid wage-setting institutions that kept real wages from rising in the face of unexpected productivity gains and monetary expansion (Blanchard and Wolfers 2000; Bertola, Blau, and Kahn 2002a). Our book *At Home and*

Abroad (Blau and Kahn 2002) summarizes existing macroeconometric evidence on the unified theory and presents some of our own as well. By and large, this work supports the theory.

While econometric evidence linking differences in labor market outcomes and institutions is consistent with the unified theory, more information is needed in order to test whether the theory helps explain why the United States has had different outcomes from other countries. For example, it is possible that Americans at the bottom of the distribution of skills are less skilled relative to the middle than is the case in other countries. This difference could conceivably explain higher levels of wage inequality in the United States. Furthermore, perhaps the skills of those at the bottom have deteriorated since the 1970s in the United States relative to those in other countries, providing an alternative explanation for the rising wage inequality in the United States relative to other countries since the 1970s. Alternatively, it is possible that the young in the United States, whose relative employment to population rates have fallen much less than those in Europe, improved their relative labor market qualifications compared to those of their counterparts in Europe. In this case, the composition of the labor force could be the explanation for rising youth unemployment in Europe relative to that in the United States during this period.

Such considerations motivate our examination of microeconomic evidence on the impact of labor market institutions on relative pay and on employment of particular groups.[5] Microdata enable us to account for the types of alternative explanations discussed earlier, through controls for individual productivity characteristics. In this chapter, we focus on the impact of unions and collective bargaining. It should be noted that, as our previous discussion suggests, a larger role for unions tends to be associated with more generous social programs and more extensive regulation of the labor market. In *At Home and Abroad* (Blau and Kahn 2002), we examine the impact of a number of other labor market institutions as well.

This chapter begins with an examination of the determinants of relative wages with a focus on the United States in comparison to other OECD countries. The unified theory suggested that real and relative wages were more flexible in the United States with respect to market forces than in other countries. We therefore investigate whether the rewards to human capital and the returns to being in favored sectors of the economy are indeed higher in the United States than elsewhere. We term these rewards "labor market prices." And we do in fact find that these rewards are substantially higher in the United States, even after accounting for the characteristics of the labor force.

Higher rewards in the United States are consistent with our more laissez-faire labor market institutions in the face of widespread economic forces, such as technology or international trade, which would increase the rewards to skill in the absence of market intervention. However, it is also possible that differences in the supply and demand conditions for skilled labor between the United States and other OECD countries could cause the observed price differences. For example, perhaps the less skilled are more abundant in the United States, a factor that would raise the price of skill. If this is true, then it is even possible that institutions do not have a major effect on relative wages, calling into question some of the logic of the unified theory. We therefore next examine direct evidence on the impact of labor market institutions on wage inequality and on employment as well. In the interests of conserving space, we focus on wage and employment inequality generally (i.e., among men or among women), although our previous work (Blau and Kahn 1996b, 2000c, 2002, and 2003) shows that general wage compression in highly unionized countries has had a significant effect in lowering the gender pay gap in these other countries in comparison to the United States.[6]

Evidence on the impact of institutions on employment is of course extremely important in and of itself. Furthermore, a finding of employment effects of collective bargaining provides indirect evidence on their wage impact as well: under a monopoly union model, we expect groups whose wages are raised the most by unions to have the most problems finding work. We examine results from both detailed comparisons of two or three countries as well as from several cases of countries in which these institutions were radically and abruptly changed. These latter studies are particularly convincing because, by definition, one is able to control for national norms and culture. We find that while institutions almost invariably affect the wage distribution, there is mixed evidence on their employment effects. In some cases, evidence of negative employment consequences of administered wages is obtained, while in others there is little evidence of such effects.

Taken together, this evidence from country studies and comparisons suggests a strong impact of collective bargaining institutions on wage inequality, and mixed evidence of their impact on relative employment of particular groups. This conclusion is bolstered by a review of results from statistical analyses of cross-sectional data from a large number of countries that examine the effects of institutions on wage inequality and relative employment of different skill groups while controlling for market forces (i.e., supply and demand). We conclude that there is strong evidence that collective bargaining has an influence through its effect on labor market prices and that, overall, collective bargaining is negatively associated with the relative employment of lower skill men (where skill embodies both experience and schooling), with weaker effects for women, other things being equal. Further examination indicates that the negative employment effects of collective bargaining are concentrated on the young; in contrast, collective bargaining is not found to have a statistically significant effect on the relative employment of the less educated.

Does the United States Have Higher Labor Market Prices Than Other Countries?

In order to know whether wage setting and other labor market institutions have affected the U.S. distribution of pay compared to that in other countries, we need to know how the labor market rewards stack up here versus elsewhere. Even if it is true that rewards are higher in the United States, as much evidence abundantly shows, this outcome could have been caused by supply and demand or by unions and other institutional interventions, or combination of both. A first step toward evaluating the importance of these factors is to determine whether the U.S. labor market does indeed yield higher returns to education or experience as well as to employment in favored sectors in the economy. We can then investigate the effect of unions and market forces on these returns.

Evidence on Labor Market Prices Controlling for Individual Characteristics

In assessing the role of labor market prices in affecting wage inequality in different countries, we can decompose international differences in wage inequality into three components. First, there is a portion due to differences in the distribution of productivity characteristics. A country might have a more dispersed distribution of pay because the qualifications of its working population are more diverse. In one country, for example, the age of the workforce may be largely concentrated between thirty and fifty years old, while in another, workers' ages may range more widely. Because wages rise with experience in every country, this difference in the age distribution would produce a difference in wage inequality.

Second, wage inequality may be affected by measured labor market prices. For example, in one country, the rate of return to an additional year of schooling may be 9 percent, while in another it may only be 4 percent. Or, working in a high-paying industry like transportation may provide workers with a 15 percent pay premium in one country but only a 3 percent premium in another country. Both of these cases are examples of labor market prices. And, adjusting for the distribution of workers by education level and industrial employment, these price differences will produce differing levels of wage inequality. Labor market prices are crucial to the workings of the economy because they provide workers with incentives to acquire skills and firms with incentives to hire various types of workers. For example, we might expect incentives to attend college to be low if there is a small wage return to attending college and jobs are plentiful for people without a college education. At the same time, if the relative price of highly skilled workers falls, then we expect employers to demand relatively more of them. As we will show later on, both of these outcomes appeared to characterize Sweden in the 1970s and early 1980s (Edin and Holmlund 1995; Edin and Topel 1997).

Third, there may be unexplained differences in wage inequality across countries. For example, we may not be able to adequately measure workers' ability and motivation or know the size of firm a worker is employed in. And we would expect more able workers and those working in large firms to earn more than others, all else being equal (Neal and Johnson 1996; Brown and Medoff 1989). Differences in both the distribution of these unmeasured factors and in the labor market prices associated with them will contribute to international differences in wage inequality. One country may have a more concentrated distribution of firm sizes or individual worker motivation than another. And one country may have especially large interfirm wage differentials or a high-wage return to motivation. Thus, in some sense this unexplained component combines the quantity and price aspects of the first two, however, for factors that are not explicitly measured.[7]

In measuring the contributions of these three factors to the higher U.S. levels of wage inequality, we make use of a statistical decomposition technique devised by Chinhui Juhn, Kevin M. Murphy, and Brooks Pierce (1993) in their study of rising American wage inequality from the 1960s through the 1980s. Table 7.1 (see p. 176–177) shows the results of this decomposition from a study we conducted (Blau and Kahn 1996a), which addressed the question of whether the United States had higher labor market prices among men in the 1980s than was the case in a sample of nine other countries. The study is based on several nationally representative microdata sources. Earnings, work hours, age, marital status, schooling, industry, occupation, and union membership are measured in comparable ways, and we can thus parcel out the effects of population heterogeneity and labor market prices in affecting the wage structure across countries.[8] We separately examined wage compression at the bottom (50–10) and at the top (90–50) of the distribution because of the importance of wage floors in highly unionized countries. Moreover, we measure labor market prices on the basis of two specifications for wage determination. First, we estimated a "human capital specification" (Table 7.1, panel A), in which we controlled for education, potential experience, and marital status in our underlying wage regressions. Second, we estimated a "full specification" (Table 7.1, panel B), in which we augmented these human capital variables with industry, occupation, and union status indicators. Comparison of the results across the two specifications can highlight the importance of industry, occupation, and union wage effects in explaining the higher American level of wage inequality.

Panel A in Table 7.1 shows that the United States in the 1980s had a far larger male 50–10 wage gap than was true of other countries. The average differential of 0.576 log points corresponds to a ratio of 1.8, meaning that the 50–10 ratio in the United States was 1.8 times the 50–10 ratio elsewhere. In contrast to the large difference in the 50–10 gap, the 90–50 gap was only slightly larger in the United States than elsewhere. The OECD data for the 1980s also show that U.S.-other country differences in the men's 50–10 wage gap were larger than the 90–50 differences. However, since the mid-1980s, wage inequality in the United States has risen especially rapidly at the top of the distribution. By the 1990s, the difference between the U.S. 90–50 gap and those in other countries had increased, although the U.S. other country contrasts for the 50–10 gap continued to be even larger (OECD 1996).

The importance of population heterogeneity in explaining the higher level of U.S. wage inequality is given in the "measured characteristics effect" column. The entries there show the differences in log wage differentials that would exist between the United States and the indicated other country if both countries had the same measured labor market prices and distribution of residual wage inequality, but had their actual distribution of productivity-related characteristics. The "wage coefficients effect," shown in the next column, tells us how inequality would differ between the United States and the indicated other country if both had the same distribution of measured characteristics and wage residuals, but had their own actual wage coefficients. Finally, the "wage equation residual effect" indicates the differences in inequality that would exist between the United States and the indicated country if both had the same distribution of characteristics and the wage coefficients, but each had their actual distribution of wage residuals.[9]

Looking first at the measured characteristics effects, the positive effects for the 50–10 differentials for both specifications indicate that the U.S. distribution of measured characteristics widens the 50–10 gap compared to that in each country. These effects—0.245 log points for the human capital specification and 0.207 log points for the full specification, on average—are large indeed. A comparison of the results for the two specifications indicates that it is the U.S. distribution of human capital characteristics that is relevant in explaining the international differences, with the U.S. distribution of industry, occupation, and union status slightly

Table 7.1

Decomposition of the U.S.-Other Country Differences in the 50–10 and 90–50 Differentials in Male Log Wages, 1980s

	U.S. differential-other country differential	Measured characteristics effect	Wage coefficients effect	Wage equation residual effect
A. Human capital specification				
50–10 Log wage differential				
Germany 85–88	0.584	0.312	−0.019	0.291
Britain 85–89	0.446	0.083	0.089	0.274
Austria 85–87, 89	0.649	0.299	−0.005	0.355
Switzerland 87	0.576	0.254	0.053	0.269
Sweden 80	0.658	0.385	0.034	0.239
Norway 82	0.668	0.331	−0.013	0.350
Australia 86	0.285	0.069	0.068	0.148
Hungary 86–88	0.578	0.158	0.038	0.382
Italy 87	0.562	0.246	0.041	0.275
Norway 89	0.816	0.338	−0.037	0.515
Sweden 84	0.518	0.225	0.018	0.275
Non-U.S. Average (unweighted)	0.576	0.245	0.024	0.307
90–50 Log wage differential				
Germany 85–88	0.013	−0.183	0.095	0.101
Britain 85–89	−0.131	−0.134	−0.043	0.046
Austria 85–87, 89	0.044	−0.199	0.121	0.122
Switzerland 87	−0.225	−0.300	0.046	0.029
Sweden 80	0.100	−0.075	0.078	0.097
Norway 82	0.170	−0.132	0.086	0.216
Australia 86	0.113	−0.067	0.054	0.126
Hungary 86–88	−0.109	−0.190	0.208	−0.127
Italy 87	0.066	−0.151	0.114	0.103
Norway 89	0.027	−0.104	0.065	0.066
Sweden 84	0.158	−0.190	0.152	0.196
Non-U.S. Average (unweighted)	0.021	−0.157	0.089	0.089

lowering the 50–10 gap compared to other countries.[10] On average, measured characteristics are estimated to account for 35.9 to 43.4 percent of the higher U.S. 50–10 differential. In contrast, the distribution of measured characteristics *lowers* the 90–50 wage differential in the United States compared to other countries. The unweighted average effect is about –0.16 log points in both specifications.

The findings for the measured characteristics effects imply that a consid-

Table 7.1 (continued)

	U.S. differential-other country differential	Measured characteristics effect	Wage coefficients effect	Wage equation residual effect
B. Full specification				
50–10 Log wage differential				
Germany 85–88	0.584	0.301	0.067	0.216
Britain 85–89	0.446	0.010	0.192	0.244
Austria 85–87, 89	0.649	0.208	0.144	0.297
Switzerland 87	0.576	0.218	0.170	0.188
Sweden 80	0.658	0.294	0.205	0.159
Norway 82	0.668	0.370	0.057	0.241
Australia 86	0.285	0.127	0.046	0.112
Hungary 86–88	0.578	0.145	0.174	0.259
Italy 87	0.562	0.233	0.092	0.237
Norway 89	0.816	0.212	0.129	0.475
Sweden 84	0.518	0.164	0.104	0.250
Non-U.S. Average (unweighted)	0.576	0.207	0.125	0.243
90–50 Log wage differential				
Germany 85–88	0.013	−0.177	0.091	0.099
Britain 85–89	−0.131	−0.149	−0.056	0.074
Austria 85–87, 89	0.044	−0.151	0.093	0.102
Switzerland 87	−0.225	−0.231	−0.049	0.055
Sweden 80	0.100	−0.091	0.080	0.111
Norway 82	0.170	−0.191	0.166	0.195
Australia 86	0.113	−0.129	0.098	0.144
Hungary 86–88	−0.109	−0.206	0.196	−0.099
Italy 87	0.066	−0.108	0.048	0.126
Norway 89	0.027	−0.132	0.050	0.109
Sweden 84	0.158	−0.140	0.132	0.166
Non-U.S. Average (unweighted)	0.021	−0.155	0.078	0.098

Source: Blau and Kahn (1996a).
Notes: The human capital specification includes education, potential experience and its square, and marital status as explanatory variables. The full specification includes these variables and adds vectors of one-digit industry and one-digit occupation dummies, and a union status indicator where available (union status information was not available for Australia, Italy, or Sweden). In all cases, a U.S. equation was estimated with the same explanatory variables as the indicated country so that the decomposition could be performed. U.S. data are for 1985 to 1989.

erable portion of the wider 50–10 gap relative to the 90–50 gap in the United States is accounted for by differences in the distribution of productive characteristics. With the same distribution of measured characteristics, the average difference between the U.S. 50–10 gap and that for the other countries would decline to 0.331 to 0.369 log points (from 0.576), while the figure for the 90–50 gap would increase to about .18 (from 0.021).

These results highlight the importance of controlling for personal characteristics. The inclusion of these controls reveals the widening effect of U.S. prices for the 90–50 gap, an effect that is not apparent if one merely compares the raw 90–50 differential in the United States with that in other countries. It also reduces the likelihood of our overstating the compression at the bottom in the other OECD countries compared to the United States (that would occur if we merely examined the raw 50–10 differentials).

However, the results also highlight the importance of wage structure or labor market rewards in explaining the higher level of U.S. inequality. If we consider the part of the differential that is not accounted for by measured characteristics (i.e., the sum of the wage coefficients and wage residuals effects) as potentially due to wage structure, we find that in every case the U.S. wage structure widens both the top and the bottom of the wage distribution relative to other countries. And even after taking the distribution of productivity-related characteristics into account, the U.S. wage structure continues to widen the wage distribution more at the bottom than at the top. This is true on average and in nine (full specification) or ten (human capital specification) of eleven possible cases. Such an effect is consistent with government and trade union wage policies in other countries that have their biggest effect in bringing up the bottom of the wage distribution.

The last two columns of Table 7.1 show the effects of wage coefficients and wage residuals separately. For the 50–10 gap, the U.S. human capital wage coefficients usually have a small widening effect compared to the other countries (accounting for 4.2 percent of the U.S.-other country difference, on average), although the effect is negative in four cases. The wage coefficients effect is notably increased when the full specification is employed (accounting for 21.7 percent of the difference, on average), suggesting that it is the prices associated with the industry, occupation, and unionism variables that are particularly high in the United States. One interpretation of the rise in the size of the wage coefficients effect when we control for industry, occupation, and unionism is that, in other countries, centralized union contracts and contract extensions to nonunion workers reduce the extent of interindustry, interoccupation, and union-nonunion wage differentials relative to the United States. In both the human capital and full specifications, however, the wage residuals effect accounts for a substantial share (42.2 to 53.3 percent) of the U.S.-other country difference. In contrast, for the 90–50 gap, the wage coefficients and residual effects are generally positive and do not differ very much between the two specifications, suggesting that the impact of measured prices at this end of the distribution primarily reflects higher prices of the human capital variables in the United States. In this case, on average the coefficients and residual effects are of roughly equal size.

The results in Table 7.1 suggest that even after accounting for differences in the distribution of personal characteristics, there is substantially more wage inequality in the United States than elsewhere. Yet, even these differences in qualifications, particularly schooling, may indirectly be influenced by labor market institutions. It has been argued that welfare state benefits and programs are likely to be more extensive where wage setting is conducted on a very centralized basis (Summers, Gruber, and Vergara 1993). If this is the case, it is possible that school systems in highly unionized societies are themselves more centralized and therefore turn out a more homogenous group of graduates than in countries where wages are set in a less centralized way. Thus, at least for the 50–10 comparisons in Table 7.1, where the United States was seen to have a more diverse workforce than other countries, some of the measured characteristics effect may have reflected the ultimate impact of labor market institutions. Furthermore, while for the 90–50 gap the United States actually had a less diverse workforce than the other countries, labor market institutions may have prevented an even larger difference in the personal characteristics effect between the United States and the other countries from emerging.

Evidence of Industry Wage Effects

The decompositions in Table 7.1 show that labor market prices and the distribution of workers' characteristics both contribute to higher wage inequality in the United States. And there was some indication that prices associated with industry, occupation, and union membership were particularly important in explaining the higher degree of wage inequality at the bottom. Such outcomes would be expected in light of the presence of binding wage floors in many highly unionized countries. An additional dimension of these wage-setting institutions is the high degree of coordination of wage setting across sectors of the economy that characterizes the Scandinavian countries as well as others in continental Europe such as Austria or Germany. To the extent that wages are coordinated across sectors, we expect smaller wage effects associated with working in a relatively high-wage industry than where wage setting is decentralized as in the United States. Britain may represent an intermediate case in coordination between the United States and the countries of continental Europe.

In the absence of some coordinating mechanism such as collective bargaining, firms in different industries may choose to pay different wage levels for similarly skilled workers for several reasons. High wages allow firms to recruit higher quality workers, reduce turnover, obtain more effort from workers, and improve employee morale. For these reasons, paying above-market wage levels may be profit-enhancing for a firm, a practice that has been termed "efficiency wages," since high pay levels may improve the firm's efficiency (i.e., profitability).[11] Firms in different industries may have different incentives to pay efficiency wages to the extent that the differing production technologies across industries imply different gains to reducing turnover, recruiting high-quality labor, and so on. For example, firms in some industries may require extensive firm-specific training for their workers and thus will especially benefit from pay policies that lower workers' propensities to quit. This discussion of possible reasons for paying efficiency wages suggests that there may be many possible reasons for interindustry wage differentials, and the ultimate reasons of these wage differences are a source of controversy.[12] Nonetheless, an international comparison of interindustry wage differentials can shed light on the extent of coordination of wage setting across industries. The economy-wide importance of interindustry wage differentials may be estimated by asking how much variation there is in average industry wage levels for workers of the same level of skill.

Table 7.2 shows results from a variety of such studies. The entries are the standard deviation of industry wage effects from each study, where the industry wage effects are estimated controlling for other personal characteristics.[13] Looking first at studies in which men and women are pooled (Table 7.2, panel A), we see that the standard deviation of industry wage effects is between 0.119 and 0.140 for the United States, while for the other countries it ranged from 0.013 to 0.077, with an average effect of 0.048, which is substantially smaller than the U.S. figures. These other countries included the Scandinavian countries and Austria, all of which have traditionally had high levels of union coverage and relatively centralized wage-setting institutions compared to the United States.

When we allow the wage determination process to differ by gender (Table 7.2, panel B, which summarizes Kahn's [1998b] results), we reach a similar conclusion. Namely, industry wage effects are much larger in the United States than elsewhere. Specifically, the average of U.S. male estimates is 0.122, while for U.S. women it is 0.137. For the other countries, the average male effect is 0.057, and the average female effect is even smaller at 0.038. To assess the magnitude of these U.S.-other country differences, note that Blau and Kahn (1996a) find that, in the 1980s, the standard deviation of the log of men's wages was 0.311 log points higher (or, taking antilogs, about 36 percent higher) for American men than it was on average for Austrian, British, German, Swedish, and Norwegian men. Looking at the results in panel B for these countries, we see that the standard deviation of industry wage effects for men in the United States was about 0.065 log points higher than it was in these five countries. By this rough comparison, industry wage

Table 7.2

Estimates of the Standard Deviation of Industry Wage Effects Based on Microdata

Study	Country	Year	Standard deviation of industry log wage effects
A. Studies pooling men and women			
Krueger and Summers (1988)	United States	1984	0.140
Edin and Zetterberg (1992)	Sweden	1984	0.013
Barth and Zweimuller (1992)	Austria	1983	0.032
	Norway	1989	0.053
	U.S. union	1983	0.141
	U.S. nonunion	1983	0.119
Albaek, et al. (1996)	Denmark	1990	0.057
	Finland	1987	0.072
	Norway	1989	0.077
	Sweden	1981	0.031
B. Estimates for men and women separately			
Kahn (1998b)	U.S. men	1985–89	0.119–0.128
	U.S. women	1985–89	0.111–0.159
	Norway men	1987	0.064
	Norway women	1987	0.026
	Germany men	1985–88	0.033
	Germany women	1985–88	0.061
	Austria men	1985–87, 89	0.062
	Austria women	1985–87, 89	0.036
	Britain men	1985–89	0.088
	Britain women	1985–89	0.062
	Sweden men	1984	0.040
	Sweden women	1984	0.003

Source: Blau and Kahn (2002).

effects account for about 21 percent (i.e., 0.065/0.311) of the higher American male wage dispersion, a substantial contribution.

A further interesting point to note about Table 7.2 is that, apart from the United States, industry wage effects are largest for Britain. Compared to Germany, Austria, and Scandinavia, Britain is much less unionized and has less centralized wage setting, although not compared to the United States, which has the least and most decentralized union coverage. For example, in Germany, Austria, and Scandinavia, 69 to 98 percent of workers were covered by collective bargaining in 1994, compared to 47 percent in the UK and 18 percent in the United States. The OECD also notes that, when there is collective bargaining, wage setting is more highly centralized among these continental European countries than in the UK and more so in the UK than in the United States (OECD 1997). The ranking of industry wage effects across countries is quite consistent with these rankings of the degree of collective bargaining coverage and coordination of wage setting. Finally, while the industry wage effects were on average slightly higher for men than women in the other countries but slightly higher for women than men in the United States, the effects move together across countries. For example, industry wage effects are higher for U.S. men and U.S. women than they are for any other countries, and the same comparison holds for Britain versus the other European countries. This consistency suggests that male and female wages within a country are affected by similar economic forces.

Table 7.2 shows that industry wage differentials for similarly qualified workers are larger in the United States than in countries with more centralized wage-setting processes and more union coverage. To the extent that highly centralized wage setting results in binding wage floors, we would expect to see an especially large coordination effect in such economies for pay levels across industries at the bottom of the distribution of each industry's scale. For example, in an economy with a national wage bargain that calls for the same high wage floor for different industries, we should see a particularly small degree of dispersion of industry wage effects for the less skilled.

Kahn (1998b) analyzed these issues by using quantile regression analysis, a technique that allows one to estimate the impact of industry on wages at different points in the wage distribution, controlling for other personal characteristics. Looking at the same countries shown in panel B of Table 7.2, he compared the standard deviation of industry wage effects at the tenth percentile of the distribution of wages, conditional on the other factors that affect pay. For U.S. men, the dispersion was 0.175 log points, while for men in the other countries, it was only 0.073 log points, a larger gap than the overall U.S.-other country gap in industry wage effects that, as we have seen, averaged 0.065 log points. Thus, for men, the evidence is consistent with disproportionately more coordination of wages across industries for those at the bottom of the distribution in other countries than in the United States. However, for women, the results did not support this hypothesis. In the United States, industry wage dispersion at the tenth percentile was 0.149 log points, and it averaged 0.069 log points elsewhere, a smaller gap (0.080

log points) than for the average industry wage differentials of 0.099 log points. Perhaps, given that the female wage distribution lies below the male distribution in all countries, European women higher up in the wage distribution are also affected by industry wage floors.

The Role of Cognitive Ability in Explaining the High Level of U.S. Wage Inequality

The evidence presented in Tables 7.1 and 7.2 strongly suggests that labor market rewards in the United States serve to widen its wage distribution compared to other countries. These patterns are consistent with the idea that collective bargaining or other labor market institutions narrow the dispersion of pay in these other nations compared to the United States. However, attention has recently been focused on what could be a competing explanation for these patterns. Specifically, as will be seen later on, data from the 1990s suggest that, at a given level of education, American workers have a lower level of cognitive skills than workers in other countries and that this is particularly true at the bottom of the distribution of test performance. Furthermore, as Stephen Nickell and Richard Layard (1999) point out, countries with larger wage returns to education, like the United States, also have larger cognitive test score differentials across education groups. This raises the possibility that evidence that appears to indicate higher labor market prices in the United States may actually be due to greater variation in cognitive skills. Of course, as noted earlier, more homogenous distributions of cognitive skills in countries outside the United States may reflect the influence of union movements in influencing government policies toward the school system. But the question of whether the distribution of cognitive skills explains higher U.S. wage inequality is still extremely important in evaluating the direct influence of institutions like unions. For example, there may be interventions that change the nature of wage setting in a country without changing the underlying educational system, and we would like to know the effect of such change on the wage structure.

Recently, microdata that allow us to examine the impact of cognitive skills on the wage structure in several countries have become available in the form of the International Adult Literacy Survey (IALS).[14] The IALS is the result of an international cooperative effort, conducted over the 1994–96 period, to devise an instrument to compare the cognitive skills of adults across a number of countries. The sampling frame was similar across countries, with the target population being those sixteen years and older who were not in institutions or the military. Of unique interest in the IALS is its measurement of cognitive skills. This was accomplished through three tests that were administered to all respondents in their respective home languages. These tests were designed to measure:

(a) Prose literacy—the knowledge and skills needed to understand and use information from texts including editorials, news stories, poems, and fiction;

(b) Document literacy—the knowledge and skills required to locate and use information contained in various formats, including job applications, payroll forms, transportation schedules, maps, tables, and graphics; and

(c) Quantitative literacy—the knowledge and skills required to apply arithmetic operations, either alone or sequentially, to numbers embedded in printed materials, such as balancing a checkbook, calculating a tip, completing an order form, or determining the amount of interest on a loan from an advertisement. (Statistics Canada 1998)

Proficiency in each of the three test areas was scored on a scale of 0 to 500, after the tests were read by several graders from the respondent's own country. The IALS provides five alternative estimates of proficiency for each test, which were computed from raw test performance information using a multiple imputation procedure developed by D.B. Rubin (1987). These alternative estimates are in fact highly correlated. We find that within each of the three types of test, the five estimates of the score were correlated at 0.90.[15] Furthermore, to ensure comparability of grading across countries, an average of 9.4 percent of the tests for each country were regraded by personnel from another country; interrater agreement with respect to these regrades was 94 to 99 percent.

Although, in principle, interpreting prose or documents and using mathematics may each require different skills, we find that these skills, as measured by the IALS, are in fact highly correlated. Forming a score for each of the three tests (i.e., quantitative, prose, and document literacy) based on the average of the five available estimates, we find that these scores were correlated at between 0.91 and 0.94. Due to this high correlation, we focus on a measure of cognitive skills, which is an average of the three average test scores for each individual. However, we also estimate models with the three average test scores entered separately, with very similar results.

Table 7.3 (see p. 186) provides evidence on the distribution of cognitive test scores for men and women in the population across the full set of nine countries with test score data (panel A) and for the wage sample in the five countries for which this information is available (panel B).[16] The wage sample is comprised of full-time workers who worked at least twenty-six weeks during the year. Looking first at the full population shown in panel A, a striking pattern is the higher level of test score inequality for both men and women in the United States than elsewhere, particularly at the bottom of the distribution. Americans do substantially worse than the non-U.S. average at the bottom, about the same at the median, and somewhat better at the top. The U.S. shortfall at the tenth percentile of the test score distribution is 15.5 points for women and 23.7 points for men, while the U.S. advantage at the ninetieth percentile is 7.3 points for women and 8.3 for men. However, the 50–10 male test score gaps in Britain, Canada, and Ireland are more comparable to those in the United States than is the case for the other countries. Among women, the 50–10 gap is higher in the United States than in every other country, with Belgium, Canada, and New Zealand having the gaps closest to the United States.

When test score differentials are computed for the subset of workers in the wage sample, roughly similar patterns are obtained (panel B). However, it is notable that, for the five countries on which we have wage data, wage sample inclusion tends to be selective of individuals with higher test scores. The mean of the wage sample is higher and the standard deviation of the wage sample is generally lower than for the full population, though the extent of these differences varies considerably across countries. We will address the issue of sample selection later on.

These test score patterns roughly mirror the differences between the United States and other countries in wage distributions, at least in leading us to expect larger wage differentials between the middle and the bottom, and the middle and the top in the United States. However, test scores are likely to provide a better explanation for the greater U.S. gap at the bottom than at the top, since the difference in dispersion of test scores between the United States and other countries in the upper ranges is relatively small.

In Blau and Kahn (2000a), we shed light on the impact of the distribution of cognitive skills on wage inequality in the United States compared to other countries by using the IALS data. We focus on a comparison of the United States to Canada, the Netherlands, Sweden, and Switzerland—the countries for which wage data were available. We find that the measured return to education in the United States remains considerably higher than elsewhere, even after controlling for test score: a one standard deviation increase in schooling is estimated to raise the wages of U.S. men by 16.6 percent and U.S. women by 26.4 percent, compared to a non-U.S. average of 6.4 percent for men and 10.3 percent for women.[17] With the inclusion of test scores, the ratio of the average return to education among the other countries to the U.S. return increases only slightly from 36.9 to 38.6 percent among men, and actually falls slightly from 41.9 to 38.9 percent among women. Thus,

Table 7.3

Distribution of Individual Average Literacy Test Scores by Country and Gender

Country	Mean	Standard deviation	Percentile			Differential	
			10	50	90	50–10	90–50
A. Population							
Men							
Belgium	284.63	51.43	221.67	292.13	341.79	70.46	49.67
Britain	273.59	63.55	192.67	283.89	344.79	91.22	60.90
Canada	277.66	67.06	186.76	289.28	346.95	102.52	57.67
Ireland	264.47	59.47	185.76	273.26	329.88	87.50	56.62
Netherlands	289.13	43.97	231.60	295.47	338.00	63.87	42.53
New Zealand	273.12	57.00	200.09	279.71	340.49	79.61	60.78
Sweden	308.47	48.26	249.08	312.38	364.67	63.30	52.29
Switzerland	281.67	51.80	227.26	288.75	334.03	61.50	45.28
United States	275.60	65.54	188.13	287.05	350.89	98.92	63.85
Non-U.S. average	281.59	55.32	211.86	289.36	342.58	77.50	53.22
Women							
Belgium	270.46	57.02	194.14	282.25	334.63	88.11	52.38
Britain	261.81	58.33	187.80	267.18	329.75	79.38	62.58
Canada	281.88	60.16	204.25	288.78	349.56	84.53	60.77
Ireland	261.69	54.37	190.39	266.50	326.03	76.11	59.53
Netherlands	282.24	43.93	224.90	288.92	333.50	64.02	44.57
New Zealand	271.04	56.11	194.45	278.89	335.14	84.43	56.25
Sweden	300.17	48.70	238.98	304.97	356.93	66.00	51.95
Switzerland	271.12	50.81	212.72	278.34	324.78	65.63	46.44
United States	274.80	62.87	190.45	283.96	343.57	93.51	59.61
Non-U.S. average	275.05	53.68	205.95	281.98	336.29	76.03	54.31
B. Wage sample							
Men							
Canada	295.96	52.40	233.95	296.76	362.29	62.81	65.53
Netherlands	294.07	40.43	241.92	297.80	338.92	55.88	41.12
Sweden	311.60	46.37	256.31	313.94	365.97	57.63	52.03
Switzerland	283.79	51.32	227.65	291.01	334.86	63.36	43.85
United States	288.97	61.43	216.49	297.16	357.13	80.67	59.98
Non-U.S. average	296.35	47.63	239.96	299.88	350.51	59.92	50.63
Women							
Canada	299.11	56.19	225.92	307.46	365.08	81.53	57.62
Netherlands	300.53	34.17	251.05	303.85	340.39	52.80	36.54
Sweden	308.54	43.08	259.48	310.49	361.42	51.02	50.93
Switzerland	278.74	47.51	230.62	284.72	326.95	54.10	42.23
United States	289.56	58.79	221.53	294.54	352.88	73.01	58.34
Non-U.S. average	296.73	45.24	241.77	301.63	348.46	59.86	46.83

Source: International Adult Literacy Survey data analyzed in Blau and Kahn (2000a).
Notes: Individual scores are the average of quantitative, document, and prose test scores. Non-U.S. average is the unweighted average of the figures in the table. Wage sample includes full-time workers who worked at least twenty-six weeks.

the greater dispersion of test scores in the United States does little to account for its higher return to education. Among both men and women, education is considerably more highly rewarded in United States than in other countries, even when controlling for test score. In addition, in regression specifications that include education, the estimated U.S. returns to cognitive test scores are higher than the non-U.S. average. This is in line with higher rewards to skills in the United States than elsewhere.

While the greater dispersion in test scores in the United States suggests that cognitive skills play a role in explaining the higher level of U.S. wage inequality, how quantitatively important are they? We address this question using the same decomposition technique employed in Table 7.1 to explain U.S.-other country differences in the distribution of wages. Again, we assess the relative importance of differences in the distribution of characteristics (in this case including test scores), as well as labor market prices and residual inequality, in explaining higher U.S. wage inequality.

We find that while the greater dispersion of cognitive test scores in the United States plays a part in explaining higher U.S. wage inequality, higher labor market prices (i.e., higher returns to measured human capital and cognitive performance) and greater residual inequality still play important roles for both men and women. Moreover, we find that, on average, prices are quantitatively considerably more important than differences in the distribution of test scores in explaining the relatively high level of U.S. wage inequality.[18]

It is possible that a given test score may not mean the same for an immigrant as it does for a native, given differences in language ability and other factors. If this is the case, our results may in part reflect the native-immigrant composition of the each country's wage samples. For this reason, we examined international differences in the sources of wage inequality for a sample that was restricted to natives in each country. Our results regarding the importance of higher labor market prices in the United States in explaining higher U.S. wage inequality remained the same for these native-only samples.

As we noted earlier, Table 7.3 indicates that test scores are higher and less dispersed for full-time employed workers than for the population in general. This pattern raises the possibility that wage inequality is higher in the United States not because of higher labor market prices as we have claimed, but rather because a larger share of those at the bottom of the skill distribution are not employed in the other countries than in the United States. This means that we do not observe wages for them. To examine this possibility, we corrected our samples for selectivity. To illustrate the adjustment, consider the comparison of U.S. and Canadian men. Among the population of Canadian men, 63.9 percent were employed full time and worked at least twenty-six weeks in the past year, while the figure was 71.1 percent in the United States, or 10.1 percent higher [i.e., $(71.1 - 63.9)/71.1 = 0.101$]. To correct for selection, we first compute a predicted probability of being in the wage sample for each U.S. male in the population based on a probit model for U.S. men in which the probability of being in the wage sample is a function of age, education, and test score. Since Canadian men are 10.1 percent less likely than American men to be in the wage sample, we then exclude from the original U.S. male wage sample the 10.1 percent with the lowest predicted probabilities of inclusion. We then reestimate the U.S. wage equations on this reduced sample and perform the Juhn, Murphy, and Pierce (1993) decomposition for the selectivity-adjusted U.S. sample and the original Canadian sample. This procedure provides some adjustment for selectivity bias both in our estimate of overall wage inequality and our estimation of the wage equation itself.[19] A similar adjustment is made for each pairwise (i.e., U.S.-other country) comparison for men and for women. After correcting our samples for selectivity in this way, we obtain very similar results to those reported earlier. We conclude that the United States has higher labor market prices than other countries do, even when accounting for labor force selectivity.

Higher U.S. Wage Inequality: Transitory or Permanent?

We have presented a considerable body of evidence suggesting that at a point in time, U.S. wages are much more unequal than those in other countries and that higher U.S. rewards to skills and employment in favored sectors are an important reason for these differences. It is possible, however, that individual wage mobility over time is greater in the United States than elsewhere and thus that lifetime earnings in the United States may be no more unequally distributed than lifetime earnings elsewhere. If this were true, then we would need to reevaluate our conclusions about the degree to which the U.S. labor market delivers unfavorable outcomes for those at the bottom. One recent study on this question compares individual earnings mobility in the United States and West Germany in the 1980s (Burkhauser, Holtz-Eakin, and Rhody 1997). Workers were followed over a period of years, and the degree to which they moved up the wage distribution was assessed. The authors find a similar degree of mobility in both countries and a high level of persistence in individuals' relative earnings outcomes over time. While this study only compares the United States to West Germany, it does suggest that our focus on annual earnings inequality gives similar results to a focus on long-term earnings inequality.

Causes and Consequences of International Differences in Labor Market Prices: Collective Bargaining, Market Forces, Wage Inequality, and Relative Employment

High labor market prices in the United States could be the result of our more laissez-faire labor markets or of market forces, or a combination both. Centralized wage-setting institutions in many other countries could lead to wage compression through the negotiation of binding wage floors and could therefore lead to lower levels of wage inequality than we find in the United States. However, it is also possible that a relatively high supply of less-skilled workers in the United States, as suggested by the relatively low test scores at the tenth percentile of the test distribution shown in Table 7.3, could depress the relative pay of those at the bottom (Leuven, Oosterbeek, and van Ophem 1998). In this section, we provide some more direct evidence on institutions, focusing on collective bargaining versus market forces as factors influencing wage inequality and the employment consequences of these wage outcomes.

We begin with an examination of the role of collective bargaining in affecting wage inequality and then turn to an assessment of relative strength of collective bargaining and market forces. An important conceptual consideration in gauging these two types of explanation is to note that if wages are compressed due to institutional interventions, such as collective bargaining or minimum wage laws, and if employment is demand determined, then we expect to observe employment problems among those whose wages are raised the most. Of course, according to the theories of efficient bargaining and monopsony, wage-setting institutions can affect relative pay without affecting relative employment. But a finding that collective bargaining or minimum wages are associated with employment problems for the less skilled, as well as with wage compression, would be strong evidence that these interventions actually do affect labor market prices. On the other hand, if the market forces of supply and demand are the main factors affecting wage inequality, then groups whose wages are raised the most, for example by high relative demand, will also have abundant employment opportunities. Therefore, an examination of employment across different groups in the labor force, in addition to being of major policy interest in itself, can also shed considerable light on the question of whether institutions like collective bargaining have an important effect on the wage structure.

Accounting for the Impact of Unionization on Wage Inequality

There are several routes through which the industrial relations system can affect overall wage inequality. First, unions may increase the difference between their members' average wages and those of nonunion workers. All else being equal, the larger the union-nonunion wage gap, the larger the country's overall wage variance will be. And, as will be seen, this gap is much higher for the United States than other countries.[20]

Second, unions typically negotiate contracts that allow for less variation in pay than that which occurs in the nonunion sector (Freeman 1982; Blanchflower and Freeman 1992). Unions are much less prevalent in the United States than elsewhere; thus, the lower union variance in pay would get a smaller weight in the United States. Hence, we would expect a higher overall variance in wages in the United States, even if the variance of wages within the union and nonunion sectors were identical across countries. However, there are strong reasons for expecting both of these within-sector variances to be higher in the United States than elsewhere. These higher within-sector variances constitute a third route by which the U.S. industrial relations system raises wage inequality relative to other countries.

With respect to the union sector, as we noted earlier, collective bargaining in the United States is relatively decentralized, with an emphasis on single-firm agreements that, in most cases, are not firm-wide (Hendricks and Kahn 1982). In contrast, in many other countries bargaining is conducted on an industry-wide or even an economy-wide level. Thus, there appears to be more scope for interfirm and interindustry wage differentials in the United States than elsewhere; and a substantial portion of the wage inequality we observe in the United States is associated with such firm or industry wage effects (Blau 1977; Groshen 1991; Davis and Haltiwanger 1991; Krueger and Summers 1988).

While a lower variance in the union sector of other countries could be achieved either by raising the bottom, restraining the top, or both, centralized bargains often emphasize the setting of wage minima across diverse units. For example, in Austria, Germany, Italy, Sweden, and Switzerland (as well as in several other European countries), collective bargaining agreements, generally at the industry level, set minimum rates for the lowest pay group in a collective agreement ("Minimum Pay in 18 Countries," 1992). Such minima, to the extent they are binding, will tend to bring up the floor among workers covered by the contract. In the limiting case, a contract that covered all workers in the economy might be expected to compress the bottom of the distribution, just as would a high national minimum wage. Thus, we expect to find greater narrowing at the bottom than at the top in the union sector in most countries compared to the United States, but regard this as to some extent an empirical question.

Several factors also lead us to expect more dispersion of nonunion wages in the United States than elsewhere. These include the practice in many other countries of extending the terms of collective bargaining agreements to non-union workers. Such contract extensions blur the distinction between union and nonunion wage setting. To the extent that unions in all countries tend to compress wages at the bottom in the union sector, contract extension will not only reduce wage variation in the nonunion sector, but compress wages at the bottom as well. In addition, the higher degree of union organization outside the United States should produce more "voluntary" imitation of union pay structures by nonunion firms than in the United States.[21] Finally, the impact of these factors has been further strengthened by explicit union and government policies in some countries to bring up the bottom of the wage distribution. This appears to have happened, for example, in Sweden, Norway, and Italy, as well as in Germany (Hibbs 1990; Edin and Topel 1997; Edin and Holmlund 1995, Kahn 1998a; Erickson and Ichino 1995; Blau and Kahn 1996a).

Table 7.4 (see p. 192) presents some descriptive information on union density and wage inequality. It is based on the International Social Survey Program (ISSP) microdata for the 1990–94 period over twelve OECD countries, although, as the notes to the table indicate, the coverage of countries is not complete in each year (for a description of these data, see Blau and Kahn 2003). Several interesting patterns emerge. First, for both men and women, the variance of log wages is much greater in the United States than elsewhere. Among men, the variance is 0.603 log points in the United States and averages only 0.250 elsewhere. For women, the comparisons are similar, with the United States having a far higher level of wage variance at 0.652 log points than other countries, where this measure of inequality averaged 0.274 log points.

Second, in every country for both men and women, union wages show less dispersion than nonunion wages. This pattern supports the idea that unions tend to narrow pay differentials within their jurisdictions. Although Table 7.4 does not control for other causes of wage compression. Blau and Kahn (1996a) and Kahn (1998b) find that, when controlling for individual productivity characteristics, union members generally have less wage inequality than nonunion workers across several OECD countries, including the United States, West Germany, Britain, Austria, and Norway. (We present the results corroborating this later on.) A further important union-nonunion pattern in Table 7.4 is that the variance of wages is much higher in the United States than elsewhere among both union and nonunion workers. Moreover, the gap between the United States and other countries is larger for nonunion workers than for union workers. For example, the U.S. variance was 0.326 log points higher than in other countries, on average, among male nonunion workers, compared to 0.165 log points higher in the United States among male union workers. The corresponding comparisons for women were a 0.362 log points higher variance in the United States among nonunion work-

Table 7.4

Unions and Wage Dispersion, Descriptive Statistics (1990–94)

	Variance of log wages	Variance of log nonunion wages	Variance of log union wages	Union-nonunion log wage differential	Union density
Men					
Australia	0.351	0.495	0.199	0.032	0.486
W. Germany	0.217	0.244	0.172	0.062	0.388
Britain	0.268	0.331	0.178	0.092	0.423
Austria	0.237	0.308	0.156	0.109	0.485
Italy	0.143	0.183	0.090	0.121	0.461
Norway	0.175	0.263	0.113	0.091	0.596
New Zealand	0.272	0.313	0.183	0.033	0.319
Canada	0.261	0.297	0.173	0.066	0.296
Japan	0.316	0.381	0.205	0.027	0.365
Ireland	0.341	0.387	0.227	0.254	0.378
Sweden	0.170	0.365	0.109	0.117	0.766
Non-U.S. average	0.250	0.324	0.164	0.091	0.451
United States	0.603	0.650	0.329	0.224	0.168
Women					
Australia	0.404	0.425	0.369	0.065	0.383
W. Germany	0.204	0.225	0.124	0.057	0.217
Britain	0.296	0.313	0.249	0.212	0.428
Austria	0.230	0.255	0.154	0.237	0.374
Italy	0.217	0.242	0.128	0.230	0.321
Norway	0.215	0.324	0.144	0.197	0.653
New Zealand	0.298	0.352	0.210	0.119	0.401
Canada	0.267	0.283	0.211	0.192	0.338
Japan	0.423	0.409	0.292	0.486	0.248
Ireland	0.337	0.384	0.215	0.315	0.417
Sweden	0.127	0.315	0.104	−0.002	0.886
Non-U.S. average	0.274	0.321	0.200	0.192	0.424
United States	0.652	0.683	0.386	0.284	0.133

Source: Blau and Kahn (2002), based on authors' computations using ISSP microdata.
Notes: The following years are used: Australia (90, 91, and 94); West Germany (90–, 93); Britain (90–94); USA (90–94); Austria (91–92, 94); Italy (90, 92–94); Norway (90–94); New Zealand (91–94); Canada (92–94); Japan (93–94); Ireland (90, 93–94); Sweden (94).

ers versus a 0.186 log points higher variance among union workers. These patterns are consistent with the impact of contract extension in many non-U.S. countries, as well as the possibility that in these more highly unionized countries, nonunion firms voluntarily imitate union pay scales to a greater extent than is true in the United States.

A third important pattern in Table 7.4 is that the union-nonunion wage differential is much higher in the United States than elsewhere, a finding that also suggests greater spillovers to nonunion workers in many countries outside the United States. Finally, union density is far lower in the United States than elsewhere, a pattern also seen in OECD (1997) data.

All of these patterns—higher variances of wages within the union and nonunion sectors, a higher union-nonunion wage differential, and a lower union density—could potentially contribute to a higher wage variance in the United States than we see in other countries. Table 7.5 tells us how important each of these factors was for the 1990–94 period. In performing this decomposition, we make use of the following statistical relationship:

$$v_i = \alpha_{ai}v_{ai} + (1 - \alpha_{ai})v_{ni} + \alpha_{ai}(w_{ai} - w_i^*)^2 + (1 - \alpha_{ai})(w_{ni} - w_i^*)^2 \ (1)$$

where for country i, v is the overall variance of log wages; α_a is the fraction of workers unionized; v_a and v_n are the variance of log union and nonunion wages; w_a and w_n are average log union and nonunion wages; and w^* is the country's average log wage level.[22]

Table 7.5 (see p. 194) indicates that the overwhelming portion of the gap between the United States and other countries in the variance of wages— about 85 percent for men and 90 percent for women, on average—is due to higher U.S. variances within the union and nonunion sectors (i.e., the within-sector variance effect). Another substantial proportion, about 14 percent on average for men and 11 percent for women, comes from the within-sector composition effect. That is, a higher proportion of U.S. workers are non-union, and this sector has a larger wage variance in all countries. The higher union-nonunion wage differential in the United States causes a small widening of the U.S. variance relative to other countries, with the between-sector wage differential effect accounting for, on average, about 1.5 percent of the average U.S.-other country variance gap for men but below this for women. Finally, the between-sector composition effect, which measures the contribution to the U.S.-other country difference in the variance of wages of a higher representation of employment in the sector with wages relatively far from the average, is found to be negligible.[23]

Table 7.5 implies that the key to understanding U.S.-other country differences in wage inequality is to explain higher U.S. inequality within the union and nonunion sectors. Table 7.6 (see p. 195) provides some suggestive evidence here by comparing union and nonunion wage inequality at the bottom (50–10 gap) and the top (90–50 gap) of the wage distributions. In light of our earlier discussion of the importance of wage floors in many OECD countries, we focus particularly on the 50–10 gap. Mirroring the

Table 7.5

Decomposition of the U.S.-Other Country Differences in Log Wage Variances by Union Status, 1990–94

	U.S. variance-other country variance	Within-sector variance effect	Within-sector composition effect	Between-sector wage differential effect	Between-sector composition effect
Men					
Australia	0.2522	0.1513	0.0941	0.0079	0.0000
W. Germany	0.3860	0.3641	0.0158	0.0074	−0.0002
Britain	0.3347	0.2905	0.0391	0.0064	−0.0003
Austria	0.3661	0.3135	0.0483	0.0053	−0.0001
Italy	0.4595	0.4287	0.0273	0.0049	−0.0003
Norway	0.4275	0.3584	0.0641	0.0055	0.0007
New Zealand	0.3311	0.3046	0.0196	0.0080	−0.0001
Canada	0.3417	0.3197	0.0158	0.0075	−0.0002
Japan	0.2868	0.2451	0.0346	0.0080	0.0000
Ireland	0.2618	0.2358	0.0336	−0.0036	−0.0033
Sweden	0.4327	0.2743	0.1530	0.0014	0.0043
Non-U.S. average	0.3527	0.2987	0.0496	0.0053	0.0000
percent due to	100.00	84.69	14.06	1.51	0.01
Women					
Australia	0.2477	0.2259	0.0140	0.0085	−0.0003
W. Germany	0.4482	0.4316	0.0085	0.0089	−0.0002
Britain	0.3556	0.3390	0.0189	0.0002	−0.0019
Austria	0.4218	0.4019	0.0242	−0.0005	−0.0034
Italy	0.4354	0.4167	0.0214	0.0014	−0.0035
Norway	0.4367	0.3436	0.0933	−0.0057	0.0062
New Zealand	0.3540	0.3105	0.0381	0.0067	−0.0007
Canada	0.3855	0.3702	0.0148	0.0035	−0.0025
Japan	0.2289	0.2503	0.0135	−0.0210	−0.0137
Ireland	0.3150	0.2817	0.0479	−0.0101	−0.0047
Sweden	0.5245	0.3562	0.1590	0.0093	0.0000
Non-U.S. average	0.3776	0.3389	0.0412	0.0001	−0.0022
percent due to	100.00	89.74	10.92	0.03	−0.59

Source: Blau and Kahn (2002), based on authors' computations using ISSP microdata. For specific years of data availability, see notes to Table 7.4.

results for wage variance patterns, the 50–10 gap is much larger in both the union and nonunion sectors in the United States than for the average of the other countries. For example, among union members, the U.S. 50–10 gap is 0.109 (men) to 0.279 (women) log points higher than in other countries, while for nonunion workers, the United States has a higher 50–10 gap by

Table 7.6

Union and Nonunion Log Wage Inequality at the Bottom and the Top of the Wage Distribution, 1990–94

	Men				Women			
	50–10		90–50		50–10		90–50	
Country	Nonunion	Union	Nonunion	Union	Nonunion	Union	Nonunion	Union
Australia	0.833	0.447	0.696	0.419	0.861	0.592	0.649	0.526
W. Germany	0.530	0.405	0.532	0.410	0.539	0.381	0.587	0.353
Britain	0.688	0.471	0.707	0.553	0.593	0.656	0.786	0.601
Austria	0.579	0.414	0.651	0.469	0.560	0.379	0.585	0.576
Italy	0.438	0.264	0.446	0.407	0.651	0.347	0.557	0.402
Norway	0.609	0.321	0.449	0.379	0.857	0.420	0.491	0.363
New Zealand	0.711	0.529	0.721	0.495	0.765	0.628	0.601	0.452
Canada	0.745	0.618	0.589	0.423	0.620	0.520	0.631	0.541
Japan	0.615	0.643	0.882	0.569	0.839	0.637	0.833	0.678
Ireland	0.560	0.648	0.944	0.594	0.734	0.418	0.728	0.669
Sweden	0.831	0.374	0.762	0.564	0.723	0.434	0.610	0.238
Non-U.S. average	0.649	0.467	0.671	0.480	0.704	0.492	0.642	0.437
United States	1.036	0.576	0.842	0.531	1.110	0.771	0.792	0.624

Source: Blau and Kahn (2002), based on authors' computations using ISSP microdata. For specific years of data availability, see notes to Table 7.4.

Table 7.7

Union Membership Regression Coefficients, 1980s
(standard or asymptotic standard errors in parentheses)

| | Union effect at various levels in the conditional wage distribution | | | |
	All workers	10th percentile	50th percentile	90th percentile
United States:				
ISSP, men	0.230 (0.043)	0.377 (0.077)	0.180 (0.030)	0.108 (0.032)
ISSP, women	0.201 (0.062)	0.437 (0.151)	0.169 (0.055)	0.165 (0.055)
PSID, men	0.263 (0.027)	0.342 (0.054)	0.263 (0.029)	0.179 (0.030)
PSID, women	0.278 (0.034)	0.335 (0.071)	0.241 (0.037)	0.234 (0.046)
CPS, men	0.186 (0.004)	0.276 (0.007)	0.185 (0.004)	0.120 (0.007)
CPS, women	0.181 (0.005)	0.243 (0.007)	0.179 (0.005)	0.112 (0.009)
Average U.S. effect: men	0.226 (0.025)	0.332 (0.046)	0.209 (0.021)	0.136 (0.023)
Average U.S. effect: women	0.220 (0.034)	0.338 (0.076)	0.196 (0.032)	0.170 (0.037)
Other countries:				
Norwegian men	0.007 (0.019)	0.026 (0.031)	0.017 (0.016)	0.023 (0.035)
Norwegian women	0.019 (0.018)	0.050 (0.032)	0.017 (0.016)	−0.0001 (0.025)
German men	0.030 (0.020)	0.044 (0.039)	−0.002 (0.021)	0.017 (0.025)
German women	0.125 (0.041)	0.184 (0.083)	0.058 (0.042)	0.091 (0.054)
Austrian men	0.061 (0.025)	0.133 (0.028)	0.043 (0.026)	−0.001 (0.041)
Austrian women	0.103 (0.032)	0.090 (0.044)	0.096 (0.032)	−0.002 (0.028)
British men	0.065 (0.021)	0.085 (0.030)	0.047 (0.023)	0.072 (0.031)

(continued)

Table 7.7 *(continued)*

	All workers	10th percentile	50th percentile	90th percentile
British women	0.076	0.133	0.075	0.040
	(0.026)	(0.041)	(0.018)	(0.054)
Average non-U.S. effect: men	0.041	0.072	0.026	0.028
	(0.021)	(0.032)	(0.021)	(0.033)
Average non-U.S. effect: women	0.081	0.114	0.062	0.032
	(0.029)	(0.050)	(0.027)	(0.040)

Source: Kahn (1998b).
Notes: U.S. sources are ISSP (1985–89), PSID = Michigan Panel Study of Income Dynamics (1988); and CPS = Current Population Survey (May 1989). Norway source is 1987 Level of Living Survey. Austrian (1985–87; 1989) and West German (1985–88) source is the ISSP. The entries are based on regressions of log wages on education, potential experience and its square, marital status, and vectors of one-digit industry and occupation dummies in addition to a union membership indicator. The entries for "all workers" refer to OLS regression coefficients, while the entries for the 10th, 50th, and 90th percentiles come from quantile regressions.

0.387 (men) to 0.406 (women) log points. And, the 90–50 gaps are larger in the United States than elsewhere, but the contrasts are less dramatic than for the 50–10 gap. Specifically, for union members, the 90–50 gap is 0.051 (men) to 0.137 (women) log points higher in the United States, while for nonunion workers the 90–50 gap is 0.150 (women) to 0.171 (men) log points higher in the United States than elsewhere. This comparison of middle-bottom and top-middle wage differentials implies relatively more compression among both union and nonunion workers at the bottom of the distribution in other countries. Moreover, these contrasts show much larger U.S.-other country differences in the 50–10 gap for the nonunion sector than for the union sector.

Table 7.6 provides evidence consistent with the idea that wage compression at the bottom of the distribution among nonunion workers in other countries is a particularly salient difference between wage setting in the United States and elsewhere. While it suggests the importance of contract extensions and voluntary imitation of union contract provisions in these countries, Table 7.6 does not control for individual productivity characteristics, which could also conceivably explain the wage patterns.

Table 7.7, from a study by Kahn (1998b), provides sharper evidence on the connection between unionization and wage compression by showing the impact of union membership on log wages, when controlling for individual characteristics (education, experience and its square, marital status, occupation, and industry). It shows that the union wage effect overall ("All Workers") is much higher in the United States than it is in other countries, similar to results from previous research (Blanchflower and Freeman 1992; Blanchflower 1996). More importantly, the table shows the impact of union membership on wages at different portions of the conditional distribution of wages. The method of quantile regression, which we discussed earlier, was used to estimate these impacts. The most dramatic contrasts between the United States and other countries in the union wage impact come at the tenth percentile of the wage distribution. At this location near the bottom of the wage distribution, the effect of unions is 0.224 to 0.260 log points higher in the United States than elsewhere; in contrast, at the median (fiftieth percentile), the U.S. union wage effects are 0.134 to 0.183 log points larger, and at the top (ninetieth percentile), U.S. effects are only 0.108 to 0.138 log points larger. This pattern of especially large differences between the United States and other countries at the bottom of the wage distribution suggests the importance of wage floors for low-skilled nonunion workers in other countries.

The union-nonunion comparisons in this subsection provide some strong evidence that low-skill nonunion workers in the United States have the least wage protection by wage floors among industrialized countries. This conclusion was suggested in the descriptive data in Tables 7.4 and 7.6 and also by the regression results presented in Table 7.5, which control for worker characteristics.

Evidence on the Impact of Collective Bargaining

The previous subsection built a strong "circumstantial" case for the claim that union wage floors are an important source of greater wage compression in other countries than in the United States. In this subsection, we first review evidence from studies of the impact of episodic change in wage-setting institutions within particular countries, or regions within a country. The research designs in these studies are especially attractive, since within a country, many factors are in effect held constant (e.g., norms or workforce characteristics) when it changes one particular aspect of its wage-setting environment. A focus on changes over time allows any unmeasured characteristics of a given country that would otherwise affect its wage distribution to be "differenced out," enabling us to concentrate more precisely on the impact of the institutional change in question. Next, we examine detailed comparisons of two or three countries. Overall, these studies show strong evidence that collective bargaining affects the wage distribution but mixed evidence that it affects relative employment.

Evidence from Changes in Collective Bargaining Institutions

Sweden has experienced episodes in which institutional changes occurred that would be expected to decrease wage inequality, as well as others that would be expected to increase it, making this country particularly interesting to study. While Sweden has had relatively centralized wage setting since at least the 1950s, during the 1964–83 period, its major blue-collar union, the LO, embarked on a "solidarity wage" policy of radical equalization of pay by giving especially large increases to the lowest paid workers. This new wage policy involved equal kroner/hour wage increases instead of percentage increases and special funds to raise the wages of low-paid workers (Edin and Topel 1997). Douglas A. Hibbs Jr. (1990) shows that the coefficient of variation of blue-collar union wages took an abrupt and large downturn precisely in the mid-1960s, following an eight-year period of gradually rising dispersion. Furthermore, Per-Anders Edin and Robert Topel (1997) and Per-Anders Edin and Bertil Holmlund (1995) document the sharp decline in the returns to education in Sweden following the 1960s, while Edin and Topel (1997) and Steven J. Davis and Magnus Henrekson (2000) present evidence that interindustry wage differentials contracted sharply between 1960 and 1970. The abrupt nature of the changes in bargaining practices and the correspondingly sudden decrease in wage inequality following these changes constitute fairly strong evidence that institutional change did indeed cause changes in wage inequality.

   These studies also find important employment effects of these changes. Edin and Topel (1997) and Davis and Henrekson (1997, 2000) find strong allocative effects of Sweden's solidarity wage policy of the late 1960s and early 1970s. Specifically, relative wages in low-paying industries were sharply raised during this time and increases in out-migration from areas where these industries were located as well as decreases in relative employment in these industries were observed. Furthermore, this relationship was strongest during the period of most intense wage compression as compared to later periods, providing some further evidence that there were negative relative employment effects of this wage policy. An additional response to Swedish wage compression was low enrollments in higher education. This occurred as the wage returns to education were sharply reduced and jobs were plentiful (Edin and Holmlund 1995).

   An additional pattern related to solidarity bargaining in Sweden is that the reduction in interindustry wage differentials was positively associated with labor productivity gains. An interpretation of this finding that is consistent with the employment responses to wage compression in Sweden is that the reduction in interindustry wage differentials caused the low productivity sectors to shrink, raising the average overall level of labor productivity (Hibbs and Locking 2000). It is also possible that by reducing the differences in the marginal productivity of labor across sectors, the economy's overall efficiency was raised. However, Douglas A. Hibbs Jr. and Håkan Locking (2000) find that reducing wage differentials within industries, for example, by reducing occupational or educational differentials, was negatively associated with labor productivity. An interpretation of this finding is that by compressing market-based occupational or educational wage differentials, the solidarity wage policy hindered the allocative function of relative wages.

Perhaps in response to the strains caused by wage leveling, in 1983 the Swedes abandoned the country's economy-wide wage setting practices and moved to a system of industry-wide wage bargains (Freeman and Gibbons 1995). In principle, this structure can allow more interindustry wage variation than the more centralized system. And the Swedish wage distribution did abruptly become more dispersed following 1983 (Hibbs 1990; Edin and Holmlund 1995). Although this pattern is consistent with a real effect of changes in bargaining institutions on the wage distribution, Edin and Holmlund (1995) suggest that, in the 1980s, supply and demand were changing to the detriment of low-skilled workers and this could be a competing explanation for rising Swedish inequality during this period. However, Davis and Henrekson's (2000) findings that, after 1983, Swedish relative employment grew in the industries whose relative pay was allowed to fall (compared to similar industries in the United States), implies that institutions were an important part of the story. This pattern is the mirror image of what happened during the solidarity bargaining period from 1968 to 1983, in which the industries whose relative pay was raised the most experienced relative employment declines. If employment is demand determined, we would expect institutional wage interventions to cause relative employment to move in the opposite direction from relative pay. These findings for employment during the 1968–83 and post–1983 periods in Sweden provide some strong evidence that interventions in wage-setting institutions have important effects on wage structure and relative employment.

The Swedish experience of the 1980s illustrates a difficulty in estimating the impact of changes in wage-setting institutions when supply and demand forces go in the same direction as the institutional changes, and may in fact have contributed to the institutional changes themselves. Indeed, in the Swedish case Edin and Topel (1997) note that excess demand for skilled workers in the early 1980s, partly due to wage leveling in encompassing labor agreements, contributed to the end of economy-wide bargaining in 1983.

In contrast, the case of Norway in the 1987–91 period provides an interesting instance in which institutions changed in the opposite direction to supply and demand forces and opposite to institutions in virtually all other advanced countries (Kahn 1998a). Until 1982, Norway's collective bargaining system was quite similar to Sweden's, in that there were economy-wide centralized negotiations between national union and employer federations. And, like Sweden, as well as several other countries,[24] collective bargaining became less centralized in Norway during the 1980s. Decentralization took the same form as it did in Sweden—industry-wide bargains replaced the economy-wide agreement. However, spurred by the recession brought on by reduced oil prices after 1986, in 1988 the national government in Norway took steps to recentralize the country's bargaining system. The government's goal was wage restraint, and recentralizing negotiations with special wage increases for the low paid was deemed necessary in order to get union cooperation in the effort (Kahn 1998a). In 1988 and 1990, negotiations returned to the nationwide level, and low-paid workers received higher absolute (and therefore higher percentage) wage increases than others did.

Supply and demand for low-skilled labor in Norway changed during the late 1980s and early 1990s in ways similar to that in other countries, notably Sweden (Kahn 1998a). And, at a time when bargaining structures were breaking apart in several other countries, Norway's was becoming more monolithic. Consistent with this change, Norway was the only OECD country with a sharply narrowing gap between the middle and the bottom of the wage distribution during the 1987–91 period. And Kahn (1998a) finds that a fall in the price of skills contributed importantly to this reduction in inequality, as would be expected based on the wage policies adopted by the union federation in this period. Moreover, while the supply of and demand for skills in Norway changed similarly in both the 1980–83 and 1987–91 periods, in the earlier period, when bargaining was being decentralized, the return to skills rose. These comparisons of Norway with Sweden and of Norway during a period of recentralization with Norway during a period of decentralization provide evidence that the change in Norway's bargaining structure did narrow wage differentials.

As was the case in Sweden, this intervention in wage-setting procedures in Norway during the 1987–91 period also appears to have had relative employment effects. Specifically, less-educated workers, whose relative wages were sharply raised, suffered relative employment declines during these years. It is possible that these relative employment changes were due to the recession that occurred at that time, rather than to the wage policy. However, during an earlier recession period in which bargaining had become less centralized (1980–83), the relative wages of less-educated workers declined and their relative employment levels actually increased among men, while remaining constant among women. Again, the "differences in differences" framework provides some support for the notion that there are negative employment effects of union wage policies.[25]

Two cases in which the government passed laws that were apparently designed to reduce union power, the United Kingdom in the 1980s and New Zealand in 1991, enable us to examine the impact on employment of reductions in the extent of collective bargaining. While the United Kingdom intervention appears to have affected the wage structure, it is less obvious that New Zealand's reforms did. Furthermore, the effects of these reforms on employment are also mixed.

In the United Kingdom, the Thatcher reforms constituted a many-faceted program designed to move the economy toward a laissez-faire ideal (Blanchflower and Freeman 1994), including a variety of policy interventions, such as abolishing closed shops and limiting union picketing, as well as reducing the generosity of the welfare state by lowering the UI replacement ratio (i.e., after tax UI benefits as a fraction of after tax wages) and eliminating wages councils. The combination of many reforms along a variety of dimensions in the case of the United Kingdom makes it difficult to single out the impact of any one reform. Nonetheless, the Thatcher programs together appear to have had a strong negative effect on union coverage in the United Kingdom (Freeman and Pelletier 1990). For example, OECD (1997) data show declines in union density (the fraction of wage and salary workers who are union members) in the United Kingdom from 50 percent in 1980 to 39 percent in 1990, with an even larger absolute and relative fall in collective bargaining coverage during this time from 70 percent to 47 percent. And there is evidence of an impact on wages of these changes. David G. Blanchflower and Richard B. Freeman (1994) find that the responsiveness of wages and employment at the microlevel to demand changes increased. Moreover, OECD (1996) wage inequality data indicate a sharp increase in British inequality during this period. Using microdata that allow him to control for worker heterogeneity, John Schmitt (1995) attributes a moderate portion (13 to 21 percent) of the increase in British wage inequality in the 1980s to declining unionization.

In contrast to the evidence that the reduction in unionization in the United Kingdom raised wage inequality, there is mixed evidence on the employment effects of the Thatcher program. On the one hand, a study from the early 1990s found that this program was not successful in lowering unemployment generally or in raising transitions out of unemployment (Blanchflower and Freeman 1994). Moreover, union relative wage effects remained in the early 1990s at about 10 percent, a relatively high level by international standards, implying that the power of union members was still a force with which to contend (Blanchflower 1996).

On the other hand, a more recent study (Nickell and van Ours 2000) notes that, in the United Kingdom, the OECD-standardized unemployment rate fell from 10.9 percent during the 1983–88 period to 8.9 percent during the 1989–94 period and was further reduced by early 1999 to 6.2 percent. This is one of the largest cumulative reductions in unemployment in the OECD. The authors attribute important portions of this unemployment decline to reductions in union density and union coverage, with smaller contributions from reductions in taxes and in UI benefit replacement rates. It is possible that the Thatcher reforms had delayed effects in lowering unemployment. For example, with such a comprehensive reform program, it may have taken several years for workers' and firms' norms of wage setting to shift to the new freer market environment. Thus, developments in the UK in the late 1990s may be an example of changing social norms in response to changing economic incentives, as discussed by Assar Lindbeck, Sten Nyberg, and Jorgen W. Weibull (1999).

Like the UK experience, the New Zealand Employment Contracts Act (ECA) of 1991 appears to have substantially reduced union power. However, unlike the British reforms, while it is not clear whether the ECA has caused a widening of the wage distribution, there is some evidence suggesting that it did have positive employment effects. The ECA legislation outlawed compulsory unionism and abolished national wage awards (Maloney 1994). Union density declined precipitously after 1991, presumably in response to the legislation. For example, prior to the ECA, union density was slightly rising from 43.5 percent in December 1985 to 44.7 percent in September 1989, and then fell modestly to 41.5 percent in May 1991, the month during which the ECA took effect (Crawford, Harbridge, and Walsh 1999). However, after the passage of the ECA, union density plummeted to 28.8 percent by December 1992; by December 1998, union membership had decreased to 17.7 percent, only slightly above the U.S. level. And collective bargaining coverage plunged from 67 percent in 1990 to 31 percent in 1994 (OECD 1997).

One would of course expect this legislation to have also increased wage inequality. And there is indeed some evidence that the returns to human capital and residual inequality both increased in New Zealand over the 1984–97 period (Dixon 1998). But wage inequality overall and the returns to human capital rose substantially faster during the pre-ECA 1984–90 period than over the 1990–97 period, a comparison that does not suggest a major impact of the ECA on the wage distribution (1998).[26] It is still possible that the ECA had some effect on wage inequality, since, during the 1984–90 period, New Zealand instituted many market-oriented reforms that would themselves have been expected to raise wage inequality. For example, industrial subsidies were reduced, exchange controls were eliminated, import protection was decreased, capital markets were deregulated, and many government enterprises were privatized (Evans et al. 1996; Cowen 1993; Lang 1998). It is therefore possible that both the 1984–90 reforms and the ECA raised wage inequality, with a larger effect for the earlier legislation. But the direct evidence in favor of an effect of the ECA on wage inequality is not overwhelming.

In contrast to this mixed picture of the impact of the ECA on the wage distribution, there does appear to be some evidence that it generated employment. Since the ECA was implemented starting in May 1991 at different rates across different industries due to different contract expiration dates, one can estimate its effect by using the industries that had not yet implemented the changes as a control group. Using this research design, Tim Maloney (1994) finds that the law sharply reduced union coverage and raised employment. However, relative wages were unaffected, implying that fringe benefits or changes in work rules were the mechanism for increasing employment.

Finally, there are two additional interesting case studies examining the impact of wage-setting interventions through the collective bargaining system. First, Steve Nickell and Jan van Ours (2000) studied the steady, remarkable fall in Dutch unemployment from 10.5 percent during the 1983–88 period to 3.4 percent in early 1999. The authors attribute the largest portion of this decline to the agreement by Dutch unions in the early 1980s to practice wage restraint, an agreement whose implementation was facilitated by the Netherlands' centralized wage-setting institutions. A smaller role in explaining the falling unemployment rate there was played by a combination of the expansion of active labor market policies, a reduction in UI benefit replacement ratios, and a reduction in labor tax rates. Second, Steven G. Allen, Adriana Cassoni, and Gaston J. Labadie (1996) studied wages and employment in Uruguay from 1983 to 1991, a period before and after the 1985 relegalization of collective bargaining, which had been outlawed after the establishment of a military regime in 1973. They find that wages grew more and employment grew less in more unionized industries, a result consistent with a negative union employment effect.

Evidence from Specific Country Comparisons

Several studies on the impact of institutions make detailed comparisons using microdata for two or three countries that have different institutions or different types of changes in their wage-setting institutions. This research uses one country as a control for the country that has more interventionist institutions or has a larger increase in the degree of intervention in the labor market. One of the best examples of such analyses is work that compares Canada and United States, two countries that have similar economic and labor force structures and are major trading partners, but have very different degrees of unionization. For example, union density and collective bargaining coverage remained relatively constant at between 36 percent and 38 percent over the 1980–94 period in Canada, but fell from 22 percent to 16 percent (density) and 26 percent to 18 percent (coverage) in the United States (OECD 1997).

Thomas Lemieux (1993) studied the impact of unionization on the differences between Canadian and American wage inequality in the 1980s and in the change in inequality in the two countries over the 1980s. He finds that, among men, U.S.-Canadian differences in union coverage accounted for 40 percent of the difference in wage dispersion between the two countries in the 1980s.[27] Over the 1980s, wage inequality increased considerably more in the United States than in Canada. For example, between 1979 and 1987 the variance of the log of male full-time, full-year earnings rose by 0.034 in the United States, compared to only 0.018 in Canada (Blackburn and Bloom 1993, 254). And, as we have seen, union density fell in the United States relative to Canada over the 1980s. Using an accounting framework similar to the one underlying Table 7.5, Lemieux finds that this decrease was responsible for 40 to 45 percent of the growth in wage inequality in the United States relative to Canada. This closely matches the magnitude of his estimate of the impact of union density in explaining the difference in wage dispersion between the United States and Canada at a point in time.[28]

While Lemieux's results suggest that unionization is an important factor explaining differences in wage inequality between the United States and Canada, it is possible that the differences in the degree of unionization between the two countries represent, at least in part, the effect of different market forces. If this is true, it is thus possible that Lemieux's results are the upper bounds for the true effect of unionization. In this regard, some results for the Canada-U.S. comparison provide some reassurance. W. Craig Riddell (1993) finds that the higher degree of unionism in Canada than in the United States is primarily due to the more favorable legal environment there, rather than to differences in the structure of the economy. For this case at least, we have some confidence that there really is an independent effect of unionization.

Four comparisons of wage and employment changes across labor force groups in the United States and Germany or the United States, Canada, and France reach conflicting conclusions about whether the decentralized wage-setting environment in the United States has contributed to better relative employment outcomes for the less skilled in the United States over the 1980s and 1990s. However, they all agree that the U.S. wage-setting system contributed to faster growth in wage inequality in the United States than elsewhere. First, Richard B. Freeman and Ronald Schettkat (2000) find that, in the 1990s, low-skill male workers in Germany had high wages but low employment relative to men with middle levels of skills in comparison to the analogous contrasts in the United States. They also find that, from the 1970s to the 1990s, the relative wages of low-skill men fell in the United States compared to Germany, while their relative employment fell in Germany compared to the United States. These findings were interpreted as reflecting the effects of German unions in pushing up wages of the less-skilled but causing employment problems for them. While unions evidently had an effect on relative employment in Germany, Freeman and Schettkat (2000) find that this impact could account for only a relatively small portion of the higher overall German unemployment rate relative to the United States in the 1990s.

In contrast to Freeman and Schettkat's (2000) findings, studies by David Card, Francis Kramarz, and Thomas Lemieux (1999) for the United States, France, and Canada and Alan B. Krueger and Jörn-Steffen Pischke (1997) for the United States and Germany produce results that do not suggest negative union employment effects. The authors compare the change in relative employment and wages by skill level in the 1980s for heavily unionized and less unionized countries under the premise that the decline in the demand for low-skill workers was common to all of these nations, but that wage-setting institutions would moderate the effects of this decline. They find that relative wages were indeed more rigid in the more unionized countries (France relative to Canada and the United States; Canada relative to the United States; and Germany relative to the United States); however, relative employment of low-skill workers compared to that of high-skill workers in Canada and France in virtually every case did not fall in comparison to that in United States. In fact, relative employment for the low skilled generally fell in the United States compared to the other two countries. And low-skilled workers' relative employment actually rose in Germany, in contrast to its fall in the United States. The authors conclude that while unions can reduce or even eliminate the impact of adverse demand shifts on low-skilled workers' relative wages, based on the authors' point estimates, there was no evidence of adverse relative employment effects due to such union policies.

Finally, Blau and Kahn (2000b) also find that for young Germans and young Americans during the 1984–91 period, the less skilled in Germany did better with respect to both relative wages and employment than their American counterparts. We speculate that differences in public-sector employment could in part be responsible for this difference (we will elaborate on this point later on).

It is possible that the contradictory findings for the various German-U.S. studies discussed earlier could be due in part to differences in the definition of skill or in the samples studied. However, overall these intercountry comparisons provide mixed evidence on the employment effects of centralized wage-setting systems over the 1980s and 1990s.

The Effect of Government Intervention in Wage Setting: Wage Indexation and Minimum Wages

While collective bargaining institutions comprise the focus of our investigation, two other closely related institutions that have also apparently exerted an important effect on the wage structure bear mentioning in this context. First, Italy's system of wage indexation, the *scala mobile,* which was in place from 1975 to 1992, evidently led to considerable wage compression. This was a nationally mandated cost of living adjustment that explicitly gave low-paid workers larger relative increases than others (Erickson and Ichino 1995). Evidence of the impact of this policy is provided by comparing Italy to other countries. There was rapid inflation from 1975 to 1983 in Italy, averaging 10 to 20 percent per year, yet wage inequality fell sharply during this time, in contrast to virtually all other OECD countries (OECD 1993). Moreover, through 1987 the Italian wage distribution did not widen, in contrast to the United States and many other countries, even though supply of and demand for skills in Italy changed in qualitatively similar ways to the American experience (Erickson and Ichino 1995, 296). And wage inequality in Italy sharply increased after 1992, when the scala mobile expired (OECD 1996), again suggesting an effect of this institution on the wage structure. A study of the employment effects of Italy's indexation system would be very interesting and informative, but unfortunately has not yet been undertaken.

Second, minimum wage legislation clearly impacts the bottom of the wage distribution and therefore is expected to have a disproportionate effect on low-wage workers, including youth and women. Much evidence on the impact of minimum wages looks for spikes in the wage distribution around the legal required minimum. For example, Card and Krueger (1995) find for U.S. teenagers that, in 1989, when the federal minimum wage was $3.35 per hour, there was a spike at $3.35, which was the largest mass point in the teenage wage histogram; by 1991 when the minimum had risen to $4.25 per hour, there was again a spike in the teenage wage distribution at the new minimum wage, which was higher than any other spike in the histogram. This evidence provides a prima facie case for an effect of minimum wages on the teenage wage distribution. Furthermore, using a full-distributional simulation technique, John E. DiNardo, Nicole M. Fortin, and Thomas Lemieux (1996) attribute 30 to 70 percent of the 1979–88 period widening in the 50–10 log wage gap in the United States to falling real minimum wages. And Blau and Kahn (1997) conclude that falling real minimum wages over this period retarded the progress of low-skill women's wages relative to low-skill men's.

Similar findings are obtained in studies analyzing the impact of minimum wages in other countries. A study by Stephen Machin and Alan Manning (1994) of the impact of wage councils in the UK for the 1979–90 period finds that, when minimum wages were raised, the distribution of pay for affected workers became more compressed. Similarly, Lawrence F. Katz, Gary W. Loveman, and David G. Blanchflower (1995) conclude that rising French minimum wages in the 1980s were an important reason why France's wage distribution was stable in the face of demand shifts that were similar to those in other countries where wage inequality widened.

Other evidence that minimum wages have had an impact on the wage distribution in several OECD countries is presented by Juan Dolado et al. (1996). For example, they show that, in France, regional wage dispersion fell dramatically when the national minimum wage was raised sharply in the 1980s. In the Netherlands, between 1981 and 1983, official youth subminimum wages were substantially lowered: for example, the minimum for twenty year olds fell from 77.5 percent of adult minimum to 61.5 percent, and for sixteen year olds, the fraction fell from 47.5 percent to 34.5 percent. As a consequence, while average nominal wages rose 9 percent from 1980 to 1984 for those aged twenty-three and over, who were not affected by these changes, they fell for those less than twenty-three years old (345).

In general, the impact of minimum wage mandates on wage distributions has not been the subject of much controversy. Most economists believe that a minimum wage that is binding will bring up the bottom of the wage distribution. Considerably more controversy has surrounded the issue of the employment effects of increases in the minimum wage. Generally, the minimum wage is too low to affect major portions of the labor market, although specific subgroups such as teenagers may be more directly affected than workers in general by legislated minimum wage increases. Most of the research on the impact of minimum wages finds little evidence of negative employment effects, and when these have been found, they are generally too small to have an important effect on the labor market.[29]

Early research in a time-series framework for the United States, based on minimum wage changes in the 1960s and 1970s, finds that, for teenagers, a 10 percent increase in the minimum wage led to a 1 to 3 percent fall in teenage employment. However, this research is criticized on the grounds that the measure of minimum wage changes was itself negatively confounded with overall demand changes, since it included average wages in the denominator. This could have induced a negative estimated employment effect even if in fact minimum wages had no impact on employment (Card, Katz, and Krueger 1994; Card and Krueger 1995). More recent research looks for appropriate control groups against which to compare the employment changes of teenagers or other low-wage workers who are most likely to be affected by minimum wage increases. Much of this work finds either no effect[30] or in some cases a positive effect on employment of increasing the minimum wage (Card and Krueger 1995, 2000). Some recent research on minimum wages in the United States continues to find negative effects, including David Neumark and William Wascher (1992, 2000), Donald Deere, Kevin M. Murphy, and Finis Welch (1995), and Richard V. Burkhauser, Kenneth A. Couch, and David D. Wittenburg (2000), although only the Deere, Murphy, and Welch (1995) study reports a large disemployment effect. Specifically, the authors find that after the 1990 and 1991 minimum wage increases in the United States, youth employment fell sharply relative to adults. However, such an outcome could also have been explained by the recession of the early 1990s having a disproportionate negative effect on youth. When a positive effect on employment of increasing the minimum wage is found, it is interpreted as possible evidence of employer monopsony, as have similar findings by Manning (1996) for the employment effect of policies designed to combat sex discrimination in the UK. Of course, a zero effect on employment is also consistent with employer monopsony, but not with the conventional competitive demand model.

Minimum wage research for other countries also finds evidence of negative effects in some cases, with little reported impact in other instances. For example, John M. Abowd et al. (2000) report that French minimum wage increases in the 1980s lowered the employment of workers at the minimum relative to a control group just above the minimum. The effects on workers at the minimum were large, but since they comprised a small portion of the labor force, the impact on total employment was small. However, an alternative analysis of France during the 1967–85 period in which minimum wages were substantially raised finds that employment growth was actually higher in regions most affected by minimum wage increases (Dolado et al. 1996). While such a finding could have been caused by the relocation of businesses to low-wage regions (a long-run adjustment that could occur even if minimum wage increases affected these regions disproportionately), it does not suggest a negative employment impact of raising the minimum wage.

Some evidence compatible with negative employment effects of the minimum wage comes from the Netherlands where, from 1981 to 1983, youth subminimum wages were sharply lowered. Dolado et al. (1996) do find that relative to youth employment changes in the economy overall, youth relative employment generally rose in low-paying occupations, the ones most likely to be affected by minimum wage changes. However, as the authors note, given the aggregate level of the data used, it is not clear whether such differences were statistically significant. In addition, if changes in the minimum wages in the Netherlands had an effect on youth employment, it must be the case that employers were taking advantage of the youth subminimum. Yet, previous work on the United States and the UK finds that employers do not appear to use the subminima in those countries (Machin and Manning 1994; Katz and Krueger 1992). If employers in the Netherlands also do not in general utilize the youth subminimum, the findings reported in Dolado et al. (1996) must have been caused by some factor(s) other than the change in the minimum wage law.

Evidence consistent with a negative effect of the minimum wage was also found for Spain, which sharply raised the minimum wage for youth sixteen years and under in 1990. Dolado et al. (1996) find that this policy led to a substitution of adults for youth but, paradoxically, also to increased total employment. Mixed evidence is also obtained for Canada based on the traditional time series approach. Summarizing Canadian research, Card and Krueger (1995) report that while negative effects on teenage employment were estimated for the 1956–75 period, the effects were not statistically significant for the 1976–88 period, with a negative point estimate for males and a positive one for females. A more recent study of Canadian minimum wage effects over the 1975–93 period (Baker, Benjamin, and Stanger 1999) finds a significant, yet modest negative minimum wage employment elasticity for teenagers. Finally, Machin and Manning's (1994) findings on the impact of wages councils on employment in the UK are consistent with the recent U.S. findings of zero or even positive employment effects of minimum wage increases.

Institutions and Market Forces: Toward Some Generalizations

The research on wage and employment effects of institutions reviewed and summarized earlier has consisted, by and large, of comparisons across a small number of countries and has not infrequently obtained conflicting results particularly with respect to employment effects. In this subsection, we discuss results from four recent studies that attempt to make some generalizations about the effects of institutions and market forces on wage inequality (Brunello, Comi, and Lucifora 2000), wage and employment inequality (Kahn 2000), youth employment (Neumark and Wascher 1999), or the relative employment and unemployment of youth, older individuals, and women (Bertola, Blau, and Kahn 2002b), drawing on comparisons across a large set of countries.

First, Giorgio Brunello, Simona Comi, and Claudio Lucifora used microdata from ten European countries to attempt to explain changes in the wage return to a college degree among men between the 1980s and 1990s.[31] Pooling the changes in these returns for different cohorts and countries, the authors regressed these changes on a cohort dummy, the change in the relative supply of the education group, the growth of labor productivity, the change in a demand index for the group, indicators for whether employment protection became more strict and whether bargaining became more centralized, and union density.[32] Although the regression had only twenty observations, the authors' findings with these seven variables are remarkably strong. Falling supply, rising demand, rising labor productivity, less strict employment protection, less centralized bargaining, and falling union density each had a positive effect on the college wage premium, and these were usually statistically significant. The authors thus find evidence that both institutions and market forces influenced relative wages in the expected direction.

Second, using ISSP data for fifteen countries from the period 1985 to 1994, Kahn (2000) formed skill groups—separately by gender for each country and year[33]—that were based on such measured human capital characteristics such as education, age, and marital status. He then analyzed the determinants of wage inequality and differences in the log of the employment-to-population ratio across these skill groups. For each year, skill groups were formed using the distribution of predicted wages from wage regressions estimated on a sample of workers pooled across countries (each country received the same weight). The low-skilled group consisted of the bottom third, the middle-skilled group consisted of the middle third, and the high-skilled group consisted of the top third of the predicted wage distribution. These fractions were computed with respect to the entire multicountry sample of men or women for that year, with each country getting the same weight. Thus, for example, one country might have had more or less than a third of its men or women in the low-skill group.

Given the evidence linking union pay setting to wage floors that have their largest effects on the bottom of the pay distribution, Kahn concentrated on comparing the middle to the bottom third of the predicted wage distribution (i.e., the middle-skill to the low-skill groups).

In order to determine whether there was a general relationship between collective bargaining institutions and wages and employment, Kahn estimated a variety of regression models separately by gender. The dependent variable was either the middle-low log wage differential or the middle-low log employment-to-population ratio differential for a given country in a given year. The major explanatory variables of interest were measures of unionization, such as collective bargaining coverage, union density, and indicators of the degree of coordination of wage setting. Kahn also included a variety of control variables that allow one to place a sharper interpretation on the unionization indicators, including the overall unemployment rate, year dummy variables, characteristics of the unemployment insurance system, the degree of mandated job protection, characteristics of the retirement system, as well as indicators of the supply of and demand for workers in the two skill groups.[34]

The results of these regressions provide considerable evidence for the importance of wage-setting institutions in influencing relative wages for both men and women and relative employment, particularly for men. First, for both men and women, moving from U.S. to other country averages for union coverage, union density and coordination caused a statistically significant reduction in middle-low wage differentials in every case. Second, in most of cases, changing from U.S. values of the unionization variables to the other country averages widened the employment differential between middle- and low-skill men, all else being equal. Third, there was mixed evidence of a similar employment effect for women, with four of six effects positive but only two of them statistically significant.

The stronger effects obtained for men than women in this study may reflect stronger collective bargaining institutions in male sectors of the economy such as manufacturing and construction. In addition, while we would like to interpret the relative employment effects as indicating employer demand, it is also possible that they are influenced by movements along labor supply schedules: higher relative wages may bring people into the labor force. This effect is likely to be stronger for women, whose labor supply is known to be more elastic than men's (Blundell and MaCurdy 1999). It is thus possible that higher relative wages could actually raise their employment-to-population ratio.

In evaluating these findings, we note that it is possible that interventionist collective bargaining institutions are negatively correlated with unmeasured heterogeneity of skills of the population. If so, this could help explain Kahn's finding of a negative effect of these institutions on wage differentials. However, such reasoning cannot explain the positive of collective bargaining, coordination, and so on, on employment differentials by skill group.

Finally, Kahn finds that while the wage compression effects were very strong for both younger and less educated workers, the employment problems identified in the results described earlier were concentrated among the young for both men and women. Collective bargaining institutions did not in fact lead to relative employment problems for the less educated. These differential effects by age and education will be relevant later on, when we consider alternative public policy and market responses to employment loss.

The United States has a relatively high employment-to-population ratio for less-skilled men, which according to Kahn (2000) was 0.79 in the United States compared to a non-U.S. average of 0.68. However, it is well known that a larger fraction of U.S. men are incarcerated than elsewhere, and this difference is likely to be particularly large for those with low labor market skills (Freeman 1996; Western and Beckett 1999). Specifically, Bruce Western and Katherine Beckett (1999) estimate that during the 1992–93 period, 519 adults per 100,000 were incarcerated in the United States, compared to an average of only 78 across a sample of 13 other OECD countries. Furthermore, over 90 percent of these individuals were men. It is therefore possible that the relatively high employment-to-population ratio for less-skilled U.S. men reflects the U.S.-other country difference in prison populations rather than labor demand effects.

To see if this factor could explain his results, Kahn performed some calculations making the extreme assumptions that all inmates are low skilled and that, if they had been released from prison, none of them would have found jobs. He further assumed that all inmates were men. Under these assumptions, the U.S. employment-to-population ratio for the less skilled fell from 0.79 to 0.77, or about 18 percent of the difference in employment-to-population ratios between the United States and the other countries. Thus, even making the most extreme assumptions about the employability of the prison population, the high incarceration rates in the United States can account for at most a small fraction of its higher employment-to-population ratio. Of course, prisoners probably would have had lower wage offers as well as lower employment than those not in prison, so consideration of the incarcerated would likely raise wage differentials between the middle and low skilled in the United States, which, of course, were already quite high.

Third, Neumark and Wascher (1999) use aggregate data to study the impact of minimum wages across sixteen OECD countries over the 1975–97 period. They find that higher minimum wages reduce youth employment, particularly when these wages are set in collective bargaining agreements.

Finally, using data from seventeen OECD countries over the 1960–96 period, Giuseppe Bertola, Francine D. Blau, and Lawrence M. Kahn (2002b) studied the impact of institutions on the relative employment of youth, women, and older individuals. Regressing relative employment and unemployment outcomes on an age structure indicator, a standard set of labor market institutions, aggregate unemployment, and period and country effects, they find for both men and women that more extensive involvement of unions in wage setting significantly decreases the employment rate of young and older individuals relative to the prime-aged, with no significant effects on the relative unemployment of these groups. In contrast, a larger role for unions has insignificant effects on male-female employment differentials, but does raise female unemployment relative to male unemployment. This pattern of results suggests that union wage-setting policies price the young and elderly out of employment and drive disemployed individuals in these groups to nonlabor force (education and retirement) states. The situation for women is more complex. A possible scenario is that high union wages encourage female labor force participation, but that women who would otherwise be disemployed by high union wage floors are able to find work in unregulated sectors or are absorbed by public employment. Taken together, these results suggest that unionization leads to either lower employment or higher unemployment of so-called outsiders (groups other than prime-age men), even controlling for country-specific effects.

Policy and Behavioral Responses to Employment Problems

As outlined earlier, there is mixed evidence on the impact of wage-setting institutions on the relative employment of the less skilled. Countries differ greatly on the degree to which they use government as a tool to bolster the employment of workers who are having trouble finding work (Nickell and Layard 1999). These active labor market policies include a variety of measures to improve the chances that these workers will find employment, such as training and relocation subsidies to workers, hiring subsidies to firms, and direct job creation by the public sector.

Several country studies indicate that government employment may camouflage some of the negative effects on employment of wage-setting institutions that we would otherwise observe. Moreover, an additional response to employment problems is to share the work, and European countries appear to place a greater emphasis on work sharing than is true in the United States. Also, temporary employment contracts appear to be more prevalent in Europe than in the United States (Blau and Kahn 1999), which may provide another way to bolster employment for particular groups in the face of rigid wages. Finally, in some countries, particularly Italy and Spain, there is a very large "unregulated" sector that can serve as an outlet for workers and firms shut out of the regulated sector by the high cost of doing business by the rules. This includes both those employed in the "underground" economy where employment regulations are flouted and the self-employed who are, by and large, exempt from these regulations. European labor markets may thus be more flexible in practice than they would appear at first blush. And actual employment to population ratios may be higher in such countries than official statistics and survey data indicate.

One mark of flexibility is the degree to which labor inputs are allowed to vary in response to changes in demand. And job creation and destruction are both much less rapid in Europe than in the United States, implying less flexible labor allocation in Europe. However, Katharine G. Abraham and Susan N. Houseman (1994) and Marc A. Van Audenrode (1994) note that, in several European countries, workers can much more easily collect short-time compensation from the government than is the case in the United States. An implication of this difference is that in Europe, hours per worker adjustments are in fact more cyclically sensitive than in the United States, in contrast to the greater sensitivity of employment to demand in the United States. The result of these offsetting patterns is that, in the 1980s, the adjustment of total production worker hours was similar in West Germany, France, and Belgium to that in the United States (Abraham and Houseman 1994).

The European practice of hours flexibility may actually provide more income insurance than does the U.S. practice of employment adjustments, since, in the former, a 10 percent cut in total labor input, for example, gets shared across all workers, while in the United States, it is more likely to be concentrated on those who become laid off.[35] And, of course, as discussed earlier, European UI benefits are more generous than those in the United States. Furthermore, the greater incidence of national health insurance in Europe implies that finding work is less important for obtaining health care there.[36] Therefore, while unemployment is much more prevalent in Europe than in the United States, it appears to have less severe consequences for poverty.

While Europe appears better able to tolerate high unemployment, it is also true that European governments intervene to a greater extent in order to shore up employment than is the case in the United States. The public sector employs a larger share of workers in several European countries than it does in the United States, and many of these countries spend considerably larger amounts per unemployed worker (in relation to output per worker) on training and relocation programs than is true in the United States.[37] And, although the size of the public sector undoubtedly reflects the demand of the electorate for publicly produced services, the government has also been explicitly used in some countries to provide employment for those out of work. For example, in Sweden and Norway government employment of unskilled workers has been found to increase during periods of wage compression, in which the wages of workers at the bottom of the distribution have been raised the most. This government hiring may serve to limit the disemployment effects of union wage bargaining (Edin and Topel 1997; Björklund and Freeman 1997; Kahn 1998a). Similarly, in the late 1980s government employment has been found to be more prevalent, both absolutely and relative to other groups, among less-skilled youth in Germany than among such young people in the United States (Blau and Kahn 2000b). Again, the group most likely to be shut out by high union wages for the low end of the wage distribution was more likely to find government employment. We will return to the issue of these responses to employment problems shortly. The prevalence of these responses may partly explain why there is mixed evidence on the impact of wage-setting institutions on employment.

Can we generalize about the use of public employment for the less skilled as a way to alleviate potential employment problems where there are high wage floors? Kahn (2000) investigated this issue by estimating the effect of a country's level of unionization on the relative propensity of the young or the less educated to be employed in the government. He finds only limited evidence that such behavior characterized countries with high levels of collective bargaining coverage or union density in general. Most of the time, the effects were insignificant, but there were some positive effects in some models for young men, less-educated women, and less-educated men. The latter two findings, while not robust, may help explain why he does not find that unionization affected the relative employment of the less educated even though it raised their relative wages. The government may be picking up the slack. Nonetheless, overall the evidence that public employment is disproportionately an outlet for the young or the less educated in highly unionized countries is fragile. This response to employment problems, then, appears to be concentrated in Scandinavia and perhaps Germany.

In addition to the possibility of public employment, another possible response to problems in the job market, at least for younger individuals, is to stay in school longer. Kahn (2000) investigated this by estimating the determinants of a country's average incidence of school enrollment of men and women aged eighteen to thirty as a function of the same kinds of explana-- tory variables used to study wages and employment for these groups. Collective bargaining coverage had a large, positive effect on school enrollment that was usually statistically significant.

These results for enrollment indicate that, in more heavily unionized economies, school attendance is more prevalent among younger individuals, other things being equal. This is a striking finding given that Kahn finds strong evidence that unions raise the relative pay of young men, and some evidence that they increase the pay of young women and the less educated as well. If there were no constraints on finding a job, we would expect these wage results to lead to *less* school enrollment. As noted earlier, this appears to have happened in Sweden in the solidarity wage period (1968–83), when relatively high-paying jobs for the less skilled were abundant (Edin and Holmlund 1995).

The difference between Kahn's findings and those of Edin and Holmlund is likely due to the fact that, in contrast to the experience during the Swedish solidarity wage period, young people, especially young men, in highly union-ized economies faced severe employment problems in the OECD countries over the 1980s and 1990s. Not only is the opportunity cost of attending school lower when few jobs are available, but obtaining higher levels of education may be the only way for many to eventually get a job at all. Such reasoning applies strongly for younger men, but less strongly for younger women, for whom Kahn finds the negative relative employment effects of unionization were less often statistically significant. The basic finding that union wage setting is positively associated with school attendance is consis-tent with Jonas Agell and Kjell Erik Lommerud's (1997) theoretical model of human capital investment in an economy with high minimum (i.e., ad-ministered) wages. In particular, the authors argue that school can raise one's employability when jobs are rationed due to wage floors.[38]

Conclusion

In this chapter, we examined microeconomic evidence on the impact of col-lective bargaining on the wage structure and on the relative employment of different skill groups. We found abundant evidence that collective bargain-ing and minimum wage laws lead to wage compression and help explain the higher level of wage inequality in the United States than we see in other countries. Collective bargaining appears to have stronger effects on the overall labor market than minimum wages do. We also found that the distribution of labor market skills is more diverse in the United States than it is elsewhere and that workers with low skill levels are more abundant in the United States in relation to the demand for their services than is the case elsewhere. While these market-oriented factors are important, there is also strong evidence of an effect of wage-setting institutions on the wage structure that remains af-ter these factors are taken into account. Moreover, recent research finds a negative association across countries between unionization and inequality in family income, suggesting that the institutional effects we found on wages also apply to living standards (Bradley et al. 2002).

Our examination of the impact of institutions on employment yielded less clear-cut results than we found for the wage structure. In many cases, union- or minimum-wage–induced wage compression was seen to lower the relative employment of the less skilled. In other cases, such effects were not evident. What negative employment effects unions have appear to be concentrated on the young. And, OECD data also show that the young had lower relative employment in 1998 and more adverse changes in their relative employment over the 1979–98 period in the European Union than in the United States (OECD 1996, 2000). Increasingly in the high unemployment European economy of the 1980s and 1990s, the young were outside the protected labor markets that provide high wages and benefit levels. Integrating the young into work is a major challenge for these countries in the coming years (Blanchflower and Freeman 2000). Conversely, in the United States wage inequality has increased both absolutely and relatively over the 1980s and the 1990s and is currently the highest in the industrialized world. Raising the living standards of the less skilled in the United States, without causing major damage to the job-generation process, is thus a major challenge facing the United States.

Notes

This chapter draws on portions from Francine D. Blau and Lawrence M. Kahn, "Labor Market Institutions, Relative Wages, and Employment: Microeconomic Evidence," in *At Home and Abroad: U.S. Labor-Market Performance in International Perspective* (New York: Russell Sage Foundation, 2002). The authors thank John Heywood and conference participants for helpful comments and suggestions.

1. These figures are taken from OECD (1983).

2. The countries were Australia, Austria, Belgium, Canada, Denmark, Finland, France, Germany, Italy, Japan, the Netherlands, New Zealand, Norway, Portugal, Spain, Sweden, Switzerland, and the UK.

3. It should be pointed out that some European-style institutions may reduce the impact of shocks on unemployment in Europe compared to the United States. For example, several authors find evidence suggesting that highly coordinated wage-setting regimes (as those that occur in many European countries) may lead to wage restraint as unions take into account the effects of their wage bargains on the overall wage-employment trade-off (Nickell and Layard 1999; Blanchard and Wolfers 2000; Bertola, Blau, and Kahn 2002a). Despite this countervailing factor characterizing many European countries, Bertola, Blau and Kahn (2002a) found that, when they took the overall institutional differences between the United States and other OECD countries into account, adverse macroeconomic shocks had much larger effects in raising unemployment in other OECD countries than in the United States.

4. This argument assumes that employment is on the labor demand curve. Under some wage-setting arrangements, including efficient bargaining and employer monopsony, theory does not necessarily predict that higher relative wages lead to lower relative employment. See Farber (1986) and Card and Krueger (1995).

5. Recent work by political scientists using macrolevel data finds that union cov-

erage and centralization of wage setting are associated with lower wage inequality, other things being equal, a result that is consistent with the studies we review later on using microdata. See Rueda, Way, and Pontusson (1998) and Wallerstein (1999).

6. Until the 1990s, the United States had a higher gender pay gap than most other OECD countries, and we find that this difference was largely due to the greater wage compression elsewhere caused by union-negotiated wage floors. By the 1990s, the U.S. gender pay gap was about the same as that elsewhere, but we find that with other countries' level of wage compression, the U.S. gap would be much smaller than that in other countries. See Blau and Kahn (1996b, 2000c, 2002).

7. In addition, this unexplained portion of international differences in wage inequality includes differences in the distribution of measurement errors.

8. Union membership information was not available for Australia, Italy, or Sweden. In each case, a U.S. wage equation was estimated, in that each had the same explanatory variables as were available for the country in question, allowing for comparisons of the pay structure between the United States and each of the other countries.

9. In performing the decomposition, we used the U.S. wage coefficients and residual distribution to obtain the measured characteristics effect and the other country distribution of measured characteristics to obtain the wage equation and wage residual effects. It would also be possible to perform the decomposition using the opposite set of weights (i.e., evaluating the U.S.-other country difference in measured characteristics at the other country's wage equation and residual distribution and the wage equation and wage residual effects at the U.S. distribution of personal characteristics). When we used these opposite weights, we obtained very similar results to those presented in Table 7.1. The decomposition is described in greater detail in Blau and Kahn (1996a).

10. To some degree, union status, while treated here as a measured characteristic in panel B of Table 7.1, could be considered part of the wage setting institutions. The effects of collective bargaining are discussed in more detail later on.

11. For example, see Shapiro and Stiglitz (1984) and Krueger and Summers (1988).

12. For example, while several argue that at least a portion of these wage differentials represents unequal pay for equally qualified workers, that is, efficiency wages (Krueger and Summers 1988; Gibbons and Katz 1992), others argue that such wage differentials are largely caused by unmeasured differences in labor quality (Murphy and Topel 1990). Abowd, Kramarz, and Margolis (1999) use matched individual and firm-level data to find that much of interindustry wage differentials are ultimately due to individual rather than firm effects.

13. For further details on the technique employed to estimate these effects and consideration of related methodological issues, see Krueger and Summers (1988), Haisken-DeNew and Schmidt (1997), and Kahn (1998b).

14. For further description of the IALS, see OECD (1998).

15. All reported correlations are based on calculations using sampling weights.

16. In addition to the countries listed in Table 7.3, the IALS collected test score data on Germany, Poland, and Northern Ireland, and data on earnings were available in the IALS for Germany and Poland. We excluded Germany because, in our version of the IALS data, the sample size was extremely small for cases in which earnings data were available, East and West Germany were not distinguished, and the earnings distributions we obtained were not comparable to other sources. We excluded Poland because of its status as a transition economy. We show test scores for Britain alone rather than including Northern Ireland in order to have a more homogeneous sample.

17. These standard deviations are computed on the pooled male and female regression samples, where each country is given the same weight. That is, each individual is given a weight of $s/(Ns_a)$, where s is the individual's sampling weight; N is his or her country's sample size; and s_a is his or her country's average sampling weight. The standard deviation effects reported in the text correspond to log wage coefficients on education for the United States of 0.0469 (males) and 0.0744 (females), and averages for the non-U.S. countries of 0.0181 (males) and 0.0290 (females).

18. Similar results are reported by Devroye and Freeman (2001).

19. This correction is similar in spirit to that used by Hunt (2002).

20. Much of this higher U.S. union-nonunion wage differential is due to a higher *ceteris paribus* U.S. union-nonunion wage gap rather than to differences in the personal characteristics of union and nonunion workers (Blanchflower and Freeman 1992; Blanchflower 1996). Thus, a strong causal role for the industrial relations system is suggested.

21. This will be the case if union "threat" effects dominate any negative "crowding" effects in the nonunion sector caused by the adverse employment effects of unionism. Kahn and Curme (1987) find for the United States that, other things being equal, nonunion wage dispersion was lower in highly unionized than in less unionized industries.

22. For further details on this method of decomposing the variance, see Freeman (1980), who uses it to assess the role of unionism on U.S. wage inequality; Blau and Kahn (1996a), who use it to compare wage inequality in the United States with that in several other countries; and Juhn, Murphy, and Pierce (1993), who employ it to measure the impact of industry on wage inequality in the United States.

23. The decomposition in Table 7.5 uses specific weights in order to exhaust the U.S.-other differential in log wage variance. For example, the first term uses the U.S. union and nonunion employment proportions to weight the within-sector wage variances, while the within-sector employment term uses the other country within-sector wage variances to weight the U.S.-other country differences in union density, and so on. We obtained very similar results when we used an alternative set of weights comprised of other country union and nonunion employment proportions for the first term, the U.S. within-sector variances for the second term, and so on.

24. These countries include the United States, the UK, Italy, West Germany, and Australia (Katz 1993).

25. The fact that the 1980–83 recession was weaker than the 1987–91 slump could have contributed to the worse employment outcome for less-educated workers in the latter period.

26. Dixon (1998) does not report evidence on changes in residual inequality for the 1984–90 and 1990–97 subperiods.

27. This is much larger than the effect of union density of 5 percent implied by the results in Table 7.5 if we sum the within-sector and between-sector composition effects. One way to view this difference is that Lemieux's (1993) estimate allows for an impact of union density on within-sector wage dispersion, while the accounting in Table 7.5 holds within-sector wage dispersion constant in estimating the impact of union density. Comparing the two estimates suggests a sizable impact of union density on within-sector wage dispersion. Lemieux does not present results for women.

28. In a related study, DiNardo and Lemieux (1997) attempt to explain Canada's slower growth in male log wage inequality compared to the United States over the 1981–88 period. Using a methodology similar to that employed by DiNardo, Fortin, and Lemieux (1996), they attribute about one-third of Canada's slower increase in the

log wage variance of males to the combined effects of its greater unionization rate and its more equalizing union pay effects; another third was attributed to the declining real value of the minimum wage in the United States. Again, institutions were important in explaining the different outcomes in Canada and the United States.

29. An exception is Castillo-Freeman and Freeman's (1992) study of the U.S. decision to bring minimum wage coverage to Puerto Rico starting in 1974. By 1988, about 28 percent of workers in Puerto Rico were paid within $0.05 of the U.S. minimum wage of $3.35 per hour; on the mainland, roughly 25 percent of teenagers were paid within $0.05 of the minimum at this time (Card and Krueger 1995). And in 1987, the U.S. minimum wage was about 63 percent of the average manufacturing wage in Puerto Rico, but only 34 percent on the mainland. Thus, the high minimum in Puerto Rico had the potential to greatly disrupt its labor market. Castillo-Freeman and Freeman (1992) in fact find large disemployment effects, but Krueger (1995) finds that this result is very sensitive to econometric issues such as weighting.

30. That is, in most cases a small, statistically insignificant effect whose standard errors make an effect that is large in magnitude unlikely.

31. The countries were Austria, Denmark, Finland, France, Germany, Italy, the Netherlands, Portugal, Switzerland, and the UK.

32. The demand index was essentially a measure of the degree to which the industrial structure of the country changed in a favorable way with respect to the particular education group.

33. Data were not available for each country in every year.

34. As noted earlier, the skill groups were chosen to comprise thirds of the distribution of people pooled across countries. Therefore, in a particular country, the size of, for example, the male low-skill group can deviate from one-third of the country's male population.

35. This point applies most strongly if layoffs are randomly distributed. In fact, in the United States layoffs are distributed by inverse seniority. So, the European system could actually increase the probability of income loss for more senior workers, while providing considerably more income insurance for junior workers.

36. This is in fact likely to be an additional reason (besides less generous UI systems) for a shorter duration of unemployment in the United States.

37. For discussions of public-sector employment, see Björklund and Freeman (1997), Edin and Topel (1997), Blank (1997), Blau and Kahn (2000b), and Kahn (1998a). Public employment has a lower incidence in the United States than elsewhere (Gregory and Borland 1999), while, in 1991, relative spending on active labor market programs in the United States was last out of twenty OECD countries (Nickell and Layard 1999).

38. The positive effects of unions on enrollment suggest the possibility that higher educational subsidies in heavily unionized economies could be responsible for both the enrollment and employment effects obtained for young men. However, when Kahn (2000) excludes the enrolled from the analysis of employment, he still finds that unionization and collective bargaining were associated with lower relative employment of young men and for young women as well. In addition, since school enrollment in the ISSP refers to one's major activity, it is not likely to include those in dual apprenticeship programs if they are also currently employed, as is common in Germany. Thus, the positive effects of collective bargaining on school attendance are not being driven solely by the high incidence of apprenticeship in highly unionized countries like Germany and Austria.

References

Abowd, John M., Francis Kramarz, and David N. Margolis. 1999. "High Wage Workers and High Wage Firms." *Econometrica* 67 (March): 251–333.

Abowd, John M., Francis Kramarz, Thomas Lemieux, and David Margolis. 2000. "Minimum Wages and Youth Unemployment in France and the U.S." In *Youth Employment and Joblessness in Advanced Countries*, ed. David G. Blanchflower and Richard B. Freeman, 427–472. Chicago: University of Chicago Press.

Abraham, Katharine G., and Susan N. Houseman. 1994. "Does Employment Protection Inhibit Labor Market Flexibility? Lessons from Germany, France, and Belgium." In *Social Protection versus Economic Flexibility*, ed. Rebecca Blank and Richard B. Freeman, 59–93. Chicago: University of Chicago Press.

Agell, Jonas, and Kjell Erik Lommerud. 1997. "Minimum Wages and the Incentives for Skill Formation." *Journal of Public Economics* 64 (April): 25–40.

Albaek, Karsten, Mahmood Arai, Rita Asplund, Erling Barth, and Strøjer Marsden. 1996. "Inter-industry Wage Differentials in the Nordic Countries." In *Wage Differentials in the Nordic Countries*, ed. Niels Westergård-Nielsen. Amsterdam: North-Holland.

Allen, Steven G., Adriana Cassoni, and Gaston J. Labadie. 1996. "Wages and Employment after Reunionization in Uruguay." *Cauodernos de Economia* 33 (August): 277–293.

Baker, Michael, Dwayne Benjamin, and Shuchita Stanger. 1999. "The Highs and Lows of the Minimum Wage Effect: A Time-Series Cross-section Study of the Canadian Law." *Journal of Labor Economics* 17 (April): 318–350.

Barth, Erling, and Josef Zweimüller. 1992. "Labour Market Institutions and the Industry Wage Distribution: Evidence from Austria, Norway and the U.S." *Empirica—Austrian Economic Papers* 19:181–201.

Bertola, Giuseppe, Francine D. Blau, and Lawrence M. Kahn. 2002a. "Comparative Analysis of Labor Market Outcomes: Lessons for the U.S. from International Long-Run Evidence." In *The Roaring Nineties: Can Full Employment Be Sustained?* ed. Alan B. Krueger and Alan Solow. New York: Russell Sage Foundation.

———. 2002b. "Labor Market Institutions and Demographic Employment Patterns." Unpublished paper, Cornell University and European University Institute.

Björklund, Anders, and Richard B. Freeman. 1997. "Generating Equality and Eliminating Poverty, the Swedish Way." In *The Welfare State in Transition: Reforming the Swedish Model*, ed. Richard B. Freeman, Robert Topel, and Birgitta Swedenborg, 33–78. Chicago: University of Chicago Press.

Blackburn, McKinley L., and David E. Bloom. 1993. "The Distribution of Family Income: Measuring and Explaining Changes in the 1980s for Canada and the United States." In *Small Differences That Matter*, ed. David Card and Richard B. Freeman, 233–265. Chicago: University of Chicago Press.

Blanchard, Olivier Jean, and Justin Wolfers. 2000. "The Role of Shocks and Institutions in the Rise of European Unemployment: The Aggregate Evidence." *The Economic Journal* 110 (March): 1–33.

Blanchflower, David G. 1996. "The Role and Influence of Trade Unions in the OECD." Working Paper, no. 0310. London: Centre for Economic Performance.

Blanchflower, David G., and Richard B. Freeman. 1992. "Unionism in the U.S. and Other Advanced OECD Countries." *Industrial Relations* 31 (Winter): 56–79.

———. 1994. "Did the Thatcher Reforms Change British Labor Performance?" In

The UK Labour Market: Comparative Aspects and Institutional Developments, ed. Ray Barrell, 51–92. Cambridge: Cambridge University Press.

———, ed. 2000. *Youth Employment and Joblessness in Advanced Countries.* Chicago: University of Chicago Press.

Blank, Rebecca M., ed. 1994. *Social Protection versus Economic Flexibility: Is There a Trade-off?* Chicago: University of Chicago Press.

Blank, Rebecca M. 1997. "Is There a Trade-Off Between Unemployment and Inequality? No Easy Answers: Labor Market Problems in the United States Versus Europe." Levy Economics Institute Public Policy Brief, no. 33. Annandale-on-Hudson, NY: Levy Economics Institute.

Blau, Francine D. 1977. *Equal Pay in the Office.* Lexington, MA: Lexington.

Blau, Francine D., and Lawrence M. Kahn. 1996a. "International Differences in Male Wage Inequality: Institutions Versus Market Forces." *Journal of Political Economy* 104 (August): 791–837.

———. 1996b. "Wage Structure and Gender Earnings Differentials: An International Comparison." *Economica* 63 (May): S29–S62.

———. 1997. "Swimming Upstream: Trends in the Gender Wage Differential in the 1980s." *Journal of Labor Economics* 15 (January): 1–42.

———. 1999. "Institutions and Laws in the Labor Market." In *Handbook of Labor Economics,* vol. 3A, ed. Orley C. Ashenfelter and David Card., 1399–1461. Amsterdam: Elsevier.

———. 2000a. "Do Cognitive Test Scores Explain Higher U.S. Wage Inequality?" Working Paper. Ithaca, NY: Cornell University, June.

———. 2000b. "Gender and Youth Employment Outcomes: The U.S. and West Germany, 1984–1991." In *Youth Unemployment and Joblessness in Advanced Countries,* ed. David G. Blanchflower and Richard B. Freeman, 107–167. Chicago: University of Chicago Press.

———. 2000c. "Gender Differences in Pay." *Journal of Economic Perspectives* 14 (Fall): 75–99.

———. 2002. *At Home and Abroad: U.S. Labor-Market Performance in International Perspective.* New York: Russell Sage Foundation.

———. 2003. "Understanding International Differences in the Gender Pay Gap." *Journal of Labor Economics* 21 (January): 106–144.

Blundell, Richard, and Thomas MaCurdy. 1999. "Labor Supply: A Review of Alternative Approaches." In *Handbook of Labor Economics,* vol. 3A, ed. Orley Ashenfelter and David Card, 1559–1695. Amsterdam: Elsevier.

Bradley, David, Evelyne Huber, Stephanie Moller, François Nielsen, and John Stephens. 2002. "Distribution and Redistribution in Post-industrial Democracies." Paper presented at the Cornell University workshop on Comparative Political Economy of Inequality, Ithaca, NY, April.

Brown, Charles, and James L. Medoff. 1989. "The Employer Size Wage Effect." *Journal of Political Economy* 97 (October): 1027–1059.

Brunello, Giorgio, Simona Comi, and Claudio Lucifora. 2000. "The College Wage Gap in 10 European Countries: Evidence from Two Cohorts." Unpublished paper, University of Padova.

Burkhauser, Richard V., Kenneth A. Couch, and David C. Wittenburg. 2000. "A Reassessment of the New Economics of the Minimum Wage Literature with Monthly Data from the Current Population Survey." *Journal of Labor Economics* 18 (October): 653–680.

Burkhauser, Richard V., Douglas Holtz-Eakin, and Stephen E. Rhody. 1997. "Labor Earnings Mobility and Inequality in the United States and Germany during the Growth Years of the 1980s." *International Economic Review* 38 (November): 775–794.

Card, David, Lawrence F. Katz, and Alan B. Krueger. 1994. Employment Effects of Minimum and Subminimum Wages: Panel Data on State Minimum Wage Laws: Comment." *Industrial and Labor Relations Review* 47 (April): 487–497.

Card, David, and Alan B. Krueger. 1995. *Myth and Measurement: The New Economics of the Minimum Wage.* Princeton, NJ: Princeton University Press.

Card, David, Francis Kramarz, and Thomas Lemieux. 1999. "Changes in the Relative Structure of Wages and Employment: A Comparison of the United States, Canada, and France." *Canadian Journal of Economics* 32 (August): 843–877.

———. 2000. "Minimum Wages and Employment: A Case Study of the Fast-Food Industry in New Jersey and Pennsylvania: Reply." *American Economic Review* 90 (December): 1397–1420.

Castillo-Freeman, Alida, and Richard B. Freeman. 1992. "When the Minimum Wage Really Bites: The Effect of the U.S. Level Minimum on Puerto Rico." In *Immigration and the Work Force,* ed. George J. Borjas and Richard B. Freeman, 177–211. Chicago: University of Chicago Press.

Cowen, Penelope J. Brook. 1993. "Labor Relations Reform in New Zealand: The Employment Contracts Act and Contractual Freedom." *Journal of Labor Research* 14 (Winter): 69–83.

Crawford, Aaron, Raymond Harbridge, and Pat Walsh. 1999. "Unions and Union Membership in New Zealand: Annual Review for 1998." *New Zealand Journal of Industrial Relations* 24 (October): 383–395.

Davis, Steven J., and John Haltiwanger. 1991. "Wage Dispersion Between and Within U.S. Manufacturing Plants." Working Paper, no. w3722. Cambridge, MA: National Bureau of Economic Research.

Davis, Steven J., and Magnus Henrekson. 1997. "Explaining National Differences in the Size and Industry Distribution of Employment." Working Paper. Chicago: University of Chicago Graduate School of Business.

———. 2000. "Wage-Setting Institutions As Industrial Policy." Working Paper, no. 7502. Cambridge, MA: National Bureau of Economic Research.

Deere, Donald, Kevin M. Murphy, and Finis Welch. 1995. "Employment and the 1990–1991 Minimum-Wage Hike." *American Economic Review* 85 (May): 232–237.

Devroye, Dan, and Richard B. Freeman. 2001. "Does Inequality in Skills Explain Inequality in Earnings Across Advanced Countries?" Working Paper, no. W8140. Cambridge, MA: National Bureau of Economic Research.

DiNardo, John E., Nicole M. Fortin, and Thomas Lemieux. 1996. "Labor Market Institutions and the Distribution of Wages, 1973–1992: A Semiparametric Approach." *Econometrica* 64 (September): 1001–1044.

DiNardo, John E., and Thomas Lemieux. 1997. "Diverging Male Wage Inequality in the United States and Canada, 1981–1998: Do Institutions Explain the Difference?" *Industrial and Labor Relations Review* 50 (July): 629–651.

Dixon, Sylvia. 1998. "The Growth of Earnings Inequality 1984–1997: Trends and Sources of Change." Paper presented at the Eighth Conference on Labour, Employment, and Work, Victoria University, Wellington, New Zealand, November.

Dolado, Juan, Francis Kramarz, Stephen Machin, Alan Manning, David Margolis, and Coen Teulings. 1996. "The Economic Impact of Minimum Wages in Europe." *Economic Policy* 23 (October): 319–372.

Edin, Per-Anders, and Bertil Holmlund. 1995. "The Swedish Wage Structure: The Rise and Fall of Solidarity Wage Policy." In *Differences and Changes in Wage Structures,* ed. Richard B. Freeman and Lawrence F. Katz, 307–343. Chicago: University of Chicago Press.

Edin, Per-Anders, and Robert Topel. 1997. "Wage Policy and Restructuring: The Swedish Labor Market since 1960." In *The Welfare State in Transition: Reforming the Swedish Model,* ed. Richard B. Freeman, Robert Topel, and Birgitta Swedenborg, 155–201. Chicago: University of Chicago Press.

Edin, Per-Anders, and Johnny Zetterberg. 1992. "Interindustry Wage Differentials: Evidence from Sweden and a Comparison with the United States." *American Economic Review* 82 (December): 1341–1349.

Erickson, Chris, and Andrea Ichino. 1995. "Wage Differentials in Italy: Market Forces and Institutions." In *Differences and Changes in Wage Structures,* ed. Richard B. Freeman and Lawrence F. Katz, 265–305. Chicago: University of Chicago Press.

Evans, Lewis, Arthur Grimes, Bryce Wilkinson, and David Teece. 1996. "Economic Reform in New Zealand: 1984–95. The Pursuit of Efficiency." *Journal of Economic Literature* 34 (December): 1856–1902.

Farber, Henry S. 1986. "The Analysis of Union Behavior." In *Handbook of Labor Economics,* vol. 2, ed. Orley Ashenfelter and Richard Layard, 1039–1089. Amsterdam: North Holland.

Freeman, Richard B. 1980. "Unionism and the Dispersion of Wages." *Industrial and Labor Relations Review* 34 (October): 3–23.

———. 1982. "Union Wage Practices and Wage Dispersion Within Establishments." *Industrial and Labor Relations Review* 36 (October): 3–21.

——— 1996. "Why Do So Many Young American Men Commit Crimes, and What Might We Do About It?" NBER Working Paper no. 5451. Cambridge, MA: National Bureau of Economic Research.

Freeman, Richard B., and Robert S. Gibbons. 1995. "Getting Together and Breaking Apart: The Decline of Centralized Collective Bargaining." In *Difference and Changes in Wage Structures,* ed. Richard B. Freeman and Lawrence F. Katz, 345–370. Chicago: University of Chicago Press.

Freeman, Richard B., and Jeffrey Pelletier. 1990. "The Impact of Industrial Relations Legislation on British Union Density." *British Journal of Industrial Relations* 28 (July): 141–164.

Freeman, Richard B., and Ronald Schettkat. 2000. "The Role of Wage and Skill Differences in U.S.-German Employment Differences." Working Paper, no. 7474. Cambridge, MA: National Bureau of Economic Research.

Gibbons, Robert, and Lawrence F. Katz. 1992. "Does Unmeasured Ability Explain Inter-Industry Wage Differentials?" *Review of Economic Studies* 59 (July): 515–535.

Gregory, Robert G., and Jeff Borland. 1999. "Recent Developments in Public Sector Labor Markets." In *Handbook of Labor Economics,* vol. 3C, ed. Orley C. Ashenfelter and David Card, 3573–3630. Amsterdam: Elsevier.

Groshen, Erica L. 1991. "The Structure of the Female/Male Wage Differential: Is It Who You Are, What You Do, or Where You Work?" *Journal of Human Resources* 26 (Summer): 457–472.

Haisken-DeNew, John P., and Christoph Schmidt. 1997. "Inter-industry and Inter-Region Differentials: Mechanics and Interpretation." *The Review of Economics and Statistics* 79 (August): 516–521.

Hendricks, Wallace E., and Lawrence M. Kahn. 1982. "The Determinants of Bargaining Structure in U.S. Manufacturing Industries." *Industrial and Labor Relations Review* 35 (January): 181–195.

Hibbs, Douglas A., Jr. 1990. "Wage Compression Under Solidarity Bargaining in Sweden." Economic Research Report, no. 30. Stockholm: Trade Union Institute for Economic Research

Hibbs, Douglas A., Jr., and Håkan Locking. 2000. "Wage Dispersion and Productive Efficiency: Evidence for Sweden." *Journal of Labor Economics* 18 (October): 755–782.

Hunt, Jennifer. 2002. "The Transition in East Germany: When Is a Ten Point Fall in the Gender Wage Gap Bad News?" *Journal of Labor Economics* 20 (January): 148–169.

Juhn, Chinhui, Kevin M. Murphy, and Brooks Pierce. 1993. "Wage Inequality and the Rise in Returns to Skill." *Journal of Political Economy* 101 (June): 410–442.

Kahn, Lawrence M. 1998a. "Against the Wind: Bargaining Recentralisation and Wage Inequality in Norway, 1987–1991." *Economic Journal* 108 (May): 603–645.

———. 1998b. "Collective Bargaining and the Interindustry Wage Structure: International Evidence." *Economica* 65 (November): 507–534.

———. 2000. "Wage Inequality, Collective Bargaining, and Relative Employment 1985–94: Evidence from 15 OECD Countries." *Review of Economics and Statistics* 82 (November): 564–579.

Kahn, Lawrence M., and Michael Curme. 1987. "Unions and Nonunion Wage Dispersion." *Review of Economics and Statistics* 69 (November): 600–607.

Katz, Harry C. 1993. "The Decentralization of Collective Bargaining: A Literature Review and Comparative Analysis." *Industrial and Labor Relations Review* 47 (October): 3–22.

Katz, Lawrence F., and Alan B. Krueger. 1992. "The Effect of the New Minimum Wage Law in a Low-Wage Labor Market." *Industrial and Labor Relations Review* 46 (October): 6–21.

Katz, Lawrence F., Gary W. Loveman, and David G. Blanchflower. 1995. "A Comparison of Changes in the Structure of Wages in Four OECD Countries." In *Differences and Changes in Wage Structures,* ed. Richard B. Freeman and Lawrence F. Katz, 25–65. Chicago: University of Chicago Press.

Krueger, Alan B. 1995. "The Effect of the Minimum Wage When It Really Bites: A Reexamination of Evidence from Puerto Rico." In *Research in Labor Economics,* ed. Soloman Polachek, 1–22. Greenwich, CT: JAI Press.

Krueger, Alan B., and Jörn-Steffen Pischke. 1997. "Observations and Conjectures on the U.S. Employment Miracle." Working Paper, no. 390. Princeton, NJ: Princeton University Industrial Relations Section.

Krueger, Alan B., and Lawrence Summers. 1988. "Efficiency Wages, and Inter-industry Wage Structure." *Econometrica* 56 (March): 259–293.

Lang, Kevin. 1998. "The Effect of Trade Liberalization on Wages and Employment: The Case of New Zealand." *Journal of Labor Economics* 16 (October): 792–814.

Lemieux, Thomas. 1993. "Unions and Wage Inequality in Canada and the United States." In *Small Differences That Matter,* ed. David Card and Richard B. Freeman, 69–107. Chicago: University of Chicago Press.

Leuven, Edwin, Hessel Oosterbeek, and Hans van Ophem. 1998. "Explaining International Differences in Male Inequality by Differences in Demand and Supply of Skill." Unpublished manuscript, University of Amsterdam.

Lindbeck, Assar, Sten Nyberg, and Jorgen W. Weibell. 1999. "Social Norms and Economic Incentives in the Welfare State." *Quarterly Journal of Economics* 114 (February): 1–35.

Machin, Stephen, and Alan Manning. 1994. "The Effects of Minimum Wages on Wage Dispersion and Employment: Evidence from the U.K. Wage Councils." *Industrial and Labor Relations Review* 47 (January): 319–329.

Maloney, Tim. 1994. "Estimating the Effects of the Employment Contracts Act on Employment and Wages in New Zealand." *Australian Bulletin of Labour* 20 (December): 320–343.

Manning, Alan. 1996. "The Equal Pay Act As an Experiment to Test Theories of the Labour Market." *Economica* 63 (May): 191–212.

"Minimum Pay in 18 Countries." 1992. *European Industrial Relations Review*, no. 225 (October): 14–21.

Murphy, Kevin M., and Robert H. Topel. 1990. "Efficiency Wages Reconsidered: Theory and Evidence." In *Advances in the Theory and Measurement of Unemployment*, ed. Y. Weiss and G. Fishelson, 204–240. New York: Macmillan.

Neal, Derek A., and William R. Johnson. 1996. "The Role of Premarket Factors in Black-White Wage Differences." *Journal of Political Economy* 104 (October): 869–895.

Neumark, David, and William Wascher. 1992. "Employment Effects of Minimum and Subminimum Wages: Panel Data on State Minimum Wage Laws." *Industrial and Labor Relations Review* 46 (October): 55–81.

———. 1999. "A Cross-national Analysis of the Effects of Minimum Wages on Youth Employment." Working Paper, no. 7299. Cambridge, MA: National Bureau of Economic Research.

———. 2000. "Minimum Wages and Employment: A Case Study of the Fast-Food Industry in New Jersey and Pennsylvania: Reply." *American Economic Review* 90 (December): 1362–1396.

Nickell, Stephen, and Richard Layard. 1999. "Labor Market Institutions and Economic Performance." In *Handbook of Labor Economics*, vol. 3C, ed. Orley C. Ashenfelter and David Card, 3029–3084. Amsterdam: Elsevier.

Nickell, Stephen, and Jan van Ours. 2000. "The Netherlands and the United Kingdom: A European Unemployment Miracle?" *Economic Policy* 30 (April): 137–180.

Organization for Economic Cooperation and Development. 1983. *Employment Outlook: September 1983.* Paris: Organization for Economic Cooperation and Development.

———. 1993. *Employment Outlook: July 1993.* Paris: Organization for Economic Cooperation and Development.

———. 1996. *Employment Outlook: July 1996.* Paris: Organization for Economic Cooperation and Development.

———. 1997. *Employment Outlook: July 1997.* Paris: Organization for Economic Cooperation and Development.

———. 1998. *Human Capital Investment: An International Comparison.* Paris: Organization for Economic Cooperation and Development.

———. 2000. *Employment Outlook: June 2000.* Paris: Organization for Economic Cooperation and Development.

Riddell, W. Craig. 1993. "Unionization in Canada and the United States: A Tale of Two Countries." In *Small Differences That Matter,* eds. David Card and Richard B. Freeman, 109–147. Chicago: University of Chicago Press.

Rubin, D.B. 1987. *Multiple Imputation for Nonresponse in Surveys.* New York: John Wiley.

Rueda, David, Christopher Way, and Jonas Pontusson. 1998. "Gendered Patterns of Wage Inequality in OECD Countries." Paper presented at the annual meeting of the American Political Science Association, Boston, September.

Schmitt, John. 1995. "The Changing Structure of Male Earnings in Britain, 1974–1988." In *Differences and Changes in Wage Structures,* ed. Richard B. Freeman and Lawrence F. Katz, 177–204. Chicago: University of Chicago Press.

Shapiro, Carl, and Joseph Stiglitz. 1984. "Equilibrium Unemployment As a Worker Discipline Device." *American Economic Review* 74 (June): 433–444.

Statistics Canada. 1998. *International Adult Literacy Survey Microdata Package.* Ottawa: Statistical Reference Centre CD Rom.

Summers, Lawrence H., Jonathan Gruber, and Rodrigo Vergara. 1993. "Taxation and the Structure of Labor Markets: The Case of Corporatism." *Quarterly Journal of Economics* 108 (May): 385–411.

Van Audenrode, Marc A. 1994. "Short-Time Compensation, Job Security, and Employment Contracts: Evidence from Selected OECD Countries." *Journal of Political Economy* 102 (February): 76–102.

Wallerstein, Michael. 1999. "Wage-Setting Institutions and Pay Inequality in Advanced Industrial Societies." *American Journal of Political Science* 43 (July): 649–680.

Western, Bruce, and Katherine Beckett. 1999. "How Unregulated Is the U.S. Labor Market? The Penal System As a Labor Market Institution." *American Journal of Sociology* 104 (January): 1030–1060.

Winkelmann, Liliana, and Rainer Winkelmann. 1998. "Why Are the Unemployed So Unhappy? Evidence from Panel Data." *Economica* 65 (February): 1–15.

8

Trade Unions and International Competition

Sarah Brown and John G. Sessions

Recent years have witnessed a flurry of, predominately U.S., interest into the effects of international competition on domestic wages and employment.[1] Somewhat less conspicuous has been research into the reaction of trade unions to such competition. This is unfortunate because the union response can tell us much about what lies at the heart of their objective function. Do unionists, for example, sacrifice some wage premium in order to protect the jobs of their members? The staunch opposition of U.S. union leaders to the North American Free Trade Agreement (NAFTA) suggests that organized labor itself perceives international competition as unequivocally pernicious.[2]

There is little conclusive evidence, however, to support such consternation. Dale Belman (1988) finds variations in trade to have relatively little impact on union wages, while Colin Lawrence and Robert Z. Lawrence (1985), employing aggregate industry-level data, find a significant negative effect of import share on wages for the years 1980 and 1984, but no differential impact across union and nonunion sectors. Evidence of an asymmetric response with union, but not nonunion, wages falling in the face of import competition is observed by David A. Macpherson and James B. Stewart (1990), Richard B. Freeman and Lawrence F. Katz (1991), and Noel Gaston and Daniel Trefler (1995). The effect on union wages, however, appears to depend critically on the degree of union density, declining sharply (in absolute value) as union densities rise. Indeed, Macpherson and Stewart (1990) find evidence to suggest that imports actually raise union (and nonunion) wages in very high (70 percent) density industries, the authors attributing the result to the existence of threat and nonunion demand effects outstripping any decrease in wages due to international competition.[3]

In this chapter, we analyze the British "union-nonunion" response to international competition. Our study is one of the few to focus on non-U.S. data and is the first to investigate the implications of international competition for labor market prospects broadly defined. Previous work has only examined the effects of such competition on the union-nonunion wage differential, from which inferences regarding any employment effects have been discerned. We investigate explicitly the effects of international competition on both the earnings *and* employment prospects of such workers. The next section outlines our theoretical model; it is then followed by empirical methodology, discussion of empirical results, and our conclusion.

Theoretical Underpinning

Our theoretical analysis builds on the work of J.A. Brander (1981) and J.A. Brander and P. Krugman (1983), which demonstrates that intraindustry trade can be motivated as the reciprocal dumping outcome of oligopolistic rivalry in imperfectly competitive product markets. J.A. Brander and B.J. Spencer (1988) extend the basic model in various respects by focusing in particular on the case in which wages in one of the economies are, rather than being set exogenously, the result of a union-firm bargain. This is an important extension given the international prevalence of union bargaining (Layard, Nickell, and Jackman 1991).

The Brander and Spencer (1988) model is likely to provide an appropriate framework for the analysis of intraindustry trade between economies with relatively distinct wage determination processes. There are, for example, a number of industries within NAFTA for which there is no unionization in one country but considerable unionization in another. But there are also many examples of trade between countries, with each having similarly unionized labor markets; in such situations, the Brander and Spencer approach requires further refinement.

We develop a framework engendered by R. Naylor (1998), in which international trade occurs between economies, with each having imperfectly competitive product markets *and* unionized labor markets. We examine how the presence of unions in both countries affects the strategies of the various players, focusing in particular on the effects of reductions in trade costs on the labor market prospects of union and nonunion workers. The key intuition underpinning our model is relatively straightforward. An increase in import competition following, for example, a decline in the export costs of the foreign firm, shifts the labor demand function of the domestic firm to the left. Under the assumption that firms employ (equally productive) union and nonunion workers, we envisage two labor market responses. Nonunion pay is assumed to be set by the firm subject to some reservation constraint that such workers receive at least their reservation wage. The shift in labor demand will thus impact enti 'y on nonunion employment. Union pay, in contrast, is assumed to evolve from a "right to manage" bargain between the firm and union.[4] Providing the union cares about the employment prospects of its members, it will allow some fall in the bargained wage to alleviate the fall in employment following the shift in labor demand. We thus expect import competition to impact relatively more on the wage (employment) prospects of union (nonunion) workers.

More formally, we follow Brander and Spencer (1988) and Naylor (1998) in assuming two identical countries ($i = a, b$), within each of which there is a single firm ($j = 1, 2$ – firm 1 in Country a and firm 2 in Country b) producing some nondifferentiated commodity, x. Each firm faces a constant cost of t_i per unit of export. This may be interpreted as an index of all costs associated with international trade (i.e., transactions, transport, and tariffs). Both firms regard each country as a distinct market and choose the profit maximizing quantity of output for each market separately on the Cournot assumption that the other firm's output in each market is given.

For ease of exposition, we assume a constant marginal product of labor normalized to unity, such that output and employment may be discussed interchangeably. The profit function of firm j is thus:

$$\pi_j = \left(p^a - w_j\right)x_j^a + \left(p^b - w_j - t_j\right)x_j^b, \tag{1}$$

where p^i represents the price of commodity x in country i and w_j the wage paid by firm j. We define $x^i = x_1^i + x_2^i$, $x_j = x_j^a + x_j^b$, and $x^a + x^b = x = x_1 + x_2$. Finally, and again for simplicity, we assume linear product demands of the form:

$$p^i = \alpha^i - \beta x^i \tag{2}$$

Each union maximizes rents and does not, when bargaining over wages, take into account any implications of the bargained wage for the overall price level. Such an assumption is justified provided that the firm's output does not constitute a significant portion of the workers' consumption bundle. We assume a utilitarian union preference structure with each union having a membership of m_i members and an objective function:

$$u_j = w_j x_j + \left(m_j - x_j\right)\bar{w}_j, \tag{3}$$

where $\bar{w}_j$ represents the reservation wage available to members of union j. The behavior of each firm-union pair is modeled as a two-stage game. In stage two, the firm sets the level of output (and therefore employment), taking the bargained wage from stage one and the level of output of the rival firm as given. Formally:

$$\text{Stage Two: } \max_{x_j} \pi_j\left(w_j, x_j\right) \tag{4}$$

We define the solution to the above $x_j\left(w_j\right)$. In stage one, each firm-union pair bargains over the wage, taking as given the wage set by the other rival firm-union pair and taking into account the implications of any wage for labor demand. Formally:

$$\text{Stage One: } \max_{w_j} \Omega_j = q_j \log\left(u_j - \bar{u}_j\right) + \left(1 - q_j\right)\log\left(\pi_j - \bar{\pi}_j\right) \tag{5}$$

where $\bar{\pi}_j$ and $\bar{u}_j = m_j \bar{w}_j$ represent the firm and union fallbacks, respectively. We assume in what follows that $\bar{\pi}_j = 0$ for simplicity. The model is therefore solved by backward induction.

Considering first stage two, maximizing (A1) with respect to domestic (export) output $x_j^a \left(x_j^b\right)$ implies:

$$\frac{\partial \pi_j}{\partial x_j^a} = \alpha^a - 2\beta x_j^a - \beta x_{k \neq j}^a - w_j = 0 \Rightarrow x_j^a = \frac{\alpha^a - w_j}{2\beta} - \frac{1}{2}x_{k \neq j}^a \tag{6}$$

$$\frac{\partial \pi_j}{\partial x_j^b} = \alpha^b - 2\beta x_j^b - \beta x_{k \neq j}^b - w_j - t_j = 0 \Rightarrow x_j^b = \frac{\alpha^b - w_j - t_j}{2\beta} - \frac{1}{2}x_{k \neq j}^b \tag{7}$$

Equations 6 and 7 may be interpreted as firm j's reaction function with respect to both its rival's $(k \neq j)$ output in the relevant product market and the equilibrium wage resulting from the stage-one bargain with the union. They may therefore be solved to obtain expressions for output as reaction functions of the bargained wage, and may thus be interpreted as labor demand curves facing each union given the bargained wage:

$$x_j^d\left(w_j, w_{k \neq j}, t_j\right) = \frac{1}{3\beta}\left(\alpha - 4w_j + 2w_{k \neq j} - 2t_j + t_{k \neq j}\right) \tag{8}$$

where $\alpha = \alpha^a + \alpha^b$. In stage one, each firm-union pair will bargain over wages, taking into account the labor demand schedule of the firm. Maximizing (A5) with respect to the wage and solving implies:

$$w_j^* = \bar{w}_j\left\{1 - \frac{q_j}{q_j E_{x_j w_j} + \left(1 - q_j\right)\left[E_{\pi_j \bar{w}_j} + E_{\pi_j x_j}E_{x_j \bar{w}_j}\right]}\right\}, \tag{9}$$

where $E_{\pi_j x_j} = (\partial \pi_j / \partial x_j) \cdot (x_j / \pi_j)$ and $E_{\delta \bar{w}_j} = (\partial \delta / \partial w_j) \cdot (\bar{w}_j / \delta)$, $\forall \delta = x_j, \pi_j$. An explicit solution to (A9) is somewhat intractable. Our interest, however, lies in simply determining how union and nonunion workers are affected by changing trade effects and so an examination of the following extreme cases are adequate:

$$\lim_{q_j \to 0} w_j^* = \bar{w}_j \tag{10}$$

$$\lim_{q_j \to 1} w_j^* = \bar{w}_j \left[1 - \left(E_{x_j \bar{w}_j}^* \right)^{-1} \right] = 8^{-1} \left(\alpha + 4\bar{w}_j + 2w_{k \neq j} - 2t_j + t_{k \neq j} \right) \tag{11}$$

Intuitively, as bargaining power is divested wholly in the firm, the equilibrium "bargained" wage is chosen to maximize the firm's profits subject to the constraint that workers receive at least their reservation wage. Conversely, as bargaining power is divested wholly in the union, the "bargained" wage is marked up over this reservation wage by some complex related to the elasticity of labor demand.

The effects of a change in the level of international competition on the labor market are readily apparent from equations 10 and 11. A decline in the trade costs of the foreign firm will lead to an increase in imports from abroad and a decline in the domestic firm's output. This shift in the labor demand curve will alter the labor market equilibrium, depending on the level of union power. In the absence of union power, wages will be set by the firm at their reservation level and the impact of the increased competition will be felt entirely in terms of employment—that is, $\left. \left(\partial w_j^* / \partial t_{k \neq j} \right) \right|_{q_j = 0} > 0$. If wage bargaining power is divested entirely in a union that cares about the employment of its members, the union is both willing and able to allow a fall in wages to alleviate the strain on employment—that is, $\left. \left(\partial w_j^* / \partial t_{k \neq j} \right) \right|_{q_j = 1} > 0$. In general, we would expect the more power the union has in the wage bargain vis-à-vis the firm, and the more it cares about employment, the greater will be the differential impact of foreign competition on the wage and employment outcomes of union/nonunion workers.

The situation is illustrated graphically in Figures 8.1 and 8.2 (see pp. 234–235). Figure 8.1 depicts an initial union-nonunion equilibrium. The union is presumed to have convex preferences over wages and employment, as depicted by the representative indifference curve I_1. We assume, for ease of exposition, an extreme "right to manage" bargaining situation, in which the union has all the power in the wage bargain.[5] In such a case, the union chooses the wage by moving to its highest level of utility subject to the constraint that

Figure 8.1 **Union-Nonunion Equilibrium**

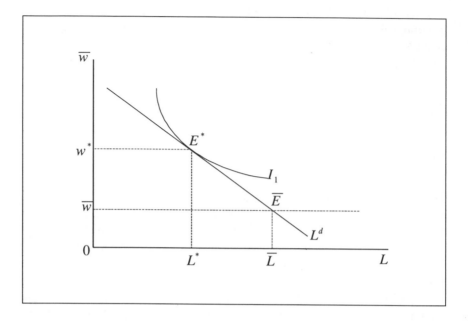

employment lies on the firm's labor demand curve, implying an equilibrium E^* with L^* workers receiving the union wage, w^*. The nonunion equilibrium is situated at $\overline{E}$, where $\overline{L}$ workers are paid the reservation wage, $\overline{w}$.[6]

An increase in imports will cause a shift to the left of the domestic firm's labor demand function, following the optimal (Cournot) response of reducing output. The "monopoly union" equilibrium in Figure 8.2 is seen to move from E_1^* to E_2^*, entailing a fall in wages of $\Delta w^* = \left(w_1^* - w_2^*\right)$ and a fall in employment of $\Delta L^* = \left(L_1^* - L_2^*\right)$. The nonunion response is the horizontal move from $\overline{E}_1$ to $\overline{E}_2$. Since nonunion workers are already paid their reservation wage, all the impact is picked up by employment, which falls by $\Delta \overline{L} = \left(\overline{L}_1 - \overline{L}_2\right)$. There is thus a differential price-quantity adjustment between union and nonunion workers, with wages falling more and employment falling less among the former. To be sure, since $\Delta w^* > \Delta \overline{w} = 0$, it must be the case that $\Delta L^* < \Delta \overline{L}$.[7]

The proposition that union and nonunion wages respond differentially to changes in trade costs accords with the work of Gaston and Trefler (1995) and Macpherson and Stewart (1990), the latter of whom find that a 10 percent rise in import shares lowered the union-nonunion differential by approximately 2 percent, with the net negative effect of any given import share on both union and nonunion wages decreasing sharply in

Figure 8.2 Union Nonunion Comparative Statics

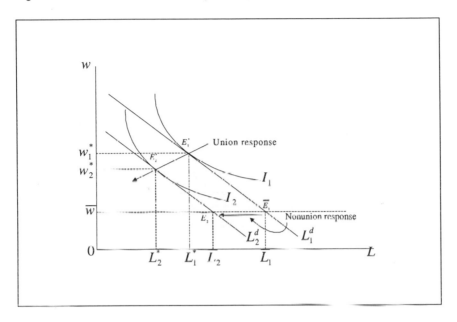

absolute magnitude as the percentage of workers organized into a union increased.

Both Macpherson and Stewart's and Gaston and Trefler's conclusions are derived from empirical analyses that, like those of other researchers, focus exclusively on the response of union and nonunion wage premia to import competition. In what follows, we infer *both* the wage *and* employment responses directly from *separate* wage and employment premia regressions.

Empirical Methodology

Our empirical methodology proceeds in two stages: First, we ascertain the relationship between an individual's labor market prospects—that is, wages and employment—and their industrial affiliation. We then ascertain the extent to which these premia are related to a measure of international competition industry trade. In detail:

Our first stage follows the interindustry wage differentials approach pioneered by William T. Dickens and Lawrence F. Katz (1987) and Alan B. Krueger and Lawrence Summers (1988). The idea is that an individual's wage depends at least as much on human capital, demographic, geographic, and occupational characteristics as it does on industrial affiliation. Our wage equation is specified:

$$\log w_{ijt} = X_{it} B_X + D_{jt} w_{jt} + \varepsilon_{ijt} \tag{12}$$

where $i = 1, 2..., I, J = 1, 2,..., J.$ w_{ijt} is the hourly wage rate of an individual i employed in industry j at time t ; X_{it} is a vector of characteristics of individual i ; D_{jt} is a vector of dummy variables indicating industrial affiliation at time t ; ε_{ijt} is an error term; and B_X and w_{jt} are parameter vectors. The latter can be interpreted as the interindustry wage differential (or wage premium) for industry j—that is, the component of an individual's wage that cannot be explained by X_{it}, but which may be explained by industrial affiliation.

A similar approach may be adopted to ascertain industrial employment probability premia. We model the probability (relative to unemployment) that an individual i affiliated with some industry j will be employed within that industry as a function of a set of personal characteristics, Z_{it} as well as industrial affiliation. In terms of the logistic specification, this estimated probability is denoted:

$$P_{ijt} = \frac{1}{1 + \exp^{-(Z_{it} A_Z + D_{jt} P_{jt})}} \tag{13}$$

where A_Z and P_{jt} are parameter vectors, the latter can be interpreted as the interindustry employment differential (or employment probability premium) for industry j—that is, the portion of an individual's employment probability that cannot be explained by observable individual characteristics, Z_{it}, but which may be explained by industrial affiliation. Taking natural logs yields the estimating equation:

$$\ln \tilde{p}_{ijt} = Z_{it} A_Z + D_{jt} P_{jt} + \mu_{ijt} \tag{14}$$

where $\tilde{p}_{ijt} = p_{ijt} / (1 - p_{ijt})$ and μ_{itj} is an error term. The left-hand side of equation 14 represents the predicted log-odds of an individual i affiliated to industry j at time t experiencing employment within that industry rather than unemployment.[8]

We selected the (X_{it}, Z_{it}) characteristics from a conventional set of variables, the latter of which have been explored extensively in Sarah Brown and John G. Sessions (1997). The Z_{it} vector comprised six of the highest educational qualification dummy variables, terms for labor market experience (and its square), five occupational dummy variables, a proxy for un-earned income, and dummy variables for share ownership, race, marital status, and sex. The X_{it} vector included four firm-size dummies as well as all the variables included Z_{it}.

Our first-stage data were derived from pooling the British Social Attitudes (BSA) Surveys over the period 1985 to 1991 (excluding 1988).[9] Our "wage" sample comprised 2,100 manufacturing employees, 986 of whom were unionized. Our "employment" sample comprised 2,447 individuals (2,100 employed and 347 unemployed) affiliated to the manufacturing sector. Since the BSA Surveys record the union status of both employed and unemployed respondents, we were able to decompose our employment sample into 1,019 unionized and 1,428 nonunionized individuals.[10]

Given our first-stage premia, we then constructed an industrial panel of data for the 1985–91 period and estimated the two premia equations:

$$w_{jt} = \beta_M M_{jt} + \beta_H H_{jt} + \varepsilon_{jt} \tag{15}$$

$$p_{jt} = \alpha_M M_{jt} + \alpha_H H_{jt} + \mu_{jt} \tag{16}$$

where $j = 1, \ldots, 20$ (industries) and $t = 1, \ldots, 6$ (years). w_{jt} denotes the wage premium and p_{jt} the employment probability premium, associated with industry j in year t. M_{jt} denotes the level of net imports as a percentage of industrial gross domestic product (both at 1985 prices) entering industry j in year t, while H_{jt} is a vector of domestic factors that might also affect interin dustry premia. ε_{jt} and μ_{itj} are error terms and (β_k, α_k), $k = M, H$, are parameter vectors. Our second-stage data were derived from the *Employment Gazette* and *Business Monitor* and our estimates were obtained from the Dynamic Panel Data (DPD) Gauss matrix program.[11]

The "domestic vector" comprises a number of variables designed to proxy the domestic influences on the industry premia. Given our interest in the relative plight of unionized workers, we focused particularly on variables that one would expect to be related to the division of industry rents, that is, firm and union fallbacks and relative "bargaining power" broadly defined. In this vein, we obtained data pertaining to the industrial five-firm concentration ratio and the industrial capital:labor ratio as proxies for the firm fallback.[12] As regards the union fallback, we follow Gaston and Trefler (1995) in deriving the wage decile for each industry—that is, the tenth percentile of the industry wage after controlling for the occupational mix of the industry (see Abowd and Kramarz 1993). We define w_{jk}^{10} as the tenth percentile of the wage distribution of occupation k in industry j, and the wage decile as

$\sum_k p_{jk} w_{jk}^{10}$, where p_{jk} is the proportion of workers employed in occupation k in industry j. The wage decile is attractive in combining features of the union-nonunion wage differential and education, given that a workers' alternative wage is largely dependent on human capital characteristics, of which education is arguably the most important component. Finally, we proxied relative bargaining power by the redundancy rate within the industry, the number of working days lost though strikes, and industrial union density. Given the probability that union premia will affect nonunion premia through threat, supply, and demand effects, we included the fallback measures into both union and nonunion premia regressions.[13]

Our estimates are compromised by the possible simultaneity of net imports, earnings, and employment. It could be argued, for example, that high unemployment rates will imply low earnings, whether via a union bargain or an efficiency wage mechanism, and that low wage costs yield a comparative advantage and thus lower net imports. Unraveling these issues is complex and made further so by the difficulty in instrumenting net exports. One possibility is to use data on nominal and effective tariff barriers, but such data are notoriously difficult to obtain for the United Kingdom (see Ennew, Greenaway, and Reed 1990). Another is the approach adopted by Ana Revenga (1992) for the United States, in which she calculates industry-specific exchange rates, the rationale being that such rates vary across industries because countries of origin vary across industries. Such an instrument is thus likely to be exogenous, because most exchange rates between—particularly large—countries are induced by macroeconomic changes that can be controlled for by time and industry-specific effects. Unfortunately, such an approach is not tenable for the United Kingdom at the level of disaggregation required by our analysis, as it is only possible to decompose imports and exports by industry or country, but not both.

Given these difficulties, we decided to adopt the simplest expedient of lagging net imports throughout. Such a strategy is far from ideal and at best will only alleviate any simultaneity—if there is any serial correlation in the errors within industries then lagged endogenous variables will still be correlated with the errors. We are thus somewhat loath to claim any causality in our results, although their apparent asymmetry would tend to suggest that any directional influence is running primarily from international competition to earnings and employment.

Empirical Results

Tables 8.1 to 8.6 (see pp. 239–244) present our six first-stage regressions for all employees (Table 8.1), union members (Table 8.2), nonunion members

Table 8.1

All Workers: Dependent Variable = Log Hourly Wage

Variable	Mean	Standard deviation	Coefficient	T-ratio
Degree level education	0.0652	0.2470	0.50450	11.718
Further education	0.1462	0.3534	0.24773	8.098
A levels	0.1224	0.3278	0.26112	8.430
O levels	0.2091	0.4067	0.18484	7.319
CSE level	0.0957	0.2943	0.11770	3.726
Other education	0.0071	0.0841	−0.05802	−0.565
No education	0.3543	0.4784	—	—
Professional	0.2495	0.4328	0.39790	11.734
Clerical	0.1276	0.3337	0.26168	7.089
Skilled manual	0.3057	0.4608	0.17485	5.825
Semiskilled manual	0.2133	0.4098	0.07055	2.250
Unskilled manual	0.0276	0.1639	—	—
Firm size: under 25 employees	0.1976	0.3983	—	—
Firm size: 25–100 employees	0.2038	0.4029	0.09430	3.469
Firm size: 100–500 employees	0.3286	0.4698	0.16255	6.280
Firm size: over 500 employees	0.2662	0.4421	0.23842	8.205
Years in labor force	22.873	13.137	0.02566	9.730
Years in labor force squared	695.65	652.69	−0.00037	−7.281
White	0.8995	0.3007	0.12970	4.145
Married	0.7386	0.4395	0.07182	3.180
Male	0.7007	0.4554	0.33792	15.500
Union member	0.4695	0.4992	0.03542	1.7459

Industry dummy variables	yes
F-statistic	228.498
R-squared	0.5406
Number of observations	2,100

Note: The approach introduced by White (1980) is adopted to produce heteroskedastic consistent T-statistics.

(Table 8.3), employment logistic regressions for all employees (Table 8.4), union members (Table 8.5), and nonunion members (Table 8.6).

The estimated stage-one coefficients (B_x, A_z) are similar in sign and magnitude to those reported by previous researchers. Our second-stage empirical results are set out in Tables 8.7 and 8.8 (see pp. 244–245). We estimated three specifications of each premia equation, namely, "all individuals," "union individuals," and "nonunion individuals." Our key finding is that net imports are significantly negatively associated with union, but not nonunion, wage premia, and with nonunion but not union, employment premia. These results accord with the argument that nonunion wages are being set competitively, with any reduction in demand impinging primarily on quantities. It also suggests, albeit indirectly, that unions care about the employment prospects of their members, sacrificing market rents for enhanced job security in the face of international competition.

Table 8.2

Union Members: Dependent Variable = Log Hourly Wage

Variable	Mean	Standard deviation	Coefficient	T-ratio
Degree level education	0.0355	0.18513	0.46949	6.241
Further education	0.1217	0.32711	0.20782	4.545
A levels	0.1237	0.32944	0.21829	5.188
O levels	0.1947	0.3962	0.13731	3.985
CSE level	0.0984	0.2980	0.13733	3.212
Other education	0.0091	0.0952	−0.02281	−0.1803
No education	0.4168	0.4933	—	—
Professional	0.1694	0.3753	0.39657	7.591
Clerical	0.0771	0.2669	0.27446	4.595
Skilled manual	0.3986	0.4899	0.23702	5.598
Semiskilled manual	0.2667	0.4425	0.15562	3.586
Unskilled manual	0.0243	0.1542	—	—
Firm size: under 25 employees	0.0862	0.2808	—	—
Firm size: 25–100 employees	0.1379	0.3450	0.13667	2.773
Firm size: 100–500 employees	0.3783	0.4852	0.21415	4.866
Firm size: over 500 employees	0.3945	0.4890	0.27625	6.084
Years in labor force	24.194	12.660	0.02819	7.124
Years in labor force squared	745.45	633.84	−0.00046	−5.933
White	0.9057	0.2924	0.20787	4.440
Married	0.7617	0.4263	0.073362	2.362
Male	0.7718	0.4199	0.33135	10.338
Industry dummy variables			yes	
F-statistic			139.317	
R-squared			0.5251	
Number of observations			986	

There is some evidence from our results that labor market prospects are inversely related to the bargaining positions of firms. To be sure, a higher capital:labor ratio, and thus a lower firm fallback, raises significantly both aggregate employment premia and aggregate decomposed wage premia.

Our results are less conclusive regarding the relationship between labor market prospects and the union fallback. The coefficient on the wage decile is correctly signed across all three specifications of the wage premia equation. The coefficient on union density, however, is significant and negative across all three specifications of the wage premia equation and across the "all" and "nonunion" specifications of the employment premia equation. This is somewhat puzzling, although remember that we are analyzing wage premia rather than wages per se. To be sure, our first-stage regressions illustrated a strong positive correlation between union membership and both

Table 8.3

Nonunion Members: Dependent Variable = Log Hourly Wage

Variable	Mean	Standard deviation	Coefficient	T-ratio
Degree level education	0.0916	0.2885	0.52213	9.180
Further education	0.1679	0.3739	0.28404	6.518
A levels	0.1212	0.3265	0.29936	6.389
O levels	0.2217	0.4156	0.22977	6.003
CSE level	0.0934	0.2911	0.12622	2.616
Other education	0.0054	0.0732	−0.08945	−0.5135
No education	0.2989	0.4578	—	—
Professional	0.3205	0.4669	0.40432	8.466
Clerical	0.1724	0.3779	0.26144	5.220
Skilled manual	0.2235	0.4168	0.13592	3.025
Semiskilled manual	0.1661	0.3723	0.00288	0.061
Unskilled manual	0.0305	0.1721	—	—
Firm size: under 25 employees	0.2962	0.4568	—	—
Firm size: 25–100 employees	0.2621	0.4400	0.09784	2.806
Firm size: 100–500 employees	0.2846	0.4514	0.15935	4.593
Firm size: over 500 employees	0.1526	0.3598	0.26206	5.9123
Years in labor force	21.704	13.442	0.02405	8.4810
Years in labor force squared	651.58	666.11	−0.00030	−4.1487
White	0.8941	0.3079	0.06048	1.3750
Married	0.7181	0.4501	0.06272	1.8415
Male	0.6490	0.4775	0.33786	10.803

Industry dummy variables	yes
F-statistic	114.324
R-squared	0.6037
Number of observations	1114

wages and employment, while the coefficients on the other second-stage explanatory variables were highly robust to the exclusion of union density. Perhaps we have omitted some factor that has impacted negatively on the relatively more unionized industries in our study. Indeed, the significant and negative coefficient on lagged working days lost in the employment premia "nonunion" specification and in the earnings premia "union" and "nonunion" specifications suggest that any industrial unrest during the period had been largely unsuccessful.

Finally and perhaps not altogether unrelated, the coefficient on lagged redundancies/employment is significant and negative in the "union" specification of the employment premia equation and significant and positive across all three specifications of the wage premia equation. Redundancies have thus been concentrated on the employment prospects of union members, although any worker, regardless of union status, who was able to sur-

Table 8.4

All Workers: Dependent Variable = Probability of Employment (Logit)

Variable	Mean	Standard deviation	Coefficient	T-ratio
Degree level education	0.0597	0.2369	0.42972	0.921
Further education	0.1320	0.3386	0.78573	2.429
A levels	0.1148	0.3190	0.61351	2.072
O levels	0.2047	0.4036	0.52110	2.442
CSE level	0.1018	0.3024	0.20867	0.869
Other education	0.0074	0.0855	0.55941	0.663
No education	0.3797	0.4854	—	—
Professional	0.2215	0.4153	1.84890	5.492
Clerical	0.1197	0.3247	1.00260	3.271
Skilled manual	4,945.2	5,831.2	0.22272	1.001
Semiskilled manual	0.3004	0.4585	−0.27894	−1.278
Unskilled manual	0.2334	0.4231	—	—
Nonearned income	0.0294	0.1690	−0.00002	−1.719
Share ownership	0.2289	0.4202	0.63659	2.772
Years in labor force	22.720	13.534	0.00373	1.762
Years in labor force squared	699.32	670.99	−0.00011	−2.761
White	0.8905	0.3124	0.69623	2.873
Married	0.7049	0.4562	0.90394	5.336
Male	0.6923	0.4617	0.00764	0.431
Union member	0.4164	0.4931	2.66667	11.419
Industry dummy variables		yes		
F-statistic		676.376		
R-squared		0.43279		
Number of observations		2,447		

vive such calamity was likely to find his or her wage prospects enhanced considerably.

Conclusion

We investigated the relationship between international competition and the labor market prospects of a representative sample of British workers. Our empirical analysis, which sets out the first explicit test of both the wage *and* employment implications of such competition, suggests that international competition affects the wage (but not employment) prospects of union workers and the employment (but not wage) prospects of nonunion workers. Such an asymmetry reinforces the results of Macpherson and Stewart (1990) and Gaston and Trefler (1995) and is consistent with the notion that nonunion workers are being remunerated at or near their reservation wage levels, with any contraction in demand impinging primarily on their employability. Union members, in contrast, are able to

Table 8.5

Union Members: Dependent Variable = Probability of Employment (Logit)

Variable	Mean	Standard deviation	Coefficient	T-ratio
Degree level education	0.0344	0.1822	3.00920	0.001
Further education	0.1187	0.3237	1.20560	0.998
A levels	0.1246	0.3305	0.17592	0.248
O levels	0.1924	0.3943	0.23008	0.319
CSE level	0.1021	0.3029	−0.61857	−0.940
Other education	0.0088	0.0936	3.12600	0.007
No education	0.4190	0.4936	—	—
Professional	0.1668	0.3730	0.58853	0.611
Clerical	0.0756	0.2644	1.20330	0.878
Skilled manual	0.4033	0.4908	−0.12855	−0.207
Semiskilled manual	0.2640	0.4410	0.60868	0.797
Unskilled manual	0.0245	0.1548	—	—
Nonearned income	4,315.5	5,122.8	−0.00007	−1.773
Share ownership	0.2316	0.4221	0.00610	0.104
Years in labor force	24.375	12.781	0.12522	1.799
Years in labor force squared	757.33	645.65	−0.00031	−2.437
White	0.9009	0.2990	0.46162	0.623
Married	0.7576	0.4287	0.53947	1.127
Male	0.7753	0.4176	−0.34909	−0.463
Industry dummy variables			yes	
F-statistic			114.084	
R-squared			0.42598	
Number of observations			1,019	

insulate themselves against such pressures by sacrificing some of their labor market rent.

These results are compromised by our inability to fully instrument for international competition and must be interpreted with caution. We nevertheless hope that they inspire further work into this important and interesting area.

Acknowledgments

We benefited from discussions with Monojit Chatterji, Michael Devereux, Lisa Grobar, Alan Manning, Chris Milner, Sunder Ramaswamy, Ian Walker, and Phanindra V. Wunnava. Helpful comments were also received from seminar participants at the Universities of Aberdeen, City, Keele, and Loughborough, and from participants at the Twenty-third Annual Conference on Economic Issues: "Changing Role of Unions," Middlebury College, April 13–14, 2002. We are grateful to Daniel Kwok for excellent research assistance. The normal disclaimer applies.

Table 8.6

Nonunion Members: Dependent Variable = Probability of Employment
(Logit)

Variable	Mean	Standard deviation	Coefficient	T-ratio
Degree level education	0.0778	0.2678	0.39298	0.795
Further education	0.1415	0.3486	0.75572	2.208
A levels	0.1078	0.3103	0.82350	2.446
O levels	0.2136	0.4100	0.54923	2.339
CSE level	0.1015	0.3022	0.45034	1.685
Other education	0.0063	0.0792	0.41550	0.432
No education	0.3515	0.4776	—	—
Professional	0.2605	0.4391	2.09640	5.599
Clerical	0.1513	0.3584	1.01630	3.116
Skilled manual	0.2260	0.4190	0.35073	1.413
Semiskilled manual	0.2115	0.4085	−0.35775	−1.502
Unskilled manual	0.0329	0.1785	—	—
Nonearned income	5,394.6	6,251.1	−0.00001	−0.933
Share ownership	0.2269	0.4190	0.81607	3.042
Years in labor force	21.540	13.932	0.00319	1.367
Years in labor force squared	657.92	685.73	−0.00009	−2.108
White	0.8831	0.3215	0.61665	2.272
Married	0.6674	0.4713	0.94431	4.966
Male	0.6331	0.4821	0.00602	0.313

Industry dummy variables	yes
F-statistic	458.908
R-squared	0.42199
Number of observations	1,428

Table 8.7

Probability of Employment Premia Regressions

Variable name	All individuals		Unionized individuals		Nonunionized individuals	
	Coeff.	T-ratio	Coeff.	T-ratio	Coeff.	T-ratio
(lag) Net Imports	−0.0601	−1.762	−0.0111	−0.268	−0.0928	−2.606
Capital : labor ratio	0.0031	2.440	0.0026	1.232	0.0020	1.007
Five firm concentration ratio	−0.0708	−0.598	0.0934	0.706	−0.1270	−0.967
(lag) Redundancies/ employment	−0.0012	−1.523	−0.0019	−1.900	−0.0009	−1.016
Industrial union density	−0.7143	−3.561	−0.3298	−1.348	−0.8112	−3.688
(lag) Working days lost	−0.0000	−0.512	−0.0000	−0.226	−0.0001	−2.522
Wage decile	−0.0673	−1.502	−0.0790	−1.196	−0.0051	−0.081
Constant	1.2431	14.351	1.1350	9.956	1.2597	12.560

N	120		120		120	
Wald statistic of joint sig. (7 df)	56.0924		11.4948		64.5324	

Table 8.8

Wage Premia Regressions

Variable name	All individuals		Unionized individuals		Nonunionized individuals	
	Coeff.	T-ratio	Coeff.	T-ratio	Coeff.	T-ratio
(lag) Net imports	0.0272	0.881	−0.1277	−3.326	0.0352	0.508
Capital : labor ratio	0.0038	9.096	0.0122	4.198	0.0072	7.094
Five firm concentration ratio	0.1742	1.604	0.1792	1.174	0.2096	1.699
(lag) Redundancies/ employment	0.0016	3.056	0.0027	2.449	0.0022	2.926
Industrial union density	−0.7123	−3.125	−1.1019	−3.067	−1.4170	−3.544
(lag) Working days lost	−0.0000	−3.480	−0.0000	−5.001	−0.0001	−2.475
Wage decile	0.1784	4.202	0.1364	3.032	0.1787	4.184
Constant	0.2126	2.934	0.3548	2.481	0.5571	3.121
N	120		120		120	
Wald satistic of joint sig. (7 df)	65.2215		37.3666		65.2807	

Notes

1. For example, see Revenga (1992), and Gaston and Trefler (1994). A summary of the evidence is set out in Lawrence and Slaughter (1993).

2. Indeed, many commentators have attributed the accelerating decline in U.S. unionism to inadequate union wage adjustment in the face of surging import competition (Freeman and Katz 1991).

3. See also Blumenfeld and Partridge (1996), who use union contract data to assess both the long- and short-run impacts of international competition on U.S. collective bargaining outcomes. Their key finding is that in the short run increases in both imports and exports reduce union wages as a result of risk aversion on the part of both unions and management, while in the long run there is little impact on average union wage settlements.

4. To be sure, this entails the two sides bargaining over wages but with the firm retaining sovereignty over employment.

5. This is the so-called monopoly union model (see Oswald 1985).

6. The more general "right to mange" union equilibrium would be determined by relative bargaining power at some point between E^* and $\bar{E}$.

7. The key exception here is if the union does not care about employment. This would imply horizontal curves and the same impact on employment as nonunion workers with wages remaining at a higher level.

8. The implicit presumption in equation 13 is that the alternative to employment within the industry of affiliation is unemployment. In reality, the situation may not be so stark, with contracting demand impacting only on the type of employment available. Unfortunately, our data offer no insight into this possibility. They do, however,

record the industrial affiliation of unemployed respondents (namely, all unemployed respondents are asked: "In what industry are you normally employed?") and thereby permit the more stringent approach outlined earlier.

9. These are an annual series of surveys started by Social and Community Planning Research in 1983, with the core being funded by the Monument Trust. The data are derived from a cross-sectional sample of adults aged eighteen and over living in private households whose addresses were included in the electoral registrar. The sampling was facilitated by selecting 114 parliamentary constituencies from among all those in Great Britain on the basis of the Registrar General's Standard Regions.

10. Individuals were also classified according to the following twenty industrial affiliations: (1) coal extraction and coke ovens (SIC 11–12); (2) extraction of oil and natural gas and mineral oil processing (SIC 13–14); (3) nuclear, electricity, gas, and other energy production and distribution (SIC 15–17); (4) metalliferous ores, metal manufacturing, and mineral extraction (SIC 21–23); (5) manufacture of nonmetallic mineral products (SIC 24); (6) chemicals and man-made fibers (SIC 25–26); (7) manufactures of metal goods (SIC 31); (8) mechanical engineering (SIC 32); (9) office machinery and data-processing equipment (SIC 33); (10) electrical and electronic engineering (SIC 34); (11) manufacture of motor vehicles and parts (SIC 35); (12) manufacture of transport equipment (SIC 36); (13) instrument engineering (SIC 37); (14) food, drink, and tobacco (SIC 41-42); (15) textiles (SIC 43); (16) manufacture of leather and leather goods, footwear, and clothing (SIC 44–45); (17) timber and wooden furniture (SIC 46); (18) paper and paper products (SIC 47); (19) rubber and plastics (SIC 48); (20) other manufacturing (SIC 49). All SIC codes refer to the Standard Industrial Classification of economic activities, 1980. Note that the dummy variable D_{jt} in equations 12 and 14 is thus a six (year) by twenty (industry) vector.

11. For details of the DPD programming technique, see Arellano and Bond (1991).

12. If no agreement is reached, then the firm will lose any rents associated with firm-specific investments in physical and intangible capital, which we proxy by the industrial capital labor ratio. The five-firm concentration ratio is included to proxy the size of labor market rents.

13. Hirsch and Addison (1986), for example, show that a higher percentage organized raises nonunion wages, implying that threat and demand effects dominate any supply effects.

References

Abowd, John M., and F. Kramarz. 1993. "A Test of the Negotiation and Incentive Compensation Models Using Longitudinal French Enterprise Data." In *Labor Demand and Equilibrium Wage Formation,* ed. J.C. Van Ours, G.A. Pfann, and G. Ridder, 111–146. Amsterdam: North-Holland.

Arellano, Manuel, and Stephen Bond. 1991. "Some Tests of Specification for Panel Data: Monte Carlo Evidence and an Application to Employment Equations." *Review of Economic Studies* 58 (April): 277–297.

Belman, Dale. 1988. "Concentration, Unionism and Labor Earnings: A Sample Selection Approach." *Review of Economics and Statistics* 70 (August): 391–397.

Blumenfeld, Stephen B., and Mark D. Partridge. 1996. "The Long-Run and Short-Run Impact of Global Competition on U.S. Union Wages." *Journal of Labor Research* 17 (Winter): 149–171.

Brander, J.A. 1981. "Intra-industry Trade in Identical Commodities." *Journal of International Economics* 11:1–14.

Brander, J.A., and P. Krugman. 1983. "A Reciprocal Dumping Model of International Trade." *Journal of International Economics* 15: 313–321.

Brander, J.A., and B.J. Spencer. 1988. "Export Subsidies and International Market Share Rivalry." *Journal of International Economics* 18: 83–100.

Brown, Sarah, and John G. Sessions. 1997. "A Profile of UK Unemployment: Regional versus Demographic Influences." *Regional Studies* 31 (September): 351–366.

Dickens, William T., and Lawrence F. Katz. 1987. "Inter-industry Wage Differences." In *Unemployment and the Structure of Labor Markets,* ed. Kevin Lang and John S. Leonard, 48–89. New York: Basil Blackwell.

Ennew, Christine, David Greenaway, and Gavin Reed. 1990. "Further Evidence on Effective Tariffs and Effective Protection in the UK." *Oxford Bulletin of Economics and Statistics* 52 (January): 69–78.

Freeman, Richard B., and Lawrence F. Katz. 1991. "Industrial Wage and Employment Determination in an Open Economy." In *Immigration, Trade and the Labor Market,* ed. John M. Abowd and Richard B. Freeman, 235–259. Chicago: National Bureau of Economic Research.

Gaston, Noel, and Daniel Trefler. 1994. "Protection, Trade, and Wages: Evidence from U.S. Manufacturing." *Industrial and Labor Relations Review* 47 (July): 574–593.

———. 1995. "Union Wage Sensitivity to Trade and Protection: Theory and Evidence." *Journal of International Economics* 39 (January): 1–25.

Hirsch, Barry T., and John T. Addison. 1986. *The Economic Analysis of Unions: New Approaches and Evidence.* Boston: Allen and Unwin.

Krueger, Alan B., and Lawrence Summers. 1988. "Efficiency Wages, and Inter-industry Wage Structure." *Econometrica* 56 (March): 259–293.

Lawrence, Colin, and Robert Z. Lawrence. 1985. "Manufacturing Wage Dispersion: An End Game Interpretation." *Brookings Papers on Economic Activity* 1: 47–106.

Lawrence, Robert Z., and Matthew Slaughter. 1993. "International Trade and American Wages in the 1980s: Giant Sucking Sound or Small Hiccup?" *Brookings Papers on Economic Activity* 2: 161–210.

Layard, R., S. Nickell, and R. Jackman. 1991. *Unemployment: Macroeconomic Performance and the Labour Market.* New York: Oxford University Press.

Macpherson, David A., and James B. Stewart. 1990. "The Effect of International Competition on Union and Nonunion Wages." *Industrial and Labor Relations Review* 43 (April): 434–446.

Naylor, R. 1998. "International Trade and Economic Integration When Labor Markets Are Generally Unionized." Coventry: Department of Economics, University of Warwick, mimeograph.

Oswald, Andrew J. 1985. "The Economic Theory of Trade Unions: An Introductory Survey." Discussion Paper, no. 211. London: Centre for Labour Economics, London School of Economics.

Revenga, Ana. 1992. "Exporting Jobs? The Impact of Import Competition on Employment and Wages in U.S. Manufacturing." *Quarterly Journal of Economics* 107 (February): 255–284.

White, Halbert. 1980. "A Heteroskedasticity-Consistent Covariance Matrix Estimator and a Direct Test for Heteroskedasticity." *Econometrica* 48, no. 4: 817–888.

V

Desire to Unionize and Union Impact on Workplace Practices and Performance

9

The Desire for Unionization, HRM Practices, and Coworkers

UK Evidence

Clive R. Belfield and John S. Heywood

Using the extensive data of the U.S. Workplace Representation and Participation Survey, R.B. Freeman and J. Rogers (1999) provide an answer to the provocative question: What do workers want? While the details of their answer are shaded, the broad outlines are clear. Two-thirds of U.S. workers want more influence at their workplace and one-third express dissatisfaction with the influence they have currently. One-third of U.S. nonunion workers desire union representation and identify better pay and working conditions as the most important thing unions could do for their members (Freeman and Rogers 1999, 40–41, 69–80). This desire for both more influence and for unions is identified as the "representation gap," a gap that fails to close largely because of the union-resistance activities of management. Moreover, advanced human resource management including, most notably, employee involvement schemes, serves to reduce the desire for unions, making the gap less than it would be otherwise (113–114).

We explore these issues using the Workplace Employment Relations Survey 1998 (WERS 98) and ask: What do British workers want? The evidence presents both similarities and differences with the U.S. conclusions outlined earlier.[1] The available questions in the WERS 98, while not identical to those asked in the United States, suggest workers are less dissatisfied with their influence over the workplace and indicate a far smaller representation gap with several of the relevant questions not even showing double-digit support for unions. Yet, the level of nonunion support for representation is not trivial and deserves further inquiry. We identify the determinants of this support using a broad set of individual and workplace characteristics. Of special interest is the extent to which human resource management (HRM) activities have a direct influence on this support. We also identify the crucial role played by good employment relations as a direct determinant of the desire for unionization and go on to show the influence of HRM practices on the quality of relations. Ultimately, this allows us to identify a direct effect of these practices and an indirect effect working through the quality of employment relations.

We also investigate directly the characteristics of coworkers who are associated with union desire. At issue is why workers desire unionization and yet are not members of a union. We argue that a worker desiring unionization sees equivalent nonunion coworkers as a threat; however, he or she also sees these coworkers as a source for support if they become unionized as well. This has been identified as the union "coordination effect"—it is good to be a union worker if all other workers are unionized. We go on to argue that nonunion workers are more likely to desire unionization in their current job if they share characteristics with a broad group of other workers at the plant. If unions give voice to the "median member," those closer to the median are more likely to favor unionization. Finally, we examine the role information revelation may play in managerial strategies to forestall unions.

In what follows, the next section outlines past research and the rationale for our study. Section three presents our data, broad descriptive statistics, and methodology. Section four presents the series of results on the inquiries outlined above and section five concludes.

The Desire for Union Representation

There exists substantial recent evidence for the United Kingdom (UK) on the effects of unions on members' wages and on firm performance/survival (e.g., see Hildreth 1999; Lanot and Walker 1998; Machin 1997; Andrews, Bell, and Upward 1998). On initial blush, the higher wages provided by unions should attract workers and the reduced performance and increased chance of failure should cause management to resist unions (Addison, Heywood, and Wei 2001; Machin and Stewart 1996; Freeman and Kleiner 1999). Yet, the picture is more complicated. Nonunion workers may fear job loss from unionization, knowing that the higher union wage is associated with reduced demand for labor (Donohue and Heywood 2000; Lawler and West 1985). Moreover, there may be important indirect effects that limit the wage advantage provided by unions: if firms dislike unions, they may offer wage supplements to reduce the threat of unionization. For the United States,

L.M. Kahn and M. Curme (1987) find that the threat effect increases non-union wage levels and that the increase is concentrated at the bottom of the nonunion earnings distribution; for the UK, in contrast, C.R. Belfield and J.S. Heywood (2001) identify no clear threat effect. The critical point is that it is inappropriate to simply assume that the pattern of the union earnings premium is sufficient to predict who will support unionization. Moreover, Freeman and Rogers (1999, 81–84) show that even a relatively long list of individual worker characteristics does not do a particularly good job of explaining the desire for union representation. They stress the combination of worker characteristics and workplace characteristics, a combination used in our current study.

More general inquiries into the desire for unionization follow one of three major avenues. First, actual elections are examined to determine the characteristics associated with voting in favor of a union (Demsetz 1993; Farber 2001; Waddington and Whitson 1997). Second, statistical analysis of broad cross-sections attempts to determine the structural determinates of those queuing for union jobs (Abowd and Farber 1982; Mohanty 1992). Third, detailed questionnaires ask workers about their preferences for a union or how they would vote in an imaginary election (Hills 1985; Heywood 1990; Freeman and Rogers 1999). This chapter falls solidly into this third category, as we use survey questions from the WERS 98 to identify individual and workplace factors that motivate support for union membership by non union workers.

Each of these approaches differs from the common statistical analysis of simply determining which worker characteristics are currently associated with representation by unions (for a review of such studies in the UK, see Mason and Bain 1993). This latter type of analysis may tell little about which non-union workers are likely to desire representation. Instead, it may simply reflect historical patterns now entrenched. These patterns are of little help for a manager facing the potential of union representation, as he or she is interested in which nonunion workers are currently on the margin of joining a union.

In addition to estimating the extent and determinants of any representation gap among nonunion workers, our inquiry helps identify the extent of the potential threat of unionization to nonunion employers. However, identification of a threat requires more detailed information than that available to many who explore the issue. Frequently, the threat is proxied by the existing extent of unionization in the industry or occupation (see Rosen 1969; Kahn and Curme 1987; Belman and Voos 1993). Again, this may well reflect historical patterns. For individual nonunion members, the decision to support a union depends on the costs and benefits. The benefits include wage premia, perhaps as much as 25 percent for some types of worker (Lanot and Walker 1998); and the costs may include a higher probability of job loss (either as the firm's financial performance is adversely affected, or the union member is replaced by a nonunion worker). The potential "tilting" of threat-induced wage supplements means that the benefits and costs may differ substantially from worker to worker. Ultimately, the threat should be measured as the extent of nonunion workers who wish to be represented. It is possible, using the WERS 98 data, to identify more precisely these workers and to isolate the influence played by managerial strategies.

Of special interest in this examination is the role played by HRM practices. The WERS 98 contains a variety of indicators of employee involvement schemes and other indicators of advanced HRM practices. These practices have been thought to enhance productivity and improve worker satisfaction (Huselid 1995; Ichniowski, Shaw, and Prennuski 1997; Cappelli and Neumark 2001). A less-tested, but very common, claim is that these practices are successful as a union substitution strategy. Firms are thought to improve workplace relations and productivity through the use of advanced HRM practices, causing the desire for union representation (and so the threat) to abate. Employee involvement schemes, in particular, may be thought to substitute for the voice role of unions and so reduce the potential benefits of unionization. While Freeman and Rogers (1999) and R.B. Freeman, M.M. Kleiner, and C. Ostroff (2000) find U.S. evidence in favor of this claim, N. Bacon (1999) presents an interesting UK case study in which the supposed gains from a comprehensive HRM approach proved illusory and the degree of management coercion increased. As a result, worker resistance toward management increased following implementation of the HRM strategy. Most would agree that additional testing of the union substitution claim is warranted.

Our particular strategy isolates determinants of nonunion workers reporting that they feel a union would best represent them (as measured across a series of particular workplace issues). We identify both a direct effect of HRM practices on the probability of supporting a union and an indirect effect working through the climate of employee relations. Isolating the indirect effect follows from our finding that when nonunion workers claim relations are good, they are far less likely to desire union representation. We also replicate this strategy with union workers to provide a contrast.

The second stage of our inquiry focuses on the characteristics of coworkers. We hypothesize that for each individual worker the anticipated advantage (or disadvantage) of unionization is a function of coworker characteristics. Following the logic of Belfield and Heywood (2001) and descriptions of typical union avoidance strategies (Lawler and West 1985), becoming a union member could jeopardize the worker's job: either the workplace might go out of business, suffer large layoffs, or replace union workers with nonunion workers. The chance of being replaced by a nonunion worker would be mitigated if equivalent coworkers were highly unionized as well. In addition, if equivalent coworkers are unionized, bargaining power is strengthened. This union "coordination effect"—it is good to be a union worker if all other workers are unionized—might show up in coworker effects. In addition, where the workforce is heterogeneous, a worker is unlikely to desire unionization because there are few equivalent workers. The voice function of unions is often viewed as a nearly democratic revelation of the median voters' preferences. Workers with preferences far away from the median may share little with the desires voiced by the median.[2] If preferences are associated with worker characteristics, workers are more likely to agree on representation when they share characteristics with coworkers. Given the unique composition of our data set, we can identify precisely which coworker characteristics lead to desire for unionization.

The final stage of our inquiry exploits simultaneous reporting by both managers and workers on the attitudes of managers toward unions. We examine the differences on the desire for unionization of alternative information strategies. In the first, managers and workers both say managers are not favorably inclined to unions. We take this to be evidence of a more traditional union avoidance strategy. In the second, managers say they are not favorably inclined toward unions, but workers believe otherwise. We associate this second combination as being more compatible with an HRM strategy of replacing unions with alternative involvement schemes. At issue is the comparison of these two alternatives in terms of worker support for unions.

Data

The data used here are from the WERS 98, which was collected in 1998 (Department of Trade and Industry 1999). The WERS 98 is a national sample of interviews with managers from 2,191 UK establishments with at least ten workers. Broadly, the survey addresses the issue of "management of employees," with detailed information on how the workplace is run and on the composition of the workforce. In addition, twenty-five employees at each workplace were randomly selected for individual survey, with questions about their work status, earnings, and education. So, the data set includes both individual and workplace characteristics. (Frequencies for control variables are reported in Appendix 9A; see p. 276.) Only full-time workers in the private sector are included in this analysis (thus, workers in the health, education, and government sectors are excluded).[3]

Specifically, workers were asked about representation within the work-

Table 9.1

Attitudes Toward Representation and Unions

Representation	Nonunion members (percent)	Union members (percent)
Ideally, who do you think would best represent you in dealing with managers here about getting increases in own pay?		
Union	15.2	77.3
Self, another employee, other	84.8	22.7
Ideally, who do you think would best represent you in dealing with managers here if you wanted to make a complaint about working here?		
Union	9.5	49.2
Self, another employee, other	90.5	50.8
Ideally, who do you think would best represent you in dealing with managers here if a manager wanted to discipline you?		
Union	12.0	73.3
Self, another employee, other	88.0	26.7
Cumulative total: Ideally, who do you think would best represent you in dealing with managers here either (i) about getting increases in own pay; or (ii) to make a complaint about working here; or (iii) if a manager wanted to discipline you?		
Union	19.9	88.4
Self, another employee, other	80.1	11.6
Do unions/staff associations take notice of members problems and complaints?		
Yes, (strongly) agree	11.4	56.9
Do unions/staff associations make a difference to what it is like to work here?		
Yes, (strongly) agree	10.7	51.5
Are unions/staff associations taken seriously by management?		
Yes, (strongly) agree	11.1	50.1
N	9,485	5,161

Note: Data are weighted by employee weights.

place: this included whether they were members of a trade union or staff association. They were also asked a series of attitudinal questions about unionization within their workplace. For our purposes, the most pertinent question from the WERS 98 is: "Ideally, who do you think would best represent you in dealing with managers here about getting increases in your own pay: (a) myself; (b) trade union; (c) another employee; or (d) some-body else?"[4] For nonunion workers, an answer of (b) represents "desire for unionization." Grouping (a), (c), and (d) responses across private-sector workers are given in the first row of Table 9.1: 15.2 percent of nonunion members think a union would be their best form of representation (along with 77.3 percent of union members). Put differently, 15.2 percent of non-union workers feel they would be best represented on issues of pay by a union, while 22.7 percent of union members feel they would be better repre-sented on issues of pay without their union.

Further information on representation is also reported in Table 9.1. Unions appear to be less well regarded for making complaints about work, with only 9.5 percent of nonunion members identifying unions as the preferred form of representation about complaints, while the majority of union mem-bers identify themselves as better represented without their union. Only 12.0 percent of nonunion workers identify unions as the preferred form of repre-sentation on issues of discipline, while 26.7 percent of union members iden-tify themselves as better represented without their union. Moreover, the workers who prefer unions in one of these areas often prefer unions in the other areas as well. Looking across all three questions, just less than 20 percent of nonunion workers prefer unions for at least one of the three is-sues identified (pay, complaints, or discipline). The respective figure for union members is 88.4 percent, which implies that 11.6 percent of union workers identify that they would be better represented without their union on *all* three issues: pay, complaints, and discipline. Even taking this very generous definition of union desire, the support in the UK appears to be less than that in the United States as identified by Freeman and Rogers (1999).[5]

Three additional questions probe workers' views of unions in the work-place. These ask whether or not unions take notice of members' problems and complaints: only one in ten nonunion members answering affirm that notice is taken, but more than half of union members answering say such notice is taken. Similarly, small percentages of nonunion workers think unions make a difference to the working environment (10.7 percent) or are taken seriously by managers (11.1 percent). Again, just more than half of union members answer positively to these questions. In short, as in the United States, it appears that to know unions (through membership) is to support them, but that support is far from monolithic. There appears to be substan-tial dissatisfaction among the UK union ranks with the nature of union rep-resentation. So, Table 9.1 establishes: (1) there is a potential threat of union formation from approximately 10 to 20 percent of the workforce, and (2) union membership is anticipated to have its strongest influence through earn-ings, and its weakest on job satisfaction.

We now turn to the role of employee involvement and union representation. Table 9.2 presents a variety of the measures of employee involvement as measured at the establishment level, while Table 9.3 (see pp. 260–261) presents a variety of measures of employee involvement as measured at the individual level. The establishment measures make clear that, if anything, the unionized workplaces make greater use of employee involvement measures. While joint consultative committees are well recognized to be more common in the union setting, the unionized workplaces hold their own in having teamworking, problem-solving groups, and briefing groups. Union workplaces also do better in formal information exchange, making more use of consultation and information exchange on a range of issues. Somewhat surprisingly given the general assumption that unions oppose explicit rent sharing, union workers are in firms that have at least as much opportunity for explicit financial participation as are nonunion workers. (Note that the dollar volume of this participation—and its availability across union and nonunion workers—is unknown.) On the other hand, the four indicators of employee-supervisor discussion indicate that union workplaces have somewhat less-reported communication.

The measures in Table 9.3 provide an alternative picture. First, nonunion workers appear more satisfied with their influence in the workplace. In a question nearly identical to one examined by Freeman and Rogers (1999), UK workers were asked about their satisfaction with the amount of influence they have at their workplace. As the first entry in Table 9.3 shows, only 13.5 percent express being (very) dissatisfied and 63 percent express being (very) satisfied. These correspond with the U.S. estimates of either 19 to 26 percent being dissatisfied and either 28 or 21 percent being very satisfied.[6] Again, the evidence of a representation gap appears more muted in the UK. Similarly, nonunion workers find their workplaces more supportive of personal growth and their managers more effective in responding to their problems. They also find their managers more communicative on all but one of the many issues listed in Table 9.3. While it is well recognized that unions may attract dissatisfied workers and that unions may encourage workers to voice their dissatisfaction (for a recent UK study, see Heywood, Siebert, and Wei 2002), it seems fair to say that UK nonunion workers are not complaining about the lack of influence when compared to union members.

Estimation and Results

Desire for Union Representation

Despite the suggestion that nonunion and union workplaces do not seem substantively different in the extent of employee involvement, the issue re-

Table 9.2

Employee Involvement Schemes

Employee involvement schemes	Nonunion members (percent)	Union members (percent)
Workplace group interaction		
Joint consultative committee	38.5	59.8
Are there committees of managers and employees at this workplace primarily concerned with consultation, rather than with negotiation?		
Briefing groups	26.8	27.9
Firm has system of briefings for any sections of workforce		
Teamworking	86.5	89.3
Employees in largest occupational group work in teams		
Problem-solving groups	47.9	57.4
Groups at the workplace that solve specific problems or discuss aspects of performance or quality		
Workplace information exchange		
Information sharing	23.9	38.0
Does management regularly give employees, or their representatives, any information about: internal investment plans; the financial position of establishment/ organization; or staffing?		
High levels of consultation	61.7	71.3
Management consults with employees using regular meetings, management chains, suggestion schemes, newsletters		
Workplace financial incentives		
Performance-related pay	16.7	20.2
Have 60 percent or more of nonmanagerial employees received performance-related pay in last 12 months?		
Financial participation	83.7	86.7
Employees receive profit-related payments or bonuses, deferred profit-sharing scheme, employee share-ownership, or group performance-related schemes		
Direct employee-supervisor discussion during last 12 months		
Discussed performance	62.2	57.5
Discussed promotion	27.0	23.2
Discussed training opportunities	48.5	51.4
Discussed pay	42.8	26.8
Cumulative total: discussed at least 3 of performance, promotion, training, or pay	33.3	26.0
N	9,790	5,161

Note: Data are weighted by employee weights.

Table 9.3

Worker Involvement at the Workplace

Indicator of involvement	Nonunion members (percent)	Union members (percent)
How satisfied are you with the amount of influence you have over your job?		
(Very) satisfied	63.0	52.7
Neither satisfied nor dissatisfied	23.5	26.5
(Very) dissatisfied	13.5	20.8
How often are you and others working here asked by managers for your views on future plans for the workplace?		
Frequently/Sometimes	42.5	51.7
Never/Hardly ever	57.5	48.3
How often are you and others working here asked by managers for your views on staffing issues, including redundancy?		
Frequently/Sometimes	31.5	30.1
Never/Hardly ever	68.5	69.9
How often are you and others working here asked by managers for your views on pay issues?		
Frequently/Sometimes	32.5	29.5
Never/Hardly ever	67.5	70.5
Cumulative total: How often are you and others working here asked by managers for your views on at least 2 of plans, staffing, or pay issues?	34.1	31.3
People working here are encouraged to develop their skills:		
(Strongly) agree	52.9	45.6
Neither agree nor disagree	24.2	23.9
(Strongly) disagree	22.9	30.5
How good would you say managers here are at keeping everyone up to date about proposed changes?		
(Very) good	41.3	35.5
Neither good nor poor	27.7	27.8
(Very) poor	31.0	36.9
How good would you say managers here are at providing everyone with the chance to comment on proposed changes?		
(Very) good	29.5	22.1
Neither good nor poor	30.3	29.0
(Very) poor	40.2	47.9

(continued)

Table 9.3 *(continued)*

Indicator of involvement:	Nonunion members (percent)	Union members (percent)
How good would you say managers here are at responding to suggestions from employees?		
(Very) good	33.7	22.9
Neither good nor poor	34.5	33.1
(Very) poor	31.8	43.9
How good would you say managers here are at dealing with problems you or others may have?		
(Very) good	48.8	38.6
Neither good nor poor	28.7	30.6
(Very) poor	22.5	30.8
N	9,790	5,161

Note: Data are weighted by employee weights.

mains as to whether among nonunion workplaces involvement matters. Our initial inquiry is to estimate, for the nonunion sample, the determinants of desire for union representation over pay.[7] Column 1 of Table 9.4 (see pp. 262–263) reports a probit estimation, where desire for unionization takes the value of 1 (and 0 for no desire). For this estimation, and all subsequent estimations, marginal effects are reported. The results indicate that those with lower hourly pay and those in temporary work are more likely to desire union representation. There are strong occupational and sector influences, and those in firms with only one establishment are less likely to desire representation (other plausible variables, such as workers' education levels, were not significant influences). The greater the mean deviation in pay, the lower is the desire, but larger firm size plays a role in increasing the desire for representation. Also of interest is that the presence of a union at the establishment makes nonunion workers more likely to be sympathetic to unions. We take this as support of the union coordination view to which we will devote more discussion later. Moreover, where management is perceived as being supportive of unions or takes them seriously, nonunion workers are also more likely to be sympathetic to representation.

More immediate for our discussion is the role of good relations, which emerges as a large and strongly negative determinant of union support. This may not be surprising, as it would seem to be capturing some of the same discontent as support of unionization does. Also, workers satisfied with their influence are less likely to support unionization. Thus, there appears to be a general role for variables logically associated with HRM. However, many specific measures of such management fail to be individually significant: of the variables capturing group interaction, information exchange, and finan-

Table 9.4

Desire for Union Representation for Pay (probit estimation)

	(1) Desire for union rep.		(2) Good relations		(3) Desire for union rep.	
	Marginal effects	(SE)	Marginal effects	(SE)	Marginal effects	(SE)
Log pay per hour	-0.0537	(0.0113)**	-0.0519	(0.0176)**	-0.0527	(0.0104)**
Ethnic minority	0.0381	(0.0250)	-0.0654	(0.0361)	0.0279	(0.0205)
Temporary worker	0.0456	(0.0286)	0.0151	(0.0493)	0.0447	(0.0268)
Occ.: managerial	-0.1014	(0.0100)**			-0.0897	(0.0098)**
Occ.: professional	-0.0680	(0.0128)**			-0.0765	(0.0100)**
Occ.: semiprofessional	-0.0452	(0.0132)**			-0.0371	(0.0120)**
Occ.: clerical	-0.0573	(0.0108)**			-0.0593	(0.0097)**
Occ.: craft	-0.0140	(0.0136)			-0.0116	(0.0142)
Occ.: sales	-0.0214	(0.0221)			-0.0035	(0.0241)
Occ.: services	-0.0284	(0.0138)			-0.0305	(0.0130)*
Mean deviation of pay	-0.1263	(0.0473)*			-0.1235	(0.0422)*
Single establishment	-0.0251	(0.0106)*	-0.0747	(0.0278)**	-0.0346	(0.0089)*
Org. size: 50–99	-0.0017	(0.0180)	-0.0738	(0.0279)**	-0.0109	(0.0156)
Org. size: 100–249	0.0198	(0.0196)	-0.1188	(0.0282)**	0.0034	(0.0156)
Org. size: 250–499	0.0318	(0.0196)	-0.1221	(0.0317)**	0.0198	(0.0165)
Org. size: 500–999	0.0809	(0.0250)**	-0.1093	(0.0355)**	0.0620	(0.0213)**
Org. size: 1,000–3,999	0.0595	(0.0273)*	-0.0827	(0.0492)	0.0558	(0.0238)
Org. size: 4,000+	0.0397	(0.0342)			0.0226	(0.0294)
Sector: manufacturing	-0.0707	(0.0123)**			-0.0651	(0.0103)**
Sector: construction	-0.0521	(0.0146)**			-0.0458	(0.0126)**
Sector: wholesale	-0.0515	(0.0134)**			-0.0448	(0.0118)**
Sector: hotels/catering	-0.0687	(0.0124)**			-0.0586	(0.0122)**
Sector: transport	-0.0348	(0.0157)			-0.0092	(0.0161)
Sector: other business	-0.0544	(0.0134)**			-0.0503	(0.0114)**
Good relations	-0.0650	(0.0094)**				
Good relations (pred.)					-0.0566	(0.0086)**
Union taken seriously	0.0861	(0.0190)**			0.0606	(0.0151)**

	(1)		(2)		(3)	
Union favored	0.1242	(0.0284)**			0.0782	(0.0202)**
Union at workplace	0.0341	(0.0123)**			0.0626	(0.0113)**
Teamworking	-0.0212	(0.0138)	-0.0254	(0.0211)	-0.0051	(0.0111)
Quality circles	-0.0073	(0.0116)	-0.0250	(0.0187)	-0.0054	(0.0103)
JCC	0.0111	(0.0094)	-0.0311	(0.0155)	0.0054	(0.0083)
Problem-solving groups	0.0271	(0.0144)			0.0086	(0.0123)
Consultation	-0.0104	(0.0141)	0.0280	(0.0173)	-0.0026	(0.0118)
Information provision	0.0125	(0.0107)	-0.0193	(0.0171)	0.0040	(0.0090)*
Profit-related pay	-0.0274	(0.0084)**	0.0028	(0.0146)	-0.0113	(0.0078)**
Performance-related pay	-0.0163	(0.0105)*	-0.0179	(0.0189)	-0.0066	(0.0098)*
Satisfaction with influence	-0.0346	(0.0094)**	0.0930	(0.0154)**	-0.0339	(0.0085)**
Discussion (3+)	-0.0295	(0.0093)**	-0.0081	(0.0150)	-0.0256	(0.0078)**
Asked opinion (2+)	-0.0264	(0.0096)*	0.0856	(0.0154)**	-0.0310	(0.0086)**
Male	0.0105	(0.0097)	-0.0252	(0.0144)*	0.0049	(0.0084)
Change in employment			0.0001	(0.0001)		
Values supported			0.0363	(0.0093)**		
Respect at work			0.1248	(0.0080)**		
Encouraged at work			0.0827	(0.0084)**		
Pride in job			0.0931	(0.0094)**		
Tenure			-0.0154	(0.0054)**		
Tenure sqd			0.0006	(0.0003)*		
Education: gcse			0.0507	(0.0197)*		
Education: alevel			0.0599	(0.0232)*		
Education: graduate			0.0984	(0.0233)**		
Kept up to date			0.1655	(0.0076)**		
Asked to do other tasks			-0.0179	(0.0189)		
Workers have discretion			0.0074	(0.0148)		
No security			0.0269	(0.0256)		
Disputes resolved at hq			-0.0439	(0.0219)		
Consulted			0.0280	(0.0173)		
Briefing groups			-0.0108	(0.0161)		
Share ownership			-0.0017	(0.0217)		
Pseudo R-sqrd	0.1347		0.3617		0.1382	
Observations	8,842		7,788		7,788	

Notes: Robust standard errors in parentheses. Constant term included in each estimation. *significant at 5 percent; **significant at 1 percent.

cial incentives at the establishment level, only the last of these has any impact on union desire (whereas the presence of problem-solving groups actually raises desire). The worker-level measures of involvement are more influential: however, reductions in union desire are obtained both from more worker-supervisor discussion (based on the cumulative total variable reported in Table 9.2) and from more managerial requests for workers' opinions (based on the cumulative total variable reported in Table 9.3).

We readily recognize that issues of endogeneity plague any attempt to isolate significant determinants.[8] In particular, the strong role of good relations seems particularly likely to be essentially capturing the same things as union desire. We attempt to instrument this more as a way of tracing out indirect effects than with any confidence that we can present an unbiased estimate. Thus, in the second column the determinants of good relations are presented as a first step to providing a predicted value of the good relations variable.

The determinants of good relations are of interest in their own right. Large firm size appears a negative determinant of good relations. Several of the involvement variables play expected roles. Thus, being satisfied with one's influence is positively associated with good relations, but financial performance does not appear to influence relations. When management asks for workers' opinions on firm policy, good relations are more likely. In addition, there appears to be an important role played by congruence of worker and management values, and where workers are treated with respect and are encouraged. Individual characteristics suggest the more educated and women are more likely to report good relations.[9]

Again, there appears to be a meaningful role played by indicators of management behavior regarding information sharing and consultation. Nonetheless, it is also the case that many specific indicators played no significant role in determining whether or not good relations were reported.

The predicted value of the good relations variable was then returned to the estimation of the desire for union representation using otherwise the same specification as before. Many of the same results carry over. Indeed, the coefficient on the predicted value of good relations is almost equivalent to the actual value, and it retains the same level of significance. Note that explicit financial performance and discussions with management, which played no role in determining good relations, continue as strongly negative determinants of union support in column 3. We identify these as direct effects. Satisfaction with influence and management asking opinions of workers appear to sit in both camps: they are significant determinants of good relations, which reduces the likelihood of union support, and continue to be direct negative determinants as well.

Table 9.5

Predicted Probability of Union Desire and Good Relations

	Union desire			
	Good relations excluded	Good relations included	Good relations	Good relations estimated
No employee involvement	0.226	0.291	0.500	0.243
Employee involvement	0.072	0.058	0.611	0.067

Notes: These projections hold all variables other than those involvement variables that are statistically significant at their sample means. See the text for more details.

The magnitudes involved are very large. Using the estimated equations in Table 9.4, we made a number of predictions to show the influence of the involvement variables. Under the most conservative estimate, we do not consider the quality of relations to reflect involvement. Thus, we use the third column of Table 9.4 holding all variables at their means except the statistically significant involvement variables: satisfaction with influence, discussion with management, opinion asked, performance-related pay, and profit sharing.[10] Setting all five of these variables at zero, we estimate the predicted probability of support for unionization. As shown in the first entry in Table 9.5, that probability is 0.226. We then predict the same probability after setting all five variables to values of 1. The resulting probability of desiring representation on issues of pay is only 0.072. At the other extreme, if we assume that quality of relations does reflect involvement, we can undertake the same estimates now using six significant variables. As the results in the second column show, the influence of involvement is much greater.

Perhaps most reasonably, we can use our estimated influences (EI) of involvement on good relations to capture an intermediate result. First, using the two significant EI variables in the good relations estimation and undertaking similar predictions, we find that with involvement the predicted probability of good relations is 0.611, but in the absence of involvement, the predicted probability of good relations is 0.500. We build this effect into our estimates again using the third column. We then set the five variables at 1 but set good relations at 0.611 and make a prediction. We still set the five variables at 0 (zero) and set good relations at 0.500 and make a second prediction. The final column in Table 9.5 shows that without involvement the predicted support is 0.243, but with involvement the predicted support for unionization is 0.067. Decomposing this difference reveals that approximately 10 percent is due to the indirect effect, with the remainder due to the direct effect.

Thus, the role played by the involvement variables is substantial. The final estimates above indicate that the use of the significant EI strategies can reduce the desire for unionization to around a quarter of its previous level (0.067/0.243). It is interesting to note that the informal measures of involvement and the financial measures of involvement show the primary influence. Teamworking, quality circles, and consultation take the expected negative signs but JCC [= 1 Joint Consultative Committee present, 0 otherwise], problem-solving groups, and information provisions take paradoxical positive signs. It remains possible that these more formal systems help generate some of the informal responses, but the data seem unlikely to allow this connection to be satisfactorily explored.

Union Members' Views About Union Effectiveness

A similar analysis can be performed for union members. In this case, the "desire" variable reflects the extent to which union members regard their union as effective at bargaining over pay. Recall from Table 9.1 that slightly more than three-fourths of union members felt the union would best represent them on issues of pay. Table 9.6 (see pp. 268–269) reports an equivalent set of estimations to those in Table 9.4, but now they are limited to union workers. Comparing the two tables, there are some differences in the impact of the coefficients. There is no clear effect of pay on union effectiveness for union workers; occupational effects are stronger for union members, but industry differences are weaker. However, the good relations variable has no direct influence on union effectiveness, nor does the variable measuring satisfaction with influence. There is limited impact of the HRM variables. Discussion continues to play a negative direct effect on the desire for unionization. Moreover, those more satisfied with their influence and who have been asked their opinion are more likely to report good relations.

Union Desire and Coworker Characteristics

We now turn directly to the identification of coworker characteristics that predispose a given worker to desire unionization. We know from Table 9.4 that where a union already exists at the workplace, desire for union status by remaining nonunion workers is higher. This fits with the notion that union status is more desirable (less costly) when the extent of organization within the firm is greater. We also have an initial indication that heterogeneity is important: where the mean deviation in pay is higher, the desire for union status is clearly lower. In order to further test if coworker characteristics influence the desire for unionization, we introduce variables that capture the position of an individual worker relative to coworkers. When a worker shares characteristics with the broad center of the distribution of workers, he or she will more likely report a desire for unionization. If, as approximately representative institutions, unions reflect the preferences of the median worker, the voice function will echo the center of the distribution (Freeman and Medoff 1984).[11] Thus, a worker substantially different from that center may well have a lower desire for unionization. An exception may be the role played by age and tenure as we will suggest shortly.

Table 9.7 (see p. 270) reports selected coefficients from a single estimation that includes the variables from Table 9.4, but also new variables to capture "coworker homogeneity." First, we introduce a variable that takes the value 1 if the individual worker is paid the same as 20 percent or more of the establishment's workforce. This homogeneity has a strong positive impact on desire for unionization. Second, we introduce a variable that takes the value 1 if the individual worker is in the same occupational group as 30 percent or more of the establishment's workforce. This variable also has a strong positive influence on the desire for unionization. Third, we introduce a set of personal characteristics, relative to the workforce. First, we measure the effect of being female but working in a mainly male workplace. As shown, and expected, this reduces the desire for unionization independent of the broader role of gender. Such a female worker might see herself alienated from other workers if she were to join a union. She might fear a "male union voice" that might not reflect her own preferences. Together, these variables suggest that working in a homogeneous workplace increases the desire for unionization.

The effects of age do not cohere as readily with this argument. Older workers are likely to have greater tenure, all else being equal, and tenure is often a critical element of union contracts. Often, on issues of job assignment and layoffs, seniority is a critical dimension. Thus, one would anticipate that those workers more likely to enjoy seniority benefits would be more supportive of unionization. We create a variable indicating whether or not the observation represents an older worker in a workplace where the average age is less than the median age of workers across all workplaces. In line with the role of seniority, such workers are much more likely to report a positive desire for a union. On the other hand, for younger workers in establishments with an older workforce, there is no effect. There is also no effect on union desire either if the worker posts more than the workplace average hours or if the workplace has a high proportion of part-time workers (as our samples are all full-time workers, this variable captures heterogeneity). Thus,

Table 9.6

Union Desire for Representation for Pay: Union Workers Only (probit estimation)

	(1) Union desire		(2) Good relations		(3) Union desire	
	Marginal effects	(SE)	Marginal effects	(SE)	Marginal effects	(SE)
Log pay per hour	0.0446	(0.0313)	0.0189	(0.0488)	0.0327	(0.0345)
Ethnic minority	−0.0552	(0.0510)	0.0604	(0.0791)	−0.0622	(0.0614)
Temporary worker	−0.0726	(0.0859)			−0.0933	(0.1017)
Occ.: managerial	−0.3424	(0.0675)**			−0.3487	(0.0743)**
Occ.: professional	−0.3002	(0.0570)**			−0.3067	(0.0607)**
Occ.: semiprofessional	−0.2126	(0.0535)**			−0.2338	(0.0576)**
Occ.: clerical	−0.1413	(0.0379)**			−0.1633	(0.0414)**
Occ.: craft	0.0180	(0.0269)			0.0076	(0.0300)
Occ.: sales	−0.2106	(0.1118)*			−0.2093	(0.1236)
Occ.: services	−0.1410	(0.0584)**			−0.1845	(0.0644)**
Mean deviation of pay	−0.3651	(0.1484)*			−0.3879	(0.1620)*
Single establishment	−0.1934	(0.0376)**			−0.1877	(0.0418)**
Org. size: 50–99	−0.0020	(0.0564)	−0.0148	(0.0577)	0.0434	(0.0535)
Org. size: 100–249	−0.0007	(0.0507)	−0.0195	(0.0550)	−0.0064	(0.0572)
Org. size: 250–499	0.0446	(0.0485)	−0.0299	(0.0532)	0.0255	(0.0543)
Org. size: 500–999	0.0456	(0.0488)	−0.0642	(0.0522)	0.0409	(0.0536)
Org. size: 1,000–3,999	0.0608	(0.0484)	−0.0966	(0.0518)	0.0553	(0.0528)
Org. size: 4,000+	0.0829	(0.0492)	−0.1251	(0.0530)*	0.0662	(0.0543)
Sector: manufacturing	−0.0416	(0.0327)			−0.0523	(0.0344)
Sector: construction	−0.0986	(0.0428)*			−0.1084	(0.0483)*
Sector: wholesale	−0.0510	(0.0446)			−0.0451	(0.0462)
Sector: hotels/catering	−0.1545	(0.0787)*			−0.1681	(0.0886)*
Sector: transport	0.0398	(0.0331)			0.0634	(0.0338)
Sector: other business	−0.0004	(0.0398)			−0.0095	(0.0433)
Good relations	−0.0365	(0.0198)				
Good relations (pred.)					−0.0192	(0.0244)
Union taken seriously	0.1042	(0.0205)**			0.1079	(0.0223)**

Variable	(1)	(2)	(3)
Union favored	0.0859 (0.0213)**		0.0825 (0.0231)**
Union at workplace	0.0629 (0.0311)*		0.0435 (0.0327)
Teamworking	0.0146 (0.0309)	0.0356 (0.0312)	0.0392 (0.0362)
Quality circles	-0.0232 (0.0258)	0.0254 (0.0234)	-0.0255 (0.0287)
JCC	-0.0027 (0.0183)	-0.0591 (0.0201)**	-0.0004 (0.0197)
Problem-solving groups	-0.0194 (0.0293)	-0.0235 (0.0250)	-0.0124 (0.0304)
Consultation	0.0284 (0.0306)	-0.0182 (0.0185)*	0.0199 (0.0316)
Information provision	-0.0014 (0.0201)	0.0182 (0.0136)	-0.0040 (0.0216)
Profit-related pay	-0.0169 (0.021)	-0.0096 (0.0221)	-0.0136 (0.0227)
Performance-related pay	-0.0468 (0.0240)*	0.0441 (0.0189)*	-0.0505 (0.0260)*
Satisfaction with influence	-0.0335 (0.0189)	-0.0282 (0.0200)	-0.0322 (0.0217)
Discussion (3+)	-0.1045 (0.0258)**	0.0675 (0.0199)**	-0.0970 (0.0270)**
Asked opinion (2+)	-0.0262 (0.0216)	0.0001 (0.0001)	-0.0288 (0.0248)
Change in employment		0.0442 (0.0123)**	
Values supported		0.1416 (0.0099)**	
Respect at work		0.0570 (0.0106)**	
Encouraged at work		0.0987 (0.0113)**	
Pride in job		-0.0107 (0.0084)	
Tenure		0.0003 (0.0005)	
Tenure sqd		-0.0027 (0.0221)	
Education: gcse		-0.0143 (0.0281)	
Education: alevel		0.0648 (0.0301)*	
Education: graduate		-0.0257 (0.0206)	
Male		0.1788 (0.0097)**	
Kept up to date		0.0234 (0.0185)	
Asked to do other tasks		0.0047 (0.0188)	
Workers have discretion		-0.0142 (0.0199)	
No security		-0.0156 (0.0191)	
Disputes resolved at hq		0.0288 (0.0216)	
Consulted		-0.0027 (0.0203)	
Briefing groups		0.0248 (0.0217)	
Share ownership			
Pseudo R-sqrd	0.1340	0.3804	0.1380
Observations	4,894	4,403	4,193

Notes: Robust standard errors in parentheses. Constant term included in each estimation. *significant at 5 percent; **significant at 1 percent.

Table 9.7

Union Desire, Coworker Characteristics, and Employee Involvement

	Marginal effects	(SE)
Coworker characteristics:		
Pay level same as > 20 percent of workforce	0.0281	(0.0087)**
Occupation same as > 30 percent of workforce	0.0197	(0.0093)*
Female worker—mainly male workplace	−0.0426	(0.0122)**
Older worker—mainly young workplace	0.0276	(0.0131)*
Younger worker—mainly older workplace	−0.0125	(0.0101)
Full-time worker—ratio part-time workers	0.0177	(0.0094)
Hours worked > mean for workplace	0.0213	(0.0254)
Workplace employee involvement schemes:		
Teamworking	−0.0296	(0.0147)*
Quality circles	−0.0060	(0.0121)
JCC	0.0105	(0.0097)
Problem-solving groups	0.0267	(0.0149)
Consultation	−0.0128	(0.0145)
Information provision	0.0081	(0.0109)
Profit-related pay	−0.0266	(0.0087)**
Performance-related pay	−0.0188	(0.0107)
Log likelihood	−3281.79	
Wald chi(2)	595.12	
Pseudo R-squared	0.1288	
N	8,802	

Note: Estimation includes all the variables as used in Table 9.4; column 1 (p. 262).

while not uniform, the results generally support a pattern of union desire reflecting either a favored position with the distribution (seniority) or being in the center of the distribution (earnings, occupation, and gender).

It is interesting to note that including the coworker effects is associated with one of the explicit EI variables becoming statistically significant. Specifically, workers employed by those workplaces using team-working are significantly less likely to desire union representation in this estimation. The role of the financial involvement variables persist and the individual indicators remain significant as well (satisfaction with say, discussion and asked opinion).

Workers' Perceptions of Union Opposition

Finally, we investigate perceptions of workers about the views of management. As indicated in Table 9.4, workers who anticipate management opposition are much less likely to report desire for a union. However, it is possible

Table 9.8

Preferences About Unionization

	Workers' views of managers' preferences about unions			
	Against	Neutral	In favor	N
Managers' stated preferences about unions:				
Against	998	762	26	1,786
Neutral	2,282	2,739	226	5,247
In favor	173	707	218	1,098
N	3,453	4,208	470	8,131
Accord between managers and nonunion workers		48.6%		
N		8,131		
Accord between all workers and union representatives		36.1%		
N		5,788		
Accord between managers and union representatives		51.9%		
N		6,064		

that workers will anticipate managers' views incorrectly and perceive more (or less) opposition than in fact exists. As well, workers will form their perceptions in the light of HRM practices implemented in the workplace. HRM practices and the perceptions of workers about the costs of unionization may be jointly determined. Thus, managers may use a combination of HRM practices and the revelation of their views on unionization as a way of forestalling unionization and influencing workers' opinions about unionization.

In the WERS 98, managers, workers, and—where present—union representatives are asked about management's view about unions (in favor, neutral, or against). Table 9.8 reports cross-tabulations on the preferences for and against unionization, as declared by the managers and as perceived by the workers. Only 48.6 percent of workers accurately perceive the preferences of managers regarding unions. Workers tend to overestimate the "antiunion" sentiments expressed by managers. Only 22.0 percent of workers have a manager expressing sentiments against unions, but 42.5 percent of workers think their managers are against unions. Similarly, 13.5 percent of workers have a manager in favor of unions, but only 5.8 percent of workers think their manager favors unions. (An alternative interpretation is that managers understate their antipathy to unions. However, the percentage of workers who misperceive managers' views is broadly uniform across all workplaces.) Interestingly, the perceptions of the union representatives are no more accurate than those of the workers (when both union and nonunion workers are included); and, if anything, the perceptions of the union representatives are more in accord with those of the managers than those of the workers.

Our earlier estimations indicate the strong role played by worker perceptions that managers favor unions. These perceptions are relatively rare and in the majority of cases are not accurate (only 218 of 470 as shown in Table 9.7). In light of these findings, two alternatives come to mind. First, "antiunion" managers may tell workers that any attempts to unionize will be dealt with harshly, implying threats of closure or layoffs. Such implied threats clearly reveal managerial attitudes and one would anticipate all workers to be aware of these attitudes (Lawler and West 1985). Second, managers who identify themselves as antiunion may undertake actions that lower worker desire for unionization but that may not reveal managerial attitudes. These could include improving the job characteristics, the quality of relations, or HRM practices in ways unmeasured by our variables but that attempt to replace traditional functions of unions. The difference between the reported position of managers and workers' perceptions of that position provides at least some leverage on this point.

First, we attempted to examine the determinants of perceptions: which nonunion workers are more likely to perceive that management is in favor of unionization? This was uninformative. We performed a logistic estimation in which the dependent variable takes the value 1 if the worker thinks—rightly or wrongly—that management is in favor of unions. Plausibly, workers are more likely to think managers are in favor if there is a union at the workplace, but other than that, none of the variables of our focus emerged as statistically significant.[12] Thus, none of the HRM practices are correlated with perceptions of managerial support and, overall, it is difficult to identify any characteristics within the workplace that cultivate the perception of managerial support for unions.

Yet, it is plausible that managerial attitudes toward unions will have different effects when recognized by workers. If workers misperceive the attitudes of managers (especially when they are antiunion), one would anticipate that the attitudes might be borne out in different practices or strategies than in those cases in which workers correctly perceive managerial attitudes. The role of worker knowledge of managerial strategies has been found to be critical. For example, F. Fakhfakh and V. Pérotin (2002) find that profit-sharing schemes increase the value added of firms, but only when known about by workers. Otherwise, equal profit-sharing schemes that were poorly understood or not even recognized by workers had no influence on firm performance. To test for the effect of misperception of managerial attitudes, we reestimate column 1 of Table 9.4 by dividing the variable "management favors unions" into four components: the first component is "management favors unions according to both workers and managers"; the second component is "management favors unions according to workers only"; the third is "management favors unions according to management only"; and the fourth—default—component is "management does not favor unions according to either management or workers." Two estimations are reported in Table 9.9.

The strongest desire for union representation in workplaces exists where both managers and workers record that managers are in favor of unions. The weakest desire exists when both workers and managers report managers are not in favor of unions (the vast majority, and the default category). Workers who misperceive managers' preferences as positive are still more likely to want representation. Yet, the extent of the preference is significantly less than that when workers accurately perceive a positive managerial preference (column 1). Thus, to the extent that the information pattern is not random and reflects managerial strategy, the case of attitudes not in favor of union recognized by workers results in the lowest probability of union desire, while that of attitudes in favor of union recognized by workers results in the highest probability of union desire. A clear middle ground exists when antiunion managers undertake strategies that make the workplace sufficiently "friendly" that workers misperceive their attitudes. We take these to be the circumstances in which managers foster practices that replace traditional union functions without appearing hostile to unions. The evidence suggests these practices may, indeed, reduce the desire for unions even holding the objective variables constant.

Finally, where managers say they favor unions, but this is not perceived by workers, there is no effect on the desire for union representation (column 2). This result is plausible, but if managers are truly in favor of unionization, it taxes credulity that they would not express this to workers (so we wonder about the veracity of these managers' declarations). Nonetheless, the previous results from column 1 carry over.

Conclusion

This analysis investigated workers' attitudes toward unions in great detail, using individual and workplace-level survey responses. We identified a nontrivial "representation gap" among UK workers, albeit one much smaller than that found for the United States. But, we also established that this gap may depend on several important characteristics.

First, the representation gap may be reduced by workplace employee involvement schemes and more general worker engagement. Thus, the desire

Table 9.9

Desire for Union Representation for Pay (probit estimation)

	(1) Desire for union rep.		(2) Desire for union rep.	
	Marginal effects	(SE)	Marginal effects	(SE)
Log pay per hour	−0.0521	(0.0112)**	−0.0521	(0.0112)**
Ethnic minority	0.0378	(0.0250)	0.0377	(0.0250)
Temporary worker	0.0455	(0.0286)	0.0445	(0.0286)
Occ.: managerial	−0.1025	(0.0099)**	−0.1022	(0.0099)**
Occ.: professional	−0.0688	(0.0127)**	−0.0687	(0.0127)**
Occ.: semiprofessional	−0.0463	(0.0130)**	−0.0463	(0.0130)**
Occ.: clerical	−0.0620	(0.0097)**	−0.0615	(0.0097)**
Occ.: craft	−0.0141	(0.0136)	−0.0140	(0.0136)
Occ.: sales	−0.0213	(0.0223)	−0.0229	(0.0219)
Occ.: services	−0.0310	(0.0134)	−0.0304	(0.0134)
Mean deviation of pay	−0.1244	(0.0472)*	−0.1216	(0.0473)*
Single establishment	−0.0255	(0.0106)*	−0.0255	(0.0106)*
Org. size: 50–99	0.0017	(0.0180)	0.0024	(0.0180)
Org. size: 100–249	0.0199	(0.0196)	0.0206	(0.0196)
Org. size: 250–499	0.0319	(0.0196)	0.0323	(0.0196)
Org. size: 500–999	0.0808	(0.0251)**	0.0810	(0.0250)**
Org. size: 1,000–3,999	0.0584	(0.0273)*	0.0568	(0.0271)*
Org. size: 4,000+	0.0397	(0.0340)	0.0421	(0.0343)
Sector: manufacturing	−0.0714	(0.0122)**	−0.0705	(0.0123)**
Sector: construction	−0.0509	(0.0147)**	−0.0503	(0.0148)**
Sector: wholesale	−0.0518	(0.0134)**	−0.0508	(0.0134)**
Sector: hotels/catering	−0.0696	(0.0123)**	−0.0683	(0.0124)**
Sector: transport	−0.0343	(0.0157)	−0.0342	(0.0157)
Sector: other business	−0.0551	(0.0133)**	−0.0551	(0.0133)**
Good relations	−0.0652	(0.0094)**	−0.0646	(0.0094)**
Union taken seriously	0.0853	(0.0190)**	0.0851	(0.0189)**
Union favored by managers (accord of workers/managers)	0.1682	(0.0486)**	0.1774	(0.0498)**
Union favored by managers (according to workers)	0.0889	(0.0309)**	0.0954	(0.0318)**
Union favored by managers (according to managers)	—		0.0198	(0.0148)
Union at workplace	0.0339	(0.0123)**	0.0292	(0.0127)*
Teamworking	−0.0220	(0.0140)	−0.0224	(0.0140)
Quality circles	−0.0073	(0.0116)	−0.0070	(0.0116)
JCC	0.0107	(0.0094)	0.0105	(0.0094)
Problem-solving groups	0.0275	(0.0144)*	0.0273	(0.0144)
Consultation	−0.0109	(0.0141)	−0.0119	(0.0141)
Information provision	0.0119	(0.0107)	0.0124	(0.0107)

(continued)

Table 9.9 *(continued)*

	(1) Desire for union rep.		(2) Desire for union rep.	
	Marginal effects	(SE)	Marginal effects	(SE)
Profit-related pay	−0.0269	(0.0084)**	−0.0268	(0.0084)**
Performance-related pay	−0.0171	(0.0103)	−0.0169	(0.0103)
Satisfaction with influence	−0.0347	(0.0094)**	−0.0348	(0.0094)**
Discussion (3+)	−0.0294	(0.0093)**	−0.0293	(0.0093)**
Asked opinion (2+)	−0.0261	(0.0096)*	−0.0264	(0.0096)*
Observations	8,842		8,842	

Notes: Robust standard errors in parentheses. Constant term included in each estimation. *significant at 5 percent; **significant at 1 percent.

for unionization is reduced by the presence and strength of these alternative forms of "representation." This happens both directly and indirectly. The latter reflects the fact that involvement appears to be associated with better relations in the workplace, which further reduces the desire for union status.

Second, the representation gap depends on the characteristics of coworkers. The net benefits of union status are likely to be higher for those near the "median worker." We confirm plausible links between union desire and an individual worker's position in the distribution of coworker characteristics. Workers who share characteristics with a large portion of their coworkers are more likely to favor unionization.

Finally, the representation gap—as perceived by workers—appears open to interpretation and manipulation by managers, who can persuade workers that they are "against unions" and so raise the expected costs to workers of being unionized. Here, the analysis is more speculative: we find few clear factors that workers rely on to declare management is in favor of unions. But, we also find that the representation gap is strongly increased where managers and workers agree that management is in favor of union status. There is also the intriguing case in which workers are not in favor of unions, but workers believe otherwise. Workers in this case are more likely to support representation than in the case of agreement that management is opposed. Yet, workers are much less likely to support unionization than in the case where managers truly favor unions. This structure is consistent with the notion that the representation gap can be reduced by HRM practices that emphasize the functions of unions rather than unions themselves. Finally, for those workers in pro-union workplaces, a question for future research

Appendix 9A

Frequencies

Individual worker variables	Mean	(SD)	Workplace-level variables	Mean	(SD)
Log pay per hour	1.893	(0.506)	Mean deviation of pay	0.290	(0.091)
Ethnic minority worker	0.041	(0.199)	Single establishment	0.238	(0.426)
Temporary worker	0.024	(0.153)	Org. Size: 50–99	0.205	(0.403)
Occ. 1: managerial	0.178	(0.383)	Org. Size: 100–249	0.217	(0.412)
Occ. 2: professional	0.135	(0.341)	Org. Size: 250–499	0.237	(0.425)
Occ. 3: assoc. professional	0.098	(0.297)	Org. Size: 500–999	0.133	(0.340)
Occ. 4: clerical	0.213	(0.410)	Org. Size: 1,000–3,999	0.079	(0.270)
Occ. 5: craft services	0.094	(0.292)	Org. Size: 4,000+	0.028	(0.166)
Occ. 6: personal services	0.022	(0.147)	Sector: manufacturing	0.252	(0.434)
Occ. 7: sales	0.080	(0.271)	Sector: construction	0.091	(0.288)
Tenure (years)	5.677	(5.198)	Sector: wholesale	0.193	(0.394)
Education: gcse	0.384	(0.486)	Sector: hotels/catering	0.072	(0.258)
Education: a-level	0.166	(0.372)	Sector: transport	0.065	(0.246)
Education: graduate	0.256	(0.436)	Sector: other business	0.213	(0.410)

Male	0.606	(0.489)	Profit-related pay	0.383	(0.486)
Good relations between managers and workers "(strongly) agree"	0.554	(0.437)	Union at workplace (recognized for collective bargaining purposes)	0.296	(0.456)
Worker "shares values of organization"[a]	2.420	(0.836)	Disputes resolved at headquarters	0.121	(0.326)
Worker "satisfied with respect from managers at work"[a]	2.457	(1.098)	No security (no guaranteed job security for any occupational group)	0.921	(0.270)
Worker "proud to say who works for"[a] share-ownership	2.611	(0.969)	Workers given discretion over how they work	0.636	(0.481)
			Change in employment (increase in workforce over previous year)	8.001	(67.686)
			Workers asked to do other tasks	0.481	(0.500)
			Quality circles	0.204	(0.403)
			Consulted via regular meetings	0.334	(0.472)
N workers	8,842		N workplaces	1,331	

Notes: [a] 1–3 scale, 1 = (strongly) disagree, 2 = neutral, and 3 = (strongly) agree. See also frequencies reported in Tables 9.1–9.3 (see pp. 256, 259, 260).

Notes

1. There are many reasons to expect differences between the U.S. and UK analysis and results: there are substantial distinctions between the two countries in how their labor markets operate, in how unions and managers behave, and as to what workers value at the workplace.

2. This is especially true when the preferences of workers are not monotonically increasing in a particular attribute. Thus, for example, workers may have different preferences on the temperature in their work environment and being too cold is as bad as being too hot. Here, it is the "distance" from the ideal that matters (see Duncan and Stafford 1980).

3. The sample was further limited by eliminating managers, but this did not substantially change the results. The results are available from the authors on request.

4. This question lends itself to a number of more subtle interpretations, depending on what "ideal" the worker might have in mind. So, the ideal workplace might be one where all workers are unionized and so best represented by their union; but in the real workplace of less than complete unionization, a worker may prefer to represent him- or herself.

5. The relevant question in the Worker Representation and Participation Survey (WRPS) asks explicitly whether or not workers would vote for a union if an election were held that day. On the one hand, this represents a specific action of support for unions but, on the other hand, it does not identify any of the specific roles that unions play.

6. The difference in the U.S. estimates comes from a unique facet of the WRPS, in which the same question was asked before and after discussing specific issues of influence. The large dissatisfaction percentage follows the discussion of influence (Freeman and Rogers 1999, 41).

7. We undertook similar estimates for the other two dimensions of representation and obtained broadly similar results. These are available from the authors on request.

8. Although the results are not materially affected when the dependent variable is either the desire for union representation for disputes, for union representation for complaints, or for any of the three services typically provided by unions (i.e., the cumulative response variable).

9. The role of women may reflect the fact that women sort into workplaces with better relations as women are known to value such relations more then do men (see Bender, Donohue, and Heywood 2001).

10. Payment schemes are designed to align the interests of workers and the firm, which we take as an element of financial involvement, so we include them as elements of overall employee involvement.

11. Another channel of coworker influences might follow from the arguments of R. Gomez and M. Gunderson (2002): union membership is often promoted through "word of mouth" recommendations of those workers who have already unionized. Where there are more coworkers who are union members, an individual worker—with similar characteristics to the coworkers—might be more willing to join the union.

12. Again, this estimate is available from the authors on request.

References

Abowd, J.M., and H.S. Farber. 1982. "Job Queues and the Union Status of Workers." *Industrial and Labor Relations Review* 35: 354–367.

Addison, J.T., J.S. Heywood, and X.D. Wei. 2001. "Unions and Plant Closings in Britain: New Evidence from the 1990/98 WERS 98." Working Paper. Birmingham, UK: Department of Commerce, University of Birmingham.

Andrews, M.J., D.N.F. Bell, and R. Upward. 1998. "Union Coverage Differentials: Some Estimates for Britain Using the New Earnings Survey Panel Dataset." *Oxford Bulletin of Economics and Statistics* 60: 47–77.

Bacon, N. 1999. "Union Derecognition and the New Human Relations: A Steel Industry Case Study." *Work, Employment and Society* 13: 1–17.

Belfield, C.R., and J.S. Heywood. 2001. "Unionisation and the Pattern of Nonunion Wages: Evidence for the UK." *Oxford Bulletin of Economics and Statistics* 63: 577–598.

Belman, D., and P. Voos. 1993. "Wage Effects of Increased Union Coverage: Methodological Considerations and New Evidence." *Industrial and Labor Relations Review* 46: 368–380.

Bender, K.A., S.M. Donohue, and J.S. Heywood. 2001. "Job Satisfaction and Gender Segregation in the US and UK: Are Women Happier Together?" Working Paper. Milwaukee. Graduate Program in Human Resources and Labor Relations, University of Wisconsin.

Cappelli, P., and D. Neumark. 2001. "Do 'High-Performance' Work Practices Improve Establishment-Level Outcomes?" *Industrial and Labor Relations Review* 54: 737–775.

Demsetz, R. 1993. "Voting Behavior in Union Representation Elections: The Influence of Skill Homogeneity and Skill Group Size." *Industrial and Labor Relations Review* 47: 99–113.

Department of Trade and Industry. 1999. *Workplace Employee Relations Survey. Cross-section 1998*, 4th ed. Colchester: The Data Archive, 22 December. SN: 3955.

Donohue, S.M., and J.S. Heywood. 2000. "Unionization and Non-union Wage Patterns: Do Low Wage Workers Gain the Most?" *Journal of Labor Research* 21: 489–502.

Duncan, G., and F. Stafford. 1980. "Do Union Members Receive Compensating Differentials?" *American Economic Review* 70: 355–371.

Fakhfakh, F., and V. Pérotin. 2002. "France: Weitzman Under State Paternalism." In *Paying for Performance: An International Comparison,* ed. M.B. Brown and J.S. Heywood, 90–114. Armonk, NY: M.E. Sharpe.

Farber, H.S. 2001. "Union Success in Representation Elections: Why Does Unit Size Matter?" *Industrial and Labor Relations Review* 54: 329–348.

Freeman, R.B., and M.M. Kleiner. 1999. "Do Unions Make Enterprises Insolvent?" *Industrial and Labor Relations Review* 52: 510–527.

Freeman, R.B., M.M. Kleiner, and C. Ostroff. 2000. "The Anatomy of Employee Involvement and Its Effects on Firms and Workers." Working Paper, no. 8050. Cambridge, MA: National Bureau of Economic Research.

Freeman, R.B., and J.L. Medoff. 1984. *What Do Unions Do?* New York: Basic Books.

Freeman, R.B., and J. Rogers. 1999. *What Workers Want.* Ithaca, NY: Cornell University Press.

Gomez, R., and M. Gunderson. 2002. "The Experience Good Model of Trade Union Membership." Twenty-third Annual Middlebury Conference on the Future of Unions, mimeograph.

Heywood, J.S. 1990. "Who Queues for a Union Job?" *Industrial Relations* 29:119–127.

Heywood, J.S., W.S. Siebert, and X.D. Wei. 2002. "Worker Sorting and Job Satisfaction: The Case of Union and Government Jobs." *Industrial and Labor Relations Review* 55, no. 4: 595–609.

Hildreth, A. 1999. "What Has Happened to the Union Wage Differential in Britain in the 1990s?" *Oxford Bulletin of Economics and Statistics* 61: 5–31.

Hills, S. 1985. "The Attitudes of Union and Non-union Male Workers Towards Representation." *Industrial and Labor Relations Review* 38: 89–102.

Huselid, M. 1995. "The Impact of Human Resource Management Practices on Turnover, Productivity and Corporate Financial Performance." *Academy of Management Journal* 38: 635–672.

Ichniowski, C., K. Shaw, and G. Prennushi. 1997. "The Effects of Human Resource Management Practices on Productivity." *American Economic Review* 87: 291–313.

Kahn, L.M., and M. Curme. 1987. "Unions and Non-union Wage Dispersion." *Review of Economics and Statistics* 69: 600–607.

Lanot, G., and I. Walker. 1998. "The Union/Non-union Wage Differential: An Application of Semi-Parametric Methods." *Journal of Econometrics* 84: 327–349.

Lawler, J.S., and R. West. 1985. "Impact of Union Avoidance Strategy in Representation Elections." *Industrial Relations* 24: 406–420.

Machin, S. 1997. "The Decline of Labour Market Institutions and the Rise of Wage Inequality in Britain." *European Economic Review* 41: 647–657.

Machin, S.J., and M.B. Stewart. 1996. "Trade Unions and Financial Performance." *Oxford Economic Papers* 48: 213–241.

Mason, B., and P. Bain. 1993. "The Determinants of Trade-Union Membership in Britain: A Survey of the Literature." *Industrial and Labor Relations Review* 46: 332–351.

Mohanty, M.S. 1992. "Federal and Union Job Queues: Further Evidence from the U.S. Labour Market." *Applied Economics* 24: 1119–1128.

Rosen, S. 1969. "Trade Union Power, Threat Effects and the Extent of Organization." *Review of Economic Studies* 52: 185–196.

Waddington, J., and C. Whitson. 1997. "Why Do People Join Unions in a Period of Membership Decline?" *British Journal of Industrial Relations* 35: 515–546.

10

Unions and Establishment Performance

Evidence from the British Workplace Industrial/Employee Relations Surveys

John T. Addison and Clive R. Belfield

One surprise in the British industrial relations literature is the seeming fail
ure of established relationships in the principal data set available to researchers—the Workplace Industrial Relations Surveys (WIRS) and the Workplace
Employee Relations Surveys (WERS)—to hold up through time; specifically, when effecting a comparison between the 1980s and the 1990s. Although the major focus of interest has been the attenuation of union effects,
for which there are a number of potential explanations, there are other empirical irregularities concerning such factors as information and consultation, participation, and financial involvement that are fundamentally more
opaque and that therefore continue to cast a shadow on easy interpretations
of the former.

In this chapter, we focus on the union argument. We first examine union
effects on financial performance, labor productivity, aspects of employment,
and the climate of industrial relations. Since our intention is to uncover
changes in union impact through time, we have also to consider evidence on
the union premium. We round off our survey of these (disparate) effects
with a discussion of union impact on plant closings. This might seem appropriate for either of two reasons: first, because evidence of plant closings
could explain why negative union effects, where observed, need not prove
pathological; and, second, because it could substantiate interpretations of
sources of observed changes in other union effects. As we shall see, the

sparse plant closings literature does neither in any obvious manner. Rather, it raises new sets of issues, and in particular whether weakened unionism is consistent with improved performance. A new strand of the unions-and-economic-performance literature, exploiting collective voice and the agency role of unionism, argues that strong unions imply better performance. Interestingly, this is echoed in the German literature, where it is argued that collective agreements reached at industry or regional level hold in check distributional bargaining at the workplace, allowing the works council (the vehicle of workplace representation in Germany) to focus on issues having more to do with the size of the cake, rather than matters of its distribution (e.g., see Hübler and Jirjahn 2001). In the second part of this chapter, therefore, we investigate whether more powerful unions are more responsible unions. Here, we reconsider the same performance outcomes reviewed earlier, but also link the new union construct to data on worker perceptions.

A final section offers an interpretation of our findings. On balance, we conclude that many though not all of the associations considered here are after all consistent with a weakening in union influence—and hence with a reduction in the disadvantages of unionism—brought about by man-made and economic forces. But the separate contributions of legislation and heightened product market competition are not easily quantifiable. Furthermore, it would be idle to pretend that we understand the sources of changes in the impact of other variables also evident in the WIRS-WERS. Finally, it is important to note that we are not discussing the macroeconomic role of unions. And this is the one area above all in which beneficial effects on employment and unemployment have been attributed to unionism or, more accurately, to coordinated wage bargaining (e.g., Nickell 1997). On the other hand, the standard industrial democracy case for unionism does not receive ringing endorsement when we attempt to go behind the collective voice argument.

Union Effects on Establishment Performance Across the WIRS-WERS

There is no doubt that unions declined in Britain after 1979, following a period of substantial growth. At that time, some 53 percent of workers were union members, but by 1999 this had fallen to 28 percent. Correspondingly, there has also occurred a sharp fall in the share of employees whose wages are set by collective bargaining: from 70 percent in 1980 to around 45 percent in the mid-1990s. Moreover, all indicators of union presence point in the same direction, and for all sectors other than the public sector (Machin 2000).

Since 1980, there have also been some profound changes in observed union effects, some of which are more controversial than others. We preface our presentation of establishment performance outcomes with some brief remarks on the course of the union-nonunion differential, one of the more controversial areas. It has been conventional to report that the union premium remained more or less stable during the 1980s but declined fairly precipitously during the first half of the following decade for a variety of union measures (see, respectively, Stewart 1995; Hildreth 1999). Today, it is often argued that the premium has evaporated (other than for specific groups such as women). The initial source of controversy was a dissonance between studies based on individual rather than workplace data, the former showing a persistent premium of around 10 percent, ceteris paribus (e.g., Blanchflower 1997). But more recent work using individual-level data seems to confirm the workplace findings (e.g., Machin 2001). So, after all, the evidence does tend to favor a marked decline in the union differential.[1]

Turning to our first outcome indicator—profitability—almost all of the early British studies pointed to negative effects of various indicators of union presence on financial performance/profitability. Some of the more recent evidence is reported in Table 10.1 (see pp. 284–285). The starting point is the study by Stephen Machin and Mark Stewart (1996) that identifies a sharp decline in the union effect on profitability over the first three WIRS. Note the finding that by 1990 any negative effect was confined to closed shop or analogous situations in conjunction with some degree of market power. Row 2 contains the results of a replication of the previous study by John T. Addison and Clive R. Belfield (2001), using the most recent WERS. If anything, it points to a sharper retardation in the effect of union recognition.

The study in row 3 of the table is of interest because it attempts to capture the effects of financial participation and employee involvement practices on financial performance. Identifying the union effect is secondary to this main concern. In particular, it is argued that employee involvement will be more capable of yielding a dividend where it is associated with financial participation—and, furthermore, that different types of employee involvement and financial participation will vary in their impact on financial performance. Mixed effects are duly reported for union recognition: unions have positive impact where the organization practices downward and upward communication, but in the absence of such schemes, the union effect is negative and statistically insignificant. However, Addison and Belfield's (2000) replication of this study (row 4) finds no statistically significant effect of union recognition for any concatenation of employee involvement and financial participation. Moreover, these authors also report different effects for the key variables in the empirical model (as do Addison and Belfield 2001, in replicating Machin and Stewart 1996).

Table 10.1

Union Effects on Profitability

Study	Data set/Methodology	Outcome measure	Union variable	Findings
1. Machin and Stewart (1996)	WIRS 80, WIRS 86, WIRS 90. Ordered probit	Financial performance	Union recognition (manual), closed shop/management recommends unionism (manual)	Negative effect of union recognition halved during the 1980s. By 1990 a significantly negative effect was confined to the closed shop. Moreover, that effect was conditional on presence of market power (as proxied by relative size of the establishment).
2. Addison and Belfield (2001)	WERS 98. Ordered probit	Financial performance	As above	Coefficient estimates for union recognition and closed shop/management recommends unionism variables statistically insignificant throughout.
3. McNabb and Whitfield (1998)	WIRS 90. Probit	Financial performance better than average	Union recognition	Union effect hinges on interaction with financial participation and employee involvement mechanisms. Union effect statistically insignificant in conjunction with financial participation. Union effect is positive and statistically significant in the presence of employee involvement schemes, and is negative and statistically significant in establishments where such schemes are absent.

Study	Data/Method	Dependent variable	Union measures	Results
4. Addison and Belfield (2000)	WERS 98. Probit	As above	As above	Coefficient estimate for union recognition statistically insignificant irrespective of employee involvement and financial participation mechanisms.
5. Booth and McCulloch (1999)	WIRS 90. Ordered probit	Financial performance	Union recognition, closed shop; manual and nonmanual union recognition, manual closed shop, nonmanual closed shop	Positive and statistically significant effect of union recognition; negative and statistically significant effect of closed shop. But these overall effects hinge on union type. Co-efficient estimates for recognition and closed shop are statistically significant only for nonmanual unions, where they are negative.
6. Conyon and Freeman (2001)	WERS 98. Ordered probit	Financial performance	Union recognition	Coefficient estimates for union recognition negative and statistically significant throughout.
7. Menezes-Filho (1997)	Sample of 494 firms, 1984–90. Pooled regressions, and fixed effect specification	Rate of return on sales	Union recognition/ derecognition; bargaining structure	Coefficient estimates for union recognition negative and statistically significant but declining through time. Strongest negative effects observed in single establishment firms and where different unions bargain jointly with the firm at the industry level. Fixed effects specifications show that derecognized firms have faster increases in profitability. Also fragmentation of bargaining structure associated with higher profitability.

Note: Unless otherwise indicated, financial performance is based on a five-element categorical measure derived from the manager respondent's assessment of the financial performance of the establishment relative to others in the same industry.

The study in row 5 of Table 10.1 widens the definition of a union. Specifically, Alison L. Booth and Andrew McCulloch (1999) distinguish between unions of manual and nonmanual workers. For the latter type of union, the effect of "recognition only" is negative and statistically significant and the presence of a closed shop increases the absolute value of the union effect. In contrast, manual worker unions have no discernible impact on financial performance, even in the presence of a closed shop. We note parenthetically that the main focus of this study is on bargaining over redundancy pay, which is not found to have any material effect on financial performance other than in nonmanual union regimes where the effect is strongly positive. In other words, firing constraints in the United Kingdom (UK) are relatively unimportant in impacting labor market flexibility.

The principal concern in the study by Martin J. Conyon and Richard B. Freeman (2001) (row 6) is the role of (four types of) financial participation in influencing financial performance, so that the union effects for the 1998 WERS cited in the table are secondary—and, interestingly, never commented on in the paper. As can be seen, the association between union recognition and financial performance is negative and statistically significant throughout (i.e., irrespective of the form of financial participation). Unlike the row 3 study, it is argued that employee involvement and financial participation are complementary.

The final study by Naercio Menezes-Filho (1997) (row 7) is notable for its use of objective financial data and incorporation of bargaining structure (and theory). The main result is that although union firms have lower profitability overall, that effect narrowed between 1984 and 1990 and had all but disappeared by the end of the sample period. That being said, profitability remained distinctly lower where unions were strongest. Union bargaining power is reported to be greatest—and profitability to be lowest—in firms with only one establishment (vis-à-vis multiestablishment undertakings) and where different unions bargain jointly with the firm at the industry level.

For their part, improvements in profitability are allied to union derecognition, the decrease in the number of establishments recognizing unions, and, consistent with the previous evidence, to changes from joint to separate bargaining and to decentralization of bargaining. Nevertheless, each result is conditional on increasing profitability due to the decreasing union recognition effect over time, so that restructuring of the bargaining relation is secondary.

The sparse early British evidence points to negative effects of unionism on firm and establishment productivity, despite contemporaneous estimates of the union wage premium of around 10 percent (e.g., Machin 1991). As before, the more recent evidence is surveyed in Table 10.2 (see pp. 288–289). The dominant theme of the newer literature is that unionized firms/plants increased their productivity most at the end of the 1980s (and arguably from 1979 to 1984, too) and/or that there is no longer evidence of a productivity shortfall in union firms/establishments. The evidence is not overwhelming, however, so that it would be premature to claim more than what has been observed is a reduction in the disadvantages of unionism. The relevant factors here include the possibility that the least productive unionized undertakings may have been evolved out of the system (for this reason, the empirical suggestion that the union effects were most positive in situations where competitive pressures were more acute is not altogether compelling), the fact that the strongest productivity gains are actually reported for union derecognitions, and to some degree the odd timing of the observed spurts of improvement. As in the case of parallel developments in profitability, reviewed earlier, it is conventional to ascribe the observed changes to the impact of the Margaret Thatcher reforms in conjunction with heightened competitive pressures. Thus, Paul Gregg, Stephen Machin, and David Metcalf write that "the gains are the cumulative result of a regained managerial right-to-manage (bolstered by union weakening and increased competition)" (1993, 895). On this view, union derecognitions are a signal to the workforce of a greater assertiveness on the part of management. At issue of course is whether the observed changes will persist (see the discussion later on). Also worrying is the apparent shift in the effects of other covariates—not just the union argument—on the productivity outcome indicators in the WIRS-WERS. In this case, however, there is supportive evidence for at least the union effect from the non–WIRS-WERS studies summarized in Table 10.2.

We turn next to the evidence of union effects on employment, which is broadly interpreted. There is reasonable agreement in the WIRS-WIRS on the apparent role of unions in retarding employment growth or exaggerating employment reduction. As can be seen from the first panel of Table 10.3 (see pp. 292–293), there is the suggestion that unionized establishments in the 1980s tended to grow by 3 percent less per year than their nonunionized counterparts. (Remarkably, a tendency of similar magnitude is observed in U.S. and Australian data—see, respectively, Leonard 1992; Wooden and Hawke 2000.). There is some disputation as to these results reported by David G. Blanchflower, Neil Millward, and Andrew J. Oswald (1991) for the 1980–84 period because of the concern that unionized firms at this time were more likely to see an erosion of restrictive practices (partly linked to overmanning arrangements and craft/job demarcations), and hence more likely to be shedding labor. But this criticism does not seem to be unduly damaging. First, the organizational change measure in the WIRS used to proxy such reform of working conditions does not overturn negative impact of the union den-

Table 10.2

Union Effects on Productivity and Changes in Productivity

Study	Data set/Methodology	Outcome measure	Union measure	Findings
1. Gregg, Machin, and Metcalf (1993)	328 trading firms from EXSTAT, 1984–89. Production function estimated using panel regression methods	Growth in log real sales	Union recognition, changes in union status	For union recognition alone, the union effect is negative and statistically insignificant for 1984–87, but positive and statistically significant for 1988–89 (+ 3 to 4%). For changes in union status, repudiation of the closed shop has no incremental impact over (favorable) effect of union presence (1988–89) but derecognitions considerably elevate differential productivity growth of union sector.
2. Conyon and Freeman (2001)	(i) 284 firms, 1995–98. Fixed effects production function estimates	Log real sales	Union recognition	Union effect negative but statistically insignificant throughout.
	(ii) WERS 98. Ordered probit	Relative labor productivity	Union recognition	Union effect negative but statistically insignificant throughout.
3. Moreton (1999)	WIRS 98. Ordered probit	Relative labor productivity and union density	Union bargaining power, proxied by separate multiunionism and firm endorsement of union membership, inter alia.	Multiunionism associated with significantly lower productivity. Where management recommends unionism there is a positive effect on labor productivity. Also some suggestion that union effect might be positive where labor demand elasticity is higher.

4. Fernie and Metcalf (1995)	WIRS 90	(i) Relative labor productivity	Union recognition alone. Pre-entry closed shop, post-entry closed shop, management recommends union membership, union recognition only	For the one-dimension measure, the union effect is negative but only marginally significant. For the fuller representation, no hierarchy of effect beyond union recognition only, which is negatively signed and highly significant.
		(ii) Labor productivity improvement, 1987–90	As above	For the one-dimension measure, the union effect is negative but only marginally significant. For the fuller representation, only the pre-entry closed shop is associated with significantly lower productivity growth.
5. Addison and Belfield (2001)	WERS 98	(i) As above	As above	Coefficient estimates for each union measure are negative but statistically insignificant throughout.
		(ii) As above	As above	For union recognition alone, the union effect is positive and statistically significant. For the fuller representation, no hierarchy of effect beyond union recognition only, which is again positively signed and strongly statistically significant.

Note: The relative labor productivity measure is a categorical variable based on management perceptions of labor productivity of the workplace compared with other similar workplaces (WIRS 90) or workplaces in the same industry (WERS 98). The labor productivity improvement measure is a categorical variable based on management perceptions of the level of labor productivity at the survey date relative to three years earlier (WIRS 90) or five years earlier (WERS 98).

sity measure on employment for the specific time period under consideration; that is, union density is negative and statistically significant when interacted with the absence of organizational change and in estimations for separate samples of establishments with and without organizational change.

Second, Booth and McCulloch (1999) (row 2) report for later intervals that the effect of union recognition on employment is robust to the inclusion of organizational change measures. Subject to obvious limitations—the data-driven failure to model the dynamics of the employment adjustment process—there is a large measure of accord in repeated cross-sections of the workplace surveys to the effect that unions slow job growth.

Not shown in the table, however, is the ambiguity surrounding other correlates of employment change. Thus, for example, Addison and Belfield (2001) (row 4) report very different findings for financial participation arguments than do Sue Fernie and David Metcalf (1995) (row 3). On the other hand, neither finds evidence of a hierarchy of union effects, namely, slower employment/stronger employment decline in circumstances where unions are more powerful. In this connection, Alex Bryson (2002b) argues that stronger unions are more likely to bargain over employment, so that one should not expect to see declines in employment for this subset of unions.

Finally, Table 10.3 contains information on union impact on quits and absenteeism rates. Here, there is no disagreement as between studies based on successive workplace studies as to the role of unions in reducing quits (rows 5 to 6), even if the WIRS-WERS data are less than ideal. Rather, disagreement instead centers on absenteeism rates: Addison and Belfield (2001) report sharply higher absenteeism rates in union regimes for WERS 98, whereas Fernie and Metcalf (1995) report no such association for WIRS 90 (rows 7 to 8). There has been no investigation in Britain of the effect of quits in improving productivity and of absenteeism in reducing it. Another outcome indicator that has attracted some scrutiny is the climate of industrial relations. Table 10.4 (see p. 294) provides results from just three studies, each using management responses (those of employees are examined in the next section).

As can be seen, the negative effects of union presence in its various guises detected in the WIRS 90 are not reflected in the successor WERS 98. It is not altogether clear whether we should regard the "climate" of industrial relations as a determinant of economic outcomes or as a separate indicator. The standard approach has followed the latter route, sometimes treating it explicitly as an intervening variable to differentiate between types of management processes (e.g., see Ramsay, Scholarios, and Harley 2000).

The study by Stephen Wood and Lilian de Menezes (1998) in row 1 of the table is of especial interest because of its attempt integrate the plethora of employee involvement and participative mechanisms used in many of the studies contained in Tables 10.1 through 10.4. Specifically, the authors test whether the schemes form a unity and can be used as indicators of a high commitment orientation on the part of management. Wood and de Menezes use latent variable analysis to search for identifiable patterns in the use of twenty-three such practices. Although they cannot identify high commitment management as a well-defined continuous variable, they are able to fit a latent class model to the data; that is, identify a progression of four types of high-commitment management (HCM). The progression is high HCM, medium-low HCM, low-medium HCM, and low HCM.

As far as unionism is concerned, the authors first examine the association between union recognition and high commitment management. Neither high HCM nor low HCM workplaces are distinctive with respect to unionism. This suggests among other things that the tendency of the industrial relations literature to treat nonunion workplaces as "bleak" and authoritarian is erroneous. Second, having confirmed that HCM is not replacing unionism, as it were, the establishment's HCM class is entered as an argument in conventional performance equations alongside unionism and controls for workplace characteristics and industry affiliation (there are three dummies, the default being high HCM plants). Row 1 in Table 10.4 simply reports results for the union covariate. As for the proproductive role of HCM, the findings are disappointing not only with respect to the climate of industrial relations, but also for the other outcome indicators (levels of and changes in labor productivity, financial performance, employment growth, quits, and absenteeism). In no case do high HCM plants perform better than all the others on any performance criteria. Thus, for example, although plants characterized by high HCM do have greater employment growth and better financial performance than the two medium HCM categories, this does not hold vis-à-vis low HCM establishments. The implicit suggestion that different types of firms can perform differently according to the outcome measure is also encountered in the other studies reviewed here (see, in particular, Fernie and Metcalf 1995). The final outcome indicator we examine is plant closings. On this occasion, all the extant studies are summarized in Table 10.5 (see pp. 296–297). The evidence is again mixed. Studies based on WIRS 84 reveal scant evidence of any association between unionism and plant closings, irrespective of the union measure (see rows 1 and 2 of the table). Note also the absence of a hierarchy of union effect: more powerful unions, as proxied by the magnitude of the wage premium or presence of the closed shop, have no discernible incremental effect on closings.

The plot thickens when we come to consider the more recent evidence. Broadly speaking, the sign of the coefficient estimate for the union variable

Table 10.3

Union Effects on Employment, Quits, and Absenteeism

Study	Data set/ Methodology	Outcome measure	Union measure	Findings
Employment				
1. Blanchflower, Millward, and Oswald (1991)	WIRS 84. OLS	Log employment (effectively an employment change equation as coefficient estimate on lagged dependent variable approximates 1)	Union recognition; union density; post-entry closed shop, pre-entry closed shop, union membership	Coefficient estimate for union recognition is negative and statistically significant. Effect of density is better determined. Together the recognition and density results imply that union establishments contract 3 percentage points more per year than their nonunion counterparts. Allowing for different union types, union membership and pre-entry closed shop are associated with lower employment growth (though the latter variable is poorly determined) while the effect of the post-entry closed shop is positive and statistically significant.
2. Booth and McCulloch (1999)	WIRS 90. OLS	Change in log employment, 1989–90 and 1987–90	Union recognition	Coefficient estimate for union recognition is negative and statistically significant throughout. The union-induced reduction in employment growth is 2.6% (5.7%) for 1989–90 (1987–90).
3. Fernie and Metcalf (1995)	WERS 90. OLS	Change in employment, 1984–90	Union recognition only; pre-entry closed shop, post-entry closed shop, management recommends unionism, recognition alone	For union recognition only, the association between employment change and union recognition is negative and statistically significant. For the fuller characterization of unionism, the coefficient estimates for all but the post-entry closed shop are negative and highly statistically significant. No hierarchy of effect.

Study	Data/Method	Dependent variable	Union measure	Findings
4. Addison and Belfield (2001)	WERS 98. OLS	Change in employment, 1993–98	As above	For union recognition only, the association between employment change and union recognition is negative and highly statistically significant. For the fuller characterization of unionist, only the two weaker measures of union presence are associated with a material reduction in employment change.
Quits				
5. Fernie and Metcalf (1995)	WIRS 80. OLS	Resignations (plus retirements and deaths) as a proproportion of total employment. Annual percent over year ending with survey date	As above	Union recognition only variable is associated with statistically significant reduction in quits measure. The same results hold for each of the four measures of union presence but again no hierarchy of union effect.
6. Addison and Belfield (2001)	WERS 98. OLS	As above	As above	Union recognition only variable is associated with statistically significant reduction in quits measure. But for the (three) measures of union presence only, the weakest is associated with a statistically significant reduction in quits.
Absenteeism				
7. Fernie and Metcalf (1995)	WIRS 90. OLS	Proportion of employees sick or absent, monthly rate	As above	No discernible impact of unionism on absenteeism irrespective of union measure.
8. Addison and Belfield (2001)	WERS 98. OLS	As above, annual rate	As above	Union recognition only variable is associated with statistically significant increase of absenteeism. Also true for union recognition alone for wider measures.

Table 10.4

Union Effects on the Climate of Industrial Relations

Study	Data set/Methodology	Outcome measure	Union measure	Findings
1. Wood and de Menezes (1998)	WIRS 90; Employers' Manpower and Skills Practices Survey. Ordered probit	Quality of management/ employee relations	Union recognition	Coefficient estimate for union recognition is negative and statistically significant.
2. Fernie and Metcalf (1995)	WIRS 90. Ordered probit	Quality of management/ employee relations	Union recognition; pre-entry closed shop, post-entry closed shop, management recommends unionism, and union recognition only	Coefficient estimate for union recognition alone is negative and marginally statistically significant. Of the four more detailed measures of union presence statistically significant negative coefficients are reported for the pre-entry closed shop and union recognition only.
3. Addison and Belfield (2001)	WERS 98. Ordered probit	Quality of management/ employee relations	As above	In all cases, the coefficient estimate for the union variable is positively signed but statistically insignificant.

Note: The quality of management/employee relations dependent variable is based on management responses on a seven-point scale ranging from "very good" to "very poor." In each of the above studies, the seven-point scale is collapsed to a five-point scale by combining the last three categories into one on frequency of response grounds.

is positive and statistically significant in the two studies using WERS 98 (rows 3 to 4). But this broad result hides as much as it reveals. Although reporting a material and robust positive association between either of two measures of unionism—recognition for collective bargaining purposes and union coverage—John T. Addison, John Heywood, and Xiangdong Wei (2003) find that this holds only for establishments that are part of larger (i.e., multiestablishment) undertakings. For single-plant entities (here firms), the direction of the association is reversed. (All studies support the more general result that single independent plants are less likely to close than their counterparts that are part of multiestablishment undertakings.) The authors interpret the former result as consistent with a decline in union bargaining power in the wake of a decade of antiunion legislation (attacking union immunities and regulating union governance), either by emboldening employers in multiplant enterprises to close unionized establishments or by weakening union influence over employment in such settings (see Manning 1993).[2] The single plant result, on the other hand, is rationalized in terms of (differential) union concessions in conjunction with rents.

While not contesting these findings, the recent study by Bryson (2001) (row 4) offers a different interpretation of the positive association between plant closings and unionism. He argues that union weakness—presumably accentuated by the legislation—underpins the sea change in union effect detected in the more recent workplace survey, but contends that this development is deleterious, whereas it is implicit in the previous study that the rate of plant closings was earlier suboptimal. Bryson argues that weak unions are less able to fulfill the collective voice function. Collective voice can provide a mechanism for overcoming many of the public goods aspects of the workplace. By aggregating worker preferences, unions can thereby enable firms to choose a more efficient mix of wage and personnel policies. Union voice may also open creative channels of communication with management and enhance management decision making. Furthermore, unions that have a say in how worker information is used by management may stimulate the disclosure of proproductive private information by workers.

Bryson (2001) reports that where unions are strong the coefficient estimate for unionism in the plant closings probit equation is no longer statistically significant. Strong unions are variously defined by the presence of the closed shop, and a combination of high union density, extensive bargaining coverage, and accompanying on-site lay union representatives, inter alia. In short, the converse situation defines unions that are too weak to be an efficient instrument of collective voice for workers. Interestingly, Bryson also suggests that strong (weak) unions may be an efficient (inefficient) agent for management as well. Here, he is apparently exploiting another public

Table 10.5

Union Effects on Plant Closings

Study	Data set/Methodology	Union variable	Controls	Findings
1. Machin (1995)	1984 WIRS; using the WIRS 1984–90 panel to identify plants that subsequently closed. Probit model	Union recognition	Log number of employees, proportion nonmanual workers, single plant, manufacturing dummies, below average financial performance, operating well below capacity.	Union recognition effect statistically insignificant both overall and by type of union (manual and non-manual), and in the presence or otherwise of the closed shop. Result robust to inclusion of one-digit industry dummies.
2. Stewart (1995)	As above. Probit model	Predicted mean union wage differential	Log number of employees, proportion nonmanual workers, operating well below capacity, manufacturing dummy.	Union wage differential statistically insignificant throughout.
3. Addison, Heywood, and Wei (2003)	1990 WIRS; using the WERS 1990–98 panel to identify plants that subsequently closed. Probit model	Union recognition; union coverage	Establishment size, establishment age, proportion female, proportion manual, proportion professional/technical, pro-portion short-term contracts, wide range of employee-involvement and participa-tion mechanisms, industrial relations climate, technology variables, flexibility at workplace, change in ownership, market power, layoff experience, export exposure, regional unemployment rate, one-digit and more detailed (three- or four-digit) industry controls.	Robust positive and statistically significant association between union measures and probability of plant closure. But the result is driven by plants that are part of multiestablishment undertakings. For single-establishment firms, the union effect(s) is negative and generally statistically insignificant.

| 4. Bryson (2001) | As above. Probit model | Union recognition; union strength (3 measures); union type; number of unions; bargaining arrangements (e.g., single vs. joint bargaining); and bargaining scope | Industry-level union density, log number of employees, proportion non-manual, single plant, (10) regional dummies, (18) two-digit industry controls, degree of competition, use of flexible contracts, financial performance better than average, operating considerably below capacity, increase in employment. | Union measure(s) positively associated with plant closure. But magnitude and significance of the effect is sensitive to form of measure. Statistically significant effects where union is weak, for manual worker unions, single unions, and where union bargains over physical working conditions. |

goods dimension of the workplace that arises when there are important complementarities in the production process, even if joint determination of effort does not necessarily imply that the union will be the employer's monitor of the employees. A final result is worth noting: although Bryson downplays the corollary of strong unionism—rent seeking—he nonetheless reports that where unions bargain over physical working conditions, the likelihood of closure is increased.

This review of the literature on union effects has uncovered evidence of seemingly important shifts in union impact over time. The evidence is largely consistent with reduced union bargaining power stemming from a decade of antiunion legislation in the 1980s and heightened product market competition. (However, we have cautioned that other associations evident in earlier WIRS data have also proved unstable, and we have altogether less compelling priors for these changes.) As cases in point, we can cite the decline in the union wage premium and the improved financial performance and productivity of unionized plants vis-à-vis their nonunion counterparts. It would be stretching things too far to claim the same for the seeming disappearance of a negative union effect in the climate-of-industrial-relations equations, given the lack of variability in the outcome measure. Equally, the presence of some constants in the empirical literature—such as the role of unions in blunting employment growth and, more controversially, in elevating absenteeism—would underscore the claim that one is speaking of an ongoing reduction in the disadvantages of unionism, rather than a complete transformation of the entity.

Nevertheless, the recent plant closings literature has raised new questions, occasionally hinted at in parts of the performance literature, by virtue of the positive association between union presence and establishment dissolutions in the WERS 98. Although this positive association is by no means inconsistent with the improvement-in-performance story, the notion that union weakness is a culprit is seductive and needs to be addressed. In the next section, we subject this claim to much closer scrutiny for other performance measures.

Effects of Union Strength on Establishment Performance

We now address directly the argument that the effects of unions vary according to union strength, using data on private-sector workplaces from the WERS 98. The WERS 98 follows closely the format of the earlier WIRS surveys (1980, 1984, and 1990), albeit with some differences (see Cully et al. 1999). It is a national survey of 2,191 UK establishments with at least 10 workers (previous WIRS only include establishments with at least 25 workers). The main focus of the survey is a "management questionnaire" that provides detailed information on the composition of the workforce, management of the personnel function, representation at work, consultation and communication, payment systems and pay determination, workplace flexibility, and (largely qualitative) information on workplace performance. In addition, twenty-five employees at each workplace are randomly selected for individual survey. This "employee questionnaire" component of WERS 98 seeks information from the worker respondent on the nature of the job, attitudes to work, representation at work, as well as on broad educational level and earnings. Unlike earlier WIRS, therefore, the WERS 98 data set includes information on both individual and workplace characteristics. For the purposes of this investigation, it contains fairly rich information on the role, behavior, and influence of unions at the establishment level across the UK economy.

Formally, the hypothesis to be tested is that stronger unions enhance establishment performance through effective "voice" (and agency), while weaker unions may actually impair performance (Bryson 2002a, 2002b). We test this hypothesis using various definitions of union strength. Table 10.6 (see p. 300) reports on various definitions of union "strength" across the 1,404 workplaces in the sample. Of the workplaces, 636 (45 percent) have at least one union that is recognized for pay bargaining purposes; the convention in the literature detailed earlier is to classify these as union workplaces (UNION). Within this sample of union workplaces, however, we can also identify unions that have relatively strong representation. Thus, for example, 521 union workplaces have an on-site union representative (REP), 270 workplaces have at least 75 percent workforce representation (union density, DENSE), while just 10 workplaces report a closed-shop agreement (CSHOP).

Union strength may also be proxied by union involvement in workplace decisions and practices. In this connection, 188 unions are reported to negotiate across a range of issues rather than simply over pay (RANGE). In ninety-eight workplaces, managers explicitly attributed a recent workplace change to a union decision or to union negotiation (CHANGE). And in forty-three workplaces, it is reported (again by the manager respondent) that unions had resisted workplace change (RESIST). In addition, we can identify workplaces where unions are welcomed by management and so have "influence": 309 union workplaces have managers who declare that they "favor unions" (FAVES), while management in a further 42 workplaces recommend union membership to their workers (REC).

Finally, we can identify the number of unions at the workplace: 343 units have more than one union (MULTI 1), of which 127 practice separate bargaining (MULTI 2). Apart from their effects on workplace performance

Table 10.6

Types of Union, Private Sector

	Number of workplaces	Percent
Recognition for pay bargaining purposes (UNION)	636	45.3
On-site union representative (REP)	521	37.1
Multiple unions (MULTI 1)	343	24.4
Management "favors unions" (FAVES)	309	22.0
75 percent + union density at workplace (DENSE)	270	19.2
Union negotiates across range of issues (RANGE)	188	13.4
Multiple unions with separate bargaining (MULTI 2)	127	9.0
Union decided or negotiated workplace change (CHANGE)	98	7.0
Union resisted workplace change (RESIST)	43	3.1
Management strongly recommends unionization (REC)	42	3.0
Closed shop (pre- or post-) (CSHOP)	10	0.7
No union recognition, but other employees act as representatives in dealing with management (NONUREP)	127	9.0
N	1,404	100.0

Note: Unweighted data from WERS 98.

through work rules, multiple unions may exert greater influence than single unions by offering more power and voice for different workers. More narrowly, where workers are complements, separate bargaining in multiunion settings implies stronger unions. Even if the opposite holds true where workers are substitutes, the fact that employers have increasingly favored joint bargaining might imply that the MULTI 2 category is still stronger unions. Accordingly, the hypothesis is that both MULTI 1 and MULTI 2 are indicative of greater union power.

In short, we can test the effects of union strength (as proxied by union types) on the range of outcome measures. Most of the workplace outcome measures can be examined: profitability; productivity and changes in productivity; employment, quits, and absenteeism; and the climate of industrial relations (closings information is not available for use with the 1998 data).[3]

In addition, we test for effects at the worker level by using responses from the "employee questionnaire." Across the 1,404 workplaces, information is available on approximately 18,000 individuals. For these employees, the outcome measures selected are their reported sense of achievement from work, loyalty toward the organization (plus shared values and pride in the organization), and the log hourly wage. The first four of these measures

capture worker attitudes and so approach more closely the notion of voice
that is emphasized in the literature. Although workers may be more dissatisfied, they need not of course be less productive and so the workplace and
worker-level estimations should be considered together. The full range of
outcome measures is described in Table 10.7 (see p. 302).

We estimate ten separate equations per outcome indicator to identify the
effects of unions (models 1 to 10). For each outcome, the more general
specification is:

$$Y = a_0 + a_1 U + a_2 Z \tag{1}$$

In equation 1, the outcome Y is related to U, the dummy variable capturing
union recognition (recall that unions are recognized in 636 of the 1,404
workplaces), and to a vector Z of workplace characteristics (detailed at the
foot of each appendix table). The sign, size, and significance of coefficient
a_1 has been the primary focus of the literature. Estimation of this coefficient
forms the basis of our model 1, and indicates the impact of unions on UK
workplace performance in 1998.

To estimate the effects of different union types, the specification in equation 1 is modified as follows:

$$Y = a_0 + a_{1S} U_S + a_{1W} U_W + a_2 Z \tag{2}$$

Here, the effect of union status is dichotomized into U_S and U_W, to represent
the nine types of unions in their strong and weak versions. These are models
numbered 2 to 10. In the case of model 2, for example, U_S takes the value of
1 if the workplace has a union with a union representative (as is the case in
521 workplaces) and U_W takes the value of 1 for the balance of the union
workplaces. To repeat, we simplify the exposition by referring to union types
as "strong" if they possess the characteristics listed in Table 10.6. Therefore, a strong union is one where there is a local representative, where union
density exceeds 75 percent, and so on. Note that because of a small number
of closed shops in the WERS 98, we combine this argument with the management recommends unionism variable (to form REC/CSHOP); also, we
should be cautious in our interpretation of the quit rate, although here we
invoke the standard argument that lower quits are beneficial. The specification in equation 2 serves two functions. First, it indicates whether unions—
strong or weak—affect workplace outcomes and worker attitudes and wages
($a_{1S} > 0$, $a_{1W} > 0$). Second, it allows us to see whether a strong union has
different effects from a weak union ($a_{1S} \neq a_{1W}$).

The coefficients a_1, a_{1S}, and a_{1W} for each model are reported in the ap-

Table 10.7

Outcome Measures, Private Sector

Workplace/Worker level	Definition	Mean	SE
Financial performance	Better than average = 3	59.9	
	About average = 2	33.0	
	Worse than average = 1	7.1	
Labor productivity	Better than average = 3	51.5	
	About average = 2	42.1	
	Worse than average = 1	6.4	
Labor productivity change	Better than average = 3	46.3	
	About average = 2	38.0	
	Worse than average = 1	10.7	
	A lot worse than average = 0	5.0	
Change in employment	(Emp 1998 − emp 1993)/emp 1993	0.62	6.93
Climate (reported by managers)	Binary variable, 1 = good relations between workers and managers	0.12	
Quit rate	Quits 1997–98/employment 1998	0.22	0.31
Absenteeism rate	Percent of work days lost 1997–98	4.24	4.66
Log hourly wage		1.847	0.527
Climate (reported by workers)	Binary variable, 1 = good relations between workers and managers	0.22	
Sense of achievement	Binary variable, 1 = (strongly) agree that the worker gets a sense of achievement	0.59	
Loyalty to the organization	Strongly agree = 5	15.3	
	Agree = 4	49.2	
	Neither agree nor disagree = 3	24.0	
	Disagree = 2	7.8	
	Strongly disagree = 1	3.6	
Shared values	Strongly agree = 5	7.2	
	Agree = 4	41.6	
	Neither agree nor disagree = 3	35.6	
	Disagree = 2	11.9	
	Strongly disagree = 1	3.7	
Pride in organization	Strongly agree = 5	15.6	
	Agree = 4	39.3	
	Neither agree nor disagree = 3	32.7	
	Disagree = 2	8.1	
	Strongly disagree = 1	4.4	

Note: Unweighted data from WERS 98.

pendices. They capture the effect of each union type in its strong and weak versions, relative to a workplace with no union. The hypothesis—stronger unions are relatively beneficial—can be examined by looking at the differences between coefficients a_{1S} and a_{1W}. However, a strict test is where the coefficient on a strong union is statistically significant and different from the coefficient on weak union. We perform this strict test by estimating the models 2 to 10, but using weak union status as the default category instead of nonunion status. With this specification, the coefficient on strong union status indicates a statistically significant effect relative to a weak union. In addition, we perform two weaker (less informative) tests. The first simply compares the absolute value of the point estimates to see which of a_{1S} or a_{1W} is the greater (ignoring significance levels). The second test is based on estimation of models 2 through 10, but now for the 636 union workplaces alone. A dummy variable is used to identify the stronger type of union, so that the sign and significance of its coefficient estimate indicates the relative effect of stronger unions in the union firmament.

Equations 1 and 2 are fitted for each of the workplace and worker outcomes. Robust regression, probit, and ordered probit estimation techniques are used, as appropriate for each outcome variable. For the worker-level estimations, the union coefficients identify the impact of being in a firm where the union is recognized (irrespective of the individual's own union status). Detailed controls for individual worker characteristics are included. But note in particular that the wage equation is simplified and does not adjust for differential selection of workers into unionized workplaces.

Summary findings for the key union measures across the ten models are given in Tables 10.8 and 10.9 (see pp. 305–306). (The coefficient estimates that indicate union effects are reported in Appendix 10A through Appendix 10D; see pp. 310–316.) Table 10.8 deals with the (seven) workplace outcomes. For each outcome, row 1 shows the direction and significance of the union recognition effect (coefficient a_1). Rows 2 and 3 report the results of the strict test. Row 2 reports union types where the coefficient on the stronger version is "beneficial" relative to the weaker version ($p < 0.05$). If the revisionist notion holds, we would expect stronger unions to be identifiable in this row. Row 3 reports those union types where a strong union has an "adverse" effect, relative to a weak union ($p < 0.05$).

This row should indicate where unions have a monotonic effect: stronger unions having "worse" effects than weaker unions. Overall, although the results are not fully consistent, the evidence tends toward rejection of the revisionist notion that strong unions are better for performance than toward acceptance of it.

For profitability, the general union effect is negative but not statistically significant (row 1). Nevertheless, the type of union that resists change does have a statistically significant adverse effect on profitability: the stronger union type has a more adverse effect, and so the recherché notion is rejected (row 2).

For labor productivity, there is again no clear general effect of unionism (the coefficient estimate in row 1 is only significant at the 0.10 level). Yet, there are four union types where a stronger union has a clearly adverse effect (and a weaker union does not). These are circumstances where the union resists change, where union density is above 75 percent, where the union bargains over a range of issues, and where multiple unions bargain separately. This evidence cautions against the idea that stronger unions are more effective. And there is no support for the revisionist notion in terms of labor productivity change. Instead, we do observe that the higher is union density, the slower is productivity growth.

For employment growth, union presence in general has deleterious effects that are statistically significant: coefficient a_1 is negative and well determined. Interestingly, where the union is "weakened" by the absence of a workplace representative, this adverse effect on employment growth is not observed. On the other hand, in workplaces where the union resists change, there is apparently no adverse effect either.

For quits and absenteeism, the results in general show quits to be lower and absenteeism to be higher in all union workplaces. As noted earlier, lower quits are conventionally viewed as a positive outcome and although we remain agnostic on the issue—since quits could be too low in union regimes—we follow the convention and treat reduced quits as beneficial. It can be seen that quits are further reduced in union plants with local representatives, in multiple union settings, and in circumstances where union density is high. For its part, however, absenteeism is further elevated where management favors unions or where union density is higher. Finally, with respect to the climate of industrial relations, there are essentially no differences as between workplaces without unions, with strong unions, or with weak unions. Only in one case—where the union is strong enough to resist change—is the workplace climate impaired to a significant extent.

Table 10.9 provides a corresponding summary of the employee results, although it will be recalled that the union variable is again measured at workplace level. Row 1 shows an interesting and persuasive result: all the worker satisfaction measures are lower in union workplaces, but the wage is higher. From the perspective of management, we can denote them as "worse." When we look at differences according to the strength of the union, there are some distinctions. Seemingly, the negative impact of unions on loyalty and pride can be obviated if the workplace has a closed shop or management recom-

Table 10.8

Strength of Union Effects on Outcomes—Workplace Level

	Profitability	Labor productivity	Labor productivity change	Employment growth	Quits	Absenteeism	Climate
Effect of union recognized for pay bargaining	-ve, not sig.	-ve, not sig.	+ve, not sig	-ve, $p < 0.05$	-ve, $p < 0.05$	+ve, $p < 0.05$	-ve, not. sig
Type of union where stronger version is beneficial($p < 0.05$), relative to weaker version				RESIST	REP, MULTI 1, DENSE		
Type of union where stronger version is adverse($p < 0.05$), relative to weaker version	RESIST	RESIST, DENSE, RANGE, MULTI 2	DENSE	REP		DENSE, FAVES	RESIST
N	1,236	1,196	929	986	1,299	1,075	1,393

Notes: See Appendix tables (pp. 310–316) for full information on estimations.

Union types: REP = on-site union representative; MULTI 1 = multiple unions; FAVES = management favors unions; DENSE = 75 percent + union density at the workplace; RANGE = union negotiates across range of issues; MULTI 2 = multiple unions with separate bargaining; RESIST = union resisted workplace change.

Table 10.9

Strength of Union Effects on Outcomes—Worker Level

	Climate	Sense of achievement	Loyalty	Shared values	Pride in organization	Log hourly wage
Effect of union recognized for pay bargaining	−ve, p < 0.01	−ve, p < 0.01	−ve, p < 0.01	−ve, p < 0.01	−ve, p < 0.01	+ve, p < 0.01
Type of union where stronger version is beneficial (p < 0.05), relative to weaker version			REC/CSHOP		REC/CSHOP	
Type of union where stronger version is adverse (p < 0.05), relative to weaker version	REP, MULTI 1, DENSE, RESIST, RANGE, CHANGE	REP, MULTI 1, DENSE, RESIST	DENSE, MULTI 1, MULTI 2	REP, MULTI 1, RESIST	DENSE, MULTI 1, MULTI 2	REP, MULTI 1, DENSE, RESIST, RANGE CHANGE, REC/CS HOP
N	18,051	18,349	17,943	17,219	17,968	17,333

Notes: See Appendix Tables for full information on estimations.
Union types: REP = on-site union representative; MULTI 1 = multiple unions; DENSE = 75 percent + union density at the workplace; RANGE = union negotiates across range of issues; MULTI 2 = multiple unions with separate bargaining; CHANGE = union decided or negotiated workplace change; RESIST = union resisted workplace change; REC/CSHOP = management strongly recommends unionisation or closed shop (pre- or post-).

mends union membership. That said, there is a strong link between adverse outcomes and the strength of the union for each of the worker measures (row 3). The negative union impact on worker attitudes is exacerbated by having a stronger union, particularly one that has a higher density, a local union representative, or multiple unions. Similarly, the higher the union wages, the stronger the union.

Overall, the strict test shows only the most limited support for the recherché notion that strong unions are beneficial and weak ones are not. This conclusion is supported by the two other weaker tests that we performed, where both tests do not include the quit rate outcome because of its ambiguity. The first weak test indicates the impact of union strength through a comparison of the coefficients for strong and weak unions across each of the twelve outcomes for each of nine union types based on specification (2) above (see the appendices). In 89 of these 108 comparisons, the coefficient on the stronger version of the union is "worse" than the coefficient on the weaker version of the union. The second weak test involved comparison of the coefficient on "strong union status" in estimations applied only to union firms. In 36 of the 108 comparisons, the coefficient for the strong union is statistically significant with an adverse effect ($p < 0.05$), whereas in only 3 cases was the coefficient statistically significant with a beneficial effect. Taken together, our results support what is to us the more plausible conclusion that the adverse effects of unions increase with the strength of the union.[4]

Interpretation

In this chapter, we discussed changes in the impact of unionism on establishment performance, inter alia, as revealed through analysis of successive WIRS-WERS, and examined the modern notion that the decline in union influence has downside efficiency consequences. Our findings may be summarized as follows. First, there is evidence of a diminution of union effects on wages, financial performance, and productivity through time. As the measures are not commensurate, we cannot quantify the degree of efficiency improvement stemming from these changes in unionized regimes. Arguably, the economic impact could have been small, but we incline to the view that more than redistribution (from workers) has been involved. But by the same token, certain unfavorable effects of unionism persist (e.g., slower employment growth and higher absenteeism) and so it is also appropriate to conclude that there has been a reduction in the disadvantages of unionism, not a reversal. Larger efficiency gains are likely to have accrued from the decline in union density and the ability of newly formed enterprises to avoid union organization.

Second, we found little direct support for the revisionist notion that the reduction in union power is responsible for worse outcomes. The argument that unions have to be strong to be an effective vehicle of proproductive voice and to act as an authoritative agent of the employer principal is, we submit, pushing things too far. We provided evidence against this notion for all of the outcome indicators earlier considered in our survey of the literature and, for completeness, for a variety of employee attitudes as well. The specific case of plant closings requires more attention. Given that there is no evidence of a union effect on plant closings in the WIRS 84, why should the reduction in union power have yielded a significantly positive association between union recognition/density and plant closings in the WERS 90? The Bryson (2001) argument would be that the legislation led to weaker unions that could neither deliver proproductive voice nor act as a responsible agent of the employer. We favor the alternative efficiency argument that there were too few closings in earlier years. In other words, we would argue from the finding for multiestablishments in the literature (see Table 10.5, row 3) that management in such undertakings have taken the opportunity to rid themselves of inefficient plants. This contention gels with the reasoning of Alan Manning (1993), who argues that the requirement for prestrike ballots (under the Conservative administration's Trade Union Act of 1984) may have led to a loss of union influence over employment. Unions, so the argument goes, had hitherto kept open unprofitable plants by threatening to strike profitable ones. The new need to ballot members destroyed the credibility of this mechanism because workers whose jobs were not in jeopardy would not vote for a strike.

Caveats attach to the interpretation that the workplace surveys unambiguously reveal evidence of a decline in union influence. In the first place, although we have not dwelt on variables other than unionism, major changes in the effects of such factors as employee involvement and financial participation are also evident in the data. These are a cause for some concern because we have few priors for the observed shifts. It is true that there were some differences in question design as between WIRS 90 and WERS 98 (e.g., more detailed questions on employee involvement), but it seems unlikely that there were major differences in the composition of the workplaces. It is of course possible that in the case of employee involvement and participation that WIRS 90, for example, disproportionately sampled the innovators and WERS 98 the second movers. Moreover, the focus on individual employee involvement schemes rather than the bundles suggested by more recent research may mean that like has not been compared with like. Again, by analogy with conventional payment-by-results schemes, individual employee involvement mechanisms may be subject to a cycle of emaciation and decay. That being said, there is also the issue of a changed impact of certain economic as opposed to industrial relations measures on the outcome indicators (e.g., in the effect of market power on financial performance).

And there remain specific concerns with the union results themselves. For example, in an analysis of the WERS 98 panel, not reported here, we found some contradictory evidence (Addison and Belfield 2002). First, a standard fixed effects approach using first-differences did confirm that changes in union recognition had no discernible impact on two main outcome indicators of (changes in) financial performance and labor productivity. Second, however, when we relaxed this overly restrictive form by allowing for changes in union recognition in both directions and unchanged union status (the default being no recognition at any time), the coefficient estimate for the latter variable was both negative and statistically significant. For their part, the introduction and abandonment of unionism led to neither deterioration nor improvement in the outcome indicators. Of course, there are unsettled issues such as the effects of sample attrition in the panel of establishments over time and the difficulty of measuring changes in performance on the basis of categorical measures. Nevertheless, these findings provide some further grounds for caution.

A final and necessarily unresolved issue is the future course of union impact. New legislation in the form of the 1999 Employment Relations Act favors unionism in a number of ways, most obviously perhaps by establishing a statutory recognition procedure for all firms employing more than twenty workers (e.g., see Wood and Godard 1999). Firms are required to recognize a trade union if a majority in the relevant bargaining unit vote in favor and at least 40 percent of the unit supports the union. There is also a procedure for automatic recognition where 50 percent of the unit workforce is already union members. The legislation also gives the right for all workers to be accompanied by a trade union representative in grievance and disciplinary proceedings, relaxes the laws on strike balloting, and extends special protection against dismissal to strikers. It is widely accepted that these measures will facilitate unionism and increase union bargaining power. If, however, the new economy is viewed as a powerful constraint on unionism, then pan-European legislation may offer a much more important crutch to the British union movement. We refer in particular to new European Union mandates that favor general systems of worker representation, such as the recently passed directive on national systems for informing and consulting workers. For a number of reasons, then, we have grounds for anticipating future iterations of the workplace survey with more than the usual interest.

Appendix 10A

Impact of Unions on Financial Performance, Labor Productivity, Labor Productivity Change, and Employment Growth, WERS 98

Union type	Financial performance		Labor productivity		Labor productivity change		Employment growth	
	Coefficient	SE	Coefficient	SE	Coefficient	SE	Coefficient	SE
#1: Union	−0.0457	0.0876	−0.0928	0.0865	0.1558	0.0937*	−0.2934	0.1146**
#2: Union and rep	−0.0263	0.0950	−0.0287	0.0938	0.1466	0.1016	−0.3322	0.1242***
#2: Union—no rep	−0.1017	0.0137	−0.2772	0.1345**	0.1545	0.1553	−0.1706	0.1897
#3: Union and faves	−0.1051	0.1043	−0.1341	0.1030	0.0676	0.1163	−0.3095	0.1397**
#3: Union—no faves	0.0052	0.1003	−0.0578	0.0989	−0.3095	0.1397	−0.2810	0.1302**
#4: Union and dense	−0.1682	0.1172	−0.2618	0.1149**	0.0025	0.1267	−0.3363	0.1531**
#4: Union—no dense	0.0081	0.0943	−0.0166	0.0933	0.2248	0.1015**	−0.2736	0.1239**
#5: Union and range	−0.1350	0.1263	−0.0955	0.1273	0.0488	0.1367	−0.2985	0.1661*
#5: Union—no range	−0.0185	0.0920	0.0922	0.0902	0.1880	0.0984*	−0.2920	0.1202**
#6: Union and multi 1	−0.1426	0.1141	−0.2106	0.1121*	0.1393	0.1266	−0.3436	0.1527**
#6: Union—no multi 1	0.0145	0.0989	−0.0182	0.0979	0.1646	0.1041	−0.2652	0.1279**

#7: Union and multi 2	-0.1020	0.1442	-0.3167	0.1412**	0.1012	0.1628	-0.3481	0.1993*
#7: Union—no multi 2	-0.0356	0.0900	-0.0526	0.0890	0.1651	0.0964*	-0.2846	0.1176**
#8: Union and change	0.0594	0.1609	-0.1108	0.1561	0.0404	0.1661	-0.4135	0.2074**
#8: Union—no change	-0.0580	0.0889	-0.0907	0.0880	0.1724	0.0958*	-0.2779	0.1168**
#9: Union and resist	-0.5204	0.2065**	-0.6399	0.2090***	0.0041	0.2229	-0.2143	0.2740
#9: Union—no resist	-0.0243	0.0881	-0.0692	0.0871	0.1635	0.0942*	-0.2974	0.1153**
#10: Union and rec/cshop	-0.1448	0.1889	-0.2844	0.1833	0.2036	0.2070	-0.4019	0.2422*
#10: Union—no rec/cshop	-0.0303	0.0891	-0.0661	0.0881	0.1288	0.0950	-0.2815	0.1167**
Observations	1,236		1,196		929		986	

Notes: Private-sector workplaces only. Unweighted data; weighted results are broadly equivalent (details available from the authors). Dependent variables are ordered, from 0 to 2. Higher numbers indicate superior financial performance or labor productivity. Controls for workplace estimations are: firm size, organizational size, industrial sector (8 dummies), ratio manual workers, training, log of employment size, briefing groups, consultation, influential JCC, information provision, problem-solving, share ownership, profit-related pay, performance-related pay, and establishment age. *significant at 10 percent; **significant at 5 percent; ***significant at 1 percent.

Appendix 10B

Impact of Unions on Quit Rate, Absenteeism Rate, and Climate, WERS 98

Union type	Quit rate		Absenteeism rate		Climate (manager reports)		Climate (worker reports)	
	Coefficient	SE	Coefficient	SE	Coefficient	SE	Coefficient	SE
#1: Union	-0.0489	0.0117***	0.8557	0.1407***	-0.0724	0.1119	-0.1955	0.0176***
#2: Union and rep	-0.0586	0.0125***	0.9174	0.1501***	-0.0956	0.1190	-0.2426	0.0190***
#2: Union—no rep	-0.0185	0.0186	0.6387	0.2316***	0.0129	0.1888	-0.0485	0.0291*
#3: Union and faves	-0.0596	0.0138***	1.2099	0.1650***	0.0014	0.1343	-0.2238	0.0206***
#3: Union—no faves	-0.0397	0.0133***	0.5436	0.1597***	-0.1327	0.1262	-0.1670	0.0209***
#4: Union and dense	-0.0808	0.0159***	1.2683	0.1840***	-0.0851	0.1484	-0.2478	0.0224***
#4: Union—no dense	-0.0348	0.0125***	0.6654	0.1504***	-0.0668	0.1199	-0.1643	0.0196***
#5: Union and range	-0.0526	0.0168***	1.0659	0.1945***	-0.1513	0.1560	-0.2538	0.0252***
#5: Union—no range	-0.0478	0.0122***	0.7781	0.1491***	-0.0463	0.1179	-0.1751	0.0187***
#6: Union and multi 1	-0.0788	0.0153***	0.9978	0.1850***	-0.0610	0.1441	-0.2593	0.0211***
#6: Union—no multi 1	-0.0313	0.0130**	0.7683	0.1589***	-0.0796	0.1257	-0.1411	0.0209***
#7: Union and multi 2	-0.0760	0.0198***	0.9257	0.2360***	-0.0377	0.1855	-0.3445	0.0289***
#7: Union—no multi 2	-0.0449	0.0119***	0.8447	0.1439***	-0.0779	0.1142	-0.1669	0.0182***

#8: Union and change	-0.0682	0.0210***	1.-101	0.2432***	0.0392	0.1999	-0.2651	0.0324***
#8: Union—no change	-0.0466	0.0119***	0.8197	0.1434***	-0.0867	0.1137	-0.1850	0.0180***
#9: Union and resist	-0.0782	0.0287***	1.-858	0.5303***	-0.5467	0.2478**	-0.3564	0.0447***
#9: Union—no resist	-0.0478	0.0117***	0.8412	0.1413***	-0.0486	0.1130	-0.1875	0.0177***
#10: Union and rec/cshop	-0.0666	0.0257**	1.-171	0.3148***	0.1051	0.2637	-0.1764	0.0429***
#10: Union—no rec/cshop	-0.0478	0.0119***	0.8304	0.1430***	-0.0848	0.1136	-0.1982	0.0179***
Observations	1299	1075		1393		18051		

Notes: Private-sector workers and workplaces only. Unweighted data; weighted results are broadly equivalent (details available from the authors). Dependent variables are ordered. Managers' views of good relations are binary, where 1 represents good relations. Workers' views are ordered, from 0 to 4, where higher numbers represent better relations. Controls for workplace estimations are: firm size, organizational size, industrial sector (8 dummies), ratio manual workers, training, log of employment size, briefing groups, consultation, influential JCC, information provision, problem-solving, share ownership, profit-related pay, performance-related pay, establishment age. Controls for worker estimations are: occupation, gender, experience (squared), age (squared), education, marital status, household composition, temporary work, fixed term work, training, log of employment size, briefing groups, consultation, influential JCC, information provision, problem-solving, share ownership, profit-related pay, and performance-related pay. *significant at 10 percent; **significant at 15 percent; ***significant at 1 percent.

Appendix 10C

Impact of Unions on Sense of Achievement, Loyalty, Shared Values, and Pride in Organization, WERS 98

Union type	Sense of achievement		Loyalty		Shared values		Pride in organization	
	Coefficient	SE	Coefficient	SE	Coefficient	SE	Coefficient	SE
#1: Union	−0.1293	0.0215***	−0.1815	0.0180***	−0.0709	0.0182***	−0.1957	0.0177***
#2: Union and rep	−0.1533	0.0233***	−0.1924	0.0196***	−0.0965	0.0197***	−0.2012	0.0193***
#2: Union—no rep	−0.0537	0.0354	−0.1478	0.0293***	0.0092	0.0298	−0.1783	0.0288***
#3: Union and faves	−0.1495	0.0254***	−0.1765	0.0213***	−0.0551	0.0215**	−0.2048	0.0209***
#3: Union—no faves	−0.1088	0.0254***	−0.1866	0.0214***	−0.0869	0.0216***	−0.1865	0.0210***
#4: Union and dense	−0.1875	0.0278***	−0.2202	0.0235***	−0.0891	0.0237***	−0.2257	0.0230***
#4: Union—no dense	−0.0944	0.0239***	−0.1585	0.0200***	−0.0599	0.0203***	−0.1778	0.0198***
#5: Union and range	−0.1406	0.0309***	−0.1561	0.0262***	−0.0726	0.0265***	−0.1795	0.0259***
#5: Union—no range	−0.1253	0.0228***	−0.1904	0.0191***	−0.0703	0.0194***	−0.2013	0.0188***
#6: Union and multi 1	−0.0996	0.0250***	−0.2233	0.0224***	−0.1154	0.0225***	−0.2485	0.0220***
#6: Union—no multi 1	0.3199	0.1103***	−0.1460	0.0209***	−0.0324	0.0213	−0.1506	0.0207***
#7: Union and multi 2	−0.1955	0.0359***	−0.2472	0.0311***	−0.1121	0.0312***	−0.2557	0.0303***
#7: Union—no multi 2	−0.1165	0.0222***	−0.1691	0.0185***	−0.0629	0.0188***	−0.1842	0.0182***

#8: Union and change	-0.1864	0.0390***	-0.1921	0.0342***	-0.0812	0.0340**	-0.2019	0.0328***
#8: Union—no change	-0.1206	0.0220***	-0.1799	0.0184***	-0.0693	0.0187***	-0.1947	0.0182***
#9: Union and resist	-0.2683	0.0543***	-0.1111	0.0466**	-0.1596	0.0479***	-0.2173	0.0453***
#9: Union—no resist	-0.1223	0.0216***	-0.1851	0.0181***	-0.0665	0.0183***	-0.1946	0.0178***
#10: Union and rec/cshop	-0.0813	0.0499	-0.0822	0.0441*	-0.0002	0.0449	-0.0716	0.0420*
#10: Union—no rec/cshop	-0.1341	0.0218***	-0.1886	0.0182***	-0.0770	0.0185***	-0.2048	0.0179***
Observations	18,349		17,943		17,219		17,968	

Notes: Private-sector workers only. Unweighted data, weighted results are broadly equivalent (details available from the authors). Dependent variables are ordered. Sense of achievement is a binary variable, taking the value 1 where there is (very) high sense of achievement. Loyalty is ordered, from 0 to 4, where higher numbers indicate greater loyalty. Controls for worker estimations are: occupation, gender, experience (squared), age (squared), education, marital status, household composition, temporary work, fixed term work, training, log of employment size, briefing groups, consultation, influential JCC, information provision, problem-solving, share ownership, profit-related pay, and performance-related pay. *significant at 10 percent; **significant at 15 percent; ***significant at 1 percent

Appendix 10D

Impact of Unions on the Wage Premium, WERS 98

Union type	Wage premium log hourly wage	
	Coefficient	SE
#1: Union	0.0373	0.0061***
#2: Union and rep	0.0470	0.0065***
#2: Union—no rep	0.0069	0.0102
#3: Union and faves	0.0389	0.0070***
#3: Union—no faves	0.0356	0.0071***
#4: Union and dense	0.0748	0.0075***
#4: Union—no dense	0.0148	0.0068**
#5: Union and range	0.0636	0.0083***
#5: Union—no range	0.0282	0.0064***
#6: Union and multi 1	0.0999	0.0070***
#6: Union—no multi 1	−0.0162	0.0072**
#7: Union and multi 2	0.0955	0.0093***
#7: Union—no multi 2	0.0261	0.0063***
#8: Union and change	0.0805	0.0099***
#8: Union—no change	0.0307	0.0063***
#9: Union and resist	0.0838	0.0146***
#9: Union—no resist	0.0350	0.0061***
#10: Union and rec/cshop	0.0663	0.0146***
#10: Union—no rec/cshop	0.0380	0.0062***
Observations	17,333	

Notes: Private-sector workplaces only. Unweighted data, weighted results are broadly equivalent (details available from the authors). Dependent variable is log hourly wage. Controls for worker estimations are: occupation, gender, experience (squared), age (squared), education, marital status, household composition, temporary work, fixed term work, training, log of employment size, briefing groups, consultation, influential JCC, information provision, problem-solving, share ownership, profit-related pay, and performance-related pay. *significant at 10 percent; **significant at 15 percent; ***significant at 1 percent.

Notes

1. A recent study by Bryson (2002a) adopts a semiparametric worker-matching approach to measure the union premium. It is reported that only in already covered workplaces are union members in receipt of a wage premium and then only if the workplace is more than 50 percent organized or the plant is aged twenty-one years or more. The postmatching differential for the entire private sector is a statistically insignificant 3.5 percent.

2. Manning (1993) argues that the requirement for prestrike ballots—introduced under the 1984 Trade Union Act—has led to a decline in union influence over employment. The argument is straightforward. In multiplant undertakings, unions could in earlier times keep open unprofitable plants by threatening to strike profitable ones. Requiring unions to ballot members destroys the credibility of this mechanism because workers whose jobs are not in jeopardy are unlikely to vote for a strike.

3. We are conscious that our definition of strong and weak unions is not without controversy. We largely justify our choice of indicators on the basis of conventions that have been adopted in the literature. Thus, for example, it is customary to regard management support of union membership as the modern version of the now-outlawed closed shop and hence indicative of union strength—rather than illustrative of the failure of the union in question to constitute a threat to the firm's management structure and objectives. But clearly some of the indicators we employ are ambiguous. This is perhaps most evident in the case of multiunionism. For example, a regime of multiunionism with separate bargaining is hardly indicative of union power in circumstances where the labor inputs are substitutes in production. Moreover, there are further theoretical subtleties having to do with bargaining level that apply here and that are ignored in our simple characterizations of union strength (see, in particular, Menezes-Filho 1997, 661–662). We would simply argue that: our tests reflect constructs used in the literature, be viewed in the round, and be understood as offering an obvious first-pass empirical procedure in assessing a likely popular (in post-Thatcher Britain) revisionist interpretation of union impact.

4. Our results remained unaffected after a substantial array of sensitivity tests were applied. These sensitivity tests fall into three categories. First, the WERS 98 includes survey response weights, derived so as to make the entire survey of public- and private-sector workplaces representative of the UK economy. The results we report here are for the unweighted data. They were largely unchanged when we applied the weights—full details are available from the authors on request. Second, individual earnings may influence worker satisfaction (and climate) and be collinear with the impact of union status on these variables. However, including individual wage levels in the worker-level estimations (as given in Table 10.2, column 4, and Tables 10.3 and 10.4) does not materially alter the results. Third, unionization may be endogenous: both a worker's decision to join a union workplace and the workplace's "decision" to be unionized may be endogenous. Such endogeneity can be addressed by instrumenting for these decisions. For a worker's decision to join a union, we used the entire range of personal characteristics and the sector of employment as instruments. This instrumentation inflated the coefficients on the union variables, but did not alter the relative sizes of the coefficient estimates across weak and strong unions. (In addition, we instrumented for a worker's decision to join a strong union, relative to joining a

weak one. Again, the relative sizes of the coefficients were unaffected.) For a workplace's decision to be unionized, we used industry sectors and organizational size as instruments. Overall, in none of the sensitivity tests were the results contrary to those reported here.

References

Addison, John T., and Clive R. Belfield. 2000. "The Impact of Financial Participation and Employee Involvement on Financial Performance: A Re-estimation Using the 1998 WERS." *Scottish Journal of Political Economy* 47 (November): 571–583.

———. 2001. "Updating the Determinants of Firm Performance: Estimation Using the 1998 WERS." *British Journal of Industrial Relations* 39 (September): 341–366.

———. 2002. "The Impact of Unions and Employee Involvement on Workplace Performance: Panel Data Evidence from the United Kingdom." Unpublished paper, University of South Carolina.

Addison, John T., John Heywood, and Xiangdong Wei. 2003. "New Evidence on Unions and Plant Closings: Britain in the 1990s." *Southern Economic Journal* 69 (April): 822–841.

Blanchflower, David G. 1997. "Changes over Time in Union Relative Wage Effects in Great Britain and the United States." Unpublished paper, Dartmouth College.

Blanchflower, David G., Neil Millward, and Andrew J. Oswald. 1991. "Unionism and Employment Behavior." *Economic Journal* 101 (July): 815–834.

Booth, Alison L., and Andrew McCulloch. 1999. "Redundancy Pay, Unions and Employment." *Manchester School* 67 (June): 346–366.

Bryson, Alex. 2001. "Unions and Workplace Closure in Britain, 1900–1998." Unpublished paper, Policy Studies Institute.

———. 2002a. "The Union Membership Premium: An Analysis Using Propensity Score Matching." Unpublished paper, Policy Studies Institute.

———. 2002b. "Unions and Workplace Performance: What Is Going On?" Unpublished paper, Policy Studies Institute.

Conyon, Martin J., and Richard B. Freeman. 2001. "Shared Modes of Compensation and Firm Performance: U.K. Evidence." Working Paper, no. 8448. Cambridge, MA: National Bureau of Economic Research.

Cully, M., S. Woodland, A. O'Reilly, and G. Dix. 1999. *Britain at Work: As Depicted by the 1998 Workplace Employee Relations Survey.* London: Routledge.

Fernie, Sue, and David Metcalf. 1995. "Participation, Contingent Pay, Representation and Workplace Performance: Evidence from Great Britain." *British Journal of Industrial Relations* 33 (September): 379–415.

Gregg, Paul, Stephen Machin, and David Metcalf. 1993. "Signals and Cycles? Productivity Growth and Changes in Union Status in British Companies, 1984–9." *Economic Journal* 103 (July): 894–907.

Hildreth, Andrew. 1999. "What Has Happened to the Union Wage Differential in Britain in the 1990s?" *Oxford Bulletin of Economics and Statistics* 61 (May): 5–31.

Hübler, Olaf, and Uwe Jirjahn. 2001. "Works Councils and Collective Bargaining in Germany: The Impact on Productivity and Wages." Discussion Paper, no. 322. Bonn: Institute for the Study of Labor.

Leonard, Jonathan S. 1992. "Unions and Employment Growth." *Industrial Relations* 31 (Winter): 80–94.

Machin, Stephen. 1991. "The Productivity Effects of Unionism and Firm Size in British Engineering Firms." *Economica* 58 (November): 479–490.

———. 1995. "Plant Closures and Unionization in British Establishments." *British Journal of Industrial Relations* 33 (March): 55–68.

———. 2000. "Union Decline in Britain." *British Journal of Industrial Relations* 38 (December): 631–645.

———. 2001. "Does It Still Pay To Be in a Union or Join a Union?" Unpublished paper, University College London.

Machin, Stephen, and Mark Stewart. 1996. "Trade Unions and Financial Performance." *Oxford Economic Papers* 48 (April): 213–241.

Manning, Alan. 1993. "Pre-strike Ballots and Wage-Employment Bargaining." *Oxford Economic Papers* 45 (July): 422–429.

McNabb, Robert, and Keith Whitfield. 1998. "The Impact of Financial Participation and Employee Involvement on Financial Performance." *Scottish Journal of Political Economy* 45 (May): 171–187.

Menezes-Filho, Naercio. 1997. "Unions and Profitability over the 1980s: Some Evidence on Union-Firm Bargaining in the United Kingdom." *Economic Journal* 107 (May): 651–670.

Moreton, David. 1999. "A Model of Labor Productivity and Union Density in British Private Sector Unionized Establishments." *Oxford Economic Papers* 51 (April): 322–344.

Nickell, Stephen. 1997. "Unemployment and Labor Market Rigidities: Europe Versus North America." *Journal of Economic Perspectives* 11 (Summer): 55–74.

Ramsay, Harvie, Dora Scholarios, and Bill Harley. 2000. "Employees and High-Performance Work Systems: Testing Inside the Black Box." *British Journal of Industrial Relations* 38 (December): 501–531.

Stewart, Mark. 1995. "Union Wage Differentials in an Era of Declining Unionization." *Oxford Bulletin of Economics and Statistics* 57 (May): 143–166.

Wood, Stephen, and Lilian de Menezes. 1998. "High Commitment Management in the U.K.: Evidence from the Workplace Industrial Relations Survey, and Employers' Manpower and Skills Practices Survey." *Human Relations* 51 (4): 485–515.

Wood, Stephen, and John Godard. 1999. "The Statutory Recognition Procedure in the Employment Relations Bill: A Comparative Analysis." *British Journal of Industrial Relations* 37 (June): 203–244.

Wooden, Mark, and Anne Hawke. 2000. "Unions and Employment Growth: Panel Data Evidence." *Industrial Relations* 39 (January): 88–107.

VI

U.S. Union Organizing
Any Hope for a Rebound?

11

Can Increased Organizing Reverse the Decline of Unions in the United States?

Lessons from the Last Quarter-Century

Henry S. Farber and Bruce Western

In 1956, one in three private sector workers were members of labor unions. By 2001, fewer than one in ten were members of unions. In stark contrast, the union membership rate among public-sector workers increased from 12 percent to 38 percent over the same period.

While the increase in public-sector unionism appears well understood, there is substantial disagreement about reasons for the sharp decline in the private-sector union membership rate. A wave of legislation at the state level was passed between the late 1950s and the 1970s that permitted and regulated unionization of public-sector workers (Farber 1988). With this legislation in place, public-sector workers were able to organize, largely because the political process gives employers neither the tools nor the incentives to resist organization effectively (for an analysis of the growth of labor unions in the public sector, see Freeman 1986). Many observers have argued that the legal and political support for organizing new union members in the private sector deteriorated through the 1970s and 1980s. Some focus on the intensified opposition to unions by employers (e.g., Freeman 1988; Weiler 1983). Others emphasize changes in the administration of the National Labor Relations Act (NLRA) due to changes in composition of the National Labor Relations Board (NLRB) (Levy 1985). Others claim that changes in the U.S. economic environment substantially reduced the attractiveness of unions to workers and the acceptability of unions to employers.

In this view, the economic environment became increasingly open to foreign competition in product markets and capital became more mobile internationally. Consequently, unions could no longer guarantee their workers higher wages while maintaining reasonable levels of job security.

In this study, we contrast two explanations for the decline of union membership in the private sector. The first explanation emphasizes legal and institutional factors affecting union organizing activity. The second is based on differential employment growth rates in the union and nonunion sectors. Our goal is to evaluate the prospects for an increase in organizing activity sufficient to reverse the downward spiral of labor unions.

Although our analysis focuses on the twenty-nine years from 1973 to 2001 using data from the Current Population Survey (CPS), we begin by presenting the facts on the union membership rate over the last century, from 1880 through 2001. In the third section, we investigate trends in NLRB election activity. Administrative data show that the quantity of organizing activity since 1973 was always small relative to the size of the nonunion workforce, but the number of elections declined sharply in late 1981. Although this decline is often linked to President Ronald Reagan's showdown with the air traffic controllers' union (Professional Air Traffic Controllers Organization [PATCO]) in August 1981 and the installation of a Republican majority on the NLRB in May 1983, we find little evidence that either event precipitated the downward trend in organizing activity. In the fourth section, we investigate whether changes in the public policy environment related to labor relations can account for the decline in election activity. The fifth section takes an alternative approach by presenting an accounting framework that decomposes the change in the union membership rate into components due to (1) differential growth rates in employment between the union and nonunion sectors or (2) the level of the union new organization rate (through NLRB-supervised representation elections). We find that most of the decline in the union membership rate is due to differential employment growth rates in the union and nonunion sectors and that it would take extremely large increases in union organizing activity to significantly influence the union membership rate. Finally, the sixth section offers some rough calculations of the financial resources required to mount an organization effort of sufficient scale. The resources required, particularly on a per-union-member basis, are quite large.

We conclude in the seventh section that the decline in the private-sector union membership rate was due primarily to changes in the economic environment that made union representation of less value to workers and/or more costly to employers. Increased global competitiveness and mobility of capital were likely important contributing factors. The decline in union organiz-

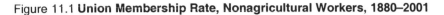

Figure 11.1 **Union Membership Rate, Nonagricultural Workers, 1880–2001**

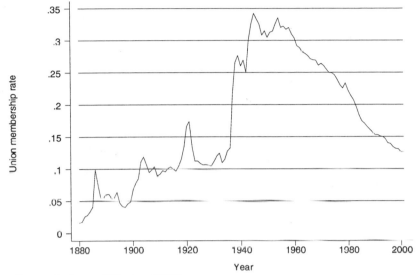

Source: Farber and Western (2001).

ing activity through NLRB-supervised representation elections was a marginal contributor to the decline in the union membership rate. In order to yield a substantial increase in the union membership rate in the long run, the level of union organizing activity would have to increase dramatically. This would require either a substantial change in the economic environment (perhaps as a result of a partial withdrawal of the United States from the global economy) or a drastic modification of the NLRA (well beyond the modest reforms that have failed to win adequate political support in over the last twenty-five years). The prospects for either of these scenarios are dim, and we are forced to conclude that a resurgence of labor unions in the private sector in the foreseeable future is unlikely.

The Decline in the Union Membership Rate

The Long Historical Record: 1880–2001

Figure 11.1 contains a plot of union membership rates among nonagricultural employees from 1880 to 2001.[1] This figure shows a rather remarkable pattern. The union membership rate was less than 5 percent in the early 1880s, and, with advances and retreats, rose to peaks of 34.2 percent in 1945 and 33.5 percent in 1954. The record since that time has been one of steady decline to a low of 12.6 percent in 2001. Richard B. Freeman (1998) characterizes the early record (through the early 1950s) of union growth as a series of discontinuous spurts followed by periods of decline. On that basis, the period since 1954 is best characterized as a long decline after the large spurt (or set of spurts) from the mid-1930s through the mid-1950s. Freeman's conclusion is that, in general, unions grow in spurts and not through slow and steady additions to membership over long periods of time.[2] These spurts originate in periods of intense social unrest (the 1930s) and wars (World War II and Korean War). But later wars (Vietnam War) and periods of social activism (the 1960s) have not resulted in spurts of organization. So, while future union growth may depend on another spurt occurring, we have little guide to what might trigger such an episode of dramatic growth.

Union Membership and Coverage in the Private and Public Sectors

Using data from the CPS, we can calculate distinct union membership rates in the private and public sectors over the 1973–2001 period.[3] Figure 11.2 verifies the well-known fact that union membership rates in the private and public sectors have followed very different paths over the past quarter-century. The private- and public-sector union membership rates were approximately equal in 1974 at about 25 percent and have diverged since. The public-sector union membership rate increased rapidly through 1980 to about 36 percent and has increased only slightly since.[4] In contrast, the private-sector union membership rate declined over the entire period to a low of 9.3 percent in 2001, though it appears that the rate of decrease in the membership and coverage rates was largest between 1980 and 1985.

Figure 11.2 also contains plots of the union coverage rate (the fraction of workers who are either members of a union or are covered by a collective bargaining agreement on their main job) from 1978 to 2001.[5] It is interesting to note that the free-rider rate (the fraction of covered workers who are not union members) is much larger in the public sector. The free-rider rate in the private sector has been steady at about 8 to 9 percent since 1978. The free-rider rate in the public sector was about 17 to 18 percent in the early 1980s and has decreased to 12 to 13 percent since that time. The free-rider rate in the private sector reflects, at least in part, the presence of right-to-work laws in nineteen states (in 1976). Based on the CPS data, the free-rider rate in the private sector between 1978 and 1998 was 15.0 percent in states with right-to-work laws and 7.5 percent in states without right-to-work laws.[6]

Given the closeness with which the coverage and membership series move

Figure 11.2 **Private- and Public-Sector Unionization Rates, 1973–2001**

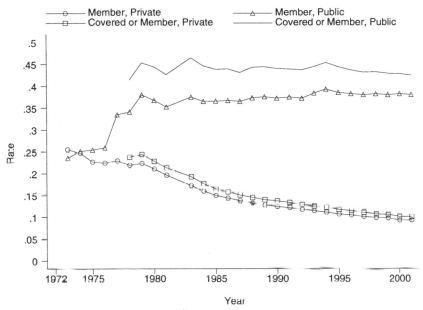

Source: Farber and Western (2001).

and the fact that a consistent series on membership is available since 1973, we proceed using union membership rates for our analysis of the decline in private-sector unionization.

The long time series in Figure 11.2 understates the decline in the private-sector union membership rate since 1973, because it combines the public and private sectors. Still, it is clearly the case that, by studying the period since 1973, we are joining the middle of a longer run process. The union membership rate has been declining since at least the early 1960s. Nonetheless, examining the processes affecting the union membership rate since 1973 has important implications for the longer time series.

The Decline in Union Organizing Activity

The NLRA provides the central mechanism through which jobs become unionized. The NLRA, passed in 1935, guarantees the rights of workers to organize and bargain collectively with their employers. The act also specifies a procedure for unions to become recognized as the exclusive bargaining agent of workers. The procedure is initiated when a large proportion (at least 30 percent) of workers show interest in union representation by signing authorization cards. The union then petitions the NLRB to conduct a representation election. Employers and unions campaign among workers from the time of the petition until the election. The NLRA also defines a set of unfair labor practices (ULPs) that limits the use of threats, dismissals, and coercion to influence the vote or the organizing process more generally. Violations can be remedied by bringing ULP charges before the NLRB.

In the early post-NLRA years, substantial organization happened outside the NLRB election process through the use of "recognition strikes" and "card checks." The definition of the former is self-evident. Organization through card checks occurred when employers agreed, without an election, to recognize a union and bargain following a strong show of interest by workers through signed authorization cards. While systematic evidence on the quantity of organizing through these mechanisms is difficult to come by, the general perception is that they have become less important in new organizing.

The Quantity of Election Activity

The left-hand plot of Figure 11.3 presents the number of NLRB-supervised representation elections held each year from 1940 to 1999. The large spurts of election activity in the early 1940s and early 1950s are clearly evident. Additionally, the number of elections increased rapidly during the 1960s before leveling off in the mid-1970s. This was followed by a sharp decline in the early 1980s. Since 1983, the number of elections has held steady at a relatively low level. The right-hand plot of Figure 11.3 presents the total votes cast in representation elections over the same period. While the spurts are evident in this series, there is a fairly steady decline in the total votes cast from the mid-1940s through the late 1950s.[7] The level of voting was fairly stable through the 1960s and 1970s before dropping precipitously (along with the number of elections) in the early 1980s. The total votes cast has remained steady at a very low level since the mid-1980s.

Figure 11.3 strikingly illustrates the sharp decline in union organizing activity in the early 1980s. The number of elections held fell by almost 50 percent from about 8,000 in 1980 to about 4,400 in 1990. The number of votes eligible to be cast fell from about 512,000 to about 221,000 over the same period, a drop of over 50 percent.

Union Success in Elections Held

Even the small number of workers voting in representation elections overstates actual new union organization since unions do not win all elections. The probability of a union win declined between 1940 and 1975.

Figure 11.3 **Quantity of NLRB Election Activity, 1940–99**

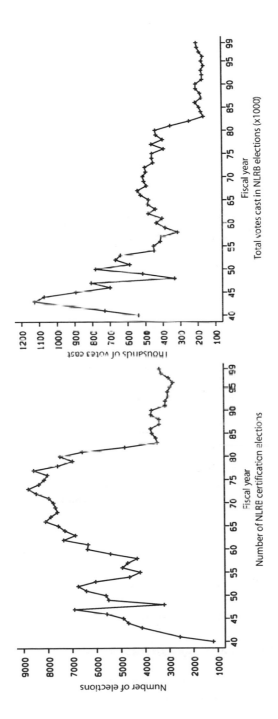

Source: Farber and Western (2002).

Figure 11.4   **Union Win Rates and Vote Share in NLRB Elections, 1940–99**

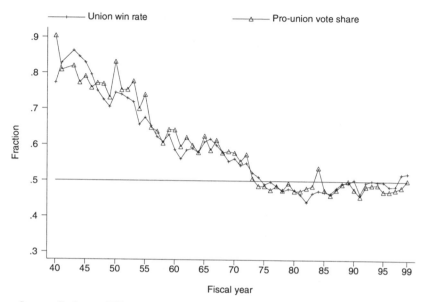

Source: Farber and Western (2002).

Figure 11.4 plots the union win rates and pro-union vote share in representation elections held between 1940 and 1999.[8] In the early 1950s, unions won 72 percent of all representation elections, but by the late 1970s the union win rate had dropped to 49 percent. Since the mid-1970s, the union win rate has been steady at slightly less than 50 percent.

An additional factor intervening to reduce the effective amount of new organization is the increased difficulty newly organized workers have had in negotiating a first contract with employers. While there are no systematic data on representative samples of union-won elections, Paul C. Weiler (1984) analyzes a small number of surveys and finds that the fraction of union wins yielding first contracts fell from 86 percent in 1955 to 63 percent in 1980.[9] Thus, even the already small new-organization rate based on the number of workers in potential bargaining units where unions won elections overstates the number of newly organized workers.

The New-Organization Rate: Two Definitions

It is clear that union organizing through NLRB elections is small relative to the labor force. In order to measure this more precisely, we define the new-organization rate, denoted ψ_t, as the product of the election rate (e_t) and the union win rate in elections held (w_t):

$$\psi_t = e_t \, w_t. \tag{1}$$

The union win rate (w_t) is defined as the fraction of workers eligible to vote in representation elections who are in units where the union won the election.[10] The win rate is appropriately computed by dividing the number of eligible voters in union-won elections by the total number of eligible voters that year. However, the number of eligible voters in union-won elections is not available prior to 1973, so we use the pro-union vote share as a proxy when constructing our long time series.

The definition of the election rate (e_t) depends on the purpose for which it is used. Because the pool of potentially unionizable workers consists of the nonunion workforce, it is reasonable to define e_t as the fraction of nonunion workers in period t who are eligible to vote in NLRB elections. This measure indicates how intensively unions are organizing potential members.[11] We rely on this definition in most of our analysis.

Alternatively, the election rate might be defined as the ratio of the number of workers eligible to vote in representation elections divided by union employment. This alternative measure highlights the extent to which unions "tax" themselves to organize new members. Since unions derive organizing resources from their members, normalizing the level of organizing activity this way helps describe the "tax rate" levied on union members to finance new organization.

The data requirements for computation of the new organization rate by either definition are substantial. Information is required on the number of individuals eligible to vote in representation elections, the number of individuals eligible to vote who were in units where the union won the election, private-sector employment, and the fraction of private-sector employment unionized. All of these measures can be calculated using microlevel data available since 1973 from the NLRB and the CPS. However, mportant components are not available prior to 1973. In order to provide some evidence on movements in the new-organization rate over the longer time period, we developed an admittedly imperfect time series on the new organization rate that covers the period from 1940 to 1997. We describe the construction of that series in Appendix 11A.

When using the microdata over the 1973–97 period, we use the NLRB data directly to measure the number of workers who voted in elections and the number in union-won elections. We compute employment levels in the union and nonunion sectors in three stages. First, we use data from the U.S. Bureau of Labor Statistics (BLS; Series ID LFS11000000) on monthly civilian employment to compute annual employment levels as the average of the monthly values in each year. Second, we compute the fraction of employment in each year that is in the private sector and the fraction that are union members within the private sector. These fractions are computed using the May CPS from 1973 to 1981 and the merged outgoing rotation group CPS data from 1973 to 1998.[12] Third, employment in the union and nonunion sectors in year t is then given by:

$$U_t = r_t \, p_t \, L_t \tag{2}$$

$$N_t = (1 - r_t) \, p_t \, L_t \, , \tag{3}$$

where r_t is the adjusted union membership rate, p_t is the fraction of employment that is in the private sector, and L_t is total employment. These employment levels are then used in calculating the new-organization rates by the two definitions.

We make no explicit adjustment in our analysis for the fact that certain groups of private-sector workers, managers most importantly, are explicitly exempted from coverage/protection under the NLRA. However, it is clear from exploratory analysis that our results would not be affected in any important way by excluding noncovered workers.

The Decline in the New-Organization Rate

With all of the components of the election rate and the union win rate in place, we calculated the new-organization rate using both the nonunion and union basis for computing the election rate. The top panels in Figure 11.5 contain the nonunion- and union-based new-organization rates over the 1940–98 period. This long perspective clearly shows the large spurt in organization in the 1940s and the smaller spurt in the early 1950s. But the record since that time is one of steady decline in the new-organization rate. Given that the union membership rate is declining, the union-based new-organization rate (with union, rather than nonunion, employment in the denominator) is substantially higher and does not show as much decline as the nonunion-based rate.

The bottom panels in Figure 11.5 contain the nonunion- and union-based new-organization rates over the 1973–98 period. The figure plots the approximate series estimated for the entire 1940–98 period and the more reliable series from the CPS. The two measures covary closely, offering us greater confidence in the longer time series. Substantively, the nonunion-based new-organization rate has been very small since 1973, but it declined substantially in relative terms in the early 1980s from over 0.3 percent in the late 1970s to about 0.1 percent by the late 1980s. Most of this decline happened between 1981 and 1983. Strikingly, union organizing activity was some forty times higher during the period of union expansion in the 1940s

333

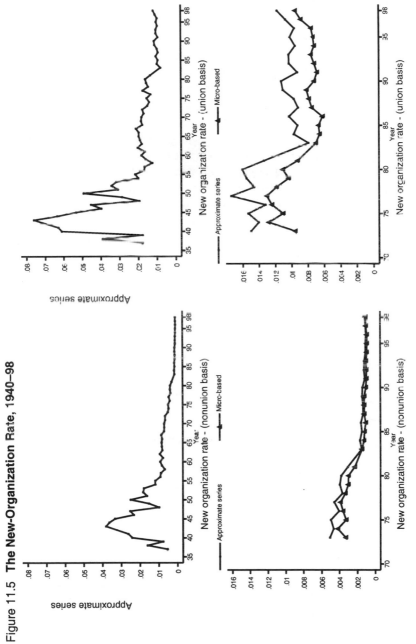

Figure 11.5 The New-Organization Rate, 1940–98

Source: Farber and Western (2001).

compared to the contemporary period. The union-based new-organization rate is clearly much higher than the nonunion-based rate, not surprisingly given the small share of union employment in the private-sector workforce. The union-based series also shows the sharp decline in the early 1980s even more clearly than the nonunion-based series.

The sharp decline in the new-organization rate in the early 1980s is due to reduced election activity (Figure 11.3), rather than a decline in union electoral success (Figure 11.4). This is consistent with a simple economic model of union decision making, where unions decide whether to undertake elections based on (1) the costs of the organizing campaign, (2) the expected probability of winning, and (3) the benefits of winning. Such a model suggests that, when the organizing environment becomes less hospitable to unions (as it likely did in the 1980–83 period), unions contest only those elections where a "reasonable" chance of success remains. The result will be a sharp decline in the election rate, but relatively little change in the union win rate.[13]

We turn now to a closer analysis of the post–1973 period in order to investigate the continuing decline of unions in the private sector in general and the decline in new-organization in the early 1980s in particular.

Is Public Policy the Culprit?

The Legal Context of Union Organizing

A large research literature argues that labor law has contributed significantly to the postwar decline in U.S. unionization. The main framework for labor law is provided by the NLRA. The original act of 1935 was passed to quell industrial unrest and encourage collective bargaining. Through a system of government-run elections, the NLRA created an enforceable procedure for union representation based on majority vote within bargaining units. Employer conduct was tightly regulated during elections, and the use of threats and dismissals to influence the vote was prohibited. Violations could be remedied by bringing ULP charges before the NLRB.

Changes in administration of the labor law allowing stronger employer opposition was viewed as a key determinant of American union decline. The employer opposition account was based on three key observations. First, the probability of a pro-union vote declined between 1945 and 1980 (Figure 11.4). Second and as noted earlier, even when unions obtained certification their success in obtaining a first contract has fallen over time. Third, the number of ULP charges against employers increased sixfold over this same period (Weiler 1983, 1984).

Many observers interpret this evidence as suggesting that employers increasingly adopted illegal tactics to defeat union organizing. Labor law was implicated by failing to protect workers' rights to a fair certification process, free of employer coercion.[14] Various links in the chain of this argument received detailed empirical treatment. There is mixed evidence that ULP charges adversely affect the probability of a union election victory.[15] There is fairly strong evidence that delays incurred by filing objections to the campaign process are associated with a lower probability of union success.[16] This led to calls for expedited procedures where the representation decision would happen within a short time after a petition is filed. This could be done either through an "instant election" or "card check" as is used in Canada (Flanagan 1987; Weiler 1990). Either of these options would limit the opportunity of employers to discourage pro-union sentiment through delay or commission of ULPs. The fact that unions have had increased difficulty translating election victories into first contracts has been used to argue that employers are not "bargaining in good faith" as required by the NLRA. This led some to propose "first-contract arbitration," a requirement that arbitration be used to decide the terms of a first contract if the parties fail to agree voluntarily (Weiler 1984).

More recently, a number of legal scholars claim that the Reagan-appointed labor board of the early 1980s established an "active regulatory constraint" on collective bargaining (Weiler 1990) that "accelerated the decline of unionism" (Gross 1995, 255; see also Levy 1995). Seats on the five-member labor board are filled by presidential nominees serving five-year terms. Because of the term length, the political complexion of the board changes slowly. A time line of the composition of the labor board shows that a Reagan-appointed majority was slow to develop (Figure 11.6; see p. 336). A few months after Reagan's inauguration in January 1981, Jimmy Carter appointments John C. Truesdale and John A. Penello stepped down. In August 1981, these openings were filled by President Reagan's first two appointments to the board: John Van de Water and Robert Hunter. The Carter majority served through 1982, and a Reagan majority was finally formed under the new chairman, Donald Dotson, when Patricia Diaz Dennis joined the board in May 1983.

The Dotson appointment broke tradition, coming from outside the usual pool of labor-relations professionals supported by business and union representatives (Moe 1987, 268). Dotson, a former steel-industry attorney, brought both a staunchly antiunion stance and an abrasive personal style to the labor board. The new chairman attracted controversy, becoming involved in public disputes with other NLRB officals. In addition, while past chairs had relied on the legal resources of the board's general counsel, Dotson hired as board solicitor an offical from the National Right to Work Committee—an antiunion lobby group (Gross 1995, 253).

Figure 11.6 **Composition of the NLRB, 1980–85**

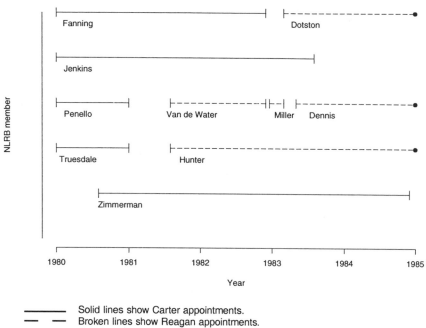

Solid lines show Carter appointments.
Broken lines show Reagan appointments.
Fanning, Van deWater, Miller, and Dotson served as chairs.

Source: Farber and Western (2002).

Critics claim that unions received prejudicial treatment, while scrutiny of employer conduct was significantly relaxed under the Dotson labor board. Unions faced increased obstacles to contesting elections as representation petitions were increasingly dismissed for failing to specify appropriate bargaining units. Where elections were held, employer conduct was substantially deregulated. Under a line of Dotson board rulings, employers obtained greater latitude to interrogate union supporters, made misleading campaign statements, speculated about the adverse effects of unionization, and discharged union supporters. In Paul Alan Levy's review, "The centerpiece of the Board's strategy is to uphold elections marred by unfair labor practices, while legalizing employer practices which interfere with, restrain or coerce employee free choice in elections" (1985, 293; see also Moe 1987, 269). Beyond the election process, employers' obligation to engage in good-faith bargaining was weakened, and employer reprisals against strikers were deregulated. During this time, the board accumulated its largest ever backlog of unprocessed ULP claims, which delayed elections and first-contract bargaining (Gross 1995;

Levy 1985). Dotson vacated his chair of the NLRB in December 1987, and a new chairman, James Stephens, was named in January 1988. Subsequent labor boards, although not as activist as the Dotson board, affirmed the weakened commitment to collective bargaining established during the mid-1980s.

Like research on employer opposition, legal analysis of Reagan's first labor board often views union organizing activity as an important cause of union decline. Although the link between ULPs and elections has been studied in detail, the impact of the Reagan labor board on quantity of union organizing activity has not been extensively analyzed. A key implication of the legal writing is that the number of elections contested and the union win rate would both decline under the first Reagan board. Although the win rate is the focus of earlier research, the major constraint on new organizing (and the variable showing greatest variation over the last thirty years) is the number of elections contested. Of course, as demonstrated by the model presented earlier, the frequency of elections and the probability of union victory are closely related in the sense that unions will only contest elections they believe they can win.

The influence of the Republican administration on the NLRA may be difficult to detect because the industrial relations climate was changing in many ways as Reagan nominees were joining the labor board. In particular, the air traffic controllers' strike of 1981 has been viewed as a key watershed in U.S. labor relations (Northrup and Thornton 1988; Traynor and Fichtenbaum 1997). Following strike action through the summer of 1981, air traffic controllers were fired by President Reagan and nonunion replacements were hired. The strikers' union, PATCO, lost its representative role and the hiring of permanent replacements became a highly visible employer strategy for deunionization. Analyses of strike data thus show the high use of permanent replacements in the 1980s in contrast to earlier decades' (LeRoy 1995; Wachter and Carter 1989). Thomas L. Traynor and Rudy H. Fichtenbaum (1997) claim that the rate of union wage growth also slowed under the new labor relations regime ushered in by the PATCO strike. Although it chiefly highlighted the role of permanent replacements, the PATCO strike is viewed as initiating a more general employer offensive against labor unions (Shostak and Skocik 1986; Kochan, Katz, and McKersie 1986). From this perspective, a shift in employer behavior rather than labor law has driven the decline in organizing activity.

It is likely that these changes in the legal and political contexts of union organizing, as well as changes in employer behavior, have affected all three characteristics highlighted in the model in ways inimical to union organizing. It is likely that the costs of union organizing (C_i) increased during the 1980s while the benefit of union organizing (R_i) has decreased. At the same time, it is likely that the probability of a union win in a typical potential bargaining unit declined during the same period. The result is the sharp drop in union election activity coupled with a slight increase in success in elections held.

We turn now to an examination of the timing of changes in election activity and how it is related to some specific changes in the political and regulatory environment.

Analyzing Trends in Election Activity

Our analysis studies trends in the monthly count of certification elections, relating these to the PATCO strike and the appointment of the Dotson labor board. If the PATCO strike (August 1981) or the appointment of Chairman Dotson (March 1983) influenced organizing activity, we would expect this would result in changes in the trend of the election series around the time of these events. A simple model of this idea fits the election data to a linear spline function with two knots corresponding to each event. In other words, the model fits the election data as three connected linear segments, the first and second segments connected at the first knot, and the second and third connected at the second knot. The locations of the knots, $\{k_1, k_2\}$, are parameters that can be estimated by searching over pairs of monthly time points. Specifying $k_1 < k_2$ restricts the search to unique pairs of knots. Admittedly, this is a rough test because the influence of the Reagan board grew over time as case law accumulated. Still, the two events provide convenient reference points for summarizing the election time series.

More formally, the spline function for the count of elections in month t is:

$$e_t = a_0 + a_1 t + u_t, \, t = 1974(1), 1974(2), \ldots, k_1$$
$$e_t = b_0 + b_1 t + u_t, \, t = k_1, \ldots, k_2$$
$$e_t = c_0 + c_1 t + u_t, \, t = k_2, \ldots, 1999 \, (12), \tag{4}$$

where u_t is an error term. The six parameters $(a_0, a_1, b_0, b_1, c_0, c_1)$ must satisfy the pair of constraints that the segments of the spline function meet at the knots. These constraints are that:

$$a_0 + a_1 k_1 = b_0 + b_1 k_1$$
$$b_0 + b_1 k_2 = c_0 + c_1 k_2 \tag{5}$$

Visual inspection of the series in Figure 11.3 shows a relatively large number of elections in the 1970s, a dramatic drop in election activity in the early 1980s, and a generally low level of election activity through the 1980s and 1990s. In order to fit the spline function, we use monthly data on the number of elections held in each of the 304 months from January 1974 through June

1999. These data are derived from the election-level data collected by the NLRB. We assume the error follows a normal distribution, and we estimate the change points, k_1 and k_2, with likelihood methods using a grid search over the parameter space. If the PATCO strike and the political complexion of the NLRB are fueling a decline in new union organizing, these events should predate our maximum likelihood estimates of k_1.

Results for the analysis are reported in Figure 11.7. The left-hand panel of Figure 11.7 (see p. 340) shows the monthly number of elections and the regression line from the maximum likelihood esitmate of the spline model. The two vertical lines indicate the timing of the dismissal of the PATCO air traffic controllers in 1981 and the formation of a Reagan majority on the NLRB in 1983.

Our estimates indicate that the sharp downturn in election activity predates the PATCO strike by a few months. By the time Reagan appointees dominate the labor board, union election activity had already fallen from its pre-1981 average by about 50 percent. In short, declining union election activity is set in motion before the two most spectacular political developments in labor relations: the PATCO strike and the Reagan labor board.

We can take the analysis a step further by estimating the probability that the earliest discontinuity in the election series arrives after the PATCO strike. We form a marginal distribution of k_1 by integrating over k_2, and, after appropriate scaling of the likelihood, we interpret this marginal likelihood as a marginal posterior distribution with a uniform prior over k_1 and k_2. We use this posterior distribution to calculate a probability that the first change point in the series follows the PATCO strike. The probability density for the location of the first knot in the spline model is shown in the right-hand panel Figure 11.7. The vertical line in this figure indicates the timing of the PATCO strike. The probability is that the decline in the election series August 1981 is less than 0.1 percent.

The model fit illustrates that k_1 and k_2 occur very close in time, providing little evidence for the distinct effects of the air traffic controllers' strike and the Dotson labor board on organizing activity. Additionally, these data record the number of elections held in each month. These elections reflect filings for every election made, on average, about two months earlier. Thus, it is unlikely that Reagan's treatment of PATCO in August 1981 could have an effect on the number of elections held until approximately October 1981. This strengthens our conclusion that the decline in union organizing activity predates the public watershed event of labor relations in 1980s. In sum, while the PATCO strike and President Reagan's first labor board may have contributed to a hostile labor relations climate, we find little evidence that these events sharply reduced union organizing activity. Indeed, the trend to declining organizing activity was already in place before the most visible political offensives against organized labor had begun.

Figure 11.7 **Union Elections Filed Monthly with the NLRB and Spline Fit, 1974–99** (left-hand side)

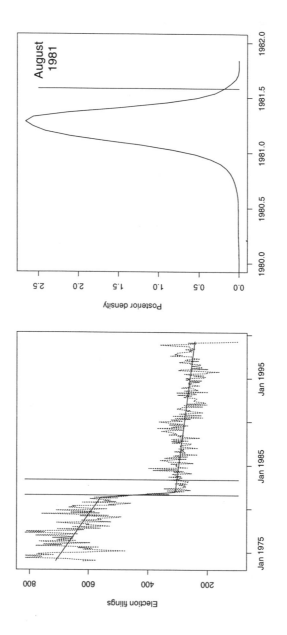

Source: Farber and Western (2002).

The vertical lines indicate the PATCO strike and the appointment of the Reagan NLRB. Probability density of the first knot in the spline models (right-hand side).

Accounting for the Decline in the Union Membership Rate

Even though institutional change does not coincide with changes in organizing activity, is the decline in organizing responsible for the decline in the union membership rate since the 1970s? In this section, we use a simple accounting framework to decompose the decline in the union membership rate into components due to the level of union organizing and the differential in the rates of employment growth between the union and nonunion sectors.[17] We define the union membership rate in year t as r_t. This is:

$$r_t = \frac{U_t}{U_t + N_t} , \tag{6}$$

where U_t and N_t are period t employment levels in the union and nonunion sectors respectively. We can express the evolution of employment in the two sectors as:

$$U_t = (1+\theta_t)U_{t-1} + \psi_t\,(1+\phi_t)\,N_{t-1} \tag{7}$$

$$N_t = (1+\phi_t)\,N_{t-1} - \psi_t\,(1+\phi_t)\,N_{t-1}, \tag{8}$$

where θ_t and ϕ_t are the growth rates between $t-1$ and t of union and nonunion employment respectively and ψ_t is the new-organization rate defined in equation 1 (the fraction of [potential] nonunion employment in period t that unions organized successfully).[18]

These expressions highlight the sources of growth of union and nonunion employment. Growth in the union sector includes growth of employment in unionized establishments at the rate θ_t and organization of nonunion workers at the rate ψ_t. Growth in the nonunion sector includes growth of employment in nonunion establishments, plus employment in new establishments (at the composite rate ϕ_t) net of new organization $(-\psi_t)$.[19] In this framework, total employment in period t is:

$$L_t = U_t + N_t \tag{9}$$

$$= (1+\theta_t)\,U_{t-1} + (1+\phi_t)\,N_{t-1} \tag{10}$$

and is independent of the quantity of union organizing activity.

Using equations 7 and 8, the current unionization rate (r_t) can be expressed as a function of past employment in the two sectors and the new organization rate (equation 1). This is:

$$r_t = \frac{(1+\theta_t)U_{t-1} + \psi_t(1+\phi_t)N_{t-1}}{(1+\theta_t)U_{t-1} + (1+\phi_t)N_{t-1}} \qquad (11)$$

$$= \frac{(1+\theta_t)r_{t-1} + \psi_t(1+\phi_t)(1-r_{t-1})}{(1+\theta_t)r_{t-1} + (1+\phi_t)(1-r_{t-1})} \qquad (12)$$

$$= \frac{r_{t-1} + \psi_t(1+\delta)(1-r_{t-1})}{r_{t-1} + (1+\delta_t)(1-r_{t-1})} , \qquad (13)$$

where δ_t is the rate of employment growth in the nonunion sector relative to the rate of employment growth in the union sector defined:

$$1+\delta_t = \frac{1+\phi_t}{1+\theta_t} \qquad (14)$$

Since union and nonunion employment growth rates are generally small (< 0.1), a reasonable approximation to the relative rate of employment growth is:

$$\delta_t = \phi_t - \theta_t \qquad (15)$$

The steady-state union membership rate at any level of new organization and employment growth rates is derived by setting $r_t = r_{t-1}$ in equation 13 and solving for r. The result is:

$$r_{ss} = \psi_t \frac{1+\delta_t}{\delta_t} , \qquad (16)$$

where r_{ss} is the steady state union membership rate. The required new-organization rate for any given steady state is:

$$\psi_t = r_{ss} \frac{\delta_t}{1+\delta_t} \qquad (17)$$

If the two sectors grow at the same rate ($\delta_t = 0$), no new organizing is needed to maintain union density. However, if employment in the union sector grows less rapidly than in (or falls relative to) the nonunion sector ($\delta_t > 0$), positive union organizing is required to maintain the union membership rate. It is also clear that the required new-organization rate in a steady state is directly related to the union membership rate.

   This framework allows us to measure the relative roles of (1) differential rates of employment growth between the union and nonunion sectors and

(2) low levels of new union organization in accounting for the decline in the private-sector union membership rate between 1973 and 1998. We now turn to this analysis.

Measuring the Relative Employment Growth Rates

The union and nonunion employment growth rates (θ_t and ϕ_t, respectively) are defined implicitly in equations 7 and 8. Solving these relationships for θ_t and ϕ_t yields:

$$\theta_t = \frac{U_t - U_{t-1}}{U_{t-1}} - \frac{\psi_t}{(1-\psi_t)} \frac{N_t}{U_{t-1}} \tag{18}$$

and

$$\phi_t = \frac{N_t - N_{t-1}}{N_{t-1}} + \frac{\psi_t}{(1-\psi_t)} \frac{N_t}{N_{t-1}} \tag{19}$$

These are based on the measured employment growth in each sector adjusted for union organizing (measured by ψ_t).[20] If there were no union organizing ($\psi_t = 0$), then:

$$\theta_t = \frac{U_t - U_{t-1}}{U_{t-1}} \tag{20}$$

which is the measured rate of employment growth in the union sector, and.

$$\phi_t = \frac{N_t - N_{t-1}}{N_{t-1}} \tag{21}$$

which is the measured rate of employment growth in the union sector and the measured rate of employment growth in the nonunion sector. In fact, as we showed earlier, the union organizing rate has been less than 0.005 per year since 1973, so the organizing adjustment is very small and will be ignored here.

The left-hand panel of Figure 11.8 (see p. 342) contains the time series of measured employment growth rates in the union and nonunion sectors between 1973 and 1999. There is a substantial differential in growth rates, with union employment shrinking by an average of 2.5 percent per year and nonunion employment growing at an average of 3.2 percent per year. The growth rate of union employment was much more volatile than the growth rate of nonunion employment. The standard deviation of the union growth rate was 4.0 percentage points, while the standard deviation of the nonunion growth rate

Figure 11.8 **Employment Growth Rates by Sector, 1973–99**

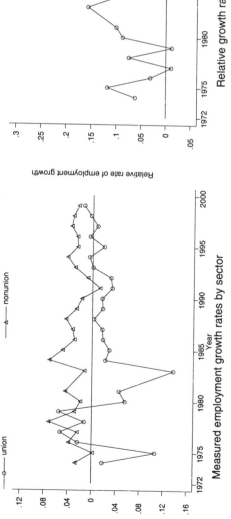
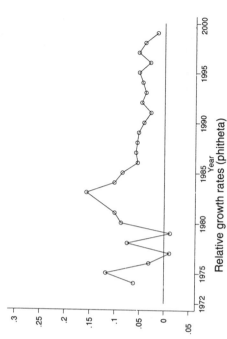

Source: Farber and Western (2001).

was only 1.9 percentage points. The relatively high volatility of the union growth rate is due to large fluctuations prior to 1984. Since 1984, both sectors have had comparable variability in growth rates with standard deviations of about 1.5 percentage points.

The right-hand panel of Figure 11.8 contains the relative employment growth rate, δ, which is usefully approximated by the difference in the adjusted employment growth rates $(\phi-\theta)$. This plot verifies the consistently higher employment growth rate in the nonunion sector than in the union sector. In fact, there is only one year in the sample where the union growth rate exceeded the nonunion growth rate (1979), and there are only five years between 1973 and 1999 where the union growth rate was even positive. In contrast, the nonunion employment growth rate was positive in all but one year, 1991.[21] On average, the relative employment growth rate was 0.056 between 1974 and 1999, and it averaged 0.046 since 1985 and 0.039 since 1990. Thus, there is a consistent, though declining, differential in employment growth rates over the entire period.

How Important Is New Organization?

Given the consistently higher employment growth rates in the nonunion sector relative to the union sector documented in Figure 11.8, it is clear that substantial new union organization would be required to maintain the union membership rate at the level of the previous year. On a year-by-year basis, the quantity of union organizing required to maintain the union membership at the level of the past year is defined in equation 17.

The left-hand plot in Figure 11.9 (see p. 346) contains the actual union-organizing rate and the rate required to maintain the steady-state year by year (e.g., the rate of organization required in 1974 to maintain the union membership rate at the 1973 level given the 1974 union and nonunion employment growth rates and the rate of organization required in 1994 to maintain the union membership rate at the 1993 level given the 1994 union and nonunion employment growth rates). The required organization rate exceeds the actual organization rate in all but two years, and the average difference is substantial. The required organization rate averages 0.9 percent between 1974 and 1999, while the actual organization rate averages only 0.18 percent over the same period. The required union organizing rate falls steadily from the mid-1980s because the union membership rate has been falling, and from equation 17, the required organization rate is directly related to the level of the union membership rate.

The right-hand plot in Figure 11.9 contains the actual union-organizing rate and the rate required to maintain the steady-state union membership

Figure 11.9 Union Organizing Rate Required in Steady-State, 1973–99

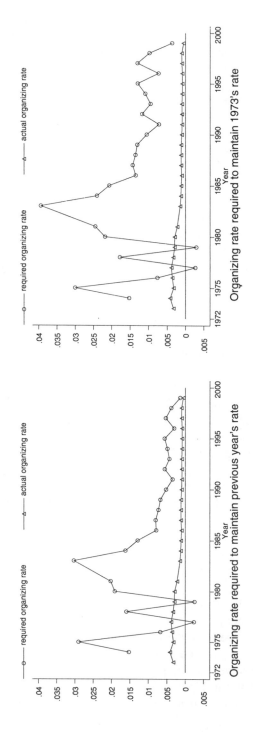

Source: Farber and Western (2001).

rate at the 1973 level (25.5 percent) in each year given the union and non-union employment growth rates prevailing each year. This is computed directly from equation 17, assuming that $r_{ss} = 0.255$, and, because the actual union membership rate is declining over time, it is higher than the organization rate required to maintain the union membership rate at the previous year's level. It is clear that substantial new organizing is required to maintain the 1973 union membership rate in the face of the large difference in employment growth rates.

Figure 11.10 (see p. 348) offers another view of the effect of increasing union organizing activity on the union membership rate, given observed union and nonunion employment growth rates. The left-hand plot shows the predicted union membership rate by year, based on equation 13, under various assumptions regarding the level of union organizing activity. The assumed values range from the observed level of union organizing activity to organization of 2.2 percent of the nonunion workforce each year. Three hypothetical levels of the new organization rate are included in the figure: 0.4 percent, 1.0 percent, and 2.2 percent, along with the actual new-organization rate.

The actual organization rate yields the bottom series on the union membership rate. This series starts at 25.5 percent in 1973 and falls to 9.7 percent by 1999. While not shown in the figure, if there had been no organization, the union membership rate would have fallen only an additional 2.0 percentage points by 1999 to 7.7 percent. This illustrates that the total quantity of new union organization since 1973 has had only a minor effect on the union membership rate.

If unions were able to organize 0.4 percent of the nonunion workforce each year (slightly more than double the actual organization rate), the union membership rate would have been 3.7 percentage points higher in 1998 at 13.4 percent. While this is a clear improvement over the actual rate of 9.7 percent, it is still nowhere near the level of union membership that prevailed in the 1970s and it implies that the union membership would have continued to decline through the 1990s.

A new-organization rate of 1 percent per year (more than five times the actual organization) would have had a much larger effect. The union membership rate would have been 21.5 percent in 1998, more than double the actual rate in that year. Perhaps more interestingly, a new-organization rate of 1 percent per year would have resulted in a stable union membership rate since 1985 of about 20 percent. However, to put this in historical context, a new-organization rate of 1 percent has not been seen since 1955, at the tail end of the last spurt of union growth (Figure 11.5). If the union membership could have reached 20 percent, as suggested by this counterfactual, a new-organization rate of 1 percent of nonunion employ-

Figure 11.10 **Hypothetical Union Membership Rates at Assumed Levels of Organizing Activity, 1973–99**

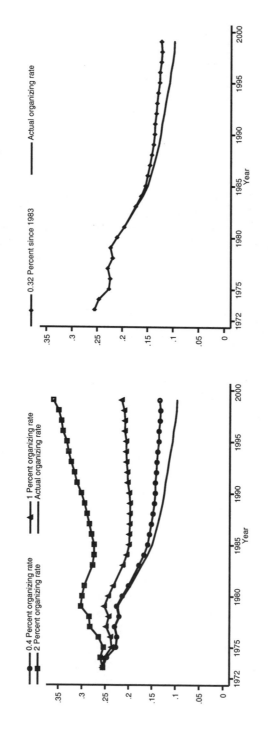

Source: Farber and Western (2001).

ment would translate into a new-organization rate of 4 percent of the union workforce. Even this rate of resource commitment by the union sector is larger than any value observed since 1950 (Figure 11.5). And, at the current rate of union membership of 9.7 percent, the 1 percent nonunion organization rate translates into a new-organization rate of over 9 percent of the union workforce.

Our most optimistic counterfactual is a new-organization rate of 2.2 percent, corresponding to the average new-organization rate over the high-growth 1940–55 period. This is more than twenty times the actual new-organization rate observed over the 1973–99 period, and it would have yielded a union membership rate of 36.0 percent by 1999. Sustaining a new organization rate of 2.2 percent of the nonunion workforce with a union membership rate of 36 percent would require a resource commitment by the union sector sufficient to organize over 4 percent of the union workforce each year. This is larger than any value seen since 1950. Given the current union membership rate of about 9.7 percent, a new-organization rate of 2.2 percent of nonunion employment translates into a new-organization rate of over 22 percent of the union workforce. This rate of resource commitment by the union sector is three times that observed even at the peak of the 1940s' growth spurt (Figure 11.5).

The conclusion we draw from the analysis of the counterfactual organization rates in the left-hand panel of Figure 11.10 is that a sustained dramatic increase in organizing could increase the union membership rate. But the per union member resources required at current low levels of union membership are likely to be prohibitively large.

Our review of union election data showed a sharp drop in union organizing activity in the early 1980s. The new-organization rate was 0.3 percent in 1980 and fell sharply to 0.15 percent in 1983 and 0.12 percent in 1984. The new-organization rate never reached even 0.13 percent subsequently. Earlier, we discussed changes in the administration of the NLRA in the 1980s that may have played some role in this decline. In this context, an interesting counterfactual is to compute union membership rates since 1983, assuming that the new-organization rate held steady at 0.32 percent per year since 1983 rather than falling below 0.13 percent. This counterfactual is presented in the right-hand plot in Figure 11.10.

Holding the new-organization rate at the 0.3 percent level does have some effect on the union membership rate. The actual union membership rate fell from 19.6 percent in 1981 to 9.7 percent in 1999. If the new organization rate had held at 0.3 percent between 1983 and 1998, the union membership rate would have fallen to 12.3 percent. Thus, about 26 percent of the decline in the union membership rate between 1983 and 1998 (2.6 of 9.9 percentage points) can be accounted for by the drop in the new-organization rate since the early 1980s.

Where Are the Resources for Increased Union Organizing?

It is clear that without a very substantial increase in union organizing activity (perhaps an order of magnitude increase from the current level of 0.09 percent per year), employment growth in the union sector needs to be almost as large as in the nonunion sector (δ close to zero) in order to achieve any meaningful increase in the union membership rate. But the barriers to increasing organization by labor unions in the private sector are enormous. Many workers are skeptical that unions can provide real value in the workplace without sacrificing job security, employers actively resist union organizing efforts, and the NLRA, as currently administered, makes the organization process drawn out, expensive, and uncertain. In this section, we use the sketchy data available to make some crude projections of the costs of increasing new organization.

The union-based new-organization rate we defined in equation 1 is computed relative to the size of the union sector. This is the appropriate measure to use when considering the resources required for new organization. We presented the union-based new-organization rate in the right-hand panels of Figure 11.5. Given that union employment is substantially lower than nonunion employment, the rates computed on a union basis are much larger than those computed on a nonunion basis. And, since the union membership rate declined sharply from about 25 percent in 1973 to 9.3 percent in 2001 (Figure 11.2), the gap between the rates computed on a union and nonunion basis has grown over time. Because of the decline in the union membership rate, the time-series behavior of the union-based election and new-organization rates differs substantially from those computed on a nonunion basis. The union-based series actually shows a small increase since the mid-1980s, while the nonunion-based series show a decrease over the same period.

This suggests a reinterpretation of the view that union organizing efforts have declined over time. While this is certainly true in absolute terms, it appears that new organization *per union member* has been roughly constant since the early 1970s. Unions have not cut back on organizing relative to their resources (proportional to their membership). However, since union employment is shrinking, unions would need to increase new organization per union member simply in order to maintain the new-organization rate (per nonunion worker) at recent historic levels. In order to return the nonunion-based new-organization rate to the levels enjoyed in the 1970s (0.34 percent), unions would have to sustain a union-based new-organization rate of 3.3 percent at the current union membership rate (9.3 percent). The investment per union member to achieve such a level of organization activity has not been seen since the growth spurts of the 1940s and early 1950s. The maximum union-based new-organization rate between 1955 and 1997 was 2.2 percent in 1955.

In order to increase the quantity of organization from its current low level, one of two things must happen, either the cost of organization per unit (per newly organized worker) must decrease or the resources that labor unions devote to organization must increase. The cost of organization depends to a large extent on the legal structure governing organization. As we discussed earlier, the NLRA as currently administered has been criticized for not adequately protecting the rights of workers to organize and for imposing large costs on both the workers and unions involved in organizing. This is why the labor movement has lobbied extensively for labor law reform designed to streamline the organization process and to protect the rights of the workers involved. However, it appears that the prospects for meaningful labor law reform are dim.

This leaves unions the option of devoting more resources to organization. However, the sums required for a meaningful increase in organizing activity are quite large relative to the "taxable" population (unionized workers). Paula B. Voos (1984a), in an analysis of the costs of union organizing, finds that it cost about $2,100 per new member (in 1998 dollars) on the margin to organize workers between 1964 and 1977.[22] It is unfortunate that more recent data are not available, but this estimate is likely to be a lower bound, given that the organizing environment has become more hostile to union organizing since 1977 and it has become harder to find promising targets for organization.

How much will increased organization cost? With private-sector employment running at about 110 million workers, there are about 101 million nonunion workers and about 9 million union members. In order to return the nonunion-based new-organization rate to the levels enjoyed in the 1970s (0.34 percent), unions would have to organize 374,000 workers per year—much more than their current organizing effort through the NLRB election process of 0.09 percent of the nonunion workforce each year (99,000 workers). Our lower-bound estimate of the increase in organizing expenditures is $575.5 million per year (275,000 workers times $2,100 per worker). This is about $64 per union member ($575.5 million divided by 9 million union members). While this does not appear to be a large amount, increasing the new organization rate to its 1970s' level would result in a steady-state union membership rate (equation 16) of only 9.1 percent (assuming the 1990s' average relative employment growth of $\delta = 0.039$ prevails).

In order to achieve a steady state with 12.75 percent union membership (half the 1973 rate), a union organizing rate of 0.48 percent per year would be required at current employment growth rates ($\delta = 0.039$). This implies that almost 500,000 workers be organized each year for an increase of 400,000 per year over the current level. The marginal cost of this increase would be about $840 million per year or about $84 per current union member per year.

Currently, unions are spending considerably less than this per worker on organizing. Voos (1984b) examines the organizing expenditures of a sample of unions representing approximately half of the private-sector union workforce. Her analysis shows that unions were spending about $20 per union member per year (expressed in 1998 dollars), representing about 20 percent of total union expenditures, on union organizing in the early 1970s. Using information, provided by Marick F. Masters (1997), on total expenditures of unions representing 79 percent of private-sector union members and Voos's (1984b) finding that about 20 percent of union expenditures were on organizing, our crude estimate of the aggregate amount that unions spent on organizing workers in the private sector is $265 million (1998 dollars), or about $29 per union member. Thus, in order to achieve a new-organization rate that is sufficient to achieve a steady state union membership rate of 12.75 percent, our lower-bound estimate is that unions would have to increase expenditures on organizing by about 300 percent ($84/$29). Given the assumption that current expenditures on organization are 20 percent of total union expenditures, this increase implies that union organizing expenditures would have to increase over half the total current union expenditures.

Caveats and Implications

Throughout this analysis, we were motivated to identify policies that might reverse the long-standing slide of private-sector unionism. To this end, we separated the relative growth in union employment from the effect of new organizing and viewed policy as chiefly influencing the organizing process. This approach has two limitations. First, our estimates of the level of organizing activity come from NLRB administrative records, so organizing efforts outside the framework of the NLRA are not accounted for. Historically, unions did organize substantial numbers of workers outside the NLRB framework through organization strikes and card checks, but these mechanisms declined in importance over time. Some argue that unions may now be moving to organize outside the NLRB procedure (Bronfenbrenner et al. 1998, 69–119). Our estimates of current organizing activity would be biased downward as a result. Union membership records might provide information about nonboard organizing activity, but such records are themselves subject to a variety of biases (Bain and Price 1980, 5). In any event, any underestimate of the level of organizing is likely to be small compared to the massive effect of sectoral differences in employment growth.

Second, we treat sectoral differences in employment growth as a product of structural forces, not policy context. However, the PATCO strike and the Reagan labor board may have influenced differential employment growth in at least two ways. Some research indicates that the PATCO strike led to increased use of permanent replacements in the 1980s and this would add to labor shedding in the union sector (Cramton and Tracy 1998). Strike rates are now so low, however, that this effect is again likely to be small. A sequence of NLRB decisions in the early 1980s weakened employers' duty to bargain, specifically in relation to plant relocation and subcontracting (Gross 1995, 258–262; cf. Miscimarra and Schwartz 1997). We know of no research that estimates the effects of these changes in labor law on the level of union employment. Still, it does appear that the costs of shifting production from a union to a nonunion basis are lower in the 1980s and 1990s than in the 1970s.

Overall, this is a very pessimistic analysis from the perspective of the union movement. It is clear that labor unions in the private sector are caught between the proverbial rock and hard place. On one side, employment growth rates are much lower (even negative) in the union sector relative to the nonunion sector. On the other side, unions have not been able to muster a meaningful amount of new-organizing activity. The bleak picture is summarized by our calculation of the steady-state union membership rate (equation 16) of only 2.6 percent, assuming current rates of relative employment growth ($\delta = 0.039$) and new organization ($\psi = 0.001$).

Notwithstanding recent changes in labor law, the causes of the divergence in employment growth rates between the union and nonunion sectors are fundamentally related to the structure of the U.S. economy. Employment has shifted away from the sectors in which unions were strongest, such as manufacturing, transportation, and communications. In manufacturing, the opening of the U.S. economy to global competition undoubtedly has played a role. Capital is extremely mobile, and it is unlikely that owners of capital are willing or able to pay a wage premium that union workers might command. In transportation and communication, there has been substantial deregulation that has made it harder for firms to pass along the union wage premium (e.g., Rose 1987). This is at least part of the reason why nonunion workers have become less likely to demand union representation

(Farber 1990; Farber and Krueger 1993), making it harder to organize. It is also part of the reason why new manufacturing capacity is disproportionately located in regions of the country that have historically not been friendly to labor unions.[23]

From a more general perspective, the relative rate of union employment growth can be viewed as an institutional effect, because the U.S. system of labor relations focuses the costs of unionism on union workplaces. This is unusual from a comparative point of view. In Europe, for example, collectively bargained wages are commonly extended to nonunion firms by employer associations or government regulation (Traxler 1994). Consequently, the labor costs of European employers do not depend so strongly on the union status of their employees. The European experience suggests policy instruments are available to equalize labor costs and control differential employment growth across the union and nonunion sectors. Obviously, though, the possibility of adopting European-style contract extensions seems unimaginable—if not bizarre—in the current American context.

Consequently, new union organizing bears a massive burden. The rate of job creation in the United States is large (about 2 percent per year), and most new jobs are born nonunion. The current rate of new organization (0.1 percent of the nonunion workforce) is sufficient to organize only 5 percent of the *new* jobs, let alone organize many existing jobs. The quantity of organizing activity required to make a substantial difference in the steady-state unionization rate is simply staggering, particularly when measured as a fraction of existing union employment. With the current union membership rate of about 9 percent, union-based new organization rates are ten times higher than the nonunion-based organization rates (0.91/0.09), holding the absolute quantity of new organization fixed. We determined earlier that, at current levels of relative employment growth, the new-organization rate would have to increase by five times (from 0.09 percent to 0.48) percent) to yield a steady-state union membership rate of 12.75 percent. But this would require that the unions organize each year new members equal to about 5 percent of their current membership.

It is hard to conceive of a reform of the NLRA that would yield such a substantial increase in new organization, even in the short run. Our examination of the 1980s' experience shows that marginal changes in the administration of the NLRA had no discernible impact on organizing activity. Suppose that a very substantial change to the NLRA were enacted, such as a move to recognition based on card checks, however politically unlikely this seems. Suppose we assume that this could double new union organization in the short run. Could this be kept up in the long run as unions try to organize less favorable targets over time? This seems to us unlikely. And a doubling of the new-organization rate from its current level, given current relative employment growth rates, will have very little impact on the steady-state union membership rate.

The first-contract problem, which is ignored in our analysis, implies that actual new-organization rates are about one-third lower than our already-low measure, which is based on election wins. If we assume a reform of the NLRA that provides for first-contract arbitration, then we simply get back to the pessimistic picture painted by our analysis.

Historically, American unions have grown during extraordinary periods of social or economic upheaval—most recently during depression and wartime—that resulted in massive new organizing efforts. Absent such upheaval, a resurgence of the labor movement in the private sector must rely on bringing the union and nonunion employment growth rates into rough equality, coupled with an increase in organizing activity. This can only happen if the union movement is transformed in a way that makes owners of capital indifferent between investing in the union and nonunion sectors. To the extent that unions transfer wealth from owners of capital to workers (a reasonable interpretation of union goals and actions), it is hard to see how this will happen, and it seems inevitable that the union membership rate in the private sector will continue to erode.

Appendix 11A

Derivation of the New-Organization Rate Series

Total nonagricultural employment is derived from BLS Series EEU00000001 and total public-sector employment from BLS Series EEU90000001. These are then used to compute the fraction of total employment in the public sector and total employment in the private sector. Freeman's (1998) historical series on union density (described earlier) covers both the public sector and the private sector. We use data on the union membership rate in the public sector, available from the CPS since 1973 and read (approximately) from Figure 11.1 of Freeman (1986) for the period from 1956 to 1972.[24] Freeman's figure shows that approximately 12 percent of public-sector workers were union members in 1956, but there are no data available prior to this date. We proceeded making two alternative assumptions: (1) that the public-sector union membership rate was zero prior to 1956 and (2) that the public-sector union membership rate was 10 percent prior to 1956. The results are not at all sensitive to these alternatives, and we proceed using the 10 percent assumption. Noting that the overall union density is an employment-weighted average of the public- and private-sector union densities, the data on public- and private-employment shares, the public-sector union membership rate, and Freeman's union density series were then used to compute a consistent private-sector union membership rate time series covering the 1940–98 period.

Since 1972, data on NLRB election activity are available electronically at the election level. But prior to this period, we are forced to rely on the published tables in the NLRB annual reports. These tables include information on the number of elections, the total number of workers who voted in elections, the total number of pro-union votes, and the number of elections won by unions. However, the tables contain no information on the number of workers in units where the unions won elections (the number newly organized). We proceed by using the number of pro-union votes as our consistent measure of the number newly organized.

We then compute two new-organization rate series over the 1937–98 period. The first is the ratio of the number newly organized divided by private-sector nonunion employment. The second is the ratio of the number newly organized divided by private-sector union employment. We also compute alternative versions of these series over the 1973–98 period based on the more appropriate microdata from the NLRB and the CPS.

We can compare our approximate time series on the new-organization rates to the series derived from the microdata over the 1973–98 period. The nonunion-based series are very close. The mean of the microbased series is 0.0019 and the mean of the approximate series is 0.0023. The two series are highly correlated ($\tilde{n} = 0.971$). The union-based series are also quite close. The mean of the microbased series is 0.009 and the mean of the approximate series is 0.012. The two series are fairly highly correlated ($\tilde{n} = 0.873$).

Notes

Earlier versions of some of this work by the authors was published as "Accounting for the Decline of Unions in the Private Sector, 1973–1998," *Journal of Labor Research* (22 [Summer 2001]: 459–485), and as "Ronald Reagan and the Politics of Declining Union Organization," *British Journal of Industrial Relations* (40 [September 2002]: 385–401), a special issue of this journal titled *Union Decline and Prospects for Revival: Editor's Introduction,* ed. Anil Verma, Stephen Wood, and Tom Kochan. Phanindra V. Wunnava would like thank the editors of these journals (James Bennett [*Journal of Labor Research*] and Stephen Wood [*British Journal of Industrial Relations*]) for giving him the permission to reprint parts of Farber and Western's published work. This work was started while Western was a visiting fellow at the Russell Sage Foundation. Useful comments on the earlier version were received from participants in workshops at the Federal Reserve Bank of New York, Harvard University, McGill University, Princeton University, the University of Chicago, and the University of Toronto.

1. It is no trivial exercise to derive a consistent series on union membership rates over such a long period of time. We use the series developed by Freeman (1998, Table

8A.2) for the 1980–95 period. These data are derived from a variety of sources, described in detail by Freeman. In order to extend the series for the 1995–2001 period, we used predicted values from a regression of Freeman's union membership series from 1973 to 1995 on our own series on annual union membership rates from the CPS over the 1973–95 period. This regression fits very well over the 1973–95 period ($R^2 = 0.953$). We then use our data on annual union membership rates from 1996 to 2001 in conjunction with the estimated parameters of this regression model to predict values for Freeman's series from 1996 to 2001.

2. There is a large literature investigating the process of union growth. Some contributions include Barnett (1933), Davis (1941), Dunlop (1948), Bernstein (1954), and Ashenfelter and Pencavel (1969).

3. These data are derived from the May CPS from 1973 to 1981 and from the merged outgoing rotation group files of the CPS from 1983 to 2001.

4. The increase in the public-sector union membership rate early in the period is due largely to new organization following enactment of laws in many states guaranteeing the rights of public-sector employees to unionize. Farber (1988) presents an analysis of the evolution of public-sector bargaining laws. In the same volume, Ichniowski (1988), Saltzman (1988), and Freeman and Valletta (1988) present analyses of the effect of public-sector bargaining laws on the union status of public-sector workers.

5. There is no information on union coverage available from the CPS prior to 1978. The CPS questions since 1977 (but not on the public-use data file until 1978) first ask if an individual is a union member. If the response is "no," then the individual is asked if he or she is covered by a collective bargaining agreement on his or her main job.

6. The free-rider rate in the public sector over the same period was 26.0 percent in states with right-to-work laws and 12.8 percent in states without right-to-work laws. Since right-to-work laws only apply to private-sector workers, this reflects a correlation between the state laws governing public-sector unionization and the existence of right-to-work laws.

7. The difference in time-series behavior between the elections series and the votes series reflects the fact that the average election size fell over this period.

8. Farber (2001) presents an analysis of the decline in union success that focuses on the fact that union success fell more sharply in large units than in small units.

9. See also Prosten (1978) and Cooke (1985). The NLRA provides that unions have one year from the date of certification as the bargaining agent of the workers to negotiate a contract. If no contract is negotiated in that time, the union is no longer recognized as the bargaining agent.

10. The lack of data requires that we ignore the fact, as noted earlier, that unions have not been able to negotiate a first-contract in many cases where they have won a representation election.

11. We ignore the fact that not all nonunion workers are covered by the NLRA. The most notable group not covered are managers.

12. We exclude the unincorporated self-employed from the calculations of the fractions from the CPS. All shares are computed using the CPS final sampling weights.

13. Farber (2001) develops a model of union organizing activity with these implications.

14. For example, see Freeman (1988) and Weiler (1984, 1990).

15. See LaLonde and Meltzer (1991). Even analyses of the same data lead to

dramatically opposed conclusions. Getman, Goldberg, and Herman (1976) use data on employer behavior and individual votes in a sample representation election to conclude that ULPs have little influence on individual votes. A reanalysis of these same data by Dickens (1983) reaches the opposite conclusion. Dickens finds that ULPs by employers substantially reduce the probability of a union election victory despite having a relatively small effect on any individuals vote. Flanagan (1987) reviews this literature.

16. For example, see Roomkin and Block (1981) and Cooke (1983).

17. Our framework is similar to that presented by Freeman (1988). Dickens and Leonard (1985) also present a related framework for understanding union decline.

18. The rate of "deunionization" of existing union jobs through NLRB-supervised decertification elections is trivial as a fraction of union employment and is subsumed in the sector-specific employment growth rates.

19. The assumption is that all new establishments are nonunion and must be organized in order to become union.

20. Measured employment growth in the union sector overstates growth in existing union workplaces because it includes newly organized workers. Measured employment growth in the nonunion sector understates growth in that sector because some nonunion jobs were organized. The adjustments take account of this new organization.

21. An extreme example of the difference in employment growth rates is that in 1983 union employment fell by 14.3 percent while nonunion employment grew by 1.4 percent, which implies a value of 0.157.

22. Voos (1984a) reports that the marginal cost of organization ranged from $580 to $1,568 per worker in 1980 dollars, depending on the particular statistical controls used. We used the midpoint of this range and adjusted to 1998 dollars using the Consumer Price Index-Urban (CPI-U).

23. For example, a number of the foreign automobile manufacturers who have built production plants in the United States have chosen to locate in the South: BMW in South Carolina, Toyota in Tennessee, and Mercedes-Benz in Alabama.

24. Freeman's data cover only even years. We interpolate his data to cover the odd years.

References

Ashenfelter, Orley, and John H. Pencavel. 1969. "American Trade Union Growth: 1900 1960." *Quarterly Journal of Economics* 83: 434–448.

Bain, George Sayers, and Robert Price. 1980. *Profiles of Union Growth: A Comparative Statistical Portrait of Eight Countries.* Oxford: Blackwell.

Barnett, George E. 1933. "American Trade Unionism and Social Insurance." *American Economic Review* 23: 1–15.

Bernstein, Irving. 1954. "The Growth of American Unions." *American Economic Review* 44: 301–318.

Bronfenbrenner, Kate, Sheldon Friedman, Richard W. Hurd, Rudolph A. Oswald, and Ronald L. Seeber, eds. 1998. *Organizing to Win: New Research on Union Strategies.* Ithaca, NY: ILR Press.

Cooke, William N. 1983. "Determinants of the Outcomes of Union Certification Elections." *Industrial and Labor Relations Review* 36: 402–414.

———. 1985. "The Failure to Negotiate First Contracts: Determinants and Policy Implications." *Industrial and Labor Relations Review* 38: 163–178.

Cramton, Peter, and Joseph Tracy. 1998. "The Use of Replacement Workers in Union Contract Negotiations: The U.S. Experience, 1980–1989." *Journal of Labor Economics* 16: 667–701.

Davis, Horace B. 1941. "The Theory of Union Growth." *Quarterly Journal of Economics* 55: 611–637.

Dickens, William T. 1983. "The Effect of Company Campaigns on Certification Elections: 'Law and Reality' Once Again." *Industrial and Labor Relations Review* 36: 560–575.

Dickens, William T., and Jonathan S. Leonard. 1985 . "Accounting for the Decline in Union Membership, 1950–1980." *Industrial and Labor Relations Review* 38: 323–334.

Dunlop, John T. 1948. "The Development of Labor Organization: A Theoretical Framework." In *Insights into Labor Issues,* ed. Richard A. Lester and Joseph Shister, 163–193. New York: Macmillan

Farber, Henry S. 1988. "The Evolution of Public Sector Bargaining Laws." In *When Public Sector Employees Unionize,* ed. Richard B. Freeman and Casey Ichniowski, 129–166. Chicago: University of Chicago Press.

———. 1990. "The Decline of Unionization in the United States: What Can be Learned from Recent Experience?" *Journal of Labor Economics* 8: S75–S105.

———. 2001. "Union Success in Representation Elections: Why Does Unit Size Matter?" *Industrial and Labor Relations Review* 54: 329 348.

Farber, Henry S., and Alan B. Krueger. 1993. "Union Membership in the United States: The Decline Continues." In *Employee Representation: Alternatives and Future Directions,* ed. Bruce Kaufman and Morris Kleiner, 105–134. Madison, WI: Industrial Relations Research Association.

Farber, Henry S., and Bruce Western. 2001 " Accounting for the Decline of Unions in the Private Sector, 1973–1998." *Journal of Labor Research* 22 (Summer): 459 485.

———. 2002 "Ronald Reagan and the Politics of Declining Union Organization." *British Journal of Industrial Relations* 40 (September): 385 401.

Flanagan, Robert. 1987. *Labor Relations and the Litigation Explosion.* Washington, DC: Brookings Institution

Freeman, Richard B. 1986. "Unionism Comes to the Public Sector." *Journal of Economic Literature* 24: 41–86.

———. 1988. "Contraction and Expansion: The Divergence of Private Sector and Public Sector Unionism in the United States." *Journal of Economic Perspectives* 2, no. 2: 63–88.

———. 1998. "Spurts in Union Growth: Defining Moments and Social Processes." In *The Defining Moment: The Great Depression and the American Economy in the Twentieth Century,* ed. Michael D. Bardo, Claudia Goldin, and Eugene N. White, 265–295. Chicago: University of Chicago Press.

Freeman, Richard B., and Robert G. Valletta. 1988. "The Effects of Public Sector Labor Laws on Labor Market Institutions and Outcomes." In *When Public Sector Employees Unionize,* ed. Richard B. Freeman and Casey Ichniowski, 81–106. Chicago: University of Chicago Press.

Getman, Julius G., Stephen B. Goldberg, and Jeanne B. Herman. 1976. *Union Representation Elections: Law and Reality.* New York. Russell Sage Foundation.

Gross, James A. 1995. *Broken Promise: The Subversion of U.S. Labor Relations Policy, 1947–1994.* Philadelphia: Temple University Press.

Ichniowski, Casey. 1988. "Public Sector Union Growth and Bargaining Laws: A Proportional Hazards Approach with Time-Varying Treatments." In *When Public Sector Employees Unionize,* ed. Richard B. Freeman and Casey Ichniowski, 19–40. Chicago. University of Chicago Press.

Kochan, Thomas A., Harry C. Katz, and Robert B. McKersie. 1986. *The Transformation of American Industrial Relations.* New York: Basic Books.

LaLonde, Robert J., and Bernard D. Meltzer. 1991. "Hard Times for Unions: Another Look at the Significance of Employer Illegalities." *University of Chicago Law Review* 58: 953–1014.

LeRoy, Michael H. 1995. "The Changing Character of Strikes Involving Permanent Striker Replacements, 1935–1990." *Journal of Labor Research* 16: 423–437.

Levy, Paul Alan. 1985. "The Unidimensional Perspective of the Reagan Labor Board." *Rutgers Law Journal* 16: 269–390.

Masters, Marick F. 1997. *Unions at the Crossroads.* Westport, CT: Quorum.

Miscimarra, Phillip A., and Kenneth D. Schwartz. 1997. "Frozen in Time—The NLRB, Outsourcing and Management Rights." *Journal of Labor Research* 18: 561–580.

Moe, Terry. 1987. "Interests, Institutions, and Positive Theory: The Politics of the NLRB." *Studies in American Political Development* 2: 236–302.

Northrup, Herbert R., and Amie E. Thornton. 1988. "The Federal Government As Employer: The Federal Labor Relations Authority and the PATCO Challenge." Labor Relations and Public Policy Series, no. 32. Philadelphia: Wharton School, Industrial Research Unit.

Prosten, Richard. 1978. "The Longest Season: Union Organizing in the Last Decade, a/k/a How Come One Team Has to Play with Its Shoelaces Tied Together?" Proceedings of the Thirty-first Annual Meeting of the Industrial Relations Research Association, Madison, Wisconsin, 240–249.

Roomkin, Myron, and Richard N. Block. 1981. "Case Processing Time and the Outcome of Representation Elections." *University of Illinois Law Review:* 75–97.

Rose, Nancy L. 1987. "Labor Rent Sharing and Regulation: Evidence from the Trucking Industry." *Journal of Political Economy* 95: 1146–1178.

Saltzman, Gregory M. 1988. "Public Sector Bargaining Laws Really Matter: Evidence from Ohio and Illinois." In *When Public Sector Employees Unionize,* ed. Richard B. Freeman and Casey Ichniowski, 41–80. Chicago: University of Chicago Press.

Shostak, Arthur B., and David Skocik. 1986. *The Air Controllers' Controversy: Lessons from the PATCO Strike.* New York: Human Sciences.

Traxler, Franz. 1994. "Collective Bargaining Levels and Coverage." In *OECD Employment Outlook,* 167–194. Paris: Organization for Economic Cooperation and Development.

Traynor, Thomas L., and Rudy H. Fichtenbaum. 1997. "The Impact of Post-PATCO Labor Relations on U.S. Union Wages." *Eastern Economic Journal* 23: 61–72.

Voos, Paula B. 1984a. "Does it Pay to Organize? Estimating the Costs to Unions." *Monthly Labor Review* 107: 43–44.

———. 1984b. "Trends in Union Organizing Expenditures, 1953–1977." *Industrial and Labor Relations Review* 38: 52–63.

Wachter, Michael, and William Carter. 1989. "Norm Shifts in Union Wages: Will 1989 Be a Replay of 1969?" *Brookings Papers on Economic Activity,* no. 2: 233–264.

Weiler, Paul C. 1983. "Promises to Keep: Securing Workers' Rights Under the NLRA." *Harvard Law Review* 96: 1769–1727.

———. 1984. "Striking a New Balance: Freedom of Contract and the Prospects for Union Representation." *Harvard Law Review* 98: 351–420.

———. 1990. *Governing the Workplace.* Cambridge, MA: Harvard University Press.

12

What Can We Learn About the Decline in U.S. Union Membership from International Data?

Solomon W. Polachek

What is common knowledge regarding union membership? A quick read of several elementary textbooks indicates not only a declining U.S. union membership since the 1950s, but also diminishing union membership in the United Kingdom (UK) beginning in the late 1970s.[1] However, these trends in American and British unionism were not necessarily typical worldwide.[2] As shall be illustrated very shortly, although the rate of union membership was deteriorating in a number of countries, such as Canada, France, Spain, Chile, and Kenya, it was increasing in Norway and Sweden, as well as a number of developing countries (e.g., Mexico, Korea, and Taiwan). So not all countries mirror the U.S. and UK decline in union membership.[3]

In an exceedingly interesting analytical and econometric chapter of this volume, Henry S. Farber and Bruce Western provide an explanation for the decline in U.S. union membership. They argue convincingly that in the United States the nonunion sector is growing far more quickly than the union sector. This asymmetric growth implies that nonunion employment is increasing while union employment is shrinking. As such, the proportion of the workforce that is union is declining. Put simply, the economy is divided into two parts: a union segment that appears to be shrinking, and a nonunion segment that in contrast is expanding.

Farber and Western's chapter relies solely on U.S. data to prove its point. Yet, declining union membership patterns are not the norm for all countries.

Thus, it is not obvious the same conclusions would be reached if international data were explored. But even if similar conclusions were reached, it would be instructive to see if international data shed light on the reasons why separate union and nonunion sectors emerged in the first place. The purpose of this chapter is to use international data, albeit with a different empirical methodology, to see if conclusions similar to Farber and Western's are attained. In addition, this chapter suggests an interesting reason based on international relations research why certain economic sectors tend to be union, while others tend to be nonunion.

International Data

Because of the nonuniform international trends in union density, I believe it instructive to examine the international data more carefully, particularly assessing what one can learn about secular changes in union density. As is it turns out, the task is made easier because Walter Galenson (1994) compiles data on eleven variables for twenty-five countries over most of the 1980–90 decade.[4]

The Galenson data include: industrial status, gross domestic product (GDP) growth, the percentage change in manufacturing employment, the percentage change in employee earnings in manufacturing, the average annual price inflation, the average annual unemployment rate, the proportion of nonagricultural female employment, and government attitudes toward unions. Only for developed countries are Social Security benefits data available. They are measured as Social Security benefits as a proportion of GDP. Appendix 12A (see p. 374) contains the full set of data.

The union density is given for 1980. Union growth rates are from 1980 to 1988. About half the countries Galenson includes are industrial, and about half are developing. The GDP annual growth rate is for the 1980–89 period, as is the change in manufacturing employment. As will be shown, this latter variable is important because the manufacturing sector tends to be union. Also key to the Farber-Western hypothesis is the proportion of females in the economy, since female sectors tend to be nonunion.

Galenson's measure of the government attitude toward unions is an assessment he computed himself based on his institutional knowledge of each country. The ranking goes from one to five, where five is most favorable. The United States achieves a two, which is the lowest in the data. This ranking is shared with the UK, Chile, Kenya, Taiwan, and Thailand. On the other extreme are Australia, Norway, and Sweden with a ranking of five, the most favorable toward unions. The variable means are given in Table 12.1 (see p. 364).

Galenson divides the union membership data into two groups: industrial and developing countries. I replicate these in Table 12.2 (see p. 365).[5] It is

Table 12.1

Descriptive Statistics Based on Data Reported in Galenson (1994)

	N	Minimum	Maximum	Mean	Standard deviation
Industrial dummy	25	0.00	1.00	0.5200	0.5099
Growth in trade as percent of GDP	23	−2.80	6.20	0.3565	2.3263
Union density	25	3.20	80.00	32.5880	20.4473
Union membership growth rate	25	−36.80	52.20	−8.6840	22.2840
GDP annual growth	25	−0.30	9.70	3.4520	2.2189
Percent change in manufacturing employment	22	−25.00	57.40	−6.0227	17.7507
Annual price inflation	25	1.30	334.80	31.7520	77.9002
Unemployment rate	18	2.10	17.50	6.5722	3.8057
Proportion female in nonagricultural employment	25	−0.40	24.10	11.0826	6.6040
Government attitude toward unions	25	2.00	5.00	3.2000	0.9574

Note: See Appendix 12A (p. 374) for variable definitions.

obvious union density declined in each industrial country, with the exception of Sweden and Norway. Thus, these patterns are generally consistent with the United States. But for the developing countries, the story is a bit more mixed. Some countries increase union density, whereas some decrease union density. Kenya and India exhibit significant declines in union membership. Union membership rates are declining in the South American countries, but the rates vary from −36.4 percent for Chile to −7.2 percent for Brazil. Kenya's decline is 36.1 percent. On the other hand, the Philippines' union density is increasing 4 percent. Mexico's is increasing 21.9 percent, Taiwan's by 40.8 percent, and Korea's by 52.2 percent.

Though Galenson does not perform statistical analysis relating the variables, his book serves as a data compendium. These data can be used to reach conclusions based on the statistical tests that are performed in this chapter. But first, more specifics with respect to the approach.

Modeling Union Membership Change

Farber-Western use an accounting framework to decompose the U.S. decline in union membership into two components: (1) the level of union

Table 12.2

International Differences in Union Density

Country	Union density	1980–88 Percent change
Australia	49	−14.3
Canada	35.1	−1.4
Denmark	76.5	−4.3
France	19	−36.8
Germany	37	−8.6
Italy	49.3	−19.7
Japan	31.1	−13.8
New Zealand	55	−23.5
Norway	56.9	0.4
Spain	22	−27.3
Sweden	80	8.8
United Kingdom	50.7	−18.1
United States	23	−28.7
Argentina	33	−8.7
Brazil	13.6	−7.2
Chile	37	−36.4
Egypt	27	−5.9
India	30	−35
Kenya	7.2	−36.1
Korea	12.8	52.2
Malaysia	10.6	−4.7
Mexico	23.4	21.9
Philippines	11.4	4
Taiwan	20.9	40.8
Thailand	3.2	−12.5

Source: Walter Galenson, *Trade Union Growth and Decline* (Westport, CT: Praeger), 1994, Tables 1.1 and 1.2.

Galenson's data sources are: Jelle Visser, "Trends in Union Membership," OECD, *Employment Outlook*, Paris, 1982, 1985–91; U.S. Department of Labor, *Country Labor Profile* and *Foreign Labor Trends*; and *Taiwan Statistical Data Book*, 1988.

organizing and (2) the differential in employment growth in union and nonunion sectors.

Accounting for Union Density

To account for the decline in union density, Farber and Western model the proportion of the workforce unionized. They define this proportion at time t to be:

$$r_t = \frac{U_t}{U_t + N_t}, \tag{1}$$

where U_t and N_t depict time t employment in the union and nonunion sectors, respectively. They go on to define dynamic adjustment equations defining how union and nonunion employment evolves based on each sector's prior period's employment, U_{t-1} and N_{t-1}, evolutionary parameters θ_t and ϕ_t depicting union and nonunion employment growth, as well as a new-organization rate parameter ψ_t portraying the fraction of potential nonunion employment unions to successfully organize. These formulations lead to an expression for the required union new-organization rate (ψ_t) that is necessary to maintain a steady-state rate of unionization (i.e., the ψ_{tss} necessary to maintain, r_{tss} defined as the r_t to occur when $r_t = r_{t-1}$):

$$\psi_{tss} = r_{tss} \frac{\delta_t}{1+\delta_t} \qquad (2)$$

The variable δ_t is the rate of employment growth in the nonunion sector (ϕ_t) relative to the rate of growth in the union sector (θ_t). Thus, δ_t is defined as,

$\delta_t = \left(\dfrac{1+\phi_t}{1+\theta_t} - 1 \right)$, which has a positive value when the nonunion sector grows

more quickly than the union sector (and a value of zero when both sectors grow equally fast). Since $\dfrac{\partial \psi_{tss}}{\partial \delta_t} > 0$, the rate of union organizing needs to

rise in order to maintain a steady state rate of unionization as relative nonunion employment climbs. Indeed as already mentioned earlier, Farber and Western show that unions would have had to organize at a rate twenty times the current rate to yield union membership rates equal to those in the 1950s, given current levels of δ_t. But given current organizing costs, achieving these rates of union organizing are prohibitively expensive. Hence, Farber and Western's pessimistic view on the future of U.S. unionization arises because of the high nonunion sector relative employment gains δ_t.

Is the Farber-Western explanation applicable to the previously mentioned patterns of international union membership change?

As seen, Farber and Western argue that union membership expansions and contractions are based on nonneutral economic growth. Union sector employment is shrinking relative to nonunion sector employment. Consistent with this story are four factors that underlie the decline in the union sector: (1) the expansion of the service and trade industries, which are typically nonunion, (2) the influx of traditionally nonunion women in the workforce, (3) the rise of the South, and (4) the growth in white-collar occupations. With the exception of the third point, which is unique to the United

States, Galenson's international data can be used to test these implications of the Farber-Western hypothesis.

In the analysis to follow, I look primarily at the factors that correlate with union membership change. I concentrate mostly on factors related to industrial shifts, but I also look at general economic variables such as inflation, employment and social services, and income. If Farber and Western are correct, then primarily industrial-shift-type variables would be related to union membership changes. Of the variables in the data set, these include the percentage change in manufacturing and the percentage change in female employment.

I begin with the Farber-Western hypothesis regarding the importance nonunion employment gains. Essentially, I model how δ_t affects r_t. Using the Farber-Western notation:

$$r_t = \frac{r_{t-1} + \psi_t(1+\delta_t)(1-r_{t-1})}{r_{t-1} + (1+\delta_t)(1-r_{t-1})} \tag{3}$$

As indicated in equation 3, the current unionization rate r_t is a function of the past unionization rate r_{t-1} and the current relative rate of employment growth in the nonunion sector relative to the union sector δ_t, given the current level of new union organization ψ_t. One can show that:

$$\frac{\partial r_t}{\partial \delta_t} = \frac{\psi_t(1-r_{t-1})}{r_{t-1}+(1+\delta_t)(1-r_{t-1})} - \frac{(r_{t-1}+\psi_t(1+\delta_t)(1-r_{t-1}))(1-r_{t-1})}{(r_{t-1}+(1+\delta_t)(1-r_{t-1}))^2} < 0 \tag{4}$$

for relevant values of r_{t-1}, ψ_t and δ_t. I test whether equation 4 holds with international data. To test equation 4, I specify equation 3 as follows:

$$r_{i,t} = f(r_{i,t-1}, \delta_{i,t}, \psi_{i,t}) + \varepsilon_{i,t}, \tag{5}$$

where i indexes a particular country and t a particular time period, and where ε_{it} depicts country-time specific errors. Of course, one can take the first difference of equation 5 to net out the country-specific effects.

But before presenting the analysis, a word regarding the relationship between the Farber-Western notation and the Galenson variables is in order. First, Galenson's union density is synonymous with r_t, and the 1980–88 union growth rate is synonymous with the first difference of r_t. Second, the Farber-Western variable δ denotes relative nonunion-to-union employment growth, which reflects increased employment in nonmanufacturing and male-dominated industries. In addition, the Galenson data contain two related variables: the proportion of nonagricultural female employment and the percentage change in manufacturing employment. The proportion of nonagricultural female employment is positively related to δ_t, and the percentage change in manufacturing employment is inversely related to δ_t. Thus:

$$\delta_t = \delta_t(L_F, L_M) \tag{6}$$

where L_F and L_M represent the proportion of nonagricultural female employment and the level of manufacturing employment, respectively.

Third, none of the Galenson variables directly measure union organizing. However, the percentage change in manufacturing earnings ($\dot{Y}_M$), the percentage change in GDP ($\dot{Y}$), the average annual inflation ($\dot{Y}_R$), the unemployment rate (U), and government attitudes toward unions (G) are all related to the costs and benefits of organizing ψ_t. Based on my notions of models describing union organizing, my best guess is that one can define:

$$\psi_t = \psi_t(\dot{Y}_M, \dot{Y}, \dot{Y}_R, U, G) \tag{7}$$

such that $\dfrac{\partial \psi_t}{\partial \dot{Y}_M} > 0, \dfrac{\partial \psi_t}{\partial \dot{Y}} > 0, \dfrac{\partial \psi_t}{\partial \dot{Y}_R} > 0, \dfrac{\partial \psi_t}{\partial U} < 0,$ and $\dfrac{\partial \psi_t}{\partial G} > 0$. Hence, the Galenson variables are applicable to test Farber and Western's model.

To set the stage, I first do a simple correlation to find the variables related to union growth. These are presented in Table 12.3. Following this (also in Table 12.3), I perform regression analyses with the union growth rate as the dependent variable. Because countries were diverse and varied so much in size, I performed various types of regression analyses with several weighting schemes. The results were consistent no matter what weights I used. Thus, the analysis presented here is unweighted.

Union Membership and Sector Growth

Begin with the simple correlations (Table 12.3, column 1). First, there is a positive relation between the percentage change in manufacturing employment (L_M) and the growth rate in unionization $\dot{r}_t$. As the manufacturing sector grows, union density increases. This finding is consistent with the Farber-Western story, since $\partial \delta_t / \partial L_M < 0$. Also consistent (though one could question the level of significance) is that the negative relation between the proportion of females in the economy and the lower the rate of union growth. This is because the female sectors tend to be nonunion, or in Farber and Western's notation, $\partial \delta_t / \partial L_F > 0$. Thus, at least using international data, these two findings are consistent with Farber and Western's U.S. results.

Substituting equations 6 and 7 into equation 5 and subtracting the lagged union membership to get at the change in variable analyzed by Farber and Western yields the estimable equation 8 utilizing the Galenson variables:[6]

$$r_{i,t} - r_{i,t-1} = g(L_{F_{i,t}}, L_{M_{i,t}}, \dot{Y}_{M_{i,t}}, \dot{Y}_{i,t}, \dot{Y}_{R_{i,t}}, U_{i,t}, G_{i,t}) + \varepsilon_{i,t}. \tag{8}$$

Table 12.3

Covariates of Union Density Growth, Dependent Variable: Union Density Growth Rate

Variable	description	(1) Simple correlation	(2) Coefficient (t-statistic)	(3) Coefficient (t-statistic)	(4) Coefficient (t-statistic)
L_M	Percent change in manufacturing employment	0.477	0.475 (0.5)	0.519 (2.0)	0.461 (1.6)
L_F	Proportion female in nonagricultural employment	-0.156	-0.778 (-0.7)	-1.138 (-1.6)	-1.544 (-2.1)
Y_M	Percent change in real relative manufacturing income	0.330	0.400 (0.1)	2.098 (0.9)	1.753 (0.7)
Y_R	Annual price inflation	0.038	0.856 (0.6)	0.007 (0.8)	0.004 (0.5)
Y	GDP annual growth	0.378	5.184 (1.4)	3.468 (1.2)	1.979 (0.6)
G	Government attitude towards union	0.037	4.806 (0.8)	7.789 (1.9)	0.007 (0.1)
U	Unemployment rate	-0.525	-0.710 (-0.5)		
Constant			-30.91 (-1.2)	-37.112 (-2.2)	
N			16	22	22
R^2			0.614	0.538	0.521

The exact estimation technique should be based on various assumptions regarding the functional form g as well as the error structure. Parameter estimates assuming a linear specification are presented in Table 12.3.

Column 2 presents results with each independent variable in a specification including the constant. But to increase sample size, the unemployment variable is omitted in column 3. (Note that according to Table 12.2 there are seven countries with missing values.) Finally, in column 4 the specification follows a first-difference type specification and omits the constant.[7] Consistent with the simple correlation results already presented, L_M is positively related to union membership growth, and L_F is negatively related to union membership growth. These results are consistent with Farber and Western. Also, the predictions of equation 7 are borne out in the results. As can be seen, the percentage change in manufacturing earnings ($\dot{Y}_M$) is positively related to union membership growth. The percentage change in GDP ($\dot{Y}$) is positively related to union membership growth. The average annual inflation ($\dot{Y}_R$) is positively related to union membership growth. The unemployment rate (U) is negatively related to union membership growth. And finally, positive government attitudes toward unions (G) are positively related to union membership growth.

Why Is Union Density Sector-Specific? Applying International Relations Literature to Get an Answer

What can be learned from these results? First, there is some evidence that variables pertaining to the costs and benefits of organizing new union members matter. Second, there is some consistency with the story that asymmetric sector-specific economic growth has implications for union membership. Both Farber and Western and the international data presented indicate that union membership expansion is linked to growth in the manufacturing sector. Growth in female-dominated industries lessens union membership growth. So, the underlying changes in union density within the United States and across countries seems to be related to asymmetric sector-specific economic growth. Growth in manufacturing tends to increase unionization, while industrial growth in sectors concentrated by women tends to lessen unionization. Thus, it makes sense that to better comprehend the unionization process, one needs to figure out why unions pervade manufacturing more so than other sectors. To do that, one should examine union density by economic sector.

In this vein, I assess the percent change in total union membership by industry. Table 12.4 contains the data for the United States and Canada.[8] Despite strong consistency between the United States and Canada, espe-

Table 12.4

Percent Change in Union Membership, 1978–89

	United States	Canada
Automobiles	35	12
Steel	−71	−21
Clothing and textiles	−47	−17
Ladies' garments	−50	−32
Rubbery linoleum	−36	−18
Building	−21	−9
State and local government	6	49
Teaching	32	20

Source: Galenson, p. 18 (Pradeep Kumar, Industrial Relations in Canada and the United States 1991, p. 14).

Table 12.5

Percent Labor for Unionized, 1976 by Occupation

Occupation	Union membership	Union coverage
Professional	13.1	14.5
Managerial	5	8
Clerical and sales	16.7	20
Craft	30.3	32.5
Operative	50.7	53.2
Laborer	24.4	28.6
Farmers	0	0
Miscellaneous	33.3	33.3
Total	18.6	20.4

Source: PSID Data.

cially in public-sector union membership rates, one can see very big differences across industries. Slight differences pervade in the auto industry, probably because some manufacturing might have moved to Canada from the United States. To exemplify these sector differences (Table 12.5), I present union membership and union coverage data by occupation.[9] Clearly, unionization varies dramatically. Operatives have twice the rate of union membership as laborers and craftsmen, 51 percent versus 24 percent. Clerical and sales workers are somewhat unionized at 17 percent. Farmers are barely unionized at all. If one treats these occupations as sectors, then these data are consistent with the sector-specific unionization patterns alluded to earlier. But the real challenge is to address the issue of why there are sector-specific unionization rates. I know of no direct literature on this—but the question regarding why union membership rates differ by sector is important. I believe one can analyze this question using tools from international relations.

One strand of international relations literature seeks to explain why a particular country, for example, the United States, has poor relations with a given country, such as North Korea, better relations say with China, and very good relations with a country like Canada or England. This literature links conflict and cooperation to economic trade. The logic is simple: If conflict leads to a cessation of trade, then the cost of conflict (all else being constant) is the lost gains from trade.[10] The higher these gains from trade losses, the more important is trade in deterring conflict and promoting peace. Thus, country pairs with the most trade tend to exhibit the most cooperation and the least hostilities between themselves. Empirical work tends to support this contention.[11]

Is there an analogue between occupations and union membership rates? Clearly, all workers and firms trade. Workers provide a service, and firms bestow a wage. But some employers and employees trade more than is indicated by a simple fee-for-service transaction. These are the workers and firms that receive and provide specific training. For these workers and firms, not only is there the traditional fee-for-service transaction, but there is a sharing of the costs and benefits of training.[12] Such sharing brings about incentives for neither the employee nor the employer to interrupt the investment process with a premature quit or layoff. Some occupations are more amenable to this type of training than others, as are some industries. If the theory of conflict and trade is applicable, then those occupations (or industries) with the most specific training should see the least unionization and strike activity. Considering union membership to be related to specific training is consistent with "union membership being an experience good."[13]

There are very little data on specific training. However, one proxy is the tenure-wage gradient. The more quickly wages rise with tenure, the greater the specific training. In turn, the greater the specific training, the lower the union membership and strike activity. To test this proposition, I examined tenure gradients for each occupation.[14] Using these gradients, I estimated a logit predicting union membership for each occupation. The proportion of intraoccupation union differences predicted by these gradients is given in Table 12.6. As can be seen, worker-firm trade explains 10 percent or more of the union membership differences in twenty-three of the twenty-eight possible interoccupation categories.

Table 12.6

Proportion Interoccupational Unionization Differences Explained by Trade

	Manager	Sales	Service	Clerical	Craft	Laborer	Operative
Professional	10	0	100	100	46	81	43
Manager		0	100	100	52	92	48
Sales			21	35	22	33	22
Service				0	22	63	23
Clerical					10	30	13
Craft						0	25
Laborer							1

Source: Polachek (2002).

Conclusion

The Farber-Western results are important. They show that union density in the United States declined because of asymmetric growth between the union and nonunion sectors. The nonunion sector grew more quickly than the union sector. Changes in union organizing to stimulate new membership had little effect to moderate this decline. These results stimulate one to think more deeply why union densities differ by sector.

This chapter consisted of two parts. First, I corroborated the Farber-Western hypothesis by using international data. I showed union density to increase in countries that are experiencing manufacturing growth. Second, I borrowed from international relations research on war and peace to develop a cogent reason why union density differs by sector. In this vein, I applied a model primarily used to describe bilateral country interactions to figure out why workers often engage in hostile activities such as strikes. In doing so, I look at the contentious rather than cooperative "face" of unions.

The conflict-trade model in international relations research claims that gains from trade motivates friendly political interactions among trading partners. As gains from trade rise, the dealings become more affable. Analogously in industrial relations, worker-firm relations fortify themselves as workers and firms augment their own trade dependencies. One form of trade dependency is specific training, in which workers and firms share the costs and benefits of corporate specific training. This chapter shows that specific training differences among workers explains a significant portion of observed union density differences between occupations.

Appendix 12A

Galenson International Union Data

Country	Industrial status	Union density 1980	Union growth rate 1980–88	GDP annual growth 1980–89	Percent change
Australia	1	49	−14.3	3.5	−21.2
Canada	1	35.1	−1.4	3.3	−14.4
Denmark	1	76.5	−4.3	2.2	−11.3
France	1	19	−36.8	2.1	−19.3
Germany	1	37	−8.6	1.9	−7
Italy	1	49.3	−19.7	2.4	−15.9
Japan	1	31.1	−13.8	4	−4.5
New Zealand	1	55	−23.5	2.2	−25
Norway	1	56.9	0.4	3.6	−25
Spain	1	22	−27.3	3.1	−17.6
Sweden	1	80	6.6	1.7	−9.9
United Kingdom	1	50.7	−18.1	2.6	−7.3
United States	1	23	−28.7	3.3	−20
Argentina	0	33	−8.7	−0.3	−999
Brazil	0	13.6	−7.2	3	−5.4
Chile	0	37	−36.4	2.7	5
Egypt	0	27	−5.9	5.4	−999
India	0	30	−35	5.3	−4.9
Kenya	0	7.2	−36.1	4.1	−7.1
Korea	0	12.8	52.2	9.7	12.2
Malaysia	0	10.6	−4.7	4.9	−3.7
Mexico	0	23.4	21.9	0.7	57.4
Philippines	0	11.4	4	0.7	−2.8
Taiwan	0	20.9	40.8	7.2	−999
Thailand	0	3.2	−12.5	7	15.2

Key:
Industrial status: 1 represents industrial country, and 0 represents developing country.
Union density is union membership as a proportion of employed wage and salaried workers.
Union growth is the 1980–88 percent change in union density.
GDP annual growth 1980–89 is the average annual growth. Galenson's source is World
    Bank, *World Development Report*, World Tables, 1991.
Government attitude toward unions: 1 = unions banned or under government control; 2 =
    employers favored by government.
* −999 = data not available.

Percent growth	Average annual price inflation	Average annual unemployment rate	Average nonagricultural unemployment female	Government attitude toward unions	Social Security benefits as percent of GDP 1986
0.2	7.8	7.5	12.9	5	9.1
0.4	4.6	7.3	10.6	3	15.6
0.5	6	8.9	0.1	3	25.5
1.2	6.5	9	8.2	4	27.2
1.7	2.7	5.9	4.8	3	22.7
0.8	10.3	9.5	8.7	3	10
1.7	1.3	2.5	9.3	3	11.5
−1	11.4	5.1	10.8	4	17.4
1.7	5.6	2.7	9.5	5	29.5
0.8	9.4	17.5	19.9	4	17.2
0.6	7.4	2.5	3.4	5	30.1
2.8	6.1	10	10.9	2	19.4
1.8	4	7.2	24.1	2	12
1.4	334.8	−999	−999	3	−999
0	227.8	−999	14.6	3	−999
−1.7	20.5	−999	7.1	2	000
0.5	11	−999	−999	3	−999
3.4	7.7	−999	17.7	4	−999
−0.1	9	−999	14.3	2	−999
5.9	5	3.8	12.5	3	−999
4.4	1.5	7.4	23.1	3	−999
−5.2	72.7	−999	4.6	4	−999
4	14.8	6.6	−0.4	3	−999
6.9	2.7	2.1	17.5	2	900
6.3	3.2	2.8	9.8	2	−999

Notes

I would like to thank Jeff Xiang for valuable research assistance and Richard B. Freeman for important comments.

1. Textbooks with data on these trends include Borjas (2000), Ehrenberg and Smith (2000), Kauffman (1994), and Polachek and Siebert (1993). Monographs include Hirsch-Addison (1986), Booth (1995), and Aldcroft and Oliver (2000). One of the early studies on the subject (Dickens and Leonard 1985) attributes the decline to structural changes, particularly occupational, educational, and gender distribution of the workforce. Ironically, this study on union membership *decline* builds on a literature analyzing American trade union *growth* (Ashenfelter and Pencavel 1969).

2. Freeman (1988) alludes to these international differences.

3. One could ask whether union membership is the appropriate variable when considering the general topic of union power. Indeed, one easily may argue that the decline in union membership understates the decline in union power for two reasons: First, data on strikes (UK) are down. Second, data presented in this volume by Barry T. Hirsch, David A. Macpherson, and Edward J. Schumacher imply that U.S. union success in achieving wage gains diminished. So one question is: How important is union membership in assessing union power? I am not going to look at this question. Instead, I am going to look at the question Farber and Western actually addressed on union density in an international context.

4. Whereas Galenson discusses qualitatively how each data series relates to unionization, he never performs a rigorous statistical analysis relating each time series.

5. Not all Galenson's data represent eight-year (1980–88) growth rates. Thus, in Table 12.1, I extrapolated Galenson's data when the full eight-year period was not given in his original table.

6. I also augmented the model by introducing a dummy variable representing countries with union-managed unemployment schemes (Ghent countries). These constituted Denmark and Sweden in the Galenson sample. The coefficient came out positive (as in Blaschke 2000) though statistically insignificant.

7. Unlike the typical first-difference approach, not all independent variables are differenced because time-series changes were not available.

8. The proportion (rather than the change in proportion) of the industry that is unionized would have been a more appropriate statistic, but Galenson's book does not provide that data.

9. Rates of unionization vary by workers' education levels and industry. However, for now I treat occupations as sectors and concentrate on them.

10. The same argument applies when conflict leads to a weakening of the terms of trade, rather than a complete cessation of trade. See Polachek (1980).

11. For evidence pro and con, see Mansfield and Pollins (2003).

12. See Kuratani (1973) and Hashimoto (1981).

13. See Rafael Gomez and Morley Gunderson, chapter 4, in this volume.

14. This analysis is preliminary because in computing the tenure-wage gradient, I did not take account of (1) the correlation between individual differences and both wages and mobility, and (2) the correlation between overall job experience, tenure, and job match quality.

References

Aldcroft, Derek, and Michael Oliver. 2000. *Trade Unions and the Economy: 1870–2000.* Aldershot, UK: Ashgate.

Ashenfelter, Orley, and John Pencavel. 1969. "American Trade Union Growth: 1900–1960." *Quarterly Journal of Economics* 83 (August): 434 448.

Blaschke, Sabine. 2000. "Union Density and European Integration: Diverging Convergence." *European Journal of Industrial Relations* 6:217–236.

Booth, Alison. 1995. *The Economics of the Trade Union.* Cambridge: Cambridge University Press.

Borjas, George. 2000. *Labor Economics.* New York: McGraw-Hill.

Dickens, William, and Jonathan Leonard. 1985. "Accounting for the Decline in Union Membership, 1950–1980." *Industrial and Labor Relations Review* 38 (April): 323–334.

Ehrenberg, Ronald, and Robert Smith. 2000. *Modern Labor Economics.* 7th ed. Reading, MA: Addison Wesley Longman.

Freeman, Richard. 1988. "Contraction and Expansion: The Divergence of Private Sector and Public Sector Unionism in the United States." *Journal of Economic Perspectives* 2 (Spring): 63–88.

Galenson, Walter. 1994. *Trade Union Growth and Decline: An International Study.* Westport, CT: Praeger.

Hashimoto, Masanori. 1981. "Specific Training As a Shared Investment." *American Economic Review* 71 (June): 475–482.

Hirsch, Barry, and John Addison. 1986. *The Economic Analysis of Unions: New Approaches and Evidence.* Boston: Allen and Unwin.

Kauffman, Bruce E. 1994. *The Economics of Labor Markets.* Fort Worth, TX: Dryden.

Kuratani, M. 1973. "A Theory of Training, Earnings and Employment in Japan." Ph.D. diss., Columbia University.

Mansfield, Edward D., and Brian M. Pollins. 2003. *Economic Interdependence and International Conflict: New Perspectives on an Enduring Debate.* Michigan Studies in International Political Economy. Ann Arbor: University of Michigan Press.

Polachek, Solomon. 1980. "Conflict and Trade." *Journal of Conflict Resolution* 24 (March): 55–78.

———. 2002. "Trade-Based Interactions: An Interdisciplinary Perspective." *Conflict Management and Peace Science* 19 (Fall): 1–21.

Polachek, Solomon, and W. Stanley Siebert. 1993. *The Economics of Earnings.* Cambridge: Cambridge University Press.

Major Themes

Private-sector unionism is in decline, with little prospect for a resurgence of unions in their traditional form, given structural changes in jobs, the competitive world economy, current labor law, and the costs of union organizing. Recent surges in unionism have involved major shocks and shifts of attitudes (world wars and depression). One cannot reliably predict the occurrence or form of future shocks. However, if the Internet is used effectively, it may bring down the cost of organizing. So, there is a glimmer of hope that the future of unions may not be as bleak as some researchers are predicting.

Left unmet is a sizable demand among workers for employee involvement in a cooperative environment. This demand is not likely to be satisfied by traditional unions. The emergence of other institutions to satisfy worker demand is uncertain, but potentially can provide large gains.

Unionism is like an "experience good" that must be experienced in order to understand its attributes. This means that unionization "decline begets further decline" as people are less likely to experience unionization. It also means that inducing young people to experience unionization may foster further unionization.

Alternative institutions or employee programs appear to be more substitutes for rather than complements to traditional unionism. Nonunion programs promoting positive human resource management partly close the involvement gap without unions. As with unionization itself, forms of employee involvement (EI) are "experience goods," suggesting that forms of EI that work well could evolve and be sustained over time.

Other forms of employee associations or information centers are likely to emerge, although the exact form is uncertain. The Internet lowers the cost of information and communication. It is uncertain whether unions, firms, or third parties will emerge as the most reliable source of such information. Better information to workers will improve their voice within union and nonunion companies (e.g., IBM), although the nature and impact of these forms of voice are likely to be heterogeneous.

Absent major shifts or legal changes, we are likely to be surprised by idiosyncratic union successes and failure (e.g., Justice for Janitors in Los Angeles). These occurrences will make sense ex post but not be readily predicted ex ante.

Unions have real impacts on compensation levels and the earnings structure (inequality). The wage impact has declined over time in the United States and Europe. Whereas both the union wage premium and management resistance to unions are large in the United States, both now appear small in the United Kingdom.

Unions have real impact on firm performance. In the UK, negative effects on financial performance have lessened as union power has weakened (plant closings an exception?). Similar evidence for the 1990s and beyond is not available for the United States and Canada.

Union density in the United States is declining mainly due to nonneutral employment growth, which is taking place mostly in the nonunion sector relative to the union sector. This decline is further accelerated by the high costs of organizing. However, declining union membership patterns are not the norm for all countries. One could hope that the lessons learned from the success stories of union organizing across the globe serve as a springboard to turn the tide in favor of higher rates of U.S. union organizing leading into the twenty-first century.

Contributors

John T. Addison
Hugh C. Lane Professor of Economic Theory
Department of Economics, University of South Carolina

Clive R. Belfield
Associate Director, National Center for the Study of Privatization in Education; Adjunct Professor
Teachers College, Columbia University

Francine D. Blau
Francis Perkins Professor of Industrial and Labor Relations and Labor Economics
School of Industrial and Labor Relations, Cornell University

Sarah Brown
Lecturer
Department of Economics, University of Leicester

Christopher L. Erickson
Professor of Human Resources and Organizational Behavior
Anderson School of Management, University of California, Los Angeles

Bradley T. Ewing
Associate Professor
Department of Economics, Baylor University

Henry S. Farber
Hughes-Rogers Professor of Economics
Department of Economics, Princeton University

Catherine Fisk
Professor of Law; William Rains Fellow
Loyola Law School

Richard B. Freeman
Herbert Ascherman Chair in Economics
Department of Economics, Harvard University

Rafael Gomez
Lecturer
London School of Economics

Darien Grant*
Program Coordinator Health Care Administration
Health Care Administration, University of Texas, Arlington

Morley Gunderson
Professor
Department of Economics, University of Toronto

John S. Heywood
*Professor; Director of the Human Resources and Labor Relations Gradu-
ate Program*
Department of Economics, University of Wisconsin, Milwaukee

Barry T. Hirsch
Stevens Distinguished Professor of Economics
Department of Economics, Trinity University

Lawrence M. Kahn
Professor of Labor Economics and Collective Bargaining
School of Industrial and Labor Relations, Cornell University

Bruce E. Kaufman
Professor; Senior Associate
Department of Economics; W.T. Beebe Institute of Personnel and
Employment Relations, Georgia State University

David A. Macpherson
Abba Lerner Professor of Economics
Department of Economics, Florida State University

Ruth Milkman
Professor; Director of the University of California Institute for Labor and Employment
Department of Sociology, University of California, Los Angeles

Daniel J.B. Mitchell
Ho-su Wu Professor
Anderson School of Management and School of Public Policy and Social Research, University of California, Los Angeles

Solomon W. Polachek
Distinguished Professor
Department of Economics, State University of New York, Binghamton

Sunder Ramaswamy*
F.C. Dirks Professor
Department of Economics, Middlebury College and Madras School of Economics

Edward J. Schumacher
Associate Professor
Department of Health Care Administration and Department of Economics, Trinity University

John G. Sessions
Reader
Department of Economics, University of Bath

Bruce Western
Professor
Department of Sociology, Princeton University

Kent Wong
Director
Center for Labor Research and Education, University of California, Los Angeles

Phanindra V. Wunnava
Professor
Department of Economics, Middlebury College

* Served in the capacity of a discussant

Name Index

Subject Index

CHALLENGING HISTORY

BRITAIN IN THE 20TH CENTURY

Liz Petheram

First published in 2001 by:
Nelson Thornes Ltd
Delta Place
27 Bath Road
CHELTENHAM GL53 7TH
United Kingdom

20 00003 120

01 02 03 04 05 / 10 9 8 7 6 5 4 3 2 1

A catalogue record for this book is available from the British Library.

ISBN 0-1744-5233-0

Printed and bound in Croatia by Zrinski d. d. Cakovec

Edited by Nick Brock
Designed by Multiplex Techniques
Illustrated by Multiplex Techniques
Picture research by Zooid Pictures Ltd

Dedication

To Peter

Contents

Preview: A New Century

'DAWN OF THE CENTURY'.

'PUNCH ALMANACK'.

TALKING POINT

What attitudes towards the new century are conveyed by the poster and the cartoon shown here?

TASKS

1 Consider these events and sources.
  What reminds you of:
  a the 19th century
  b the 20th century?
2 Make a list of things one could do at the end of the 20th century which would not have been possible in 1900.

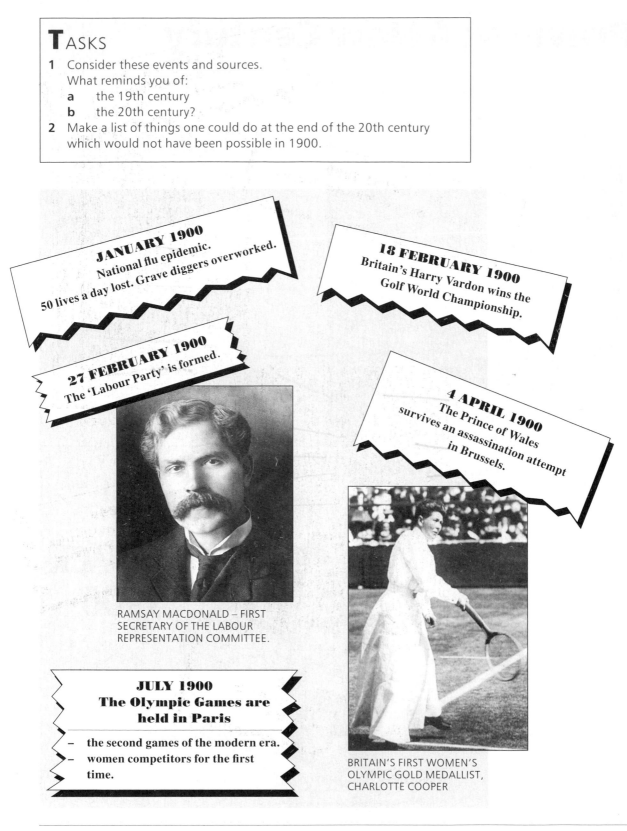

JANUARY 1900
National flu epidemic.
50 lives a day lost. Grave diggers overworked.

18 FEBRUARY 1900
Britain's Harry Vardon wins the Golf World Championship.

27 FEBRUARY 1900
The 'Labour Party' is formed.

4 APRIL 1900
The Prince of Wales survives an assassination attempt in Brussels.

RAMSAY MACDONALD – FIRST SECRETARY OF THE LABOUR REPRESENTATION COMMITTEE.

JULY 1900
The Olympic Games are held in Paris

– the second games of the modern era.
– women competitors for the first time.

BRITAIN'S FIRST WOMEN'S OLYMPIC GOLD MEDALLIST, CHARLOTTE COOPER

27 AUGUST 1900
First weekly long-distance bus service: London–Leeds 2 days.

31 AUGUST 1900
Coca-Cola goes on sale in Great Britain.

COCA-COLA ADVERTISEMENT.

OCTOBER 1900
Conservatives win the General Election. The Marquess of Salisbury is returned as prime minister.

THE THIRD MARQUESS OF SALISBURY.

OCTOBER 1900
London crowds greet troops returning from the war in South Africa.

1 The First Five Years of a New Century

PREVIEW

As Britons celebrated New Year 1900, most would have found future developments inconceivable. Who could have predicted that their familiar world would be shattered by two world wars and revolutionised by such rapid technological progress? Although the 20th century was to be a period of great change, in the first five years much of the 19th century remained. Victoria was still on the throne – until 1901 at least – after 63 years as Queen. The Conservative government was led by the aristocratic Salisbury and parliamentary opposition still centred around the Liberal Party. The class system was deeply entrenched and the same social assumptions dominated. It was a slow start to the 1900s, yet in these early years some clear changes can still be identified. The old Queen died, the Liberals re-emerged as a progressive party yet formed their last administration ever and the new Labour Party was established. The transformation from the 19th to the 20th century had begun.

FOUR GENERATIONS OF MONARCHY. QUEEN VICTORIA WITH HER SON EDWARD, HER GRANDSON GEORGE AND HER GREAT-GRANDSON EDWARD.

---

22 JANUARY 1901
Death of Queen Victoria
Surrounded by her large family, Queen Victoria died at Osborne House on the Isle of Wight. She was 81 years old and had reigned for over 63 years, 40 of them as a widow after the death of her husband Prince Albert.

TALKING POINT

Each of the three princes in this picture were later to become king – when? What were their titles? How is Britain's present monarchy related to the baby in the picture?

Edwardian Britain – two contrasting views

With the accession of Edward VII to the throne on the death of Victoria in 1901, it is tempting to see this as the beginning of a new era – particularly as it occurred at the start of a new century. It forms a natural break – a convenient line drawn under the 19th century. However, this Edwardian period – which took its name from the new monarch – offers a far more complex reality. Sharply contrasting images converge in the Edwardian period. It can be viewed as an epilogue to the 19th century, where society reflected Victorian problems, values and assumptions. Alternatively, there is much evidence to suggest this was the prelude to a 20th century age of modernity.

A modern age or a by-gone era?

TRAFFIC IN THE STRAND C.1900.

AN ADVERTISEMENT FOR DESICCATED SOUP.

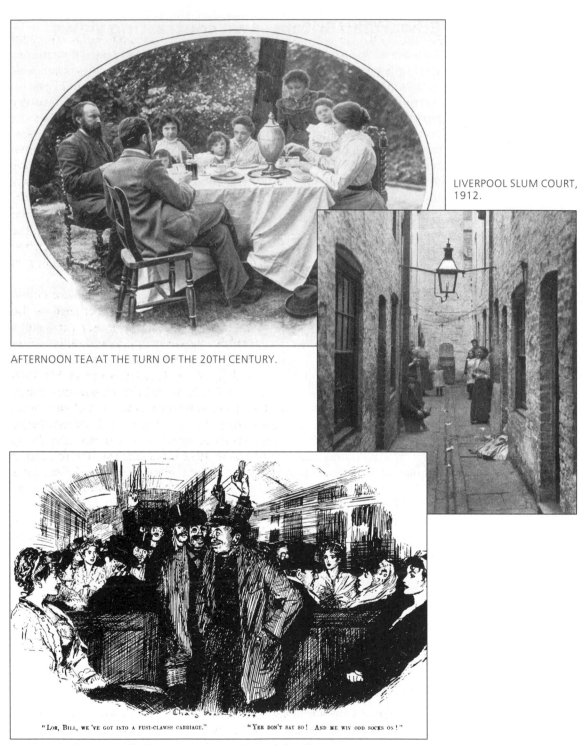

LIVERPOOL SLUM COURT, 1912.

AFTERNOON TEA AT THE TURN OF THE 20TH CENTURY.

"Lor, Bill, we've got into a fust-clawss carriage."   "Yer don't say so! And me wiv odd socks on!"

PUNCH CARTOON 1909.

What type of society do the sources suggest existed in Edwardian Britain?

Prosperity and progress

Edwardian Britain witnessed the arrival of new material benefits. The 20th century consumer society was appearing in the form of domestic toiletries such as the toilet roll and soap, and processed food, including Cadbury's Dairy Milk, ready prepared soups and milk in a bottle. A new style of shopping emerged with the establishment across the country of grocery chain stores such as Sainsburys and Liptons. Department stores offered a variety of shops under one roof – Gordon Selfridge opened his first store on Oxford Street in 1909. Edwardians also enjoyed more leisure time – the reality of one week unpaid holiday was materialising for many, together with opportunities to follow the increasingly popular spectator sports such as cricket and football. Music halls, concerts, theatres and restaurants were patronised by those who could afford them. Parks and libraries offered opportunities for all classes. By 1914 there were 3500 'picture palaces' – the early name for cinemas – in Britain. Blackpool Tower had opened in 1894 and the first Blackpool illuminations were switched on in 1912.

There was also rapid development in both transport and communication. City travel consisted of both old modes of transport such as the horse-drawn bus and the newer trams and buses. The motor car – still a luxury – provided a new found freedom for some upper- and middle-class families. It necessitated raising the speed limit to four miles per hour and its tax-raising potential was seized upon by Lloyd George in his 1909 Budget. The telephone, typewriter and radio were becoming more familiar in homes and the workplace. The development of a mass circulation press gave people a greater awareness of events in Britain and abroad. Major events were reported to wider social groups. In this period the *Daily Mirror* overtook the *Daily Mail* and in 1912 it became the first to reach a circulation of one million. Newspaper headlines proclaimed Christmas 1913 to be 'A Christmas of Gold' with 'More money than ever being spent'. The *Daily Mail* declared it to be 'The Richest Christmas'.

Another clear sign of a modern 20th century world emerging was the increasing number who became town or city dwellers. Between 1871 and 1901 the number of British towns with a population of over 50,000 doubled. In 1901, 77% lived in cities, by 1911 80%. As Masterman, a leading figure in the early 20th century Liberal Party, explained:

> ... now at the opening of a new era it is necessary to recognise that we are face to face with a phenomenon unique in the world's history ... a new race, hitherto unreckoned and of incalculable action, is entering the sphere of practical importance – the 'city type' of the coming years; the 'street' bred people of the 20th century; the new generation knocking at our doors ...

This rather threatening image of the inner city population was, however, eased by another modern image which was becoming increasingly prevalent – that of 'suburbia'. Town and city boundaries spread outward, providing pleasant areas of housing displaying better standards of house building and providing comfortable homes with the office easily accessible via new modes of transport. Satellite urban areas grew up such as

Smethwick to the west of Birmingham, Croydon in South London and Wallasey across the Mersey from Liverpool. Journeys out from the towns, however, revealed a vast regional difference. Rural life still seemed to encapsulate the notion of a pre-industrial society – with horse-drawn ploughs still common. One important sign of progress was that average life expectancy for Edwardians was much improved – at 52 years for a male and 54 for a female, although this 'average' disguised the wide differences between rich and poor.

This view of Edwardian society suggests prosperity enjoyed as a result of a 19th century industrial pre-eminence and a confidence and security borne of the prestigious international standing of the British Empire. Yet this society displayed much ambiguity in its attitudes – a complacency for having 'made it' as a nation, but also an exuberance to build on past success and move towards a new Britain of technological advance, modern conveniences and mass consumerism.

An alternative view: Poverty and conflict

The other picture of Edwardian Britain was one of poverty and deprivation. The contrast between rich and poor was most striking, particularly because it was becoming increasingly visible through a spate of published surveys and reports, the spread of cheap national newspapers and improved transport and communication. In his *Riches and Poverty* (1905), Leo Chiozza Money, the Liberal MP and economist, estimated that out of a total population of 43 million, just under half of the national income went to only 1.25 million people. Seebohm Rowntree found that in York in 1899 15% of the working class lived in 'primary poverty', despite over half of these being in regular employment. Another 22% had insufficient income for a larger family. The situation at the turn of the century worsened during the Edwardian period – real wages fell by 13% according to a 1913 Board of Trade Survey.

The term 'primary poverty' was used to describe a situation in which an individual or family did not have enough money to live at a subsistence level.

British industry began to suffer considerably from growing foreign competition – particularly from the USA, Japan and Germany – in addition to a lack of investment in our traditional industries such as coal. The resulting unemployment led to industrial tension, but it was from 1910 onwards that workers felt more confident to seek improvements in wages through striking. Between 1910 and 1912 a wave of strikes spread across Britain, focusing on the contemporary perception that the rich were getting richer and the poor poorer. The number of strikes, the organisation and growing membership of the trade unions and the escalation of violence on picket lines presented the Liberal government with a critical situation in industry. Other conflicts arose to test the governments of the day. The Boer War showed serious chinks in Britain's imperial armour, women's demands for political emancipation radicalised with the emergence of the Women's Social and Political Union (Suffragettes). In addition to the franchise issue, the role of the non-elected House of Lords led to a protracted crisis resolved in 1911, a year after Edward VII's death. Conflict again emerged in the perennial Irish question which also became far more critical in the pre-war years. This scene has been disguised by a sentimental nostalgia for an Edwardian Britain enjoyed by only certain classes.

In fact, as in Victorian Britain, the class divide clearly existed. The lifestyle of the poor contrasted starkly with the so-called 'Golden Age' of the affluent upper and middle classes. Edwardian country weekends with hunting, shooting and fishing were only seen by the working class at close quarters if they happened to be in domestic service. Carefree Edwardian summer afternoons, with games of croquet, tennis and delicate tea-time refreshments, differed sharply from the diet of most of the working class. A labourer's family would be sustained on very little variety and repetitive portions of bread, potato and tea. Individuals of any class were fully aware of their social status and this determined their expectations and values.

TASK

Consider the evidence offered for the two contrasting views of Edwardian Britain.

Identify aspects of society about which Edwardians could feel

a secure

b concerned.

The Conservatives in crisis, 1900–05

In the five years between 1900 and 1905 the Conservatives declined rapidly from a position of apparent political dominance to a party split from top to bottom and forced to resign, losing the January 1906 General Election to a landslide Liberal victory. What had gone wrong? To what extent did Conservatives suffer internally from the divisions over their quest for national efficiency or the failings of their leader, Arthur Balfour? Alternatively, had the 20th century ushered in developments such as a competitive economic climate, a new era of class-based politics, a fresh look at the Liberal Party and a new Labour Party, which the Conservatives were unable to withstand?

1900 General Election – Conservative dominance confirmed?

The Conservatives won the 1900 General Election convincingly with 334 seats. Together with the support of 68 Liberal Unionists, Lord Salisbury formed a government once more. It was the third general election victory in a short period for the Conservatives and Liberal Unionist Party – following successes in 1886 and 1895. The Liberals seemed to be permanently in opposition, unable to drive a wedge through the broad support the Conservatives had developed over the past 15 years. They were still traditionally the party of the landed classes, the upper middle class, and the defenders of the Anglican Church and Empire. Their appeal had, however, been extended to attract much more support from the growing middle-class suburbs and, with their image projecting Tory Democracy powerfully combined with jingoism, had won over considerable working-class support. The election of 1900 was called on the back of an apparent victory in the Boer War being fought by the British in South Africa since 1899. Chamberlain had declared 'A vote against this government was a vote for the Boers'. This imperialistic and patriotic reminder served to invigorate the Conservative's campaign and return

Lord Salisbury as Prime Minister. The election campaign had also demonstrated an effective party machinery – extended and improved over the 1890s due to the professional competence of Captain R.W.E. Middleton, who was their national agent from 1885. Under his stewardship, the Conservative National Union was rationalised and divided into nine regions, and the National Society of Conservative Agents was formed in 1891. Conservative Working Men's Clubs flourished and many more were attracted by the new craze of cycling to the Conservative Cycle Clubs. New initiatives were also launched by older institutions such as the Primrose League to propagandise the Conservative message.

In June 1902 Salisbury, old, ill and heartbroken over his wife's death in 1899, retired. He was succeeded by his nephew, Arthur Balfour. Within three-and-a-half years, the Conservative Party's period of political dominance had come to an end. It was a collapse from which Conservatism struggled to recover – a Conservative government was not formed again until 1922.

A search for National Efficiency

As the first nation to prosper from the beneficial effects – as well as some of the harmful ones – of an industrialised economy, Britain in 1900 bathed in a warm glow of prosperous superiority which bred a worrying and damaging complacency. In exports and overseas investments Britain still had a large share of world trade. Her economy benefited from an increased supply of South African gold, a diversification into tertiary industries such as shipping, insurance and world banking and from the continued growth of total industrial production. However, to the more astute contemporary observers there were warning signs of national decline.

TALKING POINT

In what ways can it be argued that the Conservative Party is the natural political party for Britain?

ECONOMIC WARNING

1 Competition threatened from industrial countries such as Germany, Japan and the USA.
2 Economic rivals were enjoying a faster rate of economic growth, supported by rapidly growing populations and the exploitation of new industrial techniques.
3 British industries, particularly textiles, suffered from the protective tariffs imposed by Germany and the USA to guard their own industrial base.
4 Britain was dependent on old traditional industries which were very conservative and lacked investment and innovation.

MILITARY WARNING

1 The Boer War 1899–1902, although a victory, highlighted serious weaknesses in the British Imperial machine.

2 The war cost Britain £200 million.

3 Militarily it was a long campaign with the loss of over 20,000 British lives which highlighted a serious lack of competence on the part of the Army Command.

4 The physical condition of new recruits to the British army caused a scandal and prompted the appointment of a committee to investigate the problem.

5 Criticism arose over the use of concentration camps for non-combatants. As a result of the crowded and insanitary conditions, disease spread, killing many women and children. The Liberal leader, Campbell-Bannerman, denounced the policy, accusing the government of using 'methods of barbarism'.

6 Britain's isolated position was revealed by the formation of alliances among other major European powers – namely Germany with Austria-Hungary and France with Russia.

SOCIAL WARNING

1 Despite calls for a wide package of social reforms to deal with poverty, governments had failed to deliver.

2 Standards in education were questioned.

3 The 1904 Report of the Interdepartmental Committee on Physical Deterioration highlighted the extent of social degeneracy amongst Britain's urban population.

Tasks

1 Explain why the call for National Efficiency had developed in Britain.

2 Explain, on a chart similar to the one opposite, how National Efficiency could be tackled by the following methods:

As a result of these warning signs a demand for National Efficiency grew in Britain.

Methods	Benefits
1 Expansion of education particularly at secondary school level.	
2 Widespread social reform to tackle poverty amongst the working class.	
3 An end to a Free Trade policy and the introduction of protective tariffs.	
4 Investigation and reform of the armed forces.	

FOCUS

1.1 To what extent was Balfour (1902–1905) responsible for Conservative decline?

ARTHUR BALFOUR.

When Balfour was forced to resign in December 1905 and the Conservatives lost the General Election of 1906 so dramatically, the role of this Prime Minister came into question. Historians have debated the extent of his responsibility for Conservative collapse.

Issues for DEBATE

A Character and background
B Education policy
C Foreign and defence policy
D Licensing law
E Trades unions
F Chinese slavery

Notes for the DEFENCE

A A good administrator and excellent debater. Never married after the tragic death of his fiancee. As nephew of Lord Salisbury, Balfour had been brought up close to politics and government circles. Aimed to maintain Conservative unity. Had a very clear mind, an interest in scientific and technological developments and was acutely aware of Britain's new position in the world.

B The Education Act 1902 was a great achievement for British education. It abolished the 1870 School Boards, establishing instead the Local Education Authorities in charge of administering and financing both Church schools and the old Board schools. Thus it standardised a very ad hoc system and was also successful in dealing positively with secondary education.

C Diplomatic isolation was brought to an end by the signing of a Japanese Alliance (1902) and the Anglo-French Entente (1904). The new Committee for Imperial Defence initiated a major reorganisation of the army and navy. The First Sea Lord, Sir John Fisher, began revolutionary changes in the navy.

D The Licensing Act 1904 provided for the closure of public houses where numbers seemed excessive. Publicans who lost trade were compensated by a levy on those remaining in business.

E The Taff Vale Case was brought by the Southern Wales Railway Company. The company claimed compensation from the trades unions for damages incurred by a recent strike. It reached the House of Lords who declared in favour of the employers. From Balfour's point of view, this was a matter for the courts to decide.

F Balfour approved the request of Alfred Milner, the British High Commissioner in South Africa, to import Chinese labour into the gold mines in the Rand. The Prime Minister believed this was a simple solution to improve output in the gold mines, much needed after the disruption of the Boer War. He also argued that the Chinese would certainly earn more than at home.

Notes for the PROSECUTION

A Balfour was too intellectual and wealthy to fully understand the deep social problems of the time. He seemed aloof and uninvolved. His cold detachment meant he was not a popular politician. Although he was able to identify clearly the long-term needs of both Britain and the Conservative Party, Blake, historian of the Conservative Party, states that 'Balfour, however, had his blind spots, and their effects on the electoral fortunes of his party were considerable.'

B The Education Act proved to be a major political problem as the Nonconformists across the country were outraged that rates would support a variety of Church schools, most worryingly Roman Catholic and Anglican. A campaign was set up by Dr Clifford, a London Baptist Minister, the debate was particularly bitter in Wales and the Liberals, traditionally supporters of Nonconformism, were able to attack the government with a united voice. Up until the summer of 1902 the Tories had won nine out of 10 by-elections – shortly after this Act, they lost North Leeds and Sevenoaks in quick succession.

C Foreign and defence policy was limited in actual achievements and was not greatly advantageous as a vote-catcher.

D This, as with the Education Act, offended the Nonconformist conscience. It was felt to be an inadequate reform and the Temperance lobby was disappointed.

E Balfour made no attempt to address the increasingly powerful pressure coming from the trades unions. His non-intervention in the Taff Vale Case gave the working class the impression that the Prime Minister did not understand trades union agitation and anyway chose to remain aloof.

F Over the issue of 'Chinese Slavery' in South Africa Balfour demonstrated extreme insensitivity and the government was involved in a storm of protest. The Chinese labourers were accommodated in overcrowded camps and the moral issue was raised of inhuman treatment. Secondly, the policy was seen by organised labour in Britain to threaten the possibility of white jobs in South Africa.

TASKS

Class Debate

1 Prepare for a debate by dividing the class into those prosecuting and those defending Balfour's record. Individual students can speak on the separate issues in the debate.
2 Complete further research on areas A–F.
3 Debate the question and finally determine the majority decision in the class.

Conservative split over Tariff Reform

Issues such as the Boer War, Education, Licensing and Chinese slavery politically damaged the Conservative Party, but it was Joseph Chamberlain's proposal for Tariff Reform which caused a Cabinet crisis in 1902 from which the party was unable to recover before the 1906 Election.

Who was Joseph Chamberlain?

The son of a shopkeeper who had made his fortune as a Birmingham manufacturer, Joseph Chamberlain became mayor of that city and in 1876 one of its MPs. He broke from the Liberal Party in 1886, denouncing Home Rule for Ireland and causing the party to split. As a member of the Conservative and Unionist Cabinet, he held the post of Colonial Secretary from 1895 to 1903. He left the Colonial Office in 1903 to campaign for Tariff Reform – a policy which split the Tories and contributed to their electoral defeat .

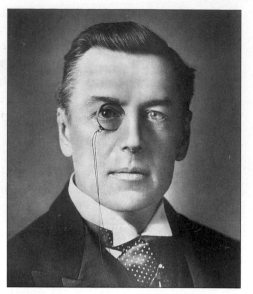

JOSEPH CHAMBERLAIN.

What was Tariff Reform?

This was a policy to abandon the traditional 19th century free trade of goods in and out of the country and adopt a system of tariffs in order to protect business interests at home. These tariffs were to be lower for goods within the British Empire (the system of imperial preference).

How did the crisis develop?

1902 Hicks Beach, Lord Salisbury's Chancellor, reimposed a registration duty on imported corn as a means to raise revenue to pay off the deficit from the Boer War. The Canadian Prime Minister – Laurier – proposed a special and reciprocal arrangement for Canadian corn entering Britain and British manufactured goods exported to Canada.

Hicks Beach retired at the same time as Salisbury and was replaced at the Treasury by Ritchie, a convinced Free Trader and critic of imperial preference. His budget reflected his economic stance.

1903 On 14 May Chamberlain made a highly significant speech in Birmingham, proposing that the Conservatives adopt Tariff Reform with the imperial preference.

By September it was clear that the government was split over the issue. Ritchie and the Free Traders were dismissed, followed by the Duke of Devonshire's resignation two weeks later. The newly constructed Cabinet – devoid also of Chamberlain, who had moved out with Balfour's blessing to pursue his cause – seemed lacking in substance.

1904–5 The question of Tariff Reform became a national issue – dividing Conservative politicians and the country. A Tariff Reform League was set against the Free Food League. Posters were produced and debates were held. Appalled by his party's new stance, Winston Churchill decided to cross the House to join the

The Free Food League was a campaigning group established by a number of Conservative MPs.

Liberals. A weakened Conservative Party did not unite behind Balfour's compromise position and he was finally forced to resign on 25 November 1905. Tariff Reform had split the Conservatives but united the Liberals.

Would Tariff Reform stop the rot of national economic decline?

Arguments FOR

1 Tariffs would protect British industry in a similar way to the system employed in Germany and the USA.
2 Protected industry would result in more jobs.
3 Revenue from tariffs would help to fund necessary measures of social reform – an important social and political consideration.

4 Imperial preference would unite and strengthen the Empire against continental power.
5 A strengthened British Empire was the key to national survival in the 20th century.
6 Tariff Reform was an attractive policy to many industrialists and farmers feeling the pinch from foreign competition.

Arguments AGAINST

1 Free Trade was a deeply rooted economic principle associated with the prosperity of 19th century Britain.
2 The orthodoxy in the Treasury at Whitehall was in favour of the policy of Free Trade.
3 Tariff Reform would cause prices to rise, particularly on food. Many were alarmed at the prospect of the 'little loaf'.
4 Tariff Reform was politically disastrous because the Conservatives were divided over the issue, the Liberals reunited over their 19th century belief in Free Trade and many in the public at large hated the idea of protection.

TASK

Identify the social group to which you might have belonged in 1904 and write a brief explanation of whether you would have favoured Tariff Reform or not.

The Labour Party – a new departure in British political life

The new century ushered in a new political party – one which was to become highly significant during the following years. After a faltering start, the Labour Party eventually replaced the 19th century Liberal Party as the voters' alternative to the Conservatives. Founded as the Labour Representation Committee in 1900, it did not take its now familiar name until after the 1906 Election. The formation of this new party took place at the Memorial Hall in London on 27 February 1900 where a conference had been convened by the Trades Union Congress with invitations issued to trades unions, co-operative societies and socialist groups, including the Fabians, the Social Democratic Federation (a Marxist group) and the Independent Labour Party.

THE RED FLAG

'The people's flag is deepest red,
it shrouded oft our martyred dead,
and ere their limbs grew stiff or cold,
Their heart's blood dyed in every fold …

With heads uncovered swear we all,
To bear it onward till we fall,
Come dungeon dark, or gallows grim,
This song shall be our parting hymn,

Then raise the scarlet standard high!
Within its shade we'll live and die,
Though cowards flinch and traitors sneer,
We'll keep the Red Flag flying here!'

Written in 1889 by Jim Connell, the Irish Socialist, in memory of the European Socialist dead. It has always been associated with British Labour gatherings.

AGENDA

1 OBJECT OF THE CONFERENCE

A resolution in favour of working-class opinion being represented in the House of Commons by men sympathetic with the aims and demands of the Labour Movement.

From the report of the Conference on Labour Representation in February 1900.

TALKING POINT

What do you understand by the term Socialist?
What role do the trades unions play in society today? Are they part of the democratic process?
What is the position of the modern-day Labour Party and what are its policies?

Explanations for the rise of the Labour Party

Argument 1   Was it the inevitable consequence of a developing working-class consciousness?

A developing class consciousness amongst the working class had begun in the earliest stages of industrialisation. Working men became more aware of their common bonds, their position and the influence of their labour within the prospering, capitalist society. In the second half of the 19th century other changes bred further working-class awareness which led to the establishment of a political party to protect and promote working-class interests.

Educational development: After 1870 elementary schools were provided nationwide. Levels of literacy Increased.

Political change: Many working-class men gained the vote in the reform acts of 1867 and 1884.

Late 19th century working-class consciousness

Economic Impact: During the late 19th century falling prices and continued profits for many men with jobs meant real wages rose and a better standard of living was experienced.

Technological advance: This ended the sharp distinction between skilled and unskilled work. The working class as a whole were a group distinct from the middle class.

TALKING POINT

What is meant by a 'class consciousness'?
How did these factors contribute to a growing class consciousness amongst the workers?

Argument 2 Was it a pragmatic response to a combination of diverse social, economic and political factors?

The Labour Party resulted from a combination of developments in the wider labour movement itself and difficulties the enfranchised working men had in identifying themselves with the existing political parties.

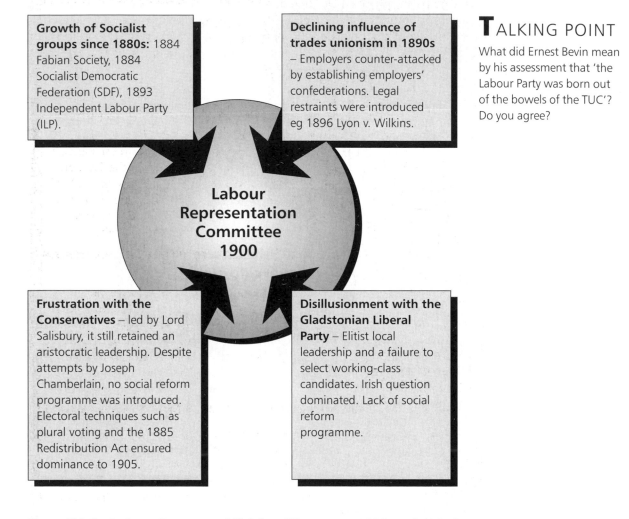

Growth of Socialist groups since 1880s: 1884 Fabian Society, 1884 Socialist Democratic Federation (SDF), 1893 Independent Labour Party (ILP).

Declining influence of trades unionism in 1890s – Employers counter-attacked by establishing employers' confederations. Legal restraints were introduced eg 1896 Lyon v. Wilkins.

Labour Representation Committee 1900

Frustration with the Conservatives – led by Lord Salisbury, it still retained an aristocratic leadership. Despite attempts by Joseph Chamberlain, no social reform programme was introduced. Electoral techniques such as plural voting and the 1885 Redistribution Act ensured dominance to 1905.

Disillusionment with the Gladstonian Liberal Party – Elitist local leadership and a failure to select working-class candidates. Irish question dominated. Lack of social reform programme.

TALKING POINT
What did Ernest Bevin mean by his assessment that 'the Labour Party was born out of the bowels of the TUC'? Do you agree?

How did the Labour Party establish itself between 1900 and 1906?

Although a general election in 1900 was a difficult challenge for the Labour Representation Committee only months after its formation, it fielded 15 candidates and returned its first two MPs – Keir Hardie and Richard Bell. In the course of the next six years, the party grew significantly. What factors encouraged the early establishment and growth of the young Labour Party?

TASK
Explain how each of
these steps contributed
to the growth of the
LRC.

LABOUR PARTY
The new name adopted
for the Labour Represent-
ation Committee.

1906

GENERAL ELECTION
LRC won 29 seats out of 50
candidates, polling 323,195 votes.

1903

LIBERAL–LABOUR PACT
In this electoral pact – between Ramsay
MacDonald, the secretary of the LRC, and
Herbert Gladstone, the Liberal's Chief
Whip – the LRC were given a clear run in
30 seats against the Conservatives.
Liberals were to benefit financially.

1901

TAFF VALE CASE
As a result of the House of Lords ruling against the
railway union in favour of the employers,
membership of the LRC rose to 861,000 and the
number of affiliated trades unions from 65 to 127. A
political levy was raised from these unions.

1900

OCTOBER – GENERAL ELECTION
The LRC won two seats out of 15 candidates, polling 63,304
votes. They were financially and numerically weak with only
12 affiliated trades unions and 375,951 members from the
unions and socialist societies. There was no individual
membership.

1900

FEBRUARY – LABOUR REPRESENTATION COMMITTEE
'They had formed only a confederation composed of organisations, not
a party to which individuals might directly adhere' (Philip P. Poirier, *The
Advent of the Labour Party* (1958) quoted in Paul Adelman's *The Rise
of the Labour Party 1880–1945*).

Examining the Evidence

The early years of the Labour Party

Source A

An account of a representative at the conference called to launch the Labour Representation Committee, 1900.

> I was present at the Conference representing the I.L.P. Other I.L.P. delegates were Keir Hardie, J. Ramsay MacDonald, F.W. Jowett and J. Burgess. This was the first time I had come in contact with the Trade Union Leaders. They struck me as being a very commonsense lot, probably quite competent at their own job, but hardly the kind of men you would expect to find at the barricades when the Social Revolution came … the Conference emphatically rejected the proposal that only working men should be regarded as competent to represent the working class.
>
> Quoted in Paul Adelman, *Rise of the Labour Party 1880–1945* (1972).

From Source A:
1 How does the account view the trades unionists?
2 What does this indicate about the social composition of the LRC?

Source B

Jesse Herbert to Herbert Gladstone, 6 March 1903.

> The LRC can directly influence the votes of nearly one million men. They will have a fighting fund of £100,000. (This is the most significant new fact in the situation. Labour candidates have had hitherto to beg for financial help, and have fought with paltry and insufficient funds.) Their members are mainly men who have hitherto voted with the Liberal Party. Should they be advised to vote against Liberal candidates, and (as they probably would) should they act as advised, the Liberal Party would suffer defeat not only in those constituencies where LRC candidates fought, but also in almost every borough, and in many of the Divisions of Lancashire and Yorkshire. This would be the inevitable result of unfriendly action towards LRC candidates. They would be defeated, but so also should we be defeated.
>
> If there be good-fellowship between us and the LRC the aspect of the future for both will be very bright and encouraging.
>
> Quoted in Lawrence Butler and Harriet Jones,
> *Britain in the 20th century (1994)*, vol.1.

From Source B:
1 What advantages for the Liberals were there in this electoral pact?
2 Why do you think the LRC agreed to the pact?

Source C
1906 The Labour Electoral Manifesto.

To the Electors –

This election is to decide whether or not Labour is to be fairly represented in Parliament.

The House of Commons is supposed to be the people's House, and yet the people are not there.

Landlords, employers, lawyers, brewers, and financiers are there in force. Why not Labour?

The Trade Unions ask the same liberty as capital enjoys. They are refused.

The aged poor are neglected.

The slums remain; overcrowding continues, whilst the land goes to waste. Shopkeepers and traders are overburdened with rates and taxation, whilst the increasing land values, which should relieve the ratepayers, go to people who have not earned them.

Wars are fought to make the rich richer, and underfed school children are still neglected.

Chinese Labour is defended because it enriches the mine owners.

The unemployed ask for work, the Government gave them a worthless Act, and now, when you are beginning to understand the causes of your poverty, the red herring of Protection is drawn across your path.

Protection, as experience shows, is no remedy for poverty and unemployment. It serves to keep you from dealing with the land, housing, old age and other social problems!

You have it in your power to see that Parliament carries out your wishes. The Labour Representation Executive appeals to you in the name of a million Trade Unionists to forget all the political differences which have kept you apart in the past, and vote for – (here is inserted the name of your Labour candidate).

Quoted in Paul Adelman, *Rise of the Labour Party 1880–1945* (1972).

From Source C:
1 What similarities with Liberal Party views do you notice in this source?
2 To what extent can this manifesto be called 'socialist'?
3 To whom is the manifesto targeting its appeal?

The re-emergence of the Liberal Party

The dominant force of 19th century Liberalism had taken a battering over the last 15 years of that century. Gladstone's great Liberal Party had split over the question of Ireland in 1886, haemorrhaging a splinter group, the Liberal Unionists, who joined with the Conservative Party. The Liberals were returned with a modest victory in 1892, only to be heavily defeated three years later by the Conservative and Liberal Unionists, who returned 411 seats compared to Rosebery's Liberals' 177. The Conservative ascendancy left the Liberals in the shadows, floundering over policies, finances, leadership and party organisation. Liberal determination to cling to the traditional philosophy of individualism made an appeal to the mass electorate more difficult, whilst tensions emerged amongst the party members' attitudes to Empire and foreign policy. The party's organisation was less effective and Gladstone's retirement in 1894 inevitably raised the divisive question of the succession to the leadership. Furthermore finances had been sapped by the removal of the Liberal Unionists, many of whom were wealthy industrialists and former benefactors to the party. A symptom perhaps of these Liberal difficulties was the significant decline in profits of the provincial radical press, the mouthpiece of Liberalism earlier in the century.

However, as the Conservative Party began to suffer from the problems outlined earlier in this chapter the Liberals began to re-group and prepare themselves as a realistic challenge to the Conservatives at the next general election. There were four main features in this re-emergence:

1   New Liberalism
2   Party reorganisation and the Lib–Lab Pact of 1903
3   19th century Liberal principles reunited the party
4   Defeat of the Relugas Pact 1905

What was New Liberalism?

This was a radical new departure in the attitudes of many key Liberals of the younger generation, such as Hobson, Samuel, Masterman and Lloyd George. They believed that it was the responsibility of government to intervene to improve the material conditions of society. Problems such as poverty were too entrenched to be tackled on an individual basis. Laissez-faire should be abandoned in favour of government action to solve major social problems. It was previously thought that excessive government intervention limited personal freedom. New Liberals suggested the opposite. The government needed to legislate to put in place a society which offered positive freedom and opportunity.

This more progressive attitude drew much of its intellectual justification from the theories of T.H. Green, an Oxford don who sought to redefine the notion of Liberty. Liberal policies based on these new principles included a major social reform package financed by a shift in fiscal policy to tax the wealthy. At a time when major social problems were being discussed, researched and seemingly ignored by Conservative administrations, New Liberalism was a clear indication that many in the Liberal Party were adapting to the demands of the 20th century.

'Self reliance is a powerful force, but not powerful enough to cure unaided the diseases that afflict society. Liberty is of supreme importance, but State assistance, rightly directed, may extend the bounds of liberty.'

Herbert Samuel, 'Liberalism' (1902), quoted in K.O. Morgan, *The Age of Lloyd George: the Liberal Party and British Politics 1890–1929* (1971).

How was Liberal Party organisation improved?

In his period as Liberal Chief Whip (1899–1905), Herbert Gladstone did much to modernise the organisation of the party. Local associations were rationalised and revitalised. Seats were targeted and radical Liberal candidates were placed in winnable seats, sometimes in receipt of financial assistance. As a result only five Conservatives stood unopposed in the 1906 election – compared with 153 in 1900.

In order to avoid a split in the anti-Tory vote between the Liberals and the newly formed LRC, a strategy developed that there should be some form of electoral understanding between these parties of the left. In 1903 a secret electoral pact was signed between Herbert Gladstone and Ramsay MacDonald (the Secretary of the LRC). It was agreed that Labour could freely contest 30 seats without a Liberal candidate standing. The Liberals were also to have access to the LRC's £100,000 election fund. A list of mainly working-class constituencies where an electoral arrangement would be beneficial was drawn up by MacDonald and Gladstone used his financial control over the local party associations in those constituencies to suggest that they refrained from nominating a Liberal candidate.

Some historians have suggested that it was reckless for the Liberals to have tacitly accepted a party which could replace them – and the long-term implications of such a strategy have to be considered. However, in the short term the Liberals benefited from extra financial help, the idea of a Progressive Alliance on the left of politics and most significantly from achieving the main object of the pact – defeat of the Conservatives.

In what ways did the Liberals reunite on traditional principles?

When the Liberal Party electioneered for support in January 1906, they were able to unite behind traditional issues. Temperance came to the fore once more in their opposition to the Tories' Licensing Act and similarly Nonconformity as a sectional appeal reappeared in the debate over the Education Act. In addition the Liberals' humanitarian concern for the freedom of individuals was professed loudly over the issue of Chinese slavery in South Africa. However, it was Chamberlain's Tariff Reform campaign that, most importantly, not only split his own party but enabled the Liberals to re-emerge united behind their great 19th century passion, Free Trade. Thanks to the problems encountered by the Conservative administration, 19th century Liberalism appeared relevant to 20th century politics.

This strength of support for old Liberal principles in addition to the more progressive ideas in the party enabled the Liberals to fight the 1906 Election on a broad range of issues which appealed to both class and other sectional interests in society.

Why was the defeat of the Relugas Pact significant?

The question over Liberal Party leadership and their prime minister in waiting could have been highly damaging. Liberal factions – namely, the Gladstonian Liberals led by Campbell-Bannerman and the Liberal Imperialists who looked to Rosebery for leadership – existed, differing particularly over defence and foreign policy. There was a conspiracy (the Relugas Pact) between Asquith, Grey and Haldane – three Liberal

Imperialists – to either remove Campbell-Bannerman to the House of Lords or possibly replace him with Rosebery as their chosen prime minister. The intrigue was defeated by Campbell-Bannerman acting decisively to win over Asquith to his side with the promise of the post of Chancellor of the Exchequer and Balfour's unexpected decision to resign rather than go to the country in December 1905. This was significant to the Liberal Party as Campbell-Bannerman took a firm grip over a potentially divided party leadership and formed a Cabinet which incorporated both factions. It was this broad-based and decisively led Liberal Cabinet which called the election of January 1906 and won.

REVIEW

The 1906 Election: Liberal victory or Conservative defeat?

1906 Election results		
Liberals	400 seats	49% of vote
Conservatives and Liberal Unionists	157 seats	43.6% of vote
Labour	30 seats	5.9% of vote
Irish Nationalists	83 seats	0.6% of vote

The 1906 Election resulted in a memorable landslide victory for the Liberal Party – the largest overall majority since 1832. The Liberals increased their number of MPs to 400 – having won only 184 in 1900 – and conversely the Conservatives sank from over 400 seats in 1900 to 157 in 1906. Why did the Liberals win such a decisive electoral victory?

This is a difficult question for historians to answer because election results only show the way the electorate cast its votes, not the motives behind its decision to vote for one party or the other. The picture is further blurred by our first-past-the-post voting system which does not allocate seats in Parliament in a manner directly proportional to the number of votes cast.

TASKS

1 What different conclusions can you draw from the number of seats won in 1906 compared with the percentage of votes cast for the parties?
2 With reference to pages 9 to 24:
    List reasons why people might have voted positively for the Liberals in 1906.
    List reasons why people might have voted against the Conservatives in 1906.
    Give evidence to show how strong the new Labour Party was at this election.

3 Plan and write an essay:
   'Why did the Liberals win the 1906 election?'
   WHY? – This type of essay, sometimes called a list essay, requires you to put a series of reasons forward. Each paragraph should be introduced with a sentence offering a reason why the Liberals won. The remainder of the paragraph should contain evidence to prove the argument.

REASON:	EVIDENCE:
E.g. A reason for Liberal success in 1906 was the split in the Conservative Party over Tariff Reform.	• Balfour's resignation on 25 November 1905 because the party split over Tariff Reform and refused Balfour's compromise solution. • Tariff Reform initiated by Chamberlain in his Birmingham speech of 1903. • Free Traders dismissed from Cabinet. • Establishment of a Tariff Reform League and a Free Food League. • Liberals united against tariffs in favour of their traditional policy of Free Trade.

- Complete this analysis chart with other reasons and substantiating evidence.
- Decide if one reason or a group of reasons – perhaps the appeal of the Liberals or an anti-Tory vote – are more important than the others and try to explain why.
- Place your arguments in an order which ensures coherence.
  Now you should be sufficiently organised to write this essay.

2 Liberals in Power, 1906–1914: Achievement and Conflict

PREVIEW

HERBERT ASQUITH, LIBERAL PRIME MINISTER FROM 1906.

WILLIAM EWART GLADSTONE – THE DOMINANT FIGURE IN THE LATE-19TH CENTURY LIBERAL PARTY.

By the outbreak of the First World War in 1914 the Liberals had been in government for eight years. It was a period which was crucial both for Britain as an international player and for the Liberal Party, an accepted force in the country's political system. The record of this administration is notable both for its achievements and its failures. On the positive side the Liberals achieved an unprecedented scale of social reform, a long sought-for reform of the House of Lords and a developing relationship with organised labour. However, this record was severely overshadowed in

TALKING POINT

What aims do you associate with the 19th century/ 20th century Liberal Party? Consider the position of the Liberal Party today. Explain your answer.

1914 by a failure to extend the franchise to all men and women, a lack of foresight to tackle some major economic problems, an Irish problem not only unsolved but in fact left on the brink of civil war and finally entry into the First World War – an event which was to have unforeseen consequences on all aspects of British life.

Liberal achievements

TALKING POINT

Why is poverty generally a difficult term to define? What are the main causes and consequences of poverty? How would you define the poverty prevalent in Britain in the early 20th century?

Liberal social reform – did this lay the foundations of the Welfare State?

The Liberal government returned in the 1906 Election had no clearly defined social programme. Social reform had been referred to in election addresses yet the thrust of their campaign emphasised the failings of the Tory government rather than any radical state interventionism. However, the administration carried through a massive package of social reform before the outbreak of the First World War. Through their actions in government, the Liberals were moving away from their old beliefs of freedom of the individual and laissez faire. Instead they increasingly advocated government intervention in both social and economic policy. Many historians argue that the package of social legislation introduced by Asquith's Liberal administration laid the foundations of the Welfare State, with the government taking responsibility for the most vulnerable groups in society and financing means to help them.

Who benefited – and how?

CHILDREN

1906 Education (Provision of Meals) Act – school dinners were to be provided for needy children paid for by a $\frac{1}{2}$d rate. However, not all local authorities complied and a government grant was not awarded until 1914. Even then, this only covered half the cost.

CHILDREN WAITING OUTSIDE A HALL FOR FREE DINNERS, 1912.

1907 Education (Administrative Provisions) Act – a medical department was set up at the Board of Education to ensure the provision of a school medical service. School clinics were introduced.

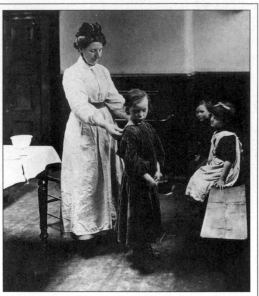

SCHOOL CHILDREN UNDERGOING A MEDICAL CHECK C.1912.

1908 Children Act – formally established the legal rights of a child. Parental negligence was made illegal. Borstals, remand houses and juvenile courts were set up to deal with young offenders. This was largely a rationalisation and codifying Act, which clarified the existing situation.

THE ELDERLY

THE NEW YEAR'S GIFT.

1908 Old Age Pensions Act – a noncontributory scheme for payment of 5s per week at the age of 70 (7s 6d for a married couple). Pensions, paid through the Post Office, were kept deliberately small and not intended to replace savings. They were paid only to those with incomes less than £31 p.a. who also passed a type of 'character test'. The estimated cost in 1908 of £6 million rose to £12 million by 1913.

PARTRIDGE, 'THE NEW YEAR'S GIFT'.

1909 Trade Boards Act – set up trade boards consisting equal numbers of employers, employed and officials for certain trades (tailoring, lace work, box makers and chain makers). These boards were to fix minimum rates for timework and piecework. Employers who paid less were to be fined. This Act covered some 200,000 workers, of whom 140,000 were female, but was criticised for curtailing the freedom of master and workers to negotiate rates voluntarily

1909 Labour Exchanges Act – provided places for workers to go to claim benefits and to obtain help in seeking work.

1911 National Insurance Act – Part I Health – provided compulsory insurance against sickness for all earning up to £160 p.a. Employee to pay 4d, employer 3d and state 2d. Entitlement was 10s sickness benefit and free medical care. Maternity benefit – 30s and help to end TB sanatoria. However, this made no provision for hospitals and failed to include dependants. It was criticised for making deductions from already low wages.

1911 National Insurance Act – Part 2 Unemployment – established compulsory insurance against employment in certain trades such as building, engineering and iron manufacture. Employer and employee paid $2\frac{1}{2}$d per week plus $1\frac{2}{3}$d from the State. Entitlement was 7s per week for 15 weeks. This scheme provided small amounts of benefits for a limited period and was not extended until 1920.

TASKS

1 Identify the groups in society vulnerable to poverty who were not covered by this legislation.
2 Analyse the impact of this social reform by listing its successes and limitations.
3 What do you understand by the phrase 'Welfare State'?
4 How far do you consider the Liberal social reforms 1906–11 contributed towards the establishment of a Welfare State in Britain?

FOCUS

2.1 Was Liberal Social Legislation Motivated by either Humanitarian Concern or Political Pragmatism?

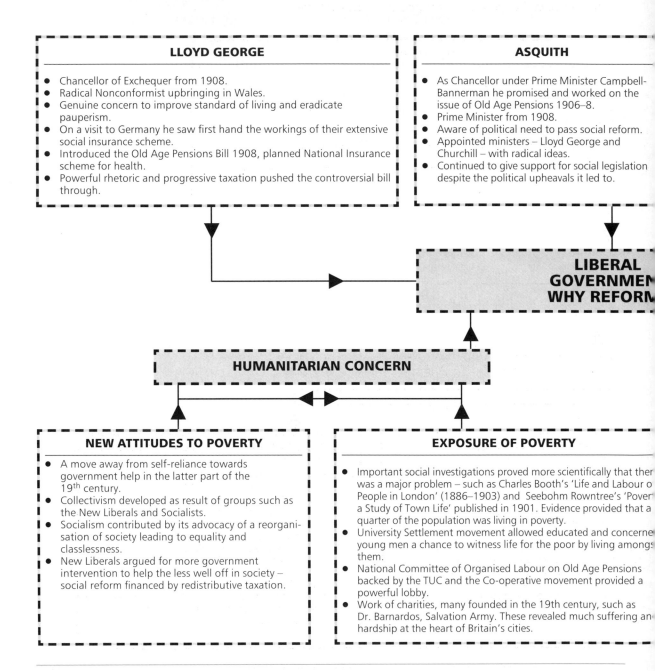

LLOYD GEORGE

- Chancellor of Exchequer from 1908.
- Radical Nonconformist upbringing in Wales.
- Genuine concern to improve standard of living and eradicate pauperism.
- On a visit to Germany he saw first hand the workings of their extensive social insurance scheme.
- Introduced the Old Age Pensions Bill 1908, planned National Insurance scheme for health.
- Powerful rhetoric and progressive taxation pushed the controversial bill through.

ASQUITH

- As Chancellor under Prime Minister Campbell-Bannerman he promised and worked on the issue of Old Age Pensions 1906–8.
- Prime Minister from 1908.
- Aware of political need to pass social reform.
- Appointed ministers – Lloyd George and Churchill – with radical ideas.
- Continued to give support for social legislation despite the political upheavals it led to.

LIBERAL GOVERNMEN[T] WHY REFORM[?]

HUMANITARIAN CONCERN

NEW ATTITUDES TO POVERTY

- A move away from self-reliance towards government help in the latter part of the 19th century.
- Collectivism developed as result of groups such as the New Liberals and Socialists.
- Socialism contributed by its advocacy of a reorganisation of society leading to equality and classlessness.
- New Liberals argued for more government intervention to help the less well off in society – social reform financed by redistributive taxation.

EXPOSURE OF POVERTY

- Important social investigations proved more scientifically that ther[e] was a major problem – such as Charles Booth's 'Life and Labour o[f] People in London' (1886–1903) and Seebohm Rowntree's 'Pover[ty] a Study of Town Life' published in 1901. Evidence provided that a quarter of the population was living in poverty.
- University Settlement movement allowed educated and concerne[d] young men a chance to witness life for the poor by living amongs[t] them.
- National Committee of Organised Labour on Old Age Pensions backed by the TUC and the Co-operative movement provided a powerful lobby.
- Work of charities, many founded in the 19th century, such as Dr. Barnardos, Salvation Army. These revealed much suffering an[d] hardship at the heart of Britain's cities.

TASKS

1 Divide the class into two groups. Using the information in the diagram each group should prepare a presentation on the importance of either HUMANITARIAN CONCERN or POLITICAL PRAGMATISM as motives for Liberal social reform. The issue could then be debated.

2 Prepare a speech or a private diary entry written by Asquith, Lloyd George and Churchill in which they explain their motives for supporting social reform.

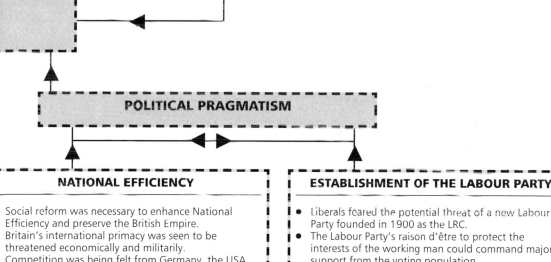

CHURCHILL

- Minister at the Board of Trade from 1908.
- Aristocratic upbringing yet a genuine concern for the poor shown in early speeches and articles.
- Advocated a National Minimum standard in his article 'The Untrodden Fields in Politics' in *The Nation* (1908).
- Particularly concerned with problem of unemployment.
- Influenced by progressive advisers at the Board of Trade, Llewellyn-Smith and Beveridge.
- Introduced his Labour Exchange Bill 1909.
- Planned scheme for Unemployment Insurance to be presented together with Health Insurance.

POLITICAL PRAGMATISM

NATIONAL EFFICIENCY

Social reform was necessary to enhance National Efficiency and preserve the British Empire. Britain's international primacy was seen to be threatened economically and militarily. Competition was being felt from Germany, the USA and Japan. The Boer War had demonstrated deficiencies in British defence, administration and foreign policy. Furthermore, the poor state of health amongst the working-class recruits prompted a call for action. Germany, a growing force economically and militarily, was underpinned by an exemplary social insurance scheme.

ESTABLISHMENT OF THE LABOUR PARTY

- Liberals feared the potential threat of a new Labour Party founded in 1900 as the LRC.
- The Labour Party's raison d'être to protect the interests of the working man could command majority support from the voting population.
- By 1906 the Labour Party had grown both in MPs in Parliament and national membership.
- Financially and in terms of pressure on government the Labour Party was supported by the trades unions.
- The Liberal's parliamentary majority was severely weakened in the elections of 1910 – not necessarily by the Labour Party but sufficiently to fire warning notes to politically aware ministers.

Examining the Evidence

Liberal social reform

Source A

The provision which is made for the sick and unemployed is grossly inadequate in this country, and yet the working-classes have done their best during 50 years to make provision without the aid of the State. But it is insufficient. The old man has to bear his own burden, while in the case of a young man, who is broken down and who has a wife and family to maintain, the suffering is increased and multiplied to that extent. These problems of the sick, of the infirm, of the men who cannot find means of earning a livelihood are problems with which it is the business of the State to deal; they are problems which the State has neglected too long.

Lloyd George – speech to Parliament, 15 June 1908.

Source B

March 24th. Last night Dr. Shirley Murphy, Medical Officer to the L.C.C., organised an expedition to the shelters and common lodging-houses of S.E. London, for the information of the members of the Physical Deterioration Committee. I and four of my colleagues left the Headquarters of the Medical Department about 9.30, and, under adequate escort, proceeded first to the Salvation Army shelter in Southwark. The picture presented on entering the large Hall had a peculiar touch of horror. In four rows, stretching away into an infinite perspective, appeared what on first sight one took for coffins, each with its occupant in some forced and unnatural attitude. Never did sleep visit suffering mortality in forms that stereotyped more cruelly the broken struggles of life. Not one lay in a position that suggested repose: or, rather, it seemed as if slumber had overtaken each of them in some phase of the convulsive agitation which is all they know of life. As we passed down the lines and flashed lanterns on the recumbent figures, not an aspect of human misery remained unrevealed; all the impotent terror, the haggard despair, the truculent brutality of the human animal in the lowest stages of its degradation were there depicted; thought could hardly realise the waste of material so collected, the wrecks of existence thus for a moment drifted into some kind of haven, the awful conglomerate of vice and poverty that lay at our feet.

Sir Almeric Fitzroy, *Memoirs*, vol. 1 (1925), p. 195.

Source C

The life of a labourer is marked by five alternating periods of want and comparative plenty. During early childhood, unless his father is a skilled worker, he probably will be in poverty: this will last until he, or some of his brothers or sisters begin to earn money and thus augment their father's wages sufficiently to raise the family above the poverty line. Then follows the period during which he is earning money and living under his parents' roof: for some portion of this period he will be earning more money than is required for lodging, food, and clothes. This is his chance to save money. If he has saved enough to pay for furnishing a cottage, this period of comparative prosperity may continue after marriage until he has two or three children, when poverty will again overtake him. This period of poverty will last perhaps for ten years, i.e. until the first child is fourteen years old and begins to earn wages; but if there are more than three children it may last longer. While the children are earning, and before they leave the home to marry, the man enjoys another period of prosperity – possibly, however, only to sink back again into poverty when his children have married and left him, and he himself is too old to work, for his income has never permitted his saving enough for him and his wife to live upon for more than a very short time...

Seebohm Rowntree, *Poverty: A Study in Town Life* (1901).

Source D
Churchill to Asquith, 29 December 1908.

I have been revolving many things during these few days of tranquillity & I feel impelled to state to you the conviction that has for a long time past been forming in my mind. There is a tremendous policy in Social Organisation. The need is urgent & the moment ripe. Germany with a harder climate and far less accumulated wealth has managed to establish tolerable basic conditions for her people. She is organised not only for war, but for peace. We are organised for nothing except party politics. The Minister who will apply to this country the successful experiences of Germany in social organisation may or may not be supported at the polls, but he will at least have left a memorial which time will not deface of his administration. Here are the steps as I see them.

1 Labour Exchanges & Unemployment Insurance:
2 National Infirmity Insurance etc:
3 Special Expansive State Industries–Afforestation–Roads:
4 Modernised Poor Law i.e. classification:
5 Railway Amalgamation with State control and guarantee:
6 Education compulsory till 17.

I believe there is not one of these things that cannot be carried & carried triumphantly & that they would not only benefit the state but fortify the party. But how much better to fail in such noble efforts, than to perish by slow paralysis or windy agitation.

I say – thrust a big slice of Bismarkianism over the whole underside of our industrial system & await the consequences whatever they may be with a good conscience…

R.S. Churchill, *Winston S. Churchill*, vol. II, companion, part 2 (1969), pp. 863–4.

Source E

Edwardian ownership and income distribution				
Class	Total number	Percentage of the population	Percentage of national wealth	Income per year (£)
(i)	300,000	1	55	1,000–1,500 (or more)
(ii)	600,000	2	25	400–1,000
(iii)	2,500,000	8	11	160–400
(iv)	16,500,000	56	8	60–160
(v)	11,000,000	33	1	Under 60

(i) rich; (ii) upper middle class; (iii) lower middle class;
(iv) skilled working class; (v) casual and agricultural labour

TABLE BASED ON FIGURES CONTAINED IN *RICHES AND POVERTY* BY L.G. CHIOZZA MONEY, LIBERAL MP AND ECONOMIST (1905).

Source F

Three causes, then, combined to convert Liberalism from the principle of State abstention. Three causes made possible the adoption of a programme such as that of the recent Liberal Government. It was seen that the State had become more efficient and its legislation more competent, and laws of regulation were found by experiment neither to lessen prosperity nor to weaken self-reliance in the manner foretold. It was realised that the conditions of society were in many respects so bad that to tolerate them longer was impossible, and that the *laissez faire* policy was not likely to bring the cure. And it was realised that extensions of law need not imply diminutions of freedom, but on the contrary would often enlarge freedom.

Such are the facts and arguments which brought about this change. In them we find the answer to those who use the doctrine of the old Liberalism to attack the policy of the new. The State is not incompetent for the work of social return. Self-reliance is a powerful force, but not powerful enough to cure unaided the diseases that afflict society. Liberty is of supreme importance, but State assistance, rightly directed, may extend the bounds of liberty.

From Herbert Samuel, *Liberalism* (1902).
Quoted in K.O. Morgan, *The Age of Lloyd George*, p. 132.

Source G

FORCED FELLOWSHIP.

Suspicious-looking Party. "ANY OBJECTION TO MY COMPANY, GUV'NOR? I'M AGOIN' YOUR WAY." (*aside*) "AND FURTHER."

'FORCED FELLOWSHIP', *PUNCH*, 1909.

Source H

Socialism wants to pull down wealth. Liberalism seeks to raise up poverty ...

Socialism assails the maximum pre-eminence of the individual – Liberalism seeks to build up the minimum standard of the masses.

Churchill speech, 1908.

1   What reasons are given in each of these primary sources for the social legislation of Asquith's Liberal government?
2   Using these sources and your own knowledge, how adequately do Sources A–H explain the motives for Liberal social reform?

Liberal problems

How satisfactorily did the Liberals deal with the domestic problems which beset them?

The Liberals' remarkable achievements in the field of social legislation contrasted starkly with the considerable problems which the government faced between 1909 and 1914. It was a period when social tensions led to significant conflicts which acted together exert pressure on a government which had to confront a worsening international situation. Optimistic historians will suggest that from these conflicts the Liberal Party gained positive achievements and sufficient success to suggest it was a party secure in the 20th-century political system. However, others have offered these problems as a full or at least partial explanation of the Liberal Party's demise. Why did the Liberals never form another government in the 20th century?

The four major problems were:

Problem 1   The 1909 Budget and the constitutional crisis

a crisis which questioned not only the financial implications of social reform but also the role of the House of Lords in the political system.

Problem 2   Industrial unrest

a strike wave which questioned the relations between employer, trade unionist and government.

Problem 3   Suffragette protest

a period of militancy by some women which questioned fundamentally their role in society and their rights within a democracy.

Problem 4   Irish crisis

a conflict involving Irish Nationalists, Irish Unionists, both major political parties and the monarch. It led Ireland to the brink of civil war by 1914 (see Chapter 5).

Problem 1

The 1909 Budget and the constitutional crisis

On 29 April 1909 Lloyd George, the Liberal Chancellor, introduced a budget to raise increased revenue for social reform and defence. The controversial nature of the Budget led to its rejection by the House of Lords, a move unprecedented in over 200 years. This in turn prompted a constitutional crisis over the powers of the unelected Upper House. After two years of wrangling which involved political parties, media, two monarchs and two general elections the matter was finally resolved by the passing of the Parliament Act of 1911.

Main proposals of the 1909 Budget:

1 Increase in income tax by 2d to 1s 2d in £ on unearned income over £700 and earned incomes above £2,000.
2 Supertax of 6d in £ on incomes over £5,000 payable on the income above £3,000.
3 20% tax on the unearned increased value of land when it changes ownership.
4 1d in £ tax on capital value of all land worth over £50 an acre.
5 3d levy on a gallon of petrol and introduction of licences for motor-cars.
6 Higher taxes on tobacco and spirits (a bottle of whisky rose from 3s 6d to 4s).
7 Rise on cost of liquor licences paid by publicans and brewers.
8 Additional death duties.

---

1 How was this Budget a break from traditional fiscal policy?
2 Can you suggest why the House of Lords rejected it?
3 What was the power of the House of Lords in 1909? *Why?*

Three contemporary views of the Budget

'Lloyd George Speech at Newcastle, 1909

The dukes have been making speeches recently. One especially expensive duke made a speech, and all the Tory Press said "Well, now, really, is that the sort of thing we are spending £250,000 a year upon?" Because a fully-equipped duke costs as much to keep up as two "Dreadnoughts," and they are just as great a terror, and they last longer. As long as they were contented to be mere idols on their pedestals, preserving that stately silence which became their rank and their intelligence, all went well, and the average British citizen rather looked up to them, and said to himself, "Well, if the worst comes to the worst for this old country, we have always got the dukes to fall back on".

But then came the Budget. The dukes stepped off their perch. They have been scolding like omnibus drivers purely because the Budget cart has knocked a little of the gilt off their old stage coach. Well, we cannot put them back again. That is the only property that has gone down badly in the market. All the rest has improved. The prospects of trade are better, and that is the result of a great agitation which describes the Budget as an attack on industry and on property.'

Quoted in H. du Parcq, *Life of David Lloyd George* (1913), vol. IV, 687–8, 696.

1 What was the significance of Lloyd George contrasting the cost of 'a fully equipped duke' to that of two Dreadnoughts?
2 What did Lloyd George mean by 'But then came the Budget. The dukes stepped off their perch'?
3 Explain why the Budget meant that 'All the rest has improved. The prospects of trade are better…'.
4 From the source, what do you consider Lloyd George's reasons were for introducing such a budget?
5 How does this speech help explain why the rejection of the Budget in 1909 led to a constitutional crisis?

'Balfour Speech at Manchester, November 1909

No man who looks at the world in which we live thinks, at all events in November 1909, that there are before the country other than these two alternatives – the Budget or fiscal reform … you may say truly of this Budget that it is a combination of bad finance and muddle-headed Socialism. It is bad finance because, for instance, it has raised the tobacco duties to a point perfectly preposterous, and it has destroyed the spirit duties as a fiscal engine. It has imposed a gigantic burden upon the taxpayer in order to carry out a universal land survey, which is not going to bring in anything in the immediate future, and, as I believe, very little in the remote future. Some of its provisions seem to be directly calculated – some of its purely financial provisions I mean, such as the great augmentation of the old death duties – seem to be directly calculated to produce unemployment in many parts of the country…

The object of a second Chamber is not, and never has been, to prevent the people, the mass of the community, the electorate, the constituencies determining what policy they should pursue; it exists for the purpose of seeing that on great issues the policy which is pursued is not the policy of a temporary majority elected for a different purpose, but represents the sovereign conviction of the people for the few years in which it carries their mandate … its mission and great function is to see that the Government of this country is a popular Government…'

The Times, 18 November 1909.

A 'fiscal engine' would be a measure – such as duty on wines and spirits or petrol – designed to produce revenue for the government. Raising the rate of duty, Balfour suggests, will reduce consumption, and therefore the amount of tax payable to the Exchequer.

1 Why does Balfour consider this Budget to be 'bad finance and muddle-headed Socialism'?
2 How and for what reasons do Lloyd George and Balfour's attitudes to the role of the House of Lords differ?

'Asquith's Speech at the Albert Hall, London, December 1909

Sickness, invalidity, unemployment – these are spectres which are always hovering on the horizon of possibility, I may almost say of certainty, to the industrious workman. We believe here also the time has come for the State to lend a helping hand. That is the secret, or at least it is one of the secrets, of the Budget of this year... it was a Budget which sought by taxes on the accumulations of the rich and the luxuries of the well-to-do, and by a moderate toll on monopoly values which the community itself has, either actively or passively, created, to provide the sinews of war for the initiation and the prosecution of what must be a long, a costly, social campaign. That was the Budget put forward on the authority of a united Cabinet – passed after months of by no means fruitless discussion by the House of Commons – rejected in a week and at a single blow, by the House of Lords. And that, gentlemen, is primarily why we are here to-night.

The immediate, the actively provoking cause of what is rightly called a constitutional crisis is the entirely new claim put forward by the House of Lords, not only to meddle with, but, in effect, to control and to mould our national finances ... This year, by one stroke, they have taken upon themselves to shatter the whole fabric of the year's taxation. This, I repeat, is a new and entirely unexpected danger to popular liberties. Two years ago it was as undreamt of as would have been, and as it is to-day, the revival by an arbitrary Minister of the veto of the Crown....'

The Times, 11 December 1909.

1 According to Asquith, what was the main reason for the 1909 Budget?
2 What is Asquith's opinion of the Lords' decision to reject the Budget?
3 How and to what extent is Asquith's attitude similar to that of Lloyd George and Balfour?

TALKING POINT

Would you have supported or opposed the reform of the Lords in 1909–11? Give your reasons.
Do you think there should be a second house as part of the legislature within a democracy? Why?
Who do you think should sit in a second chamber?

In order to overcome the power of veto which the Lords had exercised throughout the 19th century – and fatally over the Budget in 1909 – the government introduced the Parliament Bill in April 1910. This proposal to curtail the power of the Lords was passed only as a result of the support of George V (Edward VII having died in mid-crisis in May 1910) The monarch only acquiesced after two general elections returned a Liberal government, albeit with a much-reduced majority. Once the Budget and the Parliament Act had been passed, the National Insurance Bill could then complete its passage to law later in 1911.

Under the provisions of the Parliament Act of 1911:

1 The Lords were not allowed to reject or amend a finance bill. The Speaker of the Commons was to decide which were finance bills.
2 The Lords could amend and reject other bills until they had passed the Commons three times – then they would become law.
3 General elections were to be held every five years instead of every seven.

In another reform in the same year, members of Parliament were awarded salaries.

A sign of the times? Industrial unrest, 1910–13

Unrest amongst the industrial workforce in Britain presented the Liberal government with significant problems in the period 1910–13. The economy at the time displayed positive signs: the balance of payments enjoyed a healthy surplus; total industrial production was growing and reached a peak in 1913; and the economy had benefited generally from diversification into tertiary industries, and an increased supply of South African gold – maintaining its centrality in international trade. However, there were worrying signs – problems which translated into the loss of jobs or reduced hours for the working class in Britain. The old traditional industries such as textile, mining, iron and steel suffered on two accounts: firstly, there was lack of investment and innovation due to a tendency to rely on the technological success of the past; secondly, competition was developing fast from Germany, the USA and Japan. In 1913 iron and steel output stood at: Britain 5 million tons; the USA 13 million tons; Germany 13 million tons. Mining export figures were also worsening – in 1913 output in Britain stood at 287 million tons per annum and in the USA 500 million tons. The picture in the agricultural sector was similar – investment decreased, output stagnated and the contribution to the national income fell. By 1895 77% of the wheat consumed was imported and this figure increased in the years leading up to the First World War.

The extent of the problem	
Number of stoppages/strikes	
1906 – 478	1913 – 1459
Working days lost	
1907 – 2,150,000	1913 – 40,890,000

TALKING POINT

Why do industrial strikes tend to increase when unemployment is falling?

1910	
February–November	Miners' strike. 30,000 men involved. Rioting broke out.
July	Railway strike in Tyneside.
September–December	Boilermakers' strike in Tyneside.
1911	
June	Seamen and firemen on strike – began in Southampton. Lasted 10 days.
August	Dock strike – began in London. 20,000 men out for 11 days. Rioting broke out – two men killed in Liverpool. National rail strike – rioting broke out – two men shot dead by troops in South Wales.

December	Textile workers' strike. 126,000 weavers came out. Women sweatshop workers strike in Bermondsey. 15,000 involved.
1912 March–April	Miners' strike – called by the Miners' Confederation over the issue of the minimum wage. Two million men called out.
May	Dock strike in London – lasted a month.
1913	Transport workers in Dublin on strike. Small-scale disputes in the Midlands metal trades.

How successfully did Liberals tackle this problem?

SUCCESS	FAILURE
<ul><li>The government developed a policy of maintaining law and order in addition to arbitrating in disputes.</li><li>Permanent conciliation boards were established.</li><li>An industrial council was set up in 1911 as a national body to bring together employers' and trades unions' representatives.</li><li>Government-appointed mediators, led by G.R. Askwith, Chief Industrial Commissioner from 1911, negotiated settlements in many disputes.</li><li>Personal interventions by Lloyd George and Churchill were often skilful and conciliatory.</li><li>The government passed significant legislation to strengthen the legal status of trades unions: 1912 Miners' Minimum Wage Act – a compromise piece of legislation between miners' and employers demands. 1913 Trade Union Act – reversed the much criticised Osborne Judgement. It allowed trades unions to raise a political levy which workers had to contract out of rather than into.</li></ul>	<ul><li>An increased awareness amongst workers of the power of unionised labour continued to develop.</li><li>Membership of trades unions continued to increase – from $2\frac{1}{2}$ million in 1909 to 4 million in 1913.</li><li>Centralised organisation developed in this period 1910 – National Transport Workers' Federation. 1913 – National Union of Railwaymen. This would enable unions to utilise the strike tool more effectively across Britain.</li><li>The philosophy of Syndicalism spread amongst more radical unionists. Its aim was to gain control of industry for workers through the use of a 'general strike'. It was a development which could cause concern to any government.</li><li>Government's handling of the strikes in South Wales and Liverpool and the decision to call out the troops was much criticised.</li><li>Arguably compromise settlements over disputes made by government agencies postponed the problem but did not solve the deep-rooted causes of Industrial unrest.</li></ul>

Problem 3

The Suffragettes – how serious a challenge?

By 1900 there was increasing support amongst both men and women in Britain for the principle of female suffrage. A women's suffrage movement had developed, centred around the National Union of Women's Suffrage Societies (NUWSS) which had been founded in 1897 by Millicent Fawcett. This group were constitutionalist suffragists believing in non-violent methods, such as discussions, public meetings, processions and lobbying of MPs, to achieve their objectives. Their role was significant throughout the period up to the First World War, yet it has been overshadowed in historical accounts by the smaller, more radical group of Suffragettes led by Emmeline Pankhurst set up in 1903 as the Women's Social and Political Union (WSPU). The moderate NUWSS grew and by 1914 boasted 500,000 members, over 400 societies and an annual income of £45,000 – it always enjoyed a much more widespread base of support than the WSPU.

A CARTOON OF THE TIME ILLUSTRATES THE SUFFRAGETTES' CASE.

REASON: Women's legal and political status had changed

- Since 1875 divorce was possible through the courts.
- 1880s Women could keep their money and property after marriage.
- Women could be elected to School and Poor Law Boards.
- Women could vote at municipal county council and county borough elections.

REASON: Girls' education had improved

- Since 1870 both boys and girls were able to attend primary schools set up across the country
- Educational reform resulted in the setting up of academic schools for middle-class girls preparing them for a career rather than domestic duties.
- Cambridge and London universities opened to women.

WHY HAD SUPPORT FOR FEMALE SUFFRAGE INCREASED BY 1900?

REASON: Changes in the working life on women

- Increased number of women joining the professions
- Rapid increased of women in banking, Civil Service, Post Office and commerce.
- Decline in traditional women's work.

REASON: Attitudes to family life were slowly changing

- Traditional attitude of woman's place being in the home still prevailed
- But increased use of birth control meant more independence for women – families began to be smaller in size.

As the historian Martin Pugh argues, if the principle of female suffrage had largely been won by 1900 why were women not given the vote by this Liberal government?

- There had not been an extension of the male franchise since 1884 – the issue of female suffrage could not easily be separated from the question of males who still could not vote.
- Extension to the franchise was not only a matter of principle. Politicians were always concerned about the implications for their party of a cohort of new voters. Women's suffrage can be included in this consideration. Methods of determining voting patterns were far less sophisticated at the beginning of the 20th century and consequently an enlarged electorate was a 'leap in the dark' for any government in power.
- The prewar Liberal government was following a very time-consuming agenda. The legislative overload caused by social reform turned into a parliamentary log-jam for two years from 1909–11 during the constitutional crisis. There was very little time, as well as little genuine enthusiasm, to tackle such a political 'hot potato'.
- Anti Suffragist arguments still prevailed. It was still believed by many that separate spheres existed which determined the different roles in society for males and females – the latter being domestic, housebound and dutiful to the former, women it was thought were mentally and physically inferior – this inhibited their ability to exercise a democratic right. Finally and more subtly it was argued that women did not want the vote – the suffragists did not represent accurately the views of the majority.
- Arguably the Suffragettes' militancy harmed their own cause. Those men who may have supported female suffrage in the next parliamentary reform were dissuaded from this by the violent and much publicised actions of the WSPU.

TALKING POINT

Do militant tactics ever help a pressure group achieve its aims?

EXCELSIOR !

SUFFRAGIST. "IT'S NO GOOD TALKING TO ME ABOUT SISYPHUS: HE WAS ONLY A MAN!"

'EXCELSIOR!', *PUNCH*, 13 JULY 1910.

Examining the evidence

Did the Suffragettes hinder more than help their cause?

Source A
An entry from Austen Chamberlain's diary, 26 March 1909.

> Just back from the Anti-Suffrage meeting – no trace of lumbago left, whether as the result of aspirin or not I do not know. A very good meeting with a sprinkling of noisy suffragettes to emphasise their unfitness for political power. Why do some women suppose that inability to control themselves proves their right and fitness to control others?

Source B

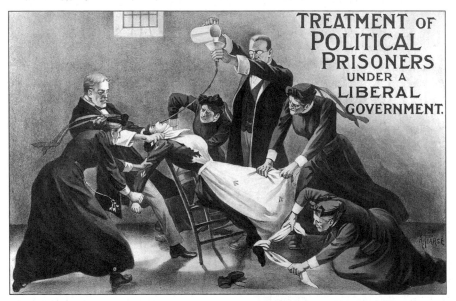

FORCED FEEDING MADE GOOD PROPAGANDA FOR THE SUFFRAGETTES' CAUSE.

Source C
Letter from Herbert Gladstone to a Suffragette, Mrs Ennis Richmond, 22 September 1909.

> All these militant tactics, at any rate in their later development, are not only lost labour, but now are most seriously putting obstacles in the way of a solution. I am afraid the outlook is thoroughly bad …
>
> Honestly, I believe the great majority of both political parties are willing and ready to co-operate for the solution of this question; But no one will lift a finger now because of these absurd tactics, which are intensely exasperating without being effective.

TASK

Identify the contemporary
views each of these
sources illustrate about
suffragette militancy.

Source D

This was the beginning of a campaign the like of which was never known in England, or for that matter in any other country …

What good did it do? We have often been asked that question. For one thing our heckling campaign made women's suffrage a matter of news – it had never been that before. Now the newspapers were full of us.

Emmeline Pankhurst, *My own story* (1914).

Source E

Just before one o'clock this morning smoke was seen issuing from the grandstand at Hurst Park Racecourse, Hampton Court, and in a few minutes the structure was almost completely enveloped in flames.

Subsequently it was reported that the stables, situated at some little distance from the stand, were also alight.

Incendiarism by Suffragettes, the Press Association states, is suspected.

The Daily News and Leader, 9 June 1913.

It was discovered yesterday that corrosive acid had been poured on some of the greens of the Rossington golf links, near Doncaster. No rain fell, so the damage was not so great as it otherwise might have been.

The Manchester Guardian, 3 June 1913.

Railway telegraph wires have been found cut between Magor and Llanwern, in Monmouthshire and near the spot was found Suffragist literature. The telephone wires at the Taff Vale Station, Cardiff were cut yesterday, the outrage being attributed to Suffragists.

The Times, 31 May 1913.

THE SHRIEKING SISTER.

The Sensible Woman. *"YOU HELP OUR CAUSE? WHY, YOU'RE ITS WORST ENEMY!"*

Source F

'THE SHRIEKING SISTER', *PUNCH*, 1906.

REVIEW

How strong was the Liberal Party by 1914? – A historical debate

The pre-First World War Liberal administration was the last ever formed by this party in the 20th century. After the remarkable electoral victory of 1906, the popularity of the Liberals steadily declined up to and during the War. In the 1920s they were replaced by the Labour Party as the main parliamentary opposition to the Conservatives. In 1924 the Liberals returned only 40 seats and in 1929 59. They had fallen to third-party status in what was essentially a two-party system.

TASKS

After careful reading of this chapter:
1 How successful was the Liberal government in handling the problems they faced in the period 1910–1914?
2 What evidence is there to suggest that the Liberal government were irreparably damaged by 1914?

The fact of Liberal demise has prompted historians to ask why this happened and when decline became irreversible. As with most historical problems, historical interpretation differs.

What the historians say

Source A

Despite all the shortcomings of the arrangement, the national understanding between Liberalism and Labour was a considerable advantage to both sides; its rupture would have been a considerable disaster on both sides…

Thus the first quarter of the twentieth century saw two sorts of change in British politics. The first sort centred upon the emergence of class politics in a stable form; the second sort upon the effective replacement of the Liberal Party by the Labour Party. But the first does not in any simple way explain the second. For one thing, the chronology is wrong. By 1910, the change to class politics was substantially complete. That from Liberalism to Labour had not really begun. It was not a light thing to overturn one party and make another to put in its place. At the beginning of the second decade of the twentieth century it looked as though both Labour and Liberalism would be subsumed in progressivism. It seemed that social democracy in England was bound up with the prospects of the Liberal Party; and in the generation after its downfall the social democratic record is not one of achievement.

From P.F. Clarke, *Lancashire and the New Liberalism* (1971), pp. 339, 406, 407.

Source B

It is easy to criticise the Labour Party of the 1910–14 period. Its M.P.s were divided in their views on a number of important issues – most notably National Insurance – and they could hardly impress the observer of the parliamentary scene. Mrs Webb's view, though obviously that of a dissatisfied socialist, was not really untypical.

> The Labour M.P.s seem to me to be drifting into futility… J. R. McDonald has ceased to be a socialist. The Trade Union M.P.s never were socialists, Snowden is embittered and Lansbury is wild. At present there is no co-operation among the Labour M.P.s themselves nor between them and the Trade Union leaders.

Yet the difference between the Labour Party and other political parties was that its principal strength lay in its extra-parliamentary organisation, and in this period that organisation was constantly strengthened. Between 1906 and 1914 the number of affiliated trade union members rose from 904,496 to 1,575,391, with a consequent improvement of party funds. If this very largely reflects the growth of trade unionism in the country, the actual expansion of political influence is exemplified by the increase in the number of affiliated trades councils and local Labour Parties, which rose from 73 in 1905/6 to 177 in 1914. The number of persons elected as Labour members of local government authorities advanced from 56 in the year 1907 to 184 in 1914… among the workers who were not Syndicalists nor even Socialists – and they were still by far the majority – a sort of undogmatic 'Labourism' was establishing itself, which consisted in little more than the opinion that the Labour Party, and not the Liberal, was the party for working men to belong to. This was of course particularly the case now with the miners, whose political solidarity was unmatched by other occupational groups.

From H. Pelling, 'Labour and the Downfall of Liberalism', published in *Popular Politics and Society in Late Victorian Britain* (1968), pp. 117–18.

1 How does Clarke's view of the future prospects of the Liberal and Labour Parties differ from that of Pelling?

2 Imagine you are writing an interpretation of a past event one day, one year, ten years and 50 years afterwards. What would affect your explanation? What factors can influence an historian's view of the past?

3 Suggest reasons why these two historians above differ in their views of the Liberal and Labour Parties before the war.

3 Why did Britain go to War in 1914? British Foreign Policy, 1890s–1914

PREVIEW

Decision to go to war

Sir Edward Grey's Speech to the House of Commons, 3 August 1914:

> '... If Belgium is compelled to submit to allow her neutrality to be violated, of course the situation is clear ... If her independence goes, the independence of Holland will follow. I ask the House, from the point of view of British interests, to consider what may be at stake ... I believe, when the country realises what is at stake, what the real issues are, the magnitude of the impending dangers in the west of Europe ... we shall be supported throughout, not only by the House of Commons, but by the determination, the resolution, the courage and the endurance of the whole country'.

SIR EDWARD GREY.

This speech – an hour long in total – by the Liberal Foreign Secretary, Grey, effectively took Britain into the First World War. This decision was justified on the basis of protecting Belgian neutrality and British interests.

Was it simply the protection of Belgium neutrality which sent so many British soldiers to fight in Europe? Or was this just the official line – the excuse to fight in order to prevent German domination or to protect Britain's wider interests? This latter position had been outlined by Sir Eyre Crow in his memo to Grey on 25 July 1914:

Should the war come, and England stand aside, one of two things must happen.

(a) Either Germany and Austria win, crush France and humiliate Russia... What then will be the position of a friendless England? Or
(b) France and Russia win. What would then be their attitude towards England? What about India and the Mediterranean?

UNCONQUERABLE.

THE KAISER. "SO, YOU SEE—YOU'VE LOST EVERYTHING."
THE KING OF THE BELGIANS. "NOT MY SOUL."

'UNCONQUERABLE' (PARTRIDGE, 1914, REPRODUCED FROM *PUNCH*).

From isolation to war, 1890s–1914:
A revolution in British foreign policy?

ROUTE TO WAR

Date	Event	Position of Britain
1890s	Triple Alliance (Germany, Austro-Hungary, Italy)	In Isolation
1901	Hay–Pauncefote Treaty	Emergence from Isolation
1902	Anglo-Japanese Alliance	
1904	Anglo-French Entente	
1905	Morocco Crisis – Renewal of Anglo-Japanese Alliance	Growing Involvement
1907	Anglo-Russian Convention	
1908	Bosnian Crisis	
1911	Agadir Crisis	
1912	First Balkan War	
1913	Second Balkan War	
1914	Assassination in Sarajevo	Commitment to War
1914	**Outbreak of the First World War**	

Why did Britain emerge from isolation, 1900–04?

'alliances, especially continental alliances, are not in accordance with our traditions'

Sir Edward Grey.

Despite this commonly held view, by the start of the 20th century Britain had begun to form agreements with other countries (see table on p. 50). She was beginning to feel the effects of economic competition, military and imperial rivalry and the shifting sands of international relations. These factors combined to breed an insecurity and loss of confidence in the primacy of the British Empire.

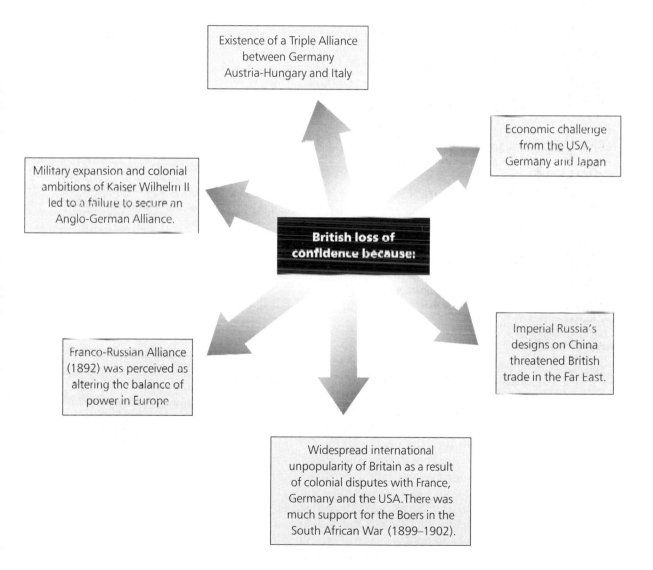

Existence of a Triple Alliance between Germany Austria-Hungary and Italy

Economic challenge from the USA, Germany and Japan

Military expansion and colonial ambitions of Kaiser Wilhelm II led to a failure to secure an Anglo-German Alliance.

British loss of confidence because:

Imperial Russia's designs on China threatened British trade in the Far East.

Franco-Russian Alliance (1892) was perceived as altering the balance of power in Europe

Widespread international unpopularity of Britain as a result of colonial disputes with France, Germany and the USA. There was much support for the Boers in the South African War (1899–1902).

Growing involvement, 1906–14: two areas of tension

Area 1: Morocco

France, along with Great Britain, considered the Mediterranean to be of special commercial and strategic importance. Her Empire already included Algeria and Tunisia, in addition to controlling much of the North African coast. Her dominant influence over Morocco was an accepted truth.

A crisis developed in 1905 when Kaiser Wilhelm II claimed that Germany would guarantee Moroccan Independence – this was an immediate challenge to the Anglo-French Entente (1904) which had agreed to French influence in Morocco. At a special conference held in Algeciras, Spain a year later France received strong support from Britain when it was agreed that Morocco should remain independent but France retain its position.

Again in 1911 Germany sent a gunboat to Agadir to protest at French troops arriving in Morocco. They feared a take-over of this North African state by France. A warning was issued to Germany and Morocco remained independent. Hostility towards Germany had increased but so had the strength of the Anglo-French Entente.

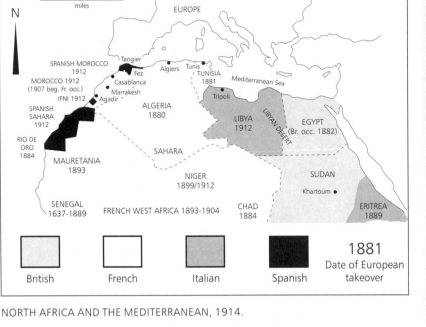

NORTH AFRICA AND THE MEDITERRANEAN, 1914.

> **TASK**
>
> Why did these trouble spots have such serious implications for each of the major European powers?

Area 2: Balkans

Austria's acquisition of Bosnia and Herzegovina in 1908 had encouraged the growth of Slav Nationalism, particularly in the ambitious state of Serbia. Russia increased her support for Balkan nationalists and encouraged the formation of the Balkan League – she feared Austrian expansion into the declining Turkish Empire at her expense. In the First Balkan War (1912), the Balkan League rose up against their rulers, the Turks. Flushed with some initial success and nationalist passions high, the Serbs turned against their ex-ally Bulgaria in the Second Balkan War (1913) and gained a significant amount of territory. All European governments were aware that the balance of power in Europe was tipping.

THE BALKANS, 1914

Britain's decision to go to war in 1914 – two alternative views?

Events in Europe had escalated following the assassination of Archduke Ferdinand of the Austro-Hungarian Empire on 28 July – Germany had declared war on Russia who refused to demobilise and also on Russia's ally, France. Yet the assassination – an event of such significance – had little effect in Britain beyond an expression of sympathy to the Austrians. The British government was embroiled in the Irish crisis and planning the end of the parliamentary session. Ironically, only five days earlier Lloyd George made a speech in the Commons suggesting economies in the Budget because relations with the Germans were improving. However, the threat of war was very real and had divided the Cabinet into the 'doves' and 'hawks', a further problem for Grey and Prime Minister Asquith. Grey admitted with resignation 'I used to hope that I was meant to keep the country out of war. But perhaps my real business was to bring her into it unitedly'.

Finally, Grey acquired Cabinet authorisation to utilise the British fleet for protection should the German fleet come up the Channel or through the North Sea threatening the French coast. On 3 August, as news broke of the German ultimatum to Belgium, the British Cabinet sanctioned mobilisation. Britain was at war against Germany and her allies.

Either

> **A** **A preventative war** – the Germans were a growing menace, distrusted and threatening the European balance of power. She was ruled by a militaristic and expansionist Kaiser. Her economy was strong and still growing. The Schlieffen Plan to knock out France quickly at the outbreak of war in order to concentrate on the other fronts suggested practical preparations for war to extend German control. Britain's principal aim was to prevent German hegemony.

Or

> **B** **A war of self-interest** – the British government considered it necessary to primarily defend British interests – her prosperity and Empire – from worldwide pressures. The defence of Belgian neutrality and the Anglo-German naval race were political tools to divert from the vulnerability of the Empire.

Examining the evidence

A preventative war

Source A

The German Empire had only been formed in 1871 – its creation due in part to the strong Prussian Army. Its geographical position within Europe is central and its economy industrialised and growing was facilitated by trade routes along the Rhine and railways across the Empire. During the late 19th century German nationalists had pressed for and gained colonial expansion . By the 1890s Germany's interests were strengthened by the Triple Alliance – a power bloc dominating Central Europe.

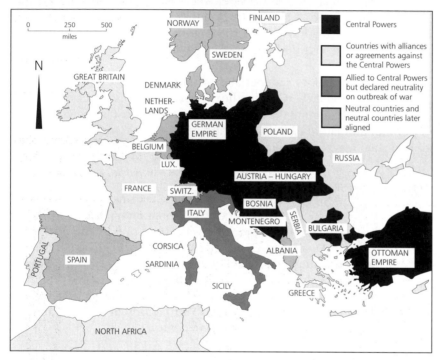

EUROPE AT THE OUTBREAK OF THE FIRST WORLD WAR.

Source B

　... If, merely by way of analogy and illustration, a comparison not intended to be either literally exact or disrespectful be permitted, the action of Germany towards this country since 1890 might be likened not inappropriately to that of a professional blackmailer, whose extortions are wrung from his victims by the threat of some vague and dreadful consequences in case of a refusal. To give way to the blackmailer's menaces enriches him, but it has long been proved by uniform experience that, although this may secure for the victim temporary peace, it is certain to lead to renewed molestation and higher demands after ever-shortening periods of amicable forbearance. The blackmailer's trade is generally ruined by the first resolute stand made against his exactions and the determination rather to face all risks of a possibly disagreeable situation than to continue in the path of endless concessions. But, failing such determination, it is more than probable that the relations between the two parties will grow steadily worse.

Either Germany is definitely aiming at a general political hegemony and maritime ascendancy, threatening the independence of her neighbours and ultimately the existence of England:-

Or Germany, free from any such clear-cut ambition, and thinking for the present merely of using her legitimate position and influence as one of the leading Powers in the council of nations, is seeking to promote her foreign commerce, spread the benefits of German culture, extend the scope of her national energies, and create fresh German interests all over the world wherever and whenever a peaceful opportunity offers …

Eyre Crow, Senior Clerk at the Foreign Office, memorandum on British relations with France and Germany, 1 January 1907 (PRO FO 371/257).

What do you think Crow is referring to by likening Germany to a professional blackmailer?

Source C

In 1900 Kaiser Wilhelm proclaimed: 'Just as my Grandfather re-organised his Army, I shall unswervingly complete the task of re-organising my navy so that it shall be in a position, internationally to win for the German Reich that place which we have yet to achieve…'

UNCLE EDWARD (TO WILLIAM): 'YOUR LITTLE MARINE MASTERPIECE IS TOO AMBITIOUS; KEEP IT AS A STUDY.'

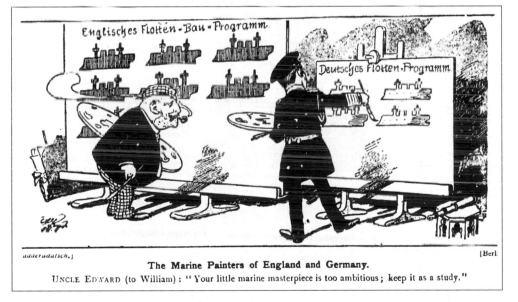

The Marine Painters of England and Germany.
UNCLE EDWARD (to William) : " Your little marine masterpiece is too ambitious ; keep it as a study."

Source D

With every rivet that von Tirpitz drove into his ships of war, he united British opinion … The hammers that clanged at Kiel and Wilhelmshaven were forging the coalition of nations by which Germany was to be resisted and overthrown.

W.S. Churchill, *The World Crisis*.

Source E

'And we aren't ready for her', Davies would say; 'we don't look her way. We have no naval base in the North Sea, and no North Sea Fleet. Our best battleships are too deep in draught for North Sea work. And, to crown all, we were asses enough to give her Heligoland, which commands her North Sea coast. And supposing she collars Holland; isn't there some talk of that?'

That would lead me to describe the swollen ambitions of the Pan-Germanic party, and its ceaseless intrigues to promote the absorption of Austria, Switzerland, and – a direct and flagrant menace to ourselves – of Holland.

'I don't blame them', said Davies, who, for all his patriotism, had not a particle of racial spleen in his composition. 'I don't blame them; their Rhine ceases to be German just when it begins to be most valuable. The mouth is Dutch, and would give them magnificent ports just opposite British shores. We can't talk about conquest and grabbing. We've collared a fine share of the world, and they've every right to be jealous. Let them hate us, and say so; it'll teach us to buck up; and that's what really matters.'

Erskine Childers, *The Riddle of the Sands*, (1903) pp. 119–21.

Source F

'THE MATCH-MAKER MALGRE ELLE', *PUNCH*, 1905.

THE MATCH-MAKER MALGRÉ ELLE.

M<small>LLE</small>. L<small>A</small> F<small>RANCE</small> (*aside*). "IF SHE'S GOING TO GLARE AT US LIKE THAT, IT ALMOST LOOKS AS IF WE MIGHT HAVE TO BE REGULARLY ENGAGED."

What message is the cartoonist trying to convey in Source E?

COPYRIGHT EXPIRES.

GERMAN TAR. "WE DON'T WANT TO FIGHT, BUT, BY JINGO, IF WE DO,
WE'VE GOT THE SHIPS, WE'VE GOT THE MEN, WE'VE GOT THE MONEY TOO."
JOHN BULL. "I SAY, THAT'S MY OLD SONG."
GERMAN TAR. "WELL, IT'S MINE NOW."

'COPYRIGHT EXPIRES', PUNCH, 24 MARCH 1909.

TASK

1 Discuss these sources individually – how reliable are they for a historian studying Anglo-German relations before 1914?

2 How do they support the view that Britain entered the First World War through a fear of Germany and an attempt to prevent further German expansion?

A war of self-interest

Source H

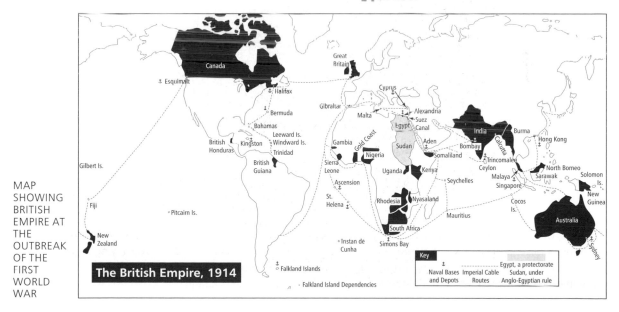

MAP SHOWING BRITISH EMPIRE AT THE OUTBREAK OF THE FIRST WORLD WAR

The British Empire, 1914

Source I

Now, for my own part, if the reader will excuse some egotism, I wish to make a personal explanation. I have never held a brief for Sir Edward Grey, and do not propose to do so now. It is generally difficult for an outsider to form a considered opinion on a complicated question of foreign affairs. It is doubly difficult if your own bias of character inclines you to differ from the persons who have most knowledge. But in me that bias of character has been strong, and has resulted in pretty definite political predilections. I have been unhappy about Morocco and Persia; profoundly unhappy about our strained relations with Germany; sympathetic in general towards the Radical and Socialist line on foreign policy; and always anxious to have the smallest Navy vote that a reasonable Government would permit.

I have never till this year seriously believed in the unalterably aggressive designs of Germany. I knew our own Jingoes, and recognised the existence of Germany Jingoes; but I believed that there, as here, the government was in the hands of the more wise and sober part of the nation. I have derided all scares, and loathed (as I still loathe) all scaremongers and breeders of hatred. I have believed (as I still believe) that many persons now in newspaper offices might be more profitably housed in lunatic asylums. And I also felt, with some impatience, that though, as an outsider, I could not tell exactly what the government ought to do, they surely could produce good relations between Great Britain and Germany if only they had the determination and the will.

G. Murray, *The Foreign Policy of Sir Edward Grey 1906–1915* (1915).

---

1 What is the author's attitude to Germany?
2 How does this differ the views expressed in Sources B, D and F?

Source J

From 1904 Sir John Fisher, First Sea Lord, reformed with great enthusiasm the organisation and armament of the Royal Navy. In 1906 the Dreadnought was launched – a ship which outclassed all existing battleships – this it was thought would maintain British supremacy. In 1909 the planned four Dreadnoughts per year was raised to eight – 18 were laid down between 1909 and 1911.

In addition R.B. (later Lord) Haldane, the Secretary of State for War, increased the Army's efficiency whilst reducing costs. Provision was made for the rapid mobilisation of twenty divisions, seven of which formed an Expeditionary Force. The Territorial Army was formed as well as the Officer Training Corps.

A DREADNOUGHT BATTLESHIP

Source K

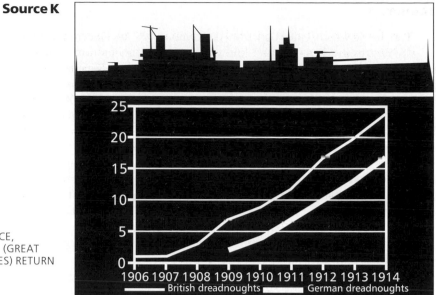

THE ANGLO-GERMAN NAVAL RACE, 1906–14 (DERIVED FROM FLEETS (GREAT BRITAIN AND FOREIGN COUNTRIES) RETURN 113, PP LIV, 1914).

Source L

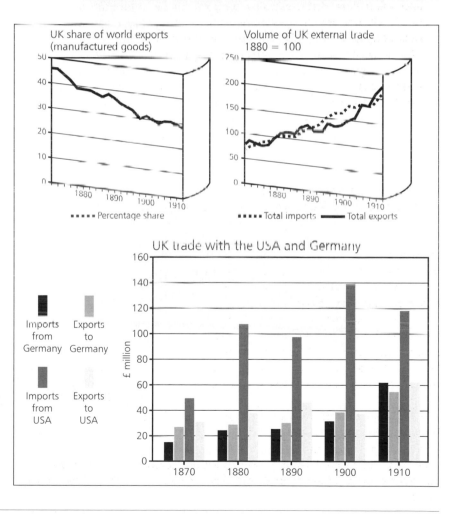

UK TRADE STATISTICS, 1870–1914.

Source M

The week which extended from December 10th to December 17th, 1899, was the blackest one known during our generation, and the most disastrous for British arms during the century. We had in the short space of seven days lost, beyond all extenuation or excuse, three separate actions. No single defeat was of vital importance in itself, but the cumulative effect, occurring as they did to each of the main British forces in South Africa, was very great. The total loss amounted to about 3,000 men and twelve guns, while the indirect effects in the way of loss of prestige to ourselves and increased confidence and more numerous recruits to our enemy were incalculable.

It is singular to glance at the extracts from the European press at that time and to observe the delight and foolish exaltation with which our reverses were received… Never again, I trust, on any pretext will a British guinea be spent or a British Soldier or sailor shed his blood for such allies. The political lesson of this war has been that we should make ourselves strong within the empire, and let all outside it, save only our kinsmen of America, go their own way and meet their own fate without let or hindrance from us… Such was the wave of feeling over the country that it was impossible to hold a peace meeting anywhere without a certainty of riot.'

Arthur Conan Doyle, *The Great Boer War: A Two Years' Record, 1899–1901* (1901), pp. 195–7.

TASK

1 How do these sources support the view that Britain entered the First World War to protect her own national interest?

2 Summarise the two alternative views – a war to prevent German expansion – a war to protect British interests.

3 Hold a class discussion on this debate and then decide which you consider the overriding motive of the British government.

REVIEW

Write the following structured essay:

'(a) How and (b) why did Britain's relationship with Germany change from harmony in 1890 to hostility in 1914?'

This is a challenging question but a fairly familiar type of essay at AS/A2 level. Always follow the

THINK!
READ!
PLAN!
WRITE!

routine when preparing an essay.

THINK!

- Think about the question carefully – it contains a lot of clues for a good essay.
- What is the range of information required? 1890–1914 Anglo-German relations.
- What are the instruction words?

HOW?		WHY?
Description/Narrative of change through the events	**What do they require?**	Explanation Causation Reasons

This immediately tells you there are two parts to your essay – be systematic, deal with **HOW?** then **WHY?**

What is central to this question? **Change** and **reasons for change**

READ!

- Read through your notes and textbook chapter on Anglo-German relations 1890–1914.
- What happened which had anything to do with this topic?
- Do you need to research further, to fill in any gaps in your knowledge?
- Begin to consider the question as you assimilate the information.
- You may need to read this through a few times.

PLAN!

QUESTION A

HOW did Britain's relationship with Germany change from

1890 HARMONY		evidence?
1895–1905?	–	evidence?
1906–1913?	–	evidence?
1914 HOSTILITY	–	evidence?

Fill in the gaps in this chart – this should give you a description of the change from 1890 to 1914.

First section of essay planned!

Now you have a PLAN – allocate a paragraph to

1. HOW?
2. REASONS – German-led.
3. REASONS – Britain-led.
4. REASONS – International.

QUESTION B

WHY did Britain's relationship with Germany change?

List all the reasons you can think of with supporting evidence

	REASON	EVIDENCE
1.		
2.		
3.		
4.		
etc.		

Sort these reasons into three categories

German-based Factors	Britain-based factors	International factors

Check before you write that you have:

a. covered the period 1890–1914.
b. discussed only issues connected with Anglo-German relations.
c. you have four paragraphs which each start by referring to the question.

WRITE!

- Write a brief introduction to your essay which defines the question and suggests your answer.
- Follow the plan you have, paragraphs 1–4 for each section – a and b.
- Make sure you select detailed but relevant facts to prove your opinions/arguments.
- Write clearly, using good spelling and grammar.
- Conclude by drawing together the strands of your essay into a final judgement on the changing relationship between Britain and Germany 1890–1914.

4 Britain During the First World War, 1914–1918

Preview

For this is now a war for peace. It aims straight at disarmament. It aims at a settlement that shall stop this sort of thing for ever. Every soldier who fights against Germany now is a crusader against war. This, the greatest of all wars, is not just another war – it is the last war!

H.G. Wells, 'The war that will end war!' (1914), pp. 10–11.

KITCHENER 'YOUR COUNTRY NEEDS YOU'.
POSTER DESIGNED BY ALFRED LEETE.

FIRST WORLD WAR GRAVES.

Task

Research some of your own family history. Were any members of your family killed whilst fighting in the First or Second World Wars?

Search for your family names on the Commonwealth War Graves Commission Website. The address is www.cwgc.org

First World War – Timeline

		MILITARY EVENTS	POLITICAL EVENTS
1914	August	GB declared war on Germany The British Expeditionary Force (BEF) sent to France Battle of Mons	Liberal government under Asquith Conservatives in opposition
	September November	Battle of the Marne – stalemate GB declared war on Turkey First battle of Ypres Coastal raids by German ships on British towns	
	December	Battle of the Falkland Islands First German air raid on GB (Dover)	
1915	January	Western Front trenches stretch from English Channel to Switzerland	
	March April	GB offensive at Neuve Chapelle Second battle of Ypres Allied landing at Gallipoli	Shell scandal
	May	Lusitania sunk by German U-boat Italy entered war on Allied side	Formation of Asquith Coalition with Conservative and Labour
	September–October December	Third battle of Artois British forces withdrew from Gallipoli	Conscription crisis
1916	February April May–1 June 1 July–18 November December	Massive French losses at Verdun German naval raids on Yarmouth and Lowestoft Battle of Jutland Battle of the Somme (British losses 400,000 overall) First aeroplane raid on London	Easter Rising in Dublin Asquith resigned Liberal Party splits Formation of Lloyd George's Coalition with Conservative and Labour
1917	April 6 April	German U-boat campaign reaches climax USA declared war on Germany Battle of Arras	
	June July–November	Battle of Messines Third Battle of Ypres (Passchendaele 400,000 troops lost for no gain over five miles)	
	August	British troops sent to Italy Battle of Cambrai Supreme Allied War Council set up	Henderson (Labour leader) forced to resign from War Cabinet
	November–December	British took Jerusalem	Bolshevik Revolution in Russia
1918	February–March	First US troops arrived in France Ludendorff offensive held by Allies	Representation of the People Act gives votes to all men over 21 and women over 30
	August	Battle of Amiens Second Battle of the Somme	
	September– October 29 September 30 October 3 November 11 November	Battle of the Argonne and Ypres German High Command demanded an end to war Surrender of Turkey Austria-Hungary surrendered Germany surrendered	
	December		General Election – victory for Lloyd George Coalition

Tasks

1 From the timeline, describe the changes to the Liberal, Conservative and Labour Parties during the First World War.

2 Can you suggest how military events, either defeats or victories for the Allies, contributed to political change in Britain.

Asquith's Liberal government at war, August 1914–May 1915

Britain's official declaration of war against Germany was accompanied by cheering crowds in London. A blind patriotism, totally unaware of the horrors to come, swept the country. The Privy Council, meeting at Buckingham Palace, had sanctioned a proclamation of war with Germany if the ultimatum had not been met by 11 p.m. on 14 August 1914. It was not met – Britain was at war.

Despite much Cabinet division during the foreign policy crisis of the past few months, Asquith's government took Britain into the war as a united front. Morley and Burns resigned but the rest of the Cabinet remained intact, being much strengthened by the eventual decision of Lloyd George, the Chancellor, to support the war effort. Lord Grey remained at the Foreign Office, Churchill at the Admiralty and Lord Kitchener was appointed to the War Office. The government were united largely because the perceived threat of an over-ambitious Germany; a respect and trust for Lord Grey, foreign secretary, particularly after his pivotal role at the 1913 London Conference over the Balkan question; and finally because the defence of Belgian neutrality was for many a convincing justification. Furthermore Asquith's Liberals enjoyed initial support from other parties. The Labour Party – itself torn over the issue of war and with Henderson as leader after the resignation of the pacifist Ramsay MacDonald – rallied to the cause together with the Irish MPs. The Conservative Party took on the role of patriotic opposition by agreeing to a party truce involving the temporary suspension of by-election contests and the restraint of Conservative leaders in the Commons. Although they became increasingly uncomfortable in this role, Balfour, Bonar Law, Austen Chamberlain and Walter Long all became involved in official work such as government advisory committees.

Immediate government action

Despite Churchill's labelling of this period – 'business as usual' – which was more a call to restrain any panic than a comment on the nature of the wartime activity – the government necessarily took some important decisions.

Finance

One of the urgent considerations on the declaration of war was that of finance. The Chancellor, Lloyd George, acted promptly and extended the Bank Holiday for another three days in order to restore the credit system and bolster confidence. The government proclaimed a moratorium, took over responsibility for bills on neutral and enemy countries in addition to the insurance of war risks on shipping. The bank rate was cut to 5 per cent and to prevent the feared hoarding of gold sovereigns the Treasury were empowered to issue £1 and 10s (the 'Bradbury') notes. Financial panic was avoided and Lloyd George's main task in the budget of November was to increase government income for the needs of war. He raised both income and super tax, placed duties on tea and beer, and raised an initial war loan. It was a start but Britain never covered the cost of war and her debt was substantial by 1918.

Trade

The Board of Trade took over the railways although they were still headed by the same boards of directors. Interestingly two thirds of British sugar came from Germany and Austria-Hungary. From 20 August the government took over the buying and selling of sugar and regulated its distribution.

The Defence of the Realm Act (D.O.R.A.)

The Defence of the Realm Act was passed in August 1914 which gave the state wider powers to deal with war generated issues such as the restriction of aliens. The press in Britain, under the control of Lord Beaverbrook, owner of the *Daily Express*, became increasingly censored.

Army recruitment

Army recruitment was initially very successful and the voluntary principle was maintained much to the relief of Liberals who feared the restriction of individual rights should conscription be introduced. Britains responded to the initial patriotic hype which swept the country – Kitchener's poster, shown on page 62, went down in history. However, the problem of insufficient troops became a reality as it was apparent that this war would not be over by Christmas.

Legislation finalised

Government, of course, had unfinished business to complete and during the Autumn Parliamentary session both Welsh Disestablishment and Irish Home Rule came onto the statute book accompanied by an Act suspending their operation until six months after the war.

The decision to form a coalition government

By April–May 1915 Asquith and his government were rapidly losing the confidence of early supporters. They had failed to marshal the country to war. The military setbacks in the early months were followed by the revelation that there was lack of ammunition for the soldiers. The shells scandal hit the press and as a realisation dawned that a quick victory was unlikely the Conservatives lost faith in the Liberal government they had been supporting. Lloyd George, who was on the Cabinet Shells Committee and had a clear understanding of the problem of recruits, munitions and labour in the factories, began to push for a coalition form of government.

Asquith himself came under attack – C.P. Scott, editor of the Liberal-supporting newspaper, the *Manchester Guardian*, had written to Lloyd George on 3 August 1914, 'No man who is responsible [for embarking on war] can lead us again'. Asquith's personality seemed increasingly unsuited for what was developing into a massive wartime commitment by Britain's government. As A.J.P. Taylor comments, 'Asquith the Prime Minister was a strong character, unshakable as a rock and like a rock incapable of movement'. The problems for Asquith's government were overcome by the formation of a coalition with the Conservatives who by May 1915 were ready to take some sort of decisive action.

TALKING POINT

Is it fair to describe Asquith's wartime Liberal government as a 'wait and see' administration?

The Asquith coalition,
May 1915–December 1916

Despite the doubts expressed about Asquith's leadership capabilities, as Prime Minister he formed a coalition Cabinet in 1915. Bonar Law, the Conservative leader, was given the Colonial Office despite his preference for the Treasury and Balfour replaced Churchill at the Admiralty. Lloyd George was replaced as Chancellor by the Liberal McKenna and himself put in charge of the Ministry of Munitions. Lloyd George was not convinced that this post had sufficient room for him to vent his energies – however, it was to prove a significant political step in his move to the top. Finally Lord Kitchener remained at the War Office. It was a group wrought with tension from the start – Lloyd George conflicted with McKenna, Bonar Law had always been cautious of Lloyd George and no one got on with Kitchener. The problem of this coalition grew over the next 18 months and by December 1916 the Conservatives had completely withdrawn their support for Asquith and conspired together with Lloyd George to form a new wartime coalition headed by Lloyd George himself and including both Conservatives and a representative of Labour, Henderson.

Why did Asquith's coalition fail?

There were four main reasons:
1   The problem of conscription
2   Mounting wartime expenditure
3   Lloyd George's role at Munitions
4   The inadequate leadership of Asquith

The military demands of the war led to problems which undermined both Asquith's position and the Liberal philosophy which his party was based upon.

The problem of conscription

From the start of the War recruitment was voluntary. By January 1915 two million men between the ages of 17 and 45 years had joined up. During that year a further 1.28 million was added. However, by mid-1915 it had become apparent that the voluntary principle was not providing sufficient men at the front. The stalemate of trench warfare and unsuccessful offensives, along with a noticeable fall in the numbers of voluntary recruits, led to a growing demand for conscription. By the end of 1915 all except a few hardcore Liberals had been persuaded that compulsory recruitment was the only answer. This was an agonising decision for Asquith but reluctantly in January 1916 the Military Service Act introduced conscription for unmarried men from 18 to 41 years. As a result the Liberal, Simon, resigned from the Cabinet. By June 1916 compulsory enlistment was extended to all males.

Mounting wartime expenditure

The problem of raising sufficient income for an increasingly expensive war fell in this government to McKenna, the Chancellor. His decision was to

TALKING POINT

Why did these policies of conscription and finance damage the Liberal Party so much?

raise direct taxation through income tax to avoid indirect taxes being paid on the price of goods. Furthermore he placed 33% duty on luxury goods such as motor cars, clocks and watches. The McKenna duties marked a Liberal Party abandonment of the policy of free trade. To quell concern that war would offer many industrialists and entrepreneurs an opportunity to 'get rich quick', the Chancellor taxed war profits by placing a 50% duty on wartime profits which were in excess of those before the War. However, increased taxes meant increased expenditure and Britain's National Debt rose from £625 million to £7,809 million over the course of the War. War loans at an interest rate of 5% increased, and prices rose so that by 1919 £1 bought only one third of the 1914 amount. Furthermore, wages in real terms fell during the War.

Lloyd George's role at the Ministry of Munitions

In contrast to Asquith's failing leadership, Lloyd George's work at the Ministry of Munitions was a significant achievement. He tackled the closely related problems of munitions production and labour with immense energy and dynamism, cutting through red tape and tradition in order to overcome a crisis which threatened the security of Britain. In these actions, he was helped by his Parliamentary Secretary, Dr C. Addison and a representative from the Board of Trade, Llewellyn-Smith. He drafted in businessmen such as Sir Eric Geddes to help and he without apology clashed endlessly with Kitchener at the War Office. By the end of the War this ministry employed 65,000 staff. The result of his initiatives and direct approach were significant.

- Machine gun production rose from 6,000 in 1915 to 33,000 by 1916
- The monthly output of shells increased from 20,000 in May 1915 to 1 million in July 1916.
- The Stokes Light Mortar – a gun turned down by the War Office was produced with financial help from an Indian maharajah.
- The tank was developed and first used at the Somme in the summer of 1916.
- Steel was requisitioned for government use.
- 20,000 small factories were built.

DELIVERING THE GOODS.

'DELIVERING THE GOODS', PICTURE EXTRACTED FROM *MODERN HISTORY REVIEW*, DECEMBER 1998.

He tackled the problem of labour with similar effectiveness, in order to increase production levels.

- Alcohol consumption was controlled by the Central Liquor Board who controlled sales and transport and cut drinking hours. Beer was diluted and the price increased. In February 1915 Lloyd George declared 'We are fighting Germany, Austria and Drink, and so far as I can see the greatest of these deadly foes is Drink!'
- Between 1915 and 1916 200 factories were brought under state control.
- The Rent Restriction Act helped migrant munition workers.
- The Treasury Agreement in July 1915 saw trades unions promising not to strike and to accept dilution of labour.
- Women workers were encouraged and in engineering 80,000 were recruited in the first year.
- Working conditions in factories were improved and factory canteens, for example, were set up.
- County Agricultural Committees were set up in 1916 to enforce production targets on farmers.

The inadequate leadership of Asquith

A.J.P. Taylor has described Asquith's wartime government as 'the last experiment in running a great war on the principles of laissez-faire'. It was not an entirely laissez-faire government, but Asquith failed to adjust fully to the demands of total war. The decision-making process remained leisurely and based upon committees. The Prime Minister's attitude was calm and opposed to putting the nation on a complete wartime footing. He did not see the need for total mobilisation and deeply disliked the compulsion of conscription. Military matters were left to the generals. Asquith was seen as being too complacent – aspects of his character which had been a strength in peacetime had become a liability in war. In 1916 Churchill complained to his brother 'Asquith reigns sodden, supine, supreme'. The horrors of the Somme disaster on 1 July 1916 – where 13 British divisions went over the top unsuccessfully with the loss of 19,000 lives – further drained confidence in the Prime Minister. The summer and autumn saw much complex political manoeuvring instigated by the Conservative leader, Bonar Law and Lloyd George, who had been moved into the War Office after Kitchener had drowned when HMS *Hampshire* sank off the Orkneys in June. Bonar Law became increasingly critical of Asquith and furthermore saw his own association with him as undermining his position with the Conservatives.

Asquith's downfall, December 1916

Bonar Law and Lloyd George together demanded a streamlined war council under the chairmanship of Lloyd George, with Asquith remaining as Prime Minister but not in the Cabinet. This attempt to speed up the decision-making process and most probably sideline Asquith was, unsurprisingly, rejected by the Prime Minister. At this point Lloyd George threatened resignation, prompting the Conservatives to ally with him more strongly and force the issue. Asquith's position had become untenable and on 5 December 1916 he resigned.

TASKS

1 Research further Asquith and Lloyd George during this period.

2 Compare their personalities and attitudes.

3 Why did a split between these two Liberal leaders emerge and why was it so damaging to their party?

Examining the Evidence

Lloyd George and the downfall of Asquith's Coalition, December 1916

Study Sources A–C below and then answer the questions which follow.

Source A

We have thrown away opportunity after opportunity, and I am convinced, after deep and anxious reflection, that it is my duty to leave the Government in order to inform people of the real condition of affairs and to give them an opportunity, before it is too late, to save their native land from a disaster which is inevitable if the present methods are persisted in. As all delay is fatal in war, I place my office without further parley at your disposal.

Private letter from Lloyd George to Asquith, 4 December 1916.

Source B

'D.' is David Lloyd George.

B. Law, Carson and D. have drawn up a memo on the reconstitution of the War Committee and its new powers, and a copy of it has been sent to the PM. If the PM refuses to accept it, then there will be a smash. The only weak spot will be Bonar Law, who cannot make up his mind to strike. If D. strikes alone, it will mean his forming an opposition, but if he and Bonar strike together it will mean the smashing up of the government. Asquith has great influence over Bonar and is using it to full advantage. D. says that the PM is absolutely devoid of all principles except one – that of retaining his position as Prime Minister. He will sacrifice everything except No. 10.

Diary of Frances Stevenson, Lloyd George's mistress, December 1916.

Source C

I have spent a fortnight in London and such a fortnight. The coalition government destroyed from within by an infamous conspiracy between Lloyd George, Bonar Law and the Northcliffe press.

I am overjoyed at finding the Liberal leaders, almost to a man, free from the coalition and its degrading compromises and I believe the mass of the Liberal Party in the House of Commons are not really sorry. LG has behaved scandalously – and the section of the Liberals he takes with him are certainly not men conspicuous for their character. The new administration is essentially Tory. Think of the Marconi business. LG is now surrounded by men who slandered him – having betrayed those who strained their consciences to protect him. Think of Limehouse and the Budget. I wonder how it will turn out. My prophecy is peace followed by Tariff Reform.

Diary of R.D. Holt, Liberal MP for Hexham, December 1916.

1 What devices of language and style does Lloyd George use in Source A to present himself in a favourable light?

2 To what extent does Source B offer support for the claim made in Source C that Lloyd George has engaged in a 'conspiracy' with Bonar Law?

3 Sources B and C are extracts from private diaries. In what ways do these extracts illustrate both the strengths and weaknesses of private diaries as source material for the historian studying the career of Lloyd George?

4 Using Sources A, B and C, and your own knowledge, account for the downfall of Asquith's coalition government in December 1916.

The Lloyd George Coalition, December 1916–July 1918

The downfall of Asquith and the formation of this coalition under Lloyd George signalled a fatal split in the Liberal Party which never healed. Lloyd George was supported not only by the Conservatives but also by about half of the Liberals, canvassed by Addison. The Labour Party also was represented in this government – retrospectively a significant turning point also for this political party. The long over-due general election (one should have been held at latest January 1915) was finally held in July 1918. In this so-called Coupon Election, Lloyd George was returned as Prime Minister in another coalition, for peace-time, with the Conservatives. By 1918, Lloyd George had been dubbed 'the man who won the war'.

THE NEW CONDUCTOR.
OPENING OF THE 1917 OVERTURE.

'THE NEW CONDUCTOR', *PUNCH*, DECEMBER 1916.

Why was Lloyd George labelled 'the man who won the war'?

There are four main features of his wartime leadership which help explain this accolade.

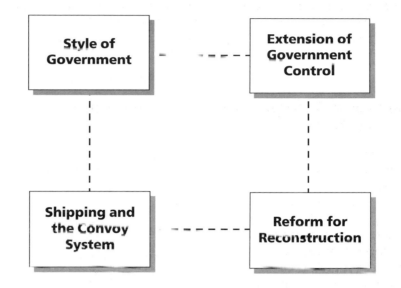

Style of government

In order to speed up the decision-making process and get policies acted upon more quickly, Lloyd George made changes which constituted a revolution in government. His critics argued that his premiership circumvented Parliament too readily and moved towards a dictatorial style of government undermining democracy.

New ministries

To address the areas of society particularly affected by war, new ministries were created: shipping, food, national service, pensions, labour, air and, later, reconstruction.

War Cabinet

Lloyd George formed a small War Cabinet of five members. He was the only Liberal on this, sitting alongside Bonar Law (leader of the Conservatives), Curzon, Milner and Henderson (leader of the Labour Party). Their tasks were to make the major decisions and appointments to head ministries. Meetings were held frequently – once a week to begin with – and usually involved more than just the five members. Advisers from industry, academia, the press and the armed forces were brought into consultation. Balfour, as Foreign Secretary, often joined in and in 1917 Smuts and Carson were added permanently.

Cabinet Secretariat

This was an initiative set up in 1916 which still exists as the Cabinet Office. It was to organise all Cabinet business and Sir Maurice Hankey was set to lead it with four assistant secretaries. For the first time minutes of Cabinet meetings were taken formally, agendas were sent out, decisions of the Cabinet were circulated to the appropriate departments and memoranda from departments to the War Cabinet were handled. This government innovation was successful in increasing efficiency.

'Garden Suburb'

Lloyd George also formed a private secretariat which at first met in the garden huts of No. 10 Downing Street – hence its name. This gave Lloyd George and others an opportunity to discuss issues with a broad range of independent advisers, by-passing bureaucrats, civil servants and MPs. The Prime Minister built up considerable knowledge from these meetings and by what Hankey called 'sucking the brains of the best men he could get on every subject. This was a continuous process. At breakfast, lunch, dinner and between meals, whenever the opportunity offered, Lloyd George was engaged in picking up knowledge from every sort and kind of person.'

Lloyd George had three private secretaries – Frances Stevenson (also his mistress), J.T. Davies and Sir William Sutherland. His informality with people encouraged a flow of ideas and he never allowed a set agenda to get in his way if he suddenly felt the need to discuss new ideas with his colleagues.

It was felt, however, that a great deal of power and government activity emanated from this group with Lloyd George at the helm, giving a distinctly presidential style to government during the war.

TALKING POINT

What is the difference between a prime minister and a president? Why was Lloyd George accused of adopting a presidential role and to what extent was this necessary?

Extension of government control

Lloyd George had seen early on in the war the need to put Britain on a total wartime footing to meet both military and domestic needs. His coalition saw a massive extension of government control – interventionism which had been so debated before the war in terms of social reform now became the norm – at least for wartime.

The coal industry was nationalised and all merchant shipping came under government control. The ministry of National Service oversaw conscription, jobs at home and women in the labour market. Food was a major problem to be tackled by the new Ministry of Food headed by Lord Devonport, a food chain magnate. Farmers were ordered under the Corn Production Act to cultivate extra land and control of prices was introduced. Lord Devonport although from a relevant background was less effective than expected. He experimented with meatless days and voluntary rationing but was replaced in June 1917 by Rhondda who immediately provided state subsidies for basics such as bread and potatoes. By early 1918 in response to the mounting bread queues, compulsory food rationing was introduced which changed the diet but maintained the nutrition levels.

Government by this time had taken control of the press and propaganda use under Lord Beaverbrook.

To ensure sufficient manpower in the factories, Geddes at the Ministry for National Service set an absolute limit on army recruits for the spring

1918 offensive. It was a risk which Lloyd George supported him on. The factories in this way were able to keep producing.

Shipping and the convoy system

Shipping and maintaining open supply routes to Britain became a serious concern when the Germans unleashed a policy of unrestricted submarine warfare in an attempt to starve its enemy out of the conflict. This reached a peak in April 1917 when 430 British ships were lost and only six weeks of corn supply was left.

Lloyd George insisted upon adopting the idea of a 'convoy system' despite arguments from the Admiralty. A large number of merchant ships were to sail together protected by warships. This plan had great success and reduced losses at sea noticeably. The German gamble had failed.

In military terms, however, Lloyd George was restrained both by pressure from the Conservatives and the Army Commanders, from making decisions. He failed to extend control over the Army and even his appointment of Lord Derby to the War Office was frustrated when the latter clearly became a tool of the generals. Disasters such as Passchendaele with its 250,000 casualties were not prevented. The only success in this arena came when Lloyd George having continually criticised such men as Haig and Robertson eventually had Marshal Foch appointed as Supreme Allied Commander.

Open confrontation between the Prime Minister and the Army broke out in May 1918 when General Maurice from the War Office accused Lloyd George in the House of Commons of lying about the numbers of men sent to the front on the Spring offensive. The Maurice debate voting was significant as it witnessed Asquith's Liberals split from Coalitionist Liberals in the lobby.

Reform for reconstruction

Domestic reforms were introduced under the Minister of Reconstruction, Dr Addison, from late 1917 to 1918. Two key pieces of legislation were:

---

1 *1918 Fisher's Education Act*
H.A.L. Fisher, the historian, was commissioned to look into education provision and as a result of the Act the school leaving age was raised to 14 years and more secondary education was to be provided.

---

2 *1918 Representation of the People Act*
There had not been an extension of the franchise since 1884. War gave much impetus to the campaign for all male and female enfranchisement (see later in the chapter). Lloyd George skilfully gained Conservative support for this act by promising that plural voting would be kept. As a result of this act, the electorate was tripled – all men over 21 and women over 30 were now included. The electorate now stood at over 21 million. The next General Election of 1918 was to be an interesting event given the new unknown female electorate, the extended male suffrage and a realignment of party politics.

TASK

Read through the pages concerning the wartime ministries carefully.

1 Identify the main political changes that occurred between 1914 and 1918.

2 Suggest reasons why these changes came about.

3 How successful was Lloyd George as a wartime leader?

Focus

4.1 David Lloyd George – some biographical notes

LLOYD GEORGE BY S. CONSTANTINE
(UKC CARTOON CENTRE)

A Welsh Upbringing — 1863–1890

1863 Born in Manchester.

1864 Moved to Llanystumdwy to live with uncle Richard Lloyd. Welsh radicalism was often discussed in his uncle's shoemaking shop.
Brought up in zealous Nonconformist home – his uncle was an unpaid minister, a strong character and powerful preacher.

1884 Passed law examinations – began career as a solicitor. Acted on behalf of Welsh working people against privilege.

Late 1880s Became an enthusiastic Liberal activist. Campaigned for Welsh Disestablishment.

1886–7 Became secretary of Caernarvon Anti-tithe League

1888 Married Margaret Owen

1890 Elected MP for Caernarvon in by-election – age 27 years.

New Liberal Reformer — 1906–1914

1906 Liberals win the General Election.

1906–8 Sees through Merchant Shipping Act, Patents Act, Companies Act.
Education Bill blocked by the Lords.
Set up Port of London Authority.

1908 Became Chancellor of the Exchequer. Old Age Pensions introduced.

1909 People's Budget to raise revenue for social reform. Constitutional crisis where Lloyd George passionately argues for reform of the House of Lords. Successful by 1911.

1911 National Insurance Act – a challenge to the new Labour Party.

1912 Welsh Disestablishment Bill.

1912–13 Supports votes for women.

1913 Frances Stevenson becomes his mistress.

1914 Eventual support for war against Germany.

Liberal Backbencher — 1890–1905

1891 Attacked Conservative Education Bill for providing support to Church of England schools.

1895 Agitated for Welsh Disestablishment.

1895 Conservatives won General Election. Lloyd George in opposition.
Attacks on Conservative Land and Education bills.

1898 Forms Welsh National Liberal Council. Member of Parliamentary Committee on Aged Deserving Poor.

1899 Opposed Boer War.

1902–3 Campaign against Education Act and Tariff Reform

1905 Appointed President of Board of Trade in new Liberal government.

'The man who won the war' 1914–1918

1915 Treasury Agreement with trades unions. Minister of Munitions in Asquith's wartime government.

1916 July – became Secretary of State for War.
Loss of confidence in Asquith.
December – Forms coalition government with Conservatives and Labour.

1918 Food rationing – Education Act – Franchise Act.

December – General Election – coalition continues.

Postwar prime minister 1918–1922

Forms a government with Conservatives.
Asquith leads separate Liberal Party.
Paris Peace Conference.

1920

1921 Unemployment Insurance Act.

Economic depression.
Public expenditure cuts.
Irish Treaty.

1922 The sale of honours by the Prime Minister's representatives angered the Conservatives.
The Chanak Crisis – British support of the Greeks against the Turks raised fears of British overcommitment.
October – Carlton Club Meeting – Conservatives withdraw their support.
November – General Election – Conservative government formed.

Out of power 1922–1945

1923 Formally returned to the Liberal Party.

1926 Succeeded as leader.

1927–9 Revival of Liberalism via Liberal Summer School and 500-page Liberal Industrial Enquiry

1929 General Election – Liberal election slogan 'We can conquer unemployment'.
Increased their percentage of the vote, but only returned 59 seats.

1930s National Governments – Lloyd George was not invited to join.

1936 Met Hitler. Lloyd George praised his economic policies.

1941 Death of wife.

1943 Married his long-time mistress, Frances Stevenson.

1945 Made an Earl. Died.

TASKS

A political profile of Lloyd George. From the biographical notes on pp. 74–5.

1 1864–90
Explain how Lloyd George's years in Wales may have shaped his character
and political beliefs

2 1890–1905
Describe what types of issues Lloyd George was campaigning for as a backbencher.
Why might this period have benefited his political career?

3 1906–14
What do Lloyd George's achievements in this period illustrate about

a his character?
b his political pragmatism?
c his social concern?

4 1914–18
With reference to the biographical notes and pages 70–3, how far do you accept that Lloyd George was 'the man who won the war'?

5 1918–22
What difficulties did Lloyd George face in this period?

6 1922–45
Lloyd George died, age 82 years, in 1945. Write a brief obituary identifying his most significant achievements.

A shift in British party politics

The impact of the First World War on the Liberal and Labour parties, 1914–18

The First World War split the Liberal Party as we have outlined earlier in this chapter. For the Labour Party the impact of war was a very different experience. In 1914 there had been division between those in favour of war and the pacifists. Ramsay MacDonald had resigned immediately, declaring the incompatibility of war and socialism. However, the onslaught of four years of total war did strange things to the British political system and ultimately the Labour Party benefited greatly. By 1918 the Liberals were irrevocably divided, whereas the Labour Party was united and strengthened.

TASK

From the diagram, explain why the War benefited the Labour Party and disadvantaged the Liberals.

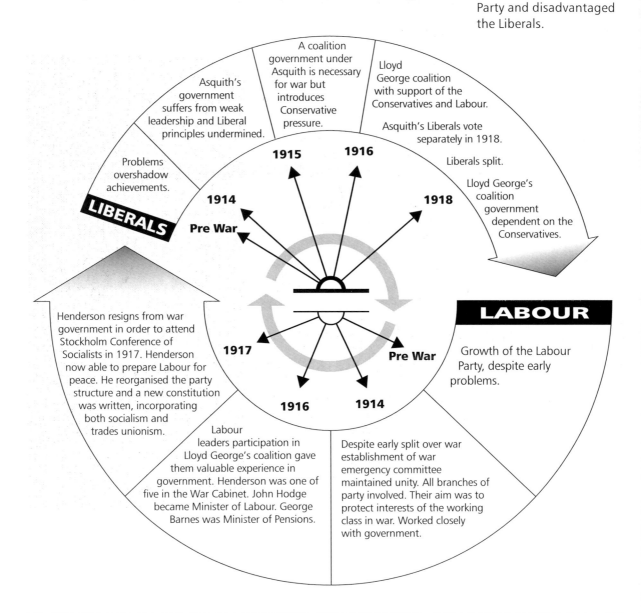

TALKING POINT

What was the importance of Clause IV to the Labour Party?
Does it still exist in the Party's constitution?

To secure for the producers by hand or brain the full fruits of their industry and the most equitable distribution thereof that may be possible upon the basis of the common ownership of the means of production, and the best obtainable system of popular administration and control of each industry or service.

Clause IV of the Labour Party Constitution adopted in 1918.

Women at War: Did the First World War change women's role in society?

Two views

Traditional interpretation	Traditional interpretation challenged
YES	**NO**
• Women's role in society was changed dramatically by the war. • This war, with its need for a supportive home front, emphasised the domestic sphere. The importance of a woman's place in the home was recognised. • By 1918 women over 30 could vote for the first time and were regarded as capable of holding down jobs in more male-dominated workplaces. • These political and social changes were also influenced due to women's significant contribution to the war effort: munitions, shipyards, aeroplane construction, drivers, nurses and a vast amount of war charity work. • The government acknowledged this contribution and rewarded women with both male approval and the vote.	• The war alone cannot explain the change of women's role in society – many developments had already occurred – legally, politically, in education and the workplace. • Women gained the vote in 1918 as an appendix to the main legislation which enfranchised all 21-year-old males. • The vote was given only to women over 30. • Many women on the wartime production line were too young to gain the vote and found that they lost their jobs in favour of demobilised soldiers. • Social attitudes which recognised a woman's place to be in the home were still very prevalent after the First World War.

Examining the Evidence

The traditional interpretation of women's role during the First World War

Source A

'DON'T WASTE BREAD!'
MINISTRY OF FOOD POSTER.

Source B

Sailors' and Soldiers' Recreation Rooms

In September, 1915, Miss Edith Carr and Miss Kathleen Taylor, as a personal enterprise of their own, opened rooms at 42, High Street, Croydon, for the benefit of soldiers billeted in the town and the men in the six large military hospitals. The rooms were from the first well patronised and the numbers steadily increased until towards the end fully 5,000 men came in each week in winter.

From ten in the morning till half-past nine at night, light refreshments were served at a very cheap rate (2 cups of tea, coffee or cocoa for 1d., cake 1d., eggs at cost price, and so on). Large quantities of stewed fruit and custard also were consumed. Although everything was so cheap the work was practically self-supporting after the initial expense. No cards were allowed, but billiards, chess and draughts were all free, and there was always plenty of music. The men always seemed thoroughly happy, and often said what a great boon the place was to them. They came not only for food, but stayed on to rest and read and write – notepaper being provided free.

From Croydon and the Great War: The Official History of the War Work of the Boroughs and its Citizens from 1914–1919 (1920).

Source C

BRITISH WORLD WAR 1
PROPAGANDA POSTER.

Source D

AN OMNIBUS
CONDUCTRESS IN
THE FIRST WORLD WAR.

WOMEN WAR
WORKERS IN
MANCHESTER
MUNITIONS FACTORY
1918.

Source F

A NURSE SERVING
TEA TO WOUNDED
BRITISH SOLDIERS.

Source G
Evelyn Goodyear – in a munitions factory.

During the First World War, at the age of 19, Evelyn answered an advertisement in the newspaper, to work at a Munitions Factory at Quedgley, near Gloucester. She shared a room and bed with another friend from Salisbury. 'When she was at work, I was a'bed and when I was at work, she was a'bed. In the sitting room we only had deck chairs like they have at the seaside, to sit in. In Winter, the cordite in the factory froze and as it thawed the gas it gave off made us faint. I was only there for six months; I had some salmon which I kept in a tin and nearly poisoned myself and that's why I come back home again.'

Once recovered, Evelyn went to work at Lipton's in the grocery trade and then went on to Bon Marche, the drapers in Fisherton Street, Salisbury. 'I remember stock taking time, when we had to unroll each bale of cloth to measure it and put in a ticket before rolling it up again.'

Bill Goodyear, Evelyn's fiance, was injured badly in the First World War. He was blown up and buried alive in the trenches of Northern France. 'His parents had a telegram to say he'd been killed and then a few weeks later had another telegram to say he was in hospital in Norwich.' Bill recovered and he and Evelyn were married at St. Paul's Church in Salisbury in 1924.

Source H

A GROUP OF NATIONAL MOTOR VOLUNTEERS LINE UP FOR INSPECTION IN FRONT OF THEIR VEHICLES.

Source I
Croydon Women Patrols.

During the War there were about forty Croydon women-patrols under the Patrol Leader, Miss Brodie, M.B.E. They patrolled in couples for two hours in the evening. Their uniform was a heavy blue coat and skirt, black hat with the badge N.U.W.W., and a distinctive armlet bearing their registered number under the Metropolitan Police. They carried a police whistle and lantern. Their work was purely voluntary and unpaid with the following few exceptions:-

From January 1917 to September 1918, some of the women-patrols worked for three hours at night instead of two, and were paid at the police rate. In June, 1918, four of them were specially trained to do whole time police work of seven hours a day, and were paid by the Metropolitan Police. They continued this work till the Metropolitan Women-Police were started early in 1919.

From Croydon and the Great War: The Official History of the War Work of the Borough and its Citizens from 1914–1919 (1920).

Source J

Undoubtedly the large part taken by women during the War in all branches of social service had proved a tremendous argument for their enfranchisement. Yet the memory of the old militancy, and the certainty of its recurrence if the claims of women were set aside, was a much stronger factor in overcoming the reluctance of those who would again have postponed the settlement. The shock to the foundations of existing social institutions already reverberating from Russia across Europe, made many old opponents desire to enlist the new enthusiasm of women voters to stabilize the Parliamentary machine. Above all, the changed attitude of the large public of all classes towards the position of women, which had grown up in the great militant struggle, made impossible a further postponement of our enfranchisement.

Sylvia Pankhurst, The Suffragette Movement (1931).

Source K

The moment you begin a general enfranchisement on these lines of State Service you are brought face to face with another most formidable proposition. What are you going to do with the women? I have received a great many representations from those who are authorised to speak for them, and I am bound to say that they have presented to me not only a reasonable, but I think, from their point of view, an unanswerable case. They say … If we are going to bring in a new class of electors, on whatever ground of State Service, they point out – and we cannot possibly deny their claim – that during this War the women of this country have rendered as effective service in the prosecution of the War as any other class of the community … what is more – and this is a point which makes a special appeal to me – they say when the War comes to an end …

when the process of industrial reconstruction has to be set on foot, have not the women a special claim to be heard on the many questions which will arise directly affecting their interest, and possibly meaning for them large displacement of labour? I say quite frankly that I cannot deny that claim.

Asquith, speaking in the House of Commons, August 1916.

1 From Sources A–I, list the ways in which women contributed to the war effort.
2 According to Sylvia Pankhurst in Source J, how important was the war in gaining women the vote? What other factors contributed in her opinion?
3 On what grounds is Asquith in Source K persuaded that female enfranchisement should be granted?
4 What are the strengths and weaknesses of these two sources when studying female enfranchisement?
5 In what ways do Sources A and K support the traditional view?

Traditional interpretation challenged: What the historians say

The following extracts challenge the traditional view that the war alone changed women's role in society. In Source A, Martin Pugh introduces the issues to be considered. Then, in a series of extracts (Sources B–E), Brian Harrison develops the theme.

Source A

One popular examination for the women's eventual triumph is that the deadlock was somehow resolved by the First World War. In particular it has been claimed that women's valuable work for the war effort radically changed male ideas about their role in society. This, however, seems simplistic and even erroneous. It obviously overlooks the pre-1914 changes of attitude. It is also inconsistent with the deliberate wartime policy of ejecting women from their wartime employment and, indeed, the severe backlash against their work; during the 1920s the idea that a woman's place was in the home was as strong as it had ever been. Finally one must take account of the process by which enfranchisement actually occurred during 1914–1918. Not surprisingly votes for women simply vanished from the agenda for some time. The issue returned only because the politicians grew anxious to enfranchise more men, many of whom had lost their qualification as a result of moving home for war service. It was this that led to the scheme of parliamentary reform in 1917 in which women were included.

Yet if the war had no fundamental effect, it did make a beneficial short-term impact in substituting a sympathetic Prime Minister, Lloyd George, for an anti-suffragist, Asquith, and also in creating a coalition government which wanted to find a comprehensive compromise on reform questions. Within the compromise each party got at least something that it wanted. Labour and the Liberals felt reassured by the generous grant of the vote to over eight million women – too large a number to give advantage to the Conservatives. Equally significantly, the politicians safeguarded themselves by imposing careful terms upon the women voters; they now included married as well as single women, and limited the vote to those aged 30 years or more.

Extract from Martin Pugh, 'Votes for Women', *Modern History Review*, September 1990.

Source B

Ever since 1918 people have said that it was women's war work that gave them the vote in that year. The women, it is argued, converted the public by carrying out the jobs the servicemen had left behind, manufacturing ammunition and nursing the wounded. But explanations of past events are sometimes accepted because they are convenient rather than true. This shorthand explanation is suspect if only because it flatters male conceit: it portrays women as gratefully receiving a vote bestowed as a reward for good behaviour. Besides, it leaves behind too many puzzles. First the anti-suffragist opponents of votes for women (the 'Antis', as the feminists called them) were at least as keen as the suffragists were to do war work. Indeed the 'Antis' were probably right to think that the war's opponents were more likely than its supporters to favour votes for women. There is something odd about a 'reward' bestowed so readily upon those who don't want it as to those who do. Still odder is the fact that in 1918 the vote was denied to the women under 30 who had been so prominent in the munitions factories, but granted to the women over 30 whose family responsibilities had largely kept them at home. Nor is it obvious that willingness to serve the State is the only or even the best qualification for claiming a share in governing the country

Source C

Still the war did help feminism in some ways. It soon became obvious that modern warfare had become so technical in nature that physical strength was less important for success than qualities where women were not necessarily inferior: skill, organisation and courage. The gun and the bomb have greatly reduced the importance of physical strength in warfare, and so have been great equalisers between the sexes, completely undermining the Antis' 'physical force' argument. Besides, modern warfare involves mobilising entire societies against one another thus creating a 'home front' at least as important as the fighting front. So widely was this recognised by July 1915 that the leading female Anti, the novelist, Mrs Humphrey Ward, privately told Lord Cromer, the prominent male Anti, that 'I sometimes wonder in my secret thoughts whether we are not already beaten!'

If the war was to be won, national unity was essential, and this indirectly helped votes for women. The challenge from Kaiserism was so great, British casualties were so huge, that the resources of government and the economy were strained to the utmost; any distinction from squabbles over the vote between men and women could not be risked. In 1915 the idea of extending the vote to all servicemen came up for discussion. The suffragists at once pointed out that women too were engaged in the war effort, and politicians were quick to sympathise. So votes for women re-emerged as a serious political issue in 1916 not primarily because of feminist pressure, but more on the back of a campaign to enfranchise more men.

Source D

The overriding need to defeat Germany gave both Antis and suffragettes an excuse for climbing down from the impossible positions they had taken up before the war, and accept a compromise settlement. The Antis' branch activity could quietly run down and prominent Antis like Asquith (Liberal prime minister from 1908 to 1916) could gradually adjust to the new climate of opinion. In May 1916 he privately assured Mrs Fawcett, leader of the non-militant suffragists, that he appreciated 'the magnificent contribution' women had made in the war effort, and that if the government did move towards franchise reform the question would be settled 'without any prejudgement from the controversies of the past'. At the same time the war enabled Christabel Pankhurst and her mother to climb down from a pre-war militant agitation that was merely escalating violence and making it difficult for politicians support votes for women. 'What paved the way for woman suffrage', Martin Pugh has written, 'was the virtual disappearance of the women's campaign'. Explaining in Parliament his decision henceforth to support votes for women, Asquith in March 1917 justified his change of view partly on the ground that 'we have had no recurrence of that detestable campaign which disfigured the annals of political agitation in this country, and no one can now contend that we are yielding to violence what we refused to concede to argument'.

Source E

A political system which had got the country into such a disastrous war, and which showed no signs of winning it quickly, was vulnerable. Still more so after the Russian revolution of October 1917, which was first expected to launch a world revolution. Like the French revolution of 1789, it seemed to threaten all established governments. Militant trade unionism in South Wales or rent strikes in the lowlands of Scotland reminded the authorities that the Bolsheviks might find British allies. This would be particularly dangerous if post war unemployment or discontent became widespread because for the first time in British history large sections of civilian public had been trained in the use of firearms. Hence the need to strengthen parliamentary government by placing it on a broader electoral foundation.

The democratic enthusiasm overcame one of the major pre-war obstacles to votes for women. Feminists had hitherto campaigned only against sex discrimination within the existing voting qualification. But given that this rested on ownership of property, conceding their demand would have increased property's influence within the political system. Such a reform could attract some Conservatives, but Liberals could never unite behind it. The democratic way of giving women the vote was through 'adult suffrage' – that is, through giving the vote to all adults regardless of gender. But the very thought of this had alarmed prewar Conservatives.

The war removed this blockage to reform, for it ensured that the first priority now became the defence of parliamentary government rather than the defence of property.

Extracts from Brian Harrison, 'The First World War and Feminism in Britain', *History Review.*

---

1 In Sources A and B, what arguments are put forward which contest the traditional view of the war and women's votes?

2 From Sources C, D and E, find the ways in which Brian Harrison argues the War was contributory to female enfranchisement.

REVIEW

The end of the First World War – remembered

Testament of Youth

When the sound of victorious guns burst over London at 11am on November 11th 1918, the men and women who looked incredulously into each other's faces did not cry jubilantly: 'We've won the War!' They only said 'The War is over'.

From Millbank I heard the maroons crash with terrifying clearness, and, like a sleeper who is determined to go on dreaming after being told to wake up, I went on automatically washing the dressing bowls in the annex outside my hut. Deeply buried beneath my consciousness there stirred the vague memory of a letter that I had written to Roland in those legendary days when I was still at Oxford, and could spend my Sundays in thinking of him while the organ echoed grandly through New College Chapel. It had been a warm May evening, when all the city was sweet with the scent of wallflowers and lilac, and I had walked back to Micklem Hall after hearing an Occasional Oratorio by Handel, which described the mustering of troops for battle, the lament for the fallen and the triumphant return of the victors...

But on Armistice Day not even a lonely survivor drowning in black waves of memory could be left alone with her thoughts. A moment after the guns had subsided into sudden, palpitating silence, the other V.A.D. from my ward dashed excitedly into the annex.

'Brittain! Brittain! Did you hear the maroons? It's over – it's all over! Do let's come out and see what's happening!' ...

I followed her swiftly into the road. As I stood there, stupidly rigid ... I saw the taxicab turn swiftly in from the Embankment towards the hospital. The next moment there was a cry ... for in rounding the corner the taxi had knocked down a very small elderly woman...

As I hurried to her side I realised that she was all but dead... but on the tiny chalk-white face an expression of shocked surprise still lingered... Had she been thinking... of her sons at the front, now safe?...

Late that evening... a group of elated V.A.D.s ... prevailed upon me to join them. Outside the Admiralty a crazy group of convalescent Tommies wer collecting specimens of different uniforms and bundling their wearers into flag-strewn taxis.. Wherever we went a burst of enthusiastic cheering greeted our Red Cross uniform, and complete strangers adorned with wound stripes rushed up and shook me warmly by the hand...

I detached myself from the others and walked slowly up Whitehall, with my heart sinking in a sudden cold dismay. Already this was a different world from the one that I had known during four life-long years, a world in which people would be light-hearted and forgetful, in which themselves and their careers and their amusements would blot out political ideals and great national issues. And in that brightly lit, alien world I should have no part. All those with whom I had really been intimate were gone; not one remained to share with me the heights and the depths of my memories. As the years went by and youth departed and remembrance grew dim, a deeper and ever deeper darkness would cover the young men who were once my contemporaries.

For the first time I realised, with all that full realisation meant, how completely everything that had hitherto made up my life had vanished with Edward and Roland, with Victor and Geoffrey. The War was over; a new age was beginning; but the dead were dead and would never return.

Vera Brittain, *Testament of Youth* (1933).

---

1 What war service was Vera Brittain occupied in at this time? What is the evidence for this?
2 What is meant by comparing 'We've won the War!' and 'The War is over'?
3 Why did Vera Brittain not join in enthusiastically with the celebrations in London?
4 'Already this was a different world from the one that I had known during four life-long years'. What reasons does Vera have for this reflection?

Memoirs

How useful are these to the historian?

You will already have some across memoir sources in your study of History or more informally from conversations with older generations. 'Do you remember when…?' is a familiar question. There are memoir sources for most significant periods or events in the past – particularly in the last two hundred years. They can be a very rich source for the historian provided you realise their limitations.

TASKS

1 Write a short paragraph describing the first term at your present school or college.
2 Compare this with others in your class.
   a How are these 'memoirs' similar or different?
   b Why are they different?
3 How useful would your 'memoir' be to a historian studying secondary school education of this period?
   a What would be the value?
   b What would the limitations be?
4 How valuable is Vera Brittain's memoir of the end of the First World War?
   Identify its strengths and weaknesses.

---

5 Lloyd George – Prime Minister Without a Party: Britain's Coalition Government, 1918–22

PREVIEW

'THE HATCHING' –
CARTOON BY DAVID LOW.

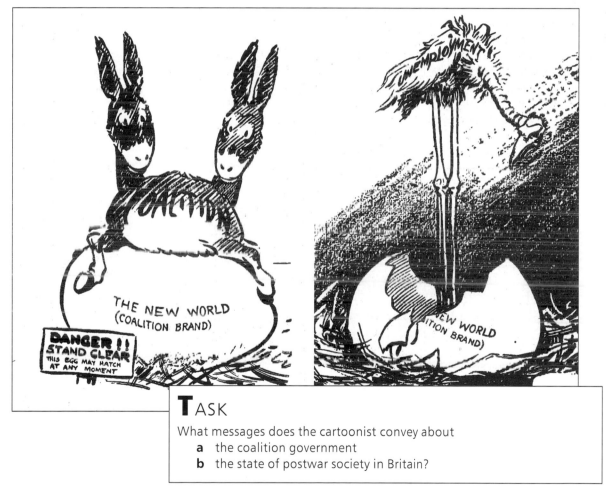

THE NEW WORLD
(COALITION BRAND)

DANGER !!
STAND CLEAR
THIS EGG MAY HATCH
AT ANY MOMENT

UNEMPLOYMENT

NEW WORLD
(COALITION BRAND)

TASK
What messages does the cartoonist convey about
    a the coalition government
    b the state of postwar society in Britain?

Examining the Evidence

The Coupon Election – 14 December 1918

Source A

An extract from a letter from Lloyd George to Bonar Law, 2 November 1918.

… If there is to be an election I think it would be right that it should be a Coalition Election, that is to say, that the whole country should be definitely invited to return candidates who undertake to support the present Government not only to prosecute the War to its final end and negotiate the peace, but to deal with the problems of reconstruction which must immediately arrive directly an armistice is signed … I am convinced also that such an arrangement will be best for the Country. The problems with which we shall be faced immediately on the cessation of hostilities will be hardly less pressing and will require hardly less dramatic action than those of the war itself. They cannot, in my opinion, be dealt with without disaster on party lines. It is vital that the national unity which has made possible victory in the war should be maintained until at least the main foundations of national and international reconstruction have been securely laid.

Quoted in John Ramsden (ed.), *Real Old Tory Politics: the Political Diaries of Robert Sanders, Lord Bayford, 1910–1935* (1984).

Source B

The 'Coupon' was a letter from Lloyd George and Bonar Law supporting coalition candidates for the 1918 General Election.

> **Polling Day, Saturday, December 14, 1918.**
>
> *The following is a copy of a letter received by Sir John Bethell :—*
>
> DOWNING STREET,
> LONDON, S.W.1.
>
> 20th November, 1918.
>
> Dear Sir John Bethell,
>
> We have much pleasure in recognising you as the Coalition candidate for East Ham, North.
>
> We have every hope that the electors will return you as their representative in Parliament to support the Government in the great task which lies before it.
>
> Yours truly,
>
> Central Liberal Coalition Committee Rooms.   339, High Street North, Manor Park, E.12.

COUPON FROM THE 1918 ELECTION.

Source C

An extract from Lloyd George and Bonar Law's Coalition Manifesto, 1918.

… We, appeal then, to every section of the electorate without distinction of party, to support the Coalition Government in the execution of a policy devised in the interests of no particular class or section, but, so far as our light serves us, for the furtherance of the general good …

The care of the soldiers and sailors, officers and men, whose heroism has won for us this great deliverance, and who return to civilian life, is a primary obligation of patriotism, and the government will endeavour to assist such members of the armed forces of the Crown as may desire to avail themselves of facilities for special industrial training and to return to civil life under conditions worthy of their services to the country. Plans have been prepared … whereby it will be the duty of public authorities and, if necessary, of the State itself to acquire land on a simple and economical basis for men who have served in the war, either for cottages with gardens, allotments, or small holdings as the applicant may desire and be suited for, with grants provided to assist in training and initial equipment…

The principal concern of every government is and must be the condition of the great mass of the people who live by manual toil. The steadfast spirit of our workers, displayed on all the wide field of action, opened out by the war – in the trenches, on the ocean, in the air, in field, mine and factory – has left an imperishable mark on the heart and conscience of the nation. One of the first tasks of the Government will be to deal on broad and comprehensive lines with the housing of the people, which during the was has fallen so sadly into arrears, and upon which the well-being of the nation so largely depends. Larger opportunities for education, improved material conditions, and the prevention of degrading standards of employment … are among the conditions of social harmony which we shall earnestly endeavour to promote…

F.W.S. Craig, *British Election Manifestos 1900–1974* (1975).

Source D

'SUPPORT THE MEN AND WOMEN WHO GAVE YOU VICTORY – VOTE LABOUR'. LABOUR PARTY ELECTION POSTER, 1918.

Source E

Among calls for 'Homes fit for Heroes' after the First World War was this call for an improved environment from Richard Reiss, an army captain. He makes the point that the country needs more 'A.1' homes if it wants to create an 'A.1' population.

RICHARD REISS, 'THE HOME I WANT'.

Coupon Election Results		
	Seats	**Vote %**
Government parties		
Coalition Conservatives	335	32.6
Coalition Conservatives (without coupon)	48	6.1
Coalition Liberals	133	13.5
Coalition Labour	10	1.5
	526	
Opposition parties		
Asquithian Liberals	28	12.1
Labour	57	22.2
Sinn Fein	73	4.5
Others	23	7.5
	181	

The actual results of this election were complicated due to party splits and the uncertainty of some MPs' allegiances. Sinn Fein MPs refused to take their seats. The coalition won a large overall majority.

Martin Pugh, *The Making of Modern British Politics 1867–1939* (1982).

TASKS

1 Compile the following lists:
   a Changes caused by the War
   b Previous developments – political, social and economic – accelerated by the War.

2 Discuss the question: 'Is it more accurate to describe the First World War as more destructive than constructive?'
   a Each student should decide on a preliminary judgement and write it down, giving reasons.
   b Divide the class into groups in which each student in turn should argue his or her case. Each individual should then arrive at a final conclusion – having changed their mind if they so wish.
   c Compile the evidence for each case and take a vote to discover the class view on the question.

1 In Source A, what reasons does Lloyd George give for a 'coalition election'?
2 From Sources C–E, what were the main issues at the 1918 election?
3 From the sources and election results, can you suggest reasons why the government elected in 1918 was vulnerable and weakened from the start?

Britain in 1918 – a changed country?

The coalition government which was returned after the 1918 Election enjoyed the advantage of an effective parliamentary majority (over 320), yet was confronted by the need for reconstruction on a massive scale. The impact of the First World War had left Britain with the scars of human suffering and immense economic damage yet witnessing notable signs of progress both politically and socially. Any assessment of Lloyd George's coalition government must be made in the context of this wartime inheritance and the many problems the government had to tackle. The impact of the War raises several questions:

● Was Britain a changed country after 1918?
● How damaging was the War to British society?
● Was the War a cause of change or an accelerator of developments already happening?

A social, economic and political sketch

HUMAN SUFFERING

▶ 745 000 Britons were killed (9% of all men under 45).
▶ Of 6 146 574 serving soldiers, sailors and airmen, 11.8% were killed.
▶ 1.6 million were wounded – many of whom were unable to work.
▶ 3.5 million orphans and widows who collected a war pension or allowance.
▶ These figures were compounded by 150 000 who died in the flu epidemic 1918–19.
▶ Balance of females in Britain rose from in 1911, 595 per thousand of the population to 1921, 638 per thousand. Proportion of widows per thousand of the population rose from 38 to 43.

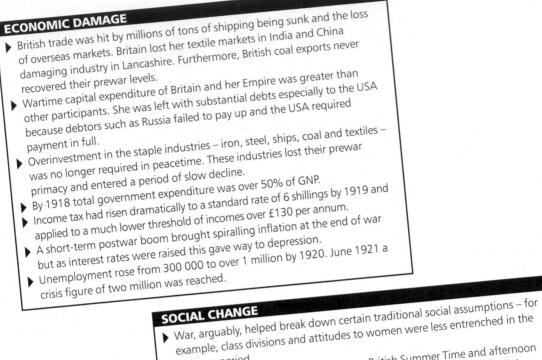

ECONOMIC DAMAGE

- British trade was hit by millions of tons of shipping being sunk and the loss of overseas markets. Britain lost her textile markets in India and China damaging industry in Lancashire. Furthermore, British coal exports never recovered their prewar levels.
- Wartime capital expenditure of Britain and her Empire was greater than other participants. She was left with substantial debts especially to the USA because debtors such as Russia failed to pay up and the USA required payment in full.
- Overinvestment in the staple industries – iron, steel, ships, coal and textiles – was no longer required in peacetime. These industries lost their prewar primacy and entered a period of slow decline.
- By 1918 total government expenditure was over 50% of GNP.
- Income tax had risen dramatically to a standard rate of 6 shillings by 1919 and applied to a much lower threshold of incomes over £130 per annum.
- A short-term postwar boom brought spiralling inflation at the end of war but as interest rates were raised this gave way to depression.
- Unemployment rose from 300 000 to over 1 million by 1920. June 1921 a crisis figure of two million was reached.

SOCIAL CHANGE

- War, arguably, helped break down certain traditional social assumptions – for example, class divisions and attitudes to women were less entrenched in the interwar period.
- War introduced two national customs – British Summer Time and afternoon closing of public houses.Cigarette smoking became more popular and the average beer remained weaker but rose in price.
- Serious decline in housing due to fewer being built yet demand increasing. This gave rise to the 'Homes fit for Heroes' campaign.
- War showed the steepest fall in infant mortality rates in the first 30 years of century. Maternity care was improved.
- Industrial canteens, subsidised meals and the provision of other facilities for workers.
- Many state benefits were extended during wartime – for example, the provision of school meals.

POLITICAL DEVELOPMENTS

- War prompted democratic progress by highlighting the question of suffrage. The Representation of the People Act (1918) gave the vote to all men over 21 and women over 30. They were 21 million electors in 1918 compared to 7.5 million male electors in 1910.
- Government intervention in the lives of British people was necessitated by war and now became the norm. Laissez-faire government had disappeared.
- The government expenditure necessary for this scale of war normalised much increased government spending. If it could be spent on fighting, why not on social reform?
- The war speeded up the Liberal Party's decline and benefited the Labour Party greatly. There were no more Liberal governments in the twentieth century. Labour replaced them as the main political opposition to the Conservatives.

Postwar reconstruction – two major successes

In terms of social reconstruction Lloyd George's past experience seemed to offer excellent credentials for the job. As Chancellor of the Exchequer in the prewar Liberal government, he had been the driving force behind the major National Insurance Act of 1911 (see Chapter 2 above). He had been credited with a political realism and sympathy for the underprivileged. During the War both at Munitions and as premier he earned his reputation for getting things done. His postwar coalition could claim solid achievement in two important areas – housing and unemployment.

TALKING POINT

What are the social consequences of homelessness?
What are the merits and problems associated with the provision of council housing?

Housing

Christopher Addison moved to the Ministry of Health from the Ministry for Reconstruction in December 1918. With much energy and enthusiasm he attempted to deliver the election promise of 'Homes fit for Heroes'. Local authorities were ordered to build an unlimited number of houses and let them at a controlled rent fixed at a 1914 level. Not allowing cost to stand in his way, Addison declared that government would meet any cost incurred which exceeded the 7d local rate. There were immediate problems. Local councils lacked housing experts, the building did not happen quickly enough and houses built under Addison's scheme for £910 per year or so later cost only £385. There was an outcry against the scheme and the Exchequer cut the housing subsidies. Addison left the Ministry of Health in March 1921. However, three main successes were:

1　213,000 houses were built – many cheap enough for lower working-class families.
2　The quality of building was good – they still remain some of the best council housing in the country.
3　In the longer term, housing became a social service. The government were now responsible for this major necessity in society.

Unemployment

Unaware that unemployment was to become an increasing problem with periods of crisis during the interwar years, Lloyd George greatly extended the 1911 Unemployment Insurance Scheme. This initial legislation provided for just three trades – building, engineering and shipbuilding. The 1920 Insurance Act provided benefits for all workers covered by the 1911 Health Insurance Act, provided they earned less than £5 a week. This extended the insurance cover to about 12 million workers. They were entitled to 15s a week for 15 weeks in one year. In 1921, there was an extension to this legislation to include benefits for those 'uncovenanted' – that is a period of insurance they had not paid for provided they were 'genuinely seeking work'. Extra payments were also made to dependents eg. 5s for a wife and 1s for each child. The main successes of this legislation were:

1　Unemployment Insurance was so extensive that it cut across the Poor Law authorities – moving the responsibility from local to central government.
2　As unemployment continued to be a problem, this insurance payment took the sting out of discontent.
3　Insurance payments were not perceived to be as humiliating as the Poor Law.

Problems for the Lloyd George Coalition

Economy and government cuts

After a short-lived postwar boom, a period of economic depression set in. Government debt was still substantial and unemployment rose during the winter 1920–1 to over one million. By June 1921 two million were without jobs. The government followed an orthodox policy of cutting expenditure. Sir Eric Geddes headed a commission which sanctioned cuts amounting to £64 million. The 'Geddes Axe' severely limited reconstruction plans. The budget of 1922 included a 12% cut in government spending.

March 1921 Addison resigned

Lloyd George's colleague at the wartime Ministry of Munitions left the Ministry of Health when the 'Geddes Axe' ended government subsidies for housing.

Worsening industrial relations

A new militancy was apparent in the trades union activity after the war. 'Red Revolution' was feared. In January 1919 the government had sent in troops to deal with 70,000 workers on strike in Glasgow. In 1921 strikes increased and 86 million working days were lost. In April 1921 a general strike seemed possible when the Triple Alliance of railwaymen, transport workers and miners threatened industrial disruption. Only the personal intervention of Lloyd George prevented this occurring.

TASK

To what extent can this government be held responsible for the problems it encountered in 1921?

Compile a list of
a criticisms of government policy
b circumstances beyond the government's control.

1921 Crisis Year

Trouble in Ireland

The government's policy of reimposing British rule in Ireland, where a republic had been set up in Dublin under De Valera, was unpopular. The war which had broken out in 1920 saw atrocities on both sides. However, Lloyd George took the blame for the excesses of British ex-servicemen – the infamous 'Black and Tans'. It was not until July 1921 that a truce was signed.

May 1921 Bonar Law resigned

Due to ill health, Bonar Law resigned from the Cabinet and leadership of the Conservative Party. This was a major blow to Lloyd George whose coalition with the Conservatives was underpinned by his good working relationship with Bonar Law. Austen Chamberlain, a critic of Lloyd George, replaced him.

Versailles Settlement

Although Lloyd George is often regarded as a moderating influence at the peace discussions in Paris, opinion at home was divided and criticism came from two fronts. Many Conservatives, along with the *Times* and the *Daily Mail*, thought him too lenient. However, liberal opinion criticised the settlement for being too harsh – permanently damaging Germany and the world economy. For the Prime Minister, the Paris peace conference was time-consuming and exhausting.

Lloyd George's fall

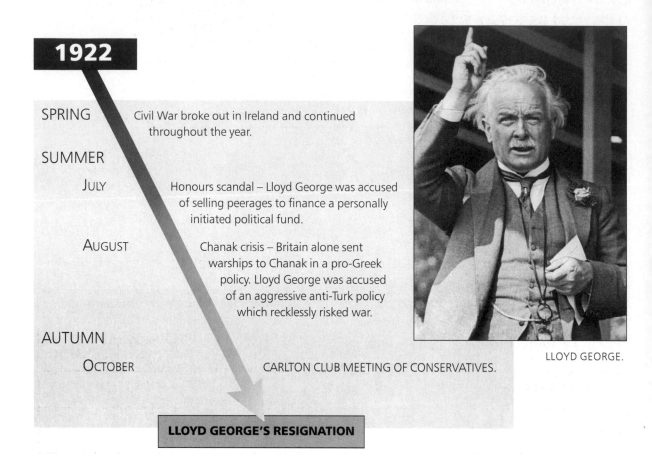

1922

SPRING — Civil War broke out in Ireland and continued throughout the year.

SUMMER

JULY — Honours scandal – Lloyd George was accused of selling peerages to finance a personally initiated political fund.

AUGUST — Chanak crisis – Britain alone sent warships to Chanak in a pro-Greek policy. Lloyd George was accused of an aggressive anti-Turk policy which recklessly risked war.

AUTUMN

OCTOBER — CARLTON CLUB MEETING OF CONSERVATIVES.

LLOYD GEORGE.

LLOYD GEORGE'S RESIGNATION

Baldwin's speech at the Carlton Club:

"I accept those words. He is a dynamic force, and it is from that very fact that our troubles, in my opinion, arise. A dynamic force is a very terrible thing; it may crush you but it is not necessarily right.

It is owing to that dynamic force and that remarkable personality, that the Liberal party, to which he formerly belonged, has been smashed to pieces; and it is my firm conviction that, in time, the same thing will happen to our party…

I would like to give you just one illustration to show what I mean by the disintegrating influence of a dynamic force. Take Mr. Chamberlain and myself … We stand here today, he prepared to go into the wilderness if he should be compelled to forsake the prime minister, and I prepared to go into the wilderness if I should be compelled to stay with him."

At the Carlton Club meeting on 19 October, the Conservatives passed a motion 187 to 87 in favour of fighting the next General Election on their own. Lloyd George resigned as Prime Minister later that day.

Lloyd George's Coalition Government – A critical assessment

A government which achieved much despite the problems of postwar Britain

A government which failed to live up to expectations of the time

An unstable coalition with insurmountable problems

What is your conclusion on the success of this government?

TASK

1 Complete the following chart with information from this chapter and your own research.

Issues 1918–22	SUCCESS	FAILURE
Composition of government		
Personality of Lloyd George		
Economy		
Unemployment		
Industrial relations		
Housing		
Foreign Policy		
Ireland		

Ireland, 1900–22

What was the 'Irish Question'?

Ireland during the 19th century and up until 1922 was ruled undivided by Britain. The Irish question presented problems to the British government throughout this period. By 1900 the nature of the Irish problem had changed – yet it still comprised three major strands:

- **Religious**
- **Economic**
- **Political**.

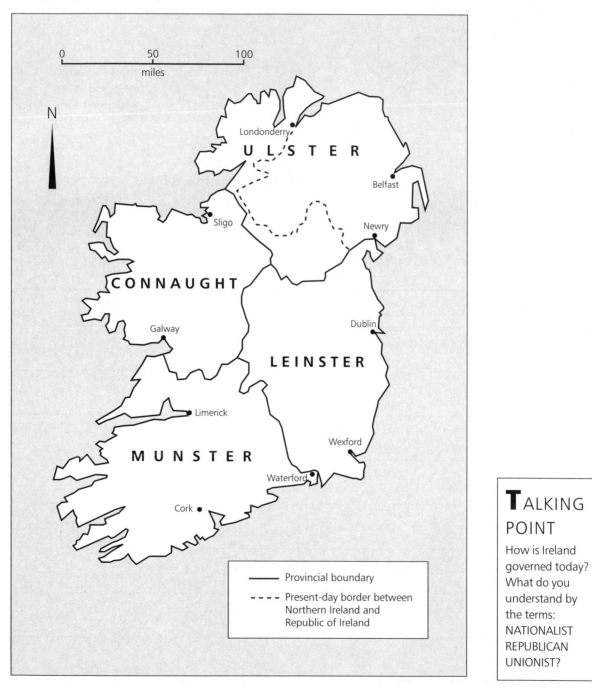

Scale: 0 — 50 — 100 miles

N

ULSTER
- Londonderry
- Belfast
- Sligo
- Newry

CONNAUGHT
- Galway

LEINSTER
- Dublin
- Wexford

MUNSTER
- Limerick
- Waterford
- Cork

—— Provincial boundary

---- Present-day border between Northern Ireland and Republic of Ireland

---

TALKING POINT

How is Ireland governed today? What do you understand by the terms: NATIONALIST REPUBLICAN UNIONIST?

Religious

90 per cent of the Irish were Roman Catholic but a minority of Protestants settled there, particularly in the North, who in the 16th and 17th centuries had been given land and privileges by the British government. The Church of England was the official Church in Ireland. Catholics were expected to pay tithes to the Protestant church at the same time as supporting their own services and priests. In 1869 Gladstone succeeded in disestablishing the Anglican Church in Ireland. However, this religious and racial division is a backdrop to the Irish question.

Economic

Agriculture: From the 1860s to the 1880s the Irish had demanded land reforms – fair rents, fixity of tenure, no eviction without compensation. A backward agricultural economy together with absentee English landlords led frequently to hunger, dissent and emigration. Gladstone by 1885 had largely solved the problems concerning land.

Industry: division between Northern, more Protestant areas of Ireland and the Southern Roman Catholic counties became more pronounced with the industrialisation of the North. There it became prosperous contrasting sharply with the underdeveloped agricultural economy of the South.

Political

1829 Roman Catholic emancipation – a campaign led by Daniel O'Connell – allowed Roman Catholics to seat in Parliament.

1860s Irish Catholic MPs began to demand some degree of self-rule from the British government. Gladstone attempted to meet these demands by his two Home Rule Bills of 1886 and 1893. Both failed but Home Rule continued to be a Liberal Party policy and was pushed for by John Redmond's Home Rule group in Parliament after 1906.

1890s Extreme Nationalists for whom Home Rule was insufficient began to work for complete independence of Ireland. Ulster Unionists developed their stance against Irish independence by calling for a maintenance of Union with Britain. The Conservatives supported them.

Home Rule for Ireland, 1910–14 – A Solution?

What was Home Rule?

Home Rule would have given Ireland a degree of self-rule. An Irish Parliament was to deal with internal affairs whereas issues such as foreign policy, trade and finance were to be decided by Parliament in London.

TIMELINE

1910
General Election (December)
– Liberals 272 / Conservatives 272 / Irish 84.

Ulster Unionists elected Sir Edward Carson, MP and lawyer, as their leader.

1911
Parliament Act (August)
– reduced the power of the House of Lords.

1912
Third Home Rule Bill (April)
– Establish two-chamber Irish Parliament to deal with internal affairs.

– 42 MPs at Westminster.

– Foreign policy, trade, finance dealt with by Westminster.

No concessions to Ulster.

1913
Lords reject Home Rule Bill twice (January and July) – Ulster Volunteer Force (UVF) established. Irish Volunteers and Irish Republican Brotherhood set up.

1914
Home Rule Bill reintroduced with Amending Bill for six Ulster Counties to opt out. Buckingham Palace Conference (July). First World War (August)

TASKS

From the 1910–1914 timeline on this page:

1 Identify and explain the attitudes of the following groups to Home Rule in the period 1910–14:
   a Irish Nationalist Republicans   c the Liberal government
   b Ulstermen   d Conservatives?
2 Explain why Ireland was on the brink of Civil War by the summer of 1914?

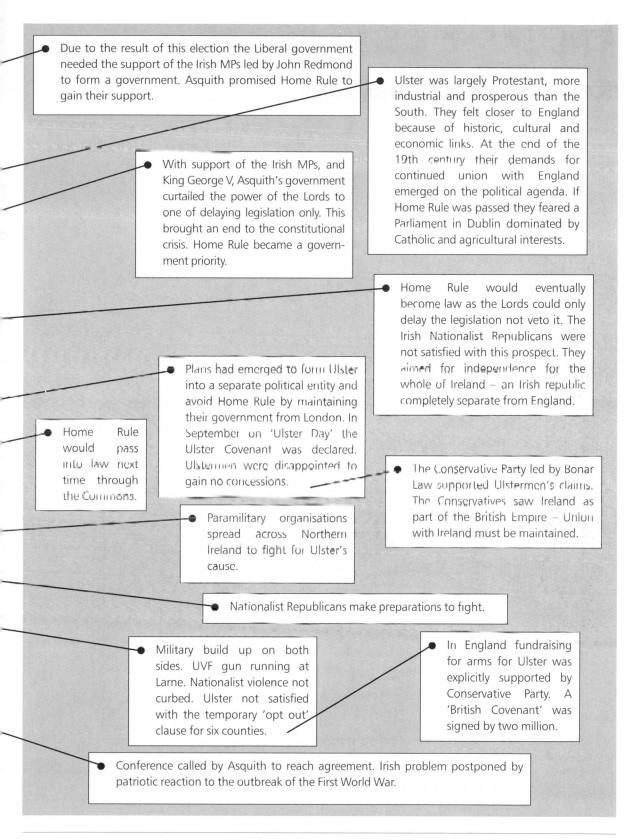

Due to the result of this election the Liberal government needed the support of the Irish MPs led by John Redmond to form a government. Asquith promised Home Rule to gain their support.

Ulster was largely Protestant, more industrial and prosperous than the South. They felt closer to England because of historic, cultural and economic links. At the end of the 19th century their demands for continued union with England emerged on the political agenda. If Home Rule was passed they feared a Parliament in Dublin dominated by Catholic and agricultural interests.

With support of the Irish MPs, and King George V, Asquith's government curtailed the power of the Lords to one of delaying legislation only. This brought an end to the constitutional crisis. Home Rule became a government priority.

Home Rule would eventually become law as the Lords could only delay the legislation not veto it. The Irish Nationalist Republicans were not satisfied with this prospect. They aimed for independence for the whole of Ireland – an Irish republic completely separate from England.

Plans had emerged to form Ulster into a separate political entity and avoid Home Rule by maintaining their government from London. In September on 'Ulster Day' the Ulster Covenant was declared. Ulstermen were disappointed to gain no concessions.

Home Rule would pass into law next time through the Commons.

The Conservative Party led by Bonar Law supported Ulstermen's claims. The Conservatives saw Ireland as part of the British Empire – Union with Ireland must be maintained.

Paramilitary organisations spread across Northern Ireland to fight for Ulster's cause.

Nationalist Republicans make preparations to fight.

Military build up on both sides. UVF gun running at Larne. Nationalist violence not curbed. Ulster not satisfied with the temporary 'opt out' clause for six counties.

In England fundraising for arms for Ulster was explicitly supported by Conservative Party. A 'British Covenant' was signed by two million.

Conference called by Asquith to reach agreement. Irish problem postponed by patriotic reaction to the outbreak of the First World War.

5.1 The Easter Rising, 1916

Thousands of Irish recruits enthusiastically joined up to fight against Germany in the First World War. They saw Ireland as important in this struggle and South Irish regiments marched together with Ulstermen to the horrors of the Western Front, proud as Nationalists of their homeland's contribution.

However, for a minority of extreme Irish Nationalists their first loyalty was the idea of a separate self-ruled Ireland. War offered an opportunity to overthrow the hated rule of the British. Leaders of this group, the Irish Republican Brotherhood, met together just after the outbreak of war. Men such as Tom Clarke,

Patrick Pearse and Sean McDermott decided on rebellion to seize power, establish a republic and force a separation from the British crown.

TALKING POINT

What do you understand by the term 'nationalism'?
What are the merits and defects of adhering to nationalism?

The Plan

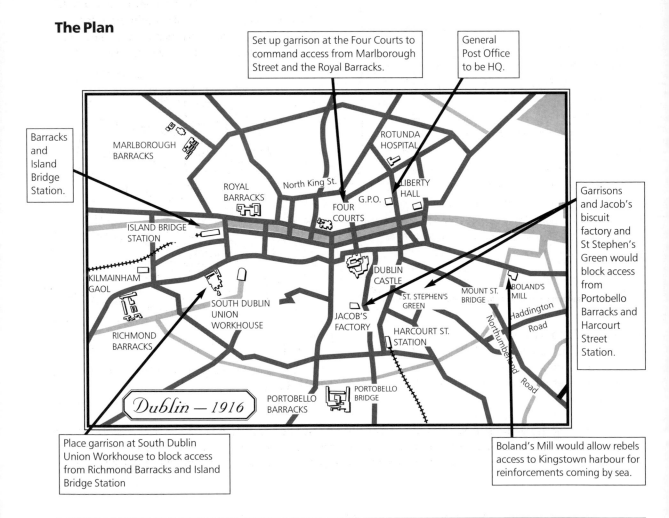

Set up garrison at the Four Courts to command access from Marlborough Street and the Royal Barracks.

General Post Office to be HQ.

Barracks and Island Bridge Station.

Garrisons and Jacob's biscuit factory and St Stephen's Green would block access from Portobello Barracks and Harcourt Street Station.

Place garrison at South Dublin Union Workhouse to block access from Richmond Barracks and Island Bridge Station

Boland's Mill would allow rebels access to Kingstown harbour for reinforcements coming by sea.

Map labels: MARLBOROUGH BARRACKS · ROTUNDA HOSPITAL · ROYAL BARRACKS · North King St. · LIBERTY HALL · FOUR COURTS · G.P.O. · ISLAND BRIDGE STATION · KILMAINHAM GAOL · DUBLIN CASTLE · SOUTH DUBLIN UNION WORKHOUSE · ST. STEPHEN'S GREEN · MOUNT ST. BRIDGE · BOLAND'S MILL · Haddington Road · Northumberland Road · RICHMOND BARRACKS · JACOB'S FACTORY · HARCOURT ST. STATION · *Dublin – 1916* · PORTOBELLO BARRACKS · PORTOBELLO BRIDGE

On Easter Monday, 24 April 1916, 1000 armed rebels joined their leaders, Pearse, Clarke and Connolly. The main body of men marched to the GPO and to a bewildered crowd an Irish Republic was declared by Patrick Pearse from the front of the building.

> ### THE PROVISIONAL GOVERNMENT OF THE IRISH REPUBLIC
>
> *'TO THE PEOPLE OF IRELAND. Irish men and Irishwomen: in the name of God and of the dead generations which she receives her old tradition of nationhood, Ireland, through us, summons her children to her flag and strikes for her freedom.*
>
> *Having organised and trained her manhood through her secret revolutionary organisation, the Irish Republican Brotherhood and the Irish Citizen Army, having patiently perfected her dis-cipline, having resolutely waited for the right moment to reveal itself, she now seizes that moment, and supported by her exiled children in America and her gallant allies in Europe, but relying in the first upon her own strength, she strikes in the full confidence of victory.*
>
> *We declare the right of the people of Ireland to the ownership of Ireland and to the unfettered control of Irish destinies, to be sovereign and indefeasible.'*

The uprising failed to gather significant support – perhaps another 800 over the next couple of days and their cause did not spread beyond Dublin city centre. By Saturday 29 April they had been defeated by the British Army, the lack of support and failed shipment of arms. Patrick Pearse surrendered, many buildings, including the GPO, had been shelled or gutted by fire, and the death toll amounted to 300 civilians, 60 rebels and 130 British troops. It appeared to have been an utter failure. However, Irish Nationalists, passionate about their cause had held out against the British army for nearly a week. Public opinion began to shift from deploring the action to feeling a sense of pride in fellow Irish men. The following actions of the British government – harsh and immediate – turned the rebels into Irish martyrs.

Executions followed rapidly despite pleas for leniency heard amongst politicians and intellectuals. The following were executed by firing squad:

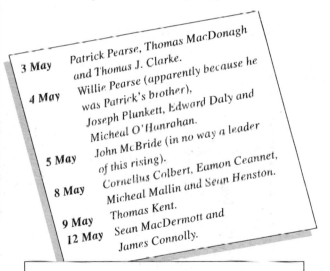

3 May	Patrick Pearse, Thomas MacDonagh and Thomas J. Clarke.
4 May	Willie Pearse (apparently because he was Patrick's brother), Joseph Plunkett, Edward Daly and Micheal O'Hanrahan.
5 May	John McBride (in no way a leader of this rising).
8 May	Cornelius Colbert, Eamon Ceannet, Micheal Mallin and Sean Henston.
9 May	Thomas Kent.
12 May	Sean MacDermott and James Connolly.

Explain how and why the First World War affected the Irish question in the following areas:
- **a** Government policy
- **b** Attitudes of the various Irish groups.

> # Talking point
>
> Do you agree or disagree with the sentences carried out?

The impact of the Easter Rising was highly significant. It radicalised attitudes, former moderates found themselves in sympathy with the extremist cause. One such, Edward Machysaght, wrote in his diary at the time: 'My heart is with them and my mind is against them.' The executions made him 'completely and absolutely pro them'.

Examining the Evidence

The Easter Rising, 1916

Source A

A speech by Pearse to his fellow rebels, Thursday 27 April 1916.

I desire now, lest I may not have an opportunity later, to pay homage to the gallantry of the soldiers of Irish freedom who have during the past four days been writing with fire and steel the most glorious chapter in the later history of Ireland. Justice can never be done to their heroism, to their discipline, to their gay and unconquerable spirit in the midst of peril and death. …

If they do not win this fight, they will at least deserve to win it. But win it they will although they may win it in death. Already they have done a great thing. They have redeemed Dublin from many shames, and made her name splendid among the names of cities. They have held out for four days against the might of the British Empire. They have established Ireland's right to be a Republic, and they have established this government's right to sit at the peace table at the end of the European War.

Source B

From our Belfast Correspondent, *The Times*, 1 May.

At 4 o'clock yesterday afternoon the Irish rebellion – an episode in Irish history which all practical and sensible people in this country regard as the most inglorious and disgraceful outbreak of organised rowdyism which ever sullied the annals of this country – came to a sudden end.

Source C

Editorial in the *Daily News* (an English paper of Liberal views), 1 May.

… But there is at least one aspect of this lamentable affair from which we may extract satisfaction. It has shown very strikingly the divorce of this wild movement from the general body of the Irish people. The outstanding fact of the whole episode is its political isolation from the spirit of the nation …

In Dublin itself the whole population was as much outraged as it was alarmed by the whole affair, and it is probable that the British soldier has never had such a cordial welcome in the Irish capital as he has had during the past few days …

In a very real sense we may say that the rising, deplorable as it is in the sacrifice of life that it has entailed, is not wholly without a gratifying side. It has revealed as nothing else could reveal the loyalty of the Irish people and the happy change that a wiser policy and a larger liberty have brought in their train.

Source D
Healey's reports for *The Times*, 2 and 3 May.

a   2 May

From J. E. Healey (in Dublin): Everywhere, amongst Unionists and Nationalists alike, one hears stern expression of the hope that the lesson of the insurrection will not be spoiled by untimely weakness. There must be no mistake about the nature of this rising. It was a brutal, savage and bloody business ... The nation must see that in return for the heavy cost it receives at least a sure guarantee of righteous punishment for the offenders and of firm, just and powerful government for Ireland.

b   3 May

With the end of the insurrection the public begin to fear that the Government may relapse into its old policy of leniency and weakness. I shall only say that Irish public opinion is absolutely unanimous in its demand that the rebellion shall be crushed and its authors and agents punished with relentless severity.

Source E
Debate in the House of Commons, 3 May.

John Redmond: Let me say in concluding with one sentence. This outbreak happily seems to be over. It has been dealt with firmly. That was not only right, it was the duty of government. But as the rebellion, or outbreak – call it what you like – has been put down with firmness, I do beg of the government, and I speak from the bottom of my heart – with all my earnestness of feeling – I do beg of them not to show undue hardship or severity to the great mass of those who are implicated and on whose shoulders lies a guilt far different from that which lies on the instigators and promoters of this outbreak. (Hear, hear). Let them in the name of God not add this to the miserable memories of the Irish people to be started up for generations.

Sir Edward Carson: With reference to the speech of the Hon. Member for Waterford (Redmond) and what he has said about these unfortunate dupes in Ireland, let me say that, while I think it is in the best interests of this country that this conspiracy of Sinn Feiners, which has nothing to do with either of the two political parties in Ireland (Hear, hear) ought to be put down with courage and determination and with an example which would prevent a revival, it would be a mistake to suppose that any Irishman calls for vengeance. (Hear, hear) It will be a matter requiring the greatest wisdom, the greatest coolness, may I say, in dealing with these men, and all I say to the Executive is, whatever is done, let it not be done I na moment of temporary excitement, but with due deliberation in regard both to the present and to the future. (Cheers).

Report from *The Times*, 4 May 1916.

Source F

Communiqué from Sir John Maxwell, Dublin, 12 May.

In view of the severity of the rebellion, its connection with German intrigues and propaganda, and in view of the great loss of life and destruction of property arising therefrom, the General Officer Commanding in Chief has found it imperative to inflict most severe sentences on the known organisers of this detestable rising, and on those commanders who took an active part in the actual fighting which occurred.

Reported in *The Times*, 13 May 1916.

Source G

The Times, 12 May.

Thirteen rebels have been shot and sentence is to be executed on two others. It is idle to represent this punishment as excessive or revengeful or to pretend, with the Nationalist Manifesto, that this 'shocks and horrifies' Ireland.

Everybody will learn with relief that the necessity for further executions of this kind is now over, but a certain number of these executions were absolutely necessary to teach the traitors who take German money that they cannot cover Dublin with blood and ashes without forfeiting their lives. We think, however, that the Government have been foolish in not stating plainly the reasons why those men were shot and we welcome Mr. Asquith's promise that any further trials for murder shall be held with the doors open …

Source H

Extract from Mr George Bernard Shaw to *The Daily News*, 10 May, 'The Irish Executions'. Shaw, the famous dramatist, was born in Dublin and took a close interest in Irish affairs. One of his best plays, 'John Bull's Other Ireland', deals with the Anglo-Irish relationship.

… But it must not be assumed that those who merely shrugged their shoulders when it was useless to remonstrate accept for one moment the view that what happened was the execution of a gang of criminals. My own view – which I should not obtrude on you had you not concluded that it does not exist – is that the men who were shot in cold blood after their capture or surrender were prisoners of war, and therefore it was entirely incorrect to slaughter them. The relation of Ireland to Dublin Castle is in this respect precisely that of the Balkans to Turkey, of Belgium or the city of Lille to the Kaiser, and of the United States to Great Britain …

1 Sources A, B and C
  With reference to the origins, content and language of these sources, how useful would a historian studying the Easter Rising find them?
2 Sources D–H
  a How do these sources differ in their opinions of how the Irish rebels should be punished?
  b What arguments are put forward for harsh treatment and for a more lenient approach?
  c Explain why these sources differ.

Poetry – as a historical source

'Easter 1916' by W.B. Yeats (1865–1939)

BRITISH TROOPS BEHIND A STREET
BARRICADE IN DUBLIN, APRIL 1916.

> ## Verse 4
>
> Too long a sacrifice
> Can make a stone of the heart.
> O when may I suffice?
> That is Heaven's part, our part
> To murmur name upon name,
> As a mother names her child
> When sleep at last has come
> On limbs that had run wild.
> What is it but nightfall?
> No, no, not night, but death;
> Was it needless death after all?
> For England may keep faith
> For all that is done and said.
> We know their dream; enough
> To know they dreamed and are dead.
> And what if excess of love.
> Bewildered them till they died?
> I write it out in a verse –
> MacDonagh and MacBride
> And Connolly and Pearse
> Now and in time to be,
> Wherever green is worn,
> Are changed, changed utterly:
> A terrible beauty is born.

1 Is literature – novels, poetry and plays – useful to a historian?
2 Discuss the message put across by Yeats in this verse.
3 How useful would this poem be to a historian studying the Easter Rising?

The Partition of Ireland by 1922

The political separation of Northern Ireland (Ulster) from Southern Ireland (Eire) came about through two legislative phases:

| STAGE 1 | **Government of Ireland Act** | **December 1920** |

This divided Ireland in two for the purpose of carrying out Home Rule as laid down in the 1914 Home Rule Bill.

a Northern Ireland – consisting of six counties (see map).

b Southern Ireland – consisting of 26 counties.

c Each was to have its own Parliament composed of House of Commons and Senate.

d The powers of these Parliaments were to deal with internal affairs as stated in the 1914 Bill.

e Supremacy of the imperial Parliament was preserved.

This legislation was accepted by Ulster Unionists with some concerns, expressed but it was rejected outright by the Irish Republicans – the fighting continued. However, it laid the basis for …

STAGE 2 **The Anglo-Irish Treaty**   **December 1921**

a   An Irish Free State was established in Southern Ireland – a self-governing dominion within the Empire (like Canada).

b   Northern Ireland could request to be excluded and retain its constitutional status within the United Kingdom. The boundary – in this case – was to be set by a commission representing all parties – the Irish Free State, Northern Ireland and Great Britain. (This clause won the support of Irish delegates for the Treaty – believing Northern Ireland would become too small to be a political unit.)

From United Ireland to Partition, 1918–1922

EAMONN DE VALERA, FIRST PRESIDENT OF THE IRISH REPUBLIC, MEETING LLOYD GEORGE IN LONDON, JULY 1921

Breakaway Republic   January 1919

In the 1918 General Election, Sinn Fein, the Irish Nationalist party, returned 73 seats. As they had contested every constituency in Ireland they would claim, with this result, to represent majority opinion in their country. Now the First World War was over, Home Rule, postponed since 1914, seemed an inevitability. Additionally, the war itself and the aftermath of the Easter Rising in 1916 had hardened nationalist resolve and won increased support through Ireland.

The 73 Sinn Feiners took the immediate action of refusing to sit at Westminster and instead proclaimed the parliament of a new Irish Republic in Dublin (the Dail Eireann). They adopted a provisional constitution, appointed delegates to attend the Paris Peace Settlement and elected Eamonn de Valera as president. He appointed a ministry of eight to effect the government of Ireland. During the following months they built up their forces in order to hold on to power. De Valera had become president of the Irish Volunteers in November 1918 – a year earlier he had taken on the leadership of Sinn Fein. Although he was court martialled after the Easter Rising, he escaped execution because he had been born in the USA. He had been released from prison in July 1917. His leadership of both the political and military wing was a significant development in the Nationalist effort.

War breaks out   1920

The newly elected British government were slow to act in the face of this
breakaway republic. They were conscious of a pro-Irish attitude in the USA which
possibly slowed down their response. However, action was taken in August 1919
when they declared Sinn Fein illegal and the following month the illegality of the
Dail. The situation for the government was further complicated by the Unionist
reaction to events. The declaration of the republic at the Dail in 1919 had claimed
the inclusion of Ulster and backed it up with the Irish Republican Army (IRA). This
stirred Unionist, sectarian passions amongst Protestant Ulstermen. Pro-Unionist
riots broke out in Belfast and elsewhere, demonstrating their fear of being
swallowed up by Republican action. Roman Catholics were driven out of their
homes by rioters and damage occurred to property and life.

War had broken out by 1920 as the Irish attempted to hold on to government
in Dublin supported by the IRA. Prime Minister Lloyd George was reluctant to
admit to a state of war but pursued a policy of reimposing British rule (referred to
as 'law and order') on Southern Ireland to curb trouble. The government relied
upon the police aided by 'auxiliaries'. These ex-servicemen, known as the 'Black
and Tans' after the uniform they wore, were to lead the attempt to break the IRA.
Martial law was formally declared in December 1920. The police and military were
given a fairly free hand in their operations, the Irish Secretary had power to
imprison without trial and with the IRA controlling activity in Ireland a war
developed where no normal rules applied. The IRA, commanded by Michael Collins
and Cathal Brughen, adopted guerilla-style tactics, with no uniforms. It was a war
of raids and ambushes. Atrocities were committed on both sides – civilians
suspected of informing to the police were shot, revenge killings took place. On 21
November 1920 'Bloody Sunday', 14 Britons were dragged into the street and
shot. British troops fired on an unarmed crowd in Dublin, 12 spectators died. In
December 1920, much of the city of Cork was burnt down by the Black and Tans.

Truce leads to Anglo-Irish Treaty   December–July 1921

By January 1921 eight counties were under martial law. The IRA had intensified
their attacks yet were beginning to realise that the military decision was impractical
as it would make normal government impossible. At the same time Lloyd George
was being blamed and shouldering responsibility for an unpopular policy. His
government had two options – either to systematically reconquer of Ireland, which
went against British opinion, or to offer terms which Republican leaders would
accept. They decided to reverse their policy and – after a personal intervention from
George V – a truce was signed and negotiations opened. Lloyd George met with
De Valera initially and this was followed in October 1921 by the arrival of Michael
Collins and Arthur Griffiths for talks in London. The Republicans came to an
agreement with the government in December 1921 – the Anglo-Irish Treaty.

Civil War in Ireland 1922

The partition and formation of an Irish Free State was rejected by the radical Irish nationalists. They wanted both a united Ireland and a republic, but had gained neither. The 1921 Treaty was only just ratified in the Dail – by 64 votes to 57. De Valera resigned and Arthur Griffiths was elected leader. Civil War broke out in Southern Ireland. Michael Collins and others were killed. The Northern division of the IRA waged a campaign of violence in the six Ulster counties. During 1922, 232 were killed, 1000 wounded and £3 million worth of property destroyed. The Ulster MP Sir Henry Wilson was assassinated in London in June 1922. By the autumn Lloyd George appeared to have failed in his Irish policy. This undoubtedly contributed to his downfall (see page 98). By the General Election of 1922, the Irish Free State had a constitution from which Northern Ireland had requested to be excluded. The constitutional settlement was formally completed in December 1922 and there was a cessation of armed resistance in early 1923. As a result, Northern and Southern Ireland now had two separate, but mutually suspicious governments.

TASK

Write an essay:
'Why did the partition of Ireland occur?'

Follow the  system.

THINK!

Think carefully about the question. The key instruction is WHY? – this requires you to offer reasons for the partition of Ireland. Each reason should be contained in a paragraph and evidenced to prove it

READ!

With reference to the Ireland section of this chapter and further research reading –
   Make sure you fully understand the partition of Ireland and can suggest reasons for the event.

Consider reasons in the following way:

LONG-TERM – The background to the Irish question is a necessary cause:
  E.g. – Irreconcilable demands of the Republicans and Ulster Unionists.
    – Pre-1914 development of the idea of separation.

MEDIUM-TERM – The First World War 1914–18 impacted on the Irish question and develops the explanation further:
  E.g. – Postponement of Home Rule.
    – Common enemy Germany stirs national pride.
    – Consequences of the Easter Rising 1916.

SHORT-TERM – 1918–1921 Events during this period forced the issue towards partition – why?
  E.g. – 1919 Declaration of the republic in Dublin.
    – 1920–1 War provided no long-term solution.
    – 1920 Partition.
    – 1921 Irish Free State.

When you are sure it is ready, write up your essay – ensuring that it is written with good grammar and spelling

REVIEW

Government changes and party alignments, 1914–22

	CONSERVATIVE	LIBERAL	LABOUR
1914	(Bonar Law) in opposition	← LIBERAL GOVERNMENT (Asquith)	(MacDonald) (MacDonald resigned – Henderson becomes leader)
May 1915	Joined government → SPLIT Withdrew support from Asquith.	ASQUITH COALITION ← ↘ Asquith Liberals	Joined government.
December 1916	Joined Lloyd George's Liberals →	LLOYD GEORGE'S COALITION ←	Joined government (Henderson – member of War Cabinet)
1917			→ Henderson resigned. Labour left coalition. ↓
1918	General Election. Maintained support for Lloyd George. Some non-coalitionists →	LLOYD GEORGE'S COALITION Asquith Liberals	LABOUR
1922	Carlton Club Meeting withdrew support from Lloyd George. ↓ CONSERVATIVE GOVERNMENT (Bonar Law).	Lloyd George Liberals. Asquith Liberals.	LABOUR

TASK

1 Work chronologically through each of the three parties between 1914 and 1922, identifying their relationship to the government of the time.

2 Can you suggest reasons for the party political shifts during this period?

3 Compare each party's standing in 1914 with that in 1922. In what ways has this period advantaged or disadvantaged the Liberal, Labour and Conservative Parties?

6 Conservative Party Dominance

PREVIEW

Conservative Governments, 1922–29

STANLEY BALDWIN SURROUNDED BY BROADCASTING CREW.

TALKING POINT

How did politicians communicate with the public before the arrival of radio?
Why do you think Baldwin considered the radio a potent political tool in the 1920s?
The media is used extensively by politicians nowadays. What do you consider the advantages and disadvantages of this?

RADIO TIMES COVER, 1923.

A timeline of three-party politics, 1922–29

1922

OCT.	Lloyd George coalition government. Conservatives voted to end coalition. Lloyd George resigned. Bonar Law – Conservative leader became Prime Minister.
15 NOV.	GENERAL ELECTION – CONSERVATIVE GOVERNMENT ELECTED

1923

MAY	Bonar Law resigned. Baldwin became Prime Minister Baldwin revived the policy of protection.
6 DEC.	GENERAL ELECTION – LABOUR MINORITY GOVERNMENT ELECTED

1924

SEPT.	Campbell case led to government resignation
29 OCT.	GENERAL ELECTION – CONSERVATIVE GOVERNMENT ELECTED Baldwin became Prime Minister

1925

Contributory old age pensions introduced
Locarno Treaty negotiated
Britain returned to the Gold Standard
Subsidy to maintain wage levels of miners

1926

Central Electricity Board and British Broadcasting Corporation set up.

4–12 MAY	General Strike

1927

Trade Disputes Act

1928

Representation of the People Act

1929

Local Government Act

30 MAY	GENERAL ELECTION – LABOUR MINORITY GOVERNMENT ELECTED

General Election 15 November 1922

Conservatives:	5,319,664 votes = 37% of total votes = 330 seats.	

Independent Coalitionist

Conservatives: 222,410 votes = 1.5% of total votes = 13 seats

Labour: 4,237,769 votes = 29.4% of total votes = 142 seats.

Lloyd George

Liberals: 1,320,935 votes = 9.2% of total vote = 47 seats.

Asquithian Liberals: 2,098,732 votes = 14.6% of total votes = 41 seats.

Other ('prefixless')

Liberals: 763,315 = 5.3% of total votes = 28 seats.

General Election 6 December 1923

Conservatives: 5,538,824 votes = 38.1% of total votes = 258 seats.

Labour: 4,438,508 votes = 30.5% of total votes = 191 seats.

Liberals: 4,311,147 votes = 29.6% of total votes = 159 seats.

General Election 29 October 1924

Conservatives: 8,039,598 votes = 48.3% of total votes = 419 seats.

Labour: 5,489,077 votes = 33.0% of total votes = 151 seats.

Liberals: 2,928,747 = 17.6% of total votes = 40 seats.

TASK

1 Explain why there are so many political parties in the 1922 election results.

2

a Outline the success/failure of the Liberal and Labour Parties over these four general elections.

b What is the significance of this period for both parties?

3 For each party forming a government after each of these elections, compare the number of seats they gained to their percentage of total votes cast. What conclusions do you draw from this?

4 From these election results, can you draw any conclusions as to why the Conservative Party dominated this period?

General Election 30 May 1929

Conservatives: 8,656,473 votes = 38.2% of total votes = 260 seats.

Labour: 8,389,512 votes = 37.1% of total votes = 288 seats.

Liberals: 5,308,510 = 23.4% of total votes = 59 seats.

Conservative government, 1922–23

Thirteen months and two prime ministers – why was this administration so short-lived?

The General Election of November 1922 was a clear victory for the Conservatives with a total of 330 seats. However, the following reasons can be argued for this government being so short-lived:

1 The election was an illustration of the disarray in party politics by 1922, with both Conservatives and Liberal ranks divided and the Labour Party more than doubled from 63 seats in 1918 to 142 in 1922, complicating a traditional two-party system as a third force.

2 The main issues at the election tended to be unclear, yet the role of the leading personalities was central. Historian A.J.P. Taylor suggests that 'the General Election of 1918 had been a plebiscite in favour of Lloyd George. The General Election of 1922 was a plebiscite against him.' The electorate seemed to be offered a choice between Lloyd George – a dynamic but tarnished figure – or Bonar Law, the Conservative leader, who offered 'tranquillity and stability both at home and abroad'. The opinion of the country in turn seemed undecided – a fact which is illustrated by the fact that each of the major parties won roughly one third of the total votes cast – if the individual Liberal factions are counted as one group. However, under the 'first-past-the-post' system of voting in Britain, the Conservatives won an overall majority of 77 seats and Bonar Law formed a new administration.

3 Churchill referred to Bonar Law's new cabinet as a 'government of the 2nd XI'. Although there were many capable ministers in the new administration, such as Neville Chamberlain (Ministry of Health) and Stanley Baldwin (Chancellor), the new Cabinet was largely unfamiliar to the public. The only minister of established reputation was Lord Curzon, who was appointed to the Foreign Office. Furthermore, the 16-man Cabinet contained seven peers, making it the most aristocratic of the century.

TALKING POINT

What authority does the prime minister in Britain have?

Do you think that the prime minister should be 'first among equals' – or should he or she adopt a more executive role in the Cabinet?

4 The leading lights of the Party – Austen Chamberlain, Balfour and Birkenhead – had rejected the Carlton Club decision and so as Independent Coalitionist Conservatives were not eligible to join Law's Cabinet.

5 The government made a constructive start in two areas: housing and foreign affairs.

At the Ministry of Health, Neville Chamberlain introduced a Housing Act which was intended to tackle the major problem of housing but also to encourage private enterprise. The government awarded a subsidy of £6 per annum for every house built for the next 20 years. The subsidy was to be available for both private and public builders so they would offer new houses for sale. However, this tended to benefit the lower middle classes rather than the working class – a discrimination which caused some resentment.

6 At the Foreign Office, Curzon successfully replaced the Treaty of Lausanne – hated by the Turks – by the Treaty of Sèvres. Relations with France, however, deteriorated due to their invasion of the Ruhr causing tension and resentment in the new German Weimar Republic. A major issue of war debts owed to the USA was dealt with and problems overcome albeit with an agreement unfavourable to Britain to pay back the debt over 62 years.

7 Bonar Law's serious decline in health – he was suffering from throat cancer – forced him to resign in May 1923. He refused to nominate a successor and no process existed to deal with this eventuality. It was left to King George V to appoint the new Prime Minister.

LORD CURZON, FOREIGN SECRETARY BUT DENIED THE POSITION OF PRIME MINISTER.

8 The King's choice was Stanley Baldwin – a surprising one, particularly for Curzon who quite expected to inherit the highest office. He was foreign secretary, had been a member of Lloyd George's war cabinet and Viceroy of India. He was a brilliant intellectual and a hardworking minister. It was perhaps his arrogance and the fact that he sat in the House of Lords which led to him being sidelined in favour of the more modest Stanley Baldwin. Privately, Curzon had called Baldwin 'a person of the utmost insignificance', yet A.J.P. Taylor considers this perhaps to have been Baldwin's greatest strength. Modest, well-balanced and honest, and widely admired in the House of Commons, he came to be seen as the embodiment of respectable postwar Conservatism. He presented himself as a simple country gentleman – a luxury afforded by his wealthy family business in iron. He was genuinely concerned with social issues and tried to establish patriarchal relations between workers and their bosses. Well-meaning, steady and conciliatory, Baldwin seemed to reflect the mood of the country after the horrors of war and the exuberance of Lloyd George.

9 The question in the Conservative Party over whether to adopt a Protectionist or Free Trade economic policy had been highly damaging (see Chapter 1). It had caused deep party rifts and lost the Conservatives the election of 1906, yet the issue had been postponed rather than solved. In October 1923 Baldwin – despite the divisive nature of the issue – declared Protection should be a government policy to be given a mandate at a General Election as Bonar Law had pledged in 1922. Why did Baldwin call for Protection?

Reasons:

a By protecting home industry, this was a policy to fight unemployment.

b If social problems were solved, class confrontation could be avoided and the capitalist economy would be reinforced.

c Baldwin, as an iron manufacturer himself, saw trade from the perspective of the home market selling more if foreign imports were curbed, but he did not fully appreciate the problem of exporters who might be faced by tariffs in other countries.

d It was a political tactic to reunite breakaway Conservatives before Lloyd George, who was thought to be moving towards Protection himself, could gain their support more permanently. This was referred to as Baldwin 'dishing the goat' – the Welsh 'goat' being Lloyd George.

10 The General Election in December 1923 was fought over the issue of Protection. Free Trade was taken up again by the Liberals who reunited behind Asquith. It also saw many Free Trade Conservatives – especially in Lancashire – emerge to lose the government vital support.

TASK

1 Read the listed reasons carefully and then categorise them under the following headings:
Political Context
Personalities
Policies.

2 To what extent was Balfour's adoption of Protection the main reason for the Conservative Party defeat in 1923?

A Labour minority government, dependent on the support of the Liberals, was formed under Ramsay MacDonald. This first Labour administration will be dealt with in Chapter 7. Baldwin, although having lost the election, had managed to reunite the Conservative Party in 1923. However, in 1924 he brought an end to Protection and, with the adoption by the Conservatives of a Free Trade policy, routed the Liberal Party.

Conservative government, 1924–29

Ramsay MacDonald, the Labour Party Prime Minister, was forced to call a general election in October 1924 when the Liberal Party withdrew their support in an anti-Socialist panic (see Chapter 7). His government, the first Labour administration in Britain, had set a remarkable precedent yet had been a minority administration, weak and totally dependent on the Liberals. It lasted less than a year and in the 1924 General Election the Conservatives won a resounding victory with 419 seats. This Conservative administration served nearly a full term of five years, achieved some successes in foreign and domestic policy, yet is most well known for its handling of Britain's only General Strike in May 1926.

Baldwin was lucky in many respects that he maintained the leadership of the Conservatives after their election defeat over Protection in December 1923. The Tories considered it too risky to change leaders given the likelihood of a Labour defeat in the short term. At 56 years of age, Baldwin's position was secured and he put forward a New Conservatism based around ideas of efficiency and moral purpose. The government's strong position was consolidated by the coalition Tories having returned to the fold – Austen Chamberlain was made Foreign Secretary. Winston Churchill, having crossed the House from the Liberals, became Chancellor of the Exchequer and stood for Free Trade. The Liberals were a spent force and Labour well and truly divided and defeated in the 'Red Scare' over the Zinoviev Letter.

WELFARE

- Legislation resulted from combined efforts of Neville Chamberlain (Health) and Winston Churchill (Exchequer)

- 1925 Contributory Old Age Pension introduced.
  In return for higher national insurance contributions, workers and wives received a pension – 10s per week at age 65 years. Widows' pensions were also introduced.

- 1925 Unemployment Insurance. Benefit could be claimed not just for two 16-week periods but indefinitely providing the worker was 'genuinely seeking work'.

LOCAL GOVERNMENT

- 1929 Local Government Act

  Awarded local authorities extra duties concerning roads, public health, maternity and childcare.

  Agricultural land, railways and industry were de-rated and government made good the loss in local government income.

  Local government was made more active but dependent on government for grants so they lost a degree of independence.

Briand   Chamberlain   Stresemann
CLASP OF RECONCILIATION

FOREIGN RELATIONS

- 1925 Austen Chamberlain signed the Locarno Treaty with Stresemann of Germany and Briand of France. This guaranteed the German border with France and Belgium. These three leaders won the Nobel Peace Prize.

- 1926 Germany joined the League of Nations – a spirit of co-operation was prevalent yet many problems remained unresolved.

FEMALE FRANCHISE

● 1928 Representation of the People Act

  Gave votes to all women aged 21 and over.

  Male and female franchise was now equal.

  Electorate increased from 22 to 29 million and there were approximately two million more women voters than men.

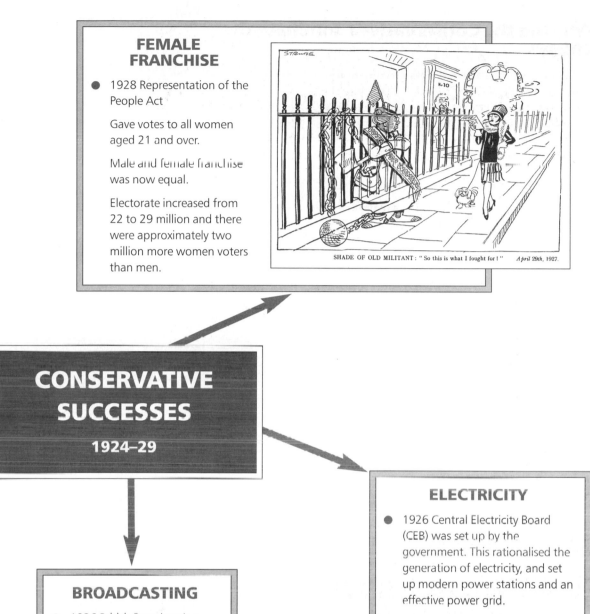

SHADE OF OLD MILITANT : " So this is what I fought for ! "   *April 29th*, 1927.

CONSERVATIVE SUCCESSES
1924–29

ELECTRICITY

● 1926 Central Electricity Board (CEB) was set up by the government. This rationalised the generation of electricity, and set up modern power stations and an effective power grid.

BROADCASTING

● 1926 British Broadcasting Corporation (BBC) was set up to replace the British Broadcasting Company which had since 1922 held the license for radio broadcasts in private hands. The BBC showed a recognition by the Conservative government of the value of public enterprise.

TASK

Devise political slogans which
a recognise Conservative achievement
b criticise its limitations.

Why did the Conservatives dominate the 1920s?

The Conservative Party were the dominant force in the 1920s – and indeed continued to be so up until the outbreak of the Second World War in 1939. Conservative influence was strong in Lloyd George's coalition from 1918–22. In 1922 they broke away from the Liberals and formed the government of Britain up until October 1929 with the exception of a brief interlude of Labour government in 1924. Nearly ten years of Conservative rule in 1920s requires an explanation.

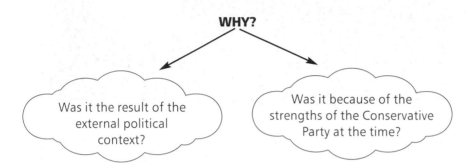

WHY?

Was it the result of the external political context?

Was it because of the strengths of the Conservative Party at the time?

Five main reasons:

1	The impact of the First World War.
2	Division of the Conservatives' opposition.
3	The social basis of Conservative support.
4	Conservative Party organisation.
5	Importance of Baldwin as prime minister.

Reason 1 – The Impact of the First World War

- The war focused attention on issues which favoured the Conservatives:
  – conscription, which wrought havoc among the Liberals
  – patriotism
  – strong defence of Britain and her Empire
- The War altered the political situation. It split the Liberal Party, advantaged the new Labour Party and brought the Conservatives into both Asquith and Lloyd George's coalitions for which they gained credit.
- 1918 electoral reform extended the franchise to men over 21 and women over 30. Many new male voters were susceptible to the Conservative appeal and women voters gave the largest share of their votes in the inter-war years to the Conservative Party.

A MOTHER VOTES FOR THE FIRST TIME.

- The redistribution of seats favoured the Conservatives by dividing many of the suburban, pro Conservative areas into two or more constituencies. Meanwhile some Liberal seats with small electorates in the West and Scotland disappeared.
- Plural voting remained, benefiting the Conservatives.
- The Irish representation in Parliament changed – no longer providing support for the Liberals. Sinn Fein refused to sit in 1918 and after 1922 only Northern Ireland was represented by Ulster Unionists who counted as Conservatives.

WHY?

Reason 2 – Division of the Opposition

- Neither the Liberal nor Labour Party were strong enough to present a viable alternative to the Conservative government.
- In certain constituencies the existence of both Liberal and Labour candidates split the left of centre vote which benefited the Conservatives.
- The Liberal Party, having split into warring factions behind Asquith and Lloyd George, continued to decline rapidly in the 1920s – despite reuniting for the election of 1923 and after. The Liberals' traditional Free Trade policy was espoused by Conservatives after June 1924. The party ran fewer candidates in 1924 than 1923. Constituency organisation was dissolving and in 1924 they lost 100 seats to the Conservatives. Asquith was defeated, leaving only 40 Liberals in the Commons uncomfortably led by Lloyd George.
- The Labour Party was growing significantly yet still not confirmed as a contender in the two-party system. Both governments of 1924 and 1929 were minorities and easily divided in the face of major issues.
- There was a surprising similarity of stance between the Conservative and Labour Party. Both agreed on the reduction of arms expenditure, international peace and security, public ownership of BBC and CEB and welfare reforms.

WHY?

- The Conservative Party drew support from a wide social spectrum. As it had done in the late 19th century support came from landowners, industrialists, middle and working class.
- Upper- and middle-class supporters gave the party both local and national prestige, public services and leadership. This broad support provided finance, favourable press coverage and good platform speakers.
- Lower middle-class support was vital, particularly within the local constituency associations. Men, women and young conservatives were involved in organisation, social events and voluntary work at election time.
- A significant number of the working class supported the Conservative Party. Between 1918 and 1940 the popular vote for the Labour Party was never greater than for the Conservatives. Working-class Conservatism varied from area to area but its broad appeal was based upon national unity, patriotism, King and empire, self-reliance and an independent enterprising spirit.
- Conservative policies appealed across class barriers. They were attractive for their moderate, constructive approach which contrasted favourably with the radicalism of both Labour and Liberals.

WHY?

Working-class Conservatism in Birmingham in the 1920s

A local study – What the historian says:

Approximately 70% of Birmingham's population was working-class yet at its peak in the late 1920s the Labour Party held just one third of the seats on the City Council and it won only 8% of the city's parliamentary elections in the interwar period. Birmingham was justly known as the 'Mecca of Unionism'.

For many, this phenomenon is explained easily by the Chamberlain Tradition. Joseph Chamberlain had made his name as a radical Liberal Lord Mayor of Birmingham before becoming one of the city's two MPs in 1876. However, in 1886 Chamberlain led the Liberal Unionist revolt against Gladstone's proposals for Irish Home Rule. Thereafter, he gradually converged with the Conservative Party around a distinctive platform of imperialism and social reform. Critically, for Birmingham politics, Chamberlain carried the local electorate with him. Even in 1906, the year of Liberal landslide, every one of Birmingham's MPs was a Unionist. Chamberlain himself suffered a stroke at the peak of this local triumph and died in 1914 but his legacy was perpetuated into the interwar period by his two sons, Austen and Neville, who both represented working-class constituencies in the city.

For many unsympathetic observers, the appeal of what may be called 'Chamberlainism' lay in a rather naïve and irrational hero-worship of an undoubtedly charismatic and skilled politician. But it is important to stress the extent to which Birmingham Unionism was a genuinely distinct and

The term 'Mecca of Unionism' refers to the prominence in the city of Birmingham of the Conservative and Unionist Association.

creative force. The 'Civil Gospel' of civic service and municipal initiative first expressed in 1850s lived on in a range of local government enterprise probably unequalled in the country in the 1920s and 1930s. Municipal baths, hospitals and health centres, more council housing per head of population than any other city, a unique Municipal Bank (founded by Neville Chamberlain) – all testify to the vitality and confidence of Birmingaham Unionism's reforming traditions…

Particular to Birmingham was the peculiar nature of the local economy. The city was renowned for its economic diversity (it was known at the time as the 'City of a Thousand Trades') and as a centre of small-scale industry (there were some 12,000 small workshops each employing under 100 workers). In this context, relations with employers tended to be close and trades unionism weak. There was, therefore, little independent working-class organisation and a weak sense of shared class consciousness.

Moreover, amongst the poorest, there was typically a fatalistic working-class mentality predicated on 'survival' with little time for 'unproductive' ideas of self-improvement or social change. This attitude was reinforced by a lack of education in Birmingham in particular, by the major institutional and ideological pillars of the local community; the pub (itself a significant target of Unionist propaganda), a strong sense of civic identity (stressed within the Chamberlain Tradition), and patriotism (exploited shamelessly by Unionism for party ends) which combined to foster an ostensibly apolitical but strongly conservative culture. In this context, Labour reformers might be as much outsiders as upper-class Unionists and, in some ways, more unwelcome as they could appear critical of the slum community and threatening of change whereas Unionists appeared to endorse local values and the status quo…

The lubricant of slum Conservatism was deference and in this context, Birmingham was, in every sense, a well oiled machine. Birmingham Unionism consciously strove to promote and perpetuate deferential attitudes amongst the working class. Central to this project was the use of charity. The notebooks of Annie Chamberlain (Neville's wife) record small gifts of flowers, food and money given to over 600 of this constituents. Smedley Crooke, MP for the 'inner ring' constituency of Deritend in the 1920s, gave half his parliamentary salary to local good works.

There was also an influential but necessarily less formal system of patronage and treating. The constituency papers of Sir Arthur Steel-Maitland, MP for Birmingham Erdington, offer a fascinating insight into this world as one tracks the anxious correspondence between MP and constituency agents calculating the political value of many requests for support: the Nechells Tug of War team, for example, was deemed worthy of 18 medals and a shield but the area's Angling Club, which Steel-Maitland was assured had only a few members, received just one guinea. Steel-Maitland himself bore the cost of 604 teas at the Westminster Lyons Tea House when his constituency party visited Parliament. Rounds of drinks at the local Unionist Working Men's Cubs were another necessary expense: as one local activist commented, 'the glass of ale still holds good for many here'…

It was the most efficient political machine in the country. The Birmingham Unionist Association enjoyed an annual income of £10,000 (at a time when the local Labour Party generally received about £750 per annum). In addition the city's Unionist MPs were expected to spend around £500 a year on their constituency parties. The Unionist Association had around 20,000 paid up members and around 15,000 in a separate women's organisation at a time when Birmingham Labour boasted just 6,500 members. All this was reinforced by a fiercely partisan local press kept in line by Neville Chamberlain. The size and range of Unionist organisation strenghtened the Party's hegemony and made it appear in local terms "the natural party of government"."

Extract from an article published in *The Historian*, no. 59, Autumn 1998 entitled 'Working Class Conservatism and the rise of Labour: A Case Study of Birmingham in 1920s' written by Dr. J. F. Boughton based on research carried out for his PhD thesis 'Working Class Politics in Birmingham and Sheffield 1918–31' (University of Warwick).

1 What is surprising when you consider Birmingham's population and voting preference in the 1920s?
2 List the main reasons given for Conservative dominance in Birmingham at this time.
3 To what extent are these Birmingham factors similar to those set out on page 126?
4 What are the strengths and limitations of this local study to a historian studying Conservatism in Britain in the 1920s?

Reason 4 – Conservative Party Organisation

- From Conservative Central Office in London to the many local Conservative associations, the party enjoyed the benefits of an effective national organisation which operated successfully in all types of constituency.
- It had greater finances than any other party.
- Candidates stood in almost every seat during this period. Those in poorer areas were helped by central funds.
- Local associations produced leaflets, posters and various publications. They organised a multitude of fundraising events. The party employed a full-time professional agent in most major constituencies.
- Many women were involved in party activities – organising bazaars, fetes and whist drives. By the end of the 1920s there were over one million women in the Conservative Party.

WHY?

Reason 5 – The Importance of Baldwin as Prime Minister

- Contemporary commentators were critical. Sir Oswald Mosley referred to Baldwin as 'a yawn who represented England asleep'. He was dubbed 'Honest Stan' – comfortable, steady and lacking appeal.
- However, the historian and Lord Blake suggested, in *The Conservative Party from Peel to Thatcher*, that 'Baldwin represented with singular accuracy the mood of a nation wearied by the suffering of war and its aftermath. He was peace loving at a time when Britain … dreaded the prospect of war. He was easy-going at a time when his fellow countrymen wanted nothing so much as to be left alone. To the public he seemed to embody the English spirit and his speeches to sound the authentic note of that English character which they so much admired'.
- Baldwin's policies did nothing to alarm or alienate either the middle or working class.
- He portrayed an image of moderation, tranquility and calm. This was particularly clear in his handling of the General Strike (see later sections of this chapter).
- He made effective use of modern media – such as radio broadcasts and cinema newsreels.
- Baldwin succeeded in uniting the Conservatives between 1922 and 1924.

WHY?

Tasks

1 Divide the class into five groups. Each group should research further one of the reasons for Conservative dominance and prepare a class presentation to illustrate the validity of their argument.
2 Each group should also list arguments against the other reasons for Conservative dominance.
3 Divide the five reasons into factors which are external or internal to the Conservative Party in the 1920s.
4 After a class discussion covering both arguments for and against each reason, each student should list the factors in order of importance explaining the priority they have selected.

Focus

6.1 The General Strike, 3–12 May 1926

The only General Strike in British history began in the early hours of Tuesday 3 May 1926 and lasted just nine days, being called off at noon on 12 May. It was industrial action taken by the miners demanding a reorganisation of the industry, increased wages and shorter hours. They were supported by the co-ordinated action of the TUC and all workers called upon went on strike – approximately two million. For these nine days, the country was divided into two camps – those on strike and those manning the essential services. It was viewed differently depending on an individual's standpoint. For many, it was an open conflict between bosses and workers, authority and idealism. For others, it was a conflict between the power of democratic government and organised labour. The General Strike was conducted much good humour and restraint, but there was some sporadic violence and disorder. The strike ended when the TUC withdrew its support for the miners. They were underprepared and misrepresented by government as attacking the Constitution. The Conservative government had the edge on the propaganda war with its control of the media – their *British Gazette* newspaper, published by Winston Churchill and its Organisation for the Maintenance of Supplies limited the public's inconvenience. As for the miners, they remained locked out until September 1926 when they were forced to accept the owners' terms.

STRIKERS DEMONSTRATE DURING GENERAL STRIKE, 1926.

TALKING POINT

Why do you think thousands of workers were prepared to come out on strike in sympathy with the miners?

Causes of the General Strike

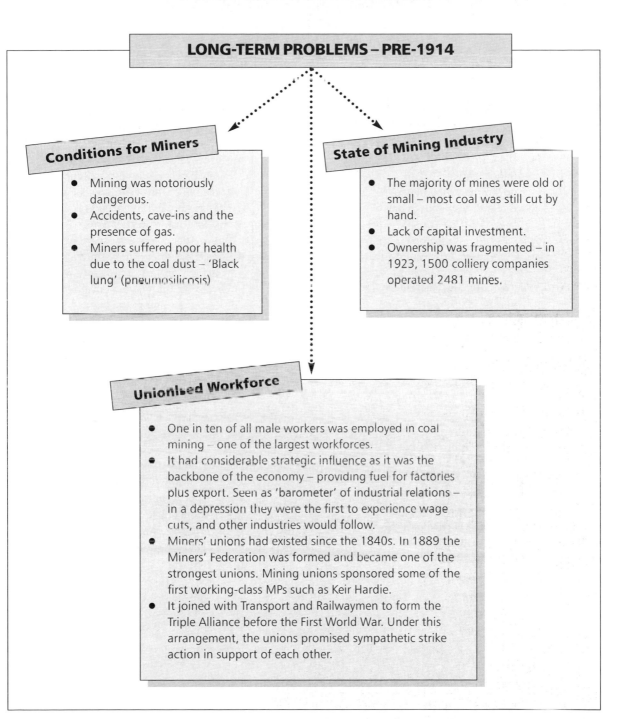

LONG-TERM PROBLEMS – PRE-1914

Conditions for Miners

- Mining was notoriously dangerous.
- Accidents, cave-ins and the presence of gas.
- Miners suffered poor health due to the coal dust – 'Black lung' (pneumosilicosis)

State of Mining Industry

- The majority of mines were old or small – most coal was still cut by hand.
- Lack of capital investment.
- Ownership was fragmented – in 1923, 1500 colliery companies operated 2481 mines.

Unionised Workforce

- One in ten of all male workers was employed in coal mining – one of the largest workforces.
- It had considerable strategic influence as it was the backbone of the economy – providing fuel for factories plus export. Seen as 'barometer' of industrial relations – in a depression they were the first to experience wage cuts, and other industries would follow.
- Miners' unions had existed since the 1840s. In 1889 the Miners' Federation was formed and became one of the strongest unions. Mining unions sponsored some of the first working-class MPs such as Keir Hardie.
- It joined with Transport and Railwaymen to form the Triple Alliance before the First World War. Under this arrangement, the unions promised sympathetic strike action in support of each other.

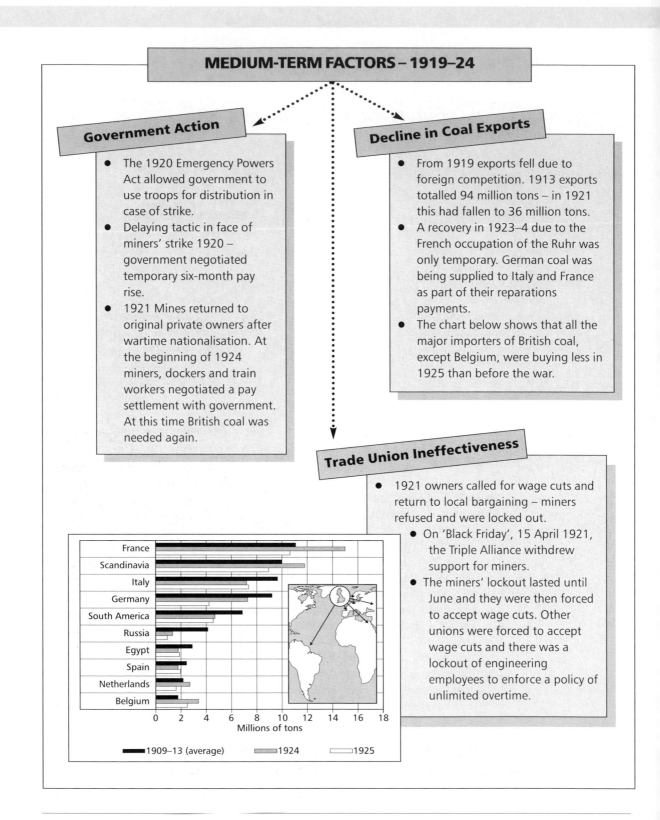

MEDIUM-TERM FACTORS – 1919–24

Government Action

- The 1920 Emergency Powers Act allowed government to use troops for distribution in case of strike.
- Delaying tactic in face of miners' strike 1920 – government negotiated temporary six-month pay rise.
- 1921 Mines returned to original private owners after wartime nationalisation. At the beginning of 1924 miners, dockers and train workers negotiated a pay settlement with government. At this time British coal was needed again.

Decline in Coal Exports

- From 1919 exports fell due to foreign competition. 1913 exports totalled 94 million tons – in 1921 this had fallen to 36 million tons.
- A recovery in 1923–4 due to the French occupation of the Ruhr was only temporary. German coal was being supplied to Italy and France as part of their reparations payments.
- The chart below shows that all the major importers of British coal, except Belgium, were buying less in 1925 than before the war.

Trade Union Ineffectiveness

- 1921 owners called for wage cuts and return to local bargaining – miners refused and were locked out.
  - On 'Black Friday', 15 April 1921, the Triple Alliance withdrew support for miners.
  - The miners' lockout lasted until June and they were then forced to accept wage cuts. Other unions were forced to accept wage cuts and there was a lockout of engineering employees to enforce a policy of unlimited overtime.

Millions of tons

France, Scandinavia, Italy, Germany, South America, Russia, Egypt, Spain, Netherlands, Belgium

0 2 4 6 8 10 12 14 16 18

■ 1909–13 (average)   ▨ 1924   ▢ 1925

SHORT-TERM PRESSURES

Return to the Gold Standard

- April 1925 Chancellor of Exchequer Churchill decided to put Britain back on the Gold Standard.
- This backing of currency with gold was associated with prewar prosperity so Churchill wished to return to this.
- The value of sterling was set at $4.86 – making the pound at least 10 per cent overvalued. Britain exports became overpriced and uncompetitive. Mine owners announced wage reductions and longer working days.

France leaves the Ruhr 1924

- Once the French occupation of the Ruhr and Germany's policy of passive resistance had come to an end – coal from the Ruhr came back on the market providing more competition for British coal.

TUC Support

- Summer 1925 the TUC promised support for the miners.

Government action to advert crisis fails

- Despite right-wing pressure to stand aside as a general strike looked certain to break out at the end of 1925, Baldwin gave a subsidy to maintain existing wage levels whilst Royal Commission investigated.
- The Samuel Report (March 1926) recommended a. re-organisation of coal industry – eventual nationalisation. b. better working conditions. c. wage reductions to make mines profitable.

... FINALLY

Compromise report was not accepted by owners nor unions. Coal owners put up lock out notices. TUC called for sympathetic strike action. Last minute government negotiation broke down.

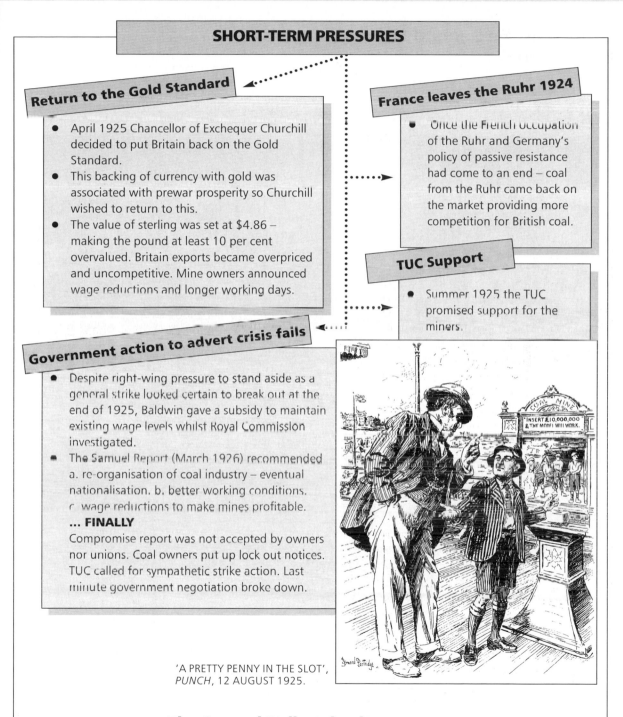

'A PRETTY PENNY IN THE SLOT', *PUNCH*, 12 AUGUST 1925.

The General Strike takes its course ...
TUESDAY 3rd MAY – THURSDAY 12th MAY 1926

Examining the Evidence

How was the General Strike viewed at the time?

Source A

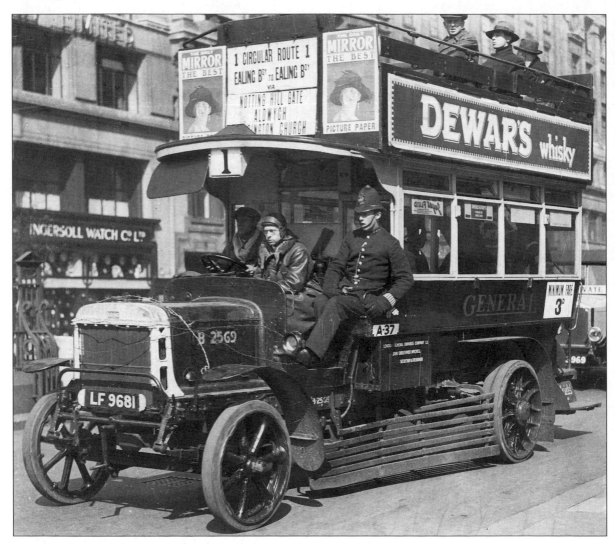

A POLICE OFFICER ACCOMPANIES A LONDON BUS DURING THE GENERAL STRIKE.

Source B

MESSAGE FROM THE PRIME MINISTER

Constitutional government is being attacked

Let all good citizens whose livelihood and labour have thus been put in peril bear with fortitude and patience the hardships with which they have been so suddenly confronted.

Stand behind the government who are doing their part confident that you will co-operate in the measures they have undertaken to preserve the liberties and privileges of the people of these islands. The laws of England are the peoples' birthright. The laws are in your keeping. You have made Parliament their guardian. The General Strike is a challenge to Parliament and is the road to anarchy and ruin.

STANLEY BALDWIN

The strike is intended as a direct hold-up of the nation to ransom … 'This moment', as the Prime Minister pointed out in the House of Commons, 'has been chosen to challenge the existing Constitution of the country and to substitute the reign of force that which now exists … I do not believe there has been anything like a thorough-going consultation with the rank and file before this despotic power was put in the hands of a small executive in London … I do not think all the leaders who assented to order a general strike fully realised that they were threatening the basis of ordered government and coming nearer to proclaiming civil war than we have been for centuries past.'

British Gazette, 6 May 1926.

Source C

FOR KING AND COUNTRY

The miners, after weeks of negotiation, have declined the proposals made to them, and the coal mines of Britain are idle.

The Council of the Trade Union Congress, which represents all the other Trade Unions, has determined to support the miners by going to the extreme of ordering a general strike.

The determination alters the whole position. The coal industry, which might have been reorganised with goodwill on both sides, seeing that some give and some take, is plainly needed to restore it to prosperity has now become the subject of a great political struggle, which the nation has no choice but to face with the utmost coolness and the utmost firmness.

We do not wish to say anything hard about the miners themselves, As to their leaders, all we need to say at this moment is that some of them are (and have openly declared themselves) under the influence of people who mean no good to this country.

The General Strike is not an industrial dispute; it is a revolutionary movement, intended to inflict suffering upon the great mass of innocent persons in the community and thereby put forcible constraints upon the Government. It is a movement that can only succeed by destroying the Government and subverting the rights and liberties of the people. This being the case it cannot be tolerated by any civilised government and must be dealt with by every resource at the disposal of the community. A state of emergency and national danger has been proclaimed to resist attack. We call upon all law-abiding men and women to hold themselves at the service of King and Country.'

Scott Nearing, *The British General Strike* (1926).

Source D

UNDER WHICH FLAG?

John Bull. ' ONE OF THESE TWO FLAGS HAS GOT TO COME DOWN—AND IT WON'T BE MINE.''

'UNDER WHICH FLAG?', *PUNCH*, 12 MAY 1926.

Source E

In answer to the "British Gazette"

UNDER WHICH FLAG?

'UNDER WHICH FLAG?', *LABOUR WEEKLY*, 22 MAY 1926.

Source F

The trade unions are fighting in defence of the mine-workers. The responsibility for the national crisis lies with the Government. With the people the trade unions have no quarrel. On the contrary, the unions are fighting to maintain the standard of life of the great mass of the people.

The trade unions have not entered upon this struggle without counting the cost. They are assured that the trade unionists of the country, realising the justice of the cause they are called upon to support, will stand loyally by their elected leaders until the victory and an honourable peace has been won.

The need is now for loyalty, steadfastness and unity.

The General Council of the Trade Union Congress appeals to the workers to follow the instructions that have been issued by their union leaders. Let none be disturbed by rumours or be driven by panic to betray the cause. Violence and disorder must everywhere be avoided no matter what the incitement. Stand firm and we shall win.

Report in the *Daily Herald*, 4 May 1926.

Source G

It is fantastic for the Prime Minister to pretend that the trade unions are engaged in an attack upon the Constitution of their country. Every instruction issued by the General Council is evidence of their determination to maintain the struggle strictly on the basis of an industrial dispute. They have ordered every member taking part to be exemplary in his conduct and not to give any cause for police interference. The General Council struggled hard for peace. They are anxious that an honourable peace shall be secured as soon as possible. They are not attacking the Constitution. They are not fighting the community. They are defending the mine-workers against the mine-owners.

British Worker, 7 May 1926.

---

1 According to Sources B and C, what is the main purpose of the General Strike?
2 What messages are conveyed by the cartoons in Sources D and E?
3 According to Sources F and G, why has a General Strike been called?
4 How useful are Sources A–G for a historian studying contemporary attitudes to the General Strike?
5 From your own research and using these sources, to what extent do you think the General Strike was a political tool to undermine the British government or simply a means to improve conditions for the miners?

Consequences of the General Strike

Failure to achieve aims

On 12 May 1926 the TUC General Council accepted a compromise solution based upon a discussion document to which the miners were not party. If the purpose of the strike was to bring the country to a standstill it failed. Similarly, the miners did not gain their demands over wages, hours and nationalisation of the coal industry.

Immediate repercussions for strikers

On their return to work many strikers found themselves forced to sign settlements accepting broken contracts for going on strike. There were some cases of demotion and loss of wages. Other strikers found they would only be reinstated if there was work for them, some jobs had been filled by volunteers.

Damage to the trades union movement

In 1927 trades union membership fell below five million for the first time since 1916 and it did not fully recover this lost ground for many years. Numbers affiliated to the TUC. fell more steeply. The strike had drained funds from $£12\frac{1}{2}$ million to $£8\frac{1}{2}$ million in a year. Many unions owed debts to their friendly funds. The strike cost both the NUR and the TGWU over £1 million each. Unions were in no position to support strikes. In the four years before 1926, between 400,000 and 600,000 workers were involved in strikes each year. In 1927 and 1928 the comparable figures were a little over 100,000.

The 1927 Trade Disputes Act

1 Outlawed sympathy strikes, thus making any further general strikes illegal.
2 Restricted picketing.
3 Allowed for the sequestration of union funds in times of dispute.
4 Reinstated the principle of 'contracting-in' for the payment of the political levy to the Labour Party.

Effect on the Conservative Government

Although the government was considered by many to have handled the General Strike very effectively, the trades union legislation introduced in 1927 embittered many workers. It caused much hatred of Baldwin and the government among organised labour and contributed to the Conservative defeat in the 1929 General Election.

REVIEW

Stanley Baldwin – A biographical assessment to 1929

Robert Blake, the historian of the Conservative Party, writes:

> At the beginning of the decade no one could have predicted that the worthy and unremarkable Stanley Baldwin would become leader of the Conservative Party – far less that he was to become for millions of Britons the personification of the country and civilisation they believed in.

Why did Baldwin survive as prime minister for so long?

TASK

1 Research and make notes on Baldwin's background, character and early years from other books in your library.
2 Re-read this chapter carefully – considering Baldwin's role in these two Conservative governments.
3 Compile evidence to support the following aspects of Baldwin's career to draw up an assessment of his success in surviving so long.
    a Luck
    b Political skill
    c Personality
    d Successes
    e Failures
    f Alternatives.

7 Labour Governments in the 1920s

PREVIEW

Labour form their first government

Nearly twenty-four years after its formation in 1900, the Labour Party formed a first minority government with the support of the Liberals. Ramsay MacDonald had only resumed the leadership of the Labour Party in 1922 and was somewhat taken by surprise when Baldwin unexpectedly called a General Election over Tariff Reform in December 1923.

Source A

'GREET THE DAWN', LABOUR ELECTION POSTER 1923.

GREET THE DAWN:
GIVE LABOUR ITS CHANCE

1923 Election Results

Conservatives	258 seats
Labour	191 seats
Liberals (reunited)	158 seats

Source B

On Wednesday the twenty Ministers designate, in their best suits … went to Buckingham Palace to be sworn in; having been previously drilled by [Cabinet Secretary] Hankey. Four of them came back to our weekly MPs lunch … they were all laughing over Wheatley – the revolutionary – going down on both his knees and actually kissing His Majesty's hand; and C.P. Trevelyan was remarking that the King seemed quite incapable of saying two words to his new Ministers; 'he went through the ceremony like an automaton!'

TASKS

1 What appeal is being made in this poster?

2 Explain why Labour formed a government when the Conservatives were the largest party.

3 What impressions do you gain about Labour's first days in power from Beatrice Webb?

'S.' in the extract refers to Beatrice Webb's husband, Sidney. Sidney Webb (later Lord Passfield) served as President of the Board of Trade in Labour's first administration.

Meanwhile I am living a distracted life which does not please me. I have taken over S.'s unofficial correspondence and dictated forty letters in twice as many minutes. What is far more troublesome is acting as the 'Doyenne' amongst Ministers' wives, in the organisation of their social intercourse within the Party and with outsiders like the Court. Just at present there are two questions – clothes and curtseys. A sort of underground communication is going on between Grosvenor Road and Buckingham Palace which is at once comic and tiresome.

Beatrice Webb, diary, 19 January 1924 (in Margaret Cole (ed.), *Beatrice Webb's Diaries*, *1924–1932* (1956), pp. 1–3).

Labour's first administration, January–October 1924

'A weak short-lived government beset with problems' – Is this the only possible verdict on this government?

Problems v. Policies

DEPENDENCY ON THE LIBERALS
MacDonald's government had only 191 seats – insufficient to defeat the Tories. They were dependent upon the Liberals for survival. This limited their ability to introduce any radical domestic legislation.

CABINET
MacDonald was both Prime Minister and Foreign Secretary. Others appointed were well respected, moderate politicians, such as Snowden as Chancellor, Henderson at the Home Office and included two former Conservatives. John Wheatley at the Ministry of Health was the only representative of the radical wing of the party.

INEXPERIENCE

'THE LATEST CRY IS THAT LABOUR MINISTERS WILL LACK EXPERIENCE'. THE *DAILY HERALD* CARTOONIST 'A.G.' PORTRAYED A SUCCESSION OF ESTABLISHMENT FIGURES DERIDING LABOUR'S SUPPOSED INEXPERIENCE.

RECORD ON SOCIAL REFORM

Old age pensions and unemployment benefits were raised. State scholarships to universities were revived. The most important piece of legislation was Wheatley's 'Housing Act' which provided government aid in building council houses. Houses to rent would directly benefit the working class.

RELATIONS WITH THE TRADES UNIONS

The Labour Party Constitution gave unions the voting power via block votes based on membership with which they could dominate party conferences. Unemployment in 1924 led to poor industrial relations during the lifetime of MacDonald's government – for example, there was a national dock strike in February 1924.

RELATIONS WITH THE ILP

The Independent Labour Party (ILP), a group within the party yet outside Parliament, had moved further to the left wing. The ILP demanded more radical Socialist measures which would end inequality, exploitation and injustice more quickly.

FOREIGN POLICY

Relations with France improved during this year. MacDonald had made overtures to the French leader Poincaré but warmer relations developed with his successor Herriot. A conference was held in London to secure acceptance of the Dawes Plan which eased German reparations payments and arranged a US loan. Despite a certain ambivalence, MacDonald attended a League of Nations meeting in September 1924 and participated in a move towards collective security.

FEAR OF LABOUR PARTY LINKS WITH COMMUNIST RUSSIA

Fears were increasing by Labour's unconditional recognition of the Soviet government and the agreed £30 million loan in return for compensation for British assets seized in the Bolshevik revolution of 1917. An anti-Soviet propaganda campaign, supported by the Conservatives, frightened the Liberal ranks. Their support for the Labour Government wavered. The Campbell Case which followed brought the government down. In this, Campbell, the editor of a small Communist newspaper, had a prosecution case brought against him by Sir Patrick Hastings, the Attorney General, for an article published which was thought to be seditious. When the prosecution was suddenly withdrawn, the Labour Government were attacked for left-wing interference in the judicial system. A combined Conservative and Liberal vote defeated the government and MacDonald decided to dissolve Parliament.
A General Election was called.

TASKS

1 Describe what you think people would have expected of this first Labour Government.
2 Identify the successes this government achieved.
3 How far did these meet expectations?
4 Explain the problems they faced.
5 Did the successes of this administration outweigh its failures?
6 Why was it such a brief administration?

FOCUS

7.1 The Zinoviev Letter – A Forgery?

Zinoviev was a leading member of Lenin's Soviet government in Russia and President of the Comintern. A letter supposed to have been written by him came into government hands four days before the General Election. It urged British workers to make preparations for revolution. The letter's authenticity was questioned at the time by a suggestion that a Tory Establishment in Britain had forged it in order to bring down the government. It proved highly inflammable in the hands of a Conservative newspaper such as the *Daily Mail*.

Report on the Zinoviev Letter, *Daily Mail*, 27 October 1924.

BRITAIN ROUSED BY REDS.

SHOCKED BY PLOT OF CABINET'S MASTERS.

PREMIER SAYS NOTHING.

'FORGERY' SMOKE SCREEN.

MOSCOW SECRETS FORCED OUT BY 'DAILY MAIL'.

The only thing left to do is to vote Conservative.

Polling Day: the day after tomorrow.

The publication of the 'Very Secret' Moscow letter of instructions to Communists in Britain (who are the Socialist Government's masters) to take steps to paralyse our Army and Navy and to plunge England into civil war has profoundly shocked the whole country …

Throughout the week-end a storm of criticism has been directed against Mr MacDonald and his Ministers, because it was they who signed the treaty to 'lend' British money to these Moscow murderers. These criminals sent their civil war orders over here, despite their solemn undertaking in the treaty to cease all such poison plots…

There is one thing left to be done. The general election takes place on Wednesday. Vote Conservative and rid the country of the Government that is controlled by the Communists who take their orders from Moscow, the home of wholesale murder and starvation.

VOTE FOR MACDONALD AND ME

ON THE LOAN TRAIL.

[In a document just disclosed by the British Foreign Office (apparently after considerable delay), M. Zinovieff, a member of the Bolshevist Dictatorship, urges the British Communist Party to use "the greatest possible energy" in securing the ratification of the Anglo-Russian Treaties. In order to facilitate a scheme for the armed insurrection of the British proletariat.]

PUNCH CARTOON ON THE ZINOVIEV LETTER.

QUESTIONS

1 What is meant by 'shocked by plot of Cabinet's masters', '"Forgery" smoke screen'?

2 On what grounds does the *Daily Mail* attack the Labour government?

3 With reference to the language and content of this newspaper article, how useful is it to a historian studying the events of September/October 1924?

4 The General Election which followed was a resounding victory for the Conservative with 419 seats (Labour 151 and Liberals 40). Do you think the Zinoviev letter affected the voting and why?

Case Re-opened 75 Years Later – February 1999

TASKS

1 By using the Times newspaper website on the Internet find out the explanation of the Zinoviev Letter given by a Foreign Office historian in February 1999.
Find the Website: http://www.the-times.co.uk
Select 'Back issues'
Select 'February 4, 1999'
Find on the index 'Zinoviev'.

2 Discuss in class:
   a The explanation offered.
   b The sources used by the historian.
   c Which British government commissioned this historian to re-investigate the Zinoviev letter? What might their motives have been?

Did the first Labour administration achieve anything?

Source A

In this letter to George V, Ramsay MacDonald made a strong defence of his government's record in office.

> They have shown the country that they have the capacity to govern in an equal degree with the other parties in the House ... and, considering their lack of experience ... have acquitted themselves with credit in the House of Commons. The Labour Government have also shown the country that patriotism is not the monopoly of any single class or party. Finally, they can justly claim that they left the international situation in a more favourable position than that which they inherited. They have in fact demonstrated that they, no less than any other party, recognise their duties and responsibilities, and have done much to dispel the fantastic and extravagant belief which at one time found expression that they were nothing but a band of irresponsible revolutionaries intent on wreckage and destruction.
>
> MacDonald to the King, 10 October 1924, Geo. V K 1958/26, quoted in
> M. Cowling, *The Impact of Labour 1920–24* (1971), p. 359.

Source B

Henry Pelling, a historian of the Labour Party, offers the following assessment of MacDonald's 1924 administration.

> On the whole the first Labour government had performed creditably; and the return of Labour's main opponent in the election was only to be expected after a period of minority rule. But MacDonald had taken too much on to his shoulders, and he had made one or two errors of tactics notably in dealing with the Campbell case and the Zinoviev letter. He had also shown himself very hostile to criticism, particularly from the ILP. Both he and his ministers had also signally failed to maintain effective liaison with the TUC and the machinery of the National Joint Council had hardly been used ...
>
> Extract from Pelling and Reid, *A Short History of the Labour Party*, 11th edition.

---

1 In what ways do these assessments agree and disagree?
2 What reasons can you suggest for the differences?

The 1929 General Election

TALKING POINT

What messages is the cartoonist conveying by this cartoon?

'JOAN BULL'S VALENTINE', *EVENING STANDARD*, 13 FEBRUARY 1928.

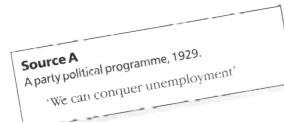

Source A
A party political programme, 1929.

'We can conquer unemployment'

Source B
An election slogan.

'Safety First'

Source C

Source D

Source E

Socialism is neither a sentimental aspiration for an impossible Utopia, nor a blind movement of revolt against poverty and oppression ... It is a conscious, systematic and unflagging effort to use the weapons forged in the victorious struggle for political democracy to end the capitalist dictatorship in which democracy finds everywhere its most insidious and most relentless foe.

Extracted from Robert Pearce, *Britain: Domestic Politics 1918–1939 (1992)*, p. 58.

Source F

The word written today on the hearts of British people and graven on their minds is *unemployment*. For eight years more than a million British workers, able and eager to work, have been denied the opportunity ... what a tragedy of human suffering; what a waste of fine resources; what a bankruptcy of statesmanship ... At the moment individual enterprise alone cannot restore the situation within a time for which we can wait. The state must therefore lend its aid and, by a deliberate policy of national development, help to set going at full speed the great machine of industry.

Ibid.

Source G

The long-awaited opportunity has now come for the Nation to give its verdict on the present government. By its inaction during four critical years it has multiplied our difficulties and increased our dangers. Unemployment is more acute than when Labour left office. International relations are worse. Vast areas of the country are derelict ... In the face of such a state of things this Tory government has sat supinely with folded arms without a policy, without a vision, waiting for Providence or charity to do its work.

Extract from Lawrence Butler and Harriet Jones,
Britain in the 20th Century (1994), p. 216.

Source H

... In spite of all obstacles, we have fulfilled the pledges given in 1924 to an extent which no Government has equalled, and as a result of our administration the Empire is more firmly united, the prestige of the country stands higher. The prosperity and welfare of our people is greater than ever before in our history.

Ibid.

'THE CONSERVATIVE SUN-RAY TREATMENT'. CONSERVATIVE ELECTION POSTER, 1929.

Source J

The party stands for a system of taxation which will distribute the burden fairly according to 'ability to pay'.

Ibid.

The Conservative government under Baldwin were becoming increasingly unpopular by 1929. Little concerted effort had been made to reduce unemployment, which was by now standing at more than one million. Unemployment benefit was reduced and stringent tests were introduced to decide who would qualify. Economic recovery was slow, trades unionists had been hit by the reintroduction of 'opting-in' after the General Strike. The Conservatives were once again divided between Tariff Reformers and Imperial preferencers, Baldwin standing as the main unifying factor. The Liberals approached the election with a very positive set of proposals for public works and housing. Labour's promises were similar in 'Labour and the Nation' (1928), although party conferences attacked this moderate line.

In the election of May 1929 the Labour Party won 288 seats, the Conservatives 260 and the Liberals 59. Baldwin refused to allow the Liberals to hold the balance of power – so he resigned. MacDonald became Prime Minister for the second time.

TASKS

1 Read and think about the sources carefully. Match the political parties **a–c** to the appropriate election poster, slogan, electoral address and promises:
   a the Conservative Party
   b the Liberal Party
   c the Labour Party.
2 What are the main issues addressed during the 1929 Election?
3 Describe the ways in which each party is attempting to appeal to the electorate.
4 Which party would you have voted for in 1929 – and why?

Labour's second administration, 1929–31

'A tenant with a lease'

TALKING POINT

What did MacDonald mean by these comments? Why do politicians use political metaphors and how useful are they to the historian?

On coming to power for a second time, MacDonald is meant to have privately remarked that in 1924 he had been a squatter in constant danger of eviction, whereas in 1929 he was more a 'tenant with a lease'.

Because of the inconclusive nature of the election and his overriding belief in gaining credibility for Labour as a party for government in Britain, MacDonald determined to pursue a moderate policy similar to that which his government has adopted in 1924. He said 'We should consider ourselves more as a Council of State and less as arrayed regiments facing each other in battle.' These words were later interpreted as meaning that he was already thinking of coalition government (see pp. 154–63 for a discussion of the 1931 crisis). He was helped in this aim by the fact that more than half the Labour MPs who had been elected were not trades unionists and also because some ILP candidates left the ILP because they disagreed with the split in the Labour Party. The composition of the new Cabinet was moderate and cautious. Philip Snowden was made Chancellor, Arthur Henderson Foreign Secretary, J.H. Thomas Lord Privy Seal and the first female Cabinet member, Margaret Bondfield, became the Minister for Labour.

In domestic policy, a Coal Mines Act (1930) was passed which reduced the working day to $7\frac{1}{2}$ hours without wage reductions and a Housing Act concentrated on slum clearance.

Foreign affairs – a successful record

TALKING POINT

How far does this foreign policy of the second Labour government reflect the Socialist goals of
a   peace?
b   self-government?
c   socialist brotherhood?

Although Henderson was now Foreign Secretary, Prime Minister MacDonald still remained involved with the USA and naval disarmament. He immediately cut the British naval building programme and visited Washington becoming the first British Prime Minister to address Congress. At a five-power conference held in London in January 1930, Britain, the USA and Japan agreed on reductions to their navies.

Henderson worked in other areas agreeing a commercial treaty with USSR following the resumption of diplomatic relations. The government also took an interest in the development of independence for India. 'Dominion Status' was acknowledged as the goal of British policy. The Simon Commission reported in 1930 and a round table conference on the future of India was organised for the Autumn of that year. It was adjourned because the Indian National Congress refused to take part.

In Europe a withdrawal of occupying forces from the Rhineland was agreed from 1930 some five years ahead of time and a new reparation deal for Germany – the Young Plan – was agreed at the end of 1929. Notably there was also resumption of work on the preparations for a general disarmament conference.

The 1931 crisis: Labour's second administration swept away in an 'Economic Blizzard'

An introductory outline

- A minority Labour government was elected in May 1929.
- They presided over a worsening economic and financial position after October 1929's Wall Street Crash.
- In order to restore foreign confidence in British trade and the currency which was still on the Gold Standard, the government faced an urgent need to balance the budget.
- A controversial decision arose over whether to cut unemployment benefits by 10 per cent. This split the Labour government over their basic tenet of a right to 'work or maintenance'.
- Prime Minister Ramsay MacDonald offered the government's resignation on 23 August 1931.
- At the request of King George V, and with the agreement of both the Conservative and Liberal Parties, MacDonald stayed on, with a few Labour supporters to head a National Government.
- This National Government fought a General Election as a single entity. In securing 554 seats, it achieved the largest ever electoral majority.

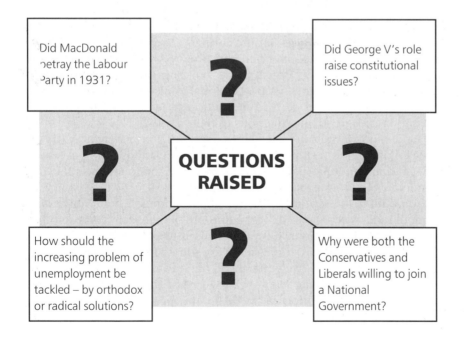

Did MacDonald betray the Labour Party in 1931?

Did George V's role raise constitutional issues?

QUESTIONS RAISED

How should the increasing problem of unemployment be tackled – by orthodox or radical solutions?

Why were both the Conservatives and Liberals willing to join a National Government?

How did the crisis develop?

1929

Unemployment was a worrying trend throughout the 1920s.
The Wall Street Crash in October 1929 led to a worldwide depression. Effects
were felt in Britain: between 1929 and 1931, the value of exports fell by half.
From November 1929 onwards, unemployment rose every month. 1929 –
1.1 million, July 1930 – 2 million, December 1930 – 2.5 million. Cost of
unemployment benefit rose as tax payments fell. 1928 – £12 million cost
rose to £125 million in 1931. Conflict arose with trades unions.

1930

In the face of a deepening crisis, a small ministerial team was formed to tackle
unemployment – led by J.H.Thomas, it also included George Lansbury and
Oswald Mosley. Government spending rose to an all-time high. May 1930 –
Mosley, finding government policy too slow, presented his own economic plan –
the Mosley Memorandum. Rejected by Cabinet. Moderates, led by MacDonald and
Snowden, clashed with radicals over proposed solutions to economic crisis. A
15-man Economic Advisory Council of industrialists and economists (including
Keynes) was formed to provide alternative ideas. The government began to fare
badly in local and by-elections. Defeat at the next General Election looked likely.

1931

May – the collapse of banks in Europe caused a further loss of British investment.

June – a Royal Commission on unemployment insurance recommended up to
30 per cent cut in benefits.

July – May Committee, set up in February, reported a deficit of £120 million and
recommended a 20 per cent decrease in unemployment benefits.

A 'run on the pound' occurred stimulated by the May Report and withdrawal of
funds by foreign investors fearing bankruptcy in Britain. By the end of July, almost
one quarter of the Bank of England's gold reserves were used up.

August – Foreign loans were necessary but these necessitated cuts. The lenders
wanted a promise of retrenchment. The Cabinet split over suggested cuts in public
spending – such as pay for the Civil Service, the Armed Forces and unemployment
benefits. Chancellor Snowden demanded a 10 per cent cut in benefits to balance
the budget and gain loans from New York and Paris. He rejected Keynes' radical
alternatives. Henderson opposed cuts because their hardest impact was on the
underprivileged – Labour's natural supporters. MacDonald
supported his Chancellor – the Cabinet vote was split 11 to 9.

23 August – MacDonald resigned.

24 August – A National Government was formed. Only four Cabinet Ministers
followed MacDonald, three of whom went into the new Cabinet.

27 October – GENERAL ELECTION.

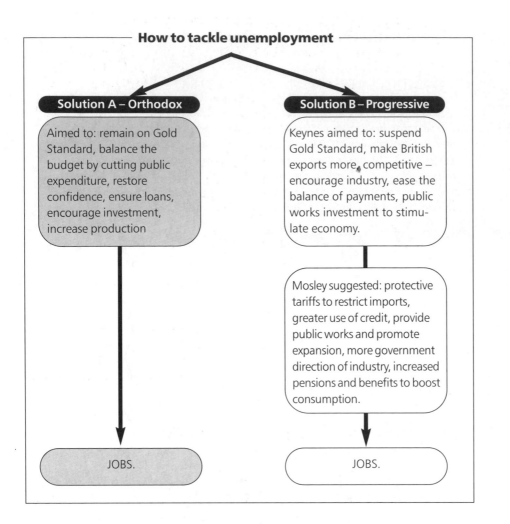

How to tackle unemployment

Solution A – Orthodox

Aimed to: remain on Gold Standard, balance the budget by cutting public expenditure, restore confidence, ensure loans, encourage investment, increase production

JOBS.

Solution B – Progressive

Keynes aimed to: suspend Gold Standard, make British exports more competitive – encourage industry, ease the balance of payments, public works investment to stimulate economy.

Mosley suggested: protective tariffs to restrict imports, greater use of credit, provide public works and promote expansion, more government direction of industry, increased pensions and benefits to boost consumption.

JOBS.

The differences between these two opposing economic creeds were laid out clearly at the Labour Party Conference in October 1930:

Source A: Oswald Mosley

They must go to parliament with an unemployment policy. If they were obstructed in parliament, then let them bring proposals before parliament to reform it, so that they could get business through … If their proposals were thrown out, they must go to the country and fight their opponents on the question of unemployment and a revision of parliament. At best, they would have their majority, at worst they would go down fighting for the things they believed in. They would not die like an old woman in bed; they would die like a man in the field – a better fate, and, in politics, one with more certain hope of resurrection.

He did not believe that the great national crisis they were living in was a menace to their Movement. It was their supreme opportunity … Let them not shrink before a great opportunity; let them seize it and use it and give the country a lead.

TALKING POINT

What does the historian Robert Pearce mean when commenting on these speeches, 'Mosley was defeated by party loyalty – so that political stability ruled out economic radicalism – and by the emotional appeal of Socialism as a visionary faith'?

Source B: Ramsay MacDonald

So, my friends, we are not on trial; it is the system under which we live. It has broken down, not only in this little island; it has broken down in Europe, in Asia, in America; it has broken down everywhere as it was bound to break down ... I appeal to you, my friends today, with all that is going on – I appeal to you to go back on to your Socialist faith. Do not mix that up with pettifogging patching – either of a Poor Law kind or of Relief Work kind. Construction, ideas, architecture, building line upon line, stone upon stone, storey upon storey; it will not be your happiness, it will certainly not be mine, to see that fabric finished ... But I think it will be your happiness; as it is mine, to go on convinced that the great foundations are being laid ... and that ... the temple will rise and rise until at last it is complete, and the genius of humanity will find within it an appropriate resting place.

TASK

Read carefully the details of the 1931 crisis on pages 154–7. Prepare presentations offering an explanation of three opposing views:

a Snowden/MacDonald – the necessity to make public spending cuts.

b Henderson – the argument against making cuts based on socialist principle.

c Keynes/Mosley – the Radical solution.

Was MacDonald a traitor to the Labour Party?

J'ACCUSE.   *September 2nd*, 1931.
"Prisoners, you have been found guilty of putting duty to the state and personal honour above party discipline. For so despicable a crime there is only one sentence—eternal banishment from our ranks!"

STRUBE OF THE DAILY EXPRESS DEPICTS MACDONALD AND J.H. THOMAS AS ARISTOCRATS CHARGED BEFORE A REVOLUTIONARY TRIBUNAL – THE GENERAL COUNCIL OF THE TRADE UNION CONGRESS BACKED BY THE RANK AND FILE OF THE LABOUR PARTY (MORRISON THIRD FROM LEFT BEHIND BALUSTRADE, LANSBURY ON STAIRS). STRUBE'S FAMOUS 'LITTLE MAN' – THE ORDINARY, HARMLESS AND BEWILDERED CITIZEN – PEEPS FROM BEHIND THE CURTAIN (SEPT. 1931).

'Here lies Ramsay Mac

A friend to all humanity,

Too many pats upon the back

Inflated Ramsay's vanity.

The Blarney stone he oft-times kissed,

But departed in his glory:

Having been born a Socialist

He died a bloody Tory.'

> R.C.Challinor, 'Letter from MacDonald to Clarke', *Bulletin of the Society for the Study of Labour History*, 27 (1972) pp. 34–5.

'We'll hang Ramsay Mac on a sour apple tree,

We'll hang Snowden and Thomas to keep him company;

For that's the place where traitors ought to be.'

> Extracted from Malcolm Pearce and Geoffrey Stewart, *British Political History*, p. 268.

1 What are the messages conveyed by the cartoon and rhymes?
2 Why do you think MacDonald and his supporters were expelled from the Labour Party?

TASK

Sort the following arguments about MacDonald's actions in forming a National Government in 1931 into
   a a case for the PROSECUTION
   b a case for the DEFENCE.

1 He agreed to lead a National Government of mainly Conservatives and Liberals.
2 MacDonald's earlier contribution to the Labour Party proved his credentials as a loyal Socialist and good party leader.
3 In agreeing to cuts in social welfare, he abandoned his Socialist principles.
4 An element of vanity played a part. MacDonald liked to be hailed as the country's saviour.
5 He had no real choice – believing in the orthodox economic approach.
6 This action, he argued, was carried out in the national interest.
7 There was a conspiracy of international bankers which MacDonald allowed to bring down the Labour government.
8 There was no bankers' conspiracy – loans based on a promise of retrenchment were normal procedure.
9 MacDonald's aim had always been and was at this point to make Labour into a nationally acknowledged party capable of government.

10 MacDonald had been corrupted by the Establishment – and is quoted as having remarked 'tomorrow every Duchess in London will be wanting to kill me'.

11 He was persuaded by the Conservatives, Liberals and King George V that this was his duty.

12 The idea of coalition government was something MacDonald had been in favour of before the crisis of 1931. He had had regular meetings over past months hatching the idea of coalition.

13 MacDonald was unable to control events and was overwhelmed by the 'economic blizzard'.

14 MacDonald's so-called 'treachery' was a useful scapegoat for a Labour Party which had failed to develop an alternative economic strategy and adopt radical policies.

Examining the evidence

Was MacDonald a traitor?

Source A

DAVID LOW 'GETTING ON', *EVENING STANDARD*, 9 OCTOBER 1930.

Source B

To dismiss MacDonald as a traitor is nonsense. His contribution in the early years was of incalculable value. His qualities as a protagonist of Socialism were of a rare standard. There has probably never been an orator with such natural magnetism combined with impeccable technique in speaking in the party's history. Before the First World War his reputation in international Labour circles brooked no comparison...

Among his people in Scotland he could exert almost mesmeric influence ... No one has ever completely explained the magnetism of MacDonald as a young man. He was the most handsome man I have ever known, and his face and bearing can best be described as 'princely' ... the people who loved him in those early days recognised it as an inborn quality. It also put him in Parliament ... Leicester was intrigued about this Labour candidate who was the sole opponent of the Tory in 1906 ... The immense Liberal vote was his from the start ... He won that election by emotionalism rather than intellect – as others before and since have won elections.

Emanuel Shinwell, *Conflict without Malice* (1955), p. 113.

Source C

The country awakens this morning to find Mr MacDonald still Prime Minister, with the prospect of a small Cabinet representative of all three parties. The former Cabinet resigned yesterday afternoon, and a statement issued last night announced that considerable progress had been made towards settling the composition of its successor, which would be a Government of co-operation formed with the specific purposes only of carrying through a very large reduction in expenditure and raising 'on an equitable basis' the further funds required to balance the Budget ...

All concerned are to be warmly congratulated on this result, so fully in accord with the patriotic spirit which has inspired a week's most anxious negotiations. The Prime Minister and the colleagues of his own party who have followed him deserve in particular unqualified credit, both for the manner in which they took their political lives in their hands by facing and forcing the break-up of the late Cabinet, and for their new decision to translate courage in the Cabinet into courage in the country. The readiness to share the responsibility – honour is perhaps the better word – of carrying through to the end the policy of retrenchment adds enormously to the prospect of its success.

The Times, 25 August 1931.

Source D

THE MASTER CHEMIST.

PROFESSOR MacDONALD. "NOW IF ONLY THESE RATHER ANTAGONISTIC ELEMENTS WILL BLEND AS I HOPE, WE'LL HAVE A REAL NATIONAL ELIXIR."

'THE MASTER CHEMIST', *PUNCH*, AUGUST 1931.

Source E

In many respects the situation which confronted the Cabinet was like that of August 1914 ... In 1914 Mr MacDonald refused to join a War Cabinet; Mr Henderson accepted. Mr MacDonald was denounced as a traitor: Mr Henderson was applauded. In leading articles in *The Times*, for instance, Mr MacDonald's patriotism is extolled, while Mr Henderson is denounced as a man who put party before country. Meanwhile, in Labour circles all over the country Mr MacDonald is being denounced ... for betraying his party ... MacDonald's decision to form a Cabinet in conjunction with the

Liberals and the Tories seems to us a mistake, just as it would have been a mistake for him as a pacifist to join a War Cabinet in 1914. For he must inevitably find himself at war with the whole of organised labour, and not only with organised labour, but with all those, in all classes, who believe that the policy of reducing the purchasing power of the consumer to meet a situation of overproduction is silly economics ... An effort is being made to represent the whole issue as merely one of a 10 per cent reduction in the dole and refusal to cut it could only be based on cowardly subservience to the electorate ... We oppose it ... because it is only the first step, the crucial beginning of a policy of reductions, disastrous, we believe for England and the rest of the world ...

New Statesman, 29 August 1931.

Source F

The failure of the 1929 Labour Government .. determined the politics of the following decade. Could that failure have been prevented? Usually criticism of MacDonald and his colleagues starts with their handling of the financial crisis of 1931 rather than with their omissions over the previous two years. But whereas between 1929 and 1931 there were plenty of effective choices open to Government, in 1931 itself there was virtual unanimity on the need to defend the gold standard ... MacDonald broke with his colleagues not over policy but over primary loyalty. As Prime Minister he considered his first duty was to the 'national interest' as it was almost universally conceived; the Labour Party saw its first duty to its own people ... The real criticism of MacDonald is not that he formed the National Government, but that under his leadership the Labour Government had drifted into a position which left it so little choice ... the Government rejected Conservative protection, the Liberal national development loan, the Keynesian and Mosleyite amalgams of both preferring instead the advice of the least progressive sections of the 'economic establishment'.

R. Skidelsky, *Politicians and the Slump: the Labour Government of 1929–1931* (1970), pp. 11–12, 425–6.

TASK

Write out a conclusion from the previous tasks on pp. 158–9, showing to what extent you consider MacDonald a traitor.

1 From each of these sources, identify the various views of MacDonald's actions in 1931.
2 Add this evidence to the case you are compiling for and against MacDonald.

Focus

7.2 King George V – His Role in the 1931 Crisis

QUESTIONS:

The formation of the National Government in 1931 raises some interesting historical problems:

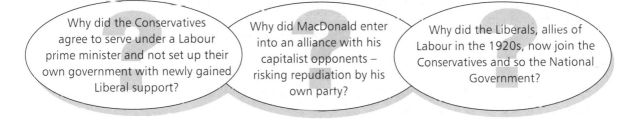

Why did the Conservatives agree to serve under a Labour prime minister and not set up their own government with newly gained Liberal support?

Why did MacDonald enter into an alliance with his capitalist opponents – risking repudiation by his own party?

Why did the Liberals, allies of Labour in the 1920s, now join the Conservatives and so the National Government?

ANSWER:

King George V intervened decisively to bring a National Government together. Is this suggestion valid?

YES

- MacDonald was seduced by royal flattery.
- The King engineered a 'palace revolution' by reappointing a prime minister who lacked the support of his own party.
- 1970s research of private documents reveal George V working hard to persuade the parties towards a National Government.
- Both MacDonald and Baldwin were persuaded by the King.
- The King held a series of separate audiences with the leaders and then a conference with all three at Buckingham Palace.

NO

- A 1950s biographer of George V showed that the King acted upon Conservative and Liberal advice.
- MacDonald acted upon his own personal belief of the nation's best interest.
- 20th-century monarchs lack the political patronage to enable them to be influential.
- Party leaders' prime consideration was to their parliamentary party, organisations and the voters generally.
- The Conservatives and Liberals both had their own reasons for supporting a National Government.
- A National Government had been discussed earlier – it was a way in which responsibility for handling the crisis could be shared.

KING GEORGE V.

TALKING POINTS

How decisive was George V's intervention?
What constitutional questions does it raise about the role of the monarch in the British political system?

REVIEW

Write the following essay:

'Why was the Labour Party able to gain, but unable to keep office on two occasions between the Wars?'

Follow the

THINK!
READ!
PLAN!
WRITE!

THINK!

- What is the instruction within the question?
- What is the scope of content to be included in this essay?

READ!

- Re-read Chapters 6 and 7 of this book
- Look carefully through your notes
- Research further areas you are unsure about.

PLAN!

- The essay requires 'reasons'/'factors' for the formation and resignation of two Labour Governments 1924 and 1929–31.
- Your essay will have two sections – decide whether there will be one section for each government in 1924 and 1929 or one section for reasons for gaining power and one section covering reasons for losing power in 1924 and 1931.
- Decide what argument will be put forward in each paragraph.
- What evidence do you have to support each argument?

WRITE!

- Ensure the introduction is brief but refers to the question specifically.
- Each paragraph should begin with a sentence which refers to the question.
- Conclude with your own historical judgement.

8 Britain in the 1930s

PREVIEW

In 1934 the novelist, playwright and social commentator J.B. Priestley published his *English Journey*:

> I had seen England. I had seen a lot of Englands. How Many? At once, three disengaged themselves from the shifting mass. There was, first, Old England, the country of the cathedrals and minsters and manor houses and inns, of Parson and Squire; guidebook and quaint highways and byways England ... But we all know this England, which at its best cannot be improved upon in this world ...

'RURAL ENGLAND'.

> Then, I decided, there is the nineteenth-century England, the industrial England of coal, iron, steel, cotton, wool, railways; of thousands of rows of little houses all alike, sham Gothic churches, square faced chapels, Town Halls, Mechanics' Institutes, mills, foundries, warehouses, refined watering-places, Pier Pavilions, Family and Commercial Hotels, Literary and Philosophical Societies, back-to-back houses, detached villas with monkey-trees, Grill Rooms, railway stations, slag-heaps and 'tips', dock roads, Refreshment Rooms, doss-houses, Unionist or Liberal Clubs, cindery waste ground, mill chimneys, fried-fish shops, public-houses ... This England makes up the larger part of the Midlands and the North and exists everywhere; but it is not being added

'INDUSTRIAL ENGLAND'.

to and has no new life poured into it. To the more fortunate people it was not a bad England at all, very solid and comfortable ... The third England, I concluded, was the new post war England, belonging far more to the age itself than to this island. America, I supposed, was its real birthplace. This is the England of arterial by-pass roads, of filling stations and factories that look like exhibiting buildings, of giant cinemas and dance-halls and cafés, bungalows with tiny garages, cocktail bars, Woolworths, motor-coaches, wireless, hiking, factory girls looking like actresses, greyhound racing and dirt tracks, swimming pools and everything given away for cigarette coupons.

'POSTWAR ENGLAND'.

1   Do you live in an area similar to one of these Englands?
2   Which industries are at the centre of the three different Englands?
3   Where would you find J.B. Priestley's three Englands today?
4   Is there now yet another England?

The Depression – What was the nature of the 1930s slump?

The National Government was the overwhelming victor of the 1931 Election, returning 554 MPs. Having expelled MacDonald, Thomas and Snowden, leading figures in their 1929 government, the Labour Party, led by Arthur Henderson, suffered heavily at the polls. They returned little more than 50 seats. The new National Government, although headed by MacDonald, was dominated by the Conservative Party. The Liberals had again split – their total vote fell to below 11 per cent. Lloyd George, leading the Independent Liberals, could only rally enough support to win four seats.

During this decade there were three National governments:

1935–7

Baldwin PM (Conservative)

1931–5

MacDonald PM (Labour)

1937–9

Chamberlain PM (Conservative)

TALKING POINT

What is the meaning of 'national government'? In what ways do economic crises affect the political context?

As with its formation, the National Government – its policies and dominant political position – can only be understood in the context of the economy of the 1930s. This period is associated with depression, unemployment and graphic images of the dole queue – however, the reality was not that simple. The 1930s depression, which seemed so cruel to many contemporaries and for many people brought much hardship, was not the only trend at this time. There was a burst of prosperity in the mid-1930s, much new industry was developing and for many working- and middle-class families the standard of living rose.

Why the Depression?

The Great Depression, known as 'The Slump', affected nearly every country between 1929 and 1939. It was triggered by the Wall Street Crash in October 1929, when stock prices on the New York Stock Exchange fell dramatically after several years of spectacular growth. The subsequent collapse of the American economy had two direct consequences for Europe:

Consequence 1

With the fall of the American market, there was a huge reduction in the demand for European exports. This led to a rapid decrease in European output and so loss of jobs.

Consequence 2

As American lenders recalled loans and US capital left Europe, there were a series of currency crises – notably in Austria, Germany and Great Britain. This forced Britain and others to leave the Gold Standard. The subsequent floating exchange rates and rising tariffs led to a reduction in world trade.

As a major exporting country, Britain was particularly badly affected by these events. From the collapse of the postwar boom in 1920 unemployment in Britain had never fallen below 1 million. During the Depression of the early 1930s, the recorded figure rose to 2.75 million – over 22.5 per cent of the insured working population. In addition, there were millions more jobless who were not insured. Keynes, the economist, declared: '"We are today in the middle of the greatest economic catastrophe – the greatest catastrophe due entirely to economic causes, of the modern world.'

In Britain it was labelled the 'devil's decade' and has generated much contemporary comment and historical debate.

What was the nature of the Depression?

The Depression in Britain in the 1930s was both cyclical and structural.

The British economy still relied heavily on the staple industries, such as coal, iron and steel, textiles and shipbuilding, which had been the engines of industrial growth in the 19th century. These were in a depressed state even at the peak of a boom and those areas which were most dependent upon them – such as south Wales, the north-east of England and the industrial belt of Scotland – were most badly affected by the depression. New industries such as electricity, house building, chemicals, motor cars and aircraft were developing rapidly and flourishing but they had not replaced the staple industries sufficiently, nor were they developing in the same parts of Britain to overcome the slump in the staple industries.

The Depression in Britain in the 1930s was a result of cyclical change happening at the same time as structural change.

TALKING POINT

Research and discuss in class the meaning of economic terms such as: cyclical and structural economic change\staple industries\consumer goods\'boom and bust'\recession\currency crisis.

Cyclical changes in the 1930s

The slump *between 1929 and 1932* saw unemployment rise dramatically to nearly three million workers and although the staple industries were most badly affected, new industries also suffered.

By late 1935, although unemployment remained high, there were signs of a booming economy such as shortages of skilled labour in key areas. The recovery continued until 1937 – unemployment fell and became an increasingly regional feature.

There were five key factors which led to recovery:

A	B	C	D	E
Low interest rates maintained by the National Government encouraged a boom in the construction industry. The building boom was nationwide and labour-intensive and increased the demand for subsidiary industry	• The development of 'new' industries and service industries. • Motor vehicles rose from 306,000 in 1932 to 586,000 in 1937 • The number of radios rose from 506,000 in 1930 to almost two million in 1937 • Manmade fibres doubled in output between 1929 and 1937 • Employment in the service industries increased by 1.2 million in the period 1931–9	There was some small improvements in staple industries, although this was inconsistent – steel did better than coal. However, exports revived patchily and contributed to recovery	Overall improvement of the world economy after 1933 helped the British economy. Exports to USA increased – from £15.1 million in 1932 to £31.4 million in 1937.	Government policy assisted recovery with innovative (but not radical) policies. Confidence was restored.

By the end of 1937, the boom broke partly as a result of a break in the American recovery. Domestic demand in Britain reached saturation level – and unemployment again increased – from 10.1 per cent in September 1937 to 13.8 per cent in June 1938. This time, the effects were particularly badly felt in the steel and textile industries.

Structural changes

Because unemployment remained at 10 per cent throughout this period the cyclical explanation for the slump is insufficient. A longer-term, gradual process was also to blame. This was the transition of the economy from old staple industries to new. This restructuring of the economy had only partially occurred in the 1930s – the shift from one type of industry to another was incomplete and limited. This made the economy at the time difficult to assess – differences of region and occupation made considerable contrast.

Britain began the 1930s overcommitted to the staple industries. The problem in this sector was two-fold – a fall in demand and where there was demand, Britain could not compete with the other producers either on cost or quantity. Attempts to limit surplus production only met with moderate success. However new industries managed to reduce costs and demand grew. By 1933 they returned to 1929 levels – producing largely for the home market with newer equipment they could compete on more equal terms.

TASKS

1 Draw a diagram to illustrate and include all the factors which affected the British economy in the 1930s.

2 Explain in a brief paragraph why the economic trends in this period are difficult to assess.

3 Identify social groups in Britain who would be winners or losers in the 1930s depression.

Examining the Evidence

The impact of the Depression on society

What was it like to live in Britain in the 1930s? The answer would, of course, depend upon who you were, where you were living and what your occupation was. There are conflicting views over the economic trends in this period and the standard of living.

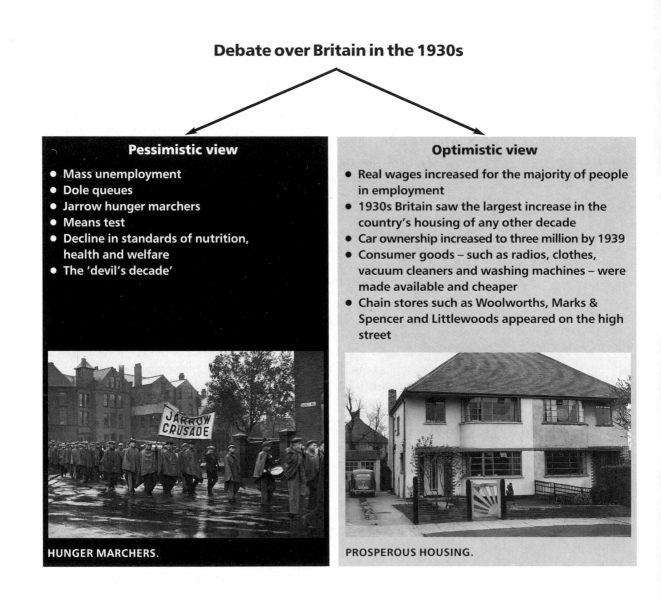

Debate over Britain in the 1930s

Pessimistic view

- Mass unemployment
- Dole queues
- Jarrow hunger marchers
- Means test
- Decline in standards of nutrition, health and welfare
- The 'devil's decade'

HUNGER MARCHERS.

Optimistic view

- Real wages increased for the majority of people in employment
- 1930s Britain saw the largest increase in the country's housing of any other decade
- Car ownership increased to three million by 1939
- Consumer goods – such as radios, clothes, vacuum cleaners and washing machines – were made available and cheaper
- Chain stores such as Woolworths, Marks & Spencer and Littlewoods appeared on the high street

PROSPEROUS HOUSING.

A debate arises due to the conflicting evidence available on this period. We need to consider the type of evidence, the date it was written, the author and the purpose. To consider the debate more thoroughly, examine the three types of evidence below:

1 **Contemporary evidence**   – memoirs
                                 – reports/surveys
                                 – literature.

2 **Statistical evidence**
3 **What the historians say.**

Contemporary evidence

Source A

We would be labouring under a delusion if we got into our heads the idea that only 31.1% of the working class population suffer from poverty. We see that 52.5% of the children under one year of age, 49.7% of those over one and under five, and 39.3% of those over five and under fifteen are living below the minimum. Since everyone who grows up has at one time been aged 0–1, that means that, of the generation of workers born in 1936, 52.5% will have been living below the minimum during the first part of their lives irrespective of what happens to them afterwards.

Report on poverty in York by Seebohm Rowntree, 1936.

Source B

H.F. Tout, 'The Standard of Living in Bristol 1938' – an investigation carried out on 104,000 inhabitants led by Tout – under the auspices of Bristol University.
Tout demonstrated that 10.7 % of families in Bristol fell below his 'needs' line, and that 25 % of children suffered from poverty.

Poverty

a   Family of eight consisting of man (aged 40), wife, six children and another expected. Boys aged 12 and 8. Girls aged 15, 14, 2 and 1.

Income: Man unemployment benefit 38s; two eldest daughters employed as learners in a factory receiving 10s 6d and 7s 6d.

Rent 11s. No travel costs. Gross income 56s.

Standard of living, 21% below needs. Extra income required to reach needs level, 11s 5d.

b   Family of one, a widow living alone (aged 47).

Income: Widow's Pension 10s; Public Assistance 3s 6d.

Rent of house 10s, but she sub-lets all but two rooms for 6s 6d.

Standard of living 11% below needs.

Extra income required to raise needs level, 1s 4d....

Source C

Stockton

Now let us consider poor Stockton. Because she had lost her initial advantages, Britain was now building a smaller proportion than ever of the dwindling amount of new shipping necessary. The north-eastern region was now building a smaller proportion of that smaller proportion. And in that region, the Tees, which was shallower and not so well equipped as the Tyne, and only suitable for the building and repairing of smaller vessels, was in the worst position. The industry had to be 'rationalized'; and the National Shipbuilders Security Ltd, proceeded to buy up and then close down what were known as 'redundant' yards. Stockton found itself woefully redundant, and said good-bye to its yards. Meanwhile, the marine engineering firms that had been monstrously over-capitalized during the short boom years, like the cotton firms, collapsed like pricked bladders with the boom itself. It was all a highly specialized industry. You cannot build motor cars in a shipyard, or make safety-razor blades in a marine engineering shop. For such a place as Stockton the game was up. Such new industries as we have had went south. Stockton and the rest, miles from London and with soaring rates, were useless as centres for new enterprises. They were left to rot. And that perhaps would not have mattered very much, for the bricks and mortar of these towns are not sacred, if it were not for one fact. These places left to rot have people living in them. Some of these people are rotting too.

J.B. Priestley, *English Journey* (1934).

The MP for Stockton was Harold Macmillan. He was greatly affected by his experiences there – and this influenced his attitude to social policies as a central figure in the post-Second World War Conservative Party, and as prime minister between 1957 and 1963 (see Chapter 12).

Source D

Twenty million people are underfed but literally everyone in England has access to a radio. What we have lost in food we have gained in electricity. Whole sections of the working class who have been plundered of all they really need are being compensated, in part, by cheap luxuries which mitigate the surface of life ... It is quite likely that fish-and-chips, art-silk stockings, tinned salmon, cut-price chocolate ... the movies, the radio, strong tea and the football pools have between them averted revolution.

That scene stays in mind as one of the pictures of Lancashire: the dumpy, shawled women, with their sacking aprons and heavy black clogs, kneeling in the cindery mud and bitter wind, searching eagerly for tiny chips of coal. They are glad enough to do it. In winter they are desperate for fuel; it is more important almost than food. Meanwhile all round so far as the eye can see, are the slag-heaps and hoisting gear of collieries, and not one of those collieries can sell all the coal it is capable of producing ...

In a working-class home – I am not thinking at the moment of the unemployed, but of comparatively prosperous homes – you breathe warm, decent, deeply human atmosphere which it is not easy to find elsewhere. I should say that a manual worker, if he is in steady work and drawing good wages – an 'if' which gets bigger and bigger – has a better chance of being happy than an 'educated' man. His home life seems to fall more naturally into a sane and comely shape. I have often been struck by the peculiar easy completeness, the perfect symmetry as it were, of a working-class interior at its best. Especially on winter evenings after tea, when the fire glows in the open range and dances mirrored in the steel fender, when Father, in shirtsleeves, sits in the rocking chair at one side of the fire reading the racing finals, and Mother sits on the other with sewing, and the children are happy with a penn'orth of humbugs, and the dog lolls roasting himself on the rag mat – it is a good place to be in, provided that you can be not only in it but sufficiently *of* it to be taken for granted.

This scene is still reduplicated in a majority of English homes, though not in so many as before the war. Its happiness depends mainly upon one question – whether Father is still in work …

Extracts from George Orwell, *The Road to Wigan Pier* (1937).

Source E

Personal recollections of working-class life during the Depression taken from Nigel Gray, *'The Worst Times'* – an oral history of the Great Depression.

When our baby was born we had to borrow a mattress from next door and spread newspapers on it. I used to feed the baby on a bottle of warm water. We put her to bed in a drawer. We made nappies out of newspaper. When I went before the Public Assistance Committee they asked me if the baby was being breast fed and when I said yes they reduced the 2/- allowance for a child. (p. 193)

I used to wait outside the same bakery every morning with a crowd of other blokes hoping someone would get the sack or would be too ill to crawl into work. One morning there was an accident at the top of my road. My mate who was a roundsman for the bakery was lying in a pool of blood. I didn't know whether to run home to tell his wife or run on and get his job. So I run on. (p. 186)

I cycled 150 miles from South Wales and went straight to the Employment Office to seek work. The clerk looked at me and he said, 'Another bloody Welshman come for his holidays.'

One man got work clearing snow for the council. So as not to lose his dole he gave a false name. When the time came for him to step up to the window for his pay he couldn't remember what name he'd given. Men would fight each other for work. (p. 185)

I was so used to cutting down dresses for my little girl. One day I told her she'd have to stop off school because she had no shoes to wear. She said, 'Can't you make me a pair out of yours?' (p. 181)

My mother seemed to think my father was not trying to get work and always seemed to be in a bad temper. Then there was a row to end rows and my father said he would not come back to the house. (p. 180)

According to Sources A–E:
1 What picture is conveyed of 1930s Britain?
2 In what ways did unemployment impact on people's lives in the 1930s?
3 Compare the usefulness of these to a historian covering this period.

Statistical evidence

Source F

WAGES, PRICES AND REAL EARNINGS 1913–38.

	Weekly wage rates (1930 = 100)	Retail prices	Average annual real wage earnings
1913	52.4	63.3	82.8
1919	–	136.1	–
1920	143.7	157.6	92.2
1921	134.6	143.0	94.1
1922	107.9	115.8	93.2
1923	100.0	110.1	90.8
1924	101.5	110.8	91.6
1925	102.2	111.4	91.7
1926	99.3	108.9	91.2
1927	101.5	106.0	95.8
1928	100.1	105.1	95.2
1929	100.4	103.8	96.7
1930	100.0	100.0	100.0
1931	98.2	93.4	105.1
1932	96.3	91.1	105.7
1933	95.3	88.6	107.6
1934	96.4	89.2	108.1
1935	98.0	90.5	108.3
1936	100.2	93.0	107.7
1937	102.8	97.5	105.4
1938	106.3	98.7	107.7

Source: D.H. Aldcroft, *The Inter-War Economy: Britain, 1919–1939.* Batsford, 1970, pp. 352, 364

These figures are drawn from the Ministry of Labour Gazette, and are based on the numbers of registered unemployed – i.e. that section of the working population that was claiming unemployment benefit

1929	1 216 000		
1930	1 917 000		
1931	2 630 000	1935	2 036 000
1932	2 745 000	1936	1 755 000
1933	2 521 000	1937	1 484 000
1934	2 159 000	1938	1 791 000
		1939	1 514 000

B.R. Mitchell and P. Deane, *Abstract of British Historical Statistics* (CUP, 1962) p. 66

Source G

UNEMPLOYMENT STATISTICS, 1929–39.

ANNUAL RATES OF
GROWTH OF OUTPUT,
EMPLOYMENT AND
CAPITAL IN SELECTED
INDUSTRIES, 1928–38.

Vehicles	Output	Output per capita	Employment	Capital
Timber and furniture	6.6	3.6	3.0	5.4
Electricity, gas and water	5.2	5.0	0.2	n.a.
Non-ferrous metal manufacture	5.0	2.5	2.5	3.3
Electrical engineering	4.8	3.6	1.2	1.4
Building materials	4.7	1.1	3.6	2.3
Food	3.7	1.6	2.1	0.5
Clothes	3.6	2.1	1.5	0.6
Mechanical engineering	2.7	2.9	−0.2	2.3
Iron and steel	1.7	3.7	−2.0	0.3
Textiles	1.1	3.5	−2.4	0.7
Mines and quarries	0.2	1.6	−1.4	−0.9
Drink	0.2	2.5	−2.3	0.7
Shipbuilding	−0.2	−1.0	0.8	0.4
All industry except agriculture	−2.7	1.9	−4.6	−0.8
	2.8	2.9	−0.1	1.4

Aldcroft, *The British Economy between the Wars*, p. 43

Infant mortality rates were carefully collated by various investigators in the 1930s. The following table was
constructed by C.E. Macnally, and is reproduced in his book, *Public Ill Health*.

	Infant mortality rates per 1000 live births						
	1928	1929	1930	1931	1932	1933	1928–33
Wigan	93	129	107	103	91	110	105.5
St Helens	98	114	80	88	89	116	97.5
Brighton	50	54	51	54	41	47	49.5
Oxford	38	64	41	44	61	32	46.7

J. Stevenson and C. Cook, *The Slump. Society and Politics during the Depression* (Jonathan Cape, 1977) p. 285

Source I

INFANT MORTALITY
RATES.

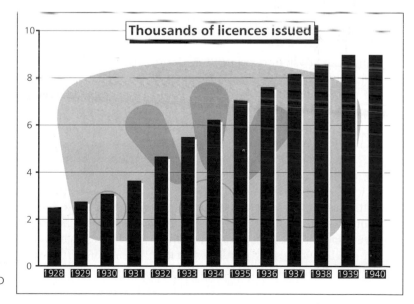

Source J

THE SPREAD OF RADIO AND
TELEVISION.

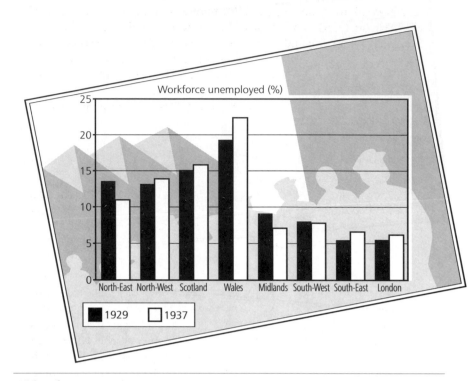

Workforce unemployed (%)

Source K

REGIONAL VARIATIONS IN EMPLOYMENT.

With reference to Sources F–K:
1 What contradictory and agreed trends are illustrated by these statistics?
2 What are the limitations of each of these sources?
3 Is it valid to assert that statistics can be used to show what you want them to?

What the historians say

Source A

I made a study of conditions in the distressed areas and met many types of men. I was deeply touched by their character and courage of outlook, by their heroic endeavour to keep on the right side of that line – by an inch or two – between sanity and despair.

They were not without help, though it didn't amount to very much in this far-stretching bog of unemployment.

The 'lucky South' adopted some of these northern towns and sent them clothes and other supplies. Local committees in touch with the National Council of Social Service did something to bring a little brightness and some purpose to these distressed areas. They taught the jobless men to take up hobbies and learn new handicrafts. They encouraged them to build village halls and playing grounds and sports pavilions. It kept them busy. It gave them a sense of doing something worth while.

Above all in value was the allotment system. Miners, and out of work factory hands, and all manner of unemployed men, worked on the land, raising vegetables and fruit, and poultry, and rabbits, and pigs, for their own families. They worked from dawn to dusk, many of them. They loved this work in the open air and could hardly drag themselves away from it for food or family life …

Sir Philip Gibbs, *The Pageant of the Years* (1946).

Source B

The same sort of problem arises at every turn. Public affairs were harsh and intense; private lives increasingly agreeable. The nineteen-thirties have been called the black years, the devil's decade. Its popular image can be expressed in two phrases: mass unemployment and 'appeasement'. No set of political leaders have been judged so contemptuously since the days of Lord North. Yet at the same time, most English people were enjoying a richer life than any previously known in the history of the world: longer holidays, shorter hours, higher real wages. They had the motor car, cinemas, radio sets, electrical appliances. The two sides of life did not join up. The public men themselves had the air of appearing in a charade. The members of the National Government may be seen in a newsreel, assembling for discussion: stern features, teeth clenched, as they face the crisis. They would hesitate at nothing to save the country, to save the pound. The result of their courage was that the children of the unemployed had less margarine on their bread. After this resolute decision, ministers dispersed to their warm, comfortable homes and ate substantial meals. Such was 'equality of sacrifice'.

A.J.P. Taylor, *English History 1914–1945* (1970), pp. 374–5, 377, 396.

Source C

Of all periods in recent British history, the thirties have had the worst press. Although the decade can now only be remembered by the middle-aged and the elderly, it retains the all-pervasive image of the 'wasted years' and the 'low dishonest decade'. Even for those who did not live through them, the 1930s are haunted by the spectres of mass unemployment, hunger marches, appeasement, and the rise of fascism at home and abroad.

Mass unemployment, more than anything else, gave the inter-war period its image as the 'long weekend'. For almost twenty years there were never fewer than a million people out of work… In the 1920s heavy unemployment reflected the special problems of the 'ailing giants', the staple export industries … Their dislocation as a result of foreign competition and the contraction of world trade led to depression and unemployment in the old industrial areas. By 1929, the depression was a major political issue. The General Election of that year was fought primarily on domestic policy and resulted in a Labour Government under Ramsay MacDonald, pledged to conquer unemployment and restore the nation's prosperity…

… In a sense the intervention of the Second World War served to perpetuate the more depressing image of the thirties, partly at least because the politics of the immediate post-war era were fought on the record of pre-war years. As late as 1951 the Labour Party campaigned with the election slogan of 'Ask your Dad!', an illustration of the way in which the emotive image of the 'hungry thirties' had become part of the repertoire of political cliché. The popular view of the 1930s as a period of unrelieved failure was undoubtedly hardened and reinforced in the years after the war; a view which became sharpened against the background of full employment and affluence of the 1950s and 1960s. Even today the ghost of the thirties stalks political platforms and the media as a symbol of economic disaster, social deprivation and political discontent … A concentration upon unemployment and social distress does not represent as accurate portrayal of the decade … It would, of course, be fatuous to suggest that the 1930s were not for many thousands of people a time of great hardship and personal suffering. But beside the picture of the unemployed must be put the other side of the case … Alongside the picture of the dole queues and hunger marches must also be placed those of another Britain, of new industries, prosperous suburbs and a rising standard of living … This was the paradox which lay at the heart of Britain in the thirties …

John Stevenson and Chris Cook, *The Slump – society and politics during the Depression* (1977), pp. 1–4.

---

1 How does the language and tone used by the historians in Sources A and B help to convey their argument about the 1930s?
2 In Source C, how is it suggested that a myth has developed about Britain in the 1930s?
3 To what extent do these contemporary, statistical and historical assessments of the 1930s agree/disagree?
4 Suggest reasons why these historians, to a certain extent, disagree.

The Impact of the Depression on the Government

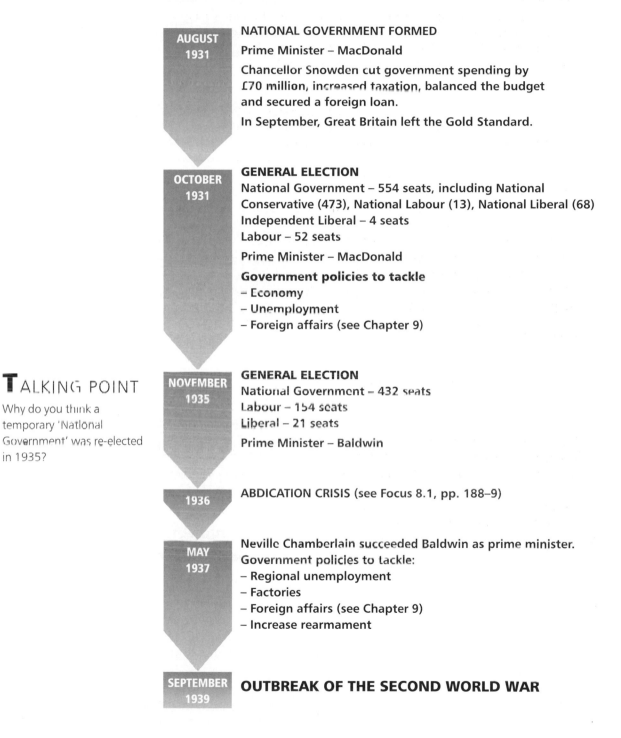

AUGUST 1931

NATIONAL GOVERNMENT FORMED

Prime Minister – MacDonald

Chancellor Snowden cut government spending by £70 million, increased taxation, balanced the budget and secured a foreign loan.

In September, Great Britain left the Gold Standard.

OCTOBER 1931

GENERAL ELECTION

National Government – 554 seats, including National Conservative (473), National Labour (13), National Liberal (68)
Independent Liberal – 4 seats
Labour – 52 seats

Prime Minister – MacDonald

Government policies to tackle
– Economy
– Unemployment
– Foreign affairs (see Chapter 9)

NOVEMBER 1935

GENERAL ELECTION

National Government – 432 seats
Labour – 154 seats
Liberal – 21 seats

Prime Minister – Baldwin

1936

ABDICATION CRISIS (see Focus 8.1, pp. 188–9)

MAY 1937

Neville Chamberlain succeeded Baldwin as prime minister.
Government policies to tackle:
– Regional unemployment
– Factories
– Foreign affairs (see Chapter 9)
– Increase rearmament

SEPTEMBER 1939

OUTBREAK OF THE SECOND WORLD WAR

TALKING POINT

Why do you think a temporary 'National Government' was re-elected in 1935?

National Government Policies – Economy and Unemployment

Government expenditure cuts

Imposed by Snowden before the 1931 Election

10 per cent reduction in unemployment benefits

Salaries controlled or cut for government employees

Expenditure cut by £70 million

Raised standard rate of income tax from 22.5 to 25 per cent

Negotiated loan from abroad

Devaluation

September 1931 Great Britain left the Gold Standard

Pound fell from $4.86 to around $3.40

Benefits from a more realistic exchange rate

'Weaker' pound made British exports cheaper and so more competitive

Low interest rates

Interest rates were lowered from 6 per cent in 1931 to 2 per cent in 1932

Government held them at this level for seven years

Encouraged expansion of private enterprise through business borrowing

1 To what extent was the gradual improvement in the economy due to the policies of the government:
   a How did government policies help?
   b What were their limitations?
   c What other factors contributed to the recovery?
2 What policies can be suggested that would have tackled the unemployment problem more directly and radically:
   a by a Communist?
   b by a Fascist?

Special areas

1935 Special Areas Act

Temporary measure to facilitate economic and social improvement of designated areas of high unemployment – such as South Wales, SW Scotland, North East, West Cumberland. The £2 million fund managed by two commissioners. Produced water supplies, sewage disposal, hospital buildings and other amenities.

Did not achieve substantially – criticised from the beginning that it was not doing enough, certain areas of need were not designated and only 50,000 jobs were created.

Economy ACTION Unemployment

Unemployment relief

1930 Poor Law Act – Poor Law renamed Public Assistance. Workhouse only for aged and infirm.

1931 10% cut in unemployment benefit. Standard rate for 26 weeks given then benefits means tested by Public Assistance Committees. In first seven weeks of operation 53 percent of claims were either disallowed or reduced.

1934 Unemployment Act. Divided relief insurance schemes into short term unemployed contributory scheme for 26 weeks and long-term unemployed assistance scheme under the Unemployment Assistance Board.

Means Test introduced – for long-term unemployed. They had to prove willing to find work and agree to an investigation of personal finances. Benefits in proportion to measured income of household.

1937 – able bodied poor, maintained up until now by Poor Law, finally absorbed into new system.

Protection

Free Trade v. Protection much debated but Conservatives in the 1930s pushed for implementation of a policy of Protection

1931 – Import duties could be imposed at short notice on goods entering in abnormal quantities

1932 – Import Duties Bill – 10% general duty on all imports except from Empire

August 1932 – Ottawa Conference – no common imperial economic policy emerged, but a measure of preference given to imperial goods

Protection was not significant in the economy's recovery

Transfers and work schemes

Transference – about 44,000 workers were encouraged to move to other towns and 30,000 men were placed on retraining courses.

An extremist response to the Depression: Communists and Fascists in 1930s Britain

The National Government continued to enjoy the support of the majority of the British public throughout the 1930s. The Liberals' political decline accelerated into oblivion and the Labour Party adjusted only slowly to the new political and economic context. However, as in Europe, the depression increased the support for extremist groups who proposed radical solutions to the economic and social problems. There was a significant growth on the extreme left wing in the shape of the Communist Party of Great Britain (CPGB) and on the far right by Mosley's British Union of Fascists (BUF).

TALKING POINT

From your own knowledge and by research, which countries in Europe were taken over by extremist dictatorships and for what reasons?

Source A

On October 4th 1936 I was 12 years old. Now if you were a youngster brought up in the East End in the 1930s you were no stranger to politics because there were political meetings on every corner. And as a kid you stood there and listened to the Communist Party, the Labour Party, and you took it all in, and the fascists had their regular meetings too. If you were a Jewish kid and you stood there listening to them belting out their message of hate, you learned to hate back, because you heard of all the attacks in the East End …

> Joyce Goodmann recollecting the events of 1936 in London 50 years later at a seminar organised by the Institute of Contemporary British History.

Source B

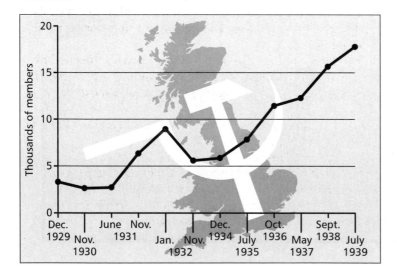

MEMBERSHIP OF THE COMMUNIST PARTY OF GREAT BRITAIN, 1929–39.

Source C

'Hurrah for the Blackshirts', *Daily Mail*, 15 January 1934.

> Because Fascism comes from Italy, shortsighted people in this country think they show a sturdy national spirit by deriding it.

This article was written by Lord Rothermere, the proprietor of the *Daily Mail* and a leading supporter of Oswald Mosley's British Union of Fascists.

If their ancestors had been equally stupid, Britain would have had no banking system, no Roman Law, nor even any football, since all of these are of Italian invention.

The Socialists, especially, who jeer at the principles and uniform of the Blackshirts as being of foreign origin, forget that the founder and High Priest of their own creed was the German Jew Karl Marx.

Though the name and form of Fascism originated in Italy, that movement is not now peculiar to any nation. *It stands in every country for the Party of Youth*. It represents the effort of the young generation to put new life into out-of-date political systems.

That alone is enough to make it a factor of immense value in our national affairs.

The Blackshirt movement is the organised effort of the younger generation to break this stranglehold which senile politicians have so long maintained on our public affairs ...

Such an effort was long overdue. The nation's realisation of the need for it is shown by the astonishing progress the Blackshirts are making, especially in the big industrial areas ... *A crusading spirit has come back to British politics* ...

What are these Blackshirts who hold 500 meetings a week throughout the country and whose uniform has become so familiar a feature of our political life? ...

Blackshirts proclaim a fact which politicians dating from pre-war days will never face – that the new age requires new methods and new men. They base their contention on the simple truth that parliamentary government is conducted on the same lines as it was in the eighteenth century, though the conditions with which it deals have altered beyond recognition. They want to bring our national administration up to date.

This purpose does not rest on theory alone. It can be justified by the gigantic revival of national strength and spirit which a similar process of modernisation has brought about in Italy and Germany.

1 From Source A, why do you think that the East End of London attracted so much streetcorner politics in the 1930s?
2 From Source B, account for the growth of Communism in the 1930s.
3 From Source C, what is the appeal of Fascism advertised here?
4 Find out the meaning of Communism and Fascism.
5 List reasons why both groups gained support at this time in Britain.
6 What sort of people do you think might support each?

Communists

Some background notes

The CPGB was formed in August 1920 with the aim of bringing about a workers' revolution. The aggressive export of Communism by Lenin in the Soviet Union came to an end in the early 1920s due to economic problems and their need to consolidate their position in Russia.

In the mid-1920s the CPGB tried to work through the Labour Party but they were marginalised and their attempts to affiliate were rejected on three separate occasions.

By 1930 the CPGB had fielded 25 candidates in the 1929 Election and had a membership of about 2,555 members – only half in fact of their original number.

Was the 1930s a 'Red Decade'?

The Depression was to the Communists' advantage – their appeal was direct and attractive to many working-class men and middle-class intellectuals. The end of Capitalism seemed near and their radical solution of a workers' revolution had a sympathetic reception. Party membership increased sevenfold to 18,000 by 1939 and their newspaper, the *Daily Worker*, had a circulation of around 80,000. They campaigned for the unemployed, rallied support against the Fascists, disassociated themselves from the failures of the Labour government between 1929 and 1931 and resumed activity through the trades union movement. Intellectuals were converted to Communism – a bevy of spies from Cambridge University included Philby, Burgess and Maclean, and notable poets such as W.H. Auden and C. Day Lewis.

From 1935 onwards the CPGB grew rapidly, partly as a result of a new 'popular front' strategy which encouraged a united front of all opponents of Fascism to work together. In an attempt to unite all forces on the left wing of British politics, in the 1935 Election the CPGB withdrew all but two candidates but another application to affiliate with the Labour Party again failed.

However, Communist success was limited. In certain areas the movement was of significance but politically it failed to make significant progress. It was more a 'minority taste' which generated interest, enjoyed some individual success, but it never posed a real challenge to the National Government.

Some areas of significance?

 Communists had some influence in established trades unions, particularly in London.

 But Communists tended not to go beyond the role of hardworking shop stewards and union officials.

 Communists highlighted the protest against Fascism.

But this tended to be in the form of street violence which was put down by the police.

 In 1936 the Left Book Club was launched by Victor Gollancz. By 1939, it had 60,000 members and over 730 local discussion groups.

This generated interest more than support.

Goodwill for Communism was gained by British Communists fighting for the Republicans in the Spanish Civil War – more than 50% of Britons killed were Communists.

However, this did not translate into active support in Britain itself.

Most significant was the CPGB's work on behalf of the unemployed via their front organisation – the National Unemployed Workers' Movement (the NUWM) set up in 1921 by Wal Hannington with the aim to provide either 'work or full maintenance'. They gave advice to the unemployed on their rights, represented them at benefit tribunals and were most effective in numerous individual cases.

 They organised hunger marches, publicity stunts and advertised the plight of the unemployed.

 But success at this level was qualified. They failed to organise the unemployed as a political force. Very few moved from the NUWM to the CPGB. In fact the NUWM served more to make the existing system bearable.

Fascists

Some background notes

- The British Union of Fascists was founded in October 1932 by a wealthy aristocrat, Oswald Mosley. It lasted until 1940.
- After Mussolini came to power in Italy in 1922 a similar group formed in Britain – always the poor relation, the British Fascists never amounted to more than a few hundred members. An Imperial Fascist League was founded in 1928 – virulently anti-Semitic but generally as insignificant as its predecessor.
- Mosley had been both a Conservative and Labour MP, finally achieving a Cabinet position in MacDonald's 1929 government. He adopted a radical solution for solving the unemployment problem, but his Memorandum was rejected by the party and he resigned in protest.
- In 1931 he formed his New Party, a short-lived political organisation which was dissolved after the election of that year having gained no seats. Mosley moved more towards the right wing and after a visit to Rome in January 1932 he founded the BUF in October closely modelled on Mussolini's Fascist party – black shirts for uniforms and many rallies and processions.

MOSLEY AND THE BLACKSHIRTS.

TALKING POINT

What was the appeal of Mussolini's Fascist regime in Italy?
What do you understand by a. 'corporate state' and b. autarky?

What were the aims of the BUF?

1 To form a strictly disciplined corporate state ruled by a small Cabinet under Mosley.
2 To limit Parliament's powers – legislative work was to be in the hands of 24 corporations representing different sections of industry.
3 To preserve a capitalist system with firm state direction and promote autarky.
4 Protectionism to maintain British goods' prices. The higher wages would stimulate demand and minimise unemployment.
5 To reorganise the position of monarchy, church and empire.
6 To encourage traditional values for gender and family.

Who joined the BUF?

Membership ebbed and flowed. In 1934 numbers rose from 17,000 members to 50,000. By the end of 1935 support had crashed to 5,000. The following year numbers recovered to 15,500 but it declined again after this.

Support shifted socially and geographically but general patterns can be established.

- Ex-servicemen, discontented professionals, ex-public school and small traders joined in areas such as the South east, East Anglia, Midlands, Yorkshire and parts of London.
- It gleaned support from the unemployed, particularly in Manchester and Liverpool.
- From 1935–8 support was concentrated in the East End of London but amongst working-class youths and anti-semites. However, support from these sections declined in the face of the BUF's increasingly pro-German line.

Why did the BUF fail?

1 The character of Mosley – although he had the capacity to inspire and was a powerful platform speaker, he was a poor tactician and administrator.
2 Financial problems – the party was always short of money, a position exacerbated by the ending of loans from Mussolini by 1937.
3 Lack of regional control – salaried staff were reduced drastically and medocrities were left in charge.
4 Division over strategy – members disagreed over whether to adopt a military or a political approach.
5 Rothermere's support – this Tory press baron withdrew his support and other media coverage was curtailed.
6 Economic recovery – this incrased support for the National Government.
7 Conservative domination of the government ensured support of the propertied classes.
8 Even after the 1931 debacle, Labour held on to its traditional strongholds where many unemployed were not attracted to extremist parties.
9 The culture of the BUF – this was intrinsically alien to Britain.
10 Many Fascist aims were antagonistic to a variety of vested interests.

TASK

As European countries such as Germany, Italy and Spain fell to Fascist dictatorships and Russia to Communist rule during the interwar period, it is worth considering why Britain did not follow the same path. As a leading industrialist exporting nation she was hit by the 'economic blizzard' following the 1929 crash yet democracy survived.

Question: Why did political extremism in 1930s Britain fail?

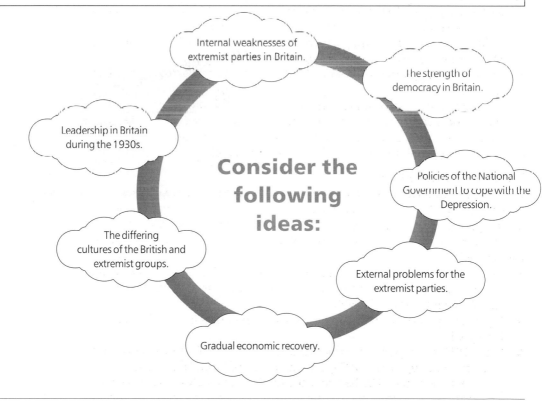

Consider the following ideas:

- Internal weaknesses of extremist parties in Britain.
- The strength of democracy in Britain.
- Leadership in Britain during the 1930s.
- Policies of the National Government to cope with the Depression.
- The differing cultures of the British and extremist groups.
- External problems for the extremist parties.
- Gradual economic recovery.

FOCUS

8.1 The Abdication Crisis, December 1936

INSTRUMENT OF ABDICATION

I, Edward the Eighth, of Great Britain, Ireland, and the British Dominions beyond the Seas, King, Emperor of India, do hereby declare My irrevocable determination to renounce the Throne for Myself and for My descendants, and My desire that effect should be given to this Instrument of Abdication immediately.

In token whereof I have hereunto set My hand this tenth day of December, nineteen hundred and thirty six, in the presence of the witnesses whose signatures are subscribed.

SIGNED AT FORT BELVEDERE IN THE PRESENCE OF

King George V had died in January 1936 and was succeeded by his 41-year-old unmarried son, Edward VIII.

1 Edward VIII decided to abdicate in order to marry Mrs Simpson a twice-divorced American. This ended a constitutional crisis lasting seven days.

2 Prince Albert, Duke of York, succeeded him as king, becoming George VI, his wife Elizabeth became Queen.

3 The instrument of Abdication was witnessed by Edward's three younger brothers.

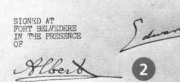

EDWARD'S MISTRESS AND CONSTANT COMPANION. DIVORCED FOR THE SECOND TIME IN OCTOBER 1936. AMERICAN. A MEMBER OF THE 'SMART SET'. THE WOMAN EDWARD SAID HE INTENDED TO MARRY.

KING OF GREAT BRITAIN AND HER EMPIRE. HEAD OF THE CHURCH OF ENGLAND. UNMARRIED. A POPULAR HEIR TO THE THRONE WITH A GENUINE CONCERN FOR THE BRITISH PEOPLE OFFSET BY A LOVE OF LIFE IN THE 'SMART SET'.

1 Why did the government, led by Baldwin, not allow the marriage?
2 A morganatic marriage could not be agreed on by either party – what would it have meant?
3 What stance did the Archbishop of Canterbury Dr Lang take in the crisis and why?
4 What does the crisis illustrate about social attitudes in Britain at the time?

The diary entries of prominent public figures at the time indicate reactions to the crisis (until 3 December 1936 the British media observed a complete news blackout – there were no intrusive zoom lens photographs of the King on his Mediterranean yacht, no speculation and very little on the Simpson divorce case in October).

Harold Nicolson, a writer, journalist and MP, wrote:

3 December 1936

The storm breaks. A fine leading article in the Telegraph and a confused muddled jumble in the Times … the other papers write in sorrow rather than anger. Down to the House. That note of feeling of expectancy which is unmistakable hangs over our dear old aquarium … Members draw in as question time draws to its end and the galleries and gangways are packed … He (Baldwin) looks ill and profoundly sad. He says that no constitutional crisis 'has yet' arisen. I dash off without dinner to Islington … The streets flame with posters 'King and Mrs Simpson' …

I do not find people angry with Mrs Simpson. But I do find a deep and enraged fury against the king himself. In eight months he has destroyed the great structure of popularity which he had raised. The Cabinet meet all day. I gather that Attlee and Sinclair have both refused to form alternative government and that the king will be forced to abdicate. The Duke of York will call himself King George VI which bedsed he is. We are all staggered with shame and distress. I never dreamt it would come to this.

Henry Channon – MP, writer and socialite often referred to by his nickname 'Chips' – wrote:

3 December 1936

The Country and the Empire now know that their Monarch, their young King-Emperor, their adored Apollo, is in love with an American twice divorced, whom they believe to be an adventuress. The whole world recoils from the shock, but very few know that she is a woman of infinite charm, gentleness, courage and loyalty, whose influence on upon the King until now has been highly salutary. … The King … is driving straight to the precipice; if he defies the government and persists with his marriage plan the Cabinet will resign and there is no alternative Government as the Socialists have refused office under the present circumstances … Wallis Simpson, a chauffeur, a detective and Perry Browlow are at this moment speeding across France and Beaverbrook is plotting at Stornoway House trying to keep up the king's courage, the courage of a broken man at bay.

1 What was the reaction of Nicolson and Channon to the news of 3 December?

2 How do they view the King, Mrs Simpson and the Prime Minister?

3 What are the similarities and differences between these two accounts?

4 How useful are the diaries of these public figures when studying the Abdication crisis?

REVIEW

How were people in Britain affected by economic trends in the 1930s?

This is a familiar type of question posed by historians. The main problem in answering it is not so much establishing 'the economic trends' as acknowledging how different groups within society had widely divergent experiences. Society can be subdvided by various criteria, which makes social history multidimensional.

Percentage of insured population

	30 and over
	25 – 29.9
	20 – 24.9
	15 – 19.9
	10 – 14.9
	5 – 9.9

Unemployment by county, June 1932

TASK

List as many social groupings as you can think of and the ways in which various economic trends might affect them
In the 1930s there were significant social groupings which were affected differently by economic trends.
From the map, can you suggest which these are?
What was the impact on their lives of the 1930s economy?

TASK

Re-read the passage from J.B. Priestley in the Preview at the start of this chapter.
Divide the class into groups of three.
Each member of the group is to prepare a report on the lifestyle of a person living in each of the three Englands during the 1930s:
- 'Old England'.
- 'The industrial England of coal, iron, steel, cotton, wool and railways.'
- 'The new post-war England'.
You will need to use the information from this chapter and your own research.

Now conduct a class discussion on the question:
'What was it like to live in 1930s Britain?'

9 Appeasement and the Outbreak of the Second World War

PREVIEW

British foreign policy in the 1920s and the 1930s

The British government's foreign policy of collective security in the 1920s and appeasement in the 1930s was an attempt, for various debatable reasons, to avoid another war. The 1914–18 conflict had been a shocking experience which had imprinted itself indelibly on people's memories. Psychologically, economically, militarily, politically and socially its ramifications had been unprecedented. Another similar war was to be avoided at all costs. However, despite the good intentions, new worldwide political institutions, visionary rhetoric and much hard work, the British governments of the 1930s failed in their aim. A second world war broke out in 1939, declared after Hitler marched into Poland on 1 September. Appeasement had failed to keep the peace.

'PEACE IN OUR TIME'. CHAMBERLAIN WAVES HIS PIECE OF PAPER, SEPTEMBER 1938.

TALKING POINT

Discuss the various portrayals of Chamberlain during the Czechoslovakian crisis on these next two pages.
Explain why he is portrayed differently. Refer to the chronology of the crisis on pages 208–9.

'MEIN KAMPF', 24 SEPTEMBER 1938.

STILL HOPE

'STILL HOPE', *PUNCH*,
21 SEPTEMBER 1938.

The international context of the 1930s

Great Britain had three areas of strategic concern – British foreign policy had to consider these simultaneously and keep them in balance.

1 The European zone

Britain's main ally here was France. Germany had been a central concern since the Versailles Treaty. As Germany's economy recovered and the Nazi system increased its hold after 1933, it was seen to be a growing problem. Among British politicians, there had been a tendency to minimise European connections in the 1920s which became more difficult to maintain in the 1930s.

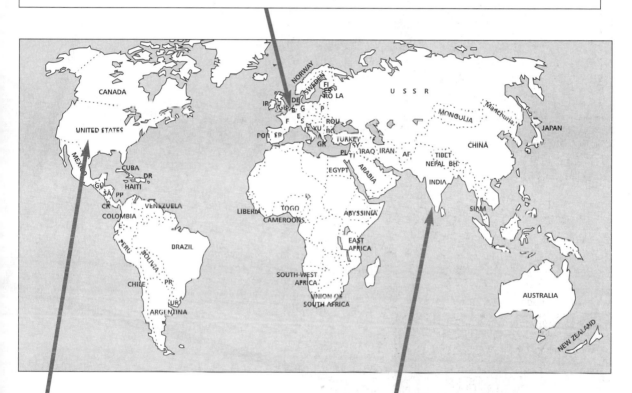

2 The USA

Britain was fully aware of the USA as a growing power. Her intervention in the First World War in 1917 had been decisive. USA in the 1920s had adopted an isolationist stance. Britain, despite the influence of some Americophobes, wished to promote relations with the USA.

3 The Empire zone

Britain was concerned to protect her existing Empire – for political and economic reasons. Dominion status in the British Commonwealth of nations was held by Canada, Australia, New Zealand, South Africa and the Irish Free State. India was providing difficulties – demands for independence increased and the Government of India Act was passed in 1935. Britain had new administrative areas mandated by the League of Nations – Palestine, Iraq and Tanganyika.

Collective security threatened

In the late 1920s and 1930s the international context changed dramatically. The arrival of three increasingly aggressive, expansionist powers – Nazi Germany, Fascist Italy and Imperial Japan – threatened democracies worldwide and impacted on all three areas of British diplomatic activity.

NAZI GERMANY

Hitler – leader of the German National Socialist Party (the Nazis) – came to power in January 1933 following the collapse of democracy, the Weimar Republic, in Germany. His main aim – set out in *Mein Kampf* – was the territorial expansion of the Nazi Third Reich. The Nazi appeal rested upon nationalist demands to revise the hated Versailles Treaty, absorb German-speaking people into the Reich and expand eastward, ultimately invading the Soviet Union, thus destroying the Communist enemy. In 1935, Hitler's political position was secure – a dictatorship existed, economic recovery was on its way. Conscription was introduced and the existence of the German Luftwaffe was announced.

- March 1936 Nazi aggression began with the remilitarization of the Rhineland. The Nazis also sent aid to Fascist General Franco in Spain.
- 1936 Hitler joined Japan and the following year Italy in an alliance, the Anti-Comintern Pact, to combat Communism, particularly in the USSR.
- 1938–9 Hitler expanded into Austria, Czechoslovakia and Poland.

HITLER AND MUSSOLINI, MAY 1938.

FASCIST ITALY

Mussolini had become the Fascist Prime Minister of Italy in 1922 – a dictatorship was consolidated over the next few years. Although Mussolini's claims had been to increase Italy's international power, during the 1920s his foreign policy was moderate. Like Hitler, he wished to revise the post-First World War settlement which for Italian nationalists had constituted a 'mutilated victory'. In the 1930s Mussolini's policy became overtly aggressive and expansionist.

- 1935 Italy invaded Abyssinia – occupying it by spring 1936.
- 1936 Mussolini signed the Rome–Berlin Axis and later in the year sent military aid to Franco in the Spanish Civil War.
- 1937 Italy signed the Anti-Comintern Pact.
- 1936–9 Increasing dependence on Hitler, signing a military pact in 1939.
- 1939 Italy occupied Albania.

IMPERIAL JAPAN

Imperial Japan

Japan's strong economic position was well developed by the late 1920s.

- 1926 Emperor Hirohito ascended the throne.
- 1927 General Tanaka, the Japanese Prime Minister, issued a memorandum which called for a positive policy of expansion and the domination of Asia by Japan. This was supported by the Japanese military who in turn provoked incidents.
- 1931 Mukden incident led to the Japanese occupation of Manchuria.
- 1933 The League of Nations declared this a violation of international law but failed to stop the establishment of the Japanese state of Manchukuo – on the Chinese mainland. Following this ruling, Japan withdrew from the League.
- 1936 Japan entered the Anti-Comintern Pact with Germany.
- 1937–45 Sino-Japanese War.

TASK

Explain the ways in which Great Britain's foreign policy concerns were impacted upon by
- **a** Nazi Germany
- **b** Fascist Italy
- **c** Imperial Japan.

QUESTION:

QUESTION: **What was appeasement?**

ANSWER:

- Appeasement was the policy followed by the British government in tackling the unfolding international crises of the 1930s in order to avoid war.
- The word 'appeasement' crept into commentators'/ politicians' vocabulary in the 1920s. At the time of the Versailles Settlement, C.P. Scott, the editor of the *Manchester Guardian*, wrote of the need for a 'peace of appeasement'.
- Appeasement, according to the historian Keith Robbins, was 'a disposition to anticipate and avoid conflict by sensible concession and negotiation'.

QUESTION: **What was the nature of appeasement?**

ANSWER:

- It was a complex mixture of moral values, political constraints, economic necessity and military realism.
- Either an active, interfering, initiating search for compromise and peace or a passive reaction, stagnation, acquiescence to extreme demands in an attempt to give in and thus avoid conflict.

QUESTION: **Was appeasement the right policy?**

ANSWER:

- This is a subject of much debate amongst contemporaries and subsequently historians.
- Were there other options? Does failure of a policy make it unjustifiable? Was appeasement in any way inevitable?

TALKING POINT

Is appeasement a policy pursued by governments today?

1 Read Sources A to N carefully and match them to the reasons for appeasement given in the table opposite:

2 Which of these factors suggest the British government in the 1930s was acting more from motives of: a. fear. b. morality. c. practicality. d. vested interests?

Why Appeasement?

REASON		SOURCE
A	Impact of the First World War	
B	Weakness of the Versailles settlement	
C	Political context in Britain in the 1930s	
D	Interwar economy	
E	British military weakness	
F	Protection of the Empire	
G	Policy against Communism	
H	Crisis of French alliance	
I	Public opinion in the 1930s	

Source A
The Peace Ballot (July 1935).

Total population: 46,869,000.

Question: Should Britain remain a member of the League of Nations? Yes: 10,642,560 (97%). No: 337,000 (3%).

Question: Are you in favour of an all-round reduction in armaments by international agreement? Yes: 10,058,000 (92.5%). No: 815,365 (7.5%).

Question: Are you in favour of the all-round abolition of national military and naval aircraft by international agreement? Yes: 9,157,145 (85%). No: 1,614,159 (15%).

Question: Should the manufacture and sale of arms for private profit be prohibited by international agreement? Yes: 10,002,849 (93.1%). No: 740,354 (6.9%).

Question: Do you consider that if a nation insists on attacking another the other nations should combine to compel it to stop by economic and non-military measures? Yes: 9,627,606 (94.1%). No: 607,165 (5.9%).

Question: Do you consider that, if a nation insists on attacking another, the other nations should combine to stop it by, if necessary, military measures? Yes: 6,506,777 (74.2%). No: 2,262,261 (25.8%).

A. Livingstone, *The Peace Ballot: the Official History* (1955).

Source B
Chiefs of Staff report as summarised by Chamberlain, Prime Minister, 8 December 1937.

From the above Report it will be seen that our Naval, Military and Air Forces, in their present stage of development, are still far from sufficient to meet our defensive commitments, which now extend from Western Europe through the Mediterranean to the Far East ... Without overlooking the assistance which we should hope to obtain from France, and possibly other allies, we cannot foresee the time when our defence forces will be strong enough to safeguard our territory, trade and vital interests against Germany, Italy and Japan simultaneously. We cannot, therefore, exaggerate the importance, from the point of view of Imperial defence, of any political or international action that can be taken to reduce the number of our potential enemies and to gain the support of potential allies.

Source C
Lord Rothermere discussing the return of colonies to Germany, *Daily Mail*, 1934.

Though this proposal may not be so popular, I am convinced that it is wise. We cannot expect a nation of he-men like the Germans to sit forever with folded arms under the provocations and stupidities of the Treaty of Versailles ... To deny this mighty nation, conspicuous for its organising ability and scientific achievements, a share in the work of developing backward regions of the world is preposterous.

Source D
Stanley Baldwin, Prime Minister, in a speech, 31 October 1935.

We live under the shadow of the last War and its memories sicken us. We remember what modern warfare is, with no glory in it but the heroism of men. We remember forcing ourselves to read the casualty lists. Have you thought what it has meant to the world in recent years to have had that swathe of death cut through the loveliest and the best of our contemporaries, how public life has suffered because those who would have been ready to take over from our tired and disillusioned generation are not there?

Source E

The Hitler revolution is a sufficient guarantee that Russian Communism will not spread westward. The solid German bourgeois holds the central fortress of Europe. But there may be secrets in Fascism or Hitlerism, which the democracies of the West will desire, without abandoning their fundamental character, to adopt.

H.A.L. Fisher, History of Europe (1936).

Source F

In this country Conservatives prefer the German system to the Russian because it is nationalistic in spirit and does not seek to divide them on class lines against themselves.

Sir E. Grigg, Britain Looks Back at Germany (1938).

Source G

" PERHAPS IT WOULD GEE-UP BETTER IF WE LET IT TOUCH EARTH "

'PERHAPS IT WOULD GEE-UP BETTER IF WE LET IT TOUCH EARTH'.

Source H
The honourable W. Astor, MP, in a speech to the House of Commons, March 1936.

The people of this country feel, I believe, that if there is a war now, it is possible that England may lose her influence for good, through many years to come, by having her economic and social system crippled, if not destroyed.

Source I

The *Evening Standard* has long and consistently attacked the League of Nations and the principle of collective security as futile yet dangerous, and has been censured for so doing even though events have justified the attack.

But it is not enough to denounce the League and the collective system. If the League does not work, the British people must be presented with an alternative policy for the attainment of their ideal, which is to live at peace.

We have such a policy. It provides that Great Britain should adopt towards European affairs an attitude of detachment. She should not be tied by neither pact nor covenant, nor alliance to the destinies of Continental nations. She should be free.

Evening Standard, 27 March 1936.

Source J
Baldwin in a speech, 12 November 1936.

You will remember the election at Fulham in the autumn of 1933, when a seat which the National Government held was lost by about 7,000 votes on no issue but the pacifist. My position as the leader of a great party was not altogether a comfortable one. I asked myself what chance there was – when that feeling that was given expression to in Fulham was common throughout the country – what chance was there within the next year or two of that feeling being so changed that the country would be given a mandate for rearmament?

Source K

Size and distribution of British Army (1938)

Home defence	107,000.
British India and Burma army	55,000.
Indian army	190,000.
Middle East	21,000.
Far East	12,000.
West Indies	2,000.
Total	387,000.

The size of the German army (1939)

Home defence	730,000.
Trained conscripts	2,970,000.
Total	3,700,000.

Figures from P.M.H. Bell, *The Origins of the Second World War in Europe* (1986).

Source L
Rumbold, British ambassador in Germany, to Sir John Simon, Foreign Secretary, 30 June 1933.

> Unpleasant incidents and excesses are bound to occur during a revolution, but the deliberate ruthlessness and brutality which have been practised during the last five months seem both excessive and unnecessary. I have the impression that the persons directing the policy of the Hitler Government are not normal. Many of us, indeed, have a feeling that we are living in a country where fantastic hooligans and eccentrics have got the upper hand.

Ernest Bevin was to become Foreign Secretary in Clement Attlee's postwar Labour government. See Chapter 11.

Source M
Ernest Bevin, Labour MP, speech to the Executive Committee of his union, March 1937.

> From the day Hitler came to power, I have felt that the democratic countries would have to face war. I believe he was taken too cheap. We have been handicapped by the very sincere pacifists in our Party who believe that the danger can be met by resolution and prayers and by turning the other cheek. While I appreciate the sincerity, I cannot understand anybody who refuses to face the facts in relations to the happenings in China, in Abyssinia, in Spain, all virtually disarmed countries. I cannot see any way of stopping Hitler and the other dictators except by war.

Source N
Chiefs of Staff report, April 1936.

> If they [the French] think they are strong enough at the present time to undertake hostilities against Germany, we may find ourselves committed to participation against Germany with forces which are not only inadequate to render effective support, but incapable of assuring our own security, with grave consequences to the people of this country.

Why appeasement? A more detailed examination of the factors

Impact of the First World War
Many lessons were learnt from this war – as the first total, global conflict ever experienced society and, in turn, governments had had to adjust to its consequences. The transition to total war was in sharp contrast to 19th century conflicts. This required the full mobilization of a nation's resources, energy and a mass participation of the whole population – in uniform or not. Much criticism was levied against 'secret diplomacy' in the prewar foreign offices of Europe. This led to a call for open government and a more democratic control over crucial decision-making – particularly in the light of the political changes which followed the First World War. Importantly, the extension of the franchise in 1918 made all men over 21 and a significant number of women politically more influential. The

Labour Party benefited greatly from the war – and emerged as proponents of a wider democracy. The war also made government aware of the great cost involved – in both human and material terms. The enormous scale of casualties produced an intense hatred of force – propagandised by a multitude of anti-war books, films, poems and pressure groups such as the Peace Pledge Union, the Peace Society and the No More War Movement. Remembrance Sunday was to be an annual living memorial, together with the thousands of stone or wooden war memorials erected throughout Great Britain. The hatred of war as experienced between 1914 and 1918 and the growth of pacifism in society influenced the tone of British foreign policy significantly.

Weaknesses of the Versailles Settlement

There were two main weaknesses in this settlement which may have contributed to the support for appeasement – the harsh treatment of Germany and the excessive faith placed in the League of Nations.

Increasingly, commentators in the 1920s and 1930s felt that Germany had been treated too harshly. The reparations payments were initially impossible for her, the loss of land led to claims for German minorities under foreign governments and a serious diminution of economic resources. In his 'Economic Consequences of the Peace', John Maynard Keynes, the economist, suggested that the world economy would suffer as Germany's position as a leading industrial nation had been seriously undermined by Versailles. General Foch saw the Versailles Settlement as a mere 20-year armistice. Sympathy was evoked for Germany's claim to revise Versailles. The USA was active in pursuit of easing the reparations question with the Dawes and Young Plans (1924 and 1929). A blind eye was turned when the Weimar Republic went beyond the military restrictions placed upon her – by developing military bases on Russian soil in the 1920s. So appeasement contains an element of guilt concerning the harshness of Germany's treatment and an attempt to put it right by responding to 'reasonable' German nationalist demands.

At the same time governments placed a naïve faith in the effectiveness of the League of Nations as a prop to appeasers. This institution was set up with the aim of settling disputes, providing collective security and imposing sanctions on any erring state. However, by the early 1930s the supposed efficacy of the League of Nations was clearly overestimated. Her power to 'police' the international scene was not backed by a military force or by effective economic sanctions. By 1937 the only major powers to remain in side the League were Great Britain, France and the USSR – and there were no real means to enforce decisions.

The political context in Britain in the 1930s

The nature of the British political system suggested that disagreements could be overcome through debate without recourse to force. In the 1920s governments and opposition had coexisted and society did not fall apart because different parties demanded different things. This democratic principle lay at the heart of appeasement. The notion of a National Government in Britain in the 1930s takes the point further. In 1931 a National Government was formed to tackle an economic crisis which required party priorities to be subordinated to the national good. The government therefore rested upon agreement and compromise – and this, it was thought, could be seen as a commendable principle. It was felt by many that domestic behaviour could be relevant to or, in fact, emulated in world diplomacy. Differences of opinion and aims are obvious on the international stage but peaceful resolutions between reasonable parties should be possible.

The interwar economy

In 1922, Bonar Law, the leader of the Conservative Party, said 'We cannot act alone as the policemen of the world, the financial and social condition of the country makes that impossible.' The impact of First World War on the British economy was severe. There was a debt to be paid to USA, exports had decreased, imports increased and there had been a critical loss of foreign markets. Unemployment was high throughout the 1920s and soared after the 1929 Crash. It is arguable that the British economy could not afford the expenditure of war. Many politicians wanted to see public finances diverted to support social welfare programmes such as housing, healthcare and unemployment benefits. The Treasury, influential at Cabinet-level discussions, consistently opposed rearmament. In the period 1931–7 their view was that rearmament would damage economic recovery. However, it could be viewed that a policy of rearmament would also generate benefits for the economy by stimulating production.

Britain's poor economic position during the interwar years made her fearful of the cost of war but also provided an added incentive towards working with Germany and bringing her back into economic co-operation, making her a viable economic partner but not allowing her to dominate. Peace was in Britain's best economic interest. This was another significant factor towards appeasement.

British military weakness

In 1935, a secret report commissioned by the government on the condition of British armed forces advised that Britain was not capable of fighting against Germany, Italy and Japan simultaneously. Throughout this period, the military had consistently looked to the government to avoid war. By 1937–8 it still appeared as if Britain could play no effective military role in Europe to prevent Hitler's seizure of Austria (1938) and protect the vulnerability of Czechoslovakia. Therefore Chamberlain, prime minister from 1937 and chief advocate of the policy of appeasement, had very real military reasons for deterring Hitler from war – or in the last instance buying time in order to build up forces.

One of the major military problems was the rapid demobilisation from 1918 onwards. There were 2,700,000 troops in France at the peak of war and men wanted to be demobilised quickly. The Dominion forces had no wish to stay either. In 1918, 3.5 million troops were on the government payroll. By 1920 it was a tenth of that figure. Rapid demobilisation was accompanied by no appraisal of future needs, nor an attempt to develop the Armed Forces in line with the lessons of the First World War. So worryingly Britain had very small-scale armed forces for a much larger territorial commitment to provide garrisons throughout Empire and newly mandated territory.

Additionally there was some uncertainty over the roles of each separate arm within the Armed Forces. The Navy – traditionally the senior service – had earned an ambivalent reputation during the First World War, with surface fleets now seemingly vulnerable to submarine and mines. The arrival of the RAF – formally constituted in July 1918 – exacerbated rivalry amongst the Armed Forces and at the same time required substantial income for technical development and its potential to be accurately gauged and financed.

Protection of the British Empire

The Empire was a major preoccupation for Britain. The new self-governing regions, such as Canada, Australia, South Africa and New Zealand, all opposed supporting Britain in war. India was concerned with her own political development and Britain was involved with her new mandated territories in Africa and the Middle East. Britain needed her trade links with these countries, but the feeling was that war in Europe might break up this commonwealth of nations altogether.

Policy against Communism

The 'appeasers' in Britain were aware that the basic premise of Germany, Italy and Japan's Anti-Comintern Pact was the common goal to defeat Communism – and prevent its worldwide spread. Although the 1924 Labour government had formally recognised Lenin's USSR and Stalin had made a certain rapprochement in his 1930s foreign policy, there was still in Britain a deep mistrust of the 'reds' and the potential Communist world revolution. Appeasement – by meeting the demands of Hitler particularly in the 1930s – might be seen as creating a strong European buffer to the Soviet Union and Communism.

Crisis with the French alliance

France was Britain's only firm ally in 1930s, but she was suffering many economic, social and political problems. There were a succession of unstable coalition governments – three in 1932, four in 1933, and two in both 1934 and 1935. France had been slow to recover after the war and her level of unemployment was still rising in the late 1930s. The French military had developed very little and had mainly defensive tactics. There was violence on the streets between the Fascists and Socialists. French foreign policy would therefore tend to follow Great Britain – and they certainly had little desire for war.

Public opinion in the 1930s

Appeasement as a policy was reflective of much public opinion in the 1930s. This is not to say the policy did not have its critics – but the public mood seemed to be against rearmament and the use of force. This mood is perhaps illustrated by by-elections at East Fulham in October 1933 when a pacifist Labour candidate gained a seat from a Conservative in favour of rearmament. In the same year a vote held at the Oxford Union suggested after a debate that a majority of undergraduates would not fight for King and Country. In 1935 a 'Peace Ballot' was organised at the behest of the League of Nations by the Peace Pledge Union and showed an overwhelming dislike of war. It is difficult to measure the public mood and each of the above illustrations are perhaps controversial. However, it does seem that the attitude of 'Never again' did prevail amongst many groups in society.

TASK

Write an essay:

'To what extent were the consequences of the First World War an explanation for the British policy of appeasement?'

Remember to:

THINK   about the question carefully. What does it ask for – both cause and consequence – in what way? What does the 'to what extent' instruction involve?

READ   this chapter thoroughly and other reading in your own research.

PLAN   identify all the consequences of the First World War which have a causal effect on appeasement. What factors are there which led to appeasement and are not directly connected with the First World War? What will each of your paragraphs require? What order will they be in?

WRITE   ensure you refer to the question throughout. Check your explanation is clear and that spelling and grammar are accurate.

Appeasement in action

TALKING POINT

Why do you think these three characteristics of foreign policy were adopted?

1920s

In the 1920s Britain's foreign policy was characterised by retrenchment, collective security and disarmament. After the First World War, the 'Ten Year Rule' had been adopted as a guideline to financing defence. This Rule stated that Britain would not be engaged in a major war for the next ten years so armed forces estimates could be gauged appropriately. As a result of the 1920s approach, Britain was to be a signatory to measures designed to promote international co-operation – such as the Locarno Treaty 1925 and the Kellogg–Briand Pact 1928 – and was also an active member of the League of Nations.

1930s

In the early 1930s there was a reappraisal of British policy due to a variety of factors. With the ending of the Ten Year Rule, there was rising apprehension at the War Office about the state of British defence. External factors seemed to confirm a cause for concern: the Geneva Disarmament Conference failed, Japan invaded Manchuria in 1931 and Hitler became Chancellor of Germany in 1933. Gradually, the government moved towards a policy of appeasement.

SCENARIO ONE

Hitler became Chancellor of Germany in January 1933

- Unknown on the diplomatic front, his appointment raised questions about the future direction of German foreign policy.
- Despite Hitler withdrawing from the Disarmament Conference and then the League of Nations early in 1933, early signs suggested Hitler was not in the least hostile to Britain.
- Britain could not at this stage decide on no negotiations with Nazi Germany.
- 1935 Hitler announced conscription and the Luftwaffe – Britain expressed concern. It joined France and Italy in signing the Stresa Front.
- June 1935 Britain signed a naval agreement with Hitler allowing Germany a fleet 35 per cent the size of Britain's.

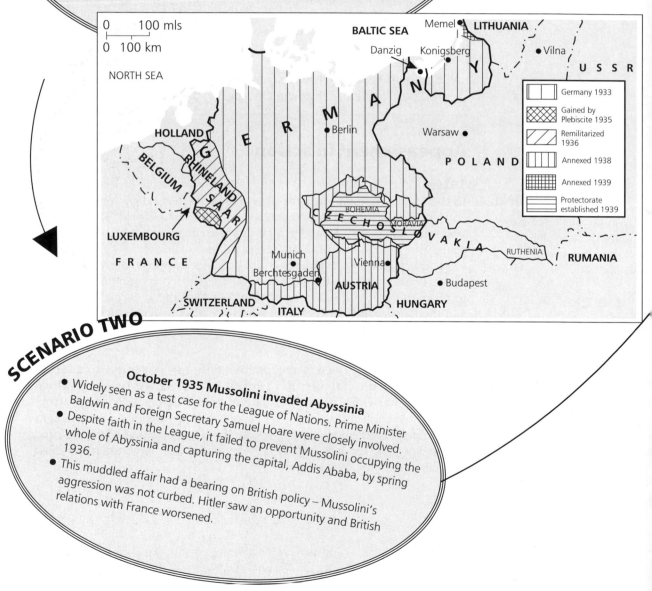

SCENARIO TWO

October 1935 Mussolini invaded Abyssinia

- Widely seen as a test case for the League of Nations. Prime Minister Baldwin and Foreign Secretary Samuel Hoare were closely involved.
- Despite faith in the League, it failed to prevent Mussolini occupying the whole of Abyssinia and capturing the capital, Addis Ababa, by spring 1936.
- This muddled affair had a bearing on British policy – Mussolini's aggression was not curbed. Hitler saw an opportunity and British relations with France worsened.

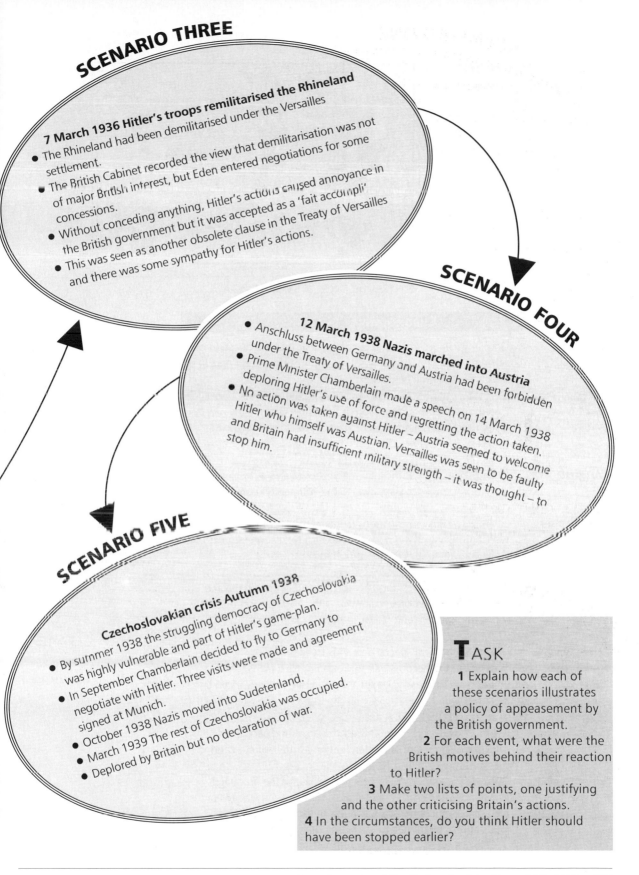

SCENARIO THREE

7 March 1936 Hitler's troops remilitarised the Rhineland

- The Rhineland had been demilitarised under the Versailles settlement.
- The British Cabinet recorded the view that demilitarisation was not of major British interest, but Eden entered negotiations for some concessions.
- Without conceding anything, Hitler's actions caused annoyance in the British government but it was accepted as a 'fait accompli'
- This was seen as another obsolete clause in the Treaty of Versailles and there was some sympathy for Hitler's actions.

SCENARIO FOUR

12 March 1938 Nazis marched into Austria

- Anschluss between Germany and Austria had been forbidden under the Treaty of Versailles.
- Prime Minister Chamberlain made a speech on 14 March 1938 deploring Hitler's use of force and regretting the action taken.
- No action was taken against Hitler – Austria seemed to welcome Hitler who himself was Austrian. Versailles was seen to be faulty and Britain had insufficient military strength – it was thought – to stop him.

SCENARIO FIVE

Czechoslovakian crisis Autumn 1938

- By summer 1938 the struggling democracy of Czechoslovakia was highly vulnerable and part of Hitler's game-plan.
- In September Chamberlain decided to fly to Germany to negotiate with Hitler. Three visits were made and agreement signed at Munich.
- October 1938 Nazis moved into Sudetenland.
- March 1939 The rest of Czechoslovakia was occupied. Deplored by Britain but no declaration of war.

Task

1 Explain how each of these scenarios illustrates a policy of appeasement by the British government.

2 For each event, what were the British motives behind their reaction to Hitler?

3 Make two lists of points, one justifying and the other criticising Britain's actions.

4 In the circumstances, do you think Hitler should have been stopped earlier?

Chamberlain and the Czechoslovakia crisis, 1938

'OUR NEW DEFENCE', *EVENING STANDARD*.

CHRONOLOGY

12 March	Germany invades Austria. It becomes clear that the question of self-determination for the Germans in the Sudetenland part of Czechoslovakia will be the next 'issue'.
20–21 May	Czechs mobilise in anticipation of a possible German invasion. Britain and France issue a stern warning to Hitler. There is no invasion.
3 August	Chamberlain sends Runciman to Czechoslovakia as his special mediator to produce a solution to the Sudetenland problem.
2 September	Litvinov, the Russian Foreign Secretary, proposes a joint French/British/Russian/Czech pact against Nazi aggression in Czechoslovakia – this comes to nothing.
4 September	Benes, the Czech President, accepts the Runciman-sponsored idea of a federated Czechoslovakia with considerable autonomy for German, Czech and Slovak regions.
12 September	Hitler's Nuremberg speech demands freedom for the Sudetenland to become part of Germany. Nazi plans for an invasion of Czechoslovakia on 1 October are well advanced by this time.
15 September	Chamberlain meets Hitler at Berchtesgaden and accepts the principle of complete self-detemination for the Sudetenland.
19 September	Anglo-French proposals to Czechoslovakia for the gradual transfer of Sudetenland territories to Germany – by means of plebiscites, international supervision of the transfers and an international guarantee to the remainder of Czechoslovakia.

What should or can 'free' nations do to influence countries in which there are repressive governments?

In other instances in which Britain or the USA have intervened against dictatorships, what has been their approach?

Do you think discussion and negotiation are the best ways of resolving international problems?

22 September	Chamberlain meets Hitler at Godesberg. Hitler raises the stakes by demanding the immediate occupation of the Sudetenland by Nazi troops by 1 October.
26 September	Britain makes it clear that she will support the French–Czechoslovakian alliance if Hitler persists with his plans for an immediate take-over. Meanwhile, both Britain and France are preparing for war.
29 September	Munich meeting of Hitler, Chamberlain, the French Prime Minister, Daladier, and Mussolini reaches agreement on the speedy transfer of the Sudetenland to Germany. War is thus avoided.
30 September	Anglo-German 'friendship agreement' is reached between Chamberlain and Hitler.

EXAMINING THE EVIDENCE

Chamberlain and Churchill

Source A

Chamberlain speaking to the House of Commons in the debate on the Munich agreement, 3 October 1938.

When the House met last Wednesday, we were all under the shadow of a great and imminent menace. War, in a form more stark and terrible than ever before, seemed to be staring us in the face. Before I sat down a message had come which gave us new hope that peace might yet be saved, and today, only a few days after, we all meet in joy and thankfulness that the prayers of millions have been answered, and a cloud of anxiety has been lifted from our hearts …

Ever since I assumed my present office my main purpose has been to work for the pacification of Europe, for the removal of those suspicions and those animosities which have so long poisoned the air. The path which leads to appeasement is long and bristles with obstacles. The question of Czechoslovakia is the latest and perhaps the most dangerous. Now that we have got past it, I feel that it may be possible to make further progress along the road to sanity …

I believe there are many who will feel with me that such a declaration, signed by the German Chancellor and myself, is something more than a pious expression of opinion. In our relations with other countries everything depends upon there being sincerity and goodwill on both sides in this declaration. That is why to me its significance goes far beyond its actual words.

Source B
Churchill speaking to the Commons in the same debate, 3 October 1938.

I will, therefore, begin by saying the most unpopular and most unwelcome thing. I will begin by saying what everybody would like to ignore or forget but which must nevertheless be stated, namely, that we have sustained a total and unmitigated defeat, and that France has suffered even more than we have ... The utmost my right hon. Friend the Prime Minister has been able to secure by all his immense exertions, by all the great efforts and mobilisation which took place in this country, and by all the anguish and strain through which we have passed in this country, the utmost he has been able to gain – (Hon. Members: 'Is peace.') I thought I might be allowed to make that point in its due place, and I propose to deal with it. The utmost he has been able to gain for Czechoslovakia and in the matters which were in dispute has been that the German dictator, instead of snatching his victuals from the table, has been content to have them served to him course by course ...

When I think of the fair hopes of a long peace which still lay before Europe at the beginning of 1933 when Herr Hitler first obtained power, and of all the opportunities of arresting the growth of the Nazi power which have been thrown away, when I think of the immense combinations and resources which have been neglected or squandered, I cannot believe that a parallel exists in the whole course of history. So far as this country is concerned with the responsibility must rest with those who have the undisputed control of our political affairs. They neither prevented Germany from rearming, nor did they rearm ourselves in time. They quarrelled with Italy without saving Ethiopia. They exploited and discredited the vast institution of the League of Nations and they neglected to make alliances and combinations which might have repaired previous errors, and thus they left us in the hour of trial without adequate national defence or effective international security.

---

1 In Source A – what was 'the question of Czechoslovakia' and why was it 'the most dangerous'?
2 What was agreed at Munich and what is the 'declaration' which Chamberlain refers to?
3 What seems to have motivated Chamberlain – according to Source A?
4 On what grounds does Churchill in Source B criticise the policy of appeasement?
5 In what ways are these sources useful to a historian studying appeasement in the 1930s?
6 With reference to Sources A and B and your own knowledge, what were the arguments for and against appeasement in the 1930s?

FOCUS

9.1 Neville Chamberlain – Prime Minister 1937–40, Appeaser, One of 'the Guilty Men'?

In the contemporary and postwar period, Neville Chamberlain's name became synonymous with the policy of appeasement. It was not, however, his policy alone and the word emerged long before his administration. Because Chamberlain was Prime Minister through the years leading up to the Second World War, he was visible in his attempt to reach agreement with Hitler (see Preview) but clearly failed when war was declared in September 1939. He has been labelled as 'guilty'. For a long time he received a bad press from contemporaries who knew him and contemporaries who did not but suffered as a result of the war he was 'guilty' of taking us into. Historians were originally harsh in their assessment, but more recently he has been seen as unfairly maligned.

A Critical View

- As a prime minister and leading appeaser, he was responsible for the failure of appeasement and so Britain's entry into the Second World War.

- He had no experience in foreign policy, but overshadowed his foreign minister, Anthony Eden, and meddled in diplomatic affairs ignorantly.

- Foreign policy was conducted like a one-man band bringing in advisers not directly connected with foreign affairs.

- His policy to which he was wholeheartedly committed was weak, short-sighted and ultimately betrayed Britain's national interest.

- He seriously misjudged Hitler, failing to comprehend the extent of Nazi ambition.

- Vanity was his major failing – a perception not helped by the use of the personal pronoun, as in 1939 'Everything I have worked for has crashed into ruins'.

- Lloyd George referred to him as 'a pin head' and suggested he would have made a good lord mayor of Birmingham in an off-year.

- Daladier, the French Prime Minister at the time of Munich, called him a desiccated stick; another critic dismissed him as 'the umbrella man'.

- Some historians have been similarly unimpressed; in his *Origins of the Second World War*, Donald Cameron Watt judged that Chamberlain was 'very difficult to like and extremely smug'. A.J.P. Taylor called him 'the least glamorous of Prime Ministers; efficient, conscientious and unimaginative'.

A Fairer View

- In contrast to his predecessor, Baldwin, Neville Chamberlain seemed energetic, efficient, brought leadership to the Cabinet. In May 1937 it looked as if he were the only man for the job.

- From the Chamberlain family – his father, Joseph, and his half-brother, Austen – his credentials were sound. Brought up in a political household, although not destined for this career, he was intelligent, a good judge of his colleagues and a quick thinker, assimilating complexities and arriving at decisions.

- His previous political achievements in social and fiscal reform were highly significant.

- Perhaps influenced by his cousin Norman's death in the First World War, he had a passionate aversion to war. He genuinely believed it to be morally wrong and felt that peace should be strived for.

- The appeasement policy he pursued between 1937 and 1940 was rational. He was at the same time aware of the growing threat from Japan, Germany and Italy and acknowledging advice given him from all sides, the Treasury, the military and the mood of pacifism amongst the public.

- The policy was a dual one of trying to achieve better relations with the Fascist powers while at the same time pushing ahead with rearmament.

- Chamberlain had conviction – a belief in his own judgement – and felt that he could do business with Hitler. He saw the evil of the Nazi regime but feared a defenceless Britain and a population in great need of social provisions.

TASKS

1 Explain why a veteran of the Second World War in 1945 might judge Neville Chamberlain differently from a student writing 50 years later.
2 What other options could Chamberlain have taken in foreign policy in the late 1930s?
3 To what extent do you consider Chamberlain to be 'guilty' of betraying the national interest?

REVIEW

Appeasement – The historians' debate

Source A

Those who supported appeasement after October 1938 did so for two reasons. Munich 'bought' a year of peace in which to rearm. It brought 'a united nation' into war by showing Hitler's wickedness beyond doubt. Both these reasons were put forward by many who could not check them. Both were false.

If a year had been gained in which Chamberlain could have strengthened Britain's defences and equipped the country for an offensive war, there should be evidence of growing strength, growing effort, and growing Cabinet unity. But while some members of the Government sought to use the 'bought' year, others did not. Chamberlain, and his closest advisers, were unwilling to allow the Minister of War, Hore-Belisha, to introduce conscription. The Air Minister, Kingsley Wood, failed to achieve the needed air parity with Germany. Machines were not lacking. Will-power was. Germany, not Britain, gained militarily during the extra year. German forces were strengthened by Czech munitions, western forces weakened by the loss of the Czech Army and Air Force …

Chamberlain and his advisers did not go to Munich because they needed an extra year before they could fight. They did not use the year to arouse national enthusiasm for a just war. The aim of appeasement was to avoid war, not to enter war united. Appeasement was a looking forward to better times, not worse. Even after the German occupation of Prague, Chamberlain and those closest to him hoped that better times would come, and that Anglo-German relations would improve. They gave the pledge to Poland, not with enthusiasm, but with embarrassment. They wanted to befriend Germany, not anger her.

M. Gilbert and R. Gott, *The Appeasers* (1963).

Source B

Though Chamberlain loathed the very idea of a great war, which was generally anticipated to produce horrors still more dreadful than those of the first, he did not rule it out on any grounds of principle. Rather, he said that he would not contemplate such a guarantee 'unless we had reasonable prospect of being able to beat her (Germany) to her knees in a reasonable time, and of that I see no sign.'

When the British and French ministers discussed the whole issue at the end of April, Chamberlain put the point in similar terms, adding that he thought a time would come 'when a gamble on the issue of peace and war might be contemplated with less anxiety that at present'. In other words, the buying of time remained a strong element in British foreign policy, as it had been for several years. This was the line which Eden had recommended to the Cabinet early in 1936; to reach agreements with Germany where they could honourably be reached, to be under no illusions that Germany would keep them when they ceased to suit her, and to accelerate British rearmament, the spending upon which was moving swiftly forward in 1938 and 1939 and which far exceeded any expenditure upon arms ever undertaken by Britain in peace time. This is not to say that the sole purpose to the policy pursued in 1938 was simply to obtain a breathing space. Chamberlain had some sympathy for German grievances, and was acutely sensible of Hitler's capacity to exploit them; he felt much doubt about the outcome of a war; he could hardly bear to think of the wanton destruction; but there is not a sign he felt any fondness for dictatorships or sneaking sympathy for fascism.

D. Dilks, *The Conservatives*, ed. Lord Butler (1977).

1 What is the interpretation of appeasement offered in these two sources?
2 What evidence is offered by each historian for his argument?
3 What reasons can you suggest for the different interpretations offered by these historians?

Source C

Chamberlain's foreign policy was an attempt to see if co-existence was possible; that it turned out not to be is no reason for condemning out of hand the only policy which promised any hope of avoiding war.

Neville Chamberlain's reputation has been blasted by a few hasty words in the aftermath of Munich, but 'peace in our time' was not an unworthy objective, and it was worth pursuing to the uttermost. Men of honour will cavil at trying to appease a dictator, while the more cynical will assert that as Hitler was bound to attack us, we were wrong to try to postpone the evil day. But most of the men of honour managed to appease Stalin after 1941, and turkeys are seldom well-advised in pressing for an early Christmas. Even Duff Cooper, who resigned from the Cabinet over the Munich agreement which consigned the Sudetenland to Germany, could not suggest any alternative policy that was viable; he simply could not stomach Munich. Chamberlain, who bore the responsibility for millions of lives, could not afford the luxury of a weak stomach. Hitler's demands were not, in themselves, unreasonable (although his methods of prosecuting them were), and Britain was hardly in any military position to veto them, had they been so.

John Charmley, writing in the *Independent* newspaper, 1989.

Source D

But where Baldwin's were sins of omission, Chamberlain's were sins of deliberate commission. He really meant to come to terms with Hitler, to make concession after concession to the man to buy an agreement. Apart from the immorality of coming to terms with a criminal, it was always sheer nonsense, for no agreement was possible except through submission to Nazi Germany's domination of Europe and, with her allies and their joint conquests, of the world ... The total upshot of (the appeasers') efforts was to aid Nazi Germany to achieve a position of brutal ascendancy, a threat to everybody else's security or even existence, which only a war could end. This had the very result of letting the Russians into the centre of Europe which the appeasers ... wished to prevent ...These men had no real conception of Germany's character or malign record in modern history.

A.L. Rowse, *All Souls and Appeasement* (1961).

1 How do the assessments of Chamberlain offered in Sources C and D differ?
2 With reference to the date of writing, author, type of source and evidence used, why are these assessments different?

Task – Chamberlain in the 'Hot Seat'.

1 Re-read this chapter carefully.
2 Prepare questions you would like to pose to Chamberlain on the outbreak of war in 1939.
3 Choose a team to prepare a defence of Chamberlain.
4 One person from the defence team should then take the 'hot seat' and field questions from the class.
5 After the 'hot seat' session each member of the class should prepare an assessment of Chamberlain's role, substantiated by evidence and attempting to counter the opposite view.

10 Britain During the Second World War 1939–45: Politics and Society

PREVIEW

1939

On the outbreak of war Britain and France were reluctant to fight until attacked and German attention did not concentrate on the West until Spring 1940. This period, called the 'Phoney War', lasted until May 1940.

1 Sept.	German invasion of Poland
3 Sept.	Britain and France declare war on Germany
29 Sept.	Surrender of Poland
30 Nov. –12 Mar. 1940	Russo-Finnish War

1940

At the start of the year, the 'Phoney War' was still in progress but the European theatre of war opened up dramatically from May. This was to prove Britain's most glorious year of the war.

9 April	Germany invaded Denmark and then attacked Norway
16–19 April	British and French forces landed in Southern Norway
3 May	Norway fell to Germany
8 May	Chamberlain resigned as Prime Minister
10 May	Germany invaded Netherlands, Belgium and Luxembourg Churchill became Prime Minister
17–21 May	Germans attacked deep into France
4 June	Evacuation of 200,000 British troops from Dunkirk
10 June	Italy declared war on Britain and France
22 June	Surrender of France – Britain severed relations with the new government
July	German occupation of the Channel Islands
10 July–15 Sept.	Battle of Britain. The German Luftwaffe failed to gain air superiority
17 Aug.	Germany announced a total blockade of Britain
7 Sept. –12 May 1941	The Blitz – bombing of London, major cities and ports
8 Dec.	Start of major Allied advance against Italians in Libya

1941

By 1941 Britain was probably secure from invasion but prone to German air attack and virtually without allies. Britain continued to fight in North Africa but was not in a position to liberate Europe.

22 Jan. –26 Feb.	British took Tobruk (Libya). Italian held Somaliland and Eritrea
6 April	British took Ethiopia – by end of year controlled Italian East Africa
11 March	Lend-Lease Act approved allowing USA to transfer goods to Britain without payment
24–27 May	German battleship *Bismarck* sank HMS *Hood* but was in turn sunk by British
22 June	Germany invaded USSR
8 Dec.	USA declared war on Japan after Japanese attack on Pearl Harbour
10 Dec.	HMS *Prince of Wales* and *Repulse* sunk by Japanese
25 Dec.	British surrendered Hong Kong to Japanese

1942

Britain now had allies, but was vulnerable to German air attack and shortage of food supplies. She was being heavily defeated by the Japanese in the Far East.

15 Feb.	Japanese capture Singapore
7 March	Japanese occupy Burma
24 April–July	Germans launch a series of air raids on historic British cities, such as Exeter, Bath, Norwich, York
June	Fall of Tobruk leads to decline in British morale and criticism of the Churchill coalition
23 Oct.	Start of British counter-offensive in North Africa. Victory at El Alamein
4 Nov.	Rommel began to retreat
12 Nov.	German and Italian forces pushed out of Egypt

1943

Britain's prospects were improving but no second front was launched into France. However, plans for this began in mid 1943.

2 Feb.	Surrender of Germans at Stalingrad
10 July	British and Commonwealth forces invaded Sicily
3 Sept.	Allies invaded Southern Italian mainland

1944

By the start of the year Britain's prospects looked better. The Battle of the Atlantic was won, North Africa and much of Italy taken. Soviet forces were moving towards Germany and British plans for invasion of France were underway. However, Germany reorganised its war machine and victory seemed an elusive goal.

4 June	Allies took Rome
6 June	D-Day landings in Normandy
25 Aug.	Allies took Paris
2 Sept.	Allies took Brussels
24 Oct.	Aachen was first German city to fall to Allies
16–25 Dec.	Battle of the Bulge – Allies held by a German counter-offensive

1945

At the start of the year, the end of the war with Germany was clearly in sight but the position in the Far East was less clear with Japan holding on tenaciously to gains.

7 March	US forces cross the Rhine at Remagen
28 April	Mussolini captured and killed by Italian partisans
29 April–1 May	German forces in Italy surrendered
30 April	Hitler committed suicide
7 May	Germany surrendered unconditionally
8 May	VE (Victory in Europe) Day
6 Aug.	USA dropped atomic bomb on Hiroshima and 3 days later on Nagasaki
2 Sept.	Japanese formally surrendered. VJ (Victory over Japan) Day was proclaimed

1   Why do you think the Second World War started with a so-called 'Phoney War'?
2   In what ways is it valid to describe 1940 as 'Britain's most glorious year of the war'?
3   Why do you think the Lend-Lease Act was agreed to by the USA?
4   Why, by the start of 1943, were Britain's prospects improving?
5   What are your opinions on the use of the atomic bomb by the USA as a means to bring victory and an end to the war?
6   With reference to the First World War timeline in Chapter 4 – what differences and similarities do you notice about the nature of these two World Wars and their impact on British politics and society?

Impact of the Second World War on Britain

SOCIAL IMPACT

An all-out six-year military struggle – this was a total, global war which required maximum use of Britain's entire resources.

The civilian population was an integral part of the war effort – far more than had been the case during the First World War.

War was experienced at home as well as at the front. (All aspects of life – housing, food, clothing, labour force, civilian defence – were embraced in the war effort.)

People's lives were affected by an unprecedented level of government control.

The war produced significant, long-term social changes.

'This country is now at war with Germany'

Prime Minister Neville Chamberlain in a radio broadcast to the British nation

3 September 1939

Chamberlain's coalition was brought down by military reversals and a loss of confidence in May 1940. This ended the period of National Government which had started in 1931.

Winston Churchill took over as prime minister and headed a wartime coalition which included both Conservatives and Labour.

The Labour Party won recognition and respect from their role in the coalition. Their victory in the 1945 Election arguably was rooted in their wartime development.

Although the two main parties differed over issues of the role of state and economic management, there was a developing centre ground where both Conservatives and Labour had policy areas in common.

POLITICAL IMPACT

TALKING POINT

In what ways can war generally be seen as a political and social accelerator? Make reference to both World Wars and other conflicts.

Political impact

Government on the outbreak of war

The National Government, first set up to cope with the economic crisis of 1931, now had to tackle the international crisis of 1939 fomented by Hitler's aggressive foreign policy. Neville Chamberlain, Conservative leader of the National Government since 1937, had worked tirelessly to avoid the outbreak of war by pursuing a policy of appeasement (covered in detail in Chapter 9). Personally devastated, he was forced to declare that Britain was at war with Germany on 3 September 1939 – two days after the Nazi invasion of Poland. A war cabinet of nine members was established immediately. It included Winston Churchill as First Lord of the Admiralty. Churchill's 'prophet of doom' stance during the 1930s had now been vindicated by international developments.

Preparations for war had been made since January 1939 and it is true that Britain was probably in a better position to fight in the autumn of 1939 than she had been at the time of the Munich crisis in September 1938. Conscription had been finally introduced in spring 1939, in July a Ministry of Supply had been set up, and because of the central importance of the labour force the government had met with trades union representatives. The government – in answer to left-wing demands – pledged to take the profit out of war and put in place agreements with the TUC and Ministry of Labour over wartime regulations and wages.

The Nazis conquered Poland in three weeks and then turned their attentions towards the Baltic and Scandinavia. Britain was at war but had entered a period known as the 'Phoney War' where it was difficult for both government and the man on the street to gauge the extent and nature of this war. The winter of 1939–40 was harsh – children had been evacuated to the country in their thousands, blackouts were in use in homes, buildings were sandbagged and everyone carried their gas masks. The government laid plans for a three-year war and military preparations were made to match this. Immediate action was also taken at home. On 8 September the party chief whips signed an electoral truce that by-elections would not be allowed to create party political divisions for the duration of the War. The National Registration Scheme was introduced on 30 September. Overall government power and control was extended beyond precedent. Homes and places of work throughout the country were directed towards the war effort. Finally, on 22 May 1940 the Emergency Powers Act was passed which gave governments unlimited authority over British citizens and property.

During the 'Phoney War' Britain's strategy was essentially passive, being limited to an economic blockade of Germany. Britain's military forces took no offensive action – they were waiting until Germany had taken the first steps. This phase of the War lasted until April 1940.

Source A

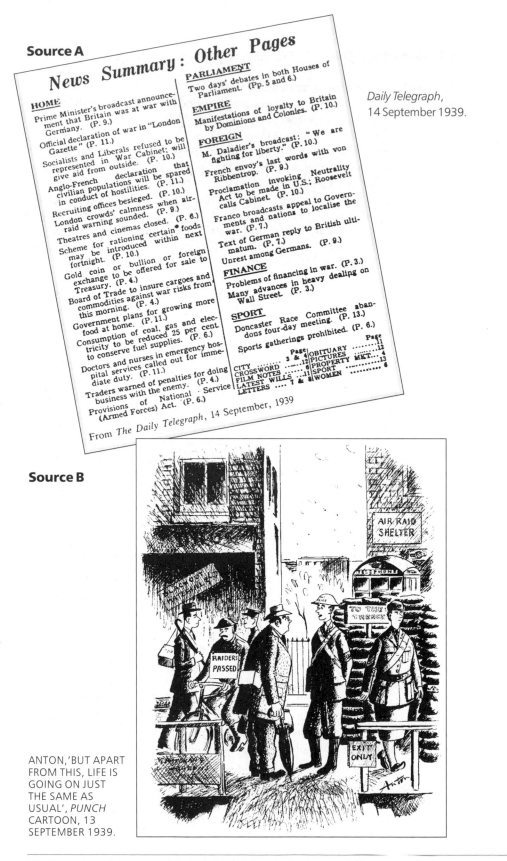

News Summary : Other Pages

HOME

Prime Minister's broadcast announcement that Britain was at war with Germany. (P. 9.)

Official declaration of war in "London Gazette" (P. 11.)

Socialists and Liberals refused to be represented in War Cabinet; will give aid from outside. (P. 10.)

Anglo-French declaration that civilian populations will be spared in conduct of hostilities. (P. 11.)

Recruiting offices besieged. (P. 10.)

London crowds' calmness when air-raid warning sounded. (P. 9.)

Theatres and cinemas closed. (P. 6.)

Scheme for rationing certain foods may be introduced within next fortnight. (P. 10.)

Gold coin or bullion or foreign exchange to be offered for sale to Treasury. (P. 4.)

Board of Trade to insure cargoes and commodities against war risks from this morning. (P. 4.)

Government plans for growing more food at home. (P. 11.)

Consumption of coal, gas and electricity to be reduced 25 per cent. to conserve fuel supplies. (P. 6.)

Doctors and nurses in emergency hospital services called out for immediate duty. (P. 11.)

Traders warned of penalties for doing business with the enemy. (P. 4.)

Provisions of National Service (Armed Forces) Act. (P. 6.)

PARLIAMENT

Two days' debates in both Houses of Parliament. (Pp. 5 and 6.)

EMPIRE

Manifestations of loyalty to Britain by Dominions and Colonies. (P. 10.)

FOREIGN

M. Daladier's broadcast: "We are fighting for liberty." (P. 10.)

French envoy's last words with von Ribbentrop. (P. 9.)

Proclamation invoking Neutrality Act to be made in U.S.; Roosevelt calls Cabinet. (P. 10.)

Franco broadcasts appeal to Governments and nations to localise the war. (P. 7.)

Text of German reply to British ultimatum. (P. 7.)

Unrest among Germans. (P. 9.)

FINANCE

Problems of financing in war. (P. 3.)

Many advances in heavy dealing on Wall Street. (P. 3.)

SPORT

Doncaster Race Committee abandons four-day meeting. (P. 13.)

Sports gatherings prohibited. (P. 6.)

	Page		Page
CITY	3 & 4	OBITUARY	12
CROSSWORD	12	PICTURES	4
FILM NOTES	6	PROPERTY MKT.	13
LATEST WILLS	11	SPORT	13
LETTERS	7 & 8	WOMEN	6

From *The Daily Telegraph*, 14 September, 1939

Daily Telegraph,
14 September 1939.

Source B

ANTON,'BUT APART FROM THIS, LIFE IS GOING ON JUST THE SAME AS USUAL', *PUNCH* CARTOON, 13 SEPTEMBER 1939.

Source C

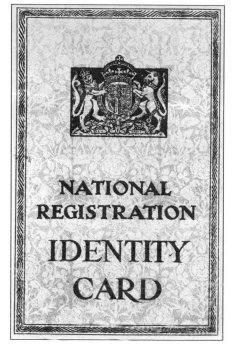

A NATIONAL REGISTRATION IDENTITY CARD.

NATIONAL REGISTRATION

IDENTITY CARD

TASK

From Sources A–C
1   What government action had been taken to prepare for war?
2   In what ways is the extension of state control illustrated?
3   What messages is the cartoonist Anton conveying about Britain in the first weeks of the War?

The end of Chamberlain's Cabinet, May 1940

TALKING POINT

In what ways is this political crisis similar to that of December 1916?

The fall of Chamberlain's government closely mirrored the fall of Asquith's First World War coalition in December 1916 (see Chapter 4). In September 1939, Chamberlain's government held 418 seats compared to Labour's 167 and enjoyed an overall majority of 200. As we have seen earlier, the Conservatives had dominated the political scene throughout the 1920s and 1930s, having won five out of seven interwar elections and enjoyed the majority of the popular vote during the 1924 and 1929 Labour governments. It seemed that the Conservatives were likely to control government throughout the War.

However, on 8 May 1940, at the end of a two-day debate on the fall of Norway to the Nazis, Labour challenged the government and called for a vote of no confidence. The Chamberlain majority fell to 81. Forty of his MPs voted with Labour and 40 abstained. The Prime Minister tried to fight on but on 10 May 1940 the Labour Party leader, Clement Attlee, phoned Chamberlain and reported that they were not prepared to serve under his leadership. Attlee had been urged to join government during a meeting with Chamberlain, Halifax and Churchill on 9 May. When the proposal was put to the Labour Party executive, it was rejected. Chamberlain's resignation came on the evening of 10 May, the day the Nazis invaded Belgium and Holland. Winston Churchill – the press and people's choice – was appointed prime minister, ahead of the other candidate, Lord Halifax – a front-runner for the job amongst many politicians.

Churchill immediately formed a five-man war cabinet, which also contained Chamberlain, Halifax and the two senior Labour men, Attlee and Greenwood. This was subsequently increased in size and the personnel changed but throughout the War the government remained predominantly Conservative in membership – Labour having 16 posts over this period compared to the Conservatives' 52.

Examining the Evidence

Chamberlain's resignation and Churchill's appointment, 10 May 1940

Source A

LOW'S VIEW OF THE CRUCIAL DEBATE, *EVENING STANDARD*, 8 MAY 1940.

1 Explain the reference to '8 years of dithering'.
2 How significant do you consider
    a Baldwin's portrait on the wall
    b the absence of other members of the Cabinet?
3 What is the message the cartoonist is conveying in this cartoon?

Source B

On the second day, May 8, the debate, although continuing upon an Adjournment Motion, assumed the character of a vote of censure, and Mr Herbert Morrison, in the name of the Opposition, declared their intention to have a vote. The Prime Minister rose again, accepted the challenge, and in an unfortunate passage appealed to his friends to stand by him ... Mr Lloyd George turned upon Mr Chamberlain.

'It is not a question of who are the Prime Minister's friends. It is a far bigger issue. He has appealed for sacrifice. The nation is prepared for sacrifice so long as it has leadership, so long as the Government show clearly what they are aiming at, and so long as the nation is confident that those who are leading it are doing their best.' [He ended] 'I say solemnly that the Prime Minister should give an example of sacrifice, because there is nothing which can contribute more to victory in this war than that he should sacrifice the seals of office ...'

I did my very best to regain control of the House for the Government in the teeth of continuous interruption ... and several times the clamour was such that I could not make myself heard. Yet all the time it was clear that their anger was not directed against me, but at the Prime Minister, whom I was defending to the utmost of my ability and without regard for any other considerations.

W.S. Churchill, *The Second World War* (1948).

Source C

During the evening [of 8 May] I saw Churchill in the smoking-room ... I wished him luck, but added that I hoped his speech would not be too convincing. 'Why not?' he asked. 'Because', I replied 'we must have a new Prime Minister, and it must be you.' He answered gruffly that he had signed on for the voyage and would stick to the ship. But I don't think he was angry with me. [And the following day ...] Rumour was rife. Some said that Chamberlain would stay. Others declared that Halifax would succeed him. Others again believed that nothing could resist Churchill's claims. It was thought that the Labour chiefs leaned towards Halifax. Churchill's long and active career had brought him many enemies as well as devoted friends.

H. Macmillan, *The Blast of War* (1967).

Source D

The morning of May 10 dawned and with it the news ... that Holland and Belgium were both invaded ... At eleven o'clock I was again summoned to Downing Street by the Prime Minister. There once more I found Lord Halifax. We took our seats at the table opposite Mr Chamberlain. He told us that he was satisfied that it was beyond his power to form a National Government. The response he had received from the Labour leaders left him in no doubt of this. The question was therefore whom should he advise the King to send for …

I have had many interviews in my public life, and this was certainly the most important. Usually I talk a great deal but on this occasion I was silent … As I remained silent a very long pause ensued … Then at length Halifax spoke. He said that he felt that his position as a peer, out of the House of Commons, would make it very difficult for him to discharge the duties of Prime Minister in a war like this. He would be held responsible for everything, but would not have the power to guide the assembly upon whose confidence the life of every Government depended. He spoke for some minutes in this sense, and by the time he had finished it was clear that the duty would fall upon me …

W.S. Churchill, *The Second World War* (1948).

1 From Sources A–D and your own knowledge, how valid is it to suggest that Churchill intended to take Chamberlain's place from the start of the debate?
2 What are the strengths and weaknesses of Sources A–D for a historian studying Chamberlain's resignation and Churchill's appointment?

What factors led to Chamberlain's resignation?

FACTOR 1

LABOUR PARTY – AN EMERGENT OPPOSITION
- During the 1930s Labour seemed weak following the 1931 crisis. The party had divided over economic and foreign policy and social reform during the 1930s.
- Labour's apparent weakness was prolonged by the existence of the National Government.
- By 1939 Labour's position had strengthened under the leadership of Attlee from 1935.
- Labour had made a U-turn from disarmament and collective security to rearmament in the late 1930s.
- Labour's concern for the preservation of parliamentary democracy was well received in the context of European dictatorship.
- During the Czech crisis 1938–9, Labour spoke of resistance to Hitler. Walter Citrine, a senior party member, said Britain and France were throwing Czechoslovakia to the wolves.
- The Labour leadership realised their clear party programme in 1918 of radical social reform and nationalisation would only be convincing if seen in practise.
- In the first months of the war, Labour Party thinking developed. Lord Boothby said 'Nothing is more certain than that this war will mark the transition from monopoly capitalism to Socialism.'
- By 1938 press sympathies had changed. The *Daily Mirror* had switched its support to Labour and the *Daily Herald* – rivalling the *Daily Express* – was funded by the TUC.
- During the first months of the war Labour were holding out for an equal distribution of power in government, but in the circumstances they would not force a General Election.
- Labour's role in the debate of 8 May was crucial – it led to the vote of no confidence against Chamberlain and their decision to work with a new Conservative leader.
- Churchill ensured their central part in wartime government.

FACTOR 2

CHAMBERLAIN'S LACK OF RAPPORT WITH THE LABOUR PARTY
- Chamberlain had an intellectual dislike of Socialist theories.
- The Labour Party leadership felt they were personally disliked by Chamberlain. Attlee recalled 'He always treated us like dirt'. Conservative Chief Whip David Margesson wrote 'He engendered personal dislike amongst opponents to an extreme almost unbelievable'.
- As the Labour Party emerged as a strong opposition and war necessitated parties working together, this lack of rapport contributed to Chamberlain's decline.

FACTOR 3

POLITICAL MISJUDGEMENTS BY CHAMBERLAIN AT THE START OF THE WAR
- Chamberlain anticipated a more limited conflict – he did not set a course for a wartime coalition government.
- Chamberlain still considered Hitler to be bluffing and the 'Phoney War' seemed to confirm this.
- The Conservatives, Chamberlain considered, could deal with this war with some co-operation from the opposition.
- He was slow to acknowledge his cool relationship with the Labour Party.

FACTOR 4

CHAMBERLAIN RESISTED DISQUIET AMONG SENIOR CONSERVATIVES
- There existed critics of Chamberlain amongst the Conservative leadership.
- Chamberlain had clashed with both Churchill and Eden over appeasement in the late 1930s, but he still brought them into his War Cabinet.
- Yet L.S. Amery, a senior party figure who had led the backbench critics of Munich, was left out of the Cabinet and his pent up indignation was a source of trouble.
- Other close political allies of the Eden clique kept in close touch with the Labour Party during the May crisis.
- Two other Conservatives Chamberlain mistakenly ignored – the highly capable General Sir Louis Spears and the ambitious Harold Macmillan.

FACTOR 5

GOVERNMENT'S FAILURE TO CO-ORDINATE THE WAR ECONOMY EFFECTIVELY
- Several departments in economic affairs were operating separately.
- Two committees co-ordinated the Ministries of Labour, Supply, Food, Shipping and Economic Warfare.
- Departments came under criticism in the period 1939–40. Ministry of Supply was criticised for half-measures and the Ministry of Economic Warfare for loopholes in the blockade against Germany.
- There was pressure from economists and civil servants, e.g. Keynes, Beveridge and Salter, who suggested the whole economy should be planned. Two agencies should be set up – one to collect data and the other to make decisions.

CHAMBERLAIN'S STYLE WAS SEEN AS INAPPROPRIATE FOR A WARTIME LEADER

- Some of Chamberlain's ministerial appointments caused a stir throughout 1939 and in April 1940.
- Unfavourable comparisons were made to Lloyd George's leadership in the First World War.
- Chamberlain failed to instil confidence amongst British industrialists.
- Lady Astor, Conservative MP for Plymouth and socialite, wrote of Chamberlain's speech to the Conservative backbench 1922 Committee in November 1939 '… I am sure he meant it to be a fighting speech, but its effect on me was to make me wish that Winston were P.M.'

TASKS

1 Explain Labour's political re-emergence in the late 1930s by reference to:

> changed attitudes within the 1930s party
> the role of Attlee as leader between 1935 and 1939
> lessons learned from the party's experiences in the 1920s and the 1931 crisis.

You will need to refer back to Chapter 7 on the Labour governments in the 1920s and complete some research on Clement Attlee's first years as Labour leader.

2 Did Chamberlain's government fall due to personal or political reasons? From the factors above, find evidence to support (a) Personal, (b) Political. What is your conclusion?

Why was Winston Churchill appointed Prime Minister?

Reason 1

Despite the doubts of some that Churchill was too unpredictable and had a record of mistakes, events in 1939 vindicated his call for rearmament and rejection of appeasement. Agitation developed to include him in the government.

Reason 2

Churchill's relations with the Labour Party had previously been problematic. Labour associated him with sending in the troops at Tonypandy (1910), government action against the General Strike (1926), criticisms of Gandhi, praise for Mussolini and intervention against Lenin during the Russian Civil War (1919). However, relations improved after 1936. Churchill and the Labour Party jointly attacked appeasement. Citrine (the General Secretary of the TUC) shared a platform with Churchill and urged he be made Minister of Supply.

The operation in Norway was disastrous Following the Nazi occupation of Denmark (8 April) and invasion of Norway (9 April), a political crisis was sparked in Britain.

WINSTON CHURCHILL'S APPOINTMENT AS PRIME MINISTER BY KING GEORGE VI ON 10 MAY 1940. THE APPOINTMENT WAS POPULAR, PARTICULARLY WITH THE PRESS AND GENERAL PUBLIC. THIS GOVERNMENT WAS TO OFFER A CONCERTED WAR EFFORT THROUGH NATIONAL UNITY.

Reason 5

Churchill held a different attitude toward Nazi Germany. Chamberlain stated the government's policy was for peace if Germany gave effective guarantees of sincerity for peace. In contrast, Churchill was unequivocal in his view that Nazism had to be destroyed.

Reason 4

Opinion polls began to move in his favour. From his base at the Admiralty, his influence extended across the Cabinet and particularly to relations with the USA. He began a correspondence with President Roosevelt through which a mutual understanding developed.

son 3

Churchill's reputation was enhanced rapidly by his role as First Lord of Admiralty. He was associated with the Battle of River Plate (Dec. 1939), the scuttling of the *Graf Spee*, the seizure of the *Altmark* off Norway (Feb. 1940) and the rescue of British sailors. Churchill gave much attention to the Admiralty's public relations via the BBC. His speeches were always scheduled at prime time and received some of the largest audiences. His role was outstanding in the War Cabinet, and he gained a groundswell of popularity around the country in addition to that of the press.

DAVID LOW , 'ALL BEHIND YOU, WINSTON', *EVENING STANDARD*, 14 MAY 1940.

TALKING POINT

What impression do the photograph and cartoon give of Churchill as prime minister?

TASKS

A comparative analysis of Neville Chamberlain and Winston Churchill.

1 Re-read the information in this chapter on the two wartime prime ministers, research them further in the library and complete the following table:

Aspects of individual	Neville Chamberlain	Winston Churchill
Political background		
Personality and style		
Views towards Nazi Germany		
Attitude to Britain's war effort		
Relations with the Labour Party		
Popular and press opinion of PM		

2 Write an essay:
   'Why was Chamberlain replaced by Churchill as Britain's wartime Prime Minister?'

Focus

10.1 Winston Spencer Churchill – some biographical notes

Background and early career

1874	Born at Blenheim Palace, Oxfordshire on 30 November – son of Lord Randolph and Jennie Churchill. His mother was the daughter of an American stockbroker.
1888	Attended Harrow School.
1893	Entered Sandhurst Royal Military College.
1896	Posted to India and involved in Battle of Omdurman.
1899	Having returned from India – sent to South Africa for the *Morning Post* and captured by Boers. He escaped in December.
1900	Elected Conservative and Unionist MP for Oldham.
1904	Crossed the house and joined the Liberal Party.

Cabinet Positions under Liberal government

1906	At the Liberal landslide election victory, elected Liberal MP for Manchester NW.
1908	President of the Board of Trade – developed a concern for social reform. Wrote in the Liberal weekly *The Nation* that social reform was 'the untrodden field of politics' (see Chapter 2). Worked to introduce the Unemployment Insurance scheme.
1910	Married Clementine Hozier. Home Secretary
1911	First Lord of the Admiralty

Government Minister and Soldier – First World War

1914	As First Lord of the Admiralty – Churchill was involved with and witnessed the British victory of the Falkland Islands (Dec. 1914) and of Dogger Bank (Jan. 1915).
1915 Feb.	Naval attack on the Dardanelles. The failed Gallipoli campaign brought about Churchill's fall from Admiralty. May – resigned office and went to the Western Front in November. Commanded 6th Battalion, Royal Scottish Fusiliers Jan.–May.
1916	
1917	Returned to Lloyd George's government as Minister of Munitions.
1919	Continued in Lloyd George's peacetime coalition as Secretary of State for War and Air.
1921	Secretary of State for the Colonies
1922	Defeated in the General Election at Dundee. Lloyd George's coalition fell.

A return to Conservative ranks – 1920s

1923	Failed to win West Leicester as Liberal
1924	Failed to win Abbey division of Westminster as Independent Anti Socialist in March. Elected for Epping as Constitutionalist and is made Chancellor of Exchequer in Baldwin's Conservative government (see Chapter 6).
1925	Returned Britain to the Gold Standard.
1926	Active government role during the General Strike.
1929	Baldwin's government fell to Labour. Elected for Epping and joined Shadow Cabinet

The political wilderness – 1930s

1931	Resigned from Shadow Cabinet over policy of Dominion Status for India
1935	Joined Air Defence Research sub-committee. Argued for increased rearmament.
1936	Supported the King against the Establishment in the Abdication crisis.
1939	Rebelled against Appeasement and the decisions at Munich. Drew on all his resources of rhetoric to criticise government appeasers.
1931–8	MacDonald, Baldwin and Chamberlain kept him out of National Government.
1939–40	First Lord of Admiralty in Chamberlain's War Cabinet

TASKS

1 What perspective on life and politics would you expect Churchill to have from his upbringing. Is this borne out in future years?

2 Identify the consistent trends through Churchill's career up to 1939.

3 What inconsistencies/ changes are apparent in his career up to 1939. Can you explain these?

4 What criticisms can be made of his career to 1939?

5 Write a curriculum vitae for Churchill, illustrating his relevant experience for the role of war leader.

Churchill – The Speechmaker Internet task

1 Access the Winston Churchill Home Page on the Internet. The web site address is http://www.winstonchurchill.org

2 There are several options here you may wish to explore.
Click on 'spoken words'. Click on 'Excerpts from speeches' – you can also read the 'complete speeches'.

3 Study the following four famous speeches of Churchill.
  a 'We shall fight on the beaches', 4 June 1940
  b 'This was their finest hour', 18 June 1940
  c 'So few', 20 August 1940
  d 'The End of the Beginning', 10 November 1942.

4 From this web site and the timeline in the preview of this chapter –

explain fully the historical context of each of these four speeches.

5 From these speeches quote phrases/ sentences which illustrate the following
  a Encouragement and praise to the British people and armed forces
  b Warning against complacency
  c The threat of Hitler to Britain
  d Importance of the moment
  e Scale of the war
  f Comparison with the First World War
  g Churchill's personal involvement and commitment
  h Understanding of ordinary Britons' lives

6 How does the language, style and tone in these speeches reinforce the message Churchill is putting across to his audience?

Churchill as War Leader or War Monger?

Churchill wrote to his wife after observing German army manoeuvres:
"Much as war attracts me and fascinates my mind with its tremendous situations, I feel more deeply every year, and can measure the feeling here in the midst of arms what vile and wicked folly and barbarism it all is".

Coalition government

Churchill initially formed a small war cabinet of five members, although this was subsequently increased in size. Two senior Labour men, Clement Attlee and Arthur Greenwood, were included along with the two Conservatives – Chamberlain and Halifax. There were changes throughout the war years, but the government remained predominantly Conservative in membership Labour having 16 posts compared to the Conservatives' 52. There were three service ministries: Alexander (Labour) to the Admiralty, Sinclair (Liberal) to Air and Eden (Conservative) to War. Other Labour leaders included Bevin as Minister of Labour and Morrison as Minister of Supply.

No one emerged during the five years to rival Churchill as leader. Churchillian rhetoric provided the nations morale booster – based upon the assumption that everyone wanted victory. His speeches made a major contribution to his leadership (see PP ....) in addition to his character. He was dogged, determined, totally committed, visible and flexible. He took on different roles through bombed ruins, on board ships, in the desert, at street corners – a different hat for every occasion and a lighted cigar. The British public viewed "Good old Winnie" with great fondness. He was very hard-working and expected the same standards from his staff. Regular hours and weekend breaks disappeared in a flurry of urgent activity. For a man in his 60s, working a 90 hour week for 5 years, and brushing off a heart attack and a bout of pneumonia – it was a massive achievement.

Command Structure

Churchill had much personal experience of fighting and military administration. He understood the problems of strategic planning, and the relations between the three services. His main achievement in terms of command structure was to centralise and integrate the two functions of policy making and military strategy. A defence committee was set up over the Chiefs of Staff Committee. Churchill was kept informed personally by his Chief Staff officer, Ismay, and took advice from various quarters.

Means of War

By 1940 Churchill was aware that Britain had neither the military nor the economic strength to win compared to Hitler's position. Throughout summer and autumn 1940 the main British effort was on survival not victory. The Prime Minister was convinced of the need for USA support. His correspondent, Roosevelt was re-elected to the White House in November 1940. The Lend-Lease Scheme, agreed in spring 1941 by USA, was a valuable contribution to Britain's means of war. USA agreed to supplies being 'lent' or 'leased' to any country whose defence was vital to the defence of the USA. When the Japanese strike against Pearl Harbour took place on 7 December 1941 the USA declared war against the AXIS powers. Their support continued to the cessation of hostilities in 1945.

Internet Task

1 Access the Winston Churchill Home Page again.
2 Click on 'Flaws and Mistakes'.
3 Make a note of the 18 criticisms made of Churchill by Richard M. Langworth, Editor, *Finest Hour*.
4 These criticisms are answered in the following section 'Not right all the time'. Make a note of the points of defence.
5 Criticisms 9–15 are particularly relevant to a wartime assessment of Churchill – how valid do you consider them?

Talking Point

With reference to the timeline on pp. 216–17 illustrate this point:

'What attitudes in the USA does the Lend-Lease Scheme reflect?'

EXAMINING THE EVIDENCE

An assessment of Churchill's wartime leadership

Source A

I think it is fitting that today I should pay tribute to one of the main architects of our victory. However we may be divided politically in this House, I believe I shall be expressing the views of the whole House in making acknowledgement here of the transcendent services rendered by the Right Hon. Gentleman to this country, the Commonwealth and Empire, and to the world during his tenure of office.

During those years he was leader of the country in war. We have seen in fascist countries a detestable cult of leadership which has only been a cover for dictatorship, but there is a true leadership which means the expression by one man of the soul of a nation, and its translation of the common will into action. In the darkest and most dangerous hours of our history this nation found in my Right Hon. Friend the man who expressed supremely the courage and determination never to yield which animated all the men and the women of this country. In undying phrases he crystallised the unspoken feeling of all. 'Words only,' it might be said, but words of great moment in history are deeds. We had more than words from the Right Hon. Gentleman. He radiated a stream of energy throughout the machinery of government, indeed throughout the life of the nation.

Many others are in the work of organising and inspiring the nation in its great effort, but he set the pace. He was able to bring into co-operation men of very different political views and to win from them loyal service. At critical times, by his personal relationship with the heads of allied States, he promoted the harmony and co-operation of all, and in the sphere of strategy his wide experience, grasp of essentials, his willingness to take necessary risks were of the utmost value ... His place in history is secure.

C.R. Attlee, speaking in the House of Commons, 16 August 1945.

Source B

While western Europe collapsed under the weight of Hitler's assault, Britain alone, against the expectations of the entire world, resisted the advance of Nazism. In that achievement Churchill's own part was inestimable. He alone, by example and exhortation, transformed a demoralised nation into one of inflexible resolution.

David Mason, *Churchill* (1973), editorial comment on the back cover of the book.

1 In what ways does Attlee evidence Churchill's war leadership record?
2 With reference to the attribution of Source A, how useful is this assessment of Churchill?
3 Compare the tone of Sources A and B. Identify the main differences in their estimations of Churchill.

Source C

Diary of Robert Menzies, 26 April 1941. Sir Robert Menzies was Prime Minister of Australia from 1949 to 1966.

Drove down to Churt to lunch with Lloyd George, who is as clear headed as ever, and has some shrewd things to say about Cabinet organisation, Winston's leadership, and the like. We found we had many ideas in common, much as follows:

1 Winston is acting as the master strategist, without qualification and without really forceful Chiefs of Staff to guide him.

2 Dill [Sir John Dill, Chief of the Imperial General Staff] has ability, but is as timid as a hare.

3 There is no War Cabinet, since WC deals with conduct of war himself, by 'directives' etc. and his Ministers just concur.

4 Beaverbrook might have some influence but he is up to the neck in the detail of aircraft construction, and simply has no time for general study and appreciation. No War Cabinet Minister here should have anything to attend to except War Cabinet.

5 War Cabinet should meet every morning. This week, this crucial and anxious week, it has met twice for an hour and an hour and a half respectively!

6 Winston should be at the helm, instead of touring the bombed areas, as he has been doing most of the week. Let the King and Queen do this. In any case they do it much better.

7 More food could be grown in this country, but there is nobody finally responsible for comprehensive policy, which must include food, agriculture, fisheries and so on. Many ministers, many opinions. Same with shipping. M/Shipping attends to the fag end – eg charter parties – Admiralty builds and mends ships, Labour control labour, Transport the getting of goods off the wharves, Supply what can be carried on the ships etc. etc. In brief, Churchill is a bad organiser.

8 A non-executive War Cabinet must contain a Dominions man, for the Dominions type of mind is essential.

9 The problem of a couple of good men to prop up Churchill is acute. He is not interested in finance, economics, agriculture, and ignores the debates on all three. He loves war and spends hours

'M/Shipping' refers to the Ministry of Shipping.

with the maps and charts, working out fresh combinations. He has aggression without knowledge or at any rate without any love for inconvenient knowledge. His advisers are presumed to have knowledge, but haven't enough aggression to convey it to Churchill.

10 Foreign policy is deplorable – eg Japan. We never have ideas, and we never beat Germany to it. Alex Cadogan [Permanent Under Secretary at the Foreign Office] is a dull dog, if not actually a dead dog.

11 Eden [Foreign Secretary] has not (trained) on [diary unclear], and John Anderson [Lord President of the Council, formerly Home Secretary] is a bureaucrat par excellence – no imagination, or sweep, or fire.

Quoted in David Day, *Menzies and Churchill at War* (1986).

1 Identify the main criticisms made of Churchill in Source C.
2 With reference to the attribution and tone of Source C, how useful is it to an assessment of Churchill?

TASK

Write a balanced assessment of Winston Churchill's role as Wartime Prime Minister, 1940–45.

The social impact of the Second World War

Both civilians' and servicemen's lives were affected in the short term by the comprehensive government controls introduced from the start of the war. Building on the experience gained from the First World War, food supplies, transport and the labour force were main considerations. The Home Front 1939–45 was made of the images and realities of rationing, shortages of consumer goods, evacuation, civilian defence, and air raids. The impact of war in the longer term led to significant plans for social reconstruction.

Source A

An eye-witness account of one of the worst bombing attacks on Coventry, 14 November 1940 – 554 people died and much devastation was caused.

When we arrived the building was well alight. All doors were locked. An iron grille delayed action by us. By the time we gained entry we realised that it was impossible to save the place from the inside so we played on the fire from a hydrant outside ... We had lost all sense of time [but] it must have been about midnight when we saw an object which appeared to be attached to a parachute falling in our direction. Four of my crew ran for shelter into Millets Stores' doorway, so Charles S, my deputy, and I took over the hose and continued to damp down the raging fires. A terrific explosion threw us to the ground and when we recovered ourselves, very dazed but not seriously hurt, we found the rest of the crew had disappeared. Charles and I tore away bricks, stone and rubble and after what seemed an interminable time we managed to free one of the buried crew. He was still alive and asked for a cigarette but before we could light it, he died. We struggled with our pump but could not get it going; it was badly damaged. Then, climbing over the piles of rubble, we found a pump at the bottom of Cross Cheaping unmanned. Using the murky water of the River Sherbourne we managed to get the pump working, only to be foiled by a leaking hose. There was nothing we could do so we decided to return to the Central Station – if it was still there.

Auxiliary Fire Serviceman George Kyrke, memories of the bombing of Coventry, 14 November 1940, recorded in N. Longmate, *Air Raid: The Bombing of Coventry* (1976), p. 114.

TALKING POINT

Can you explain the variations on the graph of civilian deaths, 1939–45?

Source B

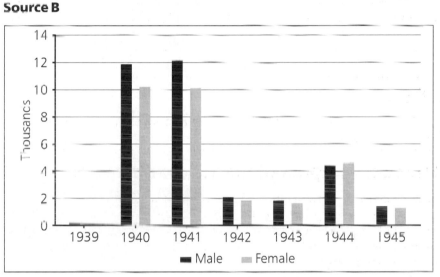

BRITISH CIVILIAN DEATHS RESULTING FROM THE WAR, 1939–45 (CHART DERIVED FROM CENTRAL STATISTICAL OFFICE, *STATISTICAL DIGEST OF THE WAR* (1951), PP. 37, 40)

Government propaganda

Through the newly created Ministry of Information, the wartime government put much effort into producing effective propaganda, using every available medium. The Ministry, based at Senate House, London University, censored all material before it was made available to the BBC, newspapers and newsreels.

The BBC increased its radio service widely during the war. In September 1939 there were 24 radio transmitters – by May 1945 the number had risen to 121. The BBC became the official voice of Britain. It was a disseminator of information, a morale booster with programmes such as Tommy Handley's show *ITMA*, and finally a means by which the Prime Minister could communicate with the vast majority of the population.

Source A

PHILIP ZEC, 'WOMEN OF BRITAIN COME INTO THE FACTORIES', UNDATED POSTER (IMPERIAL WAR MUSEUM, LONDON, PS263)

Source C

'DIG FOR VICTORY'.

Source B

'CARELESS TALK COSTS LIVES: YOU NEVER KNOW WHO'S LISTENING!'

Talking Point

What was the government's purpose behind the messages in these posters? Comment on their effectiveness.

Examining the Evidence

British Society and the Impact of War

Study Sources A–D below and then answer the questions which follow.

Source A

September 1939. At last … the evacuees arrived at their destination. Most were exhausted, thirsty, hungry and bewildered … Initially there was much animosity between the evacuees and the local children … They hurled insults and stones. As the months went by, country food and air … brought such a change that pale faces filled out and grew rosy … and many grew as much as an inch in two months. For the few, lives were made miserable by sadistic adults or those so greedy that they had only taken them in because of the boarding allowance. Some of these children were used as free labour around the house and on the land.

Anne Valery, in *Talking About the War: a Personal View of the War in Britain* (1991), a book based partly on her own recollections.

Source B

14 September 1939. The House is mainly concerned with the evacuation of children … Many of the children are verminous and have disgusting habits. This horrifies the cottagers upon whom they have been billeted … Much ill-feeling has been caused. But the interesting thing is that this feeling is not between the rich and poor but between the urban and the rural poor … The effect will be to demonstrate to people how deplorable is the standard of life and civilisation among the urban proletariat.

Harold Nicolson, MP, in his diary, 1939.

Source C

Hardly anyone has slept at all in the past week … In the poorer districts, queues of people carrying blankets, thermos flasks and babies begin to form quite early outside the air-raid shelters. The Blitzkreig continues to be directed against such military objectives as the tired shop girl, the red-eyed clerk, and the thousands of dazed and weary families patiently trundling their few belongings in perambulators away from the wreckage of their homes … The amazing part of it is the cheerfulness and fortitude with which ordinary individuals are doing their jobs under nerve-wracking conditions.

M Panter-Downes, an English woman who contributed a regular 'Letter' to *The New Yorker*, 14 September 1940.

Source D

17 September 1940. Down to the house … Everybody is worried about the East End, where there is much bitterness … Clem says that if only the Germans had had the sense not to bomb west of London Bridge there might have been a revolution in this country. As it is, they have smashed about Bond Street and Park Lane and readjusted the balance … 19 September 1940. We all refuse to face the fact that unless we can invent an antidote to night-bombing, London will suffer very severely and the spirit of our people may be broken. Already the Communists are getting people in shelters to sign a peace-petition to Churchill. One cannot expect the population of a great city to sit up all night in shelters week after week without losing their spirit.

Harold Nicolson MP, in his diary, 1940. At this time, he was Parliamentary Secretary to the Ministry of Information.

Bond Street and Park Lane are fashionable areas in London's West End.

1 What, in the context of these documents, is meant by:
   a 'The House' (Source B, line 1) and
   b 'The Blitzkreig' (Source C, line 4)?
2 To what extent do Sources C and D differ in their views on the effect of bombing on the people of London? What does the author of Source D mean by 'As it is, they have smashed about Bond Street and Park Lane and readjusted the balance' (lines 5–6)?
3
   a How do Sources A and B agree or differ in the facts they give about the state of the 'evacuees' (line 1) and their reception by their hosts?
   b How do Sources A and B differ in tone and language?
   c Discuss, with reference to their authorship and their content, which of Sources C and D is the more likely to present an accurate picture of the reaction of Londoners to the events of September 1940?

The Home Front – A Fact File

Food and Clothing

- Rationing was introduced in January 1940 to overcome the problem of limited food supplies. Although it was introduced as a temporary wartime measure, the final restrictions were not lifted until 1955.
- Ration books were distributed, different colours for different categories in society and shoppers had to register with the shops of their choice.
- Essentials, such as eggs, sugar, butter, margarine, meat, tea, cheese and fruit, were all rationed – but nutritionists checked that a balanced diet was available to all.
- Despite the National Milk Scheme, milk was in short supply and families used dried milk as a substitute.
- Special provision was made for children, pregnant and nursing mothers through the Vitamin Welfare Scheme. These groups were issued with green ration books which allowed a daily pint of milk and double egg ration.
- Cookery changed to meet availability. Soups, corned beef hash, carrot cake, toffee carrots and potato pie. Patriotic dishes such as Victory Flan and Dunkirk Delight were introduced.
- The Dig for Victory Campaign involved the digging up of famous gardens, golf courses and the moat at the Tower of London. By 1943, there were 1.4 million allotments in Britain.
- People's diets were meagre and plain but healthy and guaranteed to all the population.
- Everyone was encouraged to look after, mend and recycle clothing.
- The Utility Scheme ensured that consumer goods were produced at a price affordable to lower income families. Items such as clothes, shoes, carpets, and house paint all carried a utility mark.
- Soap and other toiletries were also rationed.

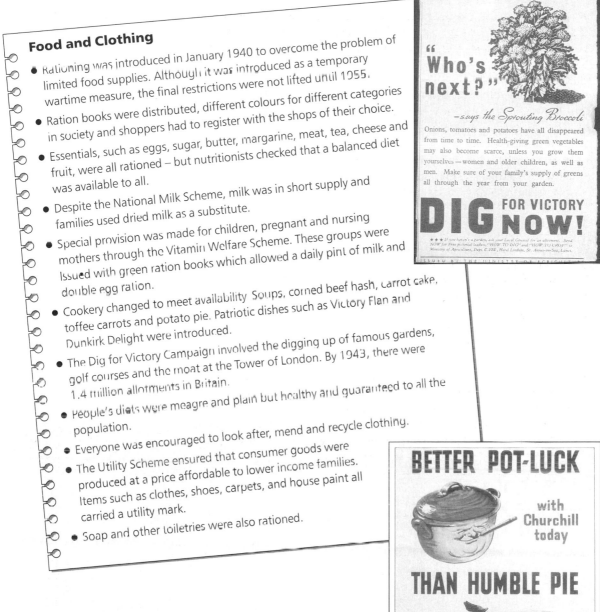

"Who's next?"
— says the Sprouting Broccoli

Onions, tomatoes and potatoes have all disappeared from time to time. Health-giving green vegetables may also become scarce, unless you grow them yourselves — women and older children, as well as men. Make sure of your family's supply of greens all through the year from your garden.

DIG FOR VICTORY NOW!

★ ★ ★ If you haven't a garden, ask your Local Council for an allotment. Send NOW for Free pictorial leaflets, "HOW TO DIG" and "HOW TO CROP" to Ministry of Agriculture, Dept. C.106, Hotel London, St. Annes-on-Sea, Lancs.

ISSUED BY THE MINISTRY OF AGRICULTURE

BETTER POT-LUCK with Churchill today

THAN HUMBLE PIE under Hitler tomorrow

DON'T WASTE FOOD!

TALKING POINT

Why has this period been referred to as the 'first food democracy'? Was it possible to achieve a full evenness of supply?

Evacuation

- 1939 brought an official recommendation that all children in the towns and cities should be moved to the country for their safety, for the protection of a next generation and to increase the numbers of women available for factory work.

- In the first wave of evacuation in 1939–40 1.5 million pregnant and nursing women and children were relocated to the countryside.

- It was a massive task involving the three ministries of Health, Transport and Education.

- The poorest areas of cities and ports were evacuated first – those nearest gas works, railways and the docks.

- Organisers were overwhelmed by the social problems they unearthed – such as malnutrition, disease and lack of clothing.

- It was a difficult experience for parents, evacuees and foster parents – all had to make considerable changes in their lifestyle, sometimes successfully, sometimes not.

- Later evacuations were more efficiently completed as the rural communities became more organised with sick bays, dormitories and canteens.

- The government were forced to witness the poverty exposed. It was discovered that between 12 and 15 per cent of poor families in Merseyside, Bristol, Sheffield and Southampton had only 4s per week for food.

- Dislocation of population generally was widespread. During the war years, there were 60 million changes of address registered in a population of 35 million.

TALKING POINT

What problems do you think were experienced by the evacuees, host families and parents during this process?
What wider social implications did it have?

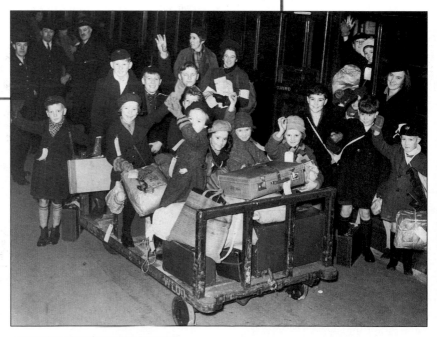

CHILDREN EVACUATING LONDON.

Civil Defence

- Air Raid Protection – ARP – became a central part of people's lives. It was essential as a counter to the German Luftwaffe.

- Government advice was issued during 1939 – the 'Phoney War' made it seem an overreaction, but the wisdom of the precautions was proved from 1940 onwards. Blackout curtains were to be put up at all windows in homes, public houses and other buildings. Dettol – a Reckitt & Sons product – was recommended for injuries.

- Air raid shelters were constructed by families. The Morrison shelter for protection inside homes by means of a steel cage or the Anderson shelter built outside.

- Local Defence Volunteers was set up on 14 May 1940 by Eden, the Secretary of State for War. This group, known as the 'Dads' Army', was for all men between 17–65 excused from military service. The age limits were extended later on. A quarter of a million men had responded in the first 24 hours and 1.5 million had volunteered by June. The Home Guard (a name it received in July 1940) trained hard, proved helpful and worked tirelessly in case of invasion despite being the butt of many wartime jokes.

- Many women joined civil defence organisations. By 1943 one in four Civil Defence workers were women. They became air raid wardens/fire guards/emergency messengers/manned First Aid Posts. In 1942 the Women's Home Defence Corps was set up with training to handle rifles and grenades.

Labour Force

- Civilians made an exhaustive effort to contribute to the war effort at their place of work.

- Munitions workers had long hours and there is much evidence of fatigue. Some jobs allowed people to take a second job e.g. vicars also worked as postmen.

- Women were seen as instrumental in gaining victory.

- December 1941 National Service No. 2 Act provided for single women over 20 years old to be taken into war service – auxiliary services or industrial workers.

- The Women's Land Army contributed to the maintenance of agricultural production.

- Women Voluntary Service offered help with First Aid, serving refreshments, taking in washing, identifying the dead and wounded.

- Many women joined the Armed Forces. Numbers increased; by 1939 all 3 female forces had 20,000. By 1945 this number was 500,000. They worked as fighter controllers, radar operators, transport drivers and code-breakers.

WOMAN WORKER AT MUNITIONS FACTORY, 1940.

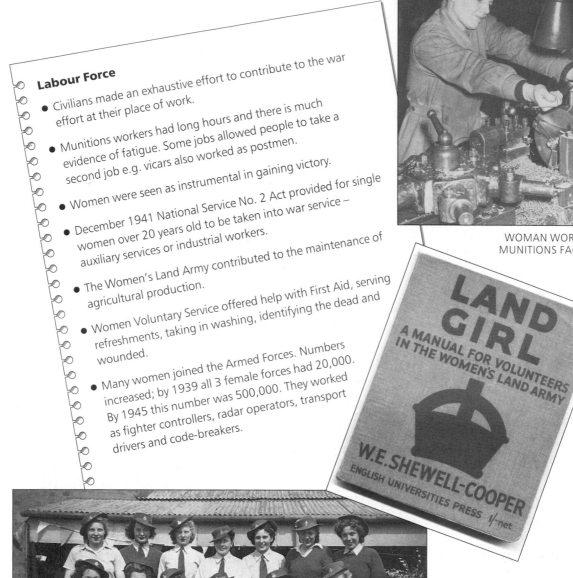

TALKING POINT

What were the social implications for women in the Second World War?

'British people were never as good as they were in World War 2.'

J.B. Priestley

'The war will bring about changes which may be fundamental and revolutionary in the economic and social life of this country.'

Anthony Eden

'Nothing is more certain than that this war will mark the transition from monopoly capitalism to socialism.'

Lord Boothby

TASK

1 List the ways in which the Home Front brought social change to Britain between 1939 and 1945.
2 Answer the question:
   'To what extent can the Second World War be seen as a levelling experience for British people?'
   Consider the situation of: (a) the armed forces, (b) women, (c) urban and rural communities,
   (d) working, middle and upper classes, (e) non-combatant men, (f) children.

Reconstruction

'Britain is being bombed into democracy' (J.B. Priestley)

I will tell you what we did for [servicemen] and their young wives at the end of the last war. We did nothing – except let them take their chance in a world where every gangster and trickster and stupid insensitive fool or rogue was let loose to do his damnedest. After the cheering and the flag-waving was over, and all the medals were given out, somehow the young heroes disappeared, but after a year or two there were a lot of shabby, young-oldish men about who didn't seem to have been lucky in the scramble for easy jobs and quick profits ...

No doubt, it's going to be all different this time, but ... the same kind of minds are still about. Among bundles of very friendly letters just lately I've been getting some very fierce and angry ones telling me to get off the air before the Government 'puts you where you belong' – the real Fascist touch. Well, obviously, it wouldn't matter very much if I were taken off the air, but it would matter a great deal, even to these Blimps, if [the] young men of the R.A.F. were taken off the air; and so I repeat my question – in return for their skill, devotion, endurance and self-sacrifice, what are we civilians prepared to do?... the least we can do is to give our minds honestly, sincerely and without immediate self-interest, to the task of preparing a world really fit for them and their kind – to arrange a final 'happy landing'.

J.B. Priestley, 'Postscript', 28 July 1940.

7 The first principle is that any proposals for the future, while they should use to the full the experience gathered in the past, should not be restricted by consideration of sectional interest established in the obtaining of that experience. Now, when the war is abolishing landmarks of every kind, is the opportunity for using experience in a clear field. A revolutionary moment in the world's history is a time for revolutions, not for patching.

8 The second principle is that organisation of social insurance should be treated as one part only of a comprehensive policy of social progress. Social insurance fully developed may provide income security; it is an attack upon Want. But Want is one only of five giants on the road of reconstruction and in some ways the easiest to attack. The others are Disease, Ignorance, Squalor and Idleness.

9 The third principle is that social security must be achieved by co-operation between the State and the individual. The State should offer security for service and contribution. The State in organising security should not stifle incentive, opportunity, responsibility; in establishing a national minimum, it should leave room and encouragement for voluntary action by each individual to provide more than that minimum for himself and his family.

Sir William Beveridge, *Social Insurance and Allied Services: Report by Sir William Beveridge* (the Beveridge Report) (November 1942).

If we speak of democracy, we do not mean a democracy which maintains the right to vote but forgets the right to work and the right to live. If we speak of freedom, we do not mean a rugged individualism which excludes social organisation and economic planning. If we speak of equality, we do not mean a political equality nullified by social and economic privilege.

The Times, 1 July 1940.

The Government have announced that they intend to establish a National Health Service, which will provide for everyone all the medical advice, treatment and care they required.

This new service represents the natural next development in the long and continuous growth of the health services of the country. Although it forms part of the wider theme of post-war reconstruction – and although it will form an essential part of any scheme of social insurance which may be adopted – it has to be seen in the light of the past as well as the future and to be judged on its own merits as part of a steady historical process of improving health and the opportunity for health among the people …

Ministry of Health and Department of Health for Scotland, *A National Health Service: The White Paper Proposals in Brief* (1944).

Given the will to plan, we could, in a quarter of a century or less, substantially transform our worst towns. Where they are black with soot, they could be at least partly green with trees and grass. We could bring the country into the town in great swathes of parkland never more than a step round the corner from the homes of the people. We could, by reorganisation, shorten the weary long journeys to work, and at the same time make the workplace itself more cheerful. We could replan and reconstruct many of our outworn public services, to stop the drain of money to no purpose.

Maxwell Fry, 'The new Britain must be planned', *Picture Post*, 4 January 1941.

The 1945 General Election

War in Europe ended on VE (Victory in Europe) Day, 8 May 1945. Debate then began over the continued existence of Churchill's wartime coalition. Having stated in the previous year that the government would end with the defeat of Germany, the Prime Minister now wished to stay in situ until Japan surrendered. However, the Labour Party were adamantly against this and on 20 May, Attlee and his colleagues resigned. Churchill formed a caretaker government, called an election for 5 July and Parliament was dissolved on 15 June. Party warfare resumed in the election campaign which followed.

GENERAL ELECTION
RESULTS, 1945.

Percentage share of the vote

Labour 47.8 — Conservative 39.8

Liberal 9.0 — Others 2.8

MPs elected

Labour 393 — Conservative 213

Liberal 12 — Others 22

The result

Why did Labour win?

Short-term factors	CONSERVATIVES	LABOUR
Party manifesto 1945	Churchill's declaration of policy to the electors included the progressive consensus on key social reconstruction issues. But it was vague on postwar economic controls, betraying Conservative divisions on this point. It was a moderate, relatively uncontroversial manifesto.	'Let us face the future' promised economic planning, full employment, the creation of a National Health Service and and a system of Social Security. Nationalisation of the Bank of England, fuel, power, transport, iron and steel. This made up a radical programme of postwar reconstruction in tune with the country's mood.
Election campaign 1945	An aggressive Conservative campaign emphasised the potential danger of a Labour government. In a broadcast on 4 June 1945, Churchill told electors that the introduction of socialism in Britain would necessitate a Nazi-style government. Attempts such as this to stigmatise Attlee's party were counter-productive.	A positive Labour campaign stressed the value of far-reaching reform for postwar Britain. Attlee was able to reply to Churchill's 'Gestapo Speech' of 4 June in a quiet, reasonable and constructive manner.
Party organisation 1945	Churchill wrote in his memoirs that Conservative party organisation was lacking. Many more Conservative Party agents were away in the armed forces whereas opponents – trades unionists in reserved trades – were on hand to campaign. Organisation had certainly deteriorated – however, during the war one of their problems was the indifferent standard of candidates.	This claim by Churchill is largely a myth. Labour organisers gave evidence that the majority of Labour agents were pressed into service at the last minute without previous experience.

Election posters 1945

Long-term factors

TALKING POINT

Can you explain the trends in these polls? Why do you think very little notice was taken of them at the time?

In his book *The Road to 1945*, Paul Addison argues that the longer-term factors are the most significant in explaining Labour's victory in 1945. He has shown that 'popular opinion swung towards Labour' and gave it electoral success. In addition to the climate of opinion producing a pro-Labour sentiment, after the formation of Churchill's coalition government in 1940, the Home Front was dominated by 'Labour's Big Three.' – Attlee, Bevin and Morrison. They were visible to Britons, gained experience and immense respect and finally pushed their ideas on 'planning', 'equality' and 'reconstruction' through their influential government positions.

OPINION POLLS, 1943–5.

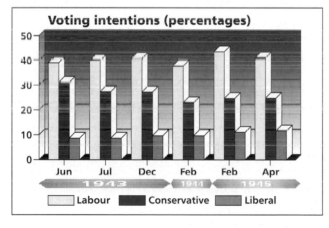

TASK

1   Re-read this chapter and complete further research and find evidence which
a   explains the changing climate of opinion in Britain during the war
b   illustrates the increasing role played by Labour in the wartime governments.
2   From the previous chapters on Britain in the 1930s, decide what the British public in 1945 would remember of the Conservative and Labour parties.
3   Using this information and the short-term factors discussed in the Review – write an essay: 'Why was Churchill ousted in the 1945 General Election?'

11 Attlee's Labour Government, 1945–51

PREVIEW

Britain at the End of the War, 1945

Human Cost of War: Numbers killed 1939–45		
	Armed Forces	**Civilians**
GB	264,433	60,595
USSR	13,300,000	7,000,000
Germany	3,250,000	3,600,000
Japan	1,000,000	2,000,000

CHURCHILL LEAVES
DOWNING STREET
TO SEE THE KING.

CLEMENT ATTLEE TO KING
GEORGE VI : 'I'VE WON THE
ELECTION'.

REPLY : 'I KNOW, I HEARD IT
ON THE SIX O'CLOCK NEWS'.

A DEMOBILIZED SOLDIER COLLECTS CLOTHES.

- By 1945 Britain's overseas debts totalled more than £3000 million.

- Between 1939 and 1941, the country's gold reserves fell from £864 million to £3 million.

- In the course of the War, one third of the country's housing stock was destroyed.

- Two-thirds of the merchant fleet was lost.

GERMAN POWS LEAVE THE PRISON CAMPS.

PRE-FABRICATED HOUSING WAS A SPEEDY SOLUTION TO THE SHORTAGE OF DWELLINGS.

VE DAY CELEBRATIONS IN TRAFALGAR SQUARE.

TALKING POINT

What problems confronted the Labour government as a result of war:

    a   in the short term

    b   in the longer term?

What would be the hopes and expectations of the British people in 1945?

Clement Attlee, Prime Minister 1945–51

Attlee was 62 years old when he became prime minister. He had been educated at Haileybury public school and Oxford. After a career in the Law, he became the Labour MP for Limehouse, Stepney in 1922. He took over the leadership of the Labour Party in 1935, succeeding the 76-year-old pacifist, George Lansbury. As a member of Churchill's wartime coalition from 1940 to 1945, he had gained valuable government experience. Churchill's total preoccupation with the conduct of war gave Attlee a virtually free hand in domestic issues. Attlee was officially Deputy Prime Minister from 1942, yet this position was overshadowed by the prestigious and dominant role of Churchill.

Source A

An *Observer* profile describes the Labour leader in 1944.

> At Cabinet meetings the Deputy Prime Minister always sits on the edge of his chair. The trick is typical of the man. It is the sign of diffidence, a lack of confidence, perhaps better, a modesty, that must be almost unique in high politics.
>
> Yet this is the man, who, on merit, is wartime Number 2 to Mr Churchill of all people. The debt owed to loyal Clem Attlee by the Prime Minister, the country and the Labour Party is big. The post of Deputy Prime Minister was literally made for him and he for it; he fills it without envy.
>
> Outside the Councils of State, too, Mr Attlee is true to type. He is almost anonymous. Slight in figure, he does not stand out in a crowd. Thin in voice, he is at a disadvantage in this Broadcasting Age. He is the forgotten Minister who four years ago brought in the forgotten Bill to put all persons and all property at the nation's disposal.
>
> How is it that he can be called the 'brace' of the Cabinet? Back in the Cabinet room, or at Party meetings, the answer is plainer. Puffing at his pipe, he puts sound points well and simply. He is no colourful figure or champion of stirring causes; he is the impeccable Chairman – at a time when both Cabinet and Party, ill-sorted and on edge, much need a Chairman. Clem Attlee is the honest broker, the good man who came to the aid of this Party. The fact is, the Labour Party distrusts leadership. The case of Ramsay MacDonald frightened it. Nor does anyone, inside or outside the party, know where it wishes to be led. All that is certain is that the motley group has somehow to be held together. Clem Attlee is neither bigot, doctrinaire, Labour boss, nor careerist. He puts the whole before the parts. He is a Party man, not a partisan…
>
> Historians will give Clem Attlee his due, even under the shadow of Churchill, for he, too, in his own, way, is equally an English worthy, though not a Great one. But they will also show how his worth to us in our tangled counsels of these days is a reflection of today's discontents and frustrations … Clem Attlee is a Fabian; it is an infinite progress to the Brave New World he believes in, but his faith is at least real; he is a man of character.

1 Explain the following references in the article above:
  a '…the Labour Party distrusts leadership. The case of Ramsey MacDonald frightened it.'
  b 'He puts the whole before the parts. He is a Party man, not a partisan'.
  c 'Clem Attlee is a Fabian'.
2 According to Source A, what are Attlee's
  a Strengths
  b Weaknesses
  as a leading politician?
3 Research Attlee's background and beliefs further.

Formation of the first majority Labour Government

'These fine men constituted a body of Ministers as talented as any in the history of Parliament' Quote from Harold Macmillan, Conservative MP and Prime Minister from 1957 to 1963.

Following a wait of three weeks while the servicemen's votes from all over the world were counted, the Election of 1945 brought a dramatic victory for the Labour Party with 393 seats – a clear majority of 146. Finally, a Labour government had been elected with a substantial majority. Pelling, a Labour Party historian, considered that although Labour had a well-written manifesto and effectively run campaign, voters tended to be influenced more by the past record of the parties – despite the wartime leadership of Churchill, the Conservatives were still associated with the period of mass unemployment and appeasement in the 1930s. This stood in sharp contrast to the valuable and responsible role played by many senior Labour figures in the Second World War coalition government.

The complexion of the new postwar Labour Party in Parliament differed substantially from earlier governments. Trade union-sponsored members totalled less than a third (although there were significant figures such as

Aneurin Bevan and Ernest Bevin among this number), a flood of young middle-class professional Labour MPs arrived at Westminster and two-thirds of Labour MPs had not been in Parliament before. However, the leading figures were older and more experienced in government.

Clement Attlee could be described as a reformist – he was an admirer of the monarchy and the public school system. He did not wish to abolish the class system, looking rather to end poverty through positive action and extend opportunities for the working class to move into middle-class ranks. He abandoned the small wartime Cabinet and attempted in his ministerial appointments to reward talent and to preserve the balance between the different ideological wings of the party. His Cabinet was a mix of right and left wing and of upper-, middle- and working-class backgrounds.

Building the Welfare State, 1944–48

The term 'Welfare State' did not become commonly used until the 1940s and it is in that decade that the beginning of the Welfare State can be pinpointed specifically. On 5 July 1948 the *Daily Mirror* announced:

> The great day has arrived. You wanted the state to assume greater responsibility for individual citizens. You wanted social security. From today you have it.

The creation of a Welfare State came as a result of a long process of changing attitudes, but the nearest to a blueprint for it was the Beveridge Report published in 1942. (See Chapter 10.)

Source A
Beveridge to the rescue.

'TACKLING THE FIRST GIANT',
DAILY HERALD, 2 DECEMBER 1945.

TALKING POINT
How important are personalities to voters?

TALKING POINT
What do you understand by the terms 'Welfare State' and 'Social Security'?

1 What techniques are used by the cartoonist in Source A to make his point?
2 Do Beveridge's '5 giants' cover all the social needs in Britain?
3 Is there an odd one out? Why do you think it is included?

What is the main point made by Bevan?

TASK

Complete the diagram below by fitting into the boxes the legislation of the Labour Government which was designed to tackle Beveridge's five giants.

'From the Cradle to the Grave'

Source B

'The eyes of the world are turning to Great Britain. We now have the moral leadership of the world, and before many years we shall have people coming here as to a modern Mecca, learning from us in the twentieth century as they learned from us in the seventeenth...'

Aneurin Bevan, Minister of Health, 4 July 1948 – the day on which the National Health Service came into being.

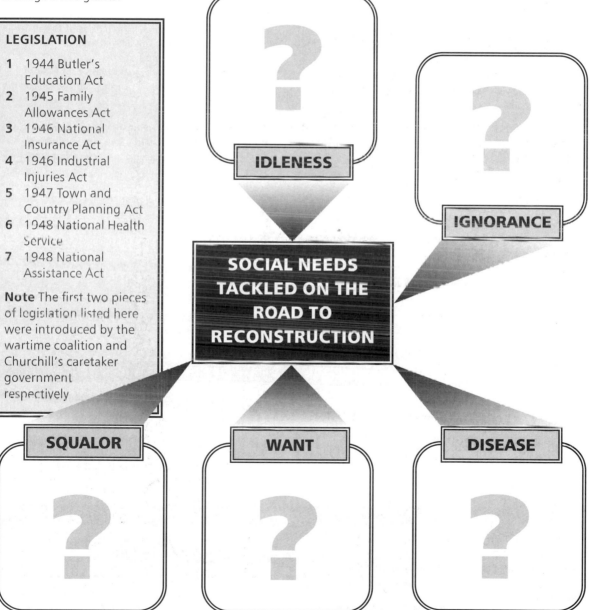

LEGISLATION

1   1944 Butler's Education Act
2   1945 Family Allowances Act
3   1946 National Insurance Act
4   1946 Industrial Injuries Act
5   1947 Town and Country Planning Act
6   1948 National Health Service
7   1948 National Assistance Act

Note The first two pieces of legislation listed here were introduced by the wartime coalition and Churchill's caretaker government respectively

IDLENESS

IGNORANCE

SOCIAL NEEDS TACKLED ON THE ROAD TO RECONSTRUCTION

SQUALOR

WANT

DISEASE

A social security system

1944 EDUCATION ACT

- Passed by Churchill's wartime coalition government under the auspices of R.A. Butler.
- The Act created a Ministry of Education with the aim of providing a comprehensive, national educational system.
- Education was split into three stages – primary, secondary and further – provided for by Local Education Authorities (LEAs).
- Free education was to be provided up to school leaving age which was to be raised to 15 years in 1947.
- A daily act of religious worship was made compulsory.
- The earlier Norwood Committee (1943) had confirmed that secondary education should be provided according to the type of pupil. Three sorts of schools – grammar, technical and modern – were made available and a pupil's suitability for a place was assessed in an 11+ examination.

11 June 1945 FAMILY ALLOWANCES ACT

- One of the final Acts passed by Churchill's administration, work led by the social reformer Eleanor Rathbone.
- Every family in Britain given an allowance of 5s a week for second and other children up to the age of 15 – or 16 years if the child was in full-time education.
- Payable without a means test.
- First Family Allowance day was August Bank Holiday Tuesday 1946 – on Day 1 2.5 million families took up the allowance.
- The amount would buy one 1lb Brooke Bond Dividend Tea, a tube of Colgate toothpaste and a Mars bar.
- Contemporary views varied – Barbara Castle, a newly elected Labour MP, called it a 'paltry sum' but Jim Griffiths, a more experienced Labour figure, calculated 'The cost to the nation was £59 million, surely one of the best investments the state ever made'.

1946 INDUSTRIAL INJURIES ACT

- Nationalised a system which had gradually built up since Joseph Chamberlain Workman's Compensation Act 1897.
- The Ministry of National Insurance took responsibility.
- The whole workforce was covered – 45s a week payment was made.
- The Act was the result of intensive lobbying from the trades unions.

Talking point

What was the significance of this allowance being payable without a means test?

1948 NATIONAL ASSISTANCE ACT

- Designed to help those who fell through the net provided by existing system.
- The Act removed the financial responsibility for the destitute out of local hands to government.
- Local authorities were responsible for providing residential accommodation and daycare centres.

HOUSING

- This was a major issue – the wartime loss of 1/3 of housing stock severely worsened an existing prewar shortage.
- The government target was 200,000 houses per annum but the lack of resources made this unfeasible.
- However, one million houses were built despite the shortages.
- 124,000 factory made pre-fabs were erected – well designed, comfortable and durable, some were still in existence 50 years later.
- The 1947 Town and Country Planning Act encouraged local authorities to undertake surveys and present plans for development.

1946	NATIONAL INSURANCE ACT

- Ministry of National Insurance set up together with National Insurance Fund with an initial £100 million.
- Annual grants were to be made from the Exchequer to supplement payments from employers and employees.
- *Unemployment benefit* – Insured employees were eligible after three days to receive a weekly payment for 180 days. Those in a job qualified for benefit but lost it after 13 weeks
- *Sickness benefit* – Payable to injured after three days' enforced leave from work. It could be drawn up to retirement.
- *Maternity benefit* – Single payment made to mothers on the birth of a child.
  - Working mothers were entitled to an allowance for 13 weeks to compensate for loss of earnings.
- *Death grant* – A lump sum awarded to cover the cost of a funeral.
- *Widows* – A widow under retirement age was entitled to an allowance for 16 weeks in addition to allowances for children up to 16 years old.
  - Widows of retirement age gained a continuing allowance.
  - To qualify a woman had to have been married for 10 years.
- *Orphans* – Guardians were to receive an allowance provided one parent at least was insured under the Act.
- *Pensions* – Men of 65 years and women of 60 years were entitled to a pension.
  - Single person 25s; married couple 42s.
  - Pensioners could continue working with reduced pension.
  - Men and women already of retirement age were paid pensions, even though they had not contributed to the scheme.
  - Pensions were not earnings-related nor inflation-linked.

TALKING POINT

What do you understand by the terms 'earnings-related' and 'inflation-linked'? What would be the ramifications of these two stipulations on pensions?

TASKS

What were the consequences for the government and people of implementing a Welfare State?

1   Refer to Chapters 2 and 8 in this book, revise the social legislation passed by (i) the Liberals 1906–14 and (ii) the interwar governments. Make a list of the ways in which the Labour Government's legislation was more extensive.

2   Groupwork – each student group should take one of the following social groups and identify from the details on legislation the costs and benefits for those people of the new Welfare State.
    a   The government, present and future.
    b   A middle-class family of four – mother, father (the only income) and two school-age children.
    c   An elderly married couple.
    d   A working-class family of seven – mother, father and five children. Father is unemployed due to an accident at work.
    e   A young married couple. The wife has just had a baby.
    Bring the details back to a class discussion.

3   The Welfare State can be described as both COMPREHENSIVE (that is, covering all social needs) and UNIVERSAL (that is, available to everyone regardless of income or social status). Discuss:
    a   How the Welfare State meets these two criteria.
    b   Whether these two principles raise problems.

4   Write an essay:
    'What were the consequences of implementing a Welfare State?'

The creation of the National Health Service

The NHS came into operation on the appointed day – 5 July 1948 – and is still in place today. Very much a central feature of the British Welfare State, it is increasingly a subject of controversy and an area undergoing change.

The Labour Government Minister of Health – an ex-miner from South Wales, Aneurin Bevan – is still associated with the creation of the NHS for all the work he did. It was an achievement in part due to him. He transformed the administration of the Ministry of Health, won over the civil servants there and showed firmness and compromise in handling the doctors. This was a remarkable achievement for a man with comparatively little administrative experience – he had previously only been involved with work for his local authority and the trade union which sponsored him – the Transport and General Workers' Union (TGWU).

ANEURIN BEVAN.

"Society becomes more wholesome, more serene and spiritually healthier if it knows that its citizens have at the back of their consciousness the knowledge that not only themselves but all their fellows, have access, when ill, to the best that medical skill can provide."

A National Health Service – 'Theoretically an Admirable Idea. In Practice – Bound by Difficulties'

Source A

HERE HE COMES, BOYS!
7th August. 1945. Mr. Aneurin Bevan's appointment as Minister of Health is not welcome in certain circles

VICKY, 'HERE HE COMES, BOYS', *NEWS CHRONICLE*, 7 AUGUST 1945.

Source B

Most people under the age of forty have grown up with the NHS. Born as NHS babies, they have learnt to rely on it in the medical emergencies of life. While critical of this or that aspect of the service they are profoundly glad of its existence and appalled by the prospect of its destruction. But however genuine, their appreciation is limited in one respect. Much as they value the NHS they do not remember what the health services were like before it started!

Paul Addison, 1985, quoted in Peter Hennessy, *Never Again* (1992), p. 132.

Source C

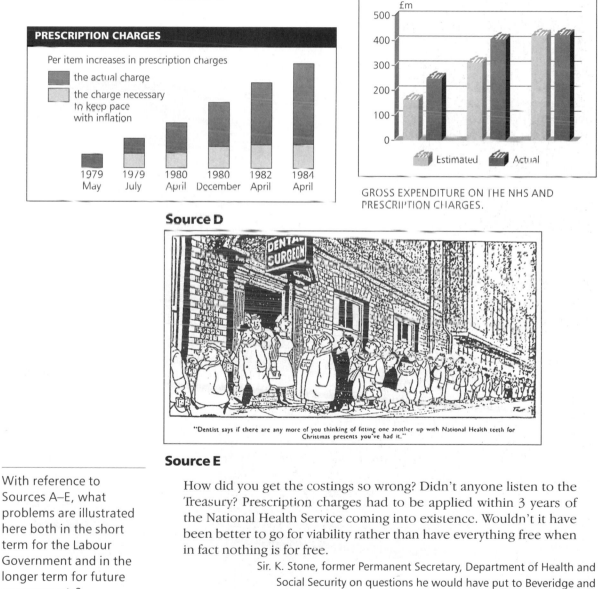

PRESCRIPTION CHARGES

Per item increases in prescription charges

- the actual charge
- the charge necessary to keep pace with inflation

1979 May · 1979 July · 1980 April · 1980 December · 1982 April · 1984 April

£m — 500, 400, 300, 200, 100, 0

Estimated · Actual

GROSS EXPENDITURE ON THE NHS AND PRESCRIPTION CHARGES.

Source D

"Dentist says if there are any more of you thinking of fitting one another up with National Health teeth for Christmas presents you've had it."

Source E

With reference to Sources A–E, what problems are illustrated here both in the short term for the Labour Government and in the longer term for future governments?

How did you get the costings so wrong? Didn't anyone listen to the Treasury? Prescription charges had to be applied within 3 years of the National Health Service coming into existence. Wouldn't it have been better to go for viability rather than have everything free when in fact nothing is for free.

Sir. K. Stone, former Permanent Secretary, Department of Health and Social Security on questions he would have put to Beveridge and Attlee's ministers, quoted in Peter Hennessy, *Never Again* (1992).

Overcoming the problems in order to build a National Health Service

PROBLEM NO. 1

Who should administer it?

TALKING POINT

What aspects of the NHS do you come in contact with? What changes to the NHS were considered as necessary in the 1990s – 50 years after its creation?

PROBLEM NO. 2

How should the hospitals be organised?

PROBLEM NO. 3

How should doctors be integrated?

- Opposition was fierce from the doctors and surgeons represented by their powerful professional body, the British Medical Association (see Source A).
- They were concerned about their payment, intrusive local authority control, conditions and their clinical freedom
- Jan. 1946 Bevan met with 16 representatives for the BMA and three from the Royal College of Surgeons.
- 1946 Rally of 1000 doctors at Wimbledon Town Hall.
- The doctors' campaign threatened to destroy the NHS and continued beyond the NHS bill gaining Royal Assent in November 1946. Bevan knew they were an essential component of the new system, but would not allow a vested interest to prevail over the general good.

SOLUTION NO. 1

Minister of Health
(responsible to government)

Central Health Services
Council (to advise the Minister)

LOCAL SERVICES	HOSPITALS	GENERAL
provided by	Administered by	PRACTITIONERS
Local Authorities	Regional Health	AND DENTISTS
Vaccination	Boards and on	Local Authority
Environmental health	a day-to-day	Executive
Clinics	basis by	Councils
Ambulances	Management	organised record
	Committees	cards; GP's
		capitation fees
		for each
		patient

SOLUTION NO. 2

- The 2000 local authority hospitals, voluntary hospitals, teaching hospitals, and cottage hospitals where GPs did some part-time surgery were: NATIONALISED AND FUNDING CENTRALISED – a move from provision by the ratepayer to the taxpayer.

SOLUTION NO. 3

- It was agreed that the sale of practices should be abolished and a GP's basic salary be provided in part by the state – with the remainder coming from capitation fees for each patient.
- Bevan compromised and enabled consultants to maintain 'pay beds' in NHS hospitals for private practice.
- Consultants, previously dependent upon private fees only, were now to be salaried.
- There was to be an extra small payment for maternity work.
- To gain a final agreement Bevan threatened to reduce capitation fees if the doctors' campaign prevented the expected 95 per cent sign-up for the NHS in July 1948.

What factors led to the Welfare State in Britain? What the historians say

Pressures leading to the Welfare State are widely debated. In his book *Evolution of the Welfare State* Derek Fraser outlines the various ways of explaining this institution.

Source A

The *whig* model of welfare history is so called because of its affinity with the 'whig interpretation of history.' This was an English school of historical interpretation, established by certain whig historians such as Macaulay in the mid-nineteenth century. Believing themselves to be possessors of a perfect liberal constitution, these historians wished to demonstrate the historical evolution of that constitution by stressing the forward-looking people and developments which had brought it about. It was a view of history characterised by a belief in progress and by an assessment of the past in terms of its relevance to the present. Similarly, in the whig interpretation of welfare history, developments in social policy are viewed as elements of progress on a path from intellectual darkness to enlightenment. As society became more sensitive to social need so the harsh excesses of the free market were curbed. Compassion and concern outweighed cruelty and indifference and progressive reform resulted.

Source B

The *capitalistic* perspective. In this model welfare measures are seen as serving the economic interests of a modernising society by bearing the social costs of industrialisation and by promoting a social organisation geared to the needs of business. This view has been much encouraged by international comparisons, which suggest that, despite some differences, all developed industrialised societies move towards common welfare systems.

Source C

The *pragmatic* model perhaps surmounts some of these difficulties by considering present social policy not so much as better but different from that of the past. As the novelist L.P. Hartley put it, 'the past is a foreign country, they do things differently there'. The pragmatic view is much closer to the German school of history personified by von Ranke who wanted to tell history 'as it really was', than to Macaulay's whig story of progress. Social policy is seen as evolving under the practical necessity of solving problems in the wake of industrialisation. In this model developments tend to be *ad hoc* and unplanned, producing more incremental and less radical, more erratic and less direct paths than in the whig view.

Source D

The *democratic* perspective views social welfare as fundamentally a response to democratic consumer demand. As working-class

TASKS

1 Read the following sources (A–E) carefully and discuss the mearning of each.

2 Match each extract up to one of the following ideas: The Welfare State came about due to …
   a benevolent, progressive reform.
   b a short-term solution to practical problems.
   c the work of officials in the bureaucracy – not politicians.
   d being an asset to industry.
   e popular demand.

3 For each of these interpretations, find evidence from this and previous chapters to support the case.

4 Which interpretation do you find most convincing and why?

5 Why do historians interpret this welfare development so differently?

consciousness developed and as institutions of working-class cohesion, such as trade unions, formulated labour demands so it became increasingly likely that governments would respond, if only for reasons of public order already cited. There was a ratio between the degree of democracy at a particular time and the centrality of social policy questions. The more the poor acquired votes in the wake of suffrage reform, the more bread and butter issues dominated the political arena, for the poor could no longer be weaned on social paternalism, they had to be wooed by electoral promises.

Source E

In carrying out whatever policy pragmatic political expediency demanded, governments increasingly came to use officials to enforce it and it is their importance which has led to the *bureaucratic* mode of interpretation. As before, humanitarians were the prime movers but they soon disappeared from the scene, as officials at all levels implemented policy, defined its future goals and became progenitors of further policy initiatives with an almost self-perpetuating momentum. This model requires us to explore in detail the specific legislation introduced, and above all its administration. Social policy changes are here best understood by analysing the role of the institutions of welfare and the officials who staffed them. Whether at local or national level these officials became professional experts, immune from political pressures and vested interests, and thus endowed with an impartial objectivity which gave their judgements great authority.

TASK

1 Write the essay:
   'What factors since the late 19th century brought about the establishment of a Welfare State in the 1940s?'
2 This is a difficult essay which requires research and planning before you attempt to write it.
   Research – Re-read Chapter 2 pages 27–35 on Liberal social reform
   – Re-read Chapter 8 page 181 on interwar reform
   – Re-read Chapter 10 on the Second World War – reconstruction.
   – Clarify what constitutes the Welfare State and try to find reasons why the legislation which is the enactment of a social security system was passed in the three periods
      a 1906–1914
      b 1919–1939
      c 1945–1948
   – Are any of these reasons for social legislation common to two or three of the periods?
3 Consider the following factors: Changing attitudes to poverty
                                    Impact of wars
                                    Work of individuals
                                    Economic pressures
   Reconsider the section 'What the historians say'. Does this provide any other ideas?
4 Plan your essay – deciding on a factor leading to the Welfare State for each paragraph – selecting evidence which supports the different arguments. Check your plan.
5 Now you should be ready to write up your answer.

Economic problems and policies of the Labour Government

It is appropriate to consider the economic
policies of the postwar Labour government
as falling into four distinct time periods:

1945
1946–47
1948–49
1950–51

1945	**'A FINANCIAL DUNKIRK' (Keynes)**

Problems

- The cost of war was enormous and Attlee's government was confronted by an immediate economic crisis.
- Vast scale of destruction – $\frac{1}{2}$ million houses/factories/shops. $\frac{1}{3}$ prewar shipping not replaced.
- Financial cost was crippling; national debt increased to £3,500 million (£500 million in 1939); Britain lost 15% of her wealth in the First World War – now it had lost another 30%.
- This cost led to the basic rate of income tax being raised to 50%, compulsory saving schemes inaugurated and selling off up to £1,000 million foreign investment.
- Adjustment to peacetime production would be difficult with only 2% of workers in export manufacture.
- Despite Labour's victories in polls, Conservatives had support amongst the elites of business/industry and the Civil Service.
- President Truman suddenly ended the Lend-Lease scheme immediately after Japan's surrender. This had been a British lifeline and the Chancellor Hugh Dalton described the resulting situation as 'very grim, grimmer than the worst nightmare'.

TALKING POINT

Explain the reference to 'a financial Dunkirk'?

Policies

1 After difficult negotiations with the USA in November 1945, Keynes secured a loan of $3750 million at 2% interest, repayments to start in 1951.
2 Despite widespread dismay, the government had to accept this loan together with the conditions:
   a Britain had to end Empire preferences.
   b Britain had to accept policies of multilateral trade and join the General Agreement on Tariffs and Trade in 1947 (GATT).
   c Britain must make the £ fully convertible to dollars within a year. This put economic recovery under pressure.
3 The Chancellor Dalton's aims, now the loan was agreed, were to re-establish a trade balance – by increasing exports to USA and keeping British imports as low as possible.

TALKING POINT

What does it mean to make sterling convertible to the dollar?

Problems

- January/February 1947 was one of the worst winters on record – the lowest temperatures for 100 years and snow lay across large parts of Britain until March – followed by the thaw and wettest March on record.
- Coal, which provided 90% of industrial and domestic energy, could not reach power stations as road, rail and sea links were disrupted.
- Industry ground to a halt and production in February fell by 50%. Domestic electricity was restricted to five hours per day.
- Unemployment rose sharply from 400,000 in January to $2\frac{1}{2}$ million by February.
- The export drive was severely curtailed.
- Agriculture suffered as 20% of sheep, 50,000 cattle and 116,000 acres of winter grain was destroyed.
- A financial crisis followed in the summer: due to convertibility to the dollar there had been a run on pound as sterling assets were changed to dollars. British reserves were dangerously low and bankruptcy loomed. The American loan was being spent faster than anticipated.

Policies

1. Emmanuel Shinwell, the Minister of Power and Fuel, did not act quickly or realistically enough. He put his faith in nationalisation (see pp. 000) to provide the answer. But this failed to solve the many immediate problems of the coal industry which were exacerbated by the severity of the winter.
2. On 20 August the Cabinet decided to suspend convertibility. It had served to emphasise the vulnerability of the British economy compared to America's. The convertibility crisis marked a downturn in Labour's fortunes and Conservatives took the lead in the opinion polls.
3. In his November 1947 Budget, Dalton aimed to renew efforts to export more and import less. Taxation was increased, government spending cut and limits on food imports led to more stringent rationing.
4. Dalton – forced to resign over a budget leak – was replaced by Sir Stafford Cripps.

TALKING POINT

Why had convertibility of sterling been to damaging to Britain?

SIR STAFFORD CRIPPS.

1948–1949   SIR STAFFORD 'AUSTERITY' CRIPPS

Problems

- During 1948 and into 1949 Britons were still fettered by food and consumer goods rationing and high taxation.
- Cripps' priorities were first to meet the needs of industry, the need for capital and lastly consumer needs.
- Society was affected by widespread austerity which made impossible a decent standard of living for most.
- Continuing dependency on the US loan to reduce war debt.
- 1949 another financial crisis resulting from signs of an American depression which reduced British exports. British reserves fell by 30% from March to September 1949.

Policies

1. In 1948 the British government gratefully received $3000 million (out of $12,000 million) from the USA's Marshall Plan. The US Secretary of State, George Marshall, decided on a vital aid programme for Europe for various reasons, including the enhancement of American trade and a tool against the spread of Communism in Europe. This failed to solve all the economic problems but it did provide a breathing space for British government.
2. It was decided during the financial crisis of 1949 to devalue the pound by 30%. The £ was reduced from $4.03 to $2.80 – the level at which it remained until 1967. Although regarded at the time as a defeat, the younger Labour proponents – Gaitskell and Wilson – were proved right. Other currencies followed and it made it easier to sell British goods. Marshall Aid could be ended in 1950 – 15 months ahead of schedule.

TALKING POINT

What are the effects on exports and imports of devaluation?

1950–1951   ANOTHER WAR? KOREA

Problems

- Overseas spending was already considered too high.
- The outbreak of the Korean War and Britain's participation became very costly.

Policies

1. Defence spending rose drastically to £4700 million between 1951 and 1954, accounted at its highest to around 14% of total national income.
2. Government had to reduce welfare provision, leading to Aneurin Bevan's resignation from the Cabinet.

TASK

An assessment of the Labour Government's economic policies.

1 Read the period 1945–1951 carefully, thinking about the problems and ensuring you understand the policies.

2 From the evidence given, complete the other side of the argument for the two problems given below:

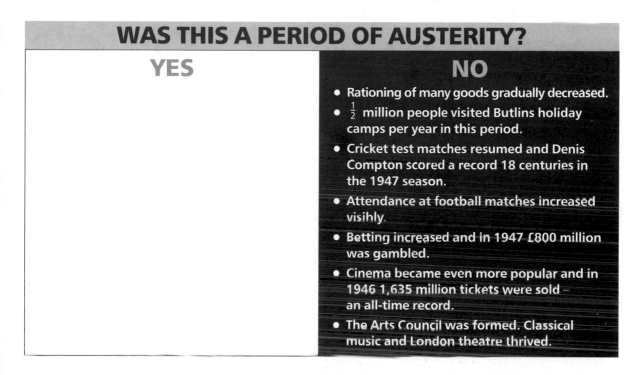

WAS THIS A PERIOD OF AUSTERITY?

YES	NO
	• Rationing of many goods gradually decreased.
	• $\frac{1}{2}$ million people visited Butlins holiday camps per year in this period.
	• Cricket test matches resumed and Denis Compton scored a record 18 centuries in the 1947 season.
	• Attendance at football matches increased visibly.
	• Betting increased and in 1947 £800 million was gambled.
	• Cinema became even more popular and in 1946 1,635 million tickets were sold – an all-time record.
	• The Arts Council was formed. Classical music and London theatre thrived.

WAS LABOUR'S ECONOMIC RECORD A SUCCESS?

YES	NO
• Unemployment averaged 1.6% between 1948 and 1950, much lower than the prewar figures.	
• Demand rose as industry needed to restock.	
• 1946–51 industrial production rose by $\frac{1}{3}$. Exports rose by 77% and imports by 15%.	
• Government avoided the inflationary boom followed by deflationary slump after the First World War.	
• Spending on welfare was pruned but not slashed as after the First World War.	
• Interest rates stayed low and encouraged investment.	

EXAMINING THE EVIDENCE

Nationalisation

Source A

In November 1945 Herbert Morrison, the minister responsible for organising the government's legislative programme, outlined his colleagues' plans for future nationalisation.

His Majesty's Government believe that it is in the public interest that they should give a general indication of the further Measures they propose to introduce during the life of the present Parliament to bring certain essential services under public ownership. This statement, which follows the clear indication of Government policy contained in the King's Speech at the beginning of the Session, will enable the Ministers concerned to enter into consultation with the industries affected.

As stated in the Gracious Speech, the Government will introduce a Bill during the present Session to nationalise the coal-mining industry. At a later stage in the lifetime of this Parliament the Government intends to introduce Measures to bring under national ownership the electricity supply industry and the gas industry. This will implement the concerted plan for the co-ordination of the fuel and power industries which were foreshadowed in the King's Speech.

It is in the intention of the Government to introduce, during the life of the present Parliament, measures designed to bring transport services, essential to the economic well-being of the nation, under public ownership and control. Government policy in regard to civil aviation and telecommunications services has already been announced. In regard to inland transport, powers will be taken to bring under national ownership the railways, canals and long distance road haulage services…

Dock and harbour undertakings will be brought within the scope of the national scheme. The most suitable form of public ownership is under examination, as is also the question of including certain appropriate ancillary activities.

It is not the intention of the Government to propose the nationalisation of the shipping industry, and we shall rely on the industry to have full regard to the public interest…

The Coalition Government invited the iron and steel industry to submit a report on the improvements required to put the industry on an efficient basis. The Government propose to await this report, which is expected shortly, before taking final decisions on the future organisation of the iron and steel industry…

The compensation payable will have regard to any extent to which an undertaking has not been maintained up to the time of transfer, and the Government will naturally take precautions in its legislation to protect the acquiring authority against any transactions entered into in the interim period, whether by way of contract of otherwise, which may prejudice that authority.

Herbert Morrison, speech to the House of Commons, 19 November 1945.

1 What does the nationalisation of industry mean?

2 According to Morrison in Source A, which industries are to be nationalised and which are not?

3 How would you describe the scale of nationalisation proposed here?

4 What problems are foreseen by the Government and solutions offered?

5 What would be the reaction to these proposals of
   a employers and
   b employees
   in the industries concerned?

Nationalisation

WHY?

A Socialist Commitment
- Clause IV of the Labour Party Constitution committed a Labour government to public ownership
- 1944 Labour Party Conference voted strongly in favour of a nationalisation programme
- 1945 Labour manifesto pledges to nationalise Bank of England, coal, gas and electricity, inland transport, iron and steel.

Early steps towards public ownership
- Before the Second World War public corporations were introduced to administer the BBC, the London Passenger Transport Board and the Central Electricity Board among others
- Many national industries had a history of state intervention
- The Second World War necessitated a sharp increase in the government's role in industry.

NATIONALISATION
- **Establishment of a 'mixed economy' with a balance between public and private ownership**
- **Government pledged fair compensation for existing owners and 'proper status' for workers in those industries. Compensation totalled £2,700 million**

HOW?

COAL (January 1947)
- Everyone, including leading Conservatives, accepted the need for nationalisation of this long-time ailing industry.
- National Coal Board was set up with limited responsibility to the Ministry of Fuel and Power.
- 850 owners were compensated with £164 million.

BANK OF ENGLAND (March 1946)
- Instead of attempting to control all banks, this would spread government influence to all in banking system.
- The Treasury had always worked closely with the Bank of England – this simply formalised the relationship.

CIVIL AVIATION
- Although not in the manifesto, this was uncontroversial.
- British Airways (BEA) and British South American Airways (BSAA) were established
- British Overseas Airways Corporation (BOAC), which already existed, was maintained and remodelled.

Solution to industries' long-term problems

- Nationalisation was advocated on the grounds of efficiency – a means to full employment and a prosperous economy
- Each industry had the 'test of national service' applied. If it failed to serve the nation, then it was deemed 'ripe' for nationalisation.
- Coal and gas had long been identified as inefficient.
- Public ownership would lead to increased efficiency and consequently lower prices.

TALKING POINT

Discuss the reasons for nationalisation.
Which do you consider the most convincing?
How are these industries run now?

IRON AND STEEL

- Conservative opposition was determined as these industries were seen as sufficiently efficient
- They feared that this would be a first step to a radical left-wing development of extensive state ownership.
- It was postponed in 1947 and finally amended so that it did not become effective until after the next election.

GAS (1948) AND ELECTRICITY (1947)

- Both these were under significant public control.
- They attracted much controversy, but the government's opposition was defeated despite tabling over 800 amendments.

TRANSPORT

- Government acquired 52,000 miles of railway track and British Rail came into operation in January 1948.
- Road haulage was contentious – finally compromises were made.
- Local bus services were exempt, as were hauliers carrying their own goods and operators in local areas up to 40 miles.
- Long-distance road hauliers were brought under the British Road Services.

CABLE & WIRELESS

- Came into operation in January 1947.
- The government bought out the stock of a company operating telecommunication links throughout the Commonwealth.

Nationalisation – An Assessment of the Results

Supporters

1 By 1951 Labour's nationalisation was complete – approximately one in ten men and women worked for newly nationalised industries.

2 Public sector industry accounted for 20 per cent of the total.

3 The 'taking over' of certain industries such as coal was a rescue act. Coal output rose significantly from 1946 to 1951 when productivity had never been higher. Cable and Wireless made healthy profits.

4 State control ensured the provision of decent standards and adequate safety levels.

5 State ownership of electricity resulted in the electrification of rural areas.

6 Government urged nationalised industries to keep prices down.

7 It was poor public relations which worked against the image of nationalisation – Labour Party fundamentalists called for a more extensive programme.

Critics

1 Aim behind nationalisation was unclear – was it industrial efficiency or was there another agenda?

2 Nationalised industries remained separate entities so no new integrated policies emerged such as for energy or transport.

3 Labour was merely propping up the capitalist system by pouring public funds into declining industries.

4 Historians Sked and Cook have dismissed the nationalisation programme as an 'administrative manoeuvre'.

5 The traditional management/worker relationship was maintained. Workers' participation in the decision-making was limited. Trades unions wished to preserve their wage bargaining role.

TASK

Write an assessment of nationalisation from the point of view of:
   a   a committed Socialist
   b   a Conservative MP
   c   a factory owner
   d   a worker.

TASK

1 Write an essay:
   'How radical were the Labour Government's economic and social policies?'
2 Consider:
a   Details of the social and economic legislation.
b   Which measures represent a radical departure from what existed before.
c   The changes made before and during the war.
d   The shortfalls in the full socialist programme.

Focus

11.1 The Festival of Britain – May 1951

NO VISIBLE MEANS OF SUPPORT

"What do you mean—symbolic?"

(The Vertical Feature for the South Bank Exhibition is now under construction.)

One hundred years after the Great Exhibition, the government decided upon a Festival of Britain aiming to dispel the gloom of postwar austerity and raise British morale. It was, like its predecessor, intended to be a showpiece of the best of British science, technology and culture. Twenty-seven acres of bombsite was cleared in order to build and house the Exhibition. Its main centre was London's South Bank dominated by the 'Dome of Discovery' and the Skylon. The exhibition's opening concert was held in the Royal Festival Hall. The cost of the festival, over £8 million, was much criticised by Conservatives and newspapers. It was dubbed 'Morrison's folly'. The public's chief complaint was that a cup of tea cost 9d!

ONE OF THE MOST POPULAR FESTIVAL INSTALLATIONS WAS THE SKYLON, A GRACEFUL ALUMINIUM STRUCTURE WHICH SEEMED TO DEFY GRAVITY. REPUTEDLY LOATHED BY CHURCHILL, IT WAS SUMMARILY BULLDOZED ON CONSERVATIVES' RETURN TO OFFICE. MEANWHILE, IT PROVIDED A METAPHOR FOR THE AILING LABOUR GOVERNMENT WHICH THE CARTOONIST ILLINGWORTH COULD NOT RESIST. HE DEPICTS ATTLEE AND MORRISON ADMIRING THE FESTIVAL SITE FROM THE NORTH BANK OF THE THAMES

Talking Point

1 Discuss what you know about the 1851 Great Exhibition, the 1951 Festival of Britain and the 2000 Millennium Dome.
2 Why are such events organised?
3 Are they worth the cost? Do they serve any useful purpose?

AERIAL VIEW OF THE FESTIVAL OF BRITAIN, 1951.

The end of the Labour Government

In the election held in February 1950 Labour struggled to a very narrow victory, being returned with an overall majority of just five seats. The government held out but were hard pressed and tired. Clement Attlee was ill. The Festival of Britain, from May to September 1951, proved to be their last high-profile event. In the 1951 October election the Conservative majority over Labour was 26. Winston Churchill, their leader, returned as prime minister.

Source A

The 1950 and 1951 General Election results.

	Total Votes	MPs Elected	Candidates	Unopposed Returns	% Share of Total Vote
23 February 1950					
Conservative	12,502,567	298	620	2	43.5
Liberal	2,621,548	9	475	—	9.1
Labour	13,266,592	315	617	—	46.1
Communist	91,746	—	100	—	0.3
Others	290,218	3	56	—	1.0
Elec. 33,269,770 Turnout 84.0%	28,772,671	625	1,868	2	100.0
25 October 1951					
Conservative	13,717,538	321	617	4	48.0
Liberal	730,556	6	109	—	2.5
Labour	13,948,605	295	617	—	48.8
Communist	21,640	—	10	—	0.1
Others	177,329	3	23	—	0.6
Elec. 34,645,573 Turnout 82.5%	28,595,668	625	1,376	4	100.0

Adapted from D. Butler and A. Sloman, *British Political Facts 1900–1979* (1980).

Source B

A memoir account of the 1951 election.

At the General Election of 1951 Labour was defeated. I held my seat at Belper, but of course I lost my job as Minister of Works and became an Opposition M.P.

The Bevanite row, which simmered on, contributed to our defeat, but the major figures of the Government, the architects of the great Labour victory in 1945, were also tired. Looking back, I'm not sure that it might not have been better for Labour to have lost the election in 1945 and to have come to power in 1950 – or in 1948 or 1949, when a post-war Conservative Government might well have had to go to the country. Our top men in 1945 had all had five

What is significant about these results?

a about the state of the four political parties named?

b about the total number of votes cast in 1951?

TALKING POINT

What reasons are given here for Labour's loss?

What other reasons can you suggest?

To what extent is a memoir source such as this useful when studying this Election?

gruelling war years. Moreover, we took office in 1945 with a lot of wartime quarrels unresolved. Aneurin Bevan, for instance, had campaigned viciously in the wartime Parliament against Bevin as Minister of Labour and against Morrison as Home Secretary in the Coalition Government, and he had shown his contempt for Attlee, whom he regarded as a Churchill stooge. It was Bevan who had campaigned most vigorously for the break-up of the war-time Coalition. Of the major Labour figures in the Coalition I think it was only Morrison who really supported him. Ernest Bevin regarded this as a betrayal, forcing Labour out of the Coalition and thereby producing a situation in which (as he saw it in the spring of 1945) the country would probably be left with a Tory Government to deal with the tasks of peace. With all that sort of conflict lying around it was hardly likely that these men would form a very harmonious team when they met around the Cabinet table.

George Brown, *In My Way* (1971).

REVIEW

Did the Labour Party take a wrong turn between 1945 and 1951?

Source A

THE UNIVERSAL UNCLES

'THE UNIVERSAL UNCLES', *PUNCH*, 25 DECEMBER 1946.

DAVID LOW, 'MAKE WAY'.

1 Explain the contrasting messages offered by the cartoonists about the Labour Government.

2 On what grounds are the Government praised and criticised?

Source C

DAVID LOW, 'I'LL ATTEND TO THE FOUNDATIONS LATER'.

TASKS

1 Identify from the extracts below which defend Attlee's record and which criticise it.

2 How do the critics of the Government differ?

3 Make a list of distinct arguments to:
   a defend the Labour record
   b criticise from a right-wing perspective
   c criticise from a left-wing perspective.

4 Why do historians differ on their assessment of the Labour Government? With reference to these sources, how might the following influence the conclusion:
   a evidence
   b political stance of the historian
   c time of writing?

What the historians say

The Labour Government after the Second World War has generated much controversy. This section includes a selection of historical comments for you to read, understand and use to arrive at your own assessment.

Source A

…by the time they took the bunting down from the streets after VE-Day and turned from the war to the future, the British in their dreams and illusions and in their flinching from reality had already written the broad scenario from Britain's post war descent to the place of fifth in the free world as an industrial power, with manufacturing output only two-fifths of West German's, and the place of fourteenth in the whole non-Communist world in terms of annual GNP per head.

As that descent took its course the illusions and the dreams of 1945 would fade one by one – the imperial and Commonwealth role, the world-power role, British industrial genius, and, at the last, New Jerusalem itself, a dream turned to a dank reality of a segregated, subliterate, unskilled, unhealthy and institutionalised proletariat hanging on the nipple of state maternalism.

C. Barnett, *The Audit of War* (1986).

Source B

What went wrong from the start? The Government, overwhelmingly right-wing in composition and outlook, far more conscious of the supposed 'enemy on the left' than of her real enemy that the electorate had sent them to power to conquer, accepted the capitalist *status quo*, political and economical, as if it were a law of nature, and never really sought to alter the class-structure of the nation, to attack the seats and sources of power, or even to weaken the ruling class. It was in reality, as Emile Burns puts it at p. 12 of *Right Wing Labour*, 'no instrument of social change, but a valuable instrument of the monopoly capitalists in damping down the post-war unease and in helping the monopoly capitalist to solve the contradictions that faced them'. It is not surprising that the ruling class soon recovered from its panic and managed; to hold a very large measure of its old power.

D.N. Pritt, *The Labour Government 1945–51* (1963).

Source C

It is easy to go too far in criticising or debunking the Attlee government. Arguments from hindsight often neglect the realities actually confronting the administration in the very different world of 1945. Critiques of that government in particular tend to underestimate the overwhelming financial and economic pressures resulting from the loss of overseas assets, the imbalance of trade, the loss of markets, the shortage of raw materials, and the vast dollar deficit which was the government's *damnosa hereditas* from the war years and from the pre-war heritage of industrial decay. In large areas of policy, the Attlee government had a clear record of achievement and of competence, which acted as a platform for successive governments, Conservative and Labour, throughout the next quarter of a century. The advent of a monetarist Conservative government under Mrs Thatcher in 1979 signalled the first real attempt to wrench Britain out of the Age of Attlee. It received a huge endorsement at the polls in 1983. Yet until late 1983 at least, the economic record of well over three million unemployed, a severe contraction of manufacturing industry, eroding public and social services, and some threat of social and racial disorder, did not suggest that this alternative ideological approach had so far provided more coherent or acceptable answers to Britain's acknowledged problems...

The Attlee government was thus unique in its structural cohesiveness and in its legislative vitality. Its legacy lived on in a broad influence over the Labour and progressive left, over political and economic thought and, indeed, over much of British intellectual and cultural life for a full quarter of a century after 1951. It was without doubt the most effective of all Labour governments, perhaps amongst the most effective of any British government since the passage of the 1832 Reform Act.

K.O. Morgan, *Labour in Power* (1984).

Source D

For the impact of the Labour Government of 1945–51, for all its promise and its vast body of legislation, was 'profoundly ambiguous'. When the rhetoric of partisan debate had died, this became quickly apparent, and was almost taken for granted by academics and commentators of the mid 1960's. There had undoubtedly been important social reforms. But power had not shifted between classes. Qualitative social transformation had not come. Nor was it any nearer for the six years of office. In essence the Labour Government of 1945–51 had not created a socialist commonwealth, nor even taken a step in that direction. It had simply created a mixed economy in which the bulk of industry still lay in private hands, and the six years of its rule had only marginally altered the distribution of social power, privilege, wealth, income, opportunity and security.

D. Coates, *The Labour Party and the Struggle For Socialism* (1975).

TASK
Class discussion.
Motion:
'The Labour Government's economic and social policies were a remarkable achievement. Discuss.'

12 Thirteen Years of Conservative Government, 1951–1964

PREVIEW

Four Conservative prime ministers

Winston Churchill 1951–55

Born in 1874 at Blenheim Palace, the son of Lord Randolph Churchill.
Educated – Harrow and Sandhurst.
Military Service – in Cuba, Malakand and battle of Omdurman.
War correspondent in the Boer War.
Previous Career – 1900 elected MP for Oldham
- 1910 Home Secretary
- 1911 First Lord of Admiralty
- Chancellor of the Exchequer, 1924–9.
- Prime Minister, 1940–5.

TALKING POINT

What similarities are there in the biographical profiles of these four Conservative prime ministers?
Do the prime ministers that you have lived under have similar backgrounds?

Anthony Eden 1955–57

Born – 12 June 1897
Educated – Eton and Oxford.
Military Service during the First World War.
Elected MP in 1923.
Foreign Secretary 1935–8, 1940–5 and 1951–5.

Harold Macmillan 1957–63

Born – February 1894 London. Mother – American. Paternal family – Macmillan Publishing House.
Educated – Eton and Oxford.
Military Service during the First World War.
Elected MP for Stockton-on-Tees.
Served in Churchill's wartime coalition and in his peacetime government at the ministries of Housing, Defence and the Exchequer.

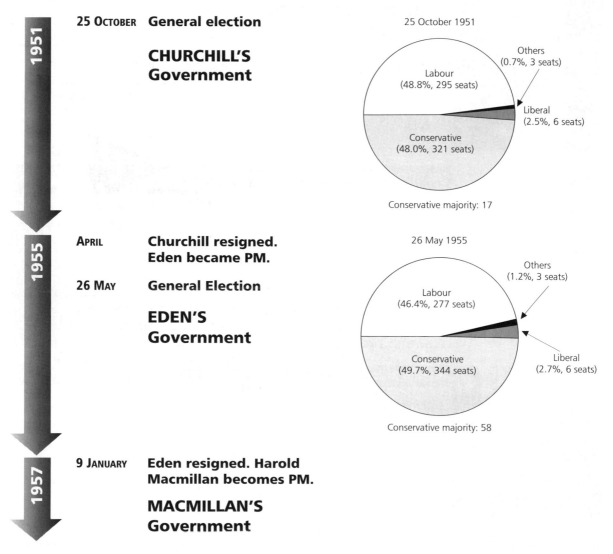

Lord Alec Douglas Home 1963–64

Born 1903 Aristocracy – 1951 became 14th Earl – owner of 96,000 acres in Scotland.

Educated – Eton and Oxford

Early Career – 1931 elected as MP.

1937–9 Chamberlain's parliamentary private secretary.

1955 entered Cabinet as Secretary of State for Commonwealth Relations.

1960 Became Foreign Secretary.

1963 Became prime minister after disclaiming his peerage.

Conservative governments, 1951–64

Four general elections – three consecutive Conservative victories

1951

25 OCTOBER **General election**

CHURCHILL'S Government

25 October 1951

Labour
(48.8%, 295 seats)

Others
(0.7%, 3 seats)

Liberal
(2.5%, 6 seats)

Conservative
(48.0%, 321 seats)

Conservative majority: 17

1955

APRIL **Churchill resigned. Eden became PM.**

26 MAY **General Election**

EDEN'S Government

26 May 1955

Labour
(46.4%, 277 seats)

Others
(1.2%, 3 seats)

Conservative
(49.7%, 344 seats)

Liberal
(2.7%, 6 seats)

Conservative majority: 58

1957

9 JANUARY **Eden resigned. Harold Macmillan becomes PM.**

MACMILLAN'S Government

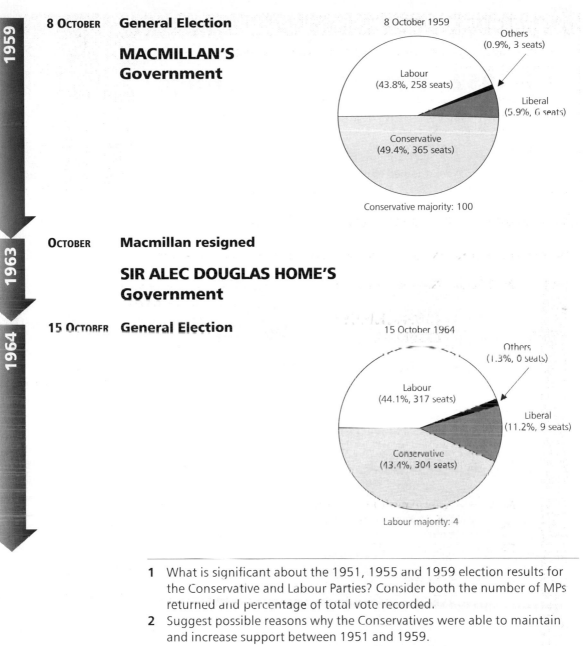

1959

8 October | **General Election**

MACMILLAN'S Government

8 October 1959

Others
(0.9%, 3 seats)

Labour
(43.8%, 258 seats)

Liberal
(5.9%, 6 seats)

Conservative
(49.4%, 365 seats)

Conservative majority: 100

1963

October | **Macmillan resigned**

SIR ALEC DOUGLAS HOME'S Government

1964

15 October | **General Election**

15 October 1964

Others
(1.3%, 0 seats)

Labour
(44.1%, 317 seats)

Liberal
(11.2%, 9 seats)

Conservative
(43.4%, 304 seats)

Labour majority: 4

1 What is significant about the 1951, 1955 and 1959 election results for the Conservative and Labour Parties? Consider both the number of MPs returned and percentage of total vote recorded.
2 Suggest possible reasons why the Conservatives were able to maintain and increase support between 1951 and 1959.
3 What is the significance of the 1964 Election result?

12.1 1952 – 'A New Elizabethan Age?'

On 6 February 1952, a few months after the Conservatives were returned to power under Prime Minister Churchill, King George VI died. The people of Britain received the news with genuine sorrow. His accession to the throne in 1936 was unexpected and unwanted. The abdication of his brother Edward (see Chapter 8) had confronted George VI with the duty of monarchy. He is remembered as a man of great sincerity, loyalty and immense affection for his countrymen. The role and moral support of George VI 's wife – Queen Elizabeth, the Queen Mother – was greatly appreciated during the War. News of the death of George VI reached the Princess Elizabeth in Kenya where she was on the first stage of a Royal Tour to Australia and New Zealand. Accompanied by her husband the Duke of Edinburgh she flew back to England where she was met by the Duke of Gloucester, Prime Minister Churchill and other Privy Councillors as Queen Elizabeth II. She was crowned the following year at Westminster Abbey amongst all the pomp and ceremony traditional in Britain. The arrival of the new monarchy helped to foster a new optimism for national recovery. However, over the next decade – despite the patriotic flag waving – Britain's position in world affairs declined and many domestic problems confronted Queen Elizabeth's successive prime ministers.

QUEEN ELIZABETH AT HER CORONATION.

Talking Point

Is it feasible to refer to the second half of the 20th century as an 'Elizabethan Age'?
Give reasons for your opinion.
What major royal occasions can you remember?

Leader-writers began to remind their readers that Britain's days of greatest glory had always coincided with the reign of a queen... The conclusion to which all this evidence pointed was that when a queen was on the throne Britain was invincible. In the weeks following the accession of the new queen, the talk was of a new Elizabethan age...

Extract from
Roy Hattersley,
Fifty Years On.

20th Century British Monarchs

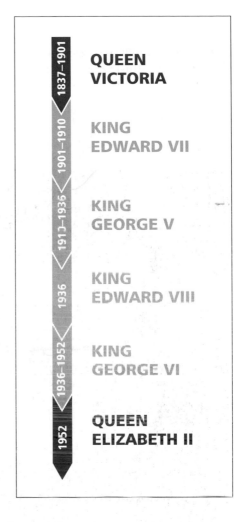

1837–1901	**QUEEN VICTORIA**
1901–1910	KING EDWARD VII
1913–1936	KING GEORGE V
1936	KING EDWARD VIII
1936–1952	KING GEORGE VI
1952	**QUEEN ELIZABETH II**

TALKING POINT

Is monarchy in Britain an outdated institution?

1 What evidence is there to suggest Britain prospers under female monarchs? What is your reaction to this comment?
2 Discuss the arguments for and against monarchy in Britain today. Take a class vote on the issue.
3 Write an essay:
'Monarchy in Britain is an expensive, outdated institution. Discuss.'

Churchill's Conservative Government, 1951–55

The elder statesman of British politics, Churchill became prime minister once more at the age of 77 following the 1951 Election. He had suffered two strokes before returning to 10 Downing Street, and he was to suffer two more in the course of this administration. His government's main aim was domestic peace, maintaining the Welfare State set up by the previous government while at the same time expressing some doubts about the extent of the nationalisation programme which Labour had carried out. Indeed, Churchill's government denationalised the iron and steel and road haulage industries in 1953.

The Cabinet

The members of Churchill's Cabinet were on the whole familiar and experienced figures – with an average age of 60. The resemblance to Churchill's wartime Cabinet was no accident – these were colleagues he had worked with before and whom he could trust. Eden returned to the Foreign Office, R.A. Butler, a progressive, was made Chancellor, and Walter Monckton and Harold Macmillan went to the Ministries of Labour and Housing respectively. Peter Thorneycroft was at the Board of Trade. Some younger MPs, such as Iain Macleod, Enoch Powell and Edward Heath (later to become prime minister himself), received their first ministerial appointments. The prime minister's first request of his Cabinet was that they should accept at 20 per cent pay cut – himself taking a 30 per cent cut. This was intended to convey the message that the country should be prepared to make sacrifices in a time of economic austerity and that the political leaders would be prepared to set an example.

Domestic policies – an inconsistent record?

Success

Economy

The Government in 1951 inherited a fragile economic situation. A balance of payments crisis saw deficits racing towards £700 million and the export market was being damaged by countries starting to buy outside the sterling area. The situation caused much alarm. However, by 1952 the government was in the black again – by £300 million and this spectacular recovery continued so that – by 1954 Great Britain was becoming increasingly prosperous. There was renewed confidence economically, with full employment and rising wages.

What policies were pursued by Butler, the Chancellor?
1. Credit restrictions were imposed.
2. Imports were reduced.
3. Government food subsidies were cut.
4. Travel allowances were reduced to £25 just when foreign travel was becoming popular.

1951 Conservative Manifesto
'The Conservative aim is to increase our national output. Here is the surest way to keep our people fully employed, to halt the rising cost of living and to preserve our social services. Hard work, good management, thrift – all must receive their due incentive and reward.'

TALKING POINT
What does this tell us about the philosophy upon which the Conservative Party is based?

TALKING POINT

How would the average citizen react to these economic policies?

5. Interest rates were raised from 2% to 4% to restrict demand.
6. Ministers' salaries were cut and the number of official cars reduced in addition to civil service staff cuts of 25,640.
7. A return to a free market was aided by the abolition of Identity Cards in February 1952 and the ending of rationing on all goods by 1954.
8. Iron and steel and road haulage was denationalised.
9. A plan to float the £ – Operation Robot – was suggested by Butler in 1952. It was never implemented due to a lack of confidence and understanding of this economic mechanism.
10. The 1955 Budget – just prior to the General Election, tax cuts included a 6d reduction in income tax plus higher personal allowances.

The economic recovery in the first years of the 1950s is thought to have been brought about by factors other than the government's policies. They made no fundamental changes to economic management but instead seemed to economise through cautious pruning. The use of interest rate increases to curb demand appeared to work, but in fact became the first 'stop' of a 'stop–go' policy throughout the 1950s. Bank rate was cut again in 1952 and 1953 only to be raised again in 1954 and 1955. In fact the Conservatives benefited greatly from what Pearce and Stewart refer to as 'a mixture of good fortune, no confrontation and inactivity'. The end of the Korean War certainly aided a reduction in spending and other external trade factors also stimulated the export market.

Housing

The government's housing policy was their one major achievement, being a personal triumph for the ambitious Minister of Housing, Harold Macmillan. Churchill had promised him: 'Every humble home will bless your name if you succeed.' The Conservatives kept faith with the major postwar policy of both parties to provide adequate housing.

What did Macmillan achieve?

1. He provided the organisation and finance to ensure building in both the public and private sectors. In 1953 327,000 houses were built and in 1954 354,000.
2. In 1952 the housing subsidy from government was increased from £22 to £35 per home.
3. Policies were implemented to encourage the provision of mortgages.
4. Local authorities were granted powers to license private builders.
5. New towns – such as Basildon, Hemel Hempstead and Crawley – were completed to house overspill from the cities.

Social services

The welfare services were left intact and social benefits rose marginally, amounting to more in real terms by 1955 than 1951. The Health Service continued to function as first implemented, although costs increased and prescription charges were raised to 2s.

Education

There was very little progress made in education. A plan for improving the technical schools was implemented by 1955 and double the number of children were staying on at school until 17 years old compared with 1951. However, education in Britain seemed to be lagging increasingly behind the provision available in other advanced industrialised European countries.

Trades unions

The moderate, cautious government of Churchill maintained a conciliatory approach to the trades unions. An Industrial Charter was introduced but was largely rhetoric as proposals for trades union legislation were talked down or postponed in Cabinet.

Immigration

This became an increasingly significant political issue in the 1950s. By the late 1950s, 26,000 migrants per year were settling in Britain from the West Indies. Their arrival raised many important social and political issues which the government at this stage were slow to tackle.

TALKING POINT

What questions are raised by an influx of foreign immigrants?

1955 General Election

By the beginning of 1955, there were a number of problems for the Conservative Party. They enjoyed only a small majority of 17, their backbenchers had proved more critical than expected and their domestic record was patchy. The major concern, however, was over the next Election and Churchill's continued obstinacy over holding on to the leadership despite ill-health and tiredness which detracted from his performance at both Cabinet and parliamentary level.

Man goeth forth unto his work and to his labour until the evening.

L.G. ILLINGWORTH, 'ON THE PREMIER'S PROBABLE RETIREMENT', *PUNCH*, 3 FEBRUARY 1954.

TALKING POINT

What messages are conveyed by this cartoon?

In April 1955 Churchill finally resigned and was succeeded by his foreign secretary, Sir Anthony Eden. An election was called immediately for 26 May 1955. It was a success for the Conservatives who managed to increase their seats from 321 to 344, giving them a more workable majority of 58.

CONSERVATIVE PARTY GENERAL ELECTION POSTER, 1955.

Why did the Conservatives win the 1955 Election?

REASON 1
Conservative Party

- Eden was a popular replacement for Churchill. He had a reputation as a distinguished Foreign Secretary and statesman.
- On the whole, the Conservative Party was united and working together. In preparing for 1955 they focused their electoral appeal on the undecided middle class – the so-called 'floating voters'.

REASON 2
Economy and Society

- There was a marked economic improvement in Britain – trade had recovered, new industries supplying consumer goods were thriving and unemployment was low.
- Butler's 1955 Budget was clearly intended to have electoral appeal – it cut taxes significantly. The country was wrapped in a mood of new Elizabethan age optimism. In 1953, England's cricketers had won the 'Ashes' from Australia and Britons were amongst the first to conquer Everest.

REASON 3
Division in the Labour Party

- Attlee's last years as leader were troubled by the demands from different wings of the Labour Party.
- The split with the left wing continued after Bevan's resignation. These MPs – over 50 in number, including Michael Foot, Crossman, Wilson, Mikardo and Bevan's wife Jennie Lee – took control of the National Executive Committee. In 1952 they refused the party whip.
- The right wing led by Gaitskell wished to revise Clause IV.
- The TUC were opposed to the abolition of Clause IV. Revisionists such as Tony Crosland put forward proposals to extend the Welfare State and fund this by growth and managerial efficiency.
- The decision by the government to develop the H-Bomb raised nuclear disarmament as an issue.

TALKING POINT

Which issues were sources of contention between the left and right wing of the Labour Party? What is meant by the 'party whip'? What was the Labour Party's Clause IV?

TASK

Write the following essay.
'It was by sheer good fortune that the Conservative Party were returned to office in May 1955.' Discuss.

REMEMBER TO

THINK!

What does the question mean?

- It requires an explanation of the Tory 1955 victory.

- It suggests 'sheer good fortune' was the only reason.

- It invites you to discuss this argument.

READ!

- Go through this chapter up to 1955 carefully.

- Research further Churchill's government.

PLAN!

- List all the evidence which supports 'sheer good fortune' consider the economic improvement, the condition of the Labour and Liberal parties, the promotion of Eden to Prime Minister.

- List all the evidence supporting other reasons for Tory victory, considering Conservative Party policies, state of the party, mood amongst the electorate.

- Organise your essay into these two sections.

WRITE!

- Introduce the essay with information on the election of 1955 and suggest the line of your discussion.

- Write up the two sections clearly, giving arguments which answer the question and are supported by evidence.

- Conclude by reaching a judgement on the extent to which good luck was a factor in the 1955 result.

Eden's Government, 1955–57

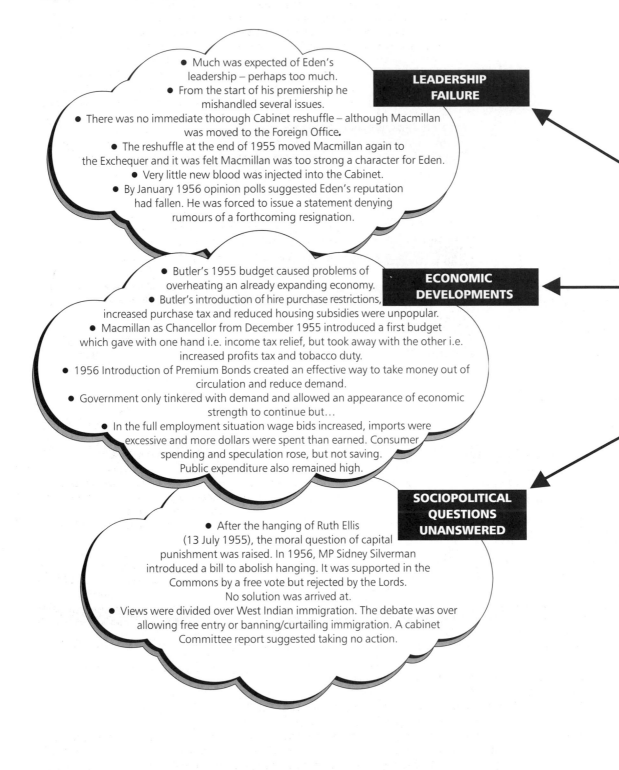

LEADERSHIP FAILURE

- Much was expected of Eden's leadership – perhaps too much.
- From the start of his premiership he mishandled several issues.
- There was no immediate thorough Cabinet reshuffle – although Macmillan was moved to the Foreign Office.
- The reshuffle at the end of 1955 moved Macmillan again to the Exchequer and it was felt Macmillan was too strong a character for Eden.
- Very little new blood was injected into the Cabinet.
- By January 1956 opinion polls suggested Eden's reputation had fallen. He was forced to issue a statement denying rumours of a forthcoming resignation.

ECONOMIC DEVELOPMENTS

- Butler's 1955 budget caused problems of overheating an already expanding economy.
- Butler's introduction of hire purchase restrictions, increased purchase tax and reduced housing subsidies were unpopular.
- Macmillan as Chancellor from December 1955 introduced a first budget which gave with one hand i.e. income tax relief, but took away with the other i.e. increased profits tax and tobacco duty.
- 1956 Introduction of Premium Bonds created an effective way to take money out of circulation and reduce demand.
- Government only tinkered with demand and allowed an appearance of economic strength to continue but…
- In the full employment situation wage bids increased, imports were excessive and more dollars were spent than earned. Consumer spending and speculation rose, but not saving. Public expenditure also remained high.

SOCIOPOLITICAL QUESTIONS UNANSWERED

- After the hanging of Ruth Ellis (13 July 1955), the moral question of capital punishment was raised. In 1956, MP Sidney Silverman introduced a bill to abolish hanging. It was supported in the Commons by a free vote but rejected by the Lords. No solution was arrived at.
- Views were divided over West Indian immigration. The debate was over allowing free entry or banning/curtailing immigration. A cabinet Committee report suggested taking no action.

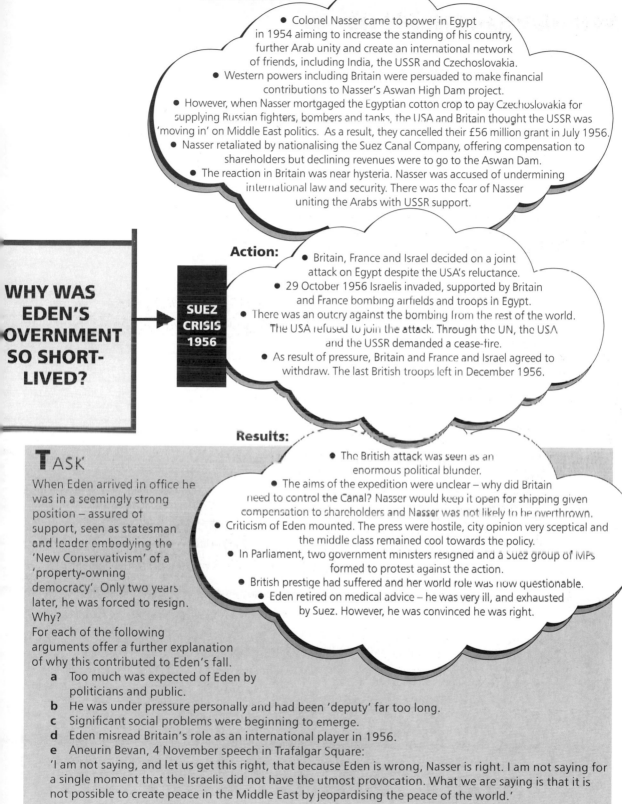

The Problem:

- Colonel Nasser came to power in Egypt in 1954 aiming to increase the standing of his country, further Arab unity and create an international network of friends, including India, the USSR and Czechoslovakia.
- Western powers including Britain were persuaded to make financial contributions to Nasser's Aswan High Dam project.
- However, when Nasser mortgaged the Egyptian cotton crop to pay Czechoslovakia for supplying Russian fighters, bombers and tanks, the USA and Britain thought the USSR was 'moving in' on Middle East politics. As a result, they cancelled their £56 million grant in July 1956.
- Nasser retaliated by nationalising the Suez Canal Company, offering compensation to shareholders but declining revenues were to go to the Aswan Dam.
- The reaction in Britain was near hysteria. Nasser was accused of undermining international law and security. There was the fear of Nasser uniting the Arabs with USSR support.

Action:

- Britain, France and Israel decided on a joint attack on Egypt despite the USA's reluctance.
- 29 October 1956 Israelis invaded, supported by Britain and France bombing airfields and troops in Egypt.
- There was an outcry against the bombing from the rest of the world. The USA refused to join the attack. Through the UN, the USA and the USSR demanded a cease-fire.
- As result of pressure, Britain and France and Israel agreed to withdraw. The last British troops left in December 1956.

SUEZ CRISIS 1956

WHY WAS EDEN'S OVERNMENT SO SHORT-LIVED?

Results:

- The British attack was seen as an enormous political blunder.
- The aims of the expedition were unclear – why did Britain need to control the Canal? Nasser would keep it open for shipping given compensation to shareholders and Nasser was not likely to be overthrown.
- Criticism of Eden mounted. The press were hostile, city opinion very sceptical and the middle class remained cool towards the policy.
- In Parliament, two government ministers resigned and a Suez group of MPs formed to protest against the action.
- British prestige had suffered and her world role was now questionable.
- Eden retired on medical advice – he was very ill, and exhausted by Suez. However, he was convinced he was right.

Task

When Eden arrived in office he was in a seemingly strong position – assured of support, seen as statesman and leader embodying the 'New Conservativism' of a 'property-owning democracy'. Only two years later, he was forced to resign. Why?

For each of the following arguments offer a further explanation of why this contributed to Eden's fall.

- **a** Too much was expected of Eden by politicians and public.
- **b** He was under pressure personally and had been 'deputy' far too long.
- **c** Significant social problems were beginning to emerge.
- **d** Eden misread Britain's role as an international player in 1956.
- **e** Aneurin Bevan, 4 November speech in Trafalgar Square:

'I am not saying, and let us get this right, that because Eden is wrong, Nasser is right. I am not saying for a single moment that the Israelis did not have the utmost provocation. What we are saying is that it is not possible to create peace in the Middle East by jeopardising the peace of the world.'

Macmillan's government, 1957–63

Situation in 1957

On becoming prime minister, Macmillan joked that his government would only last six weeks. The Conservative Party was at a very low ebb. The fallout from the Suez Crisis had been disastrous, not only for Eden's personal career but also for the Conservative Party as a whole. Labour were leading in the opinion polls by 13 points. There were serious economic problems as well. The new Chancellor, Peter Thorneycroft, reported Britain's liabilities to have increased to £4 billion, whereas assets only totalled £850 million. Finally relations with the USA had been severely damaged by the whole affair. Prospects were not good for the Conservatives, halfway though their term of office.

Situation by 1959

However, in two years Macmillan's optimistic style of leadership, and his new Cabinet team, seemed to have turned around the fortunes of the country – and with it also those of the Conservative Party. The General Election of October 1959 saw a third consecutive Conservative victory – increasing their majority further to 100. This has subsequently been seen as the high point of Tory fortunes. British voters believed what Macmillan told them – 'they had never had it so good' – but chose to ignore the following words of caution in the speech. Affluence and the consumer revolution at home, alongside improved international relations, won votes but perhaps belied the real strength of Britain's position in 1959.

Conservative policies in the late 1950s – Apparent affluence, but underlying problems?

ECONOMY	POLICIES	POTENTIAL PROBLEMS
	• By the end of May 1957 Britain's assets were £850 million but liabilities had risen to £4 billion. • The Chancellor, Peter Thorneycroft, wished to control public expenditure. In September 1957 the bank rate was raised to 7 per cent and cuts of £550 million were proposed. • Macmillan disagreed, he feared unemployment more than inflation and Thorneycroft resigned in January 1958. • The new Chancellor, Derek Heathcote-Amory, shifted policy towards expansion of economic demand. • Bank rate was gradually reduced – reaching $4\frac{1}{2}$ per cent by August 1959. • Budget 1959 – cut taxes, relaxed credit controls and wage increases – prior to the election, the economic policy was in part determined by political consideration.	**BUT** • By the 1960s Britain clearly had a problem of inflation and unsustainable growth. • Over the next ten years, government expenditure rose rapidly.

	POLICIES	POTENTIAL PROBLEMS

TRADES UNIONS

POLICIES
- Macmillan aimed to avoid industrial action.
- Unions were encouraged to work closely within government. Many union leaders belonged to Whitehall committees – some involved with economic planning
- 1957 the railwaymen were bought off by Sir Brian Robertson with a 5 per cent pay increase instead of the 3 percent proposed by an independent report. Cost amounted to £42 million to the payer. Other disputes were settled quickly.

POTENTIAL PROBLEMS

- In 1957 8.5 million days were lost due to industrial action – the highest figure since 1926, the year of the General Strike.
- In 1956 Frank Cousins (TGWU) took over as TUC leader and shifted unions to the left in their policies and demands.

DEFENCE

- Conventional defence was very costly, amounting to 8 per cent of GNP and rising.
- Government decided to reduce the armed forces and rely more on nuclear capability.
- National conscription finally ended in 1960.
- The H-bomb and new nuclear weapons would it was thought reduce defence spending and place Britain on the world stage.

- Nuclear defence costs were to quickly outstrip the cost of conventional defence with research, training and delivery system.
- 1957 The Campaign for Nuclear Disarmament was established. Protests against nuclear weapons continued.

HOUSING

- The 1957 Rent Act relaxed control of rents for landlords with the intention that they would spend the extra rents on improvement of the property.

BUT

- Considered a 'Landlords' Charter' lining the pockets of wealthy landlords and leading to the exploitation of poorer tenants.

IMMIGRATION

- The balance of net immigration rose in Britain between 1955 and 1963.
- Over 50,000 immigrants, particularly from the West Indies, Pakistan and India, arrived in Britain.
- They were often recruited for low-paid, unskilled work.
- By 1958 it had become a political issue with a series of highly publicised attacks on immigrants communities in London and Nottingham. There was widespread condemnation of these attacks in the press and by the Labour Party.
- The government decided that there should be no controls on immigration — although in 1963 it introduced new regulations requiring immigrants to have work permits.

BUT

- The race relations issue raised an intensity of feeling.
- Integration into society was problematic in immigrant areas.
- The numbers of immigrants increased, peaking in 1961–2 at over 100,000 people.

Examining the Evidence

1959 General Election

Source A

The Conservative Record.

Eight years ago was a turning point in British history. The Labour Government had failed in grappling with the problems of the post-war world. Under Conservative leadership this country set out upon a new path. It is leading to prosperity and opportunity for all.

The British economy is sounder today than at any time since the first world war. Sterling has been re-established as a strong and respected currency. Under Conservative government we have earned abroad £1,600 million more than we have spent. Our exports have reached the highest peak ever. Overseas, mostly in the commonwealth, we are investing nearly double what we could manage eight years ago. Capital investment at home, to build for the future, is over half as large again. To match this and make it possible, people are saving more than ever before.

The paraphernalia of controls have been swept away. The call-up is being abolished. We have cut taxes in seven Budgets, whilst continuing to develop the social services. We have provided over two million new homes and almost two million new school places, a better health service and a modern pensions plan. We have now stabilised the cost of living while maintain full employment. We have shown that Conservative freedom works. Life is better with the Conservatives.

In the international field, thanks to the initiative of the Conservative Government, the diplomatic deadlock between East and West has now been broken. The Prime Minister's visit to Russia in February began a sequence of events which has led to the present easing of tension. The proposed exchange of visits between President Eisenhower and Mr Khrushchev is the most recent proof of this. It is our determination to see that this process continues and to make a success of the important negotiations which we trust will follow.

The main issues at this election are therefore simple: 1) Do you want to go ahead on the lines which have brought prosperity at home? 2) Do you want your present leaders to represent you abroad?

Source B

The Labour Manifesto 1959.

(*Britain Belongs To You: The Labour Party's Policy for Consideration by the British People*)

We welcome this Election: it gives us, at last, the chance to end eight years of Tory rule. In a television chat with President Eisenhower, Mr Macmillan told us that the old division of Britain into the two nations, the Haves and the Have nots, has disappeared. Tory prosperity, he suggested, is shared by all. In fact, the contrast between the extremes of wealth and poverty is sharper today than eight years ago. The business man with a tax-free expense account, the speculator with tax-free capital gains, and the retiring company director with a tax-free redundancy payment due to a take-over bid – these people have indeed 'never had it so good'.

It is not so good for the widowed mother with children, the chronic sick, the 400,000 unemployed, and the millions of old age pensioners who have no adequate superannuation. While many of those at work have been able to maintain or even improve their standard of living by collective bargaining, the sick, the disabled and the old have continually seen the value of state benefits and small savings whittled away by rising prices. Instead of recognising this problem as the greatest social challenge of our time, the Prime Minister blandly denies it exists.

---

1 What is meant in Source A by 'Eight years ago was a turning point in British history', 'We have shown that Conservative freedom works'?
2 Who were President Eisenhower and Mr Khrushchev? What is the 'tension' referred to between the USA and USSR?
3 According to Source A, why should people vote Conservative in 1959?
4 What is the main argument advanced by Labour in Source B?
5 Which social groups would be attracted by
   a *the Conservative record*
   b *the Labour Manifesto?*
6 To what extent are these sources valuable to a historian studying the 1959 Election?
7 Assess the presentation/language and voter appeal of each of these sources. Are more recent party manifestos similar or not?

'The zenith of Conservative rule'?: What the historians say

Source C

Macmillan decided that he would wait at least till the autumn. A few days later Amory introduced a highly popular budget which took nine pence off income tax. The opinion polls gave the Conservatives a lead throughout the summer. On 7 September Macmillan asked for a dissolution, and the election was fixed for 8 October. The situation looked promising. The year 1959 was one of the few years in which low unemployment, stable prices and a favourable balance of payments coincided. The Conservatives were tipped as favourites, and their position was strengthened by a gaffe on Gaitskell's part when he claimed that the expensive programme of social expenditure promised in the Labour manifesto could be met without raising income tax. The Conservatives won 365 seats with 49.4 percent of the vote. The Labour figures were 258 and 43.8. It was widely regarded as a triumph for the Prime Minister, henceforth depicted as 'Supermac' by the cartoonist Vicki.

Lord Blake, *The Conservative Party from Peel to Thatcher* (1985), p. 284.

Source D

The election result represented a personal triumph for Harold Macmillan. He had come to power in the aftermath of Suez expecting to have to relinquish office fairly soon. Instead, he had revitalised his party and led it to its greatest post war electoral victory. It was a truly remarkable achievement and one which seemed to be full of great political significance. Was affluence undermining the whole pattern of British voting? Would the Labour Party ever again be called upon to govern Britain? It seemed as if the Conservative Party, having won three elections in a row, each time with an increased majority, had discovered the secret of eternal power. If booms could be engineered before election dates by employing Keynesian economic methods and if the Prime Minister alone was responsible for choosing the election date, why could not an intelligent prime minister – and Macmillan was certainly that – cling on to power for ever? All these questions were posed time and time again as social scientists now turned to investigate the society which had grown up in Britain since the war.

Alan Sked and Chris Cook, *Post War Britain: A Political History* (1979), pp. 178–9.

Source E

Britain entered the sixties still in confident mood, despite the legacy of divisions and tension inherited from pre-war years. The sense of national decline, even humiliation, at the time of Suez drifted away. Externally and internally, the land appeared to be thriving and self-confident, with Macmillan's curious ability to bridge old and new values highly appropriate and symbolic. Yet much of it was based on illusion and evasion. Underlying the surface of growth was a pattern whereby Britain had steadily lagged behind other western nations rising from the ashes of defeat. The upward curve of public spending masked serious discussion of the productive base whereby it could all be financed. An expanding economy sucked in imports, to an extent that the balance of payments could no longer sustain. By the end of 1960, the economic omens were distinctly less cheerful, after a year which had seen tremors in the economy, Heathcoat-Amory leave the Treasury in something less than a triumphalist glow, and a sticky mood on the stock exchange. Perhaps, after all, the Tory success in the late fifties owed more to good fortune, the fall in the cost of imports, accidents that prevented wage inflation from getting out of hand. The omens for 1961, some thought, were a downturn in the economy that might prove to be the worst since the war.

K.O. Morgan, *The People's Peace* (1990), pp. 193–4.

---

1 What reasons are given by these historians in Sources C–E for the Conservative victory?
2 To what extent do Sources C–E agree?
3 What doubts are cast in Source E about the affluence and confidence of the 1950s?
4 Do Sources A–E suggest 1959 was a zenith for the Conservatives? If so, why?

Political cartoons

Source F

TROG (WALLY FAWKES),
'WELL GENTLEMEN, I THINK
WE ALL FOUGHT A GOOD
FIGHT…', *SPECTATOR*,
16 OCTOBER 1959.

Source G

'VITAL
STATISTICS',
PUNCH, 27
AUGUST 1958.

1 What messages are put across in these cartoons about Macmillan and the 1958–9 period for the Conservatives?

2 How useful are these political cartoons to a historian assessing the Conservatives in the 1950s?

EXAMINING THE EVIDENCE

The 1950s

Source H

The Britain of the early fifties was still a tight, parochial little island, wedded to the old ways. Trams lorded over city streets, Bisto, Ty-Phoo and the good old British products stood pre-eminent … trains ran on steam, London was still often brought to a walking pace by smog; Liverpool was a city of which the rest of the country knew little…

Arthur Marwick, *Britain in Our Century* (1984), p. 150.

Source I

The policeman shown here has the features of the then Home Secretary, R.A. ('Rab') Butler. The victim is Harold Macmillan.

CUMMINGS CARTOON,
DAILY EXPRESS,
16 NOVEMBER 1960.

"Bad luck, Sir! Never mind — if I catch the scoundrels, I'll give them a sharp tap on the head with this report!"

Source J

THE 1950S COFFEE BAR
PROVIDED A MEETING
PLACE FOR YOUNG PEOPLE.

Source L

ROCK 'N' ROLL DANCING
BECAME VERY POPULAR.

Source M

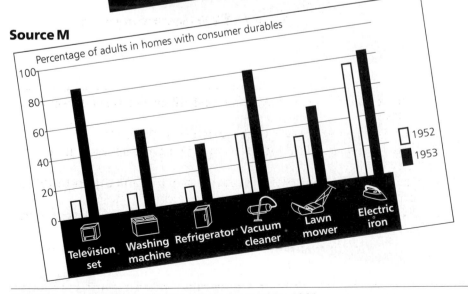

Percentage of adults in homes with consumer durables

Legend:
□ 1952
■ 1953

Source N

Between 1950 and 1955, Average weekly earnings rose by 50% (£7.10s to £11) whereas the cost of living rose by only 30%.

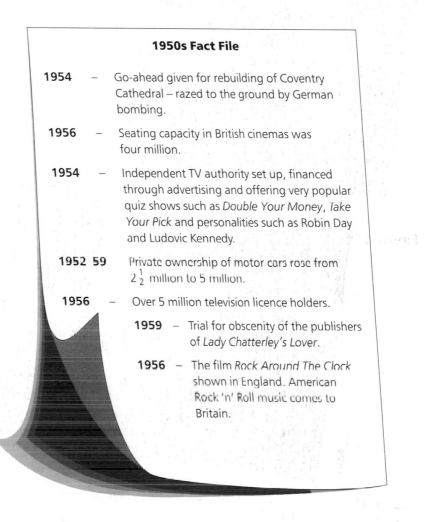

1950s Fact File

1954   –   Go-ahead given for rebuilding of Coventry Cathedral – razed to the ground by German bombing.

1956   –   Seating capacity in British cinemas was four million.

1954   –   Independent TV authority set up, financed through advertising and offering very popular quiz shows such as *Double Your Money*, *Take Your Pick* and personalities such as Robin Day and Ludovic Kennedy.

1952 59   Private ownership of motor cars rose from $2\frac{1}{2}$ million to 5 million.

1956   –   Over 5 million television licence holders.

1959   –   Trial for obscenity of the publishers of *Lady Chatterley's Lover*.

1956   –   The film *Rock Around The Clock* shown in England. American Rock 'n' Roll music comes to Britain.

1   In source H, what does Marwick suggest Britain was like in the early 1950s?

2   What is the message given by the cartoonist in Source I?

3   Consider Source J. How does this housing differ from most prewar housing?

4   How do Sources I to M demonstrate the beginnings of change in 1950s society?

5   In what ways does Source N help explain the changes in society? Can you think of other reasons for the changes in society and culture?

The Affluent Society – or 'Thirteen Wasted Years'?

Source A

Already by 1964 the appeal of the slogan 'Thirteen Wasted Years' was strong enough to give Labour a tiny majority; in the years following it has been confirmed almost as the conventional wisdom... Perhaps the period of Conservative rule will be looked upon as the last period of quiet before the storm – rather like the Edwardian age which in many respects it resembles. In that case its tranquillity will come to be valued more highly than its omissions.

The illusion with the most profound consequences was the economic one. In his book *The Affluent Society* (1958) J.K. Galbraith intended to sketch an outline of a developed society which had in large part solved the problem of production, and could concentrate its energies on other things.

Uncritical transference of Galbraith's thesis into the British context helped obscure the fact that Britain had not, in fact, solved its economic problems. The optimism of the early 1950s is, however, perfectly understandable... But this miracle was build on temporary and fortuitous circumstances. From 1955, Britain was bedevilled by a series of sterling crises which gradually forced upon the attention of politicians problems they wished to avoid.

It is now possible to see that for Britain the years 1951–64 were neither a period of continuous and uninterrupted expansion as the Conservative would have us believe, nor the 'Thirteen Wasted Years' of Labour mythology...

In 1962 Dean Acheson said, 'Britain has lost an empire; she has not yet found a role'... the failure to rethink her world role was as evident in diplomacy as in economics. Macmillan foresaw and expedited the final liquidation of Empire, but he had few ideas about what to put in its place... The special relationship with the United States was to remain the cornerstone of British policy. But without the Empire, this relationship was bound to become increasingly one between master and servant... These illusions blinded Macmillan ... to the far-reaching changes occurring in Europe...

What is the explanation for these illusions? For we are of course dealing not with one illusion but with several, which reacted upon, and reinforced, each other... At the political level these psychological factors revealed themselves in consensus. In economics, as in foreign policy, consensus reigned. Consensus is, indeed, a fundamental idea in understanding the politics of the 1950s. It signified acceptance of the mixed economy and the Welfare State. From this point of view, it did entail a real humanising and civilising of the political battle... Consensus did ensure the emancipation of politics from the ghosts of the past; unfortunately it also imposed a moratorium on the raising of new and vital issues. For consensus also signified acceptance of traditional assumptions concerning

Dean Acheson had been the US Secretary of State (an office broadly similar to that of British Foreign Secretary) from 1949 to 1953.

Britain's political choices came to be submerged in a generalised commitment to the objective of economic growth.

Economic growth was essential to the consensus. It enabled the Conservatives to offer for the first time available alternative to Socialism with their idea of property-owning democracy.

The politics to which consensus gave rise was one which reacted to events, but it was not able to provide the imaginative understanding needed to confront the future. For this the inherited framework was inadequate... For during the 1950s it was gradually discovered that the questions vital to Britain's future could not be discussed within the confines of the party system and the political conventions which surrounded it.

V. Bogdanor and R. Skidelsky, *The Age of Affluence 1951–64* (1970), pp. 7–11, 15.

---

1 What were the main illusions which the authors identify in the passage?
2 What do you understand by the term 'political consensus' and why does this help explain the 1950s and early 1960s?
3 In what ways does this Conservative period resemble the Edwardian age?

The decline of the Conservatives, 1960–4

In March 1962 the Liberal by-election victory in the suburban seat of Orpington in Kent fuelled speculation that a revived Liberalism could find a substantial constituency among the white-collar workers of the lower middle class. The Liberal surge proved to be a temporary phenomenon, however, as illustrated by contemporary opinion poll findings.

Source A

Conservative Central Office market research report on white-collar voters, satire in *Private Eye*, 6 April 1962.

> After the Orpington incident last March, it was brought to our notice that the unfortunate number of Conservative abstentions could be attributed to a certain discontent among the large quantity of so-called 'White-Collar Workers' living in the area.
>
> We received a memorandum from the Cabinet enquiring as to who these people were. But no one at Central Office, with the exception of our Mr Goldman, could ever remember having met one.
>
> It was obviously vital that, before preparing our advertising campaign for the next General Election, we should conduct a thorough investigation. We therefore called in Probes Ltd, the well-known market research consultancy which recently conducted the enquiry into 'Why the Working Classes don't use Harrods', to go down to Orpington and give us a full report. To talk to these 'White-Collar Workers' in their own homes, even to live with them for a few days, and to find out exactly what was on their minds.

Source B

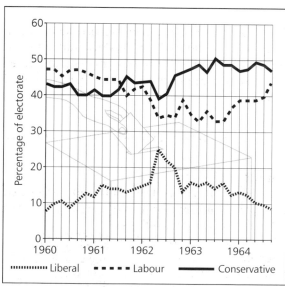

VOTING INTENTIONS, 1960–4.

Source C

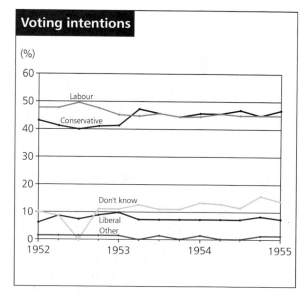

PUBLIC OPINION POLLS VOTING PREFERENCES, 1952–5.

1 What does the satirical magazine *Private Eye* (Source A) suggest about Conservative support in 1962?
2 What do Sources B and C suggest about the popularity of Conservatives, Liberals and Labour:
   a   1952–5
   b   1960–4?

Symptoms of Decline

Did voters simply want a change of government after more than ten years of Conservative government?

Defence

Criticism mounted over defence policy when the nuclear weapons programme collapsed. The Blue Streak, a medium-range missile, was abandoned on the grounds of cost. However, in December 1962 Great Britain had persuaded the USA to sell Polaris missiles to them on good terms. Both American dependency and Britain's status as a nuclear power seemed certain.

Economy

The government encountered economic difficulties in early 1961. An adverse balance of payments was countered by tax increases and public expenditure cuts. Selwyn Lloyd, the Chancellor, was dismissed and replaced by Reginald Maudling. His 1963 Budget cut taxes by £260 million, causing rapid growth which increased imports. New initiatives, such as the establishment of the National Economic Development Council, did not solve the fundamental problems. In 1963, Britain's application to join the EEC was rejected by the French president Charles de Gaulle.

Scandal

The Profumo Affair caused the Macmillan government much embarrassment. The Secretary of State for War Jack Profumo resigned in June 1963 after admitting lying to the House of Commons about his affair with the call-girl Christine Keeler who had also been involved with a Soviet naval attaché.

Opinion polls

Labour gained the lead in the opinion polls for the first time this decade.

Management of government

In 1962, concerned by adverse election results, the prime minister sacked one-third of his cabinet. Seven ministers went in the so-called 'Night of the Long Knives'. In the last 18 months of his administration, Macmillan seemed to be losing his grip. His appeal seemed dated compared to that of the new Labour leader, Harold Wilson. The press began to focus on weaknesses of the government. In October 1963 sudden illness forced him to resign.

MACMILLAN RESIGNED OCTOBER 1963

DEFENCE

ECONOMY

SCANDAL

OPINION POLLS

MANAGEMENT OF GOVERNMENT

Conservative dominance comes to an end

After Macmillan's resignation Sir Alec Douglas Home became prime minister. Not only a rather lack-lustre leader, Home inherited a party whose fortunes were flagging seriously. His task to restore the popularity of government was nearly impossible. An election was called in October 1964 which Labour won with 317 in a close-run fight when Conservatives still returned 304 seats.

Source A

"THANK GOODNESS, WE EVOLVE OUR LEADER IN OUR OWN WAY AND DON'T ELECT HIM DEMOCRATICALLY LIKE THOSE SOCIALISTS!"

TALKING POINT

What is the message Vicky is putting across both about the new Prime Minister and the election of party leaders?

Discuss how party leaders are now chosen for the three main parties. You may need to research this.

Why is this process significant in a democracy?

TASK

Write an essay:
- How accurate is it to describe the 1959 Conservative victory as the zenith of their power as a government, 1951–64?
- Zenith means 'high point' and therefore implies that the Tory position was strengthening from 1951 to 1959 and weakening from 1960 to 1964.

From the previous pages, find evidence to support:
    a The Tory position was strengthening 1951–59.
    b From 1959 to 1964 the Tories were in decline.

Now are there counter-arguments to this?
    a What were the weaknesses from 1951–59?
    b What were the persistent strengths after 1959?

REVIEW

Why did the Conservatives dominate the 1950s and early 1960s?

The Conservatives were returned to government in 1951 yet if the percentage of total votes is checked (page 278) it is clear that it was a close-run thing. The Conservatives polled 48.8% and Labour 48%. There were no realistic expectations that victory would last. However, the Conservatives governed for 13 consecutive years with four different prime ministers and increased majorities at the 1955 and 1959 elections. The early 1960s saw support for the Conservatives eroding but an explanation is still required.

TASK

'Why did the Conservatives, despite social and economic problems at the time, hold on to power for 13 years?'

1 Consider the problem above and with reference to this chapter and your own research complete the chart below:

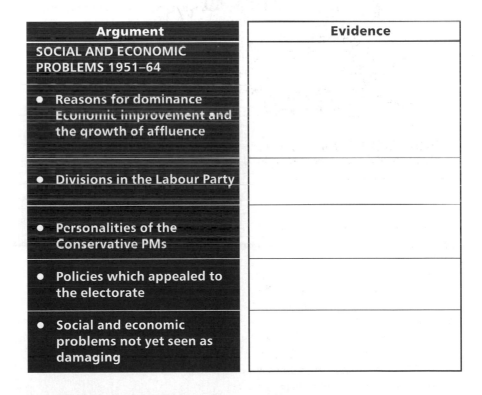

Argument	Evidence
SOCIAL AND ECONOMIC PROBLEMS 1951–64 • **Reasons for dominance** Economic improvement and the growth of affluence	
• **Divisions in the Labour Party**	
• **Personalities of the Conservative PMs**	
• **Policies which appealed to the electorate**	
• **Social and economic problems not yet seen as damaging**	

2 Class discussion – decide which factors you consider most important and justify your choice by careful use of the evidence.

13 The Wilson, Heath and Callaghan Era, 1964–1979

PREVIEW

'The swinging 60s and 70s'

The postwar younger generation had enjoyed the benefits of a rising standard of living, growing consumerism, a media revolution and wider educational opportunities than their parents or grandparents. This generation born after the war became increasingly experimental, nonconformist and challenging in their attitude towards the establishment. A trend which had begun in the 1950s reached a peak in the 1960s.

Peter Clarke described it as 'a conspicuous and noisy youth culture' which 'came to the boil in the 1960's'. It was a period of optimistic popular culture: pop music symbolised by British groups such as the Beatles, the Rolling Stones and the Kinks; new fashion trends, created by designers such as Biba and Mary Quant and modelled by icons such as Twiggy – simultaneously her name and a comment on her figure. Pirate radio stations, miniskirts, and unisex long hair and denim jeans were symbols of the age's youth. This visual revolution was matched by a deep change in social values and morals. Youth – many more than ever having experienced a full education through to university – were prepared to question and challenge the social and political assumptions of their parents. Student demonstrations of the late 1960s resulted in marches and the occupation of college and university buildings. Discontented youth, perhaps the vanguard of a social revolution, shocked and dismayed parents, teachers and taxpayers – the elder generation.

Source A

A PRO-ABORTION DEMONSTRATION.

AN ANTI-RACIST DEMONSTRATION.

Source C

ALDERMARSTON CND
MARCHERS IN LONDON.

THE ROLLING STONES.

1 What issues are the targets for protest?
2 How do the fashions, hairstyles and forms of entertainment differ from the prewar era? What do they tell you about this generation?
3 From these sources, describe the type of society the younger generation in the 1960s and 1970s were calling for.
4 What factors do you think gave rise to this social revolution?

1964–79 A political overview

Date	Government	Prime Minister	Parties in Opposition
1964 General Election	Labour (majority = 4)	Harold Wilson	
1965			Leader of the Conservatives, Sir Alec Douglas Home, resigned. The leadership contest was won by Edward Heath who defeated Reginald Maudling and Enoch Powell.
1966 General Election	Labour (majority = 96)	Wilson	
1970 General Election	Conservatives (majority = 43)	Edward Heath	Liberals remained a small party in Parliament with six seats.
1974 (Feb.) General Election	Labour (majority = 4, but no overall majority)	Wilson	Liberals, now led by Jeremy Thorpe, were reinvigorated and drew support away from the Conservatives
1974 (Oct.) General Election	Labour (overall majority = 3)	Wilson	A disappointing result for Labour but Tories in disarray.
1975			Heath's leadership challenged. Margaret Thatcher became leader of the Conservatives.
1976 (March)	Wilson resigned	James Callaghan	Jeremy Thorpe resigned as leader of Liberals and was succeeded by David Steel.
1977–78			Lib–Lab Pact agreed to overcome govt majority of 1.
1979 General Election	Conservatives	Margaret Thatcher	

Wilson's Labour government took office in October 1964 amidst a mood of some optimism... A good deal of it embodied in the new image carved out for himself by the new P.M. He offered a no-nonsense, classless style associated with modernisation ... He frequently worked in the spirit of J.F. Kennedy ... with talk of a 'new frontier' and his 'first hundred days' of positive action. His Gannex raincoat, his Yorkshire accent, his skill in television interviews, where well-timed puffs from his pipe were interspersed with shrewd political comments, gave him for a time a dominant political appeal...
K.O. Morgan, *The People's Peace*, p. 239.

Harold Wilson

... Heath's influence on the Tory Party since becoming its leader was considerable. The patrician air of landed and ducal public school educated had weakened a little to reveal the music-loving, sailing bachelor with a grammar school background – even if the Oxford connection was maintained.
Pearce and Stewart, *British Political History*, p. 490.

Edward Heath

Callaghan was in many ways an impressive figure as prime minister, no less wily than Wilson in the acts of party management but less transparently wily... Callaghan aroused less bitterness on the left... Callaghan felt that his tenure of all four great cabinet offices had given him unrivalled lessons in the hard school of experience. Statesmanlike certainly he nonetheless did not come across as aloof... or arrogant, ... instead the avuncular good sense of Jim... was widely thought reassuring.
Peter Clarke, *Hope and Glory*, pp. 350–1.

James Callaghan

TALKING POINT

How important is the image of a prime minister?
What are the images of Wilson, Heath and Callaghan as described here?
Do these images either help explain why these politicians became party leaders or why they won elections?

Reform under Wilson – An attempt at modernisation

Harold Wilson was described by his political secretary Marcia Williams as a traditionalist and throughout this time in office he concurs with and is part of the ritual of government. However, before gaining office he had written about sweeping away the 'Edwardian establishment' mentality! The governments of 1964 to 1970 saw considerable attempts to reform the political, economic and social systems of Britain.

Area 1 The Economy

- The Industrial Reorganisation Corporation was set up in 1966. This was a government-funded organisation to encourage efficient firms to take over from inefficient ones.
- The Queen's Award for Industry was introduced.
- Industrialists figured prominently on the Honours List.
- The Decimal Currency Board was established in 1966 under Sir William Fiske to work towards the introduction of decimalisation in 1971. This was carried through but weights and measures were not made metric.

TALKING POINT

What were the major social issues which would be tackled by a reformist government?
Can you suggest how the political and economic systems could have been modernised in the 1960s?

Area 2 Constitution and Political System

- Reform of the House of Lords had been an electoral pledge. The upper chamber had a built-in Conservative majority despite the introduction of life peerages in 1958. Wilson did not attempt to abolish the Lords but a 1960 white paper sought to reduce the power of hereditary peerage families and eliminate a one-party majority in the Lords. The bill to reform was defeated in the Commons.
- Morning sessions of the Commons were experimented with between 1966 and 1967 but failed to be introduced permanently.
- Specialist Committees were successfully introduced to give back bench MPs more opportunity to examine the work of government. These fulfilled useful work in areas such as Education, Science and Race Relations.
- Ombudsmen were introduced to investigate complaints from the public about the administration of the country. This attempt to make government more accountable was limited by the limited power given to these Ombudsmen.
- In 1969 the Representation of the People Act lowered the voting age for men and women to 18.
- Concern over the power, competence and efficiency of the Civil Service led to the publication of the Fulton Report in 1968. This advocated more professionally qualified entrants, more training in the service, abolition of the class system with better prospects of promotion through the ranks. Only parts of this report were implemented and a move was made to opening up the Civil Service.

- The death penalty was abolished for five years in 1965. A motion for permanent abolition was passed in 1969.
- Homosexual practice in private between two consenting adults was legalised in England and Wales under the Sexual Offences Act 1967 – a private members bill introduced by Leo Abse, a Welsh Labour MP
- The 1967 Abortion Act made abortion easier on grounds of physical and mental risk to pregnant women or existing children.
- Divorce laws were modernised in 1969 when irretrievable breakdown of marriage became the sole reason for divorce.
- 1967 National Health Service Family Planning Act ordered local authorities to provide family planning clinics – free advice and contraception to be paid for according to the means of the recipient.
- 1968 Theatre Act ended censorship of plays in London.
- The Race Relations Act was passed to prevent discrimination in employment or housing. By 1968 James Callaghan, the Home Secretary, was faced by the problem of Kenyan Asians flooding into Britain. He acted to place controls on immigrants without connections in Britain.
- Breathalyser test introduced by Barbara Castle – Minister of Transport.
- Dangerous drugs offences doubled between 1969 and 1972. This was the start of a long-term trend but no legislation was passed to deal with the problem.
- Changes in education were significant. The Robbins Report on Higher Education 1963 led to an increase in the number of universities. Labour developed the provision of polytechnics in Britain. Introduced the Open University 1969 at Milton Keynes and comprehensive secondary education.

TASK

1 Divide the class into three groups to research further
   a Economic, **b** Political and **c** Social reforms.
   Each group should identify how far implementation was taken, what problems still remained and what benefits arose as a result of reform.
2 Write an essay using the evidence in this chapter and your own research: 'How successful was Wilson's Labour government in its modernisation of British systems?'

FOCUS

13.1 The great educational debate of the 1960s: grammar schools or comprehensive schools?

How and why did 'comprehensive schools' develop?

Department of Education and Science, circular 10/65, The Organisation of Secondary Education, 12 July 1965

Introduction.

1. It is the Government's declared objective to end <u>selection at eleven plus</u> and to eliminate <u>separation in secondary</u> education...

   The Secretary of State accordingly requests local education authorities, if they have not already done so, to prepare and submit him plans for reorganising secondary education in their areas on comprehensive lines...

26. It is for the authorities ... to devise the most satisfactory plans in relations to local circumstances. In doing so, they should appreciate that while the Secretary of State wishes progress to be as rapid as possible, he does not wish it to be achieved by the adoption of plans whose educational disadvantages more than off-set the benefits which will follow flow from the adoption of comprehensive schooling...

36. A comprehensive school aims to establish a school community in which <u>pupils over the whole ability range and with differing interests and backgrounds</u> can be encouraged to mix with each other, gaining stimulus from the contacts and learning tolerance and understanding in the process. But particular <u>comprehensive schools will reflects the characteristics of the neighbourhood</u> in which they are situated; if their community is less varied and fewer of the pupils comes from homes which encourage educational interests, schools may lack the stimulus and vitality which schools in other areas enjoy. The secretary of state therefore urges authorities to ensure, when determining catchment areas, that schools are as socially and intellectually comprehensive as is practicable...

TALKING POINT

What type of school were you and your parents educated in between the ages of 11 and 16? In 1965 Anthony Crosland at the Department of Education and Science (1965–1967) issued a controversial circular which requested local authorities to submit plans for the reorganisation of secondary education on the comprehensive model.

1 Explain fully what is meant by the underlined phrases:
   a 'selection at eleven plus'
   b 'separation in secondary education'
   c 'pupils over the whole ability range and with differing interests and backgrounds'
   d 'comprehensive schools will reflect the characteristics of the neighbourhood'
2 Why do you think this is part of the Labour government's policy?
3 How are differences in ability, interests and background catered for in a comprehensive school?

Before 1965 most local education authorities organised their schools on the Tripartite System (see Butler's Act – Chapter 11) – only a few comprehensives existed.

However, public opinion began to move towards a comprehensive system as a result of the problems of the 11+ examination. A national debate followed

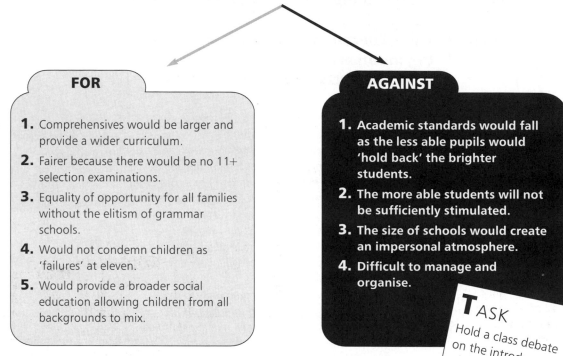

FOR

1. Comprehensives would be larger and provide a wider curriculum.
2. Fairer because there would be no 11+ selection examinations.
3. Equality of opportunity for all families without the elitism of grammar schools.
4. Would not condemn children as 'failures' at eleven.
5. Would provide a broader social education allowing children from all backgrounds to mix.

AGAINST

1. Academic standards would fall as the less able pupils would 'hold back' the brighter students.
2. The more able students will not be sufficiently stimulated.
3. The size of schools would create an impersonal atmosphere.
4. Difficult to manage and organise.

TASK

Hold a class debate on the introduction of comprehensive schools.

Steps towards implementation

Between 1965 and 1968, 66 per cent of LEAs in England and Wales had submitted plans for comprehensive reorganisation to the Department of Education and Science (DES) for approval. Three types of system were adopted:

- straight through 11–18 years
- 11–16 with transfer to Sixth Form or Tertiary College
- Middle schools for 8– 12-year-olds and upper schools for 13–18-year-olds.
- In 1970, Conservative Education minister Margaret Thatcher stated that LEAs were under no obligation to reorganise.
- In 1974, Labour reversed the Conservative policy and insisted plans be submitted.
- In the 1980s, 90 per cent of state secondary schools were comprehensives. Some LEAs continued to favour a selective system.

Economy and industrial relations, 1964–79

The economy and the problems of industrial relations dominated the agenda of British governments between 1964 and 1979. Economic problems were inherited from the war and the postwar Labour and Conservative ministries. In addition, pressures developed which gave rise to a series of crises which Cabinets had to deal with. The problems of the economy had complications throughout government policy but none so significant as with industrial relations. These problems and government policy towards them will be examined in the three chronological periods:

1. Wilson's governments, 1964–1970.
2. Heath's government 1970–1974.
3. Wilson and Callaghan's governments, 1974–1979.

Economic problems by 1964

Source A

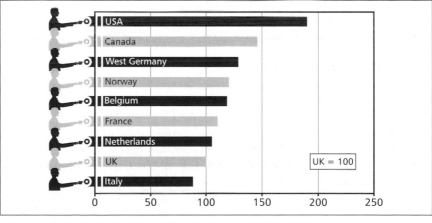

COMPARATIVE ANNUAL RATES OF ECONOMIC GROWTH, 1950–73.

OECD is the Organization for Economic Co-operation and Development – a group of the leading western industrial countries.

Source B

COMPARATIVE LEVEL OF REAL OUTPUT PER MAN-HOUR IN 1965.

1 What problems with the British economy are shown by these graphs?
2 Why do you think it was easy to believe that the 1950s to the early 1960s was a period of affluence?

By 1964

1. **Economic growth lagged behind other countries and productivity was low.** Many reasons were suggested for this; low levels of investment, inadequate research and development, bad marketing and poor industrial relations.

2. **Consequences of 'stop–go' policies of previous governments.**
   After the experience of mass unemployment throughout the 1930s, postwar governments adopted Keynesian policies. J.M. Keynes believed that unemployment could be avoided by maintaining a high level of demand in the economy – this would stimulate industry and provide jobs. The problem was to ensure tax policies maintained an equilibrium. If, as a result of a high level of taxation, there was too little demand this would lead to unemployment. However, too much demand would lead to inflation, increased imports and a balance-of-payments crisis. In order to maintain this balance, governments during the 1950s and early 1960s pursued a 'stop–go' approach to economic policy. For political reasons, the 'go' part of the cycle – reducing taxes and encouraging spending – tended to coincide with general elections.

TALKING POINT

Find out the meaning of the following terms: 'inflation', 'balance of payments', 'public expenditure', 'sterling crisis'.

The 'Stop–Go' Cycle

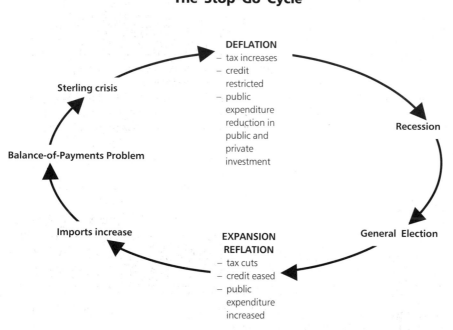

'Stop–go' policies undermined business confidence – long-term planning and investment became very difficult. As a result investment was low and comparative economic decline led to Britain becoming less competitive.

3. Economic dependency on Middle Eastern oil

Britain's energy supply relied heavily on cheap oil from the Middle East. This oil supply was controlled by OPEC – an Arab-dominated oil producers' cartel. In addition the Middle East was a politically unstable area and the Arabs in their conflict with Israel could use their power as an oil producer to exert political pressure. This later led to a cut in the oil supply and an energy crisis in Britain.

TASK

1 Re-read Chapters 7 and 8 on the economic problem of the 1920s and 1930s. How did governments during this earlier period deal with the economic problems of declining staple industries, unemployment and loss of American financial support in 1929?

2 Explain clearly the difference between classical orthodox economic policies pursued by governments before the Second World War and the Keynesian approach adopted in the 1950s and 1960s.

Wilson's economic problems and policies, 1964–1970

1964

PROBLEMS

- Lack of investment and economic growth.
- Massive and mounting balance-of-payments deficit.
- Demand to devalue the pound which would create cheaper British exports and raise the price of imports.

POLICIES

- No devaluation – it was believed politically damaging to undermine confidence in sterling.
- Chancellor's Callaghan's 'carrot-and-stick' budget and a rise in bank rate in November proved insufficient.
- April 1965 Budget was deflationary. Taxes rose and hire purchase was restricted.
- The Department of Economic Affairs (DEA) was set up to plan for economic growth.
- 1965 The National Board for Incomes and Prices was established and agreed by trades unions. Increases in income had to be related to increases in productivity.

1966

CRISIS

Caused by:
- Strike by the National Union of Seamen in July led to sharp fall in exports.
- Serious selling of sterling due to fall in US confidence.
- Bank rate was raised from 6 to 7 per cent.
- France called for Britain to devalue in order to join the European Economic Community.

POLICIES

- No devaluation.
- Introduction of a deflationary package of ten measures:
  - hire purchase downpayments were raised.
  - invoked a 'regulator' allowing the Chancellor to raise or lower indirect taxes by 10 per cent.
  - increased taxes on drink, oil, petrol and purchase tax.
  - postal charges were increased.
  - controls on building.
  - foreign exchanges rates tightened. Personal limit of £50 for foreign travel.

CRISIS	POLICIES
1967 Caused by: • Poor set of trade figures in May. • June – the Six Day War in the Middle East. It closed the Suez Canal and affected trade. • September – unofficial dock strike in Hull, Liverpool, London and Manchester. • By July, Britain's gold and dollar reserves had fallen by £36 million. • Unemployment had reached 496,000 – the highest July figure since 1940. • By October, the trade deficit was a massive £162 million.	• Devaluation of £ from $2.80 to $2.40. • Major expenditure cuts on defence. Prescription charges were increased, free milk in secondary schools was ended and the housing programme was reduced.

TALKING POINT

Why was devaluation considered a sensible move by some? Why did the government reject it?

CRISIS	POLICIES
1968 Caused by: • International monetary crisis. • Dollar value was weakening. • In March, the USA requested a close of the London Gold Market where traders were deserting dollars for gold. • By the autumn, progress was still slow. The balance of payments was still in deficit and the £ fell on the foreign exchanges.	• A bank holiday was announced for 15 March. • The March Budget was very deflationary: – severe tax increases equalling £923 million. – income tax allowances were cut. – there was a special surcharge on large investment incomes. • November – emergency measures announced by the government led to an opposition vote of 'no confidence'.

Industrial relations during the Wilson government

In 1968 Wilson appointed Barbara Castle, formerly at the Ministry of Transport, to the newly created Ministry for Employment and Productivity. She had put forward proposals to modernise industrial relations and lessen the damage they were doing to the economy.

Source A

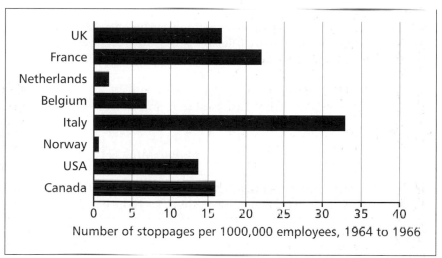

Number of stoppages per 1000,000 employees, 1964 to 1966

COMPARATIVE NUMBER OF STOPPAGES PER 100,000 EMPLOYEES, 1964–6.

Source B

What problems in industrial relations can be deduced from these graphs?

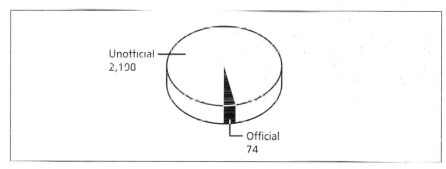

OFFICIAL AND UNOFFICIAL STRIKES IN THE UK, 1964–6.

The problem

Industrial relations were becoming difficult for two reasons – the economic problems and the Government's attempts to peg wages and prices, but also because of the problems within trades unionism itself such as:

- Aggressive trade union leaders such as Jack Jones of the TGWU and Hugh Scanlon of the AEU.
- Inter-union rivalry.
- Union opposition to equal pay for women.
- Unofficial strikes were increasing, promoted unrepresentative, militant, left-wing shop stewards organising strikes in the face of opposition from national union leadership.

The result

The rising number of strikes were damaging.

1. In 1967, 2116 disputes meant the loss of 2.7 million working days. In 1969 3116 disputes resulted in the loss of 6.8 million working days. Many of these strikes were unofficial and, as Barbara Castle commented, these were worse because unpredictable.

2. In January 1969 Castle's proposals were published in a White Paper 'In Place of Strife'. The Industrial Relations Bill which followed prepared measures to strengthen the unions:
   – a permanent committee on industrial relations was to be set up.
   – industrial boards were established to hear cases.
   – safeguards against unfair dismissal were introduced, but there was also legalisation to prevent unofficial strikes.

This was a highly controversial bill and although popular with the public, keen to see reform of the unions, many Cabinet members thought it inadvisable to take on the unions. The Labour Party was divided and the TUC issued their own programme for action. The Industrial Relations Bill was postponed. Labour had failed to reform the trades unions. The problem continued into the 1970s.

Economic problems and policies under Heath, 1970–74

POLICY 1970–71

On coming to power, the Conservative government under Edward Heath aimed to overcome inflation, suppress wage demands, and increase exports through greater productivity. According to their election manifesto, their approach was to be in contrast to the Labour government and would disband their Prices and Income Policy.

It seemed the economy by the end of 1970 had begun to stagnate so the budget of April 1971 was an attempt to encourage demand. It made tax reductions amounting to £550 million, cut corporation tax to 40 per cent, increased tax allowances for children and reduced Surtax for high earners. Another reflationary budget followed in March 1972.

a. INFLATION - retail prices rose by 8.6 per cent between 1970 and 1973.
b. RISING UNEMPLOYMENT - from 579,000 in 1970 to 899,000 in 1972.
c. DETERIORATING BALANCE OF PAYMENTS - in 1972 exports hardly rose but imports increased by 11 per cent in volume and 15 per cent in value.
   – the trade balance fell to a deficit of £700 million.
d. STERLING CRISIS - value of the £ began to plunge.

To cope with the mounting problems, the government decided on an economic U-turn and embarked upon a three-stage counter-inflation policy – reminiscent of the policies pursued by Labour during the 1960s.

Stage one:
- Money was made available for industry e.g. Rolls Royce and Upper Clyde Shipbuilders.
- An Industrial Development Executive was set up.
- A statutory Prices and Pay standstill was introduced in November 1972 i.e. freeze on prices of all goods except imports and fresh food and a standstill on all negotiated wages and salaries for 90 days.

Stage two:
- In January 1973 two new agencies were set up. Firstly a Price Commission to regulate prices, dividends and rent and secondly a Pay Board which had to give approval to wage settlements of over 1000 employees. No pay increases were to exceed £1 per week or 4 per cent of current pay.

Stage three:
- October 1973 proposals were set out which became fully operative in 1974. Similar price controls, a ceiling of £2.35 per head on wages increases and a £350 p.a. limit for all. A threshold agreement allowed this ceiling to rise up to 40p per week if the Retail Price Index rose 7 per cent above the 1973 level.

TASK

1 Explain why Heath's government decided on the change of policy in 1972.
2 How would inflation affect the following:
   a an old age pensioner
   b middle-class family of four
   c a factory worker
   d a professional couple without children?
4 In what ways did government policy between 1972 and 1973 counter inflation? What problems might result from these policies?

CRISIS OCTOBER 1973

In addition to the already mounting economic problems, Britain experienced a damaging fuel crisis in October/November 1973. As a result of the October 1973 Arab–Israeli War, the oil supply had been restricted. 50 per cent of Britain's energy depended on oil. Her imported oil was cut by 15 per cent. There were steep rises in the price of crude oil and shortages of petrol resulted in panic buying and long queues. The situation was worsened by industrial action. Miners and electrical engineers declared an overtime ban and the raildrivers' union, ASLEF, banned Sunday overtime.

GOVERNMENT RESPONSE

- A state of emergency was declared in December 1973
  - The Minimum Lending Rate (formerly called Bank rate) rose from $11\frac{1}{4}$ per cent to 13 per cent.
  - Orders were made to restrict electricity heating except in houses and other places.
  - Electricity for advertising, displays and floodlighting was prohibited.
- Refusal to make an offer to the miners.
- From 1 January 1974 a three-day week was introduced. Electricity was to be supplied to industry on three specified days per week.
- A 50 mph speed limit was introduced on all roads.
- Maximum heating limit was imposed on all commercial premises.
- Television closed down at 10.30 p.m. each evening.
- In February there came an announcement of a miners' strike. Heath's position became untenable and a General Election was called for 28 February 1974.

Industrial relations under Heath

Despite the Heath government's determination to tackle the trades unions, industrial relations worsened considerably between 1970 and 1974. It became a period characterised by what two historians, Sked and Cook, have referred to as 'the politics of confrontation'.

Why?

Reasons:
1 A rising level of unemployment and inflation.
2 Government prices and incomes policy.
3 Industrial Relations Act 1970 – made collective bargaining enforceable by law. A National Industrial Relations Court was set up to enforce the Act.
4 Government policy was seen by trades unionists as uncompromising and confrontational.

Evidence:
- Between January and March 1971, working days lost were four times those for the same period in the previous year.
- January 1972 – coal miners' strike. 280,000 miners went on strike for more pay having rejected £2 per week. In February power stations were picketed, violence broke out and railwaymen refused to work. The National Coal Board made an renewed pay offer which was accepted.
- June 1972 – dockers' strike. 30,000 dockers stopped work in sympathy with three dockers who refused to appear before the new Industrial Relations Court for picketing. An arrest for contempt was ordered. The order was quashed and government had been defeated twice.
- February – gas workers' strike. To protect their pay claim gas workers went on strike and enforced overtime bans. Four million homes experienced reductions in gas during that month and 600 industrial plants were forced to close.
- civil servants' strike. For the first time ever 200,000 civil servants went on strike over pay and conditions on 27 February.
- autumn/winter 1973 – miners, ASLEF and electrical workers banned overtime.

Economic and industrial relations policy under Wilson and Callaghan, 1974–79

Immediate action

With no overall majority, Wilson seized opportunities before another election.

1. Brought an end to the miners' strike.
2. Repealed the Industrial Relations Act.
3. Dismantled Heath's pay policies.
4. Began renegotiations for Britain's entry into Europe.
5. Two Budgets – the first increased taxation severely, but in July the Budget was more inflationary.
6. Announced the end of the pay-beds in National Health Service hospitals and an immediate full move to a comprehensive school system.

The state of the economy dominated government policies at this time.

Problems persisted:

a. Inflation hit a 29 per cent high in 1975.
b. There were continued balance-of-payment problems.
c. Low productivity, high labour costs and rising unemployment (1.5 million in 1976).
d. Pressure on sterling led to a crisis in 1976 when the pound fell from $2.024 to $1.637.

Government responded:

A. Economy – called in the International Monetary Fund (IMF) in 1977 and negotiated loans of £3900 million conditional on £3000 million of government cuts.

B. Trades unions – an agreement was reached in July 1975 to place a compulsory limit on wage increases for those on £8500 and nothing for those earning more than this.

   – In 1978, government announced a 5 per cent limit on pay increases. However there was a rising mood of militancy amongst trades unionists. Ford car workers went on strike against the 5 per cent limit. Lorry drivers in 1979 claimed 25 per cent and settled at 14 per cent. Public service workers went on strike for six weeks – eventually reaching a settlement of 9 per cent plus £1 per week. Secondary picketing emerged as a worrying development.

Source A

JOHN JENSEN, *SUNDAY TELEGRAPH*, 31 OCTOBER 1976.

Source B

Amidst overflowing rubbish bins, closed schools and undug graves the unions destroyed wantonly a government which could hardly have been gentler to them and which had steadfastly ruled out statutory restraints on pay or on the internal conduct of union affairs.

K.O. Morgan, *Labour People: Leaders and Lieutenants* (1987), p. 273.

With reference to Sources A and B, and the sections on the economy and industrial relations.

1 Explain why it might be thought by 1979 that Keynesian economics were no longer desirable in Britain.

2 List reasons why the Labour government lost the General Election on 3 May 1979.

Britain joins Europe

The creation of the European Economic Community (EEC)

The concept of an integrated Europe was not new to the 20th century. Yet it was not until the second half of the century that an organisation for a united Europe was established. Older precedents of European unity had been set by the existence of a Holy Roman Empire and the Napoleonic Empire – here national entities were suppressed but not wiped out by the political might of one ruler.

This type of political unit gave way to the idea of economic co-operation across European states such as Prussia had established in the 19th century with the Zollverein – a precursor to a united Germany.

In 1923 a Pan-European Union saw proposals for a common economic market across Europe initiated. During the Second World War, Winston Churchill was president of the European Movement – a Franco-British Union against Germany. However, it was the postwar environment which gave rise to stronger motives for European Unity. In 1946 Churchill called for a United States of Europe believing that Britain's diminished Empire could be bolstered by ties with Europe. The postwar union amongst European countries was that an integrated Europe would solve basic enmities between nations such as had been experienced in the First and Second World Wars. It would provide defence and strengthen economically the European capitalist systems against the Soviet planned economy.

The EEC came into being through a series of key stages shown on the next page.

TALKING POINT

What is the difference between economic and political union?
Does economic union encourage political union or can a separate function be maintained?

3RD STAGE

1958 The Treaty of Rome (signed in March 1957) came into force, establishing the European Economic Community and the European Atomic Energy Community (Euratom). The six signatories were France, Germany, Italy, Belgium, the Netherlands and Luxembourg.

2ND STAGE

Failure of the Pleven Plan
The French Premier Pleven proposed a European Defence Community – where national armies would be pooled with West Germany's in a common European army. Increased Cold War tensions in Europe and the Korean War suggested closer defence ties were necessary. However, the plan failed when Stalin's death in 1953 and the end of the Korean War meant the urgency had subsided. Great Britain had no wish to participate, although it did agree to the idea in principle.

1ST STAGE

1951 Treaty of Paris – established the European Coal and Steel Community (ECSC) between France, Germany and the Benelux countries. This is a development of the Schuman Plan, proprosed by Robert Schuman, the then French foreign minister, who had suggested pooling the European coal and steel industries under a supranational authority. The British Prime Minister Attlee had his own plans for nationalisation and declined the invitation.

EARLY STEPS

1960 The Organisation for Economic Co-operation and Development. developed from the body set up to run the European Recovery Programme financed by Marshall Aid through the late 1940s and the 1950s.

1948 Council of Europe established at the Hague Conference. Marshall Aid from USA was offered to all European countries. The USSR declined.

The Organisation of the EEC

EUROPEAN COUNCIL

Heads of Government meet 2–3 times a year to agree on major political issues and to resolve difficult problems referred to it by the Council of Ministers.

COUNCIL OF MINISTERS

The legislative body meets in several specialist formations and one General Affairs Council. The Council debates all matters of European interest, agrees policy and makes laws to implement policy.

ECONOMIC AND SOCIAL COMMITTEE

Represents workers, employers and civil society. Can comment on legislation but has no power to change it.

PARLIAMENT

A deliberative body, with limited power over legislation. Controls budget. Oversees Commission activities, and can dismiss it.

EUROPEAN COMMISSION

The executive body. Proposes legislation and policies to the council and implements them when passed. Represents the Union internationally.

AUDIT COURT

Examines Commission expenditure and reports to the Parliament.

EUROPEAN COURT OF JUSTICE

Interprets and gives rulings on European law. Tries difficult civil cases referred by the Commission or the courts of member states.

1 What is the difference between a legislative body, a deliberative body and an executive body?
2 MEPs representing Britain sit in the European Parliament. Find out how they are elected.
3 What is the difference between the European Court of Justice (on diagram) and the European Court of Human Rights (not on diagram)? You may need to research this.

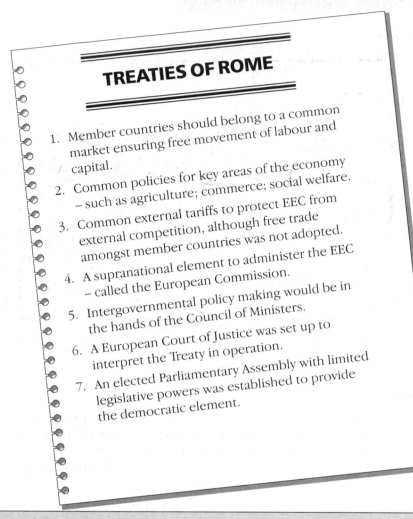

TREATIES OF ROME

1. Member countries should belong to a common market ensuring free movement of labour and capital.
2. Common policies for key areas of the economy – such as agriculture; commerce; social welfare.
3. Common external tariffs to protect EEC from external competition, although free trade amongst member countries was not adopted.
4. A supranational element to administer the EEC – called the European Commission.
5. Intergovernmental policy making would be in the hands of the Council of Ministers.
6. A European Court of Justice was set up to interpret the Treaty in operation.
7. An elected Parliamentary Assembly with limited legislative powers was established to provide the democratic element.

Task

1 List all the apparent motives of the six member countries for joining the EEC.
2 In what ways is Great Britain different?
3 What were seen as the benefits and disadvantages of Britain joining the EEC?

Britain's entry into the EEC

Source A

TALKING POINT

What messages are Low and Sir Stafford Cripps conveying about Britain and her relationship to Europe in 1948?

'I FORBID THE BANNS', DAVID LOW, *EVENING STANDARD*, 24 MARCH 1948.

Source B

> Participation in a political federation limited to West Europe is not compatible either with the Commonwealth ties, our obligations as a member of the wider community or as a world power.
>
> Sir Stafford Cripps, 1955.

Views in Britain diverged over membership of the EEC. Arguments were put forward which were both pro and anti. However, by the 1960s the government's position had become decisively pro-Europe, but it nevertheless took three applications for Britain to join.

Should Britain enter Europe?

ANTI

- The EEC's external tariffs would damage Britain's trade links with rest of world.
- Britain had to consider her role in the British Commonwealth.
- The organisation seemed too formal and structured.
- The British Commonwealth was undergoing change and ties were weakening.
- Many Europeans seemed set on supranational solutions. It was feared this would lead to a loss of sovereignty.
- Britain wished to pursue free trade but discussions with the French leader,
- De Gaulle, broke down.
- In 1959 British Conservative government established the European Free Trade Alliance (EFTA) with other countries outside the EEC – Austria, Denmark, Norway, Portugal, Sweden and Switzerland.

PRO

- The EEC would provide a larger 'home' market for declining British industries.
- British export goods would suffer from the imposition of external tariffs.
- Stiffer competition would force improvements in British industry.
- The British Commonwealth was undergoing change and ties were weakening.
- In the early 1960s the USA were prepared to back Britain's entry into the EEC.
- Relations between EFTA and the EEC were strained, leading to political tensions within Western Europe.

TALKING POINT

Which political, social and occupational groups in Britain would tend to be:

   a   anti-Europe

   b   pro-Europe?

Britain's three applications to join Europe

FAILED!

1ST APPLICATION

In August 1961 Macmillian's Conservative government announced its intention for entry. A Europe Committee under Sir Frank Lee had supported Britain's membership in its report. Most of the Labour Party opposed this. Labour leader Hugh Gaitskell called it 'The end of 1000 years of history'. The Labour Party Conference made five demands for entry to establish safeguards over our national independence to decide on foreign and economic policy. Negotiations opened in 1962 but both the West German Chancellor Adenauer and the French President De Gaulle were disinclined towards British entry. In 1963 De Gaulle vetoed British entry on the grounds that Britain was not ready.

TASK

1 What reasons did De Gaulle have for twice rejecting British entry?
2 Considering both the British economy and prevalent attitudes to Europe was De Gaulle justified in vetoing – or was it simply French intransigence?

2ND APPLICATION

In May 1967 the British Labour government under Prime Minister Wilson made another formal application to join the EEC. The Labour Party now seemed to be the party of Europe – although many of its leftwing remained opposed and signed the Tribune group's anti-market manifesto. However Wilson, George Brown (the Foreign Secretary) and James Callaghan (the Chancellor) were in favour. They believed that the EEC would bring the benefits of economic growth and improvements in social welfare. By 1967 Britain was experiencing a changing trade pattern and EFTA seemed inadequate for her purposes. The importance of trade with the Commonwealth was clearly in decline. Brown wrote that 'Britain's future rests upon her emergence as the leader of a new bloc in the world – a new European bloc'. In November 1967 De Gaulle once more vetoed Britain's entry.

SUCCESS!

3RD APPLICATION

Edward Heath, Conservative Prime Minister 1970–74, was a committed European and had been in change of negotiations for Macmillan in 1961. To the voters in 1970 he declared EEC entry was 'something to get us going again'. In October 1971 Heath gained a majority of 112 in the Commons and 393 in the Lords in support of entry into Europe. President De Gaulle's retirement in 1969 removed the major obstacle to Britain's entry. On 22 January 1972 the Treaty of Accession was signed in Brussels between the European Communities – France, Belgium, Germany, Italy, Luxembourg and the Netherlands on one side and Great Britain, Denmark, Norway and the Republic of Ireland on the other side. In September a referendum in Norway rejected full membership. In December Britain and Denmark withdrew from EFTA. Labour's attitude had been to oppose the terms on which the Tories had entered. Tony Benn, opposed to Europe, had proposed a referendum on the issue – this view was supported by Conservatives such as Enoch Powell. Wilson suggested renegotiating terms.

Wilson's renegotiations and referendum, 1974–75

The issue of Britain's membership became politically heated with splits in both the major parties. When Wilson returned to office in 1974 he immediately began renegotiating Britain's terms of entry as he had promised during the election. Wilson secured some concessions.

The four main areas for renegotiations were:
1. The Common Agricultural Policy
2. The level of British contribution to the EEC budget
3. Relations with the Commonwealth
4. Britain's ability to pursue her own industrial policies.

Wilson secured concessions for Britain on sugar beet and New Zealand dairy products plus member states' eligibility reimbursements on contributions on the basis of GNP and economic growth. The renegotiations were concluded in Dublin on 10 March 1975 and debated in the Commons in April. The package was voted through by 396 votes to 170, but the Labour Party was split 137 to 145 with 33 abstentions. Seven Cabinet members voted against their own government's proposals. It was decided a referendum should be held on 5 June 1975. The two camps – 'Britain in Europe' and 'Britain out of Europe' – were allocated equal television coverage and literature from the government to each householder at great expense. The 'Britain in Europe' lobby consisted of influential individuals and groups across the political and social spectrum. Most of the press, big business and the Establishment were in favour of continued European membership. Margaret Thatcher described the referendum a 'Contest between David and Goliath, which Goliath won' – Opponents of Europe were led by politicians such as Tony Benn, Michael Foot and Enoch Powell.

---

1 Why do you think a referendum was called?
2 Is this usual practice in Britain? Have referenda been held before or since?
3 Should referenda be used if there is an elected parliament?

Source A

The basis of Tony Benn's open letter to his constituents, 'What the Market Really means', was published in the TGWU publication *Record* in February 1975:

First, it (membership) subjects us to laws and taxes which your Members of Parliament do not enact, such laws and taxes being enacted by authorities you do not directly elect and cannot dismiss through the ballot box. Secondly, British membership means that Community laws and taxes cannot be changed or repealed by the British Parliament, but only by Community authorities not directly elected by British people. Thirdly, the EEC requires the British courts to uphold and enforce Community laws that have not been passed by Parliament, and that Parliament cannot change or amend even when such laws conflict with laws passed by Parliament, since Community law overrides British law. Fourthly, British membership imposes duties and constraints upon British governments not deriving from the British Parliament; and thus, discharging those duties ministers are not accountable to Parliament or to the British people who elect them. Fifthly, British membership, by permanently transferring sovereign legislative and financial powers to the Community authorities, who are not directly elected by the British people, also permanently insulates those authorities from direct control by the British electors, who cannot dismiss them and whose views, therefore, need carry no weight with them and whose grievances they cannot be compelled to remedy.

From Bill Coxall and Lynton Robins, *British Politics since the War* (1997), p.129.

---

1 Summarise the five arguments put forward by Benn in opposing Britain's membership of the EEC.
2 What is his underlying fear, which is the basis of all five arguments?
3 Tony Benn is a Socialist. Does this help to explain his point of view?
4 Write a response to this open letter countering Benn's views and putting forward advantages of membership?

Despite some apathy and much confusion over the economic arguments concerning wine lakes and butter mountains, the referendum vote approved Britain's membership. Of the 64.5 per cent of the electorate who voted, 17.3 million said yes as opposed to 8.4 million no. The vote was an acknowledgement of a need for friends now there was no empire, and a recognition that a heavy penalty would be exacted to leave and a preference to co-operate with Europeans who broadly had similar values, standards and problems. However, the debate has continued into the 21st century – proving to be a distinctive issue for succeeding prime ministers and party leaders.

– consider the question very carefully.
- The idea of 'wasted opportunity' implies that there were permanent solutions to Britain's problems which were missed. Is this true?
- 'On what grounds' could refer to both economic or social – they need to be covered.

READ!

Carefully re-read Chapters 12 and 13 for information in the 1960s and 1970s. Research further.

TASK
Write the following essay:
'On what grounds might the 1960s and 1970s be regarded as years of wasted opportunity for Britain?'

PLAN!

Introduction – briefly identify the context – the governments concerned, define 'wasted opportunity' and outline your overall argument which answers the questions.

Paragraph 2 – Economic
Consider the economic problems which persisted through these decades
– Industrial inefficiency
– lack of economic growth
– trade deficits
– Industrial relations
How were they tackled?
Were there missed opportunities?

Paragraph 3 – Social
Consider the social problems such as:
Immigration and race relations
Women's rights
Education
Public health and the drugs problem
Social welfare and poverty
How were these tackled?
were opportunities missed?

Paragraph 4 – International
Consider relations with the USA and Europe

Paragraph 5 – Public opinion
Individuals and pressure groups – who were they and how did they identify areas of wasted opportunity?

WRITE

After planning the essay thoroughly – write it up. Ensure that paragraphs are directed to the questions throughout. They should begin with a reference to the question and contain evidence which is accurate, detailed and relevant. In your conclusion reach a judgement which is coherent and a logical end to your analysis.

Review

Political diaries – as evidence for the historian

Labour entered the 1966 Election with a 9 per cent lead in the polls and were returned to power with an increased majority of 96. In the following months Wilson's personal standing as prime minister and Labour's popularity seemed unassailable. However, the diaries of his colleagues Barbara Castle, Tony Benn and Richard Crossman reveal deep unease over Wilson's leadership at this time.

Source A

Tony Benn, diary, 21 June 1966.

... To the Commons and this evening to Number 10 for a buffet supper that Harold had laid on. Among those who came were Peter Shore, Ron Brown [MP for Shoreditch and Finsbury], George Wallace [MP for Norwich North], Gerald Kaufman, Marcia, Percy Clark, and Dick's PPS, Geoffrey Rhodes, and members of the PLP permanent staff. Harold began by giving his usual analysis. The public 'are not interested in politics and want to play tennis and clean their cars and leave things to the Government. By contrast the party wants to do things and change things, and the main thing is to keep it on the move like a caravan so that it does not have time to stop and fight.'

The discussion roamed on for some time, so I plucked up my courage and said that if there was a conflict between what the public wanted and what the party wanted, I was on the side of the Party. Anyway, I didn't agree that the public wasn't interested in politics. They may be sick of Party bickering but they are interested in a whole host of issues that are essentially political and it was the Party's job to show the connection between issues that concerned the public and the political ideology and decisions that we expressed. It was for us to propagandise and campaign, just as it was the job of the Labour pioneers to convince the people fifty years ago that unemployment had something to do with politics.

What worries me is that Harold may be going to preside over a period of decline just as serious as occurred under Macmillan and accept the same basic philosophy of 'never had it so good' affluence that Macmillan accepted. Consensus is no substitute for putting key issues and institutions deliberately into the crucible of controversy. If we don't change things fundamentally, we shall have failed in our job even if we survive as a Government – which is not by any means certain.

Tony Benn, *Out of the Wilderness: Diaries 1963–67* (1987), pp. 436–7.

Source B

Richard Crossman, diary, 24 July 1966.

What is really wrong ... is that we have no real instrument of central decision-taking for the home front ... In its absence the P.M. has run the Government Prime Ministerially, arbitrating between George Brown and Callaghan, and in every other field retaining the right of final decision and, in this particular crisis, working direct with the Permanent Secretaries behind the backs of their Ministers. As for his own personal decisions, they've been taken in consultation with a very small inner private circle ...

This week we have had the beginnings of a collective Cabinet reaction against this Prime Ministerial method. The odd thing is that I, who wrote the introduction to Bagehot, am now busily trying to reassert collective Cabinet authority because I see how disastrous it is to allow Cabinet government to decline into mere Prime Ministerial government. It's better to get back to something much more like Cabinet responsibility; just as it is better to get back to effective Cabinet responsibility to Parliament, and the reassertion of parliamentary control over government – one of those bright ideas Harold announced during the election campaign and at the beginning of the Session but which has got entirely lost since then.

'Bagehot': Walter Bagehot, Victorian author of *The British Constitution*, often cited as a guide to parliamentary behaviour.

Richard Crossman, *The Diaries of a Cabinet Minister, Vol. One: Minister of Housing, 1964–66* (1975), pp. 582–3.

Source C

Sunday 24 July 1966

The Sundays are full of loss of confidence in Harold, both here and in America. Rees-Mogg says he should have concentrated more on the economics side and less on the political. This is what I have been saying all along – as far back as when he became Leader of the Opposition. I told him then, when he said to me he was going to be his own Foreign Secretary, that he would do better to be his own Economics Minister. I agree, too, that he seems strangely to have lost his grip of events. I first noticed it in the General Election. Is it his health? We still haven't had a satisfactory explanation as to why the blue skies for sterling changed so suddenly to storm in a matter of three weeks. And I shall never understand why we are not making more of our emphasis on science and technology. We don't give the impression as a Government of having something here the Tories hadn't got. And I don't think it is all Frank's fault. If he is wise, Harold will give his whole mind to this from now on instead of trying to strike attitudes on the world stage.

'Rees-Mogg': William Rees-Mogg, journalist and later editor of *The Times*.

Barbara Castle, *The Castle Diaries 1964–1970* (1984), p.152.

1 What criticisms are levelled against Wilson in these political diaries?
2 To what extent are the comments similar?
3 What is the value of these political diaries to a historian studying the politics of this period?
4 What limitations should a cautious historian be aware of when using such evidence?
5 How useful are the following types of sources to contemporary political historians: diaries, autobiography and memoir, biography?

14 The Thatcher Decade, 1979–1990

PREVIEW

Introducing Margaret Thatcher – the first female prime minister of Britain

Source A

Source B

IMAGE

Source C

The new regime took its cue, to a truly extraordinary extent, from the personality and outlook of the new Prime Minister. Margaret Thatcher was remarkable, of course, for being the first woman Prime Minister and she could use this factor to persuade or beguile male colleagues on occasion. But it was very seldom her femininity, but rather her image of toughness, determination, and ruthless single-mindedness that dominated public perceptions. She took office in May 1979, proclaiming on the steps of Number 10 Downing Street the healing words of St Francis of Assisi – 'where there is discord, may we bring harmony.' Yet it was not the message of saintly benevolence but the jarring note of conflict, belligerence, and confrontation which marked her style from the outset. Moderates or doubters were dismissed as 'wets' or sometimes 'wimps'.

K.O. Morgan, *The People's Peace* (1990).

Source D

The suggestion that I do not listen, particularly when it comes from ex-ministers, can, however, simply mean that I do not agree with their views. You might say I 'chair from the front'. I like to say what I think quite early on and then see whether arguments are adduced which show me to be wrong, in which case I have no difficulty in changing my line. This is, of course, not the traditional formal way of chairing meetings. My experience is that a group of men sitting round a table like little better than their own voices and that nothing is more distasteful than the possibility that a conclusion can be reached without all of them having the chance to read from their briefs. My style of chairmanship certainly nonplussed some colleagues, who knew their brief a good deal less well than I did. But I adopt this technique because I believe in argument as the best way of getting to the truth not because I want to suppress argument. In fact, I would go further: nothing is more important to successful democratic government than the willingness to argue frankly and forcefully – unless, perhaps, it is the willingness to recognise collective responsibility when the decision is made.

Margaret Thatcher, *The Downing Street Years*, p. 56.

Source E

And the very last thing I could afford was well-publicised dissent from within the Cabinet itself. Yet this was what I now had to face.

Public dissent from the 'wets' was phrased in what was obviously intended to be a highly sophisticated code, in which each phrase had a half hidden meaning and philosophical abstractions were woven together to condemn practical policies by innuendo. This cloaked and indirect approach has never been my style and I felt contempt for it. I thrive on honest argument. I am interested in practical options. And I prefer to debate my opponents rather than to undermine them with leaks. I do not believe that collective responsibility is an interesting fiction, but a point of principle. My experience is that a number of the men I have dealt with in politics demonstrate precisely those characteristics which they attribute to women – vanity and an inability to make tough decisions. There are also certain kinds of men who simply cannot abide working for a woman. They are quite prepared to make every allowance for 'the weaker sex': but if a woman asks no special privileges and expects to be judged solely by what she is and does, this is found gravely and unforgivably disorienting. Of course, in the eyes of the 'wet' Tory establishment I was not only a woman, but 'that woman', someone not just of a different sex, but of a different class, a person with an alarming conviction that the values and virtues of middle England should be brought to bear on the problems which the establishment consensus had created.

Margaret Thatcher, *The Downing Street Years*, p. 129.

1 From Sources D and E, what was Thatcher's style with her government?

BELIEFS

1 what were her main beliefs?
2 These sources are taken from Thatcher's autobiography *The Downing Street Years*. How useful to a historian are such autobiographical sources?

Source F

My father's background as a grocer is sometimes cited as the basis for my economic philosophy. So it was – and is – but his original philosophy encompassed more than simply ensuring that incomings showed a small surplus over outgoings at the end of the week. My father was both a practical man and a man of theory. He liked to connect the progress of our corner shop with the great complex romance of international trade which recruited people all over the world to ensure that a family in Grantham could have on its table rice from India, coffee from Kenya, sugar from the West Indies and spices from five continents. ... The economic history of Britain for the next forty years confirmed and amplified almost every item of my father's practical economics. In effect, I had been equipped at an early age with the ideal mental outlook and tools of analysis for reconstructing an economy ravaged by state socialism.

My life, like those of most people on the planet, was transformed by the Second World War. In my case, because I was at school and university for its duration, the transformation was an intellectual rather than a physical one. I drew from the failure of appeasement the lesson that aggression must always be firmly resisted. But how? The ultimate victory of the Allies persuaded me that nations must co-operate in defence of agreed international rules if they are either to resist great evils or to achieve great benefits. That is merely a platitude, however, if political leaders lack the courage and far-sightedness, or – what is equally important – if nations lack strong bonds of common loyalty. Weak nations could not have resisted Hitler effectively - indeed, those nations that were weak did not stand up to him. So I drew from the Second World War a lesson very different from the hostility towards the nation-state evinced by some post-war European statesmen. My view was – and is – that an effective internationalism can only be built by strong nations which are able to call upon the loyalty of their citizens to defend and enforce civilised rules of international conduct. An internationalism which seeks to supersede the nation-state, however, will founder quickly upon the reality that very few people are prepared to make genuine sacrifices for it

Source G

The 1983 general election result was the single most devastating defeat ever inflicted upon democratic socialism in Britain. After being defeated on a manifesto that was the most candid statement of socialist aims ever made in this country, the Left could never again credibly claim popular appeal for their programme of massive nationalisation, hugely increased public spending, greater trade union power and unilateral nuclear disarmament. But there was also undemocratic socialism, and it too would need to be beaten. I had never had any doubt about the true aim of the hard Left: they were revolutionaries who sought to impose a Marxist system on Britain whatever the means and whatever the cost.

The 1979 Election

The Conservative Party, led by Margaret Thatcher, won the General Election on 3 May 1979 gaining 339 seats (43.9% of the total vote) as opposed to Labour's 269 (36.9%) and Liberal's 11 seats, with an overall majority of 43. The idea of a united nation behind the government was undermined by certain worrying characteristics in the voting patterns. A North–South divide clearly existed. In the South Conservatives had 186 seats compared with Labour's 30, in the Midlands Conservatives had won 57 against Labour's 41 but in the North the Labour Party won 107 seats to the Conservatives' 53. In Scotland and Wales the Conservatives, despite some gains, were outnumbered by two to one.

However, Thatcher had a strong mandate to introduce the policies of regeneration for Britain promised in the Conservative manifesto. These promises, as yet not detailed, were particularly attractive to the voters whose memories of the so-called 'Winter of Discontent' were sharp enough to bring an end to Callaghan's Labour government. The key promises in May 1979 were:

- Control inflation and the trades unions.
- Restore incentive.
- Extend home ownership.
- Provide an improved education and health service.
- Uphold law and order.
- Strong defence policy.

This election proved to be a 'watershed' opening the way to what has been dubbed 'Thatcher's Britain'. It was the first of three consecutive election victories for the Conservatives under Thatcher – the others being in 1983 and 1987. For ten years she held power with presidential style – a record not matched in the twentieth century nor since Lord Liverpool's administration at the beginning of the nineteenth century. The decade became synonymous with the prime minister – terms such as 'Thatcherism' and the 'Thatcher era' were coined. There was during these years considerable change in economic and social policies but more fundamentally this period of Conservative government marked changes in attitudes and expectations throughout the population. An emphasis on the primacy of society's needs before those of the individual was shifted, if not indeed reversed for many. It is with some justification Thatcher was able to announce after some years in office 'I have changed everything'.

TALKING POINT

Can you explain why voting followed this pattern? What difficulties would this present to an incoming government?

MARGARET THATCHER CELEBRATING THE 1983 ELECTION VICTORY AT CONSERVATIVE CENTRAL OFFICE.

TALKING POINT

Why do you think Thatcher was considered an outsider in relation to the Conservative Party establishment?
Would this be an advantage or a disadvantage?

Thatcher's background

Margaret Roberts was brought up in a conventional middle-class family of shopkeepers in rural Lincolnshire. From grammar school, she qualified for Oxford where she studied Chemistry – she would be the first British prime minister to be a qualified scientist! After Oxford she studied Law, qualifying as a barrister, but her interest in politics was fulfilled when she was elected MP for Finchley in 1959. Despite the pressures of domestic life – marriage to a wealthy businessman, Denis Thatcher, and children, twins Mark and Carol, within two years she was a junior minister. As Minister for Education in Heath's 1970 government she earned the nickname 'Thatcher – milk snatcher' by ending free school milk. When Heath's position as leader was challenged in 1975, Thatcher was not an obvious contender for the position, having only having held more minor ministerial posts. However, in the leadership contest of that year Thatcher defeated Heath in the first ballot by 130 to 119 and in the necessary second ballot she defeated William Whitelaw, Geoffrey Howe and James Prior.

Leader of the Opposition, 1975–79

During her younger, formative years, Thatcher had not been persuaded by the leftish egalitarian call which developed after the Second World War. Instead, she was much impressed by F.A. von Hayek's *Road to Serfdom* (1944) which argued strongly against excessive government planning, intervention and welfare state provision. This, together with her own background rooted in the 'self-help' ethic of rural middle-class England, formulated Thatcher's own philosophy. Much groundwork was completed in these four years in opposition – particularly working with Sir Keith Joseph who was central to developing the 'New Right' within the Conservative Party.

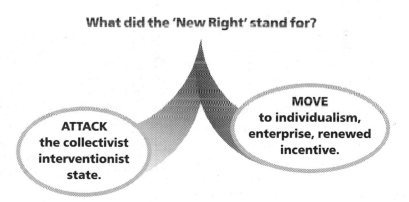

What did the 'New Right' stand for?

ATTACK the collectivist interventionist state.

MOVE to individualism, enterprise, renewed incentive.

In 1979, Keith Joseph crystallised the attack:

> the poisons ... which wreck a country's prosperity and full employment; excessive government spending, high direct taxation, egalitarianism, excessive nationalisation, a politicised trade union movement associated with luddism and an anti-enterprise culture (other countries had one or two) ... We are the only country that has all six.

TASK

1 Examine each of the six 'poisons' identified by Joseph and consider why he may argue they poison and how others on the left wing may argue they are justifiable.
2 Fill in the chart below.

POISONS	Attack by NEW RIGHT	Defence by LEFT
1 'Excessive government spending'		
2 'High direct taxation'		
3 'Egalitarianism'		
4 'Excessive nationalisation'		
5 'A politicised trade union movement'		
6 'Anti-enterprise culture'		

Thatcher – A 'conviction' not a 'consensus' politician

By declaring herself a 'conviction' politician Thatcher disassociated herself and her party from the postwar Labour–Conservative consensus politics. The historian K.O. Morgan, among many others, has suggested that 1979 was a turning point when consensus ended and conviction politics (the convictions of the New Right) started.

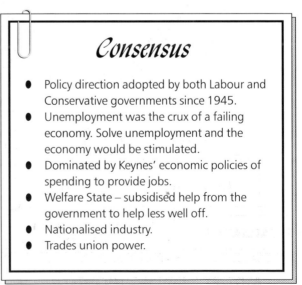

Consensus

- Policy direction adopted by both Labour and Conservative governments since 1945.
- Unemployment was the crux of a failing economy. Solve unemployment and the economy would be stimulated.
- Dominated by Keynes' economic policies of spending to provide jobs.
- Welfare State – subsidised help from the government to help less well off.
- Nationalised industry.
- Trades union power.

TALKING POINT

In what ways can each of these
sets of beliefs be seen as a
product of the events which
precede them?

Conviction

- Thatcher's convictions dictated Conservative government after 1979 – the 'New Right'.
- Inflation was the most serious economic problem.
- Monetarism – the control for the money supply – adopted as the prime economic policy.
- Control government spending.
- De-nationalise (de-regulate) industry.
- Curbs on union power.
- Encourage individualism, enterprise, thriftiness, hard work and a property-owning democracy.

'Building Thatcherism' – the Conservative administration, 1979–83

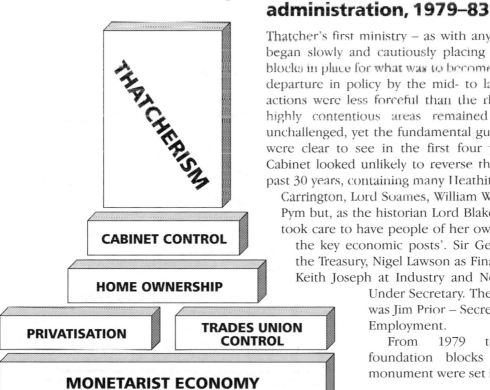

Thatcher's first ministry – as with any long innings – began slowly and cautiously placing the foundation blocks in place for what was to become a major radical departure in policy by the mid- to late 1980s. Early actions were less forceful than the rhetoric. Certain highly contentious areas remained for the time unchallenged, yet the fundamental guiding principles were clear to see in the first four years. Her first Cabinet looked unlikely to reverse the trends of the past 30 years, containing many Heathites such as Lord Carrington, Lord Soames, William Whitelaw, Francis Pym but, as the historian Lord Blake suggests, 'She took care to have people of her own persuasion in the key economic posts'. Sir Geoffrey Howe at the Treasury, Nigel Lawson as Financial Secretary, Keith Joseph at Industry and Noman Tebbit as Under Secretary. The only exception was Jim Prior – Secretary of State for Employment.

From 1979 to 1983 the foundation blocks of Thatcher's monument were set in place.

THEORY:

▨ Set out by the 'guru' of monetarism – Milton Friedman, an American economist – this economic theory stated that inflation rather than unemployment was enemy number one in a country's economy to be defeated. Inflation was a monetary phenomenon – if the supply of money was controlled, inflation would be controlled. Prices could not rise if there was less money in circulation and as a result of prices staying constant wage demands would decrease. How was the money supply to be limited? Both by adopting interest rate controls and constraining bank lending – through the correct policies, the government could encourage this.

▨ However, there were acknowledged pitfalls with this theory. Firstly there would be an inevitable time-lag before that money supply was adequately constrained, there was a difficulty in measuring precisely the supply of money and there was a danger of firms going out of business or having to reduce output, leading to unemployment. Thatcher considered these necessary evils in the pursuit of the greater good.

PRACTICE:

In June 1979 Geoffrey Howe – a late convert to monetarism – introduced the government's first budget in which the seeds of economic policy to come were sown. It had three main planks:

1 *A switch from direct to indirect taxation*:
   – Standard rate of income tax fell from 33 to 30 per cent
   – Higher rate income tax fell from 83 to 60 per cent
   – Value Added Tax (VAT) on goods was increased to a uniform 15 per cent.

2 *A sharp attack on public spending*:
   – Reduction of £1.5 billion in the Public Sector Borrowing Requirement (PSBR).
   – Government cash limits imposed another £1 billion cut.
   – Proposed sale of public assets would raise a further £1 billion.

3 *Minimum Lending Rate rose to 14 per cent.*

In March 1981 the third Conservative budget marked a triumph for monetarism against much criticism both inside and outside the party. Thatcher, who had announced famously at the 1980 Party Conference that she was 'not for turning', drove ahead with her economic adviser Alan Walters to oversee the most anti-Keynesian budget introduced in modern times:

1 £$3\frac{1}{2}$ billion was taken from the PSBR.

2 Indirect taxes soared, with a rise of 20p tax on petrol and similar rises on cigarettes and alcohol.

This drew much criticism in political and economic circles. Thatcher's popularity plummeted. The effects of early monetarist moves seemed to be damaging.

TALKING POINT

List all the problems caused by inflation.
Can it ever be beneficial?

TALKING POINT

Suggest simple definitions for the following terms:
Inflation
Money Supply
Interest Rates
Direct/Indirect Taxes
Value Added Tax
Public spending
Public assets.

TASK

1 Explain how these two budgets are pursuing the Conservatives' monetarist policies.

2 What would the effects of these budgets be on people such as: businessmen, the middle class and the working class?

BLOCK No. 2   PRIVATISATION

THEORY:

▨ This major plank of the 'New Right' aimed to withdraw government from direct contact with major sectors of the economy, thereby allowing a free market to work. It aimed also to end state intervention and government propping up inefficient businesses. It would allow ordinary people to become shareholders – a more positive interest in industry rather than through trades unionism.

▨ Finally, the sell-off would raise government money much needed to facilitate tax cuts.

PRACTICE:

Despite the rhetoric of 'rolling back the state', very little privatisation was introduced by 1983. Cable & Wireless, Amersham International and Britoil were de-regulated, but these tentative measures caused very little excitement.

BLOCK No. 3   TRADES UNION CONTROL

THEORY:

▨ During the 1960s and 1970s, the trades unions had become increasingly assertive and highly politicised (see Chapter 13). Wage demands had been impossible to meet given the profitability of the industry concerned and persistent industrial action had crippled the country and hastened its economic decline. At the same time some trades union leaders were using their organisations to pursue their own political ends. There was a widespread perception that trades union power had to be restricted.

PRACTICE:

The government did not make an immediate full-frontal attack on the unions but two Acts were passed to strengthen the government's position against the unions.

1 *The 1980 Employment Act* – James Prior at the Department of Employment. Government money was to be provided to ensure union ballots over strikes and leadership.
   Secondary picketing and sympathy strikes were outlawed.
   Closed shop arrangements were made more difficult.

2 *The 1982 Employment Act* – Norman Tebbit at the Department of Employment. Unions were made legally responsible for their actions and fined for unlawful strikes.
   Harsher penalties were set for secondary picketing.
   Compensation was to be paid to anyone dismissed through the operation of a closed shop.

BLOCK No. 4 | **HOME OWNERSHIP**

THEORY:

▓ By granting council house tenants the right to purchase their houses, it provided an incentive for the working class to work and join a property-owning democracy. The reduction in the number of council house tenants would be a financial saving.

PRACTICE:

The 1980 Housing Act

1 Required all local authorities to make property available for purchase.
2 Length of tenancy was to be taken into account.
3 Local authorities were to provide mortgages to facilitate purchase by tenants.

This proved both a successful and very popular provision. By the end of 1984 800,000 council houses had been bought.

BLOCK No. 5 | **CONTROL OF THE CABINET**

THEORY:

▓ In order to reverse the economic and social decline in Britain tough measures were required by the government. Thatcher was fully aware of the route she wished the Conservatives to take and it was important that the Cabinet was fully united behind the task. As the historian Peter Clarke says, 'In making appointments, administrative as well as ministerial, Thatcher became notorious for demanding whether the candidate was "one of us". She wanted to be served by people who believed in the mission of her government… She was to turn 10 Downing Street into a fortress staffed by loyalists on whom she could implicitly rely.' Those opposing Thatcher or even hesitant towards her policies were labelled 'wets' were gradually excluded from Cabinet.

PRACTICE:

Although she began with an ideologically mixed Cabinet, there was an important government reshuffle in September 1981 when the Conservatives were at a low ebb. Four Heathite ministers – Christopher Soames, Norman St John Stevas, Mark Carlisle and Ian Gilmour – were removed. James Prior was sent from Employment to the political exile of the Northern Ireland Office. At the same time 'New Right' figures emerged – Nigel Lawson at Energy, Norman Tebbit at Employment and Nicholas Ridley as Financial Secretary to the Treasury. Gradually during the 1980s on the formation of each new Cabinet, Thatcher hired and fired to ensure a compliant Cabinet with not a 'wet' in sight.

TASK

Read carefully the theory and aims behind each of the five policies. For each list problems that the government or public may encounter when the policies are put into practice.

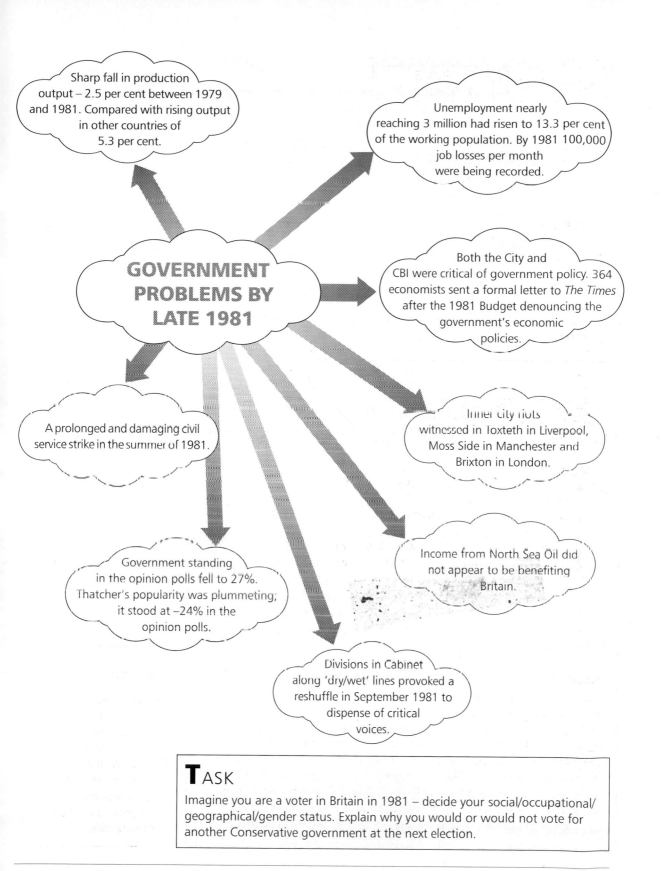

Sharp fall in production output – 2.5 per cent between 1979 and 1981. Compared with rising output in other countries of 5.3 per cent.

Unemployment nearly reaching 3 million had risen to 13.3 per cent of the working population. By 1981 100,000 job losses per month were being recorded.

GOVERNMENT PROBLEMS BY LATE 1981

Both the City and CBI were critical of government policy. 364 economists sent a formal letter to *The Times* after the 1981 Budget denouncing the government's economic policies.

A prolonged and damaging civil service strike in the summer of 1981.

Inner city riots witnessed in Toxteth in Liverpool, Moss Side in Manchester and Brixton in London.

Government standing in the opinion polls fell to 27%. Thatcher's popularity was plummeting; it stood at –24% in the opinion polls.

Income from North Sea Oil did not appear to be benefiting Britain.

Divisions in Cabinet along 'dry/wet' lines provoked a reshuffle in September 1981 to dispense of critical voices.

TASK

Imagine you are a voter in Britain in 1981 – decide your social/occupational/geographical/gender status. Explain why you would or would not vote for another Conservative government at the next election.

Why another Conservative victory in 1983?

By the end of 1981 the Conservative government were at a critically low ebb. So why were they able – within 18 months – to win the election and extend their majority from 43 to 142?

In answering this question, here are three main factors to consider:

- The state of Labour Party opposition.
- The improving economic situation in 1982.
- The Falklands War.

FACTOR A

Divisions in the Labour Party

- James Callaghan resigned as leader of the Labour Party in October 1980 and was succeeded by Michael Foot – the left-wing candidate who narrowly defeated Denis Healey.
- Foot's leadership was a victory for the left wing of the party. He was an intellectual, a radical MP – pacifist and a staunch supporter of nuclear disarmament, but never looked an effective leader.
- Debate over critical issues such as the EEC, economy, industrial relations and defence divided the party.
- The Labour Party were also infiltrated by extremists such as Trotskyites.
- Growing animosity by some of the leadership towards the leftish tendency displayed at the Wembley Conference in January 1981 led to a breakaway party being formed.
- The Limehouse Declaration was published a week after Wembley. It announced the establishment of a Council for Social Democracy. This was led by the 'Gang of Four' – David Owen, William Rodgers, Roy Jenkins and Shirley Williams – all leading figures within the Labour Party.
- On 26 March 1981, the Social Democratic Party was formed – 13 Labour MPs and one Conservative joined the initial group.
- At the election of 1983 the Labour Party was badly led, disorganised and in disarray. The Alliance of SDP and Liberals failed to make a distinct impression. However, the vote opposing the Conservatives was seriously split – a significant advantage for Thatcher.

THE SDP'S 'GANG OF FOUR' WILLIAM RODGERS, SHIRLEY WILLIAMS, ROY JENKINS AND DAVID OWEN.

FACTOR B

The improving economic situation

- The recession bottomed out in 1981.
- Growth resumed in 1982 and was nearly 4 per cent by 1983.
- Inflation was falling – including the mortgage rate by 4 per cent in the months before the election.
- The sale of council houses had been very popular.
- Unemployment was still high – at 3.2 million in January 1983 – but the government had refocussed the voters on the battle against inflation. People were increasingly accepting this high level of unemployment.

FACTOR C

The Falklands War 1982

- The Argentinian forces of General Galtieri – leader of the ruling Junta – invaded the British territory of the Falkland Islands in the south Atlantic in April 1982. Argentina had long claimed the return of their 'Malvinas Islands'.
- Despite the withdrawal of British ships such as the *Endurance* from the South Atlantic in June 1981, the House of Commons were united in their feeling to protect the British population in the Falklands. Lord Carrington, the Foreign Secretary, took the brunt of the blame for leaving the Falklands insufficiently protected and resigned.
- A task force of 10,000 were sent from Britain to recapture the islands.
- Militarily, the British task force was stretched to the limit, diplomatically it met with opposition at the United Nations but in Britain jingoism against the 'Argies' swept the country. The Prime Minister seemed intent on forcing the Argentinians to surrender rather than a negotiated settlement.
- On 2 May a British nuclear-powered submarine sank the *General Belgrano* with loss of 300 lives. It was a serious episode because facts seemed scarce at the time but the *Belgrano* was thought by many to have been outside the exclusion zone and by others to have been leaving it. Questions were asked later about this incident.
- On 26 May troops landed at San Carlos Bay and within 3 weeks Port Stanley – the capital – was captured and Britain had won the Falklands war.
- The Falklands evoked memories of Britain's imperial past and Thatcher – as she declared 'Rejoice Rejoice' – became the most popular of Prime Ministers – likened to Churchill and even Boudicea as a wartime leader.
- The victory changed the public and political climate. Opinion polls which had been making a small shift at the start of 1982 now made a surge towards the Tories.
- A general election victory now seemed a certainty for the Conservatives.

TASK

1 Research further the three factors on pages 348–9.
2 Consider the historian Lord Blake's views of the importance of the 'Falklands Factor':

> 'How the Conservatives would have fared at the next election but for the Falklands war is anyone's guess. The likelihood is that they would have won though not so overwhelmingly. It is hard to see how Labour could have recovered from its disastrous condition, war or no war.'

Using the evidence you have available, how far do you agree with Blake's assessment?

General Election 1983 – Results

	Seats	% vote
Conservatives	397	42.4
Labour	209	27.6
Liberal – SDP Alliance (17 Liberals, 6 SDP)	23	25.4
Others	21	5

How much of a victory was this for the Conservatives?

Research and answer the following questions:
1 What do the percentage vote in the results above illustrate about the four main parties?
2 In what parts of the country was the Conservative vote highest?
3 What were the unemployment figures in 1983 – how does this compare within the 1930s?
4 What has government economic policy meant for the public services from 1979–83?
5 How did our economic progress compare with that of Europe?

Thatcherism at its height: the Conservative administration, 1983–87

As a result of the increased majority the Conservative Party and its leader glowed with confidence and in the Queen's Speech there was a complete commitment to the radicalism promised in 1979 and embarked upon up to 1983. Thatcher's new Cabinet reflected this commitment and focused on the aims of the 'new Right'. Geoffrey Howe was made Foreign Secretary, Nigel Lawson, Chancellor of the Exchequer, Leon Brittan, Home Secretary – all members of this Cabinet were adherents to Thatcher's ideas and aims. The guiding principle of 'one of us' secured her a compliant team.

This government attacked with gusto the areas considered by the Conservatives to need either removing or remoulding. Privatisation of industry, control of the trade unions and centralisation of local government were accompanied by major changes in Education and the Health Service. Institutions such as the Civil Service, the Press, and the Arts also felt the new broom of Thatcherism sweep through their houses.

REMOVE
- Nationalised industry
- Power of trades unions
- High-spending local authorities

REFORM
- Civil Service
- Education
- National Health Service
- Press
- The Arts

Nationalised industry

In order to allow the free market to operate fully the government wished to end government control of the nationalised industries. This aim 'to roll back the state' was complemented by the vision of a share-holding democracy' – an industrial society invested in by individuals of all classes. There were a series of privatisations:

1984	British Telecom	Sold off for £4 billion and a new shareholding class amongst workers and trades unionists was created.
1986	British Gas	Sold off for £5,454 million.
1987	British Airways, British Petroleum, British Aerospace and Rolls Royce.	
1990	Electricity, Water	

There were criticisms of this policy. From within Conservative ranks disquiet was expressed by former Prime Minister, Macmillan, who accused the government of 'selling the family silver'. The Labour party disagreed with the reversal of the post war mixed economy and many ordinary people who had rushed to buy shares soon discovered that share prices can fall. The stock market crash of 1987 resulted in British Petroleum shares being less successful.

Power of the trades unions

One of Thatcher's main aims had always been to curb the power of the trades unions. However, the high unemployment figures of the early 1980s had already sapped their strength. Between 1979 and 1982 membership had declined by around 14 per cent. Strikes were far less frequent and the movement was at its weakest for years. There were, however, three occasions between 1983 and 1987 which provided a test of strength between the government and the unions. On each occasion, the union side suffered a heavy defeat:

1 In 1983 the National Graphical Association's strike against Eddie Shah's non-unionised printing operations in Warrington was deemed illegal. The Association incurred huge financial costs.

2 At GCHQ – the headquarters for government intelligence based at Cheltenham – union membership was declared illegal.

3 The Miners' strike April 1984 to April 1985 – described by Kim Howells MP for Pontypridd as the 'last great industrial strike'. It lasted 362 days and finally resulted in victory for Thatcher.

Why did the NUM strike?

Because: In 1984 plans were announced to close 20 pits and Cortonwood Colliery. The government, basing their decision on a 1982 Mergers and Monopolies Commission Report, considered that the closure of inefficient pits made economic sense.

Because: In 1983 Ian McGregor was appointed as Chairman of the Coal Board. He was a no-nonsense Canadian Scot whose reputation was well known. He had already slimmed down British Steel by cutting staffing levels from 150,000 to 85,000. His task was clear – reduce the number of pits and break the power of the NUM.

Because: In 1982 Jo Gormley, the President of the NUM, was succeeded by Arthur Scargill. He was a young, aggressive overtly Marxist union leader from Yorkshire. His view that 'while there's coal in the ground then it should be mined' was contrary to the government's policy. Scargill saw action by the miners also as action against Conservative trades union legislation – he felt that he was fighting for the whole trades union movement.

In April 1984 the NUM called a strike and was supported solidly by the miners. The strike was memorable firstly for its violent nature – physical confrontation, injuries on both sides, 'flying pickets' for reinforcement prevented from getting to the pits by police motorway blocks. Secondly for the hardship it meant for miners' families and the way it divided communities. The determination of the government to hold out against miners' demands finally won through. The miners voted to return to work. The union had split and between 1984 and 1987 42 pits were closed and the number of colliery workers fell from 181,000 to 108,000.

TASK

Explain clearly how policy towards each of these three areas is in line with the philosophy behind Thatcherism:

   a nationalised industry.

   b trades unions.

   c local authorities.

TASK

1 Class discussion: 'Why did the Conservative government under Thatcher pursue the extension of individuals' rights and freedoms yet extend the control of central government?'

2 To what extent would you accept that the Soviet label of 'the Iron Lady' is an accurate description of Thatcher's government?

High-spending local authorities

The government in their attempt to cut public spending identified high-spending local authorities as a serious drain on the Exchequer. Additionally local authorities – particularly those Labour-controlled ones – were often charging high rates and operating in defiance of government policy. In 1986 the Local Government Act abolished the Greater London Council (GLC) and six metropolitan counties. Additionally it curbed the power of local government in general. This was criticised widely as marking a serious decline in local democracy. It was claimed that central government was extending its control over locally elected authorities.

Thatcherism, the public services and the media

Thatcher distrusted the covert power exercised by civil servants, particularly those more senior in the administration of the country. Certain branches of the *civil service* – such as the Driver and Vehicle Licensing Centre – were separated off as self-sustaining agencies. The civil service also became far more politicised – reminiscent of Lloyd George's at the beginning of the century. Thatcher's favourite television programme *Yes Minister* (later *Yes Prime Minister*) parodied in a very funny way the compliance and complacency of the civil service permanent secretaries.

Education also experienced change at a rapid pace and at all levels. Morale amongst teachers and university lecturers hit a low ebb as they were constantly bombarded by change. GCSE examinations unified the bipartite system of GCEs and CSEs. A National Curriculum was introduced and assessment tests set at key stages in a child's education. The 1988 Education Reform Act introduced the local management of schools by governing bodies which were to include parent participation. In the Universities also management techniques and short-term profit-making strategies had to be introduced as competition and market forces came into play. These policy changes combined with continued funding cuts to produce a loss of morale and a drain of academics to Canada and the USA.

In the *National Health Service* changes were introduced in an attempt to create both financial and operational efficiency. Trusts were set up and hospitals increasingly had to run themselves along the lines of a commercial business. General Practitioners similarly found themselves having to 'manage' their practices along commercial lines.

The profit-making business ethic was introduced into the world of the *Arts Council*. The American's private funding of the arts was cited as a model to be emulated and theatres, museums and art galleries increasingly had to pay their way independently as government expenditure on the Arts declined.

Finally, constraints were placed on *the press* by the Prime Minister's increasingly influential Press Secretary, Bernard Ingham. Through the Conservatives' considerable influence with multinational newspaper empires such as that owned by Rupert Murdoch, the broad range of media opinion increasingly favoured the government.

What was Thatcherism?

Source A

'Economics are the method', said Thatcher in 1981; 'the object is to change the heart and soul.' Thatcherism was both more and less than a programme of economic liberalism, intent on maximising the freedom of choice of the individual. Thatcher was never tempted by a thoroughgoing libertarian position which enjoined laissez-faire in matters of moral, personal and sexual conduct. The 'permissive society' was reviled, along with a liberal elite whom it was the mission of Thatcherite populism to dispossess. Tebbit caught this nicely in 1990 in a diatribe against 'the insufferable, smug, sanctimonious, naïve, guilt-ridden, wet, pink orthodoxy of that sunset home of that third rate decade, the 1960's'. Even at the height of her power as prime minister, Thatcher's public posture was still that of an outsider, appealing to public opinion over the heads of her own cabinet. She would voice popular discontent as though an unspecified 'they' ought to do something about it; she would openly applaud pro-hanging speeches at Conservative Party conferences, to the embarrassment of her own Home Secretary. Thatcher's politics of moral populism, practised with a success unmatched since Gladstone, helped give her government its authentic streak of radicalism – yet its project of economic liberalism was to tempered, perhaps hampered, by her conservative instincts.

Peter Clarke, *Hope and Glory: Britain 1900–1990* (1996).

1 According to Clarke, what else did Thatcherism involve other than just a series of economic policies?
2 What does this passage suggest about Thatcher's views and style?

Source B

More than anyone, it was the Left who did Margaret Thatcher the honour of giving her policies the coherence of an ideology by inventing the term 'Thatcherism'. To a considerable extent this is a misnomer. Thatcher's policies were simply the platform of the Reaganites, adapted to Britain. Ronald Reagan was elected President of the United States in 1981, but long before this he had campaigned, as Governor of California, on a robustly free-market and anti-welfare agenda. This agenda sought to roll back the state, reducing its activities drastically by privatisation and deregulation. Private bodies, it was argued, subject to market forces, were better suited in virtually every ease to produced positive results. Deregulation was meant to increase competition and release the creative energy of individuals. The encouragement of private businesses would further this process. For the same reasons,

TASK

From studying this chapter and further research on Thatcher's governments between 1979 and 1990, list all the features of policy and personality you would associate with the term Thatcherism.

individuals should be weaned off welfare dependence and encouraged to provide for themselves. This implied measures to gradually reduced eligibility for state benefits, in order to get people back to work. Also important was the fight against inflation. Little, or preferably nil, inflation would encourage people to save and enhance confidence in the economic system. It was also part of this platform to proclaim 'Victorian values' – thrift, hard work, self-reliance and moral rectitude, though the arguments for the economic agenda were not necessarily dependent on these values. Finally, the Reagan/Thatcherites were strong on 'law and order'.

David Childs, *Britain Since 1939: Progress, Decline* (1995).

1 According to Childs, who first coined the phrase 'Thatcherism'?
2 Why does Childs consider this a 'misnomer'?
3 What features does Childs consider common to both President Reagan and Thatcher?
4 To what extent do these two historians
   a Agree
   b Disagree
   in their definition of Thatcherism?

Postwar Ireland

The Irish question in the 1950s and 1960s

During the period of Conservative government 1951–1964 the hope had been to avoid entanglements in the Irish question. The loyalists supported rule from Westminster in Northern Ireland but the Nationalist case was as follows:

- A united, free independent Ireland was still incomplete.
- Discrimination against the Catholic minority in the North must be ended. There was inequality in housing, jobs and election rigging (known as gerrymandering) in local elections to ensure Protestant control of the councils.
- Actions of the Royal Ulster Constabulary (RUC) and the B Specials were too heavy handed.
- The government could not ignore Ireland when a campaign of violence was relaunched by the IRA between 1956 and 1962. 'Flying squad' tactics were used and there were hundreds of incidents involving violence.
- However, the IRA, acknowledging their lack of success, announced a suspension of violence in 1962. The Irish Republic's government meanwhile gave priority to good relations with Britain and with the latter's support joined the United Nations in 1955. If extremism seemed to be in decline in the early 1960s, why by 1969 had the British government decided to send in troops to maintain law and order?

WHY?

16 AUGUST 1969
British troops sent to Northern Ireland

1 A more determined leadership had emerged in the IRA by 1962/3. Cathal Goulding and Roy Johnstone tried to extend its appeal, increase numbers. They adopted a more left-wing stance and rhetoric. This more left-wing approach caused a split in the IRA leading to the setting up of the Provisional Council (Provos) with violence and self sacrifice as methods to their end.

2 Outburst of civil rights campaigning in USA in 1960s spread to Europe and Ireland. Civil rights of Catholics in Northern Ireland became a major issue. In 1965 Paul Rose Labour MP set up the campaign for Democracy in Ulster.

3 Ulster Prime Minister O'Neill (1963–69) attempted gradualist reform in the province. Insufficient to satisfy many Catholics but enough to unleash Lyalist criticism.

4 1966 Republican celebrations of the 50th anniversary of the Easter Rising sparked a Loyalist backlash. The hardline views of the Reverend Ian Paisley gained much support.

5 October 1968 Londonderry Civil Rights March went ahead despite a ban and resulted in violent clashes between demonstrators and police. It gained international attention.

6 Spring 1969 IRA attacks on the utilities. Bernadette Devlin – a civil rights activist – was elected to Westminster and spoke of the 'misrule in Ulster'.

7 Violence erupted and continued from Spring to Summer 1969. The worst was witnessed in Londonderry and Belfast. Peace was threatened and Harold Wilson – Prime Minister – thought it necessary to overrule Stormont and send British troops in to maintain law and order.

RESULTS?

By shifting the responsibility for Northern Irish difficulties to Westminster it humiliated and undermined the position of the Stormont ministers, implying they could not cope. Yet Westminster was unable to solve the problem either.

The Social Democratic Labour Party (SDLP) was formed in Northern Ireland to represent the views of the more moderate Catholic minority.

Sectarian violence worsened – reaching an unprecedented height between 1970 and 1973.

Nationalist extremists   – IRA official provisional
                                    – INLA (Irish National Liberation Army)

Loyalist extremists   – UDF (Ulster Defence Force)
                                   – UFF (Ulster Freedom Fighters)

Record of violence:

1970 – 100 bomb outrages in Northern Ireland.

1971 – 1st British soldier killed by IRA.
       – British Commander in Chief resigned as government refused his request for more troops.
       – McGurks Bar bomb – killed 15 Catholics.
       – 175 deaths.

1972 – Civil Rights March in January later known as 'Bloody Sunday' – 13 civilians were killed by troops. An angry mob in Dublin protested by burning down the British Embassy. IRA reprisals led to the bombing of the Parachute Regiment in Aldershot, England.
       – 400 deaths.

1973 – 20 bombs were detonated on 'Bloody Friday' in Belfast in July. 11 were killed and 120 injured.

Government attempts to solve the problem – 1970s

Direct rule or power sharing?

In the wake of the 'Bloody Sunday' disaster in January 1972, the Conservative government under Heath passed the Northern Ireland (Temporary Provisions) Act which suspended the parliament in Belfast – Stormont – for a year. Internment was to be phased out and plebiscites held to measure public opinion in Ulster. This ushered in a period of 'direct rule' from London and William Whitelaw was sent to control and stabilise the province. Intense negotiations were held in an attempt to reach a more permanent solution – in July 1972 at Darlington, County Durham and in December 1973 at Sunningdale. The parties at Sunningdale, in the knowledge that a recent plebiscite had shown 57.4 per cent of the Northern Irish to be in favour of the union, reached an agreement. Ulster was to be left to govern itself, but Britain was to retain a security role. Communication with Dublin should be maintained via their membership of the Council of Ireland. In January 1974 'direct rule' ended and a new assembly was set up but this lasted only a year. The Sunningdale agreement had failed to win support of both the Loyalists and the Republicans. The return of the Labour government in Britain under Wilson, then Callaghan saw Merlyn Rees appointed a minister for Ireland. He pursued diligently the power-sharing policy, but progress was held back by strikes organised by the Ulster Workers' Council and the development of terrorism by the IRA who now were exporting their violence to the British mainland. The Birmingham Pub bombings prompted the passing of the Prevention of Terrorism Act.

Ireland in the Thatcher years

Situation in 1979

- Direct rule and the power-sharing experiments of the 1970s had failed to stabilise the situation.
- Callaghan's attempt to increase Ulster representation in Westminster had been overtaken by his election defeat.
- IRA violence had intensified. The 'provisional' wing displayed great commitment and personal sacrifice to their cause with the result many died in bombings.
- Government's negotiations including extremist groups had given them a degree of legitimacy and they were also gaining much publicity.
- Indiscriminate bombing campaigns continued but political assassinations of key individuals shocked the population. In 1976 the British ambassador in Dublin, Christopher Ewart-Biggs, was assassinated. In March 1979 Thatcher's close confidant Airey Neave was murdered at the House of Commons by the INLA and in August Earl Mountbatten, a member of the Royal Family, was assassinated by the IRA while fishing in the Irish Republic.

Thatcher's dual approach

Thatcher's aims were to maintain a tough line with the extremist terrorists but seek a political solution to the problem. She was perhaps more sympathetic to the loyalist cause than some of her predecessors, but felt that the Irish question should be tackled by all three sides – London, Belfast and Dublin.

In 1980 Thatcher held summit meetings with the Irish premier Charles Haughey in May and December. Unity of Ireland was agreed on but with the consent of a majority of the people in Northern Ireland. Talks were resumed in 1981 with Garrett Fitzgerald – the new Premier – and an Anglo-Irish Intergovernment Council was established for ministers to meet

What is the significance of
the 'special status'
demanded by Republican
prisoners

regularly to discuss matters of common concern. In 1982 James Prior, the Secretary of State for Ireland, set up a new Northern Ireland Assembly to resume legislative and executive powers. Its success was to be limited due to both the SDLP and Sinn Fein boycotting.

Hunger strikes, rioting and bombing

Republican prisoners mounted a 'dirty protest' for special status and began hunger strikes in October 1980. This was resumed in 1981 led by Bobby Sands who died in the Summer followed by nine other hunger-strikers. Rioting over the hunger strikes led to more than 50 deaths. On the mainland violence again emerged – in 1982 the Hyde park bombing, in 1983 just before Christmas a bomb exploded outside Harrods. This IRA campaign reached a peak in October 1984 when an IRA bomb exploded at the Grand Hotel, Brighton killing five people and narrowly missing Thatcher and the Conservative leadership assembled for their annual party conference.

THE GRAND HOTEL IN
BRIGHTON AFTER THE IRA
BOMB.

The Anglo-Irish Agreement – November 1985

This was signed by Thatcher and Garret Fitzgerald and given the status of an international treaty. It was a new attempt to secure peace and stability in Northern Ireland by reconciling the two traditions – Unionist and Nationalist. It was agreed that any change in the status of Northern Ireland should only come about with the consent of the majority living there. Their present wish was for no change in the Union, but if in the future the majority demanded changes, legislation was to be introduced into the respective Parliaments.

However, amid massive demonstrations, it was immediately denounced by the two main Unionist parties as a sell-out, while Haughey – the Irish opposition leader – called it 'a very severe blow to the concept of Irish unity'.

Between 1985 and 1989, the government continued to attempt solutions. The IRA and Sinn Fein were banned from press and television coverage. The London–Dublin axis was maintained and seen as important to progress. To further complicate a complex situation internecine fighting developed in the extremist camps, both Loyalist and Nationalist. Atrocities continued – the Remembrance Day bombing at Enniskillen killed 11 people. Political assassination continued with that of Ian Gow, a Conservative MP, in summer 1990. Old fears, rivalries and prejudices remain deeply entrenched, violence continued and a political solution had not been found.

1 Outline arguments for and against deploying British troops in Northern Ireland.

2 Summarise the views of
   a an Irish nationalist
   b an Ulster loyalist
   c the British government
   towards events in Northern Ireland during the twenty years since 1970.

Thatcher's downfall

The 1987 Election

Another well-timed election was called for 11 June 1987 – the Conservatives had recently enjoyed some good local election results, a stock market boom was complemented by a fall in unemployment figures and a 2 percent cut in income tax in March and finally Thatcher's image as a world leader was high after an April visit to the USSR. The result was historic, a third consecutive election victory for the Conservatives with an overall majority of 102 – a record not repeated since the early 19th century.

Why, then, within two-and-a-half years had Thatcher been forced to resign – challenged as leader by some of her closest political allies?

There were four main issues which brought about Thatcher's downfall:

1   Style of leadership
2   Poll Tax
3   Europe
4   The next General Election

TALKING POINT

Why did Thatcher call elections after four years instead of the constitutional five-year span?

STYLE OF LEADERSHIP

Thatcher's style had always been to lead from the front with a team in full agreement with her. However, in a third term of office a government is bound to seek scapegoats if it hits rough times. Criticism mounted from her ministers about her style of leadership. Thatcher seemed to depend excessively on her non-party advisers, was accused of bypassing Cabinet and reaching decisions via other channels. There were several serious disagreements with ministers – notably Heseltine's resignation in 1986.

POLL TAX

The Community Charge (dubbed the 'Poll Tax') was introduced in England in 1988 and Scotland in 1989. It was a highly unpopular reform of the old rate system. Tax fell on individuals rather than their property. It was seen to favour the well off in larger houses and to discriminate against the worker. There was much protest – rallies, demonstrations and even violence against the social iniquity. This provided another stick for ministers to beat Thatcher with. There was a growing rift in the party.

EUROPE

Thatcher was suspicious of European unification with all its ramifications – monetary and possibly political union. She adopted a 'Little Englander' role against mounting pro-Europe pressure at home and in Europe itself.

Conservative Party managers were already considering the possibility of a fourth election victory. This in the light of a significant Labour Party revival under their new leader, Neil Kinnock. Both policies and party organisation had been reformed. Labour now wished to accept the market economy and to show that they could run it better than the Conservatives. Within the Conservative Party there were serious doubts that Thatcher could lead the party to another election victory.

Thatcher challenged

Thatcher's leadership was challenged by Michael Heseltine in November 1990. She had already been seriously damaged by the resignation of Nigel Lawson, the Chancellor of the Exchequer, in 1989 and of her Deputy Prime Minister Sir Geoffrey Howe on 1 November 1990. His departure, followed by his damning resignation speech in the Commons, seriously damaged Thatcher on several counts.

According to the rules of the Conservative Party leadership election at the time, a winner at the first ballot had to have an overall majority and a clear 15 per cent margin over their nearest rival. Thatcher gained 204 votes of the Conservative MPs and Heseltine 152. A second ballot was called for – Thatcher, speaking from a meeting of European leaders in Paris, declared 'I fight on, I fight to win!'

However, when she consulted each of her Cabinet individually, only two considered she could win. The other nineteen were either doubtful or thought she should stand down. On Thursday 22 November, Thatcher resigned; she was succeeded – after an election within the Conservative Party – by John Major, her recently appointed Foreign Secretary.

The Thatcher years had come to an end – defeated by her own ministers rather than the decision of the electorate.

REVIEW

Assessment of Thatcher

TASK

Study the chapter and research further.
In groups draw up
   a defence
   b prosecution
case based on the evidence of Thatcher's ten years as Prime Minister.
Simulate a debate in the leadership contest between Michael Heseltine and Margaret Thatcher based upon the cases prepared.
Take a class vote on student views of Thatcher's premiership.

Index